I0827067

Center for Basque Studies
Basque Classics Series, No. 2

Anthology of Apologists and Detractors of the Basque Language

by
Juan Madariaga Orbea

Translated by
Frederick H. Fornoff, María Cristina Saavedra,
Amaia Gabantxo, and Cameron J. Watson

Center for Basque Studies
University of Nevada, Reno
Reno, Nevada

This book was published in part with the generous financial support obtained by the Association of Friends of the Center for Basque Studies from the Provincial Government of Bizkaia.

Center for Basque Studies
Basque Classics Series, No. 2
Series Editors: William A. Douglass, Gregorio Monreal and Pello Salaburu

Center for Basque Studies
University of Nevada, Reno
Reno, Nevada 89557
http://basque.unr.edu

Cover illustration: Fragment of the drawing *Sorguiñ aizia* (1990) by Julio Caro Baroja.

Library of Congress Cataloging-in-Publication Data

Anthology of apologists and detractors of the Basque language / edited and with an introduction by Juan Madariaga Orbea.
p. cm. -- (Basque classics series ; no. 2)
Includes index.
ISBN 1-877802-62-X (pbk.) -- ISBN 1-877802-63-8 (hardcover)
1. Basque language--Social aspects. 2. Basque language--Political aspects. I. Madariaga Orbea, Juan. II. Series.

PH5024.75.A58 2006
499'.92--dc22

2006001007

The Center for Basque Studies wishes to gratefully acknowledge the generous financial support of the Bizkaiko Foru Aldundia / Provincial Government of Bizkaia for the publication of this book.

Anthology of Apologists and Detractors of the Basque Language

by
Juan Madariaga Orbea

Hobe genuke euskarak maitasun gutxixeago eta begiramen gehixeago jasoko balu gugandik.

(It would be better if we loved Euskara a little less, and respected it a lot more)

KOLDO MITXELENA

Contents

Acknowledgments

First of all, I have to say that without the invaluable encouragement and friendship of Gregorio Monreal Zia this work would not have been possible. Similarly, I must acknowledge the continuous support I have received from Joseba Zulaika. Additionally, a number of friends have contributed through their critiques, suggestions, corrections, and observations to the improvement of the manuscript of this book: Jerardo Elortza, Anaje Narbaiza, Michael Judge, and Jone Azurmendi. My thanks, also, to Santiago Segura, aided by Andrés Ortiz-Osés, for their invaluable help with the translation of the Latin texts. Finally, I must also express my thanks to the team of translators (Frederick H. Fornoff, María Cristina Saavedra, Amaia Gabantxo and Cameron J. Watson) for taking on the challenge of translating into English such a diverse and complex body of texts. *Bihotzez eskertzen dizuet langintza korapilotsu eta nekez honetan egin duzuen ahalegina.*

Anthology of Apologists and Detractors of the Basque Language

FROM TUBAL TO THE *IKASTOLAK*: THE LONG DEBATE ABOUT THE EXCELLENCE OF THE BASQUE LANGUAGE DURING THE *FORAL* ERA, 1545–1876

1. The Basque Language and the Ideological Construct of the *Fuero**

How is it that the language of a small country, with few inhabitants and consequently few speakers, an inferior literature, and who were excluded

---

* The term *Fuero* refers to the pact or charter negotiated between the Spanish monarchy and the Basque provinces guaranteeing certain rights in exchange for nominal allegiance to the Crown.

T.N. In a work of this nature, spanning four centuries, two embyronic nation-states, three cultures, and several languages, coherence is a necessary, although difficult objective. For those readers familiar with the Basque Country in both France and Spain, its multiple denominations, for the region as a whole, as well as its various provinces, cities, towns, villages, rivers, mountains, and even languages, retaining the original orthography of the texts might have been an option. However, given that even in the original texts, the spelling of toponyms and even proper names differs widely, and in the interests of those readers unfamiliar with such nuances, as well as the fact that what appear in this work are not the original texts per se, but rather translations into modern American English, the orthography will, here, observe certain norms.

Following the example established by Gregorio Monreal Zia in *The Old Law of Bizkaia (1452)*, Basque Classics Series 1 (Reno: Center for Basque Studies, University of Nevada, Reno, 2005), the present study will respect the orthography established by Euskaltzaindia (the Basque Language Academy), as regards the names of Basque provinces. As such, in the northern Basque Country, Lapurdi will be used instead of the French Labourd, and Zuberoa, rather than Soule. In the southern Basque Country, Araba will be used in place of the Spanish Álava, Bizkaia instead of Vizcaya, and Gipuzkoa rather than Guipúzcoa. Two exceptions will be our use of English variants still in use: Navarre and Lower Navarre.

For the most part, the Basque orthography of place names will be used, with parenthetical references, where appropriate, to French or Spanish variants. Exceptions to this rule will be toponyms, mainly found in the southern part of the modern Basque Country, where Romance and Castilian denominations had already predominated for some time prior to the start of the present work. Proper names will, however, be rendered in their original forms.

For any questions regarding variants on place names in the Basque Country, please refer to the website of Euskaltzaindia, http://www.euskaltzaindia.net/eoda/toponimia.asp?hizkuntza=eu.

Furthermore, as if to demonstrate what in *The Old Law of Bizkaia* is termed the "flexibility" rather than "inconsistency" of orthography in Basque history and culture, the present study will frequently use the contemporary bilingual variants of certain key towns and cities: namely Donostia-San Sebastián, Pamplona-Iruña, Vitoria-Gasteiz, and Arrasate-Mondragón.

from public administration and education, has had and continues to have so much presence and has aroused so much interest and passion, and provoked such constant commentary, either to praise or to ridicule it? Over the centuries, varied opinions about the character and nature of the Basque language proliferated to an extraordinary degree. Speakers and non-speakers speculated as to its possible link with the languages of the Caucasians, Berbers, Carthaginians, Celts, etc. Even while some were claiming it originated in Babel or even Paradise and insisting on its supernatural perfection, others were treating it as a mere dialect, an amalgam, an unintelligible jargon, a barbaric language. Currently, philological interest alone would be reason enough for this interest, considering its distinct profile and its lack of connection with any of the major linguistic trunks; but at the height of the sixteenth or seventeenth century, different evaluative criteria were at work. However, behind each commonplace idea received and accepted without examination, a political motive was and still is concealed. Thus, the dramatic role played by Euskara during those centuries has more to do with the identifying characteristics of the community of its speakers than with the language itself. This identity was constructed by referencing a peculiar institutional system (the *Fueros*), by an assumption of its greater Catholicity, by certain practices and customs, and later on, even by the vindication of a specific aesthetic (with special consideration to the landscape) or to the mythology supposedly shaped during prehistoric times. Yet it was mostly constructed, as I have said, especially with reference to a language, Basque, which was in this case quite real and quite different from those around it. For centuries, authors in the service, directly or indirectly, of different powers (Spanish and French monarchies, Churches, the Company of Jesus, the administration of privileges, etc.) made use of the Basque language, denigrating or exalting it, as a tool for their ideological demonstrations that were focused simplistically around a central point: the peculiar and distinct political-juridical-administrative system of the Basque territories. Strained linguistic arguments, conditioned by ideology and religion, were modeled on a varied outpouring of theories that today strike us as extravagant. We Basques, however, are left with the sad consolation that this anthology is not the patrimony of linguistic nonsense, but that we share these ideas with the rest of Europe.

Of course, the lack of connection between the Basque language and those around it has always been perceived by outsiders to our country as a quality of strangeness, remoteness, and unintelligibility that was subject to polarization: it was considered as either a barbaric jargon that was suitable only for peasants, or an ancient, mysterious and miraculously preserved language, presumably touched by divine grace. This dichotomy was difficult to reconcile, because those who did not speak the language found any approximation taxing, and those who did speak it were faced with the problem of a meager literary production that limited their culture almost entirely to oral expression. With this, you could claim whatever you wanted because the arguments for or against would inevitably be few and lacking in force. From the first written references to the Basque language that have come down to us, we find evidence of this bewilderment, detachment, and even scorn from the foreigners who came in contact with it. Hence, the assumed barbarism of the language is linked to the presumed savagery of its speakers. The model of the traveler who comes in contact with the Basques and their language, maintains somewhat cool relations with them and then dismisses the country radically, both the inhabitants and their language, is the author of a chronicle describing his pilgrimage to Santiago in the twelfth century: Aimeric Picaud. His denigration of the Basques, apparently because of the poor treatment he received during his passage through the country, is absolute; however, this does not prevent him from providing us with the first known lexicon of Euskara in his description of the barbaric language:

> These [Basques] are fierce, and the land they live in is fierce, wild, and savage; the fierceness of their faces, matching the barbaric nature of their language, inspires fear in the hearts of those who see them . . . Basques and men from Navarre are similar in appearance and characteristics, such as food, clothing, and language . . . If you listen to them speaking, you would be reminded of dogs barking, for they have a totally barbaric language: they call our Lord, *Urcia*; God's mother, *Andrea Maria;* bread they call *orgui*; wine, *ardum*; meat, *aragui;* fish, *araigu*; the house, *echea*; the owner of the house, *iaona*; his wife, *andrea;* the church, *elicera*; the priest, *belaterra*, which is translated as 'beautiful land'; wheat, *gari*; water, *uric*; the king, *ereguia*; Santiago (Saint James), *iaona done iacuc*. These are barbaric people, unlike any other in their rites and nature; filled with malice; dark in color with harsh faces; twisted, fierce, perfidious, vain and corrupt in their faith; libidinous, drunken by habit, skilled in every kind of violence, ferocious and wild, vicious reprobates; impious and surly, furious and contentious, unlearned in other virtues, gifted in all vices and iniquities, similar to the Goths and Saracens in their malice, enemy absolute of our Gallic people. Whether they're Navarrese or Basques, they'll kill a Gaul for a penny if they can.[1]

In reality, Picaud, in his passage through Navarre, was welcomed by the Frankish community that populated the most important farming settlements, and he probably wrote all or part of the text in one of these cities, echoing the violent hostility facing the Frankish and Navarrese communities and provoking, among other things, the so-called "Navarrese War" of Pamplona-Iruña. In addition, his mentality is paradigmatic of the French ethnocentrism of his period that tended to consider anything beyond its borders as barbaric. To some extent, the history of the relations between Basques and their neighbors and visitors is the history, moderated at times, of Aimeric Picaud: repulsion and incomprehension toward a language, customs, and culture that for the most part blazed its own trail, rejecting the influence of surrounding cultures. Simply because it was different, it was thought to be inferior, primitive, and to a certain extent socially and politically dangerous. And because these negative feelings, which were produced over many centuries, were connected, more or less consciously, to the prejudice of considering the Basque people as barbaric and their language as the epitome of primitivism, the Basques had to spend a lot of time combating that prejudice and, quite logically, they chose the language itself as the primary object of vindication and apology.[2]

But all these cultural differences and failures of comprehension do not in themselves explain why dozens of writers (philosophers, politicians, historians, and pedagogues), both inside and outside the country, included in their treatises, which had little to do with linguistics in general, a chapter or at least a page or reference to the Basque language. The explanation comes, largely, from the fact that this language was transformed into an essential ingredient in the ideological edifice, constructed during the sixteenth century and maintained until the second half of the nineteenth century, which we know as the *foral* system, or the system of the *Fuero*. From the sixteenth century on, the different Basque territories found it necessary to define their inclusion within the emerging absolute monarchies of Spain and France, whether they had been brought in by force, or in fact a Navarrese king had become king of France, or because, although incorporated since ancient times, social and economic changes facilitated a more advantageous institutional link than the one prevailing during medieval times. The new juridical and political situation made it necessary, with different levels of urgency, for the different territories to justify the new conditions through the elaboration of a legitimizing myth in which the Basque language would play a key role.

Broadly speaking, this ideological construct would prove to be a good fit in the thoroughly humid Atlantic and Pyrenean territories of

Euskal Herria* (the Basque Country), and especially in those territories belonging to the Spanish Crown. This does not mean that the remaining territories would not be affected to a lesser extent by this ideological phenomenon. Bizkaia, Gipuzkoa, the Atlantic valleys of the province of Araba, and the Navarrese valleys of the Atlantic and the Pyrenees had, until the sixteenth century, an economy based on the cultivation of livestock, chestnuts, apples, and grains (wheat, millet, and barley) that altogether did not yield much and could not provide enough to support an overly dense population. This agricultural and cattle-based economy combined with other sectors that had been complementary up to that point: iron and steel production (along with its corollaries: mining, the coal industry, transportation, and the construction of arms), fishing (whales and cod), naval construction, and bureaucracy. As a result, the opportunities that the Spanish monarchy extended into these areas, in the wake of imperial construction and the opening of overseas markets, were virtually unlimited. Thus, the bid to integrate this new politico-juridical and economic space was affected by the channeling of the demographic overflow into alternative sectors of production, be they ironworks, the Church, the monarchic bureaucracy, or American enterprises. The Basques would offer the royalty of the House of Austria ships, nails, metal strips, picks, harquebuses, scriveners, accountants, members of the clergy, etc., and the monarchy would offer the Basques a market in which to place these individuals and products. This, along

---

* There are a number of ways of referring to the Basque Country:

In Basque, *Euskal Herria* is the traditional name that includes all the territories in which this language has been spoken historically, which are: Navarre (*Nafarroa* in Basque), Bizkaia, Gipuzkoa, Araba, Lapurdi, Lower Navarre (*Behe Nafarroa*) and Zuberoa. The Romance language equivalent of *Euskal Herria* would be the term *Vasconia*. In principle, the neologism *Euskadi* is also used to refer to the seven territories, but this term has of late been reserved for the territories of the Autonomous Basque Community, that is, Araba, Bizkaia, and Gipuzkoa. The same is true of the term "Basque Country," which turns out to be equally ambiguous, sometimes limited to these last three provinces, on other occasions including all seven. This is the case also in the northern Basque Country with the term *Pays Basque*, which can refer to the three northern territories or to all seven. Other denominations, finally, are also used: *Iparralde* (literally, the northern zone) to refer to the three Basque territories under French administration and *Hegoalde* (the southern zone) to refer to the four situated to the south of the Pyrenees, under Spanish administration.

As for the Basque language, depending on the dialect, we find *euskara, euskera, eskuara* or *uskara*. By contrast, any language other than Basque is called *erdera* or *erdara*. In French, *euskara* is known as *basque* and in Castilian, as *vasco* or *vascuence*. Here, for the purpose of consistency, the single term Euskara will be used as much as possible.

with the integration of American crops, especially corn, allowed those small, barren Basque regions to populate their towns and villages and to export a considerable quantity of products and services to the most powerful nation in the world at that time. In general, the key to understanding this process lies in the dependent character of the Basque territories, pressured by an unbalanced demography whose regulatory elements (industry, commerce, and the service sector) were entering a depressed external market, which explains the relative necessity of connecting with superior politico-economic entities.

This integration occurred through the construction of a peculiar politico-institutional system, the *Fuero*, which is based on a fundamental premise: a pact. Speaking in a generic way, it might be said that the different Basque territories that integrated into the Spanish monarchy were capable of maintaining a system constituted on the following terms: before it was allied to the King of Castile, the territory had possessed a kind of freedom, either real or imagined, but in any case, one that was regarded as real and therefore defended. The association was made freely through an agreed-upon commitment, in such a way that a union would be established personally between the King, who was obligated to comply with the parameters of the pact, and the subjects, who were obligated to acknowledge his authority. The list of the elements that, allegedly or actually, comprised the basis of this pact became the essence of the *Fuero*, to wit: military and fiscal exemptions; the territory's own economic laws that presumed free markets; the territory's own institutional organization rooted in its customs, and therefore based on tradition; a universal territorial nobility; an exclusive legislative system that encompassed the penal and justice systems (with a ban on torture), and public and civil domains (thereby institutionalizing the right to inheritance that protected family property). This system was by no means original or particular to the Basques; it was to be found in other territories of the Spanish Crown and in other places in Europe. What is original is the powerful ideological construct elaborated to justify it and above all, the persistence of the system up to an unusually late date in comparison to other analogous systems, given that, from an institutional perspective, the *Fuero* survived until 1876, and some of its juridical and ideological elements can be found even later in Spanish constitutional systems.

This brings us to the ideological construct formulated in the sixteenth century to legitimize the *foral* system, in which the Basque language would play a prominent role. It should be stated from the outset that the legitimizing myth of the *Fuero* was developed a posteriori, when the greater part of the political and juridical elements of the system were already in place. Well before the legitimating sanctions offered by the theorists, the *Provincia* (province, administrative district) itself and the *Señorío* (manorial lands owned by the nobility, domain, estate, Seigniory) had already included more or less finalized juridical formulations of the theory of universal nobility early on. The Old Law of Bizkaia, signed in 1452, already included an expression of this idea, which later culminated with a statement by the Chancellor of Valladolid on 26 March 1580 that established the general nobility of the Bizkaians. Likewise, the Statutes of the Military-Religious Brotherhood of Gipuzkoa, drawn up in 1397 and 1436, followed suit. In this territory, universal nobility was recognized in 1527, 1557, 1562, 1608, 1635, and 1662. The key to the system is to be found in measures to control rights of *vecindad* (association) (with provisions for the exclusion of non-nobles), regulations aimed at creating a certain demographic imperviousness to avoid the collapse of an already overly-large population, and which would be justified a posteriori through treaties and discussions. In Bizkaia (in 1511 and 1575) and Gipuzkoa (in 1527), laws were instituted prohibiting the residence of Moors, Jews, and converts in the Seigniory. Hence, although it could be said that the foundations for the *foral* system were laid in Bizkaia and Gipuzkoa in the first third of the sixteenth century, it would be another forty years before we began to see the first works produced by theorists and apologists to solidify it ideologically.

A chronology of the development of the *foral* theory, and by extension, of the attacks on and apologies for the Basque language can be formulated as follows: There is an initial period, between approximately 1570 and 1640, in which the imaginary of the Basque ideological construct begins to take shape theoretically through abundant and important contributions, partially of course through the reformulation of preexisting themes, and partially through the development of new theories. Up to the mid-eighteenth century, the already established theories abound in the work of minor writers who make no innovative contributions. Later, between 1750 and 1804, a reformulation of the myth is created on the same general bases but also as a response to other interests and other reformulated declarations. Finally, between 1835 and 1898, a new Basque myth is conceived, which in part destroys the old paradigms and puts new ones in their place, while also bringing some of the old elements up to date.

Concurrent with the theoretical construction of the *Fueros*, which is elaborated almost exclusively in Spanish and French, we see the development of literary production in Basque that assumes a de facto stance that encourages writers to use their own language. However, in many cases it also contains explicit manifestations of an acquired linguistic commitment, in some cases overtly apologist, in others, simply utilitarian. Although these two trajectories initially run parallel, their points of intersection become increasingly more frequent. Thus, we have on the one hand the *foral* theorists, who were, for the most part, lay persons who belonged to an urban bureaucracy and preferred to write in Spanish for an audience abroad, and on the other, writers who used the Basque language and were, for the most part, members of the clergy writing for a domestic audience.

2. Creating the Mythical Construct

Society's ideological construct is a reference system that consists of a collection of representations located on the border between the real and the imagined. The subtle mental structures of the imaginary construct respond to anthropological obsessions (sex, death, identity, and power) and act as powerful engines for perception. This imprecise combination of ideas conditions reactions, opinions, and behavior. The system of values in society, therefore, follows principles that are not necessarily either rational or conscious but are, nonetheless, endowed with great power. In fact, the capacity of imaginary elements to intervene in history is more enduring and more heavily weighted by inertia than those of concrete reality. Hence, we have before us a construct conceived on a nebulous foundation of rumors, legends, myths, beliefs, ambiguous texts, and authoritative sources that, notwithstanding, enjoy a certain degree of plausibility and, above all, serve particular interests. Historical developments, on the one hand, narrow the window of plausibility when certain "commonly accepted" truths start to become implausible and even ridiculous, and on the other, when changes in social, political, and economic interests make the defense of certain beliefs useless and even counterproductive. In any case, as previously stated, the inertia with which these systems of beliefs and values are endowed is enormous and can manifest itself beyond a strict chronological context even after a long period of time.

In the construction of political nationalisms, the recovery of a mythic past, a presumed "Golden Age"—that is, the moment when the conditions for a comprehensive national identity were achieved and then at some later point lost—plays an important role, and its recovery becomes imperative. Ancient kingdoms, empires, and other political formations, generally less real than imagined, make up the memory of that lost paradise. Whether the myth has pagan origins, the mechanism that inspires the entire system is of a religious nature, modeled on Paradise–Guilt–Punishment–Redemption–Recovery of Paradise. The hope of recovering this Golden Age is coupled with the millennia-old beliefs imprinted in the mental universe of Europeans.[3] In this kind of analysis, historical developments are subject to an interesting ellipsis, since the longed-for future is none other than a return to an idealized past, in which the time elapsed between the Fall and the Restoration is only transitory and negligible, something to be denied and negated. All of this occurs within a Manichean and dualistic framework that allows little room for nuance, where the terms goodness/happiness of the paradisiacal age are exclusively juxtaposed with those of evil/misfortune/sin in the Iron Age.[4]

This cyclical concept of the future implies a continuous decline and loss of the natural state of perfection and its successive recoveries (returns). With some subtle distinctions, the idea is expressed in most of the "archaic" and "pre-modern" cultures through the divine creation of human beings, who in correlation to this natural aurous state, possess the perfect faculties to act and communicate; what follows is a progressive degeneration, evidenced in the ancient Greco-Romans and in the three eras of Silver, Bronze, and Iron of Genesis; and finally, the Golden Age returns only to begin again. The cosmic cycles correspond to drastic beginnings and endings: either absolute perfection or utter chaos. The myth of Eternal Return would be the engine fueling historical regeneration preempting class warfare. Two mutually exclusive views of the future of human beings appear in opposition: one of cyclical time with the periodical regeneration of history, and the other of historical time (in the strict sense of the term) with a linear progression and a teleological view of the world. The latter concept began to acquire currency in the seventeenth century (with Bacon, Pascal, and Leibniz) and reached its maximum expression in the nineteenth century with Marxism. In any case, in the historical period we are analyzing, the concept of cyclical time that experienced a periodic regeneration was still dominant. Obviously, the formulation of a theory founded on the recovery of a mythic imagined state requires a certain re-formulation of the aforementioned original myth. In that process, a good number of the elements that figure in that construct are borrowed precisely from the foreign cultural system that brought about the Fall. These elements must be reinterpreted in order to shape a new, supposedly autonomous, original state that would be operative at the moment of effecting the move toward the Restoration.[5]

There is no shortage of references to the Golden Age among the Basque theorists. It seems this was an underlying concept in the existing culture and therefore did not require much explanation. Writing circa 1560, Juan Martínez de Zaldibia, for example, refers in his *Suma de las cosas cantábricas y guipuzcoanas* (Summary of Events in Cantabria and Gipuzkoa) to Cantabria (Vasconia) saying: "Additionally, it is well-known that this nation alone among all the provinces and kingdoms of the world preserves the natural law from before the time when Nino, King of Babylonia, perverted the Golden Age and corrupted the world with idolatry. Only this nation has maintained its original language."[6] Just a few years later, Alfonso Rodríguez de Guevara published a treatise on ancient Spain and the nobility of Cantabria, with the clear understanding that where he refers to Cantabrians he means Bizkaians, identified also as Iberians.[7] In it, he assumed the classical theory that Basque was "that primitive language spoken in Spain when it was first founded."[8] But what is of most interest to us now is the almost literal repetition of what was already stated in Zaldibia, Guevara's idea that Bizkaian nature, and by extension, Basque nature, was the recipient of the spiritual legacy of humanity's first Golden Age, with the Bizkaian law being naturally related to the Golden Age's natural law: "The notorious truth known to all is that this Bizkaian province alone among all the provinces and kingdoms of the world maintains its natural laws from before the time that Nino, King of Babylon, perverted that Golden Age."[9] This system had been transmitted in an undiluted form, since Bizkaia (i.e., Cantabria and Vasconia) had always maintained its political independence and was not conquered by foreign powers. Another curious reference to the existence of ages of gold or iron is made by the painter and historian Francisco Mendieta in his historical piece dedicated to Bizkaia, in which he refers to the civil struggles incited in the Late Middle Ages by the Abendaños—Ruiz de Arteaga, González de Butrón, and by extension all those in the lineage. This age of death and chaos would be the Iron Age, which succeeded the presumed primogenital Golden Age. But following the elimination of factions and the restoration of justice by the monarchy, a new golden age is recovered:

> The deaths in these camps were regrettable, but it was probable that those who perished had been condemned as transgressors of God's precepts and teachings, which forbid murder. And although it is true that in this day and age there is a good deal of malice and resentment, in comparison to that malevolent Iron Age, this is the time we consider the Golden Age, for we are safe from the treacherous criminals that existed at that time, who were the orchestrators of dissent and the protectors of rogues; they had to be punished and brought to justice.[10]

The author who develops a more comprehensive theory, however, is precisely the one who completes the cycle of modern thinking and opens the door to contemporary systems of thought: Agustín Chaho. He dedicated a portion of his early writings to developing a theory that would later provide the basis for the bulk of his work. According to him, the history of humanity was divided into "Eras" lasting 60,000 years each, each one passing on to the next by means of an enormous cataclysm, the last such cataclysm being the Flood. Each Era, in turn, would be comprised of five periods of 12,000 years, and each of these would be further broken down into four "Ages" of 3,000 years, the aforementioned ages of Gold, Silver, Bronze, and Iron.[11] This conception correlates with the secular confrontations of the peoples of the north and south, the former being barbarian and sanguinary, and the latter lucid and civilized. The invasions of the former would temporarily dash the civilizing gains of the latter. The noble, monotheistic culture based on peace, reason, and political liberty clashed with the violent, polytheistic culture, controlled by the tyrannical rule of kings. The two peoples would also be racially drastically different: those of the north being actual giants with pale complexions (the *tartalo* [cyclops] of Basque mythology), those of the south more proportionate in height with dark hair and skin. The passage from one age to another would always be related to invasions and the violent acts of the barbarians from the north upon the cultivated peoples of the south.

Once again, we should recall that these concepts are in the end related to language. In effect, an aurous state corresponds to a natural and perfect language innate in the human species. The notion that a natural language does not need to be acquired and corresponds to the primordial state of man was already alluded to in Astarloa and developed in D'Iharce de Bidassouet. Chaho takes it up without the slightest hesitation. Of course, it goes without saying that the natural language of man would be Basque. In Aitor's own legend, Chaho (through the bard Lara), recounts the first occurrence of the Basque language in Paradise, inspired by the natural God, whose conceptions are always laden with meaning:

> When Basque man and woman were placed in the earthly garden by the hand of God, they gazed upon each other with love, and the woman said to the man: "You are my strength. You are the man that my heart has chosen *(Zu ene arra)*." And since that time, the woman's husband has been called *senarra* in the sacred tongue. Man and woman took one another's hands *(eskua)*, and in the

> intoxication of that enchanted union, they said, *on*: It is good! Nothing is sweeter. Matrimony is known as *eskuontza* among the tribes, because the lovers were wed by the joining of hands. The newlyweds were fed honey, *ezti*, a symbol of perfect pleasure, and from then on the nuptial feasts were called *ezteya*. What other peoples were more inspired by Nature, enriching their intuitions with enchantment and simplicity?[12]

The creators and diffusers of the most effective and interesting imaginative constructs need not be the most original, serious, honest, or rigorous. Rather, they could be the best synthesizers of foreign ideas, those who rely on the most efficient methods of communication, or those who possess the best dialectical resources that provoke reactions and polemics of greatest impact, as for example, Sada or Larramendi; or, still others, who resort to certain mystifications (Ibargüen) that, nevertheless, later on have great repercussions. In some cases, communicative rigor and efficacy coincide. Among the theorists who laid the ideological and theoretical basis to create the modern Basque mythic construct were, in my opinion, Garibay, Poza, and later, Oihenart, followed by Larramendi. Ibargüen-Cachopín's chronicle represents a model for the consolidation and use of foreign materials, offering an even more literary and imaginative version that is, at the same time, much more attractive and susceptible to being mythologized.

3. The Basque Mythical Construct

To begin with, it should be noted that not all of the elements that make up the legitimizing myth of the *Fuero* are exclusive to the Basque Country, nor did they originate there. Religion, monarchy, antiquity, nobility, and Tubalism—all are terms found in the foundational myths of other nations, most notably in the myth that attempts to legitimize the Spanish monarchy. In effect, the majority of the elements that sanction as well as endow the Basque *Fueros* with a sense of timeless immortality are those it shares with the Spanish mythic system. One has the impression that the Basque theorists make a virtue of necessity, so to speak, by taking up Spanish themes and converting them into Basque ones, and through a legitimizing twist, transform the Basques into the most authentic Spaniards: if Tubal founded Spain, he began in Vasconia using the Basque language that would later spread throughout the peninsula, thus making the Basques and their language the most authentic Iberians, and the only ones capable of preserving the essence of Tubalism upon the arrival of foreigners. This theoretical myth attempted to justify the harmonious accords that integrated the Basque territories into the political and economic core of the Spanish monarchy. Although not completely exclusive to the Basque construct, the aspect of language in the theory, an aspect not as central or well developed in other legitimating systems, is certainly the most original one and one which theorists prominently promote as evidentiary in making their case.

As in other legitimating systems, the foundations on which Basque theory rests are essentially religious, relying on external authorities for legitimation. On what is the supposed distinction or superiority of one group of people over another based, according to the interpretive canons of the time? On that group's proximity to those elements assumed to be authentic and true, that is to say, foundational and divine as certified by "serious" and "ancient" authors. If a certain people had enjoyed divine privilege, it would be noted in fact, and if those facts were corroborated by authors—the more famous and older, the better—the matter was proven and settled. If, then, Garibay should cite Lucio Marineo Sículo, Florián de Ocampo, or Flavius Josephus, subsequent writers could rely, in addition to these authors, on Garibay himself, who with the passage of time, would become as ancient and serious as they were. As such, the sum of the evidentiary lists of authoritative texts in the eighteenth century became overwhelming and annoying in the case of some authors. This, however, did not discourage the frequent use of these sources as logical and rational proofs, a practice that seems rather naive and misguided from our current perspective.

What, then, were the elements that solidified the legitimizing apparatus of the Basque *Fuero* after the second half of the sixteenth century? The first such element to consider, not necessarily listed according to its degree of importance, is a sense of autochthony, of being primogenital, original, of having resided in a specific area since time immemorial. This idea is tied as a corollary to the notion of antiquity, since it follows that if the land had indeed always been occupied, then it was so since the most ancient times, or since before recorded time began. The loss of a collective, foundational memory is considered a positive value. Even in the twentieth century, Unamuno declared that "we Basques are timeless people." That "antiquity" suggests degrees or stages does not trouble theorists of that time. As such, the farther back that a family genealogy can be traced, the better. And if the family should find its nobility challenged by another, it would then be compelled to prove the seniority of its lineage to demonstrate its superiority. In some writers, like Pedro de Agramont, this is clearly illustrated:

> I dated this history of Navarre from the time when God created the world to illustrate through the ancestry of Adam and Eve, our original parents, and the holy patriarchal line of Noah, the lineage established by Tubal, founder of Spain, as universal patriarch of the original and true Spaniards, who were superior in antiquity and nobility to the Goths. The diverse customs, language, and traditions that are today preserved in the mountains of Navarre came from those original founders that accompanied him to Spain.[13]

But in addition to having always resided in this territory without outside contact with other peoples, yet another important value was guaranteed to the Basques, namely that they were pure and undefiled. This purity is established through a kind of stasis, which is to say that not only would there be no mix with regard to language or lineage, but there would also be no localized evolution through internal dynamics. Those privileged few who manage to endure unchanged from the moment of their creation, without intermixing, would thus reach a state of perfection. The Basques supposedly maintained such isolation from the rest of the world for centuries. This would explain the preservation of their language, customs, and institutions without alteration. It is not worth devoting even a single paragraph to the myth of isolation, precisely because Euskal Herria lies at an intersection of major crossroads, some of which are critical, like the one in Santiago, as well as coastlines and waterways that penetrate into the region, such as the Ebro River. In addition, the simplest way to traverse the Pyrenees is precisely through the Basque Country. It is, therefore, not surprising that the Celt, Roman, and Arab influences in the region, although not overwhelming, are nonetheless undeniable, and that the incorporation of foreign peoples and cultures is vital and on-going. In spite of arguments to the contrary, the theory, bolstered by the idea of isolation, has been used extensively by apologists to demonstrate an ethnic and linguistic purity, independent political origins, and other such matters. In his *Corografía* (Geography), Larramendi bases his discussion on this presumed isolation, where he refers to the "inherent nobility of Basque blood":

> The Basque nation and Gipuzkoa in particular has been held in higher regard by God than any other in Spain, and perhaps even in the entire world. This small nation has always kept to its northern corner of the globe and has never mixed or intermingled with any of those nations that came from the outside, neither the Moors, the Goths, the Mastiffs, the Vandals, the Romans, the Greeks, the Cartesians, the Phoenicians, nor any others. And the proof lies in

> the Basque language, which clearly distinguishes us from these other peoples. Gipuzkoa knows its blood is in no way related to that of other nations, and its origins, ancestry or genealogy are not to be found in any of them. None of them interfered with its lineage or ancestry. And trusting in these facts, it knows positively that it comes directly without any variation from the sons of Tubal, who populated Spain and whose most noble and pure blood has remained inviolate in spite of the barbarian nations that invaded the rest of Spain with incessant revolutions and wars that ruined families, provinces, nations and kingdoms, and established themselves all over Spain.[14]

Larramendi did nothing less than underscore earlier theories that more or less tied the general nobility of the Basques to what are clearly racist assertions. As an example, we might examine the Franciscan Juan de Luzuriaga's assertions that forced a connection between nobility, the sun, and the color white. As such, the Basques were descendants of the sun *(sol)*; they, therefore, called their noble houses *solares* and they constituted a pure white republic that aesthetically and cosmically counterbalanced the blacks of Ethiopia:

> The Cantabrians are notorious throughout the world for their famous *Solares*, and their *solariegas casas* [noble houses], so called because as descendents of the sun, they see themselves as illustrious as this luminous celestial body. This region is also appropriately called the Land of Whites [*Blancos*], as an antonomastic term, since there exists on earth an Ethiopia made up purely of blacks. In order to counter such a contrast to the beauty of the universe, there exists a Cantabria of pure whites; as was so well written by a Seraphic hand, nobility is to these nations as the color white is to snow.[15]

During the Enlightenment and the Romantic period, the idea of ancient isolation was tied to the concept of the noble savage and to an innate sense of goodness and purity, presumably incarnate in the Basque people. This immutability was also manifest in political terms, by ostensibly having preserved a single system independent of any outside force without any changes. An ancient defense of a sense of independence, a political naiveté coupled with the notion of never having been conquered, and having maintained a supposedly permanent and particular political framework is thus sustained. As shall be seen below, the proof required to bolster the assertion of independence, as an antonomastic term, was demonstrated through the victory over the Romans, for which Basque theorists developed the myth of Cantabrianism, but it was equally necessary to prove that the nation had never been conquered by either the Goths or the Saracens (Moors). The myth of the battle of Padura is thus transformed into the central theme of the Basque mythical construct, whereas the idea that at least Bizkaia and Gipuzkoa had remained free of Muslim control became, for Basque theorists, a recurrent theme, expressed in even more emphatic terms, if that were possible, as an attempt to prove they had not been contaminated by an "abominable" race and religion: "When the valiant Goths, conquerors of the earth, who for many years held the royal throne in Spain, suffered God's justice in the year 719, under the reign of the unfortunate king, Don Rodrigo, . . . these two provinces of Gipuzkoa [Bizkaia and Gipuzkoa] remained immune to such abhorrent destruction.[16]

This sense of immunity to contamination is expressed in terms of continuity in medieval formulations using genealogies. In the same way that medieval historians held a preference for genealogies, the Renaissance theorists, such as Garibay and Mendieta, headed by Lope García de Salazar, used the genealogical method, but instead of applying it to subjects and lineages, they apply it to specific peoples. Hence, the Basque people transmitted "knee to knee" (a Basque expression roughly meaning "from generation to generation") their political and cultural heritage without any intermixing or variation.

This brings us to a preeminent method of categorizing among the Basque people: *apellidismo* (by surnames). A surname would ostensibly provide concrete evidence of the transmission of a pure lineage through the ages, and beyond this, of the peoples themselves. The expression of the continuity and immutability of the lineage through time should tell us something of its noble origins. Accordingly, Basque surnames had to remain constant and meaningful, with an intelligibility and translatability that would correspond to the original house of nobility. The Basque theorists, from Garibay to Poza and Echave, never miss an opportunity when referring to an individual's last name to give its meaning in a Romance language. Having a name linked to a noble house is one of the greatest proofs of lineage. For Juan Huarte de San Juan, a surname is one of the conditions necessary for being ennobled: "I believe man must possess six things to be considered ennobled, and if any one is missing, he will be the lesser for it . . . The fifth thing that ennobles a man is having a good surname and an agreeable first name that is pleasant to the ear, not like Majagraças or Majadero, or others I have heard."[17] Zaldibia clearly links the noble origins of Gipuzkoa with the construction of the first homes in the land: "these houses on the outskirts of the town were built by the nobility who retain their ancient surnames and who were the first settlers of this land, never having paid tax."[18] He claims, therefore, an indissoluble union between nobility, residence, lineage, and surname.[19] Of course, in the case of surnames, and as we shall see later, place names, a device is used that with time becomes both repetitive and obsessive: etymology. Since all surnames are rooted in a house of nobility and constitute a metaphor of its identifying characteristics, they must necessarily have some meaning that alludes to the origins of the nobility that can be uncovered through its etymology. As we shall see when our focus turns to the issue of language, the etymological method becomes a central tool for theorists, regardless of whether they are linguists, and the foundation on which the Tubalist, Basque-Iberian, and Basque-Cantabrian theories rest. I will venture to say here, however, that the etymological method used by Garibay, Poza, and others as proofs in their texts, bestowed, as was common at that time, a greater weight on two sets of names: those that embodied civilization itself, representing cities, or those representing nature, either in mountains or bodies of water.

In any case, this issue of surnames is not a trivial one. Various writers underscore the relationship that exists between the evolution of surnames and the landed nobility in various Basque spaces.[20] As such, surnames during the Middle Ages were made up of three elements in their most noble form: the Christian name, unique to each individual; the patronymic, indicative of the lineage that initially changed with each generation (Pedro's son took the patronymic Pérez, while Juan's took Ibáñez) but that was eventually fixed as an eponym; and lastly, the locative that alluded to the noble house from which it originated. For instance, a complete form of medieval denotation would be: Martín González de Ibarra. In those territories that possessed universal nobility, then, the patronymic began to disappear after the seventeenth century, leaving only the locative. In the southern regions of Araba, and especially in Navarre, the opposite occurred, whereas the rest of Araba (a territory that evolved belatedly and incompletely in relation to the general nobility) was not entirely affected, retaining instead the complete form of surnames. The relation between the predominance of hereditary solidarity, the preservation of the patronymic, and territorial solidarity with the preservation of the locative, seems rather clear.

Having placed such importance on surnames, the Basque theorists, not surprisingly, use them to bolster their arguments on Basque Iberianism and universal nobility. Amid the debates between the *Historia del Búho gallego con las demás aves de España* (Fable of the Galician Owl and Other Birds of Spain) and the *El Tordo vizcaíno* (The Bizkaian Thrush) during the first third of the seventeenth century, the treatise by

Basque writer Martin, *Castellanos y vascongados* (Castilians and Basques), appears. It posits that the families of the highest Spanish nobility have surnames of Basque origin, and offers the appropriate etymologies as proof: "many houses in Castile are descended from [the Basque] and its provinces, such as Mendozas, which is the same as Mendiozas, which means cold mountain; Velascos, who are Veliazcos, which is the same as the House of Ravens; and that of the Duke of Nájera."[21] Of course, the *Tordo vizcaíno* again develops this idea in a much more tedious way:

> This nobility and valor is based on having always supported the Crown of Castile and León; . . . In the victory of Zamora over General Ugarte and in the struggle between Clavijo and Otzoërio Gueiterri over who should bear the standard, those with this surname have their origins in Bizkaia, because Otzoërio means "slayer of wolves" *Gueiterri* is the same as *montañiz*, one who always walks in the woods, and when corrupted the name becomes *Osorio Gutierrez* or *Gutierre Osorio*. And there are many other Basque surnames in Spain, although corrupted in their origins, as in Mendozas from *Mendioza*, cold mountain; Velasco, Vélez, Velásquez from *Velea*, raven; Ochoas from *Ochoa*, wolf; Arces from *Arça*, bear; Graces, García, Iñigos, Fortúñoz, Ortúñoz, Ortizes, and others; though some who are vain and curious look for their origins in other foreign kingdoms, as if the nobility of Bizkaia were lesser than that of the Goths, Germans, French and Italians, all mixed together and several times defeated, while Bizkaia, as ever, remains on top.[22]

Toward the end of the eighteenth century, the erudite Hervás y Panduro founded his argument about the ancient universal spread of Basque throughout the Iberian Peninsula on the pretense that most Spanish surnames were rooted in Basque, and to that end, he produced a tiresome list of these surnames to which he assigned real or fictitious etymologies as proof.

All of this brings us to what constitutes the original nucleus of the Basque mythic construct: the notion of universal nobility. In short, we are discussing here the passage from a classical medieval system, based on patrimony, to another, based on territorial solidarity, in which the family identifies with the noble house of residence, and by extension, with the collective nobility made up of the various individual nobles in the territory. The extension of nobility to the territory in a generalized fashion occurs in different ways in the Basque region: in Bizkaia,

Gipuzkoa, and the northern valleys of Araba and Navarre, it is ubiquitous; in Zuberoa, it occurs to a lesser extent, and in Lapurdi, it is even more subdued. The extension of nobility to all the inhabitants of a territory ended in a democratic victory resulting in a kind of juridical egalitarianism, although not social or economic. The theory developed by Poza, among others, is that the territories of the nobility in Bizkaia (or in other Basque territories) existed before the Spanish monarchy, since time immemorial, and therefore could not be subject to Spanish laws. Echave and Isasti had a similar reading for Gipuzkoa. The idea that an original nobility, and not one established by royal concession, extended to the territories and therefore to all their inhabitants in terms of equality was schematized by Garibay and Zaldibia and later developed by Echave and Isasti especially. The egalitarian theory is a myth of origins that attempts to justify a previous social order while avoiding a historical midpoint that would patently contradict the principles that inspired it, namely, in our case, the long feudal rule of the original forebears.

It appears that the egalitarian theories formulated by theorists in the second half of the sixteenth century laid the foundations for the development of a series of ideological, fraternal, and egalitarian trends (which had already begun to emerge in the early 1380s), that were more or less connected with millennial projects (such as the Beghards, the Brotherhood of the Free Spirit, etc.) which tried to form a horizontal solidarity that would stand against the dominant, vertical, lineal solidarities that tended to consolidate the authority of the Seigniory. In political terms, this meant a confrontation between the Brotherhoods and the power of the feudal lords. In some areas, the former clearly triumphed, while in others, they were defeated and in still others, a compromise was reached. In general, in Euskal Herria, the triumph of the Brotherhoods is evident during the first decade of the sixteenth century, although this does not mean to imply that the power of the lords was completely abolished. By contrast, the feudalism of the original forebears was not felled by a single blow when some members of the most combative family lines were exiled to Andalusia and their castles were brought down. Rather, it survived into the middle of the seventeenth century during which it resurfaced periodically. The economic apex of the sixteenth century, the connection with the Latin American economy, the influx of capital, the quelling of rebellions, and the end of internal strife, all permitted the rise of the bourgeoisie. From that time on, a dual system of political control (municipal and provincial) arose through the two tiers of dominant classes: the *millares* (tracts of land) controlled economically by the bourgeoisie and the security payments controlled by the nobility.

As noted above, between the fifteenth and seventeenth centuries a great number of judicial decrees were issued, aimed at formulating the generalized nobility for different territories, Bizkaia, Gipuzkoa, Baztan (Navarre), Zuberoa, etc., and restricting the rights of residence of those who were not original inhabitants and had not proven their nobility. Bizkaia, for example, in the *Fuero Nuevo* (New *Fuero*) of 1526, included a legal title that read: "In Bizkaia, no one shall reside who is of Jewish or Moorish descent, and any residents must provide proof of their lineage,"[23] along with a Royal Decree issued by Queen Juana in 1511 with the same intent. Of course, Bizkaia had to be considered in its entirety, not just the *Tierra Llana*,* but also the *villas* (chartered towns), however urban and commercial they might have been. As such, the *villas* themselves created similar agreements in their ordinances, establishing a procedure to follow in cases where the purity of the bloodline had to be determined. A case in point was Bilbao, which was at that time an important commercial center that served as the link between Castile and the territories of northern Europe, and therefore relied on a network of contacts that required a connection with people of diverse cultures and beliefs. This did not prevent the inclusion, in its ordinances of 1564, of an article stipulating the need to prevent the residence of those with impure blood and regulating in minute detail the way inquiries were to be made:

> No person of any state, quality, or condition who wishes to reside in said town should dare to take up residence or call himself a resident of this town without first presenting himself before the court and the magistrate to state that he has always been from this *villa*. After such declaration, he shall be asked to present a statement, and in said statement, he shall provide the names of his grandfather and grandmother, mother and father, and the rest of the ancestors he can recall. And he shall further state where his grandparents and parents resided or lodged and what occupation they had . . . so that it may be ascertained if they are Old Christians and of pure blood on all sides, without any intermixing of Jews or Moors, and stating

---

* Municipal organization in Bizkaia implied a complex process of uniting diverse juridical and territorial elements. In general terms, there was a distinction between, on the one hand, the twenty-one *villas* or municipalities, urban centers with an exclusive status based on a foundational charter, and on the other, the Tierra Llana (the original countdom and core of Bizkaia), areas formed by councils, valleys and *anteiglesias* (parishes) with their own system whose reference point was that of the Seigniory.

> their lineage and other qualities which said decree stipulates; and being of such and such lineage, those who present themselves shall be permitted residence, and those who do not meet these conditions, shall not be permitted to reside.[24]

The egalitarian doctrine was connected to the nobility and to the fiscal and political rights they enjoyed at that time. As such, the first inhabitants of the territory would claim the established noble houses and then transmit through well-known surnames the original nobility to their successors. Certainly, this presumed original settlement would have occurred with none other than Tubal, for which the egalitarian theorists rely on Garibay as one of their fundamental references. If one accepts this Tubalist theory, then its extension of nobility to all of these first settlers and their descendents follows, and this is precisely what Zaldibia asserts,[25] by defining the group of the first settlers who never paid tax over time and who settled in castles where the original nobility resided. The next step was to demonstrate that all the members of a territory came from the same first families without having mixed with external bloodlines, which had been the case since the middle of the sixteenth century. If, therefore, it was demonstrated that a specific territory had been settled by those of the same origins and that they had transmitted, intact and without contamination to their successors, their ethnic background and in that same territory all the bloodlines were equally pure, that territory would have a natural rather than a concessional universal nobility bestowed upon it. But in fact, by the sixteenth century the system had begun to work in reverse; because it was supposed that all the original inhabitants in the territory were nobles, proof that a territory was original lay precisely in the fact that it was inhabited by nobles. Conversely, if an alien or non-native wanted to settle, he would have to prove his nobility before being admitted. To maintain the juridical guise of universal nobility, it would not be at all convenient to have individuals residing in the territory that obviously belonged to "damned races" or simply those who were not nobles, which is why the ordinances in those areas that attained this status were careful to include strict regulations for admission to residence, placing all sorts of obstacles in the way of those not ennobled and even decreeing their expulsion.

A writer in the second half of the sixteenth century who takes on the subject of universal nobility in an original way is Juan Arce de Otalora, who was originally from Valladolid but had Basque ancestors, and was a lawyer and judge in the chanceries of Granada and Valladolid. In 1510, he published a book that dealt with the nobility of the Bizkaians.[26] As to whether nobility was universal in Bizkaia, he only considered the original forebears, made no juridical statements, and determined a single case at a time; still, he proposed a solution as original as it is absurd, but of particular interest because it is rooted in language: he established a link, making the Basques the descendants of the Goths. Because the latter were the prototype for the Spanish nobility, the Basques would also have universal nobility. The solution once again would be found in the language. Basque was the same language spoken by the Goths and was preserved in certain territories that used it to validate their universal nobility: "The language that the Goths spoke then was kept alive in those who took refuge in the Pyrenees, along the great sea, who remain in the valley of Roncal [Erronkari], Salazar [Zaraitzu], Esena, and Santisteban [Doneztebe], and their environs, and who descend into Gipuzkoa, and along the coastline into Araba and Bizkaia."[27] Following Garibay and Zaldibia, Echave clearly explicated the idea that those belonging to a noble line of descendants of the first residents were nobles, not only through family, but also because the province had a single noble house in common:

> Whence it is clear that the nobility is one, and so ancient, that it is the highest and most sacred, as some say, and uninterrupted, and that through the ages has grown and remained alive with all the requisites that a true nobility requires: These noble houses have come to the defense of the homeland, religion, kings, and princes to whom they have entrusted their loyalty. It should also be noted that not only do the renowned sons of noble blood hail from these houses, but above all, these provinces are of acknowledged nobility and renowned for their noble sons.[28]

The theorist who lays the final stone in this ideological structure is Lope Martínez de Isasti.[29] The nobility of those native and original inhabitants of the province of Gipuzkoa relied on the notion of having remained uncontaminated by foreign nations with regard to the lineages of the noble houses, the Basque language, the clothes they wore, and their way of life. This is to say that the noble house and surname, as well as the language and ethnographic features, were the foundations on which the collective nobility rested. This was a natural nobility, not one bestowed by kings, but a function of primal origins, obtained by the first inhabitants and transmitted through generations to their successors, in such a way that it would not be lost even if some of these individuals worked in lowly occupations, since their roots had already been laid. The collective Basque nobility, therefore, was compatible with professions that were not noble. In any case, in connection with this matter, the ideas that various theorists who were concerned with this subject began to develop and gradually became more attuned to the development of political and, above all, economic affairs. Zaldibia established the origins and basis of the Basque nobility. Huarte de San Juan felt that this theory was not in accord with work in servile occupations, and that in undertaking them, nobility was lost. Isasti, however, made a clear distinction between two different types of nobility, that of privilege, which is tied to a certain noble lifestyle that would be tainted by manual labor, and nobility established through lineage, that cannot be lost through these types of occupations. In addition, Isasti draws a distinction between nobility and wealth, since they might not go hand in hand. Juan Huarte de San Juan synthesizes his ideas on nobility here in a presumed dialogue between Prince Carlos and his justice of the peace in Alcalá:

> Prince: Which king in my ancestral line created your noble lineage?
>
> Doctor: None, for your highness should know that there are two types of noble houses in Spain: one of blood and the other of privilege. Those who are noble through their bloodline, as I am, did not receive their nobility through a king, but the others did . . . But we call nobles by birth men for whom there is no memory of their origin nor any written record when the lineage began or which king may have bestowed nobility on them; and this mystery is regarded by the republic as more honorable than clear knowledge to the contrary . . . The fourth thing that gives a man esteem is having an honorable profession. But on the other hand, nothing debases man as much as making his living in a servile occupation.[30]

Let us now examine the way Isasti takes up this subject again a few years later:

> The nobility of the native and original inhabitants of Gipuzkoa is well known throughout the world, since its noble houses have remained from the beginning pure and without any mixing with foreign lands, as is evidenced in its Basque language, its customs, and way of life . . . Let it be known that those of noble bloodline, especially those from Gipuzkoa, do not lose their nobility through servile, necessary occupations, even when they have fallen on extreme poverty, because nobility through bloodline did not begin with them; rather, it came from their forbears and their lineage, and it is enough that it was in effect then even if in the present it is no

> longer the case . . . Tiraquelo adds that the professions of stonemasons, carpenters, silversmiths, and blacksmiths are not vile arts.[31]

This extremely important subject of making universal nobility compatible with lowly professions was repeatedly taken up by theorists after the seventeenth and even up to the eighteenth century. The anonymous author of *El Tordo vizcaíno* approaches it from an interesting point of view by connecting it to iron work. In this way, metalworking is transformed exactly into one of the elements of Basque identity as an expression of the people's ancient heartiness and independence, which rather than undermine their nobility, actually justified it:

> Notwithstanding these fine points, some ingrate will try to debase its innocence by referring to them disparagingly as blacksmiths, since iron is the most common metal in the region, but the cause is sanctioned from the heavens above, because Bizkaia has always remained invincible, intact, and honorable. And because iron is the strongest of metals, they have also remained most true in the defense of their country, its laws, customs, and nobility; and because iron prevails over other metals, they too prevail over their enemies, without ever having suffered defeat . . . Even the presence of blacksmiths does not dull its glory, for to attain glory one must wield iron. Although these professions may seem lowly, they are very important to this nation...[32]

Like pieces of a puzzle, the various elements interconnect with one another. In this way, egalitarianism among the Basques is related to their nobility and their nobility to a racial purity and political independence. Or, conversely, an ancient independence leads to purity and from there to a general nobility, and because all are nobles, they are equals, which leads to an age-old solidarity. Solidarity among the Basques, whether real or not, was a trait perceived by outsiders, and it reappears persistently throughout the seventeenth and eighteenth centuries. Logically, it is more evident among the communities of Basques who reside in other parts of the empire: Madrid, Seville, Cádiz, Peru, Mexico, etc. As an example, we point to a paragraph on the subject in the anonymous work *El Tordo vizcaíno*, which makes a clearly racist statement: The purity derived from the lack of contamination produces a nobility and a sense of worth in all the Basques, independent of the fact that providence might make some richer or more powerful than others:

> The admirable brotherhood of the Basques results from this. There is no nation in the world that exceeds the Basque in unity, affection,

> love, or that gives greater preference to their own, holding each other in esteem, not as fellow countrymen but as true brothers. That devotion to the language and the homeland, that piety, that kindness, that brotherhood, as in the immediate offer of a handshake, are all founded on the identity of a pure bloodline. An authentic Basque will not disdain another, rather he will try to support, lend a hand, provide help, take him under his wing, and help certify his nobility, because he knows that the same blood cannot produce different results. Some may be fortunate, but the less fortunate deserve the same, for all have the same obligations and deserve the same positions, whether by merit or by luck, for some have advantages that they do not deserve and others who do deserve them, are less fortunate. This brotherhood has flourished most in the populous and rich city of Seville, from which those in the Peruvian and Mexican territories hail...[33]

A general tendency in the arguments of all theorists is the acknowledgement of an egalitarianism "since before recorded history," creating an abstraction and an ellipsis of the none-too-distant and certainly nonegalitarian ancestral domain. When on occasion those days are referred to (Zaldibia), those ancestors are presented in the guise of paternalistic tutors watching over all aspects of society. Echave refers to them as "highly virtuous" and adds: "our original forbears, for many centuries and with constant and illustrious deeds, virtue, and prudence have governed and led the other noble houses."[34] In some cases, attempts to reconcile the contradictions—feudal oppression/egalitarianism—are greater, since the theorists themselves have lineages that go back to the original forbears. Garibay as well as Zaldibia are descendants of the forbears, however indirectly, and in their works, they touch on the ancient genealogies and the situation that arose from them, the burning of Arrasate-Mondragón, the challenge to the *villas*, etc. Nonetheless, in no way are they apologists for this state of affairs. On the contrary, they support the new order of the monarchy, the Brotherhoods, the Province, etc.

Only Francisco de Mendieta, a contemporary of the aforementioned theorists, is a strong critic of the *señorial* system and its supporters, comparing it to the monarchic system in place at the time, which he characterizes as just and restorative. This unusual individual deserves further consideration. Although trained in law, he did not thrive in that realm. As a painter, he did not master the canvas, and as a writer of history, he was more of a plagiarizer. Notwithstanding all of this, Mendieta achieved an interesting ideological synthesis of the *foral* system, expressed as much in his work as a historian as in his painting. He lived in the second half of the sixteenth century, taking up residence in Bilbao in close proximity to his mentor and protector, the painter Francisco Velázquez. He painted various altars and paintings in churches in Bilbao and Bergara (Vergara), but the works in oil that interest us are those known as *Jura de los Fueros de Vizcaya por Fernando V (el Católico)* (Oath of Allegiance to the *Fuero* of Bizkaia by Fernando V [the Catholic]); *Boda de hidalgos* (Noble Wedding), and *Procesión en Begoña* (Procession in Begoña). These works represent to some degree an iconographic representation of the mental and ideological universe of the time. One might say that he was a "social" painter in that he translated onto the canvas the dominant ideas of his time. The first of the three is without a doubt the most political and deliberate of his paintings. According to various writers, the work could have been produced between 1590 and 1609, but it did not attract much attention until 1828, at the height of Romanticism, when it was placed in a prominent spot in the newly constructed *Casa de Juntas* (General Assemblies Building) in Gernika. From there, it was moved to the seat of Provincial Government and later to the Museum of Fine Arts (both in Bilbao), with a copy left in the General Assemblies Building in Gernika. The subject of the piece could not be more emblematic of the *foral* system: the pact between the king and the Bizkaians in which the former agrees to honor the *Fueros* and the latter to obey the king's authority. The oath of allegiance was taken in 1476. King Fernando is represented as the founder of a new pact or system that triumphs over factionalism: loyalty from the nobility and stability on the part of the monarchy—the nobility's pact with the king. The heraldry of the noble houses is also prominently represented, along with the women in headdresses that symbolize the various communities, and other notable individuals. The inscription above the throne where the king is seated reads: "Here, the most noble Prince that ever was swore an oath to Bizkaia beneath this oak tree to uphold the *Fuero*," and of course, the Tree of Gernika figures prominently in the composition. There is another inscription written in Basque at the foot of the tree. Here the use of the Basque language cannot be accidental as it is a clear link between the linguistic and the political, for at a time when all public documents were written in Spanish, writing an explanation in Basque cannot be unintentional. The text is as follows: "*Au da nola milla ta laureun ta yrurogueta amasei urteeta Garagarrillen ogueta amargaren egun erregue jau Fernando bosgarrena guernicaco arbolen bean bizcaitarrai confirmadu eguinezan euren foruac ta eurac berajauntçat ecutea*" (In this manner, on 30 July 1476, King

Fernando V made a pledge to the Bizkaians beneath the Tree of Gernika to uphold the *Fuero* and they to take him as their lord).

All of his historical works remained unpublished: his treatise on the noble families of Bizkaia and Gipuzkoa entitled *Erario de la Hidalguía y nobleza Española y plaza de armas de Vizcaya* (Treasure Chest of the Spanish Aristocracy and Nobility and Grand Army Square of Bizkaia), as well as *Casas Solariegas y de Apellido que ay en la Muy Noble y Muy Leal Provincia de Guipuzcoa* (The Noble and Surnamed Houses in the Most Noble and Most Loyal Province of Gipuzkoa) and his *Annales de Vizcaya* (Annals of Bizkaia), which according to the title were recorded by order of the Seigniory. These were chronicles presented to the General Assemblies of the two provinces in 1592. Most of the text has been lost. A quarter of the manuscript was preserved in the National Library and later edited by Juan Carlos Guerra at the beginning of the twentieth century.[35] This section of the work deals with the reigns of Enrique III and Juan II, from 1399–1456, and in particular, the factional wars, especially those waged by the Salazares and Marroquines. The text virtually plagiarizes the *Bienandanzas y Fortunas* (Prosperity and Fortunes) of Lope García de Salazar but with a distinctly different intellectual tone. Mendieta combines his background in art and law with his interest in genealogy, heraldry, ethnography, and philology and presents a modern vision for his time. This makes his work suggestive. Of course, Mendieta is a Tubalist[36] and a purist who is imbued with ethnic pride. On the other hand, he opposes medieval factionalism with a post-Renaissance modernity. Although Salazar describes the wars between factions without the slightest hint of moral criticism, Mendieta is at pains to discredit, condemn, and decry bitterly the destruction of the country. He presents a powerful contrast to the notion of political stability, justice, and respect for the *Fuero* offered by the Spanish kings, and especially by Felipe II:

> As the narrative of this chronicle has demonstrated, there was never a time in which Bizkaia did not experience civil war, led purely by the will to conquer and by the desire of the strong to dominate the weak, who periodically aided those of one noble lineage or another, so that all of Bizkaia was burned by continuous wars, deaths, casualties, thefts, violence, and pilfering . . . people had become like rabid dogs, killing without regard for law or reason. Many times, I have wondered how these people survived, given that the land was barren, and they were so indolent. What little they had, they burned and destroyed, so much so that it seems to me that all of Bizkaia would not suffice to provide for a group of three thousand men for

> fifteen days, not to speak of one hundred years, during which wars were so common. It is impossible that they could have survived, especially if they drank wine then the way they do today, although it is true that in those days there was no wine in Bizkaia, except in each district a variety known as *Chiriboga*, administered to the sick, while those who were well drank only cider, and they were the stronger and healthier for it. And they were no more elegant in their dress. They used linen kerchiefs, and even the highest lords wore long breeches with lined, fitted coats that went down to their thighs and bells on their sleeves. They left their heads bare, but wore a long braid that went down to below their ears, and they were clean-shaven, like clerics. They carried machetes, daggers, lances, and small spears or crossbows. For them, war was a pastime and peace was an annoyance, as Horace, Lucio Floro, and other historians have claimed. And although they were aware of it, they were on a road straight to hell and did not care, as part of a bargain struck with the original forbears, with whom they would be enjoying the fruits of their labors. Bizkaia can consider itself fortunate, for in our time it enjoys great tranquility because justice has sunk deep roots, no one need doubt that without it, those passions of the sort I have seen would be rekindled, as I have witnessed among simple people, including women, competing over which one is better, Oñez or Gamboa, as if one group were better than another, blinded by the devil . . . There were so many deaths and so much chaos in Bizkaia and Gipuzkoa on account of the original forbears, in whose interests the murderers and evil doers acted, that the common people grew weary of it and in some areas of Gipuzkoa created brotherhoods, and in the name of justice and without regard for Oñez and Gamboa, they revolted against them and overthrew all the noble houses, such as those of Lazkao [Lazcano], Ayarza, Amezketa [Amézqueta], Ugarte, Alzaga...[37]

Finally, Mendieta underscores the importance of the reforms on the *Fuero* of Bizkaia in 1452. He recounts how, before the General Assembly of Idoibalzaga, Bizkaians proclaim before the *Corregidor* (the Chief Magistrate, or principal representative of the Crown in the province) how "they had their privileges and exemptions and freedoms and other Bizkaian *Fueros* of their own free will, and that there was no record of the amount of damage, harm, and deceit that had befallen them...," and they asked that the *Fuero* be written and that the King agree to it. The *Corregidor* accepted and said that King Juan would come to Bizkaia to swear an oath to the *Fueros*.[38]

Mendieta is not by any means the only theorist who emphasizes the peace, prosperity, and justice that reigned during the rule of Felipe II, before the arbitrariness of that age of factionalism. At the heart of the theory of the *Fuero* in the sixteenth century lies this supposed pact between the community and the king and the great benefits that it supposedly grants to both parties. Monarchy and *Fuero* are the essence of the *foral* system. Poza, for example, is another supporter of the monarchy and especially of Felipe II for his rigorous support of the conditions stipulated by the *Fuero* of Bizkaia. In his *Antigua lengua...* (Ancient language...), he states that the Bizkaians "live as free and easy as they please" and in his *Ad pragmaticas...* he emphasizes again that "under these laws, [the Bizkaians] have entrusted themselves to the glorious Kings of Castile and are at present delighted and full of praise for our lord King Felipe."[39] Other Basque theorists, such as Guevara and Zaldibia, insist on demonstrating that the lineage of the kings of Spain was in part *cántabro* (that is, Basque), with which they achieved two objectives: on the one hand, the union between the monarchy and Vasconia was strengthened, and on the other, even the slightest fissure over whether the Basques had been conquered by outsiders could be avoided, since the Spanish kings themselves had Basque blood. The theorists insisted, as such, that Don Pelayo had a Goth father and a Basque mother: "His Majesty is a natural Spaniard, having descended from Tubal through the line of *cántabros*, although there are Spanish writers who say that Pelayo was of Goth lineage, as was the Bishop Don Alonso de Cartagena, in the book on the genealogy of the kings of Spain. Through the maternal line, however, it is certain that the kings of Spain were descended from the *cántabros,* who had not been completely conquered by any nation in the world."[40] Martín de Aguirre, a professor at the University of Bologna, born in Azpeitia (Gipuzkoa), is another classicist of the *Fuero* theory. His work *Responsum...* (Response...)[41] argues in defense of the rights of Felipe II to the Portuguese throne. For him, governance lay within the realm of the people's rights, and as such, it should be based on a pact between the king and his subjects. The system of government, therefore, was limited. In the Basque case, the *Fuero* precedes the king and therefore he is obligated to respect it. Were the line that founded the pact eliminated, the monarchy would revert to being elective and a new one would have to be founded.

In any case, Garibay developed the most definitive theory based on the monarchy and on Felipe II. First, in an unofficial capacity and later, from 1592 on, as the official chronicler of the Crown, Garibay became one of the most successful intellectuals to legitimate (through a genealogical methodology) the presumed rights of the Spanish monarch, and by extension, of the monarchy itself. Maintaining the same line as Zaldibia, he lays the basic groundwork of the *foral* system: universal nobility, allegiance to the Crown, and a voluntary union with Castile. He first posits that the Gipuzkoans "are in favor of maintaining the nobility, and of upholding the bloodline, and of defending their general and specific rights and privileges, as good patricians, and champions of the universal good."[42] But it is in on the subject of the voluntary union that Garibay places the greatest theoretical emphasis. If the immemorial independence of Gipuzkoa were regarded as a corollary of its universal nobility, the latter would be compromised by the process of political dependence on the kingdoms of Navarre and Castile. It would have to be "demonstrated" that the incorporation of the territory was done through a pact and voluntary unification, and because it was done independently, it was merely a personal union with the king and not with the Crown.[43] An argument so difficult to prove had no shortage of detractors, and Garibay became its apologist. So after the accountant of the Duke of Infantado, Pedro de Alcocer, published his *Hystoria, o descripción de la imperial cibdad de Toledo* (History or Description of the Imperial City of Toledo), claiming that Gipuzkoa had been conquered—a direct challenge to the proposition of voluntary unity—Garibay and Friar Juan de Alzolaraz, the general of the Jerónimos, a native of Zestoa (Cestona), were sent by the Assembly of Tolosa (16 April 1559) to debate with Alcocer, in the presence of the Duke himself. Alcocer backed off his claims and agreed to revise his works on this point.[44] By the seventeenth century, the voluntary union of Gipuzkoa with Navarre and the equally voluntary separation of the two, and Gipuzkoa's association with Castile, had become commonly accepted among the Basque theorists. The *Tordo vizcaíno* sheds more light on the process: Castile was more fertile ground for the Gipuzkoans to channel their enterprising spirit and bellicose nature in the war against the Moors: "The union of Gipuzkoa to Navarre was voluntary; it found itself needing to sever a bad relationship, because the conditions were not being honored and the Kings of Navarre became tyrannous, and their natural spirit could not be crushed. Castile was more welcoming and offered better employment for their sons, and there the wars against the Moors were more active."[45]

In the case of Bizkaia, there is an interesting trajectory in the construction of the theory of an independence from time immemorial, the voluntary unification, and the *Fuero*. It first appears in the *Livro dos linhages* (Book of Lineages) (1343) by Count Barcelos, the illegitimate son of the King of Portugal, Dionis I, and friend of the lord of Bizkaia, Juan Núñez de Lara. The book mentions the battle of Arrigorriaga in the ninth century during which the Bizkaians, led by Froom, brother of the English king, maintained their independence. From that time until the first sign of Basque nationalism in the nineteenth century, Arrigorriaga becomes the inevitable point of reference, proof of independence before the Kingdom of León. Lope García de Salazar follows later with his *Crónica de Vizcaya* (Chronicle of Bizkaia) (1454) as well as his *Bienandanzas y Fortunas* (1475), in which the leader and first lord of Bizkaia following the battle is Jaun Zuria, nephew of the Scottish king. Salazar introduces the important element of the pact: Jaun Zuria is considered lord once he agrees to take the oath granting liberties to the Bizkaians. Now, according to Salazar, this pact appears to have been made between the lord and the nobles of the Seigniory, not with all those native to the territory. Poza (in his *Ad pragmáticas*) follows this idea, but with an extremely important innovation: the pact is now made between Jaun Zuria and all Bizkaians, thereby territorializing the nobility. Zaldibia, likewise, always refers to "the Bizkaians" in a generic form and links the battle of Padura (Arrigorriaga) to the independence of the noble houses in the Seigniory: "they are quite free, pay no tax, and have great privileges; in Bizkaia there are many noble houses and nobles, referred to as the *Infanzonazgo* [Noble Land] of Bizkaia."[46]

The need of the Bizkaian and Gipuzkoan authorities to find documentary proof of the presumed foundational pact is quite interesting. Araba had such a proof: the document of the pact of the Brotherhood of Arriaga; but the other Basque territories did not. As such, the search reached the point that in the middle of the seventeenth century, the *Juntas* (Assemblies) of Gipuzkoa offered a substantial prize of 4,000 ducats for the person who could find the document. This served as motivation for Antonio Lupián Zapata (whose real name was Antonio de Nobis) in 1664 to turn over to the *Juntas* a text that turned out to be counterfeit, with the obvious objective of collecting the great prize. Yet despite its inauthenticity, the document was used widely as proof.

The theorists from Navarre, Sada, and Agramont, represent an important confluence in the relationship between the monarchy and the community: a defense of the power of the kingdom over the king. Navarre, according to these writers, had been voluntarily inserted as a distinct kingdom as long as it could maintain its *foral* status. On the other hand, although they had no intention of extending nobility to the entire kingdom, there was a concern that nobility would be granted to the territories "of the Mountain," where Tubal had settled and had left the usual legacy: Euskara, customs, dress, ...and universal nobility. Both Sada and Agramont, whose apologist bent is evident, are at pains to define nobility, to have it hark back as far as possible and apply it triumphantly to the kingdom of Navarre or at least to its mountains. As the latter states, "it will be good to situate the origins and beginning of the nobility,"[47] and by so doing, he bases it and establishes it at the origins of the world: "For which, it is known that since the origins of the world, fathers and mothers had both good and noble children and bad and villainous ones. Of Adam's children, Abel was good and noble, whereas Cain was bad and villainous. Of Noah's children, Shem and Japheth were good and Ham was bad. Of Abraham's children,..." Aside from a theological nobility that anyone can achieve with saintliness, Agramont is concerned with a political nobility, which truly establishes distinctions between men, defining it as follows: "Political nobility comes to men through lineage, or through learning, as was declared in the second of the *Siete Partidas* (the laws of Castile, established by Alfonso X), third law, title nine concerning nobility: that it comes from being erudite and observing proper customs. Finally, nobility, according to Boethius, is a result of the worth of the progenitors." But what basis does Agramont use for his argument on the superiority of the nobility in the mountains of Navarre? "The mountains of Navarre preserve the nobility, language, habits, and dress of the primitive inhabitants, the origins of the noble houses, and the castles of Spain." In sum, the argument presents a compilation of those of previous writers but with an original and interesting addition. To begin with, of course, the Basque language was brought to Navarre by Tubal, whose descendants spread it to the rest of Spain. This and other possible shared features, and inherent in the original nobility of Tubal (according to Agramont), had however been lost at some point in history on the rest of the peninsula and were to be found only in Navarre: "In Spain, no one is to be found who preserves the same clothing, language, dress and way of life that existed in the time of Tubal." Therefore, the rugged way of life of the people in the mountainous Basque-Navarre regions would serve as proof of the continuation of Tubal's legacy: they dressed in sackcloth and brogans, slept on straw mattresses, lived in rustic houses of stone and earth, and ate wild game and dried meats... "And so it is that these mountain dwellers, who left their homes for the farthest reaches of Castile, seem to be from another world, since nothing is known about the way they dress and no one can understand a word they say."

But aside from cultural differences, Agramont notes three other features worth mentioning that are characteristic of the nobility of Navarre. First, the abundance of noble estates built in Navarre before the arrival of the Goths, from which many nobles from Spain and elsewhere are descended; second, the fact that Navarre served as a refuge when needed: "These mountains are so rugged that they have always served as a sacred refuge for Catholics and their peoples, and as a place to restore the faith during all the trials that Spain has faced as has been documented in the histories of all times and all nations, in wars, droughts, and persecution, without any of these perverting or destroying the natural languages, customs, and dress of this land." But the third feature is the most original one of all: the particular customs of the people of the mountainous region of Navarre, that is, their work. In establishing the fact that these people from the mountainous region dedicate themselves exclusively to gathering fruit and especially to shepherding, Agramont also asserts that not only do they not lose their nobility by undertaking this kind of manual labor, but it is precisely this labor that constitutes a characteristic feature of their Tubalesque essence, the evidence of their natural and primitive state:

> They maintain the custom of shepherding and gathering fruit, and although they are themselves shepherds, they have not lost their nobility; rather they take pride in imitating kings, prophets and ancient patriarchs, because Moses, who became leader of God's people when God appeared in the bush, and David, whom God called king, were shepherds. And Abel was a shepherd, and shepherds were the first to arrive at Christ's birth, and Jacob and his brother-in-law Lam were shepherds. And in the time of the gentiles, shepherds were considered saints. Romulus and Remus, founders of the Roman empire that ruled the entire world, were shepherds. And from these mountains many went out and became powerful, but those who remained maintained themselves strong and free, as evidenced in their noble feats, demonstrating that they have retained their original nature, as robust and strong now as in those times.[48]

Another supposedly typical feature of the Basque character that they managed to turn in their favor as a factor underpinning their worth within the structure of the Spanish monarchy should be mentioned: their violent natures and their propensity for war. When Sebastián de Covarrubias stated in his *Tesoro* (Treasury) that "the Bizkaians are a ferocious people who are not happy unless they are waging war,"[49] he was merely expressing a point of view that was well established by the beginning of the seventeenth century. A few years later, the author of the *Tordo vizcaíno* himself shared this same view almost to the letter, when he referred to those individuals of this nature: "They cannot live without war, for they live to bear arms, and a life not spent in war is a damnable one . . . But the youth who have the strength to work, develop from birth an aversion to lighter, easier professions, and give themselves over either to the cultivation of the fields or to the rigors of Mars. All their lives are spent with arms; whether they are taming a young bull or tilling the soil with a plow, their lances never leave their hands . . . Their greatest joy is coming home each day with new spoils, and living off the game they hunt with their lances."[50] But the *Tordo vizcaíno* also indicates the direction in which so much bellicosity is channeled: in the service of the monarchy, where the Basques fought in every memorable battle and secured the borders against enemy attack, especially against the French:

> The Catholic king, Don Fernando, used the Basques against the Portuguese to repel them from Zamora, to repel the French from Perpiñan, to occupy Navarre, to conquer Granada; he used the Basques in all battles, and because of this he was undefeated, feared, and considered a peace broker in Europe. Who brought Princess Juana to Flanders, if not a Basque? Who conquered Gelves, if not a Basque? Who gathered the relics in Ravenna, if not a Basque? Who taught the Spanish to sail, if not the Basques? Where were vessels built to reach Africa, to conquer its shores, to defend the Atlantic and the Mediterranean, if not in this land? Who were the pilots, the grandmasters, corporals, and generals, if not the Basques? On land and sea, the valiant and never defeated Basques were known to be invincible, prodigious, admirable, victorious, and triumphant for themselves and their lords and kings, for whom they overcame hunger, thirst, heat, and cold, and everywhere conquered the elements, always victorious, never defeated.[51]

The ostensible ferocity of the ancient Basques (referred to as *Cántabros*), who would rather die than be conquered and were content only when fighting, apparently came from the verses of Silius Italicus: "*nec vitam sine marte parti, quippe omnis in armis / lucis causa sita, et damnatum vivere paci*"(in favor of war and not life, they clearly define their cause as an obviously armed one and refuse to live in peace).[52] And although many authors pointed to these verses as evidence of the Cantabrians' ferocity and of their independence from Rome, accepting the exaggerations about their supposedly inherent savagery and fierceness was another matter. As such, there is no shortage of theorists who put things in perspective: military capability, defense of the borders, fighting in service of the monarchy, all this, of course, was acceptable; but cruelty with a congenital predisposition for violence, was not at all acceptable. Lope de Isasti is one of the writers who make this distinction:

> The Cantabrians are naturally inclined to take up arms, so much so that at age sixteen, they are already anxious to shoot a firearm, since they practice every year at the festivals in the *villas*; and they travel widely on the seas as gunmen, which is why they are sought after for ocean armadas in the service of God and his Majesty. Silius Italicus, an ancient author, wrote the following verses about them . . . In spite of what this writer has said, it is by no means our natural inclination to seek out altercations and afflictions, although we stand quite ready to fight; the poet exaggerates about this warlike zeal.[53]

To be sure, the constant military service that the frontier Basque territories provided for the monarchy had a high price. The guarantee of protection that the people of Gipuzkoa and Navarre, in particular, offered the Crown should be interpreted as a gesture of loyalty, but the toll on lives and homes destroyed must also be taken into consideration through certain fiscal exemptions that became central to the *foral* system. The argument that continuous military assistance compensated for certain privileges appears in the work of writers such as Sada, who in this case, applies it to Baztan:

> On many occasions when the French heretics have forcefully tried to make inroads into this kingdom . . . they [the Basques] have come to her defense with such valor that they have had to retreat in shame; [the Basques] have offered protection on many occasions and for a very long time at a far greater cost than these mountains can bear, so that they are in need of exemption from paying tax, and it would be important in the service to his Majesty and in maintaining the security and peace of these kingdoms that they be well provided with everything so that they will be ready to fight off the sudden attacks that often arise, for in other parts of this kingdom where they do not have such costs, these [debts] are nonetheless difficult to pay; it would be better if this were understood in this and other frontier valleys. The people are ferocious, agile, and skillful in the handling of arms, and fortunately, before any attack, they promptly send 700 or more gunmen to the hills and mountain passes of the Pyrenees. On the many occasions when they have taken up arms against the neighboring French, they have inflicted great damage and overwhelmed them.[54]

Naturally, the concept of a Basque universal nobility and supposed egalitarianism always had its detractors among Castilians and

Spaniards in general. In the best of these cases, the incomprehensibility of this phenomenon was settled with jokes in the comedies, in which it was not rare to see the *graciosos* (country bumpkins) doing manual labor and pretending to be "Bizkaians," and by that token "noblemen." On other occasions, they were simply treated with scorn and disdain. In this spirit, Cardinal Mendoza refers to the land of Bizkaia, the mountains of Burgos and Asturias, saying "as miserable as these lands might be, no Moor or Jew ever reached them; it is true that it is the part of Spain where they were least likely to live, but even so the most noble houses of those valleys are still affected by a good number of questionable marriages and bastardy."[55] In the most debated, controversial cases, juridical and historical essays strictly denied universal nobility to the Basque territories, as was the case in the controversy surrounding the attorney general of Valladolid, Juan García or the aforementioned Pedro de Alcocer. One extremely polemical text that demystified the elements in the framework of the Basque argument is the previously cited *Castellanos y vascongados*. It responds from a Castilian perspective to two suppositions, among others, that were current among the aforementioned Basque theorists: universal nobility and the merits of securing the borders. As for the first issue, Alonso, the Castilian protagonist of the work, sums up what most of his contemporary countrymen felt, that to assume that anyone residing in a specific place or territory would automatically be a noble was sheer idiocy and intrinsically contradictory, since nobility implies subordination and without it, there is no distinction. To hammer home the argument, he goes on the attack with a case that profoundly wounded the Basque sensibilities of those in this camp: the possibility that a black who was born in Bizkaia would be considered to be as noble as the rest of his neighbors:

> Your sixth argument, that your privileges come to you not simply because of nobility but exalted nobility: I say you are noble by privilege, and what is more that nobility was instituted within the body of the government so that there would be high and low individuals, just as we have in the human body, where the head is the head and the foot is the foot, and the hand, the hand. Not every stone in a building is placed in the front; rather, the best ones are placed in the best spots and the others in lesser places. Therefore, your nobility without noble lineage is clearly outrageous. In Potosí there is a black man named Mateo Luviano, who belonged to Nicolás de Guevara; he was a fishmonger who went into bankruptcy, so his guarantor had him put in jail, and before the attorney, Ibarra, the

> lieutenant of the *Corregidor* [Chief Magistrate, the representative of the Crown], he gave testimony that he was Bizkaian, having been born in Bilbao, and so in the end he was set free. And these proceedings took place in the courtroom of Mateo de Almonaci, now presided over by Sebastián Esteban de Sagastigui, where if you wish, you may examine them. The nobility and lineage that is common to all blacks is to be lowly and to labor. Among you, then, the feet are equal to the head; this you cannot deny is true, and it is what I have aimed to prove to you.[56]

Regarding the second issue, the response could not be other than this: if the Basques contributed to the defense of the Crown from the attacks of the French, then others, such as the Andalusians, did likewise against the aggression of the Berbers without demanding compensatory privileges. In addition, in reference to the above, the Castilian soldiers would go to any border to secure it: "You cannot claim that you serve as a barricade for Spain against France, where the king sends his Castilian troops. The Andalusians have long defended Andalusia from Africa, and rest assured that Africa has Andalusia at its doorstep, especially Ceuta, the opening where the treacherous Count Don Julián allowed the Moors to enter . . . But this is not enough; we trust neither them nor you, but our reliable Castilians who protect you and your lands."[57]

With the connection of universal nobility to egalitarianism, the issue of purity comes up once again. Nobility is based in part on the pure and intact preservation of a subject through generations. What remains pure is noble. And in order to demonstrate purity/nobility we turn once again to language. Proof of the lack of contamination lies in the fact that the primordial language of Tubal is still spoken, and what is more, in an immutable form—ostensible proof that the language has remained the same in an unaltered state since its known existence. Since there are not many ancient documents written in the Basque language, it is, of course, not easy either to prove or disprove this. In any case, as will be shown extensively, the Basque language claims to be close to Hebrew, or Chaldean, in other words, to the supposedly first language of humanity handed down by God to Adam. In addition, the varied evidence relating to its antiquity and longevity goes hand in hand with an analysis of toponymy and etymologies.

Along with the issue of noble lineage and surnames, a referential element connected to the collective nobility is that of the noble house. It is no accident that precisely in those territories where there is universal nobility, noble houses possess a strong family name and profile. All the neighbors of a specific locality know the family names of each house and often refer to others by the name of the house where they live: "Echeberri's" or "Tomasena's." What is more, many famous individuals (such as writers and *bertsolaris* or Basque oral poets) come to be known by the name of their noble houses rather than by their own surnames, as in the case of Axular or Xenpelar. Conversely, in the southern regions where there were many estates, the profile of the house diminishes or disappears altogether.[58] A final element that completes the referential symbolism of family, manorial estate, lineage, noble house and surname, is the sepulture. Although located beneath the floors of churches since the fifteenth century, the family sepulture of each house creates a link between the living who are connected to that noble lineage, and those who died and were also connected to it.[59]

For the rest, the preference for territory over lineage has a strictly physical component that can be dated chronologically: the general construction of the noble estates. As such, the importance of the noble lineage and the noble house run parallel to the construction, since the end of the fifteenth century, of units of production and residency with durable materials: tile and stone, alongside less stable medieval constructions made of wood. The estates of the sixteenth century are so zealously created to endure, that in many cases they have survived to the present day. These run from a few sturdy constructions that resemble military rather than residential dwellings, with the heads of the noble houses on their towers, to the proliferation of numerous small or medium size estates in the hands of peasant proprietors. The extensive construction of estates and of houses in the *villas* coincides with the moment in time when a society that had been dominated by noble factions becomes mesocratic, dominated by agrarian proprietors and the commercial, artisanal, and bureaucratic bourgeoisie of the *villas*.

This combined system of identity and independence that lasted through the ages can only be explained through a certain supernatural intervention, or at the very least, through a "privileged relationship between the community and the divine." To this end, numerous writers attempt to demonstrate that the Basques were not only Christians since time immemorial, but were monotheistic and worshiped at the Cross since the time of Babel, that is, long before Christ was actually incarnate. In a clearly Counterreformationist context, when the monarchy defines itself as Catholic and where one of the essential elements of nobility lies in creating the greatest possible distance from "the races of the damned," the Jews and Muslims, it is no small feat to state definitively that the Basques were "always" monotheistic and were Catholics since the time it was possible to be so. To bolster this construction, it is repeatedly asserted that in the organization of the military branch of the

Counterreformation—the Company of Jesus—the participation of the Basques was decisive with two of its supporters: Saint Ignatius of Loyola and Saint Francis Xavier. We will see this line of thinking used by the majority of theorists as a model, as in the case of Lope de Isasti:

> Through the patriarch Tubal, nephew of Noah (who founded Gipuzkoa), the religion that conforms to the natural law as we pointed out in chapter two has been preserved for the continuation of the generation of first families that founded it with the same language, dress, and customs without mixing the superstitions or misconceptions of the heathens and other [religions] that have appeared on earth. It is a very special gift that our God wished to bestow on us, because to be sure, we have never had or known another God than our *Jaungoicoa*, the God on high, although not with the esteem and reverence that we should have offered: . . . After our Lord Jesus Christ died for our redemption and rose again to the heavens, he did well to send us preachers to teach us the laws of his gospel.[60]

One should not assume, however, that this desire to underscore the traditional religiosity of the Basques as an essential part of their identity was imagined by ecclesiastical writers; lay writers, like Echave, express the same ideas in identical terms. As such, when comparing the following quotation with the previous one, one might notice another habit of the classic Basque theorists, namely, that of copying each other's ideas, sometimes literally:

> Notice all the histories about the provinces of Europe, and you will find that not a single one has endured in these Cantabrian provinces through the same first generation of families that originally inhabited it, with the same language, dress, and customs, without mixing the superstitions and misconceptions of the heathens and other [religions] that have appeared on earth. It is a very special gift that our God wished to bestow on us, because to be sure, we have never had or known another God than our *Iangoicoa,* though our knowledge of him was unclear; we raised our understanding and embraced with genuine good will, the true doctrine: a principle that interested us greatly, we who are reluctant to bring in new things, and for that reason we did not allow the Christians of the primitive church to consider us heathens as they did all other nations.[61]

Putting aside the presumed timeless cult of *Jaungoikoa*, the theorists never miss an opportunity to bring up the Christianization of the country as much as possible and to mention the undying fidelity of the Basque faith in Christ. Agramont, for example, in the case of Navarre, puts it this way: "The people of Navarre have four special privileges, more than other nations: they converted, as has been mentioned, twenty-two years after the Passion of Christ, Our Redeemer, during the time of the primitive Church. Second, their conversion was benign and without resistance, without abuse from those who professed the faith. Third, they were ever constant. And fourth, they never promulgated any sort of treason."[62] The anonymous author of the *Tordo vizcaíno* also states "the Bizkaians used the Cross as a weapon during ancient times."[63]

There is a sphere in which the two areas discussed up to now are connected and together help solve the puzzle that makes up the Basque imaginary construct: the regrettable experience of the sectarian wars and the supernatural solution linked to the invincible faith of the Basque people. In effect, an interpretation of the sectarian phenomenon preferred by the clergy posits that it was not the intervention of the monarchy that resolved the problem of sectarianism in the Basque Country, as the lay theorists maintain; rather, it was the apparition of the Virgin of Arantzazu. The most complete version of this explanation is given by the Franciscan friar, Juan de Luzuriaga, who held the office of Commissary General of the Franciscan Provinces of New Spain in Mexico, where he published a text on the sighting of the Virgin Mary more than two centuries after it occurred. Luzuriaga, who picks up the Cantabrian tradition from Garibay, Zaldibia, and other theorists, insists on something that was already commonly accepted in his time: the deep-rootedness of the "true faith" among the Cantabrians from earliest times, even before Christ, and the relationship that this had with maintaining the Basques' independence and their lack of contamination with other peoples, that is to say, their nobility: "For the Cantabrians, the laws and the cult of the true God were so wedded with the inherited nobility of their elders that they were not considered two different things, but a single quality deeply held in their hearts and their beings; [they were] as noble as they were true, and as faithful to God, as nobility was to its own blood." Of course, this identity originated at that moment when Tubal gave the Basques their faith and their language simultaneously:

> The illustrious Patriarch (Tubal) founded many other settlements; and being Wise, and Holy, he used gentle meters, in their native Basque language, to teach his people and their neighbors the precepts of both laws, natural and Divine, indoctrinating them in the adoration and reverence for the one God, the true Creator of

> Heaven and earth, explaining to them the doctrine necessary for the ultimate end and eternal health of their souls. To instill perfect observation of such sovereign mysteries, he instructed them in worthy and exemplary customs, encouraging them to the exercise and practice of the moral virtues in order to turn them into true disciples of peace, and instill in them lasting harmony, in bonds of friendship with their neighbor, and with God as their only master and Creator.[64]

But something must have gone awry in the education that the Basques received from Tubal, because several centuries later, they became enmeshed in a fierce civil altercation that brought the country to ruin. In reference to the situation afflicting the Basque Country before the apparition of the Virgin of Arantzazu, Luzuriaga does not skimp on epithets or scorn: "The subject of this chapter is nothing less than horrific." The friar maintains that the civil wars are far more frightening than wars against outsiders, and the Basques, who were victorious over the Romans, the Saracens, the Goths, and all others who had attempted to conquer them, perished in the discord and divisiveness resulting from factional wars. The analysis of the origins of these wars, however, proves to be totally unoriginal, as it merely transcribes what had already been recorded by García Salazar or Zaldibia regarding the battle that took place in Ulibarri over the way candles should be carried in religious processions. As I stated, the description of the situation is quite evocative:

> There were occasions when these powerful bands fought pitched battles to the last man, in which illustrious men died. There was a time in which violent and bloody attacks occurred, leaving sumptuous, noble farmsteads in flames. The sown fields looked like battlefields, for the desire to plant and till them was absent due to the lack of workers who, fearful or driven away by the cruelty of the enemy abandoned their work, fled to the mountains to save their lives, and the fields were left barren, the lack of harvest causing hunger and deprivation in the towns that was worse than the knives and clamor of soldiers.[65]

Luzuriaga records the attempts to put an end to these terrible and protracted circumstances. At first, King Enrique IV took the usual measures against the original forebears: destruction of their castles, imposed exile to fight the Moors, and so on. But all the actions and threats of the monarchy ended in disaster; the fighting continued. Later, God sent a drought that made the rains over Cantabria disappear for two years. Yet, not even this proof of divine wrath was enough to assuage the Basques' obstinacy. And when the punishment seemed as if it would prove to be absolute and devastating, God resorted to a merciful, unassailable intervention: the apparition of the Virgin to assuage their combativeness: "opening her infinitely merciful bosom, she forgave Cantabria, correcting her benignly through the Image of Our Lady of Arançazu, who because of her eternal disposition had been reserved for such calamitous times, like a tranquil rainbow to temper the squalls and calm the tempest of violent emotions, serving as a sign that these Provinces should return to their ancient and friendly federation, free of the eternal curse that had befallen them for their sins."[66] This is the basis of the ecclesiastical theory that explains the conclusion of the sectarian wars: it was not the monarchy or the brotherhoods, but the arrival of the Virgin that brought about an end to the fighting and the restoration of peace and prosperity.

One thing that puts into perspective the purity of blood (and other purities, among them the purity of language), nobility, and religion is the relationship of the Basques with the Jews and converts. As previously stated, institutions in the territories that had established a general nobility managed by all means to avoid the residence of anyone who belonged the "the races of the damned." Because the possibility of Muslims settling in Euskal Herria by the sixteenth century was unlikely, the regulations therefore applied to Jews and *conversos* (Jews who had converted by force to Christianity). The competitive relationship between Basques and *conversos* over the control of administrative posts during the reigns of Carlos and Felipe II is well known. Garibay is representative of the Basques' hostility towards the Jews and converts. After settling down in Toledo where there were many newly converted Christians, he softened his views, demonstrating a great tolerance towards them but maintaining his aversion toward the Jews. Garibay was totally in favor of the policy of casting them out and fully supported the Inquisition.[67] He was greatly concerned about mixed marriages (of financial interest) between the nobility, and old and new Christians, which according to him, brought great dishonor to the first and to the second group somewhat less, and of course, he was in favor of preventing these unions so that each should retain his own status.[68] Garibay's complaints about and distrust of the Jews could not be more classic: usury, wealth at the expense of the Christians, and control over the medical, surgical, and pharmacological professions all to the detriment of Christians.

Withal, the most interesting polemic occurs between 1622 and 1638 in three texts: *El Búho gallego, Castellanos y vascongados* and *El Tordo vizcaíno*, which, in spite of their irregular publication, were widely distributed with remarkable repercussions. The first was published anonymously, without a license or information on the year or place of publication, that is, in clandestine form, and was likely written around the year 1620 by Pedro Fernández de Castro, the Count of Lemos. This noble Galician appears to have been well known for his defense of the Basques as well as the Galicians; this, at least, is the impression that Echave gives the reader in his dedication to his *Discursos...* (Discourses...); among the reasons that Echave offers for daring to dedicate his work to him he states: "Your Excellency is a stalwart and constant defender of a Basque nation that recognizes the good will it always receive from V.E. [*Vuestra Excelencia*, your excellency]."[69] Nonetheless, this same individual undertook a vengeful literary adventure against Galicia; the problem was that in his zeal to confer dignity on Galicia, Castro resorted to putting down and undermining the other nations that formed part of the monarchy, beginning with Andalusia and Catalonia, but especially the Basque Country.[70] The point of origin for these spiteful interethnic exchanges would have to be traced back many years. Emilio Temprano dates it back to the chronicle of Fernando del Pulgar,[71] in which he endows the Castilians with the highest virtue, while belittling those of the other groups.[72]

The arguments that interest us here are based on a double negation, namely, that the Basques are neither Christians nor Spaniards, but Jewish slaves brought to the peninsula by Vespasianus to serve the Goths. This argument is presented in *El Búho* from a presumed fifth century text by Paulo Orosio, whom he refers to as Marco Orologio, whose assertion is supposedly based on some unusual etymologies of Basque toponyms—*Haro* would have come from the name *Aaron*; *Amézqueta* would have been the site of a mosque [mezquita in Castilian] or synagogue, and *Fuenterrabía,* the rabbi's fountain. The logic here was devastating, for on the one hand, it transformed the Basques into members of the accursed deicidal race, and on the other, it turned them into slaves, useful only as servile laborers in the ironworks (that is to say, as far as one could get from the supposed ideal of nobility), and finally, it "explained" the mystery of why they spoke a language so different from those around them. Of course, it was a corrupt form of Hebrew that these Bizkaians spoke—that is, these "vice-Cains" or "almost Cains," or "imitators of Cain."[73] This theory met with some success between the end of the sixteenth and the beginning of the seventeenth centuries and is cited in Floreto[74] to explain why it was "a language so cut off from others." It also becomes the central argument in the text *Castellanos y vascogandos* of 1624. This anonymous treatise was produced in the context of the wars between the Basques and the Spaniards known as the "Guerra de los Vicuñas" (Vicuñas being a term for Creole or non-Basque Spanish landowners) in Peru between 1622 and 1625. The text was not published (although it was known) until the somewhat dubious date of 1876 by Justo Zaragoza. The anonymous author of *Castellanos* acknowledges having read this theory in *El Búho gallego*, but he insists that he does not rely on it but on Orosius' theory, in which the supposed origins of the Basques are laid out.[75] Of course, for the author of the *Búho* as well as for the author of *Castellanos*, Orosius had sufficient credibility as a "serious and ancient" writer so that such a hoax would carry the weight of fact. The argument had already been analyzed in the *Búho*, but the very act of repeating the same etymologies had the effect of giving this absurd claim greater credibility and making it accepted among the Castilian writers of the middle of the seventeenth century. The main example continues to be the etymology of "Fuenterrabía," a Castilian exonym that can be traced back to "Hondarribia," that is, "sandy ford." But now, "Fuenterrabía" was supposed to mean "the rabbi's fountain," and in fact, the very port where the first rabbinical Jews arrived. The easy-going Basque personality allowed the settlement of Moors, thus "Amezqueta" (i.e., Amezketa, "gall oak grove" in Basque), which supposedly came from the word mezquita, "mosque." The text attributed to Osorio would remain nothing more than a ridiculous joke exploited by the author of the *Búho*, and whose currency between the Basque and anti-Basque polemicists ran the risk of making it seem authentic. A few years later, a response to the *Búho* was published, likewise anonymously and semi-clandestinely: *El Tordo vizcaíno*, whose erudite author may have been Father Henao. With little effort, he dismisses the absurd assertions in the *Búho* as to the Jewish origins of the Basque people:

> He [the anonymous author of the *Búho*] calls the Bizkaians descendants of Cain, and this with absolutely no support, thus proving the axiom: "The fool's follies are fueled by confidence and imprudence." Erudite, by my faith, and versed in human and divine letters!—everyone knows that the Cainites perished in the Flood, unless perchance there was another ark besides Noah's floating around in the fantasy of our Aristarchus, preserving a few fragments of Cain to use for populating Bizkaia. And this proposition stumbles against the Faith, although there's no reason to pay any attention to the *Búho*, whose entire argument never emerges from

the fog. If you're effeminate, you censor valor. If you're born without honor, you persecute nobility.[76]

The crowning piece in the construct of the *Fuero* (which included purity, independence, antiquity, the *Fuero*, and the voluntary union with Castile) is the recurrent theme of language. In contrast to other constructions of identity in which the weight of the argument falls on historical, religious, or strictly political factors, in the Basque case, language occupies a prominent place. As previously stated, the fact that it possessed the special characteristics of a presumed antiquity, rareness, and originality even with regard to its own survival, makes it especially attractive as irrefutable proof of the central ideological arguments in support of the *Fuero*. By the second half of the seventeenth century, the assumption among Basque intellectuals regarding the antiquity and purity of Euskara based on the Tubalistic theories, is already commonplace and easily incorporated into works of all genres, from the juridical to the philosophical, as well as in works of literature and essays. The Gipuzkoan Jesuit, Miguel de Abedaño y Eztenaga (Idiazabal, 1617–1686), a professor of philosophy in Valladolid and Soria and of theology in Pamplona-Iruña and Santiago, wrote several religious works in which he discussed the classical themes surrounding the Basque ideological construct: nobility, heroism, independent origins, the voluntary integration with Castile, constant purity of faith, the lack of contamination from outsiders, loyalty to the Crown, and of course, the ancient Basque language handed down through Tubal's legacy.[77] The Franciscan friar, Bernardino de Iñurrigarro (Antzuola, Gipuzkoa, 1620), presented the Assemblies of Tolosa in 1669 with a publication in which he elaborates on the classic concerns of Tubalism, Cantabrianism, and the *Fuero*. Vardulia (or Gipuzkoa) was the site where Tubal had settled his people in the "heart of all of Spain." From Tubal came the Basque language and the religious nature of the Basque people, situating the cult of the Cross on this Cantabrian shore even before Santiago professed the gospels. The Gipuzkoans, of course, had traditionally maintained their independence against the Romans and the Goths, and their integration into Navarre and Castile had been achieved voluntarily through the creation of a pact, which he proved using the false document of Antonio Lupián Zapata. In addition, he supported the idea, as did other Basque theorists, that universal nobility would not be lost if some inhabitants were occupied in manual labor.[78]

This ideology is clearly incorporated into the compilation of laws during this era. In 1687, an anonymous author put together the *Compendio guipuzcoano* (Gipuzkoan Compendium), which was found in the private archives of Father Larramendi.[79] The theory is classic: the Gipuzkoan *Fueros* are laws that preceded the kings and so were not handed down by them; rather, they correspond to the first natural rights founded by Tubal, and the preservation of Euskara from those times was a sign of political independence. In 1696, Miguel de Aramburu, an attorney from Tolosa who on several occasions had been the elected leader of the elected head of Gipuzkoa, produced the *Nueva recopilación* (New Compilation) of the laws of the province. His prologue contains the essentials of all the ideas held by previous Basque theories with regard to the legitimizing construct of the *Fuero* in relation to the Tubalist, Cantabrian, and linguistic arguments. The continuity and political independence of the Gipuzkoans since the times of Babel was linked to the continuity of the first inhabitants in the territory, evidenced in the preservation of the Basque language as "the natural language of the first inhabitants."[80]

This does not preclude the parallel creation of the Spanish legitimating ideological construct, which is likewise rooted in Tubalism. One of its most ardent supporters was the Benedictine monk, Gregorio de Argaiz, who published between 1667 and 1669 two extensive and tendentious works: *Población eclesiástica de España...* (Ecclesiastical Population of Spain...) and *Corona real de España por España...*[81] (Royal Crown of Spain through Spain...). Laboring under a strong monarchism, he invents genealogies of kings or takes advantage of those equally false ones invented by previous writers. And he continues to spread the myths of Ocampo, Annio de Viterbo, Beroso, and Antonio Lupián, from whom he borrowed Hauberto's false chronicle, with its royal genealogies, and published it with his own interpretations. In this way, the first royalty of Spain became Adam and Eve, and passing through the heirs of Methuselah and others, we arrive at the eighth king who turns out to be Noah, and the tenth, of course, none other than Tubal, and so on.[82]

4. Tubalism, Basque-Cantabrianism, and Basque-Iberianism

The temptation to fall back upon a vision of the world organized chronologically and based on data found in the Old Testament was widespread among ancient and medieval writers. Similarly, another medieval tendency that was later inherited by Renaissance writers was to systematize lineages with no clear line of continuity, making them date as far back as possible. This applied to families as well as to noble houses and even to towns. The search in *Genesis* for the historical records of towns and the lineage of the progeny of the founding fathers up to the present day became a common exercise. The account of the origins of the Iberian Peninsula related to the patriarch Tubal is a confusing one. The Jewish historian Flavius Josephus had written in his *Antiquities of the Jews*: "Thobel established the Thobelites, who today are called Iberians." But Josephus was referring not to the Occidental or Hispanic Iberia but to the Oriental or Caucasian one. Subsequent historians, nonetheless, identify Tubal as the founder of Spain, identifying him as an immigrant from Armenia or Georgia. In the thirteenth century, the Archbishop of Toledo, Rodrigo Ximénez de Rada (who was born in Puente la Reina [Gares] and died in 1247), insists that not only is Tubal the ancestor of the Iberians but that they also first settled in the Pyrenees. The tradition continues to grow with, among others, Alonso de Madrigal (1400–1455), known as *el Tostado*, indicating that Tubal and his descendants originally resided in the Pyrenees, later founded Pamplona-Iruña, and when they grew in number, they inhabited the rest of Spain. The notion of Hispanic Tubalism had already become dogma among the late medievalists.

It was an Italian historian, however, the Dominican Giovanni Nanni (1432–1502), known as Annio de Viterbo, who would be responsible for the total diffusion of the idea of Tubalism and of the supposed progeny of the Spanish monarchy that followed. Annio held the important post that controlled permission for publication in the pontifical territories under Pope Alexander VI. When Constantinople fell to the Turks, the Pope insisted on promoting a new Crusade. His predilections in this area did not resonate well with the Christian princes, but the decidedly anti-Islamic views of Isabel of Castile and Fernando of Aragón and the fact that the Pope was a Borgia from Valencia led them to the conclusion that it was through the Spanish monarchy that the Muslims could be contained. As such, he includes in one of his works[83] a genealogy, as laudatory as it is false, of the Spanish royalty based on ancient texts but mostly on the imaginings of the Dominican. The most famous and influential is the one attributed to Beroso, who had been a Chaldean priest during the fourth to third centuries before Christ and had established the genealogies of the Babylonian kings. These lost texts, written in Latin and not Chaldean as one might logically assume, were "recovered" by Annio. He used this genealogy to make a connection with the genealogy of the Spanish royalty. It begins after the Flood with the repopulation of the world as planned by Noah, who sent his son Shem to populate Asia, and Ham and Japheth to do the same in Africa and Europe. A son of Japheth, Tubal, would populate Spain and become its first king; later he would be followed by his son Íbero, and his son Iubelda, and later Brygo (the builder of *brigas* or fortified cities), and subsequently: Tago, Beto, Gerión, etc. Of course, from the beginning, there were writers who denounced the fraud inherent in the falsification of documents, from Sabellico to Justus Scaliger, as well as Luis Vives and Juan de Mariana. But even the latter acknowledged the arrival of Tubal, although not the link to the royal genealogy. Although Annio had some detractors, he had many more supporters who, as happens in these situations, helped finish and redirect his work, basing it on this foundation: the false narrative of Beroso. Such was the case with the Sicilian humanist Lucio Marineo Sículo (1460–1533), chronicler of the Catholic Kings who relies on the work of Annio.[84] An even more assiduous follower of Annio was Florián de Ocampo (c. 1499–1558). More of a novelist than a historian, he contributed a multitude of inauthentic or simply fabricated elements, adding to the fictional list of Spanish kings.[85] The Venetian chronicler, Pero Antón (Pere Antoni) Beuter, published, first in Catalan and later in Spanish, a chronicle of Spain and Valencia,[86] in which he traced the Tubalist mythology and the assertions made by Annio, although as we shall see, with some interesting contributions and nuances. From the middle of the seventeenth century, the rationalist French and English critiques of literal readings of the Bible, with works like Richard Simon's *Histoire critique du Vieux Testament* (Critical History of the Old Testament) (1678), made any attempts to support a Japhetic genealogical analysis indefensible. But it would not be until the end of the eighteenth century in Spain, despite the partial objections of Mariana[87] and Vives, that the radical critique[88] by the Abbé Masdeu totally discredited Annio, although the Tubalist[89] narrative retained its viability for some time, especially in Vasconia.[90]

In this way, Tubal becomes the foundational Spanish myth, a part of the legitimating Hispanic construct and the necessary link between the Biblical Golden Age and the foundation of the modern political entity. The well-known narrative maintains that Tubal, grandson of Noah, left Armenia after the Flood and the confusion of tongues in Babel[91] and became the first inhabitant of one of the territories that had been destroyed by the flood waters, the Iberian Peninsula, settling down in the spot he found most pleasing, and best endowed in all the peninsula. From this point of origin, Tubal's descendants would inhabit the rest of the peninsula, but this initial site would enjoy a superior status because of its antiquity. Its civilizing and regenerative character must be emphasized, especially given the renewal implied by the Flood and the myth of Babel. The erection of the tower and its subsequent destruction along with the confusion of languages implies a before and after with links to two critical cultural constructions: language and the founding of cities, in other words, the essential differentiation of nationality. In ancient times, people presumably spoke one language, there were no cities and a general and undifferentiated cultural mire predominated. With Babel and the proliferation of urban bases came the diversity of languages and identities. The fact that this account contradicts those of the Bible does not diminish the power of its position. Many European communities, and especially those in Spain and Portugual, vied to be the original settlements of Tubal, based on toponymic, historical, logical, archeological, and other types of proofs. Cities like Setubal, for example, believed they had an almost immediate, irrefutable etymological argument. Another argument that carried weight held that since Tubal had come from the East, he had to land first on the Mediterranean coast. But Euskal Herria held the trump card: it was the only one on the Peninsula that had a non-Romance language, which implied that it predated the arrival of Latin and was therefore the oldest language and presumably the one spoken by Tubal. In this way, surprisingly, or precisely because the presence of Tubal served as the foundational element in Spain, it would also become its equivalent in the Basque case. The constitutive elements of the Basque *foral* construct—purity, primitivism, antiquity, independence, and a privileged relationship with the divine—congeal and organize around the originative narrative of Tubal.

Garibay and Mariana were Renaissance writers who spread Tubalism throughout Spain. The primary difference between them was that the writer from Arrasate-Mondragón, Garibay, did so in a Basque version, whereas the priest Mariana did so in a generalized Spanish version. Juan de Mariana (1536–1624) convincingly made the argument that Tubal, the fifth son of Japheth, was the first man who arrived in Spain the year after the Flood, and therefore, his descendants were clearly Spanish.[92] Garibay, on the other hand, asserts that the purity and nobility of the Basques is rooted in its having been the first inhabitants of Spain ("the arrival in Spain of the patriarch Tubal, its first king" and his "settlement in the region of Cantabria and the lands of Navarre"), resorting to the argument of toponymy, which Larramendi would later develop extensively.

Place names throughout the Peninsula are rooted in Basque: "the names of our rivers, or important sites common to Armenia and this part of Spain." The fundamental argument was that the Armenian immigrants had given to the new locations (cities, rivers, and mountains) the names they already knew from their place of origin. Thus, we find the Basque-Armenian coincidences in the names of the Araxes River, the Ararat mountain and the Aralar Mountains, the Basque mountain Gorbeia, and the Armenian Gordeya; these stood in opposition to those who, like Ocampo, identified Setubal as a settlement of Tubal with the Basque toponym of Tudela (Tubela, today written Tutera in Euskara).[93] Attempts to justify the idea that Tubal arrived on the eastern shores but chose not to settle there, and instead chose to settle in Vasconia, seem a bit farfetched. According to Garibay, the Pyrenees (and Cantabria, which at that time was identified with Vasconia) was then endowed with a profusion of wild fruits, corn, and mushrooms—in short, the types of foods that primitive individuals, such as Tubal and his sons, would have liked. He thus rejected the notion that Tubal could have settled in Catalonia as Maestro Esquível de Alcalá suggested, because that location would not have suited their primitive lifestyle. So, the Basques' primitivism was transformed into evidence of the Armenians' original settlement. This argument had already been seen in the work of Beuter, which disagreed with Garibay in a fundamental issue—language. The Valencian sensibly argued: "I don't believe Basque was the Spanish language spoken by the sons of Tubal, the first inhabitants of Spain after the Flood, because it is not the Aramaic spoken before the Flood, or Chaldean, nor does it resemble either of them."

Garibay's primary reference for Tubal's presumed arrival on the Iberian Peninsula was Florián de Ocampo,[94] who relied on the false account by Beroso, published by Annio de Viterbo. Ocampo resorts to using toponymy and anthroponomy to make the Tubalist argument. He connects Tubal to Setubal, Tafalla to Taballa, and Tudela to Tubela. Ocampo did not support the Basque-Iberian argument and believed that Tubal had settled in Andalusia and did not speak Basque. Mariana and Ocampo upheld the theory that had been generally accepted for centuries, whereas Garibay's reinterpretation clashed with theirs in that he made the Basques into the original Spaniards, even Iberians. Besides the question of language, another connection that worked in favor of the Gipuzkoan's thesis was the relationship of Tubal with the invention of the forge and metallurgy, which brought him closer to the Basque argument, given the association made at that time between iron production and the Basques. In effect, Tubal is considered the inventor of the forge and Spain was considered the country par excellence in Europe and most associated with metals, and within Spain, Vasconia was, second to none, iron country.[95]

Those writers who defended the Tubalist theory, with some discrepancies and contradictions, boldly put forth a chronology that tied Genesis to the "closest" history in Cantabria (Vasconia). Broadly speaking, this chronology could be seen as follows: year 0, the creation of the world in which God gives the first humans language, which was supposedly Hebrew; year 1624, the universal Flood; year 1785, the Tower of Babel and the confusion of the seventy-two languages. Tubal arrives on the Iberian Peninsula in year 1797 and his descendants inhabit the entire land (it's assumed that there were no previous inhabitants), and throughout the land, of course, Euskara is spoken. Beto's death in year 2110 is followed by a proliferation of languages in Spain. In year 3768, the Romans arrive on the Peninsula and continue the use of Euskara along with other languages, including Latin. The wars between Rome and Cantabria in year 3810 resulted in a victory for Cantabria and the disappearance of Basque in the rest of the Spanish territories. In year 3956, Christ is born, although the Basques had already been practicing a "primitive monotheism" learned from the Chaldeans.

Garibay also fomented the spread of Basque-Iberianism, which was generally accepted by most theorists until the twentieth century.[96] The line of transmission would be like this: Garibay, Poza, Echave, Moret, Astarloa, Hervás, Humboldt, Menéndez Pidal, and Hugo Schuchardt. The theory essentially upholds the association of the Basque with the Iberian, making Vasconia a foundational nucleus of Iberia (Spain), and from there, toponymy and the Basque language spread throughout the peninsula; what was Basque, therefore, was also the very marrow of Spain. Although Garibay spread this theory, it had previously been created by Lucio Marineo Sículo.[97] Garibay articulated the theory of Basque-Iberianism in *Las Grandezas de España* (The Grandeur of Spain), where he states that Tubal and his Iberian son went to live in Cantabria, that is, in Vasconia: "Tubal taught his [sons] the laws of nature, and commanded them to live well. The language of Cantabria, now called Bascongada, was the first in Spain, which may be verified through notable sources."[98]

Although Tubalism was primitive, crude, and essentially a religion-based linguistic ideology, the Basque-Iberianism rooted in Tubalism (as it attempts to defend similar objectives) has a scientific basis—especially after Humboldt—albeit an erroneous one, which frees it of the most religious and least attractive elements. After this prestigious German philologist and scientist in one way or another endorsed the connection, the confusion between the Basque and the Iberian, or the idea that Basque was a Neo-Iberian language (as per Menéndez Pidal and Gerland), or the notion that the decline of Iberia could be understood through Basque (as per Hugo Schuchardt) was well disseminated among intellectuals. However, when Gómez Moreno deciphered the Iberian characters he showed that Basque was useless in trying to understand these texts. In these inscriptions, there are only a few names and some terms, like the suffix "*-etar*" or the word "*gudua*," that are recognizably Basque—in short, too insignificant to maintain the connection. These coincidences can be explained by the contact between the two frontier languages.[99]

There is an enduring fascination with the paradoxical evolution of the notion of Basque-Iberianism with regard to its defenders and its detractors. In the sixteenth century, Garibay and his Basque followers defended the Basque-Spanish identity through this Basque-Iberian theory, while Ocampo denied it. In the seventeenth century, Echave and other Basque writers also supported it, while Flórez rejected it. In the twentieth century, the Basques who were more or less nationalists, or *foralists,* rejected Basque-Iberianism, while the Spaniards who supported unification now defended it. This is to say that in those instances when Basque theorists tried to uphold the presence and identity of the Basques within the Spanish monarchy, it was the Spanish who offered resistance to this interpretation, whereas in those instances when it was unseemly to insist on the issue, it was in Spain that theories flourished maintaining the belief that the Basques were first to arrive and therefore were the most typical and the truest Spaniards. Viewed from this perspective, one can understand how Basque-Iberianism became the bold and spirited theory that, under different guises, has survived in a lively and belligerent form to this day. Periodically, debates about this issue have sprung up, both within the academic realm as well as outside of it. After the War of the Convention between Spain and France (1793–95), when the government of Carlos IV was evaluating the loyalty of the Basque territories and preparing an attack against the framework of the *Fuero*, which consisted, in part, of a move to refute its ideology carried out by the Academia de la Historia (Academy of History), Llorente, Conde, and others, there appears in the press of Madrid a complementary and inevitable polemic over Basque-Iberianism. After the publication in 1806 of the works by Astarloa and Sorregieta y Erro, a more or less bitter exchange of letters and articles between several writers on this subject—which, of course, extends generally to the Basque language[100]—is disclosed in *La Minerva, El Diario de Madrid*, and *El memorial literario*. It is interesting to point out that this is the first time that a debate of this sort takes place through a modern system of communication, such as the press. The medium, therefore, renews itself, but the debate remains the same. Throughout the twentieth century and up to the present day, in the most politically opportune moments, there has been no shortage of Spanish theorists to recover and reenergize the Basque-Iberian argument. Although the most distinguished researchers, some Basque and others not (as in the cases of Koldo Mitxelena and Antonio Tovar), have been lowering their valuation of the Basque-Iberian identity, writers such as Julio Cejador de Frauca, Pío Beltrán, or Domingo Fletcher, continue to defend it, availing themselves of a renaissance in publications on the subject since the decade of the 1990s.[101]

On the other hand, Basque-Cantabrianism attempted to prove the naiveté or independence of the region going back to a remote time; this is why the Basque territories were shown to be assimilated into the old Cantabria, as a symbol of anti-Roman resistance. For writers in the sixteenth century, like Echave, this Cantabrian (Vasconian) secular independence was linked to the defense of Spain's independence and occurred, among other things, as a token that favored the Basques in particular: iron and with it the arms necessary for battle. A subject dear to the hearts of the *foral* theorists of that century and the one that followed was the great military service of the Basques for the monarchy:

> Is there any Province in Europe that can pride itself on greater antiquity than Cantabria? Which of them can truly say, as we can, that no foreign nation ever conquered her, passed through her, or inhabited her hills and river valleys as if they owned her? Which province can say that it has not mixed its blood with foreign blood, that it has not been ruled by foreign laws and government? Which one, finally, has been so constantly attacked by enemies and foreigners as this region, if not to conquer her, then to enter Spain through her, as we have seen until now? For this reason, from our infancy and since ancient times we have been, and still are, ready with weapons in hand and in perpetual vigil without respite or relief, whence there is no mystery why God provided us so abundantly with the strongest of metals so that from time immemorial she has been and is now the arsenal and armory of all Spain.[102]

The misunderstanding began with Zaldibia and later spread among most Basque theorists: Martín de Ibarra, Martín de Azpilicueta (who admitted to being Cantabrian and Navarrese simultaneously), and of course, Garibay, Poza, Echave, and later Larramendi.[103] But by the same token, many other non-Basque historians participated in this same pretense: Marineo Sículo, Ocampo, Vaseo, Ambrosio de Morales, Nicolás Antonio, Covarrubias, etc. Some arguments favored the association between Cantabria and Vasconia, because the two territories were adjacent to one another, were mountainous, and had resisted the Roman presence and acculturation; this allowed the two to become confused and identified with each other. What is more, by the sixteenth century, it was a commonly accepted idea that the reconquest during the Middle Ages had occurred from north to south, from the territories that were free of Saracens and therefore presumed to be free of Romans, giving rise to a naive presumption of timelessness. All the northern mountain people, the Basques, Cantabrians, and Asturians, had a single label applied, that of "barbarians," a term understood in the sense of being foreign, strange, and lacking in civilization—that is, foreign to the Roman civilization. Thus, they all ended up pigeonholed together.

Initially, Spanish writers were prudent or indifferent to the consequences implicit in this grouping together of the Cantabrian territories: since they were free of Roman influence, their language (Basque, of course) was spoken universally throughout the peninsula before the arrival of the Romans, and it only survived in the territories that remained free of their domination (the association is Basque-Cantabrianism = freedom = the preservation of the Basque language). As such, Juan de Valdés, for example, neither affirms nor denies it. But as the apologist stance of the Spaniards began to solidify, the theorists became increasingly hostile to the Basque notion that questioned the patrimony of the Spanish language. Such was the position of Ambrosio de Morales and Mariana. Also opposed to the Cantabrian position were Zurita, Padilla, Oihenart, and above all Father Flórez, who dismantled this identification definitively, at least from a scientific point of view.[104] Having said this, even after Flórez, the polemic continued to rear its head, with challenges from Basque-Cantabrianists like Ozaeta, as well as apologies from Risco.[105] This confusion, clearly rejected by the end of the eighteenth century, nonetheless remained operative until the twentieth century and many writers (such as Iztueta and Iparraguirre) continued to return to it.

The original formulation of Cantabrianism was developed by Zaldibia, using a somewhat forced interpretation of a chronicle by the Navarrese Archbishop Rodrigo Ximénez de Rada, in these terms:

> The identity of the first inhabitants and rulers of Cantabria can be clearly ascertained from the curious Chronicle written by the Archbishop Don Rodrigo de Toledo, where in Book 1, chapter 5, describing the arrival in Spain of Tubal, the son of Japheth and grandson of Noah, which occurred 143 years after the Flood and 2,174 years before the birth of Christ, he affirms that he and his companions, who were called the people of Tubal, stopped in the Pyrenees Mountains, and after their population grew, they descended to the plains and built some Navarrese and Basque towns in that territory.[106]

Because of the great number of associative elements it contains, the version of the Tubal-Cantabrian theory in the *Crónica* of Ibargüen-Cachopín, is one of the most interesting. Juan Iñiguez de Ibargüen was a scrivener from the district of Zornotza (Bizkaia). It seems his work as a historian centered in the search for original documentation in the archives; to that end, he visited the main archives that might contain information on Bizkaia, among them the archives in Simancas and Valladolid. For this reason, later historians, like Ituriza, held him in high esteem and considered him a serious and trustworthy historian. His work, *Crónica General Española y Sumaria de la Casa de Vizcaya, y su antigua fundación, y Nobleza* (General Spanish Chronicle and Summary of the House of Bizkaia, and its Ancient Founding, and Nobility), was probably written around 1588, but certainly between 1580 and 1620. Part of the manuscript is housed in the Biblioteca de la Diputación de Bizkaia (Library of the Provincial Government of Bizkaia). It consisted of some 184 notebooks, 62 of which have survived. It would appear that the author was a doctor from Laredo, García Fernández de Cachopín, whereas Ibargüen was probably merely the compiler of the materials and information. Consisting of diverse and disordered materials, among which are a multitude of fabrications and falsehoods (as in the song of Lelo), it also contains a substantial number of ideas in currency among Basque intellectuals at that time. It is a decidedly Cantabrianist text. This ancient Cantabria had an extensive reach: almost to Zaragoza, Calahorra, Navarre, Bizkaia with the *Foral* Territories adjoining the province, Gipuzkoa, Araba and Béarn.[107] And of course, it is seamlessly Tubalist, assuring the foundation of the Seigniory of Bizkaia by Tubal himself, but it offers a version that deviates from the conventional one to an extent worth mentioning. According to the *Crónica*, Noah personally went to the peninsula to see his grandson Tubal and while there, he took the time to enact the *Fuero* of Bizkaia. It was, of course, created in Basque, and transmitted through the generations in an oral form, most likely sung in the style of the Balkan bards, where the etymology for Cantabria as a name for Vasconia orginated, and Cantabria would mean "land or region of *cantares* (songs)":

> The Seigniory of Bizkaia was founded by Tubal, grandson of Noah. They never wrote down their laws because when Noah came to Spain to visit his grandson and the towns he had established, he gave them the Adoration of One God and the government of the Republic in verse so that they could more easily memorize it, and this is why Cantabria came to be called the "country and region of songs" because they sang their laws and sang of the heroic deeds of those who had died in the war and of their lineages, which they called *Heressia* [Legacy] which means "thing that gradually moves downward and descends as from great grandfather to grandfather to father to son," and then the Basques, or Cantabrians, called him Jauna, which in the Basque language means Lord because he truly

was Lord of all the world, because in his person he recuperated and was a second Adam.[108]

In other words, the following elements are linked to this Cantabria (or Vasconia): it was settled by Tubal and resettled by Noah himself, who then instituted a "Republican government." This was communicated in sung verses and transmitted through generations in oral form; these songs were furthermore related with elegies (*Eresiak*). And finally, Noah gave the Basques the cult of a single god. This citation leaves nothing out: The Basque *bertsolaris* (oral poets who improvised verses) were endowed with an orally transmitted culture and their own language, carried out funeral rites with elegiac songs, were Christian even before Christ, and were gifted with a *foral*-style democracy that goes back to the times of Babel. The rest of the Basque foundational myths also appeared in the text: Jaun Zuria, conqueror of King León Ordoño II in the year 860 in the battle of Padura or Arrigorriaga, as the first lord of the patriarchal "democracy" ("the freedom and good government they had") institutionalized by Noah. And again, the essential features of the pact: the Catholic Monarchs who restored political order just after the sectarian era and Basques who felt a loyalty so deep for their kings that they followed their laws: "and above all, they felt from their beginnings a great love and fellowship for their kings and princes and lords of Spain."[109]

Even into the nineteenth and twentieth centuries, the Cantabrian position is defended in more or less colorful ways. One is the Abbé D'Iharce de Bidassouet's absurd Cantabrian etymology, which we have already seen in the *Crónica* of Ibargüen and that is still viable even in 1825: "Of the arrival of the Cantabrians, in Basque *Khanta ver* Cantor, Singer without equal... The Romans called them Cantabri because of the excellence of their voices; thus, they provided enrichment to the theaters, as the famous Basque Garat has done in the theaters of Paris."[110] In other words, Basque-Cantabrianism was justified in accordance with one of the supposed ethnic characteristics of the Basques, that is, the notion that they were good singers. These kinds of supposed racial characterizations that had always worked well in the past, worked even better, if it is indeed possible, during the height of romanticism.

5. Apologia and Territories

As one can appreciate from the above, the practical applications of the Tubalist theory that were based primarily on a linguistic argument ran into a particular complication. Since Euskara was spoken in different territories on both sides of the Pyrenees, the political loyalties of the theorists were largely restricted to one of these specific territories. How could the Tubalist nobility be restricted to one's own territory without acknowledging that a living testimony of the language also existed in others? It should be noted from the outset that this problem is discussed among the political authors who write in the Romance languages. In the case of those who write in Euskara, the linguistic community is so obvious and political interest is so weak that, in general, the issue does not come up. Dechepare, Axular, and others who write in Basque refer to the entire region as Euskal Herria and rarely abandon their ecclesiastical agenda to venture into the political realm.

Another major distinction is the situation of those Basque apologists who write primarily in Spanish. Because the majority of them are Cantabrians, it might be seen that all their apologetics regarding excellence, antiquity, and nobility could be applied equally to all the territories that make up the presumed range of ancient Cantabria. However, in the first place, the borders of Cantabria were by no means agreed on by the various authors, and in the second place, even when they defended the spread of the Basque language and the fact of a Tubalist primogenital nobility throughout Cantabria, they succumbed to the paradox of claiming preeminence for their own territory over those of other Basque regions, with arguments that are at times rather aggressive, even towards each other.

To begin with, an issue that was responsible for more than one misrepresentation and some suspicions is the common practice of referring to Basque speakers as "Bizkaian" and the Basque language itself as "Bizkaian" well into the eighteenth century. In Castile and Latin America, anyone from Navarre, Gipuzkoa, or Araba who spoke Basque (and even when that was not the case) was referred to generically as Bizkaian. This irritated more than a few writers from other territories, especially those from Gipuzkoa, who tried to clarify the situation whenever they could. Isasti declared that "strictly speaking, the Gipuzkoans cannot call themselves Bizkaians, although in Castile and Galicia, people refer to all those who speak Basque that way.[111] But the misunderstanding persisted and continued to exasperate those who were deeply entrenched in that camp, such as Larramendi: "The habitual stupidity of the Castilians (and other Spaniards) is intolerable, when in what they say and write they refer to all the Basques as Bizkaians, giving to all three Provinces the name that is proper and peculiar only to the Seigniory of Bizkaia; and the same with the Aragonese and the Valencians, who call the Basques *Navarrese*, leading to hundreds of ridiculous assertions in history."[112]

Bizkaian and Gipuzkoan writers of the sixteenth century, who were all Cantabrians, included their respective territories under this generic rubric, but with a few nuances regarding its borders and importance. Zaldibia states literally: "It is unfair that Cantabria, being the oldest nation of Spain, should be forgotten, along with the memorable deeds of those who resided in her provinces, among them Gipuzkoa and Bizkaia, which in Castile are generally referred to as Bizkaia and their inhabitants as Bizkaians."[113] That is to say, although Cantabria itself is more extensive, interest has focused on the two coastal territories. Echave includes Araba, Navarre, Bizkaia, and Gipuzkoa within Cantabria, but he limits his praise to the latter two territories because they had persisted in the use of Euskara most faithfully. Isasti relies on Pomponio Mela, Mariana, and the zoning of provinces as determined by the Franciscan friars to chart a Cantabria from Logroño and Viana to the sea, which includes Gipuzkoa, Bizkaia, Araba, the greater part of Navarre, and La Rioja, clearly identifying Euskara as "the Basque Cantabrian language." When he refers to the nobility and to the region's perennial independence, however, he limits himself to citing Araba, Bizkaia, and Gipuzkoa, and on occasion, he restricts himself to only the latter two.

To sum up, most theorists characterize Cantabria generically but later distinguish a specific nucleus consisting of Bizkaia and Gipuzkoa. This deliberate confusion of Bizkaians and Gipuzkoans with the Basque territories to the north of the Pyrenees and the kingdom of Navarre had, of course, a political dimension. The former belonged to the Kingdom of France and the latter, although conquered and integrated into the Kingdom of Castile, remained foreign and in political competition. The differences on this subject must be noted above the issue of cultural identity. One of the writers who might best express the duality between the linguistic-cultural unit and the political diversity is the anonymous author (possibly Henao) of the *Tordo vizcaíno,* when he writes:

> . . . And I observe that the name Cantabrian included everything between the Ebro and Asturias de Santillana, as far as the Mountains, *Foral* Territories, Bizkaia, Gipuzkoa, Araba and much of La Rioja. Some would even say it extended to Guienne in France, including the Basques and almost all of the Province of Lapurdi; however, Silius Italicus makes a distinction between the Cantabrians and the [northern] Basques . . . He describes the young warriors: first the Cantabrians, then the Basques. So it should be said, that although their origins and way of speaking were the same in the time of the Romans, they were separate nations, as are the two

> Navarres, Bizkaia and Gipuzkoa today, who are bonded only in their language; in everything else they are distinct, with understandable rivalry, similar in origins but different in nobility, language, and customs, despite the misrepresentations of some outsiders.[114]

Friar Juan de Luzuriaga, who inherited the entire tradition, proclaims the existence of a "Cantabrian Region," which stretched from Asturias to the Pyrenees and from the Ebro to the Cantabrian Sea, but distinguishing between an "External Cantabria" and an "Internal" one that would coincide with the area where the Basque language is spoken: "It is commonly believed to encompass all of the Basque region, including the never conquered provinces of Araba, Gipuzkoa, the Seigniory de Bizkaia, and a large portion of the Kingdom of Navarre."[115]

Zaldibia is the perfect example of a theorist at the service of Gipuzkoan interests, in a pro-Castilian and anti-Navarrese sense. He is the creator of a good number of the semi-legendary theories that articulate a certain Gipuzkoan singularity at the expense of the prestige of the inhabitants of Navarre. Zaldibia's thesis is that, originally, the Gipuzkoans were circumscribed within the sphere of Castile, but by taking advantage of their independence, they became associated with the Kingdom of Navarre; but because there was an effort to force them to pay taxes, they freely and voluntarily decided to reunite themselves with Castile. Since the Navarrese did not accept this step willingly, they attacked and robbed them continuously until the Battle of Beotibar in 1321, which the Gipuzkoans won. Whether that actually took place and whether that was the outcome, what is most interesting here is the heroic dimension that Zaldibia gives the description of the battle and the creation of a myth that would be handed down for centuries:

> . . . And because there was constant discord between them [the Navarrese] and the Gipuzkoans, after they returned to the pristine state of being Castilians, as free, unconquered people, but under obligation to the crown of Castile, whose subjects they indeed were, they assembled a great army and swept powerfully into the Province, and what happened on their entry is described here . . . and they went around all during the week, recruiting people until as many as 70,000 warriors from Navarre, Gascony, and France were assembled, and they invaded Gipuzkoa on Friday, before the festival of Saint Matthew, and set fire to Berastegi and did much damage to its church, and on the following Saturday they reached Beotibar, and Xil López de Oñaz, Lord of the House of Larrea—which, at the time, was the principal house of the village of

> Amasa—came out to attack them with eight hundred Gipuzkoans and wiped out the entire army . . . so that the Navarrese, weeping over the destruction of Beotibar where the battle took place, describe it in an ancient lament: "*Beotibar, Beotibar hic dia dutac Martín de Oybar*" (Beotibar, Beotibar, you have Martín de Oybar), and the ancient song of the Basques says: "*Milla urte igaro eta, hura bere videan, Guipuzcoarroc sartu dira Gazteluco echean; Nafarroquin bildu dira Veotibaren pelean,*" which means: "After one thousand years, the water returns to its riverbed. Thus did the Gipuzkoans enter the House of Castile again, and they fought the Navarrese in Beotibar."[116]

In the same way, Zaldibia dwells on another conflict that the Gipuzkoans and Navarrese faced during the conquest of 1512: the Battle of Belate and the capture of Navarre's artillery, whose cannons became part of the Province's coat of arms. Another element that was included within this coat of arms, Zaldibia also notes, was the image of a crowned king sitting at his throne with a drawn sword pointed at the sky. He attributes this to the fact that a certain king of Navarre had been taken prisoner by the King of Aragón and "the courageous Gipuzkoans, seeing that the King whom they had served as confederates and lords had been defeated by the King of Aragón and taken prisoner, charged out onto the battlefield with incredible swiftness and courage and engaged the victorious army in battle and crushed and defeated the King of Aragón, restoring the King of Navarre to his freedom."[117] After Zaldibia, more than a few Basque writers, especially Gipuzkoans, returned to the subject of the Battle of Beotibar, with more or fewer details and additions, until it became commonplace and generally accepted by everyone. Father Henao, for example, dedicates two chapters of his extremely erudite *Averiguaciones* (Investigations)[118] to the battle.

The Navarrese theorists did not skimp in their apologias, and they counterattacked, albeit belatedly, defending their preeminence and greater valor. In this context, the most important work is the one published by Juan Sada y Amézqueta under the pseudonym García de Góngora y Torreblanca, with the unmistakable title of *Historia apologética y descripción del Reyno de Navarra y de su mucha antigüedad, nobleza, calidades...* (Apologetic History and Description of the Kingdom of Navarre and of its Extreme Antiquity, Nobility, and Qualities...). Essentially, it is a vindication of the Kingdom of Navarre, written in a strongly polemical tone, which presents arguments in two different veins: on the one hand, it disputes the preeminence of the Kingdom of Aragón, among others, in Spain and argues in favor of the undisputed greater antiquity of Navarre; on the other hand, it questions the myth of the Tubalist supremacy of the Basques, and particularly the Bizkaians and Gipuzkoans, that had been around since Garibay and Zaldibia. Sada, or if one prefers, Góngora, incorporates Navarre into ancient Cantabria and considers it the original territory in which Tubal settled and initiated the spread of the Basque language. Moreover, in spite of the fact that the language had been preserved in other areas, such as Bizkaia and Gipuzkoa, one should not assume that these territories possess the same degree of Tubalist heritage, for in the case of Navarre, the Euskara spoken there is more pure than in the western provinces, from which Sada deduced that it must be the original form of the language. To develop the argument that Euskara arrived in Navarre through Tubal, he uses two testimonials from previous authorities: Alonso de Madrigal and Prudencio de Sandoval. From the first he takes the Tubalist settlement of Pamplona-Iruña, and from the second, the antiquity of the city as seen in its Basque name, Iruña, pre-dating the founding of Pompeii, from which he deduced that Tubal spoke Basque, the language that he used to name the places he inhabited. On the other hand, Sada disputes what was established by Zaldibia, Garibay, and Echave (to whom he refers as Chávez) about the notion that the provinces were not conquered by the Romans and concludes, instead, that the true Cantabrians were the Navarrese, whom the Romans so greatly feared that they let them live in peace to practice their Christian cults:

> . . . Upper and Lower Cantabria contained three nations, to wit: Basques, Berones, and Varduli, and the Basques inhabited the region from Tafalla northward, whose head was Martua, or Atanagria, which is the City of Pamplona and which extended from the peaks of these Pyrenees to the River Gallego; and the Berones were in the region below Tafalla as far as Tudela, and above the Ebro River including some parts of La Rioja, which was called Austrogonia; and the Varduli, he says, who were the Gipuzkoans, Bizkaians, and Arabans, so that of the three regions into which Cantabria was divided, two of them made up Navarre, situating it in the center and most advantageous place, where it has preserved the primitive matrix language, Cantabrian-Basque, which the Patriarch Tubal brought to Spain in its original form, . . . Estevan de Garibay y Çamalloa [Zamalloa] in his historical compendium and Baltasar de Echabe, both of them Varduli, or who were the people of Gipuzkoa, Bizkaia, and Araba, writing about the journey of Don Sancho the Strong to Africa, say that during his absence when King Don Alonso de Castilla entered La Rioja, Araba and other lands,

which at the time belonged to the crown of Navarre, being in the City of Vitoria, the Gipuzkoans summoned him and they surrendered to him of their own free will, with the armies of San Sebastián, Fuente Rabia [Hondarribia], and others of the land, because they had wanted to do so for many days because of the insults and outrages they say they had committed against them and new taxes that the Kings of Navarre wanted to impose upon them, but in response to Çamalloa [Zamalloa], I say that there was no way that they could have done so, because they belonged then as now to the crown of Spain they could not give themselves to another Prince, neither could they have done so in those times, because as they were their Kings and natural Lords under whose reign and crown they were subjects as they are now to the Kings of Castile with the title of Subjects and Vassals, and they were so from the first King Don García Ximénez until the aforementioned Don Sancho for a period of five hundred years, . . . In five years that the wars of Cantabria lasted, although they conquered Araba and Navarre, and other parts of Cantabria along with the rest of Spain, they were never able to conquer Gipuzkoa and Bizkaia, and that for this reason the Basque language has been preserved in them, because fortifying themselves in the mountain of Menduria they fought so courageously with the Romans that they inflicted many injuries on them and to keep from giving them the triumph of conquering them they allowed themselves to die of hunger . . . letting it be known too that they were the true Cantabrians, with other apocryphal tales, which when I read them gave me much to ponder, . . . because it will be impossible to find any Spanish or foreign historian who mentions or says that the Patriarch Tubal, or his son King Ibero, or any other successor of his had ever made in Gipuzkoa, Bizkaia or Asturias de Oviedo any settlements until many years after his death, but only in Navarre and other regions from which, as we have stated in other parts of this work, originated all the others that were established in Spain and from which all Spaniards originate.[119]

For Sada, all the ancient denominations that could be related to the Tubalist episode, which therefore were all noble and worthy, were clearly manifested in Navarre (and only there), in such a way that these names were nothing but a succession of references to a single reality: Navarre, ". . . because before these events, these mountains had another name, just as Navarre was previously known as Iberia, Celtiberia, Vasconia, Cantabria, and by other names."[120] But in addition to the foundational myths, Sada attacks the political constructions that had been forged by the Bizkaians and the Gipuzkoans, such as the capture of the artillery in 1512:

> These same authors, insisting on praising the things of their country, refer among other things to that fabulous battle of Beotibar, where they say that 70,000 Frenchmen and Navarrese were crushed and defeated by 800 Gipuzkoans . . . concerning which many have remarked that no one could be persuaded to write such nonsense, and which is so repugnant to reason, especially since no Spanish or foreign historian could be found who would write such a thing, nor is there any written evidence of it or any authentic text, except for a single piece of paper which they say was found at the Puente la Reina [Gares], which, if it really existed, could have been forged by some Gipuzkoans and left there just so they could say that it was found in Navarre . . . Çaldibia [Zaldibia] goes on to say that when one of the Kings of Navarre was captured in a certain battle that he had with the King of Aragón, although he doesn't say which kings or where this happened, when the Gipuzkoans saw their king captured, because the army of Aragón was very powerful, with Catalonians, Valencians, and Aragonese, they charged against them so fiercely that, crushing their army, not only did they liberate the King of Navarre, but they captured the King of Aragón, and that thus the Gipuzkoans took a king by force, something that never happened nor could it ever, because as we have explained at length elsewhere, from the time the Royal house of Navarre was founded until it came under the sovereignty of that of Aragón, a period of almost three hundred years, that Province was ruled by a Count, and with this title it was under the crown of Navarre, and after the kings of Aragón were established, these two crowns were united for several years, so there could not have been any discord between Navarrese and Aragonese during all that time, nor could the imprisonments that this author refers to have occurred.[121]

And of course, Sada theorized about the kind of union that linked Navarre with the Spanish monarchy, constructing the idea of a union forged through a pact that gave limited power to the kings who had to swear to the *Fueros* in order to assume said power. He also thought that the events of 1512 did not constitute a conquest, as Garibay stated and with whom he disagrees, but a voluntary concession. According to Sada, power had been transferred from one king to another, thereby maintaining the essence of the *Fuero* from one kingdom to the next.

From there, the precedence of the kingdom over the king was established:

> . . . From which it follows that the power which the kings enjoy in Navarre is granted by reciprocal contract between them and their people, for with these conditions they elected them and gave them the oath as kings, and surrendered their lands which they had won through their valor from the Moors, and transferred the right and power which they had . . . and the King acting on his own cannot undo a *Fuero* without the Assembly and consent of the Kingdom, because if the annulment of statutes and laws depends on the jurisdictional authority of those who make them, and the power is limited in a way that cannot be ordained or decreed from outside . . . the Kings who have ruled in it, from the time of King Don Fernando, and united with Castile, have the same obligation as their predecessors to guarantee their ancient freedoms.[122]

The polemic surrounding Aragón, which generated some ideas that might be interpreted as disparagement of Navarre, was no less virulent. Góngora's tirades were such that the Diputación de Aragón (Aragonese regional government) appealed to the king to have the work destroyed, and it appears that it was in part. Basques and Aragonese alike were irate over Sada's *Apología*. Even in 1831, when José María Murga, a liberal historian from Jemein entered the Academia de la Historia as a corresponding member, he chose as his subject a critique of the *Apología*. It seems that even in the nineteenth century, inter-territorial resentments still lingered.

Pedro de Agramont insisted on assigning a preeminent position to the Kingdom of Navarre in relation to the other Spanish kingdoms. To begin with, he defended the position of the kings of Navarre, beginning with the first, García Ximénez, claiming that "he was a descendant of Tubal and his people, and that he was the first king of Navarre and an inhabitant of these mountains and of Cantabria, and therefore a native and speaker of the Basque language."[123] In addition, he argued that the Kingdom of Navarre was the first to be founded in Spain after the Muslim conquest, which would endow it with a corresponding preeminence over those instituted afterwards: "Whom the Kings of Navarre established in their monarchy, acquiring proper titles as legitimate and first born kings of Spain, and endowing their kingdom with primacy and authority throughout Spain, with priority over the others in the antiquity of royal dignity."[124] And he concludes: "Already in the other books, it has been verified and confirmed how the kings of Navarre, from their beginnings, were anointed, and that, because of this, they conserve until this day the title 'His Majesty' among all those of Spain, and it has been conferred and is even today in Navarre and even before it was incorporated into the crown of Castile. The kings of Navarre, for their antiquity, always had priority over all the others of Spain in the General Assemblies and other public acts."[125] To the Tubalist origins of Euskara in Navarre, Agramont adds the theories of Basque-Iberianism and primitive monotheism borrowed from the Basque and Gipuzkoan theorists, which are not present in Sada's text. In fact, Agramont bases the distinction and superiority of Navarre over other nations essentially on its early and enduring Catholicism. It converted before any other and without any opposition, and was constant in its preservation of the faith, without a single act of heresy within its territory.[126]

In spite of the strong territorializing of the Basque apologists of the sixteenth and seventeenth centuries, some introduced a notion that would consolidate itself in the eighteenth century: the idea that a united Euskal Herria be conceived as a cultural and idiomatic unit, if not an administrative one, and in a certain sense, a political one. Of course, the singularity of the *Fuero* will appear once again as an agglutinating and differentiating element with regard to the other territories of both monarchies. This united approach had already been clearly presented in the work of Oihenart, although he extended the analysis to the north to include all of Aquitania. After the middle of the eighteenth century, however, a good portion of those who write on Euskal Herria refer to it as a group of seven territories. Between 1761 and 1766, the Zuberoan, Jean-Philippe Bela (1709–1796), a military man, wrote a *Histoire des Basques* (History of the Basques) that was never published, in which he takes on the grouping of the country from this perspective. The constitutional bishop, Jean-Baptiste Sanadon, reworked the piece by Bela and published it in 1785 as *Essai sur la noblesse des basques...* (Essay on the Nobility of the Basques...), translated into Castilian the following year,[127] in which this cultural/national identity is proclaimed independent of the administrative borders of each territory:

> Today the name Basques includes the inhabitants of Upper Navarre, Araba, Gipuzkoa, and Bizkaia who recognize the King of Spain; and the inhabitants of Lower Navarre, Zuberoa, and Lapurdi who are subject to the Crown of France. All of these peoples speak the same language, which the Castilians call "Bascuenze"; the French "Basque"; and the natives of the Country call "Huscara" or "Euskara." Their habits and customs are the same; and there's much less difference between a Spanish Basque and a French Basque than

between two Spaniards or two Frenchmen from two different provinces, or even from two neighboring cities. For the identity of language, way of life, and customs has been considered throughout time as proof of the identity of origin.

Another Zuberoan, the schoolmaster Juseff Eguiateguy, began an unfinished and unpublished Basque history that, in spite of being based in Zuberoa, was to have included *Hüskaldunen kondaira jeneral* (General History of the Basques), that is, Basques from the seven territories. Years later, the Lapurdian priest, Jean Martin Hiribarren (1810–1866), published an extensive historical poem that likewise conceived of the entire Euskal Herria as a combined Basque culture, with the expressive title of *Escaldunak: Iberia, Cantabria, Eskal Herriac, Eskal-Herri bakhotcha eta hari darraicona* (The Basques: Iberia, Cantabria, Euskal Herria or Matters Concerning Each Basque Territory) (1853).[128]

6. The Ideological and Social Formation of the Theorists of the Modern Basque Mythical Construct

To understand the interests (personal or collective) that the creators of a specific mythic construct served, as well as their associations and their dependencies, it is necessary to develop a collective social profile of these theorists—a kind of sketch of these intellectuals, who were in service, either directly or indirectly, to specific political and juridical institutions. A close examination of the biographies of the theorists will allow us to further our understanding of their general interactions. Unfortunately, in the Basque case most of the information on many of them is rare and sketchy during this period; however, we can attempt a schematic social approximation of the best-known writers. During the foundational period of the mythic construct, we find the following:

Esteban de Garibay was a descendant of the Original Forebears, although only through a minor bloodline. Having lost the class status of his feudal origins, he became a historian, a royal chronicler, hence, the official historian of the monarchy. Moreover, because he belonged to the ruling class, he assumed political, military, and administrative positions: as ensign in the war against France, mayor of Arrasate-Mondragón, and Director of Exports for the Provincial Government of Gipuzkoa. Finally, given his absolute Catholicism, it is not surprising that he would be, as he was, a Minister of the Inquisition. Juan Martínez de Zaldibia had a similar profile. Likewise descended from the Original Forebears and having lost his original class status, he supplemented his legal training with a vocation as historian. He also held public offices; as mayor of Tolosa, he put his knowledge at the service of the province, either compiling the ordinances by order of the *Juntas* (Assemblies) or representing Gipuzkoa in Madrid. In addition to his career as an attorney, Francisco de Mendieta became a painter and a historian. His work on the Annals of Bizkaia "was compiled by order of the Seigniory," to whom he was obviously in service. He translated in iconographic terms the foundational ideas of the nobility, the *Fuero*, the pact with the monarchy, and the glorification of local religious beliefs (in the Virgin of Begoña). Poza was university trained, with an impressive background that included work in the juridical, mathematical, naval, and linguistic fields. He, as well as his family, was in the service of the monarchy in Flanders. The General Assembly of Bizkaia charged him, along with other representatives, to rebut the famous case of the Attorney General Juan García, in which the profile of Basque nobility was questioned. Juan Iñiguez Ibargüen was a scrivener who would be called a "documentarian" today. García Fernández de Cachopín was a doctor. Ibargüen took part, as did Poza, in the polemic against the prosecutor Juan García. Baltasar de Echave had a background in law, but was a writer and philologist by avocation and eventually became a highly reputable painter in Mexico. He held public offices, as Magistrate of the Royal Court in Mexico. Juan Arce de Otalora was a jurist and as such, he held the post of judge in the Chancelleries of Granada and Valladolid. Antonio Navarro de Larreategui was a typical high functionary of the administration of Asturias: accountant, secretary to King Felipe III, Secretary of the Archives of Simancas, etc. Juan Sada studied mathematics and liberal arts and worked as a teacher. Lope Martínez de Isasti was a priest, but from a family of shipbuilders who held posts in this field in the service of the monarchy. He himself served as harbormaster of the Royal Fleet. He was otherwise involved with the repression of witchcraft. Pedro de Agramont was a scrivener from a family dynasty of scriveners in Tudela. He was a classical example of the urban bourgeoisie, most likely originally a convert. Alfonso Rodríguez de Guevara seemed to have worked for the monarchy in Milan, without abandoning his Basque roots. Arnaud Oihenart was a jurist who came from a family of jurists and functionaries on both his paternal and maternal sides. The Third Estate elected him Delegate to the Silviet (Assembly) in Zuberoa and when he became affiliated by marriage with Lower Navarre, he served as a lawyer in the parliament of Navarre. Gabriel de Henao was a Jesuit from Valladolid who lived for years in Bilbao. But his real contact with the Basque Country was through the Company of Jesus. In his zeal to uphold the noble house of the Founder, he created an extremely erudite work that would prove, on the one hand, the link between Saint Ignatius and the three Basque provinces, and on the other, the excellence of these three territories. Henao was the quintessential classical and ecclesiastical intellect.

A dual incentive is evident in the work of these intellectuals. From one perspective, they responded to concrete interests: corporate, familial (whether personal or through lineage), in the service of which they establish lines of argumentation or select specific ideas to develop. From another perspective, they functioned under certain limitations, namely, the system of sponsorship, or patronage, with direct authority or economic oversight that frequently either forced or directed their arguments in specific directions, namely in the service of the lines established by the institutions or patrons in charge. Finally, their thoughts were, in some way, an expression of the commonly accepted values of their day, what was disseminated as the most widely acknowledged and practical, "what is remembered after all else is forgotten"—an intellectual magma that these theorists tried to shape and legitimate coherently.

With the exception of Father Henao, who was a Jesuit, and Isasti, a priest with family and personal connections in service to the Crown, the rest were all members of the bourgeoisie, very much allied to the interests of the Monarchy, whom they served or tried to serve through the legal profession. The majority held public offices. Several worked as advisors on legal, political, or intellectual matters in the service of their respective territories. They wrote in Spanish, although they might have been Basque and have spoken Euskara. Without a doubt, these authors were writing for an audience outside the Basque Country; they were not addressing their compatriots and so they used Latin, Spanish, or French. They defended the interests of the *Fuero* in their territories. They were members of the lay community, but they were deeply committed to the spirit of the Counterreformation, defenders of the Company of Jesus, the Inquisition, and opposed to witchcraft. In sum, they defended the monarchic state, the values of the Counterreformation, and the *foral* status of their respective territories—the Kingdom of Navarre for Sada and Agramont; the Province of Gipuzkoa for Echave, Isasti, and Zaldibia; the Seigniory of Bizkaia for Poza; and Zuberoa and Lower Navarre for Oihenart. It was the triumph of the urban, bourgeois functionary in the service of the new monarchic and *foral* institutions, to the detriment of the old powers of the Seigniory.

The loyalty of the theorists towards these institutions did not end with the responsibilities entrusted to Poza and Mendieta by the Assembly of Bizkaia, or to Zaldibia by those of Gipuzkoa, or with the translation of the New Testament by Leizarraga's group, under the auspices of Margarita of Navarre; or with the appointment of Moret as chronicler of Navarre and the creator of its History sponsored by the Crown; or with the obvious dependence of Garibay on the Monarchy or of Henao on the Company of Jesus. A more subtle system of patronage spread among the intellectuals of the time. The issue of the patronage of intellectual work at this time is very suggestive. Of course, a good many works were commissioned specifically for the consolidation of a particular intellectual, political, or religious position, etc. But in addition, some works that appear without a previous charge are assigned to specific individuals who can be counted on to render aid and support should the need for it arise; the publications of this era usually name monarchs, nobles, bishops, etc. in their dedications. This must be understood as truly a strategy of survival and not as a mere adulation. As such, we know that several works published in Euskara at the beginning of the seventeenth century in the Basque Country of the Northern Pyrenees—*Gero* (Later) by Axular, *Eliçara erabiltceco liburua* (Book to Use to Go to Church) by Joannes Etcheberry of Ziburu (Ciboure), for example—are dedicated to Bertrand de Echauz (1556–1651), a native of Baigorri (Lower Navarre), Bishop of Baiona (Bayonne) (1599–1618), and later of Tours (1618–1641). We must assume that he, whom Axular calls *Kantabres fina* (a fine Cantabrian), was a powerful defender of the Counterreformationist catechesis in the vernacular language, and that without his protection these types of manuscripts ran the risk of remaining unpublished.

In any case, there are some interesting developments within this panorama. It does not seem accidental that the earliest theorists in the last decades of the sixteenth century maintained a strict fidelity to the specific territories (Bizkaia and Gipuzkoa) that were still in the process of formation, while towards the beginning of the seventeenth century, some writers prefigure another kind of framework and solidarity. Oihenart does not have as well defined a territorial adscription; rather, he defends a cultural trans-Pyrenean identity that encompasses all of the Basque Country, while denying the Iberian connection. From his perspective, Henao is inclined toward a territorialization of the three Basque provinces. One can probably speak of a novel configuration of interests already evident by the middle of the seventeenth century.

By comparison and contrast, the second reformulation of this ideological construct formulated roughly between 1750 and 1804, presents notable differences with regard to the theorists' social and professional interests. We must consider two primary lines of thought (each with its own ramifications). The first is clearly tied to ecclesiastical interests, headed by clerics (Larramendi, Cardaberaz, Astarloa, Moguel, Santa Teresa, Hervás, Sorreguieta, and Sanadon) or laypersons (Iturriza) equally imbued with religious values; the second, by laypersons more or less amenable to the Enlightenment in its bourgeois, noble, and popular versions (Peñaflorida, Olaso, Foronda, and Iztueta), but with a shared modernizing vision of the Basque territory driven by concerns of the political and cultural institutions shared by the three Basque provinces.

The era when the modernist paradigm was being replaced by a nationalist and romantic one began with the revolutionary projects of the 1830s and 40s and ended with the rise of Aranism (followers of Sabino Arana, the creator of Bizkaian, and later Basque, nationalism). It included intellectuals with different ideologies from both lay and bourgeois backgrounds, who nonetheless had religion as a common referent that they either supported or denied depending on the specific case, but that remained an inescapable point of reference. One would have to include among them the writers of the legends—Juan Venancio de Araquistain (*Tradiciones vasco-cántabras*; Basque-Cantabrian Traditions), Antonio Trueba (*Cuentos populares*; Popular Tales), José María Goizueta (*Leyendas vascongadas*; Basque Legends), Vicente Arana (*Leyendas de Euskaria*; Legends of the Basque Country), Francisco Navarro Villoslada (*Amaya o los vascos en el siglo VIII*; Amaya or the Basques in the Eighth Century), as well as Zamácola, Nicasio Landa, Iturralde y Suit, Campión, Yanguas, and Oloriz—but giving special attention to the initiator: Agustín Chaho.

Among the many concerns of the Zuberoan native connected to the Basque system of identity, the most noteworthy is the creation of the seminal legends that gave rise to a new Basque mythic construct. In serial format, he published *Lelo ou la Navarre il y a 500 ans* (Lelo, or Navarre 500 Years Ago) in serial format in his newspaper *Ariel*, but even more important was his legend of Aitor (*Aîtor, Légende Cantabre*; Aitor, Cantabrian Legend). It was published in 1845 and later was taken up again by Francisco Navarro Villoslada and Arturo Campión, who translated and published it in the *Revista Euskara* in 1878.[129] The success of the legend was such that today Aitor is one of the most common names for children in some Basque territories. The text that appeared in *Ariel* is a narrative about the origins of the Basque people and their language, as narrated by the presumed legendary patriarch. It deals with a matter of some transcendence, since Aitor aspires to replace in the Basque mythological construct the classical-religious myth of Tubal, the unassailable legitimizing referent of the entire Basque ideological framework from the Middle Ages to the nineteenth century. Within the plan that Chaho laid out for himself for the exploration of the territorial origins of the Basques, the crowning figure was the patriarch himself, the presumed originator of the progeny. The name Chaho invented is a bit farfetched, based on an essential traditional concept: the notion of Basque nobility. As such, the equivalent in Basque for "noble" (hidalgo) would be *Aitonen semea,* literally "the son of good parents," or more liberally, "the son of nobles." Chaho pretends that the term in reality is *Aitor-en semea,* that is, "son of Aitor." The fact that it lacks any historical or linguistic foundation is unimportant. What is essential is the coherence and plausibility of the myth: a romantic discourse, not scientific, legendary, or historical, manifestly distanced from rationalist paradigms but one that nonetheless represents an effective alternative to the Biblical Tubalist myth. It provided a transition from a myth with Semitic roots to one with Basque and nationalist roots. Essentially, the legend unfolds as follows: Under the sacred oak of Gherekiz, the improvisational bard, Lara, relays to the Basques the story of their origins, their people, and their language. In it, the fundamental elements that supposedly make up the Basque soul merge: the language/people as one identity, the oral nature of the culture, and the sacred protection of the oak tree, a symbol of a secular political freedom ever inviolate. The connection between political identity and language, or if one prefers, a political nationalist project with a cultural and esoteric foundation, appears to be in this case utterly remarkable.[130]

In any case, that Chaho would attempt to replace the very heart of the traditional identity theory as manifested in the figure of Tubal with the supposed patriarch Aitor, after which the origins of the Basques and the Spaniards would no longer be identical—or in what amounts to the same thing, that he should completely abandon the notion of nationality based on a Judeo-Christian myth in favor of one that seeks validation in a presumably pagan legend—does not keep the author from Atharratze from summarizing and embodying a good part of the traditional theory. In fact, it would turn out to be his most complete and finished legacy and text. Chaho presents himself as an author/bridge who takes up the elements of Cantabrianism, Iberianism, and the Basque language itself in order to insert them into his own somewhat original theoretical system. To put it another way, although the subject remains the same from Zaldibia to Chaho, the meaning changes in the process of taking up the old arguments and placing them within a new framework. As such, the Iberianism of Garibay and the theorists of the sixteenth century, for example, was completely Spanish in nature and consistently underscored the identification of the Basque and Iberian, in the sense that the Basque was "what is genuinely Spanish." For Chaho, however, the Iberians (the primitive Basques) are the Children of the Sun, the embodiment of the golden age whose civilization was compromised and in part destroyed by the incursion of the Sythian-Celts. The Basque culture interpolated itself among the peoples of the South (Iberia, Gaul,

Latio, and North Africa) who maintained a secular struggle against the barbarians of the north, in particular the Celts. Chaho's Basque-Iberian is a national, primogenital Basque who has nothing in common with the Spain of Felipe II; he is an independent and freedom-minded Basque, who rejects any rule but that of his own traditional law derived from the natural/golden state. Euskal Herria became the repository of the values, way of life, and language of the ancient peoples of the south who had been wiped out by the barbarian invasions from the north:

> "You know as well as I, my dear Lapurdian friend, that the Basques trace their origin back to the Iberian patriarch Aitor, and that every peasant of the Cantabrian race, every heroic soldier, every free man is considered noble among us, and a son of Aitor, *Aitoren seme.*"
>
> "That's true," replied the old man. "Now I'll tell you that this name Aitor is allegorical; it means sublime, universal father, and our forefathers created it to recall the primal nobility and great antiquity of the race of the Euskaldunes. Our ancestors," said the old man, "were visionaries and learned men: they had a multitude of seers and prophets, and the Lamb shone brightly among them during the primitive epoch; their sons walked in darkness; they are sinners..."
>
> A moment of silence followed this observation by the old man from Lapurdi.
>
> "You are aware, are you not, friend from Lapurdi, that the Iberians, our grandfathers, have repopulated Spain, Gaul, and Italy following the great Flood; and that the patriarchs, on establishing their solar republic, improvised, with God's inspiration, our language Euskara, each sound a harmonious chord, each word the truth. That without any doubt the Basques, unique among all the peoples of the West, through knowledge of this divine Verb refer to themselves as *Eskualdun*; at the same time they give the name *erdara*, imperfect verb, semi-language, to the mixed dialects, to the dark jargons of the foreign peoples, making no exception even for the Spanish and French languages."
>
> "All this is true," said the old man, whose attention grew ever more intense.
>
> "Perhaps, Lapurdian friend, you have heard the story of the invasion of the peoples from the North and of the tartars that brought the golden age to an end and initiated for humanity the age of blood and darkness and the reign of the evil spirit. The victory by the barbarians drove our ancestors out of their beautiful land, and deforested throughout Iberia the oak trees of the feder-

ated republics. The land of the *Eúskaros, Eskual Herria,* which in ancient times included the entire Hispanic Peninsula and part of Gaul, was from that time reduced to the seven provinces which the Basques occupy today in the Western Pyrenees."[131]

Chaho summarizes many of the modern theorists' arguments, integrating them into his own esoteric theory; Cantabrianism, Iberianism, and the cultural elements maintained by the Basque people reveal a superior primogenital state—in language, customs, legislation, etc. Among the customs that Chaho identifies with a superior primitive civilization is the presumed practice of the couvade—the equality between the sexes among the Basques that endows women with an incomparably more equal position to men, a sense of hospitality, and a supposed historic proscription of wine:

> The identity of language, customs, laws and the testimony of history provide unanimous proof of the uninterrupted alliance binding us, the Basques, to the original Iberians through the ancient Cantabrians and Vasconians. The law that prohibited these aboriginal peoples from growing grapes and drinking wine has remained in effect from then until this century. There are valleys in this province whose inhabitants remember how infants were raised in the society: the Bizkaian women abandon them in their bed immediately after giving birth, and the man from the mountain takes his wife's place beside the newborn . . . Alongside these primitive customs, ancient institutions flourish that denote a perfect civilization: the Cantabrian woman enjoys perfect equality in the social order; she receives the title of *etxekoandre* (lady of the house) and can inherit the family home.[132]

It would be interesting to consider the proscription of wine among the Basques. As we have seen, earlier theorists, like Mendieta, allude to the subject but in a more cautious way. In comparing the sectarian era with his own Renaissance period, this writer explains that previously, wine was not consumed in Bizkaia, only cider, which kept all its inhabitants healthy and strong. A vineyard called *Chiriboga* was planted in each *Merindad* (district) for the cultivation of a medicinal wine used exclusively for the sick. Chaho, as we see, goes way beyond this and pretends that a prohibition to the planting of vineyards existed in this territory. Of course, the connection of wine to post-Babel civilization and the earlier abstinence from alcohol were characteristic particularities of the golden age. Noah, as the first to be inebriated according to biblical texts, would mark a before and after for the consumption of alcohol. Up to his time, the innocence of Paradise had made the virtues of the fermented grape unknown. And to be sure, if one were to assume that the Basques formed part of pre-Babel civilization, the lack of consumption of alcohol and indeed the prohibition of wine would be in sync with the characteristics of this civilization. By the time Chaho was writing, either his speculations on the subject of wine were completely mistaken or the original qualities of the Basques had totally degenerated.

Of course, all the symbols identifying the People of the Sun translate into national political terms that, although rooted in Oihenart, have absolutely the same intentionality: although predominantly cultural in Oihenart, they are totally political in Chaho:

> Ensconced among their mountain peaks, according to the picturesque expression of Floro, the Basques believed those crags were an integral part of their nature; it was utterly inconceivable to them, even without the perfect oneness of origin, language, customs, and laws, that the circumstance of inhabiting either the northern or the southern side of the Pyrenees would be sufficient to divide politically two peoples that adjoin and merge with each other at the intersection of the valleys. Based on this principle and on historical law, perhaps one day, the Basques will try to recover the national unity they enjoyed yesteryear. The interpolation of a small free people advocates struggles that only the close proximity of large nations can bring about. If evil influences do not stifle the voice of justice and sound policy, the independence of the Cantabrian federation will be proclaimed without resistance.[133]

The apparent contradiction that Chaho embodies—that despite being a republican and committed progressive all his sympathies turned him toward the Carlist cause—can be resolved in terms of the secular, civilizing confrontation between the peoples of the north and those of the south, between one civilization that is dark and barbaric and another that is light and cultured. For Chaho, the Basque political system, derived from the golden age, was perfectly egalitarian, representative, free, and republican. He had nothing to learn from the new liberal constitutional systems because his own was liberal and perfect before any of them. In the esoteric logic of the man from Atharratze (Tardets), there was no comparison between the Basque Republic of Visionaries and the modern republics inspired by the Revolution. For the Basques, the adoption of liberalism would represent a retreat, whereas for the peoples descended from the Visigoths and Celts (the barbarians) it represented, in effect, a great step forward. This being so, Chaho failed to see the profoundly reactionary and religious significance of Carlism, preferring to view it as a popular movement of anti-Spanish resistance and national restoration. In his texts dealing with this topic, the *Voyage en Navarre* (Journey to Navarre...) as well as his *Paroles d'un Biscaïen...* (Words of a Bizkaian...), or in articles published in *Ariel*, this interpretation is tangibly apparent:

> Know this, you liberal sophists from Madrid, the Basques always rejected and despised your bastard liberalism, looked with horror on your vile yoke. I hear you define Progress, and it makes me laugh because I know that the regeneration of savages is a hopeless convalescence. You go forward ass backwards. All Basques are equal, all Basques are free, de facto and de jure; and in your world, the wretched people, reduced to the condition of slaves, are nothing but a vile herd of men without manhood. You want to Frenchify Castile; in this, only the Spaniards can win; we Basques can only lose. For us, your progressive institutions would be reactionary. The Basques are an ideal people, who wish only to imitate the Republic of their forefathers. To whom are you talking about a Constitution? You think you've invented freedom, charlatans of yesterday—what will you be tomorrow?[134]

Or:

> *Batzuek Isabel, bertzek Karlos Montemolin; bertze gizako zuten Kantabre zaharrek bere bandera zaharrena,* Lauburua *deitzen zutena, eta arte denborako bandera berria.* Irurak-bata, *bere irur eskuekin, Eskualdunen Errepublika famatua errepresentatzen zuena. Nork oiho eginen du, azkenian, errege-erreginak eta heien partidario tontoak edo anbiziosak akazatu ondoan: Biba Independentzia¡ Biba Errepublika¡ Biba Eskual Herria!* [Some in favor of Isabel, others Carlos Montemolin; the ancient Cantabrians raised their flag, which they called *Lauburu*, in a different way, and that of modern times, *Irurak-bat*, with its three interlocking hands, representing the famous Basque Republic. Who could finally exclaim, after finishing off the kings and queens and their foolish ambitious followers: Long live independence! Long live the Republic! Long live the Basque Country!].[135]

For Chaho, the recovery of national freedom is linked to the culture and the language through the one feature that is supposedly most genuinely Basque: orality. Relegated to the Pyrenees in the face of Scythian-Celt and Tartar hostilities and lacking in written forms of expression, the Basque people were forced to maintain their language and their culture in oral form. The clearly romantic vindication of the oral as a sign of Basque identity would affirm the nobility and national will of the Basque people:

> The Basque of the Pyrenees, the Euskarian, and the Iberian with no written tradition, lost his legends, his poems, but he preserved monuments that were far more enduring: his laws, the songs of his improvisational bards that the old people repeat and the child assimilates, and, especially, a wise and virginal language, exactly as it was spoken, after having invented it, the Indian or Atlantic society in the beginning . . . And what book could be comparable to this living concert of a million voices with accents bursting with audacity and originality, singular, never comprehended, without analogies among the languages existing today, . . . what can be said of an entire people, a living people, when it rises up like a single man, armed, seeking his secular independence, to the shout of war or freedom...[136]

After Chaho, we find a pleiad of late romantic writers extending almost to the end of the century. The political landscape in Euskal Herria had changed, and the ideological context in which the literary versions of the Basque legends had been produced was notably different. With some qualifications, the majority of the romantic writers of the Basque legends were conservative, traditional if not counterrevolutionary, and proponents of the late *foral* system, a fact easily explained by the two Carlist wars between 1841 and 1876 that brought about the collapse of institutional *foralism*.[137] Araquistáin, Goizueta, Trueba, Iturralde, etc. were not folklorists who would adopt traditional themes and put them in literary form; instead, inspired by the issues raised in the treatises of the Old Regime, they imitated their style and contents and invented new legends that would serve contemporary needs. An essential difference that should be noted among the folklorists, like Jean de Jaurgain and later Azkue, and the writers of legends is that the first group compiled materials in Euskara, while the latter wrote their legends exclusively in Spanish. As such, along with the *lamia* or the Lady with Goat's Feet, the old battles and the old heroes of Basque independence (Arrigorriaga, Beotibar, Hernio, Lekobide, Lelo, Jaun Zuria, etc.) were taken up along with their single subliminal or explicit message: In the same way that the ancient Basques took up arms to defend their freedom, so too, the Carlists of today are ready to defend their institutions.

Juan Venancio de Araquistáin from Deba (Gipuzkoa) serves as a model for the school of thought on which the romantic Basque legends of the nineteenth century rely. His *Tradiciones vasco-cántabras* begins with a dedication in the old style ("*Dedicatoria a L. M. N. y L. Provincia de Guipúzcoa*" or "Dedication to the Most Noble and Loyal Province of Gipuzkoa"), which nevertheless has nothing to do with the legends of Zaldibia's day. In this text, he tries to justify the value of popular knowledge gained through traditions, stories, legends, etc.—that is, through the heritage of common wisdom. "It is true," states Araquistáin, "that this popular knowledge based on truth is also imbued with superstition, but are science and religion not so imbued in the same way?" There is no possibility of comparison between popular knowledge and historically accepted knowledge, because both are fallible and prone to contagion by superstition; historical scientific knowledge is dry, whereas popular knowledge is full of sentiment and emotion. People, and among them the Basques, have been able to maintain their "spirit," their identity, through time and revolutions, while powerful institutions have fallen. Of course, the transmission of this heritage is oral in the Basque style. The theoretical base, then, of the "popular spirit" is to be found in Herder, and the justification of its importance was based on the testimony of a Catholic and conservative historian, César Cantu:

> Popular traditions, says the illustrious Catholic philosopher and eminent historian Cantu, "although they seem trivial or perverse, proceed from some great deed, or have their origin in a profound truth; hence, for one who seeks in history, not the anecdote but the man, they cannot be regarded with indifference." Traditions and popular songs, adds Herder, "are the archives of the people, the treasury of its knowledge, its religion, and its cosmogony; they are the life of their ancestors, the annals of their history." . . . Amid the grand convulsions that have shaken Europe, dragging down and destroying great empires, robust nations, languages, monuments, and even entire races, our forefathers have known how to extract, unscathed from all those storms their nationality, their institutions, language, and customs . . . But obeying this traditional spirit, which is the characteristic seal of our race, and entrusting to it the preservation of its institutions and history, they have never bothered to transmit to their children in written form the stories of their great exploits, the secret of their robust organization, or,

> finally, the secret of their territory and wealth . . . And do you think their popular beliefs have played no part in allowing the Basque Country to rise up today unique and alone among the ruin and desolation of all the primitive peoples, with the same language, customs, and the same blood with which she lives amid those opulent empires whose memory is now vanishing from the memory of the human race? Certainly not. And whatever influence it may have succeeded in exercising elsewhere, it must necessarily have been extraordinary in a people, traditional by nature, traditional by history, and traditional in its institutions and existence. What they say is true then, that the nation that can assemble the most complete collection of traditions, songs, and popular legends would be the one that had the most perfected history. Thus, in all the states of Germany, they devote themselves with enthusiasm and zeal to the publication of this genre of studies; and in France, the government itself has assumed responsibility for this labor, as a national priority . . . Therefore, the only road open to us is the memory of our people.[138]

It is quite clear that what Araquistáin understands as "the memory of our people" is actually the memory of the theorists who created the *foral* theory: Jaun Zuria, Beotibar, Cantabria against Rome, etc. appropriated from Zaldibia, Echave, Otalora, Poza, or Guevara. The discourse of the writers of the legends attempts to become an alternative defender of the *foral* order when the traditional arguments of the theorists, along with the system, are in crisis. When it becomes difficult to sustain the struggle of the Basques and Romans in Ernio against nineteenth century historical criticism, legend, as a presumed superior form of knowledge of the popular spirit, takes it up and legitimizes it.[139]

Given that religion occupies such an important place in the entire ideological framework with which we are dealing, it would be appropriate to examine the professional evolution of the theorists who constructed the different formulations of the Basque mythic construct. Specifically, if we focus on the writers under consideration in this essay, we will see that throughout the sixteenth century, the preponderance of the lay person over the ecclesiastical theorists is extraordinary (two thirds of the former to one third of the latter); later, throughout the seventeenth, eighteenth, and the beginnings of the nineteenthth centuries, the clerics attain a slight superiority over the lay theorists (58 percent), whereas the preponderance of the lay theorists from the second decade of the nineteenth century on becomes overwhelming at 81 percent.

7. Euskara and the Vernacular Languages of the Renaissance

The commonly accepted theories on language in the Middle Ages rested on a basic premise: the divine origin of language. Logically, this would imply that at one time all of humanity spoke only one language, which most writers believed was Hebrew. The obvious diversity of languages was explained as the punishment imposed on humans for their hubristic sin of attempting to emulate God with the construction of the Tower of Babel. Apart from that, it was assumed that an intimate relationship existed between the object named and the name imposed, and that finally, language was a means of dominating nature and other men, as evidenced in Genesis in the episode in which Adam gives names to things. As a general practice, there was unanimous agreement that Latin was the vehicle for the transmission of higher knowledge.

The assertion that Hebrew had been the language of Paradise was sanctioned in the fifth century thanks to the authority of Saint Augustine (354–430), who affirmed this beyond any doubt in his *De civitate dei* (On the City of God), and this belief was generally held until the eighteenth century, although this does not mean that it was unanimously accepted. However, the majority of theories regarding the language of Paradise pointed to those languages from the Semitic family: Arabic, Phoenician, Syrian, and Aramaic. From Gregory of Nyssa to Maimonedes, through Theodore of Tyre or al-Maqdisi, some of these alternatives to Hebrew were proposed. There were, moreover, no shortage of other ideas: patriotic hypotheses about a number of other languages that attempted to challenge the privileged position of the Near Eastern theory developed by these classical writers. By the twelfth century, some held that Adam and Eve spoke a "*Teutonica lingua,*" and there would be many German writers in the following centuries who would maintain the primacy of origin of German over Hebrew. Luther himself subscribed to the idea that the Germanic peoples were descendants of Askenaz, grandson of Japheth, who was considered the primogenital offspring of Noah instead of Shem, giving the Japhetic Germans preeminence over the Semitic Jews. Johannes Goropius Becanus (*Origenes Antwerpianae...*; The Origins of Antwerp, 1569) held this same theory with reference to the Flemish. In a similar way, the following writers asserted that theirs was the original language: Olof Rudbeck with Swedish, Tycho Brahe with Danish, and Rowland Jones with English.[140] In any case, the notion of Hebrew as a proto-language from which all others were derived, was defended by, among other Renaissance writers, Guillaume Postel (1510–1581), who later provoked a veritable etymological frenzy, based purely on similarity, to prove this presumed linguistic derivation.[141]

The sixteenth century saw the revival of a debate from classical antiquity that lasted almost up to the twentieth century and that had important repercussions on the ideas of the Basque theorists: the question regarding the natural or artificial nature of man and the corresponding possibility of settling this question through the use of etymologies. In Genesis, we saw God and Adam naming things and animals, but did they impose these names arbitrarily or in correspondence with the natural or quintessential essence of each of them? The original reference that addresses this subject is the dialogue in Plato's *Cratylus,*[142] where Cratylus defends the position that the Nomothetikos designates things according to their own nature (*physis*), whereas Hermogenes holds that it is done according to a human law or convention (*nomos*). The notion that phonemes had their own meaning or that they articulated a single specific meaning, was widely held, especially with the emergence of the "philosophical languages" towards the end of the eighteenth century. This phono-symbolism negated the principle of the double articulation of phonemes that could be organized in different orders resulting in different meanings. Otherwise, as indicated above, the etymological method that predominated for centuries was eminently mimetic, relating words to one another exclusively through their likenesses.

The sixteenth century witnessed several cultural changes of transcendental importance. First, the formation of modern states challenged an unshakeable dogma of the medieval period: the monopoly of Latin (or Greek or other languages that were considered scholarly, as the case may be) for practically anything literary or scientific, or for texts related to ecclesiastical or lay administration. To position the challenge presented by the vernacular languages accurately, we must pause for a moment to consider what was meant by scholarly or learned versus oral languages at that time.

The testimony somewhat later of an individual who was involved in maintaining the orthodoxy, the general inquisitor Antonio de Sotomayor, is emblematic of the general perspective on the subject up to the dawn of the eighteenth century: "These languages—Hebrew, Greek, Latin, Chaldean, Syrian, Ethiopian, Persian and Arabic—are not common or vulgar. This is true of the original languages, which are no longer used today in ordinary speech, whereby the reader can understand that all the other languages are vernacular."[143] It should also be noted that the majority of those languages regarded as scholarly were also liturgical, a status which conferred upon them still greater dimension and power. The challenge to the high languages also took another route, namely, through a greater understanding of the linguistic diversity of the world, of totally exotic language groups in the Indo-European family, from the Americas to Africa and Asia—all because of the proliferation of voyages and expeditions towards the end of the fifteenth century. As a result, by the end of the sixteenth century, the notion of the indisputable primacy of Hebrew is called into question, and new myths arise—from Germanic, Celtic, and even Basque—challenging its status as the original language. Running parallel to this growing understanding of the world's languages are the early attempts at classification through the comparative method, in particular through the work of Joseph Justus Scaliger (1540–1609), who produced a catalogue free of nationalist abuses where he also diverged from the premise that no relationship existed among the "matrix languages" (that is, those at the top of linguistic groupings).

The debate surrounding the use of vernacular languages, quite characteristic of the Renaissance and the established monarchies in power, would be quickly resolved in their favor, between approximately 1520 and 1560. By mid-century, the dominant national languages in the various European countries had already become the languages used by their respective governments. Paradoxically, it was at this point that because of a renewed interest in classical culture, the prestige of the high/scholarly languages reached its zenith. The demise of the Church as a universal and unifying power, however, was undeniable, and in its place, secular powers based on sharp political distinctions sprang up along with their corresponding distinctive languages. Clearly, the majority of these states were multilingual, so much so that the selection of one of these languages to conduct administrative practices condemned the rest to marginalization and orality. Therefore, from the sixteenth century on, most literary production and ecclesiastical administration remained in Latin (and as the case may be, in other liturgical languages such as Arabic, Hebrew, or Slovenian), at least for a while. The various states chose one of their languages for governance and commerce, and also supported the creation of a national literature in that language. The rest were excluded from learned/scholarly use, and they became the means of communication among the popular classes in the familial and local sphere.

In France, a succession of kings, from the time of Louis XII (1498) up to Richard III (1589), decided to protect and promote the *langue d'oïl* (northern French) rather than the *langue d'oc* (southern French), although the culmination of this process occurred with the pronouncement of the Edict of Villers-Cotterêts (1539) by François I, which confirmed French as the language of governance; from that point on, all judicial pronouncements had to be "spoken, registered, and issued in the maternal language of French and in no other fashion."[144] In spite of the fact that his maternal language was Flemish, the Emperor Carlos I did not hesitate in promoting Spanish in his kingdoms as the language of governance, although according to the Crown of Aragón, Catalan remained in use in some sectors. His speech given in Naples in 1535 to this effect is quite famous.

This process culminated with a decree from Felipe II in 1583 requiring instruction in all the sciences from then on to be in the common language of Spanish instead of Latin, which had been standard and compulsory up to that time. The Tudors, in spite of their Welsh blood, followed the same model with the Act of 1536, which established that: "No one who speaks or uses the Welsh language shall have or enjoy any occupation of any kind in this Kingdom of England or Wales or in other dominion of the King, under penalty of loss of these occupations, unless he uses and employs the English language."[145]

The elevation of the vernacular tongues, which was barely developed up to that time, to the rank of literary, scientific, and administrative forms of communication conferred upon such languages another useful tool: a well ordered lexicon, and above all, a good grammar, or as it was then called, an "Art." To a certain extent, the publication of the grammars of the different European languages runs parallel to the development of those same languages as the official languages of their respective states. The earliest published grammar was the Spanish *Gramática Castellana* (Castilian Grammar) (1492). Its author, Antonio de Nebrija (a pseudonym of Antonio Martínez de Cala, 1441–1522), in a model prologue dedicated, of course, to Queen Isabel, known as the Catholic queen, clearly makes the link between the building of Empire and the scientific development of the official language and its implementation as such: "After your Highness subjugates many barbaric peoples and nations with their strange languages, and with the conquest it will be necessary for them to receive the laws which the victor imposes on defeated, and with them our language, then they will be able to learn it using this grammatical art . . . One conclusion I find indisputable: always, language accompanies empire, and so inseparably that they were born together, grew together, flourished together, and at last both went into decline together."[146]

The first Italian grammar was produced by Pietro Bembo (1470–1547), *Prose della volgar lingua* (Prose of the Vulgar [i.e. Vernacular] Language) (1525), in which political and linguistic interests were likewise connected. France saw the appearance of its "art" with John Palsgrave's *L'Esclarcissement de la Langue Françoise* (Explanation of the

French Language), published in London in 1530; Portugal's first grammar, *Grammatica da Lingoagem Portuguesa* (Grammar of the Portuguese Language), was written by Fernão de Oliveira in 1536.

No real grammar of Euskara was published until Manuel de Larramendi brought out *El Imposible vencido* (Achieving the Impossible) (with its quite expressive title) in 1726, because previous attempts, such as *Modo breve de aprender la lengua vizcaína* (Quick Method for Learning the Basque Language) (1653) by Rafael de Micoleta, were not published until the nineteenth century, although they were compiled centuries before. Practical requirements, primarily commercial ones, necessitated the creation of dictionaries quite early, but they used a non-literary vocabulary, and in many cases, they were circulated as manuscripts and never published. This was the case with dictionaries written by Nicolás Landuchio (in 1562), Silvain Pouvreau (first half of the seventeenth century), and the lost works of Melchor Oyanguren or Joannes de Etcheberri (both written in the first half of the eighteenth century).

Once again, it was Larramendi who compiled the *Diccionario Trilingüe del Castellano, Bascuence y Latín* (Trilingual Dictionary of Castilian, Basque and Latin) published in 1745, which could be considered the first dictionary actually used by later writers. Two circumstances related to this event should be noted: on the one hand, a good number of the frustrated attempts by other Basque writers to publish dictionaries and grammars were made in commercial centers, such as Vitoria-Gasteiz, Bilbao, or the Lapurdi coast, where there was obviously a practical need for them. But on the other hand, it is also clear that the public authorities did not demonstrate the slightest interest in the publication of these works, thereby reducing them to mere personal initiatives that remained unpublished because of a lack of support.

In addition to the grammars (and at times concurrent with them), defenses of the various languages proliferated. A panegyric argument was common to all the writers: no language is better or worse than any other, any subject can be expressed in any of them, and they become more sophisticated through their development and use. For Spanish, the most famous exaltations were made by Juan de Valdés (1500–1542) in his *Diálogo de la lengua* (Dialogue on Language), in 1536, Ambrosio de Morales (1513–1591) in *Discurso de la Lengua Castellana* (Discourse on the Castilian Language), and Friar Luis de León in *Los nombres de Cristo* (Christ's Names) (1585). For his part, Cristóbal de Villalón, in presenting his grammatical treatise,[147] states:

> [I reflected] . . . on many occasions about the excellence, elegance, and perfection of the Castilian language, wondering who invented

it so I could hold the creator of such a wondrous thing in the high regard and veneration he deserves. All those who study languages and their authority and power say that the perfection and value of a language should be judged by its capacity to be reduced to art. This is why everyone says that the Hebrew, Greek, and Latin languages are the most perfect. This aggrieved me so greatly that out of sheer humiliation I held my tongue . . . The language that God has given us should be no less pleasant or esteemed than Latin, Greek, and Hebrew, which are in no way superior to our language, if only we praised and preserved and refined it with the elegance and indulgence that the Greeks and others lavished on theirs. He who values the language of another more than his own is his own worst enemy.

Fernão de Oliveira expressed himself in similar terms:

Greece and Rome are all the more vital because of this, because when they ruled the world they ordered all the peoples who were their subjects to learn their languages and in them they wrote many good doctrines and not only what they understood to be written in them but also they translated into them everything good that they found in others. And in this way, they forced us to work quickly to learn and understand theirs, neglecting our own. Let's not do the same thing, but come to our senses now that the time has come and we are lords, because it's better to teach Guinea than to be taught by Rome, even if she now had all her value and worth. And let us not mistrust our language because men make languages, languages don't make men. And it's clear that the Greek and Latin languages were crude in their infancy and the men brought them to their current perfection.[148]

As a result, apologies of the French language also proliferated: Joachim du Bellay (1525–1560), *Deffence et Illustration de la Langue Françoise* (Defense and Illustration of the French Language) in 1549; Henry Estienne (1531–1598), *Précellence du langage françois* (Of the Pre-Excellence of the French Language), *Deux dialogues du nouveau langage françois italianisé* (Two Dialogues on the New Italianized French Language) and *Traité de la conformité du langage française avec le grec* (Treaty on the Similarity of the French Language with Greek); and above all, Etienne Pasquier's (1529–1615), *Recherches de la France* (Research on France), 1560. This writer, the originator of a good part of the Gaelic mythic construct, explored an interesting political-linguistic landscape. According to him, the lack of an erudite French language that is courtly (*courtizane*) was the result of political fragmentation: "but our Kingdom was broken in pieces, and there were almost as many Courts as Provinces." By his time, however, the situation had changed: "Today the circumstances are quite different. Because all the great Dukes and Counts are united with our Crown, we write only in one language that of the Royal Court which we call the French language."[149]

With this precedent, the defense for using French instead of Latin was obvious to Pasquier: ". . . I will always be on the side of those who favor their Romance language; and it is my belief that we will resuscitate the golden age when, rejecting those bastardly opinions of affecting foreign ways, we will use what is natural and innate within us, effortlessly. What? Are we to call ourselves Frenchmen, that is, frank and free men, but enslave our minds to a foreign language?"[150]

In the context of these polemics between the proponents of Latin and those of the vernacular languages, a priest from Lower Navarre, Bernard Dechepare, was the first to publish a book in Euskara in 1545. It was titled *Linguae Vasconum Primitiae* (Primitive Basque Language). Its contents could not have been more in harmony with the times: religious and love poems dedicated to the exaltation of the language in which they were written: "*heuscara*" (Euskara)—a true vindication. In the introductory poems (*Sautrela* [saltarello] and *Contrapas*), Dechepare proclaimed the motives that had led him to venture into such unknown territory: to infuse the language with the essential tonic for its conservation—self-esteem and social prestige: "*Heuscaldunac mundu orotan preciatu ciraden / Baina hayen lengoagiaz berce oro burlatzen / Ceren eceyn scripturan erideiten ezpaitzen / Oray dute iccassiren nola gauça hona cen*" [The Basques were esteemed throughout the world / but everyone made fun of their language / because it had no written form / Now everyone knows how proficient a language it is]. Moreover, he hit upon another basic element for the preservation of the language: that far from being relegated to use only by the popular sectors, it was the powerful who were developing and using it: "*Printze eta iaun handiec oroc haren galdia / Scribatus hal balute iqhasteco desira*" [Princes and great lords alike express an interest in it / They are anxious to learn and be able to write it]. Was Dechepare describing a wish or a reality during this time? The recent discovery of the so-called "Lazarraga manuscript"[151] leads us to the possibility that it was likely more the latter than the former. At least one of these "great lords," Joan Pérez de Lazarraga, did so during the years 1564–67. This is the story of a noble, the head of an important bloodline that extended its economic reach on horseback from the Aitzgorri Mountain range to the lands of the people of Oñati

(Oñate) and Araba. From his tower in Larrea, he carried on the important work of developing a genealogy of the Spanish language, which was already known. In addition, he became a poet of the Basque language, writing on subjects similar to those of Dechepare—religion, love, and pastoral poetry. For his part, the aforementioned Joannes Leizarraga restored, at just about this time, the parity of Basque with other languages when it was called on to serve as a refined and erudite instrument: "*Alabaina segur içanez ecen Heuscaldunac berce natione gucien artean ez garela hain basa, non gure lengoagez ecin eçagut eta lauda deçagun gure Iainco Iauna . . . Berce natione guciek, ceinec bere lengoagean bezala, Heuscaldunac ere berean duençat, certan iracurçen icas ahal deçan*" [Moreover, we are sure that we Basques, among all the other nations, are not so savage that we do not know our own language and praise Our Lord in it . . . Just as all other peoples, the Basques can learn to read in their own language].[152]

The defense of the vernacular languages against the prestige of Latin and Greek was not exhausted in the nineteenth century;[153] many of the most celebrated writers who wrote in the vernacular felt pressured to mount a defense of their maternal language against the use of the erudite tongues, which indicates that the battle had not yet been won. In *La Dorotea,* Lope de Vega states that "each is obligated to honor his own language," and "the poet, in my view, should write in his natural language." Nonetheless, one of the most interesting positions related to this is found in the magnum opus of literature written in the Spanish language: *Don Quixote* by Miguel de Cervantes. In the dialogue between the Manchegan Hidalgo and the Caballero del Verde Gabán (part 2, ch. 16), the latter states that he has a son "who is eighteen years old. For six years, he has been in Salamanca learning the Latin and Greek languages . . . which the modern poets who write in the vernacular do not care much about," to which Quixote responds:

> And regarding what you say, Sir, that your son has little regard for poems in the vernacular, I believe he's misguided, and for this reason: the great Homer did not write in Latin, being Greek, and Virgil did not write in Greek, being Latin. In short, all the ancient poets wrote in the language they drank in with their mother's milk, and they did not go out looking for foreign languages to express their lofty thoughts; and this being so, it would be reasonable to extend this custom throughout all nations, and not look down on the German poet because he writes in his language, or the Castilian poet, or even the Basque poet who writes in his.

This quotation is interesting for two reasons: In addition to a generic vindication of the mother tongue, and along with German and Spanish, "*vizcaína*" is mentioned, that is, Basque, although there is an "even" before it that gives away the meager literary use the language had at that time. This, nonetheless, serves as an extreme example—even the Basques, whose language was clearly marginal, had a right, according to Cervantes, to use it for literary purposes.

From another perspective, the sixteenth-century Protestant Reformation, along with the corresponding Catholic Counterreformation, signaled a new cultural stage in which different scenarios of opportunities and different threats directed at the vernacular languages emerged. The different attitude of Lutherans and Calvinists toward sacred texts and their personal interpretation implied not only the freedom of Christians to read them, but also the convenience, and indeed, the obligation to do so. This entailed a double responsibility: to make these texts available in the "vulgar" languages and to ensure that the popular masses had the minimal level of instruction that would allow them to grasp the written language. The Catholicism of the Counterreformation restricted the reading of the Bible to the clergy and to the "educated," thereby effectively eliminating any direct contact by the people with the sacred texts. For this reason, the religious bent of governing princes toward one camp or another implied a distinct cultural stance: either to promote the reading of the Bible in the vernacular or to bar the people from any contact with the written word. From very early on, those countries in North and Central Europe where the Reformation had begun, therefore, had translations of the Bible in their respective languages, usually the New Testament first and later the entire Bible.

Before the beginnings of the Reformation, of course, there had already been a multitude of translations written before the Protestant ones appeared—some partial and others complete—into Armenian in the fifth century and Bulgarian in the ninth century by the monks Cyril and Menodius. By the thirteenth century, there had been several partial translations into Anglo-Saxon, Gothic, Spanish, and French. The Bible of Guyart Desmoulins was published in French two centuries later (NT 1478, OT 1487). The monk Bonifaci Ferrer in the Valencian monastery of Porta Coeli translated the Bible into Catalan in 1478. John Wycliffe translated the Vulgate to English in 1382, which circulated in manuscript form. From the invention of the printing press until 1526, some 156 vernacular versions of the Bible were in circulation in different translations. Although Luther is credited with the first translation into German, there were several earlier versions, to be specific, fourteen in High German and four in Low German. But it is after 1522 that the momentum of

Protestantism accelerates the publication of both partial and complete translations of the Bible: Martin Luther into German (1522–1534); Olaus Petri (Olof Peterson) (1493–1573) into Swedish (NT 1526, OT 1541); Robert Estienne in 1528 and Pierre Robert in 1535 into French; Cristen Pederson (d. 1554) into Danish (NT 1529, OT 1550); Odd Gottskalksson into Icelandic (NT 1540, OT 1584); Mikael Agricola (1510–1557) into Finnish (NT 1543); William Tyndale (1495–1536) in 1526 (NT) and Miles Coverdale in 1535 into English; Jurij Dalmatin (d. 1589) into Slovenian in 1584; the Bible was also translated into Dutch in 1526, into Gaelic in 1567, and into other languages as well.

Meanwhile, translations in the Catholic countries appeared much later. A partial translation into Spanish was done by Casiodoro de Reyna (1520–1594) in 1569 (the so-called *Biblia del Oso* [Bear Bible]), but Felipe Scio de San Miguel's translation of the entire Vulgate was not completed until 1791–93. The first partial translations of the Vulgate into Italian were those of Antonio Bruccioli (1495–1566) in 1532 and Giovanni Diodati in 1607; the first complete translation, by Antonio Martini, was not published until 1769 (NT) and 1775 (OT). The translation of the Bible in Portugal also appears at about this time, 1778–90, thanks to Antonio Pereira de Figueiredo.[154] Apart from this, the early existence (in 1581) of a translation of the Bible in the orthodox liturgical language, Slovakian, could explain the long delay in the appearance of translations in other Slavic countries and languages: Russian in 1867 and Serbian in 1868.

What influence did translations of the Bible into the vernacular languages have on the rise or on the preservation of national consciousness, or to put it another way, what political role did religion assume through language? Without a doubt, these seminal questions remain unresolved. Some writers have maintained that there is a correlation between the translation of the Bible into the vernacular languages and the development of proto-nationalisms.[155] The political dimensions of the Christian religion in the sixteenth century and beyond are clear; likewise, Christianity's contribution to the preservation of national identity through the essential and indispensable instrument of Biblical translations into the vernacular languages is also irrefutable. A perfect example of this would be the case of Armenia, with translations dating back to 1666. But it is also apparent that this situation is not analogous in all religions, as most obviously seen in the case of Islam, in which the Koran cannot be translated into any other language but classical Arabic. Any role played by other translations has historically been invalidated. We should also bear in mind that if the initiative to translate the sacred texts into the vernacular languages was remarkable and required a good deal of effort, no less an effort was made to prevent the distribution of these texts. In fact, the Inquisition recalled and destroyed all but one of the editions (which has been preserved) of the Spanish Bible by Ferrer. Wycliffe was declared a heretic after his death, and his body was exhumed and thrown into the Thames in 1428. Tyndale was burned at the stake in 1536. And Casidoro de Reyna was burned in effigy in 1562 after his death in Frankfurt.

In the case of the Basque translation, the Queen of Navarre, Juana de Albret, became a follower of Calvinism and declared religious freedom in her kingdom in 1564. She commissioned and financed a translation of the New Testament into Euskara by a group led by the priest Joannes Leizarraga; the text saw the light of day in 1571 under the title *Iesu Christ Gure Iaunaren Testamentu Berria* (New Testament of Our Lord Jesus Christ). Nonetheless, the fate of the Huguenots in the kingdoms of France and Navarre after the religious wars did not permit this important aspect of the institutionalization of the written language to take hold on Basque soil. And the conversion of Enrique III of Navarre to Catholicism in 1593 definitively sanctioned this step backwards.

Some of the circumstances surrounding this Basque translation tell us much about the state of literary language and its social context. In the first place, there were problems with the use of prose for the first time in a language whose literary domain had previously been limited to the field of poetry. In addition, first time writers were faced with a basic problem—the variations in the dialects of the Basque language—and because they wanted their work to be of truly practical and general use, they needed to create a kind of unified literary Euskara. Finally, aware of the inadequacies of the people's education, they saw the need to add to the translation of the New Testament an *Abc edo Christinoen instructionea* (ABC or Instruction for the Christian), a kind of fundamental catechism with the basics for beginning readers.

In theory, the Council of Trent advocated the diffusion of Catholic orthodoxy in the vernacular languages among the popular masses, and this occasioned the publication of a multitude of catechisms and other similar works. One should qualify this, however, in the Basque case, for although it is true that many catechisms were published, mostly as translations of the *Astete*, it took quite some time for them to appear, and neither the publications themselves nor their numbers were comparable to those in the languages of the surrounding areas. It was the Bishop of Calahorra, Pedro Manso, who ordered the publication of the catechism in Basque, and from that time on as far as we know, few other catechisms from his diocese appeared besides those of the doctor Betolaza (1596) and of Martín Ochoa de Capanaga (1656);[156] we would have to wait more than a century, and only then thanks to the persistence of the

Synods of Calahorra in 1700 and to policies similar to those of Pamplona-Iruña, for the proliferation of these short works: Ochoa de Arín's catechism in 1713, and later those of Arzadun, Eleizalde, Láriz, and others.

One has the impression that the socio-linguistic circumstances of Basque during the years 1545–1571 did not differ much from other European languages that were either in the process of becoming powerful instruments in the service of the state administrations or being marginalized from this process. Nonetheless, the die had not yet been cast. Consequently, during the Renaissance, Euskara was clearly in sync with the rest of Europe with a translation of the New Testament into the vernacular, as well as noteworthy publications that proclaimed its right and its suitability for scholarly work and the need to advance its literary usage to develop a form of the language that would overcome the fragmentation caused by the dialects. But the political/religious development that Euskal Herria underwent clearly worked against the Basque language; the political fragmentation of the various Basque territories became entrenched, and indeed grew; the princes that ruled them were inclined toward Catholicism, which ensured that any impact that the reading of the Bible might have had disappeared, and in the end, the Basque language was excluded from civil government, and of course, from the liturgy, so that when the sixteenth century came to a close, its status as "vulgar" and "vernacular" was well established. It became useful solely for indoctrinating the popular monolingual masses in the spirit of the Counterreformation. This was the only, shall we say, more lofty use of the language that remained after the seventeenth century, but it did, of course, continue to be practiced in oral form in domestic and local settings.

8. The Socio-Linguistic Status of Euskal Herria in the Old Regime

During the Old Regime, many Europeans lived a diglossic existence, in which they used one language in their everyday lives but were also familiar with others employed in the liturgy, business, or government. In this way, a hierarchy of languages was established between the marginalized oral languages practiced colloquially and those used in governance and in more exclusive cultural contexts. One of the most extreme examples of this situation occurred in France. According to the evaluation made by the Abbé Grégoire, only three million out of twenty-eight million French inhabitants spoke French as their first language on a regular basis, whereas another six million had only a rudimentary understanding of it. In any case, from the middle of the sixteenth century, the status of the various marginalized languages that were relegated to popular use by the government was in no way uniform. Some, like Occitan and Catalan, were greatly promoted in the courts and in literature before this time, while others, such as Basque, had never been used in administrative or cultural contexts. The attrition of the Basque language, evidenced from the seventeenth century on, is directly connected to the relationship of the language with the social and legal circumstances of the times, which were clearly and completely bilingual. In broad terms and allowing for exceptions in different regions, we should concede that the working classes spoke Basque, whereas the ruling classes were bilingual. The latter used Basque in their dealings with the common people and Spanish in their interactions with foreigners and their peers. Anyone who wanted to succeed in government or the artistic professions, or who had business dealings abroad or with the royal courts, or who had an interest in a religious vocation needed to speak Spanish, and in many cases Latin as well, fluently. On the other hand, those who made their living off the land could live out their lives speaking only Basque. From early times, the disdain for "the vulgar Basque language" and the esteem for the Spanish language of the royal courts by the elite was notorious. A literary selection from Pérez de Montalbán demonstrates this eloquently. In a dialogue between the Castilian Lisardo and the Basque noblewoman Doña Elena, Lisardo asks: "How is it that you, a Bizkaian, speak our language so well?" to which she responds, "Because it's humiliating for a Basque woman to ever speak Basque, and it annoys the nobility, but not when she speaks correct Spanish."[157] In the business centers and in the government, this linguistic duality between the elite and the common people was quite evident. In 1572, the Italian traveler Giovanni Battista Venturino described the situation as follows: ". . . Here, you can see that the common people speak Bizkaian, or Basque, as they call it, which is a hard language to learn, although the nobles speak excellent Castilian very clearly."[158] Throughout the eighteenth century, the idiomatic deterioration of the Basque language becomes more pronounced. Initially, it was understood that the professions that provided a service directly to the people, such as priests, government officials, and doctors, would be Basque speakers in those areas where the majority of the population or indeed the entire population was also. With a minimal amount of trouble, this was the case until the middle of the eighteenth century. Whether willingly or by force, priests, scriveners, government officials, and other professionals became the linguistic intermediaries between the Basque-speaking people and the various law-making powers that functioned in Spanish or

Latin. For example, during the Offertory of the Sunday Mass, it was common for the priests to translate the municipal or provincial edicts for the general public into the vernacular language. This custom endured in the diocese of Pamplona-Iruña until 1832 when it was prohibited.[159] During the years 1765–67, government officials in Navarre who were in charge of hearing testimony during legal proceedings, whether in ecclesiastical tribunals or in non-religious settings, challenged the hitherto respected tradition of speaking in Basque when they were assigned to Basque-speaking areas, while those who worked in towns where Spanish was reasonably well known could be exclusively Spanish speakers themselves. From then on, any open positions were filled without regard to the specific linguistic characteristics of the area. At this same time, especially in Araba and Navarre, there were frequent protests over the fact that Spanish-speaking priests and doctors were assigned to Basque-speaking towns. By the 1780s, a general policy (*Ley de Cortes de Navarra* [Law of the Courts of Navarre], on obligatory attendance in school) spread to the level of basic education in these two provinces (and somewhat later in other provinces) among the various schools and teachers; it held that teaching in Spanish or French, depending on the case, was mandatory. Only catechism, or Church doctrine, was taught in Basque.[160]

This brings us to another issue. On the one hand, there was a linguistic fragmentation according to social class, which was anything but rare or exceptional in Europe before the development of nation-states in the nineteenth century. The Hungarian, Estonian, and Czech ruling classes generally spoke German; in Lithuania, they spoke Polish and in Finland, they spoke Swedish. Jan Potocki, who was a Polish patriot, was nonetheless incapable of writing in his own language and instead wrote in French. On the other hand, there was an attitude by the ruling elite toward the minority languages of the subaltern classes. Or, to put it another way, the language's level of prestige depended on the importance of the various social groups. It goes without saying that the social status of a language is what either guarantees its development or condemns it to oblivion. By the seventeenth and eighteenth centuries, the status of the Basque language had dropped so low as to be negligible among the elite, whereas the working classes continued to use it simply because they spoke no other language. Only a few sectors of the Church saw it as a useful tool for the spread of theology, and therefore, they made a special effort to write prayer books, catechisms, and to deliver sermons in the language their congregations understood.

With respect to the issue of preaching the Gospel, the Church's attitude regarding the importance of connecting with the people was quite revealing. The success of the public liturgy was based more on the prestige of the individual officiating and the staging of the ritual than on the actual substance of what was being communicated. As such, things used in the staging of religious services, such as the pulpit, the ringing of the bell, the lights, and the ornaments, were indispensable to a successful delivery, but it would appear that the question of whether the audience understood a single word of the proceedings was inconsequential. We have, therefore, from an early date, evidence of Spanish-speaking clerics who seemed to be rather disinterested in whether they were being understood by their Basque-speaking flock. Their personal charisma was enough to spread their message. This was the case with the sermons of San Francisco de Borja in Gipuzkoa (Oñati and Bergara, among other locations). Although the people did not understand a word he said, they were moved to participate totally: "In these Basque territories, San Borja delivered sermons to immense audiences, in which everyone cried and was contrite. And when asked why they cried if they did not [actually] understand the sermon, they replied that upon the sight of such a holy lord and duke in the pulpit, God spoke to them in their souls in a language that elicited tears and remorse."[161]

In an even more remarkable case, when a sermon was delivered to the Basque congregation in Spanish, the people were not just moved, but miraculously also understood what was being said. Writing about the establishment of a convent in Pamplona-Iruña in 1583, Jerónimo Gracián, an associate of Santa Teresa de Jesús, asserts: "The nuns arrived in Pamplona during the month of December, accompanied by señor Oris, who was a hermit at the time; because I had been waiting for them in the city for several days, preaching to instruct those people; and it turned out that the women, who did not understand Castilian, but only Basque, came to hear me saying that they understood what I was saying."[162]

The use of Spanish continued to spread and by the eighteenth century had become intolerable for some. It should be noted, in any case, that the preaching of the Gospel was not in a hopeful state at this point, even for those who spoke in their congregants' own languages, at least judging from the savage and exquisite critique of bad preachers made by Father Isla in his *Fray Gerundio* (Friar Gerundio). But if we add to the problem of the sermons being delivered in a language little understood if at all by the public with the further issue of clerics themselves being poorly educated, we can understand Larramendi's ire in devoting some of his finest pages to this group of *erdeldunes* (Castilian-speaking clerics) and even to Basque-speaking clerics who themselves did not dare to preach in their own language, either because they did not speak it well enough or because they spoke it so poorly that they were unable to be understood. Moreover, what has already been said about sermons also applies to confessions. Here is how Larramendi put it:

> Those who ought to be best educated in this are the ones who are worst, speaking Basque carelessly and without a trace of intelligence. These are the ecclesiastics and the religious, gentlemen, and people accustomed since childhood to Castilian or to the Latin grammar they learned . . . To force men such as these to study their language with interest and learn its grammar is like sentencing them to the salt mines, so it happens that, in their role as confessors, they are useless for hearing confessions conscientiously and with discretion for others; because as priests and preachers, they are useless for preaching and teaching the doctrine to the people, who are all Basques; because, lazy and arrogant, they are useless for carrying on conversations and discussing things in Basque . . . Because of this, the devil ensures that that no sermon in Basque can have any effect, or bear fruit, or rid people of their illusions, because a sermon poorly written and poorly translated from Castilian, addressed to the clouds and coming out haphazardly, with no coherence in the Basque language in which it is preached, profaning with such a swelter of malapropisms, with so much clownish buffoonery, without piety or sound fervor or sanctity, and without fruit or sobering effect . . . What is even more intolerable is that Basque preachers ascend to the pulpit and preach in Castilian, not daring to do it in Basque. The do not wish to work or apply themselves to master their language, or to read and write in it . . . My only consolation, if not to see that their Castilian sermons are so bad and so dry and empty of content or instruction, is that the congregation loses nothing if they don't understand them.[163]

Having said this, even Larramendi is not exempt from his own ideological position, and in spite of being such a firm promoter of the Basque language, he maintained, nonetheless, certain qualifications:

> There are occasions when a sermon should not be preached in Basque or in the common language of all the congregation, and this is when a sermon is too conscious of the wishes and interests of those who govern or rule are in power, and fail to advocate the

> common interests of the congregation, it would be better for them not to understand how poorly governed they are and all the sins committed by the men in the government who rule them, unless there's some other alternative to remedy their behavior than to simply embarrass them in public in front of all the people. I say the same about those sermons whose subject matter, preached in the maternal tongue of the congregation, would cause more harm than benefit to their souls, more risk of falling into sin than to learn and defend catholic truths.[164]

In general, the Church, like other institutions, played a negative role in relation to the Basque language. In addition to what we have seen with regard to its ministers, most of the bishops were foreigners and did not know the language. The diocese in Pamplona-Iruña, which included a good number of Basque speakers, did not have a Basque-speaking bishop until 1768—Lorenzo de Irigoyen from Baztan, to be exact. Whenever one of these bishops spoke in favor of preaching in Basque, he stood out more as an exception than the rule. But even when the bishops of the Basque dioceses attempted to approach prudently and belatedly the logic of preaching in Basque, the discussion ended in nothing more than good intentions and empty talk. In 1851, during the Concordat between the Spanish nation and the Holy See, the Bishop of Pamplona-Iruña, Severo Adriani, put forth the notion of creating a center of Basque-speaking missionaries who would devote themselves to preaching in this language. The center would even provide general training for Basque-speaking priests in the cloistered convent of Loiola (Loyola) in Gipuzkoa. But none of this came to pass. Loiola, in fact, reopened in 1852 but for the purpose of creating a center to train missionaries for overseas work.[165]

Civil institutions did not express any interest in publishing Basque works; they repeatedly denied them support or funding. Thus, many of these works remained unpublished, and in fact, some were lost. What is more, the only known policy related to language in the *foral* institutions protected Spanish and French explicitly; knowing them was a requirement for assuming any public position: mayor, alderman, delegate, etc. In fact, in order to impose their political will, the ruling minorities resorted to putting in place a series of requisites for eligible candidates in the local and the provincial governments—among them the ability to read and write Spanish. In 1571, in the General Assembly of Gipuzkoa held at Errenteria (Rentería), it was decided that this requirement should apply to those who were elected mayors in the *villas*. In the General Assemblies of Bizkaia, the same decision was made with regard to assembly members. This resulted in a constant lack of compliance, since so many towns were unable to elect representatives that knew how to speak Spanish, or what was even less likely, knew how to read it. Between the years 1624 and 1625, some representatives were thrown out of the meeting of the General Assemblies because they could not express themselves in Spanish, and still others were arrested for being recidivists. It was not until 1760, 1766, and 1833 when agreements were made to translate the Assembly proceedings into Basque so that those who did not know Spanish could understand the contents of the treaties.[166] It was obvious that the standards could not be met and were in fact not being met; although they could be put into effect any time the elite had an interest in doing so.

A case that illustrates the status of language in the Basque municipalities occurred in an important Gipuzkoan *villa*, Bergara. In a complicated dispute that took place in 1770, because of the preeminence that parish priests and members of the city authorities were supposed to have, a bitter meeting took place in which the two sides, the religious and non-religious, debated about this issue. When a survey was taken of the various participants in the discussion, which had taken place in Spanish, the only ones who had spoken were the priests, the mayor, the secretary, and one of four aldermen; of the remaining three, one vaguely understood what was being said, whereas the other two had absolutely no clue; these three therefore had remained silent.[167] If this was the case in a *villa* well disposed to commerce, with an urban profile, and the venue for the General Assembly, one can imagine what the situation was in the small *villas*, parishes, and villages. In several cases, the local authorities attempted to give the learning of Castilian or French a boost, especially during the final two decades of the seventeenth century and the first two of the next. Many town halls took measures to require educators to teach exclusively in Romance and to forbid their students to speak Basque, at least in primary schools; there is abundant testimony to this: Beasain (1730), Bera (Vera de Bidasoa) (1777), Aia (1784), Elgoibar (1789), Uztarroz (1807), among others. This was the period when the well-known ring method was used in schools to prevent children from speaking in the only language they knew.[168]

Until the 1790s, the situation of the Basque language was relatively stable within its marginalized status, with linguistic subordination and true deterioration occurring in the southernmost territories. The institutional authorities (General Assemblies, Courts, and Municipal Authorities), controlled by oligarchies consisting of noblemen and, to a lesser degree, members of the bourgeoisie, did not support the cultivation of the language of the lower classes. Neither did the Church as an institution, except for timely as well as tardy initiatives by some religious orders. Cities like Vitoria-Gasteiz had become Castilian-speaking, and regions like Tierra Estella or La Llanada in Araba went through a major process of loss regarding the Basque language. Even so, the majority of the population of Euskal Herria, including the *Foral* Territories of Bizkaia, that part of La Rioja in Araba, and the Ribera de Navarra continued to consider Basque as their rightful language. In a "*Plan de Curatos y Beneficios de la Provincia de Álava*" (Plan for the Curates and Benefices of the Province of Araba), drawn up soon after 1787, it was noted that: "Basque is spoken in many of the towns of the vicariate of Vitoria, in all of Ganboa, in most of Salvatierra [Agurain], and in [the vicariates] of Mondragón, Zigoitia, Zuia, Orduña, Ayala [Aiara], Orozko and Tudela, where any parish priest chosen in open competition who did not speak the language would be useless at best."[169]

But as I say, it was after the 1790s when the profound political changes that were about to occur would lead to a new, completely different linguistic reality. The early nineteenth-century generation was to experience an accelerated, unstoppable linguistic decline, especially in the urban areas, combined with an endemic loss of prestige for the Basque language. This resulted in a lack of cultivation and its being associated with rural areas. Juan Antonio Moguel's diagnosis could not be more explicit:

> But let us be clear: in the midst of the passion with which Basque is censured, there are, generally speaking, no people who are as indolent as we are when it comes to cultivating and perfecting our language, and so we ourselves, except for a few individuals, are its worst enemies. Our Basque society has fallen asleep on this branch of the tree, and this is why the Basque language has not had an academy or good writers who have particularly cultivated it. It lives like a stranger among the woods and solitary homesteads, where it is more than true that our rustic mountain folk know the language and speak it wonderfully well, and without the alterations noticeable in people who ought to be its repositories . . . In our times, we have observed this language becoming increasingly confined to pockets of speakers. There are villages where only the old people know Basque; their children speak Basque and Castilian, and their grandchildren only Castilian. This has been the case since the time of Augustus: how much terrain must it have lost? And if it were not for the farmsteads it would already be a dead language.[170]

9. Apologists, Scholars, and Detractors of the Basque Language during the Period of the Formation of *Foral* Ideology, 1571–1640[171]

Meanwhile, as we have seen, a group of Basque authors (Zaldibia, Garibay, and Echave) had been publishing works that were either directly apologetic regarding the Basque language or else were historical works in which proofs and arguments about aspects of the language occupied a prominent place. What, in fact, was the role that the Basque language played in the works of these sixteenth century scholars? Of course, hardly any of them present arguments in favor of the language itself as a means of communication or in defense of the right of its speakers to use it as an instrument of culture. On the contrary, as we have already seen, the language stands as the definitive argument to prove that its roots go back to Tubal. The value that Basque held for these scholars lay in the fact that it was different from other languages, was presumably extremely ancient, and that one could deduce from it (albeit rather forcedly) a multitude of etymologies that could attest to its having spread throughout the Iberian Peninsula.

Throughout the seventeenth century, authors writing in Basque were fulfilling a double task in its defense. On the one hand, its use during a clearly reactionary time gave the act a certain air of militancy. But on the other hand, these authors included pro-Basque comments that were generally expressed in prudent tones. For example, Joannes Etcheberry of Ziburu (Ciboure, Lapurdi) opens his 1627 *Manual Debozionezkoa* (Devotional Manual)[172] with a dedication to the Bishop of Baiona in which he includes the following: "Pray God, Sir Prelate, that you know Euskera as well as the languages that you master (Greek, Hebrew, Latin and *Erdera*, that is, French), so you can understand the work that I present to you." But as this could be taken as a double entendre, the simple desire for his bishop to better understand his book and the veiled criticism of the individual in charge of the diocese of Baiona for not knowing the language of his people, caused Etcheberry to immediately cover himself by going on to explain: "In any case, a man's head can't understand everything as if it had God's understanding and capacity." This same *Dedicaçionea* ends with another interesting allegation: "The king should defend his people, whether they speak one particular language or different ones."

But in 1636, Etcheberry published his *Eliçara erabiltceko*.[173] In the introduction (*Atarikoa*) to Book 3 he includes a few lines of poetry, which were initially thought to be his own but later turned out to be by Joan Klaberia, another cleric from the "School of Sara" who, in any case, expressed an opinion that was not only personal but no doubt shared by many other Basque authors of the time: that the best way to defend the Basque language was by writing in it and not, as Garibay and Echave did, by theorizing about it in Castilian. This matter can be said to have marked a clear distinction as regards the attitudes of Basque writers in the northern and southern Pyrenees, at least during the sixteenth and seventeenth centuries, because the former defended Basque in their own language and in practical ways, whereas the latter did so in Castilian and in theory.

The writer whose name is the most revered in traditional Basque language studies, Axular, left a record in his *Gero* of what the Basque linguistic problems were during his time, the middle of the seventeenth century. In first place, of course, he registers the dearth of literature in the language. Axular is very clear on this point: the Basques themselves were to blame for this situation, not any possible deficiencies in the language: "*Euskaldunek berek dute falta eta ez euskarak.*" (Basques themselves are to blame and not Euskara.) The Basque writer does not lack resources in which to express himself; the problems derive from the fact that there are few existing references, but this can be changed by working on it. Axular also declares that the fact that Basque is different from *erdera* (the generic term for any other language, most typically applied to Castilian and French) does not mean that it should be treated as inferior to it: "*Ezta ez handik segitzen gaixtoagoa dela euskara.*" (And one should not deduce from this that Euskara is any worse). On the contrary, the two languages are equally rich in and of themselves; where they differ is in their degree of cultivation. One matter that could not be missing from Axular's analysis is dialectal fragmentation and the need to attain a cultured language that all speakers could use. The prevailing linguistic diversity was so remarkable that people spoke differently "from one house to another." Of course, dialectal dismemberment was a product of the lack of political unity in the country, which was fragmented into several administrative entities: "The Basques do not possess a single law and tradition, nor the same way of speaking Basque, because they belong to different kingdoms." In the midst of all these pithy and sensible observations, Axular is not able to distance himself from the dominant opinion regarding the Basque language and introduces a thought that diminishes his otherwise prescient judgments: "The other common languages have been mixed with each other, but Basque remains in its original pure state."[174] That is to say, he upheld the immutability and clarity of Basque as a feature that distinguished it from other languages.

However, it is Juan de Beriain, a contemporary author from beyond the Pyrenees who, in my opinion, makes a few brief observations that put the defense of the language in its proper place. This Navarrese priest published a few practical works, aimed at his pastoral duties that posed two arguments justifying the reason why it was necessary to write in Basque and Romance, the two languages spoken in the Bishopric of Pamplona-Iruña. The initial argument was of a practical nature, because there was little use in preaching and performing other liturgical actions to the faithful in a language they did not speak: "If only those who speak Romance are present during a sermon preached in Basque, or if only those who speak Basque are present during a sermon preached in Romance, it is obvious that they will not understand what is being said to them." The second argument is clearly of a more assertive nature: "I write in Basque because there has not been a nation in all the world that has not taken pride in the mother tongue of its homeland, and in teaching students in its schools to read and write in it."[175] This unequivocal declaration was published in 1626, when a good part of the most erudite European authors would have completely disagreed with it. To link the identity of fatherland, nation, mother tongue, and pride in all of them constituted some high-sounding language for the time, especially if it did not refer to one of the official languages of the authoritarian monarchies, but to a modest and marginalized language belonging to rough mountain dwellers. Of course, seeking to teach Basque in the schools (and not French or Castilian which few people aspired to) at a moment in history when the ruling classes viewed any popularization of literacy with considerable distrust and when the rates of illiteracy were extraordinarily high, was a magnificent but isolated opinion, not merely in Basque circles but, as I have said, from the general European perspective.

In fact, despite what has already been said about the advance of literacy in the Protestant countries being a result of greater access to Biblical interpretation (at least in the early days), this was understood to be restricted to individuals with more education and greater social standing: clergymen, nobles, merchants, etc. But not even Luther himself was thinking in terms of farmers and tradesmen being able to read the Bible. Generally speaking, an educated person was permitted to read aloud, while the untutored merely listened. In the Protestant countries, the spread of literacy to the popular classes was not to occur for some time.[176] Complaints and suspicions could still be heard, however, from the middle of the seventeenth century and particularly throughout the next hundred years, when a greater number of schools were endowed and a small number of farmers and tradesmen began to have access to the rudiments of education.

The basic argument wielded by those against public education was that when farmhands, small businessmen, and tradesmen sent their children to become literate they were in fact distracting them from activities essential to the support of the community. They also brought up the possibility that there could be a scarcity of hands for tilling the fields or for the maintenance of workshops and a proliferation of semi-literate types doing nothing but bringing lawsuits. In 1677, for example, the *Cortes de Navarra* (Parliament of Navarre) received a memorandum whose anonymous author complained that "the abundance of schoolteachers who have taken paying jobs in the cities, towns, and villages, is so harmful . . . and in recent years this has caused depopulation throughout the kingdom, and there is nobody left to farm the properties because there are no tillers, and it is the same with all the trades and mechanical arts. And if there is one left all he does is stir up trouble in the place by bringing lawsuits, because he knows how to read and write."

An identical opinion was wielded by Boutin, the Intendant of Aquitaine, in 1760: "*Je suis bien éloigné de penser qu'il faille multiplier dan le bourgs et les villages les maîtres d'ecole, qui ne produisent souvent d'autre effect que de faire de paysans de demi'savants qui, la plupart ne profitent de l'instruction qu'ils ont reçue que pour abandonner l'agriculture ou faire des procès à leurs seigneurs*" (I am far from convinced that we need to increase the number of school teachers in our towns and villages, as their only influence is to turn peasants into pseudo-savants, most of whom do little else with the education they've been given than to leave their farms and bring lawsuits against their lords). Not even Montesquieu himself was far removed from this opinion: "*Un des grands abus qui soit dans la rouyaume est l'etablissement des demi-collèges, qui sont dans les petites villes, où les artisans envoient tous leurs enfants pour leur apprendre quelques mots de latin* . . ." (One of the worst abuses in the Kingdom is the establishment of middle schools in the small villages where the workers send their children to learn a few Latin phrases . . .)[177] Moreover, when the Real Sociedad Bascongada de los Amigos del País (Royal Basque Society of Friends of the Country) decided to implement an incentive plan by way of rewards for the furthering of public education in 1772, it received a memorandum whose author, under the pseudonym "Don Patricio de Castilla," criticized the measure on the grounds that the number of schools might multiply exponentially, which might "harm the public by increasing the number of scholars and calligraphers at the expense of agriculture and the mechanical arts." The Sociedad replied without opposing the main argument (the danger that potential farmers and mechanics might take to "the comforts of the sedentary life"), arguing that there was an excess of labor in Vasconia and that the small number of awards did not present any risk of social destabilization."[178]

Now what did foreign authors of the sixteenth and seventeenth centuries think of the Basque language? Firstly, we should attest to the fact that the Basque language did not go unnoticed by certain authors, at least among the better-known Castilians. Whether it was to draw attention to its unintelligibility, to classify it as babble, to highlight its antiquity, or to make it synonymous with ruralism and brutality, the fact is that many writers made reference to it. A good number of classical literati employed it in their works, especially for picturesque, funny, or rural characters. In any event, one has the impression that in the sixteenth century, Basque was perceived as being on a par with other vernacular languages. When the authors of the time wanted to show off how many languages they knew and introduce phrases from several languages, they frequently resorted to Basque as just another vernacular tongue. Toward the end of the century and the beginning of the next, matters had changed and the subordinate, popular nature of the Basque language became evident in comparison with those that enjoyed official status and were profusely cultivated in literature. Consequently, the first printed phrase in Basque is found in the preface to Bartolomé de Torres Naharro's work *Tinelaria* in 1513. The author, in a show of his command of languages, issues a *¡Voto a Dios!* (My God!) in several, among them Basque: "*Veréis vos: / ¡Jur a Dío! ¡Voto a Dios! / ¡Per mon arma! / ¡Bay fedea! / iobbigot y culycós / Boa fe nau canada e mea.*"[179] Lope de Vega also resorted to including Basque among several other languages when it came to making such linguistic displays.[180]

The debate over the antiquity of the Basque language is interesting. I have already quoted Juan de Valdés as one of the best-known authors to extol the Castilian language, although his works, written between 1535 and 1536, remained unpublished until the eighteenth century. This author, like the majority of those who addressed the subject of the Iberian languages at the start of the sixteenth century, maintains a fluctuating, poorly supported, and friendly attitude toward Basque matters. Valdés first describes the idea of Euskara being the primeval Spanish language as an opinion commonly held among the authors of his time and is in agreement with it. Later, however, he grants this primacy to Greek, and finally, he returns once more to the earlier idea, or at least he refrains from arguing with those who uphold it. "The belief held by most of those who feel curiosity about these matters is that the language employed today by the Bizkaians is the ancient language of Spain . . . But look, if someone wants to declare that as regards Spain, Bizkaian goes back even further than Greek, I will refrain from arguing the contrary and I will wish them all the best instead."[181] From what Valdés says about the geography of the Basque language in Navarrese territory, it does not seem that he had firsthand knowledge of the subject but relied on what other prestigious authors had to say. Of course, there is no doubt that in his time the most widespread belief was that Basque was an extremely ancient language, perhaps the oldest spoken in Spain. This is indicated, among other sources, by the scribe from Arratia, Pedro de Madariaga and in the *Gramatica castellana* (Castilian Grammar) published in 1558.[182]

But the publication in 1571 of Garibay's *Los XL Libros del Compendio* forced the debate and changed the situation. As has already been said, this work sought to limit to the Basque Country the honor of having been Tubal's first residence. Also, as he spoke Basque, his language would be Spain's first and oldest; this "proved," along with toponymy, that the Basque language had been common to the entire Peninsula. In other words, Garibay's work launched the thesis of Basque-Iberianism. In 1587, on the strength of being an accomplished linguist and the fact that that his pronouncements, misguided or not, were essentially philological, Poza reinforced the idea of Basque being Spain's oldest language. In 1607, Echave underscored yet again the arguments defended by Garibay and Poza. From that moment onward, Spanish authors began to view the alleged antiquity of Euskara with suspicion, to find fault with certain nuances of the argument, to call it into question, and even to denigrate the value of the language itself. Alonso de Madrigal, *El Tostado* (c. 1400–1455) had already upheld the idea that Castilian had arrived with Tubal, a theory to which other authors would subscribe later on. He was also a supporter of the existence of several languages in the Peninsula, among which Castilian and Basque would be found in their respective areas, therefore refuting the theory that Basque was the only Spanish language.[183] Gregorio López Madera was the most radical in his statements, going so far as to uphold Castilian as Spain's original and oldest language, predating even Latin. To him, Castilian was "one of the original tongues to coalesce into a language during the confusion of Babel."[184] Madera subscribed to the theory of the existence of a plurality of languages in the Peninsula before the arrival of the Romans, and that Castilian would be the most widespread of all. Its similarities with Latin would be explained by contact between both languages, not by one being derived from the other.

This was how the Castilian apologists, in exactly the same way as their Basque counterparts, presented their language as a metonym of their own peoples, adorned with the basic characteristics of antiquity, nobility, and purity. This nonsensical theory of "original Castilian" was maintained by such seventeenth century authors as Juan González Correas, Doctor Viana, and Francisco de Quevedo himself. However, it was Father Mariana who passed a judgment in this regard, which aside from dismissing the alleged greater antiquity of Basque did so in strongly defamatory terms. Regarding "this rough barbarian language," which some claimed to be "the oldest in Spain, and formerly common to all of it," Mariana argues that it was a vernacular exclusive to its own territory, but by no means the common language, because in his estimation a plurality of languages formerly dominated the Peninsula: "We do not deny, however, that it was one of the many languages spoken in Spain in the past. We merely suggest that it was not common to all parts of it."[185] Mariana appropriated as much credit as he could from Garibay and became the obligatory reference for detractors and defenders of both Basque and Castilian. It is no coincidence that the liberal Spanish unionists of the nineteenth century benefited from the writings of the priest from Talavera. Moreover, subsequent Basque apologists did not cease to maintain that Basque was the oldest language and common to all of Spain, an argument inseparable from the Tubalist and Iberianist theories. For this reason, nearly everyone devoted a passage or two to refute what Mariana had written. Father Larramendi was particularly vicious about his fellow priest's opinions, which he termed "*talaveradas*" (incidents or absurdities associated with an inhabitant of Talavera).[186]

Even the moderate Cervantes gives us an approximation of the Basque language and its reputed antiquity and importance that is worth savoring. In his work *La gran sultana*, Madrigal, the protagonist, is a slave who regains his freedom thanks to the possession of a magical art by which he can teach an elephant to speak Turkish in ten years. In preparation for this, he begins by making it speak other languages, Basque among them. The Qaddi, concerned about the progress of the experiment, has a conversation with Madrigal in which he inquires about the teaching of the elephant and the languages it its learning. Madrigal replies: "[It is learning] Basque, / A language that is proven / To bear the honor of being older / Than Ethiopian and Abyssinian," to which the Qaddi concludes: "This valuable language's antiquity / Alone makes it stand. / Better to teach it Spanish / Which we better understand."[187]

Nevertheless, the opinion most often put forth by Spanish authors, and the most common of perceptions, was that Basque was a difficult, alien, unintelligible, and strange language, which occasionally resulted in indications of contempt for its alleged barbarity. The aforementioned Juan de Valdés states, "I would like to know enough about Bizkaian to tell you something, but because I can neither speak it nor understand it, all I can say about it is this, that I have been told by persons who understand it, that many Latin words have gotten into this language, words that cannot be recognized because of the way they have been added and the way in which they are pronounced. This language is so different from all the others in Spain that its native speakers cannot be understood at all by speakers of the other language, nor can Basque speakers understand the others."[188] There are two things, then, that we should point out: that there was no way of making oneself understood to the Basques and no way of making them understand Castilians. The other point is that, no matter how hard it was to find them, the language contains elements borrowed from Latin, and had therefore not remained unchanged. In view of this, Basque scholars posited exactly the opposite argument: The internal order and simplicity of Euskara and the ease with which it could be learned. Garibay naively states that "It causes great wonder and mystery to find that, at least in Spain, all the children already speak it from birth . . ."[189] But above all, it refers to a subject that would later be repeated by other scholars: the ease with which the natives of the Labrador (*Ternua*, in Basque) Peninsula in present-day Canada had learned to speak Basque in a short time from the fishermen who would put in there and stay for a while.[190] In any event, the most significant of Garibay's statements with regard to the Basque language was that it could be subjected to grammatical rules that were even simpler than those of Latin.[191] To test the versatility and literary capacity of Basque, successive scholars endeavored to make sample translations and versions of prayers[192] or classical texts in the language. A fairly exemplary case of this is a rendering by Friar Bartolomé de Santa Teresa of Plautus's *Poenulus,* in which translations into Carthaginian, Basque, and Castilian were included.[193] Of course, Larramendi would turn Basque's simplicity into one of his main arguments, tying it to the internal orderliness of the language.[194]

What was a commonplace, however, was that Basque should sound so strange and alien to foreign ears, particularly its proper names. The problems faced by the Basques in having their surnames spelled and pronounced properly were often insurmountable, and not a few of those living outside the country ended up changing them. There are numerous examples of this. Most Castilian authors marveled at the peculiar accentuation and the length of the names. Father Mariana opined once more in this regard: "The accounts of ancient authors tell us that Bizkaian words, especially those referring to localities and towns, were rougher and more barbarous than in the rest of Spain, and that they could not be reduced to a Latin declension."[195] Likewise, Yanguas includes in his *Diccionario* a collection of particularly complex toponyms from Alduides to demonstrate the complexity of Basque place-names.[196] Mapmakers, travelers, and geographers had great difficulty in transcribing toponyms correctly, and their works are littered with errors and uncertainties. It is common to refer to Basque toponyms as "the place known as . . ." or "the place they call . . . " as if to divest themselves of any responsibility for employing such a word and blaming it on the natives.

Added to these denigrating elements directed at the Basque language, we might add another that was the generalized opinion among Castilians: that the Basques were rough, savage, violent, and dim-witted, which translated into their manifest inability to speak Castilian. In the literary works of Spain's Golden Age, the character of the Bizkaian *gracioso* (country bumpkin) who speaks something barely recognizable as Castilian is a constant. All the authors of the period share the notion of the rustic nature and lack of linguistic skills possessed by Basques. Quevedo summarizes this in a poem: ". . . than a Bizkaian, / whose mouth, purse, and mind / are the most closed / that the world has ever seen."[197] Basque scholars were unanimous with regard to the origin of the language: it was brought to the Basque Country by Tubal. Although some related this Tubalist language to Hebrew and others to Chaldean, still others went so far as to hint that it was the language spoken in Paradise, suggesting that its origin was divinely inspired. On the other hand, Spanish authors led by Mariana declared that it was descended from a barbaric tongue, or in any event, one without any known affiliation to the gibberish that the Basques were daring to consider a language. The most radical attack, mentioned earlier, took place in the mid-seventeenth century when *El Búho gallego*, followed by *Castellanos y vascongados*, posited something highly dangerous and poisonous for those times: a subservient Jewish origin for the Basque language.

The matter of the purity and immutability of the Basque language, which might seem so scarcely worthy of attention today, was nevertheless a key matter to the Old Regime. We have already seen the opinions of writers like Juan de Valdés regarding the evidence that Basque absorbed borrowings from other languages and therefore, at least from a lexical perspective, changed over time. However, the commonly held opinion among Basque authors was quite the opposite. Axular himself, although he acknowledged the marked variance among dialects, concluded by upholding the purity and immutability of the language. This was not a trivial affair, of course, because it was linked to, among other things, proving the validity of Basque-Iberianism. Indeed, Basque scholars sought to explain Spanish toponyms through Basque, thus proving that it had been the general language of the entire Peninsula and that, because it remained unchanged, the Basque spoken in the seventeenth century could be readily used to analyze pre-Roman place-names.

This extended to the language itself, giving rise to an effort to demonstrate, using a small number of loan words as evidence, that there was proof within Castilian that Basque had in ancient times been the language generally spoken in Spain. Ambrosio de Morales denied that terms from Spain's ancient language could be found in the Basque of his time, and that Basque was immutable. Echave joined the fray by calling attention to a group of terms, some of which appeared more Castilian than others but which he judged to be entirely of Basque origin: *mozo* (youth, servant), *bizarro* (gallant, generous), *escudo* (shield), *izquerdo* (left, left-hand), *motilar* (to cut or shave hair), *ola* (wave), *sarna* (itch, scabies), *zurdo* (left-handed), and so on.[198] Two years after Echave published his *Discursos* (Discourses), in Mexico, Mateo Alemán, also in Mexico, brought out his *Ortografía*, a work in which he addresses the question of Basque loan words in Castilian, corroborating Morales's theory and disproving Zumaia's: "Let the Cantabrians say that many of our expressions are actually theirs; let them prove it with their etymologies, deductions, and so on, and proclaim that we say, as they do, *mozo, sayo, masmordón, verde, izquierdo, guardián, bizarro, ganivete, cabo, zatico, motilar* and *asmar*—, and so on. words that are no longer in use."[199] This controversy over loan words reached its peak with Larramendi, who made the matter one of the cornerstones of his work by attempting to show that Basque was the main matrix language to come out of Babel, arguing that this was the reason why all other languages contained hundreds of terms borrowed from it, and not just absorbed into Castilian but also into Greek, Latin, French, and Italian, although it might later have appeared that inverse processes had been at play.[200]

Obviously, loan words are a sign of vitality and adaptability, qualities on which their survival depends. But in the sixteenth or seventeenth century, the concern was not so much with the communicative ease of a language, its functional capacity, or even its survival so much as with its degree of purity. A loan-free language would be one that was pure, ingenuous, and might even have been the language spoken before the confusion of the Tower of Babel. It might also be the language employed in Paradise. A matrix language would remain pure and unchanged, would be the same in every detail as that used by Iñigo Arista, Francisco Javier, or Astarloa. This leads to the purist stance of avoiding terms that are presumed to be borrowings from other languages. As we have already seen, the possibility of an internal linguistic evolution had hardly been considered, and the only changes admitted were those deriving from loans acquired through contact with other languages. So the unchanging nature of a word was seen as a sign of its purity, that is, of its never having been mixed with another language.

This disconnect between communicative capacity and purity is well evidenced in the work of Garibay. This author shows himself to be a purist in his refutation of Beuter, who considered the possibility of contact between Basque and several other languages, such as Chaldean and Aramaic. Because Beuter did not know any of these languages, Garibay opines that he had no authority in the matter. Pere Antoni Beuter, who, like other foreign authors, was more dispassionate although less well-versed in Basque, showed evidence of the variations that had taken place over time in that language, as well as influences from other languages with which it had been in contact. He also emphasized the extremely wide dialectal variety of Basque:

> This gives us reason to believe that the language is not as pure as it previously was. But it is the basis and foundation of the tongue that was first spoken in Spain, and has absorbed a number of terms from new arrivals to these shores from England and Germany, and according to the degree of contact between Basques and these foreigners, different speech patterns grew up between the Basque spoken in Bizkaia, Araba, Gipuzkoa and Ruchonia, which we call Navarre, to the extent that these variations almost seem like foreign languages.[201]

For Garibay, however, "the pure, perfect Basque language" would be that of Armenia, spoken without admixture from Latin, Greek, or Hebrew—"especially not from Hebrew." Nevertheless, he establishes a clear distinction between the vernacular or spoken language, and the cultured (Arabic, French, and Latin) or written language useful for communication and commerce. He thus compares the case of the Berber and Basque peoples. The Berbers speak Tamazight on an ordinary, day-to-day basis, but Arabic is employed for commercial and political purposes requiring contact with foreigners. The Basques, however, do the same thing with "their communications" in Spanish and French. The same situation obtained with the Bretons.[202]

Esteban Garibay was essentially a chronicler and historian, but he was very concerned with linguistic matters. Inserted among his historical writing, we find a large amount of information or reflections on languages. Whenever a Basque first name, nickname, or toponym appears, Garibay takes the opportunity to include its etymology. His fondness for the subject led him to include ancient elegiacal Basque texts that he believed should be preserved for their intrinsic interest. He explains that "they are women's laments that I decided to include here because of the need to preserve items of such antiquity." Garibay was the first to publish such a collection of old texts from the fourteenth and fifteenth centuries. These elegies, "which in Basque are called *Eresiac*," are of an indisputable dual value owing to their historical and philological content. They are laments for the death of Martín Bañez de Artaçubiaga and Doña (E)milia de Lastur, the song of the battle of Beotibar, and the song of Olaso.[203] At the behest of Juan de Idiáquez, Garibay also put together two collections of Basque proverbs, which he himself translated into Castilian together with philological annotations, thus placing the collections far ahead of their time. All these early contributions made him the first intellectual to be seriously concerned with collecting Basque philological material.[204] In fact, Garibay was the first to propose a series of analyses and methods to be followed copiously (and sometimes slavishly) by later authors.[205] As we have seen, Tubalists, Cantabrianists, and Iberianists all rest a good part of their supporting evidence for these theories on the permanence of the language within the Basque Country and on the Basque toponyms found all over the rest of the Iberian Peninsula. As was the norm during his time, Garibay frequently established relationships between words that were similar in form, and formulated forced propositions that sometimes served to strengthen the myth. This, however, was not always the case. He is correct in a good number of his proposals referring to Basque etymology, and when he is not, the terms in question are dubious and convoluted, and in some cases still have not been explained to this day.[206] For example, Garibay made advances in the etymology of *briga / ili* (*iri-uri*), assigning both toponyms to Basque: the first was equivalent to large towns and the second to smaller ones.[207] In 1812, Humboldt was to identify two separate toponymic areas in the Peninsula, attributing a Celtic origin to those of the *briga / burg* type and a Basque-Iberian one to the *iri (uri)* or *ili* group. Despite his spells of naiveté and ignorance when establishing etymologies, Garibay should be placed within the context of the linguistic development of his time, where he would not fare at all badly, and even if his work were to be compared to the nonsense that was still being defended in the eighteenth and even the nineteenth century, he would still emerge as a great deal more moderate and judicious than many of his successors.[208]

Although he defended the purity, naturalness, and individuality of the Basque language and the perfection of its characteristics, Garibay's beliefs evolved over the course of his work. In both his *Grandezas* (Grandeur)—an unedited text later studied by Julio Caro Baroja—and his *Memorias* (Memoirs), written in his old age, Garibay calls attention to an internal element in the Basque language by which he attempts to demonstrate its superiority over other tongues. He compares its structure to that of a language that is supposedly the first and most perfect of all: Hebrew. Basque, like Hebrew and unlike Greek and Latin, conjugates its verbs according to gender. He gives several examples of this, such as *veardoc / veardon*, *edandoc / edandon*, etc. "It has masculine and feminine verbs, like Hebrew, the first of the world's languages, and is very different from Greek or Latin . . ."[209] Also, in his *Memorias* Garibay plays down the idea of Basque's immutability and purity. On the contrary, he denounces its "degeneration," because it has not been subjected to a formal grammatical description and is merely a spoken language with no written form, it has suffered fragmentation and has been contaminated by its neighbors, the Romance languages. This makes it possible for a person from Bilbao to have difficulty understanding the Basque spoken by a person from Baiona: "which, like all other vulgar languages not preserved by a formal grammar, has degenerated so much that if people from within a thousand years ago were to come back to life we would barely understand each other, just as today people from Bilbao and Baiona, both important Basque-speaking areas, can only understand each other with difficulty, because the Basque of Bilbao has a great deal of Castilian influence and that of Baiona is equally mixed with French."[210]

Martínez de Zaldibia was also an eminent historian but with a merely tangential interest in linguistic matters. In 1564, he wrote the first *Historia de Guipúzcoa* (History of Gipuzkoa), which was not published until 1945, although in its time the work was circulated to some extent in manuscript form. In any case, it is interesting that Zaldibia, Garibay, and other historians should be concerned with Basque, indicating that the language had passed beyond being a mere matter of communication into the political arena. Therefore, the linguistic references in *Suma* focus on a few etymologies and on developing the Basque-Cantabrianist and Tubalist theories in vogue at the time. Zaldibia also develops the myth of the Basque Country's secular independence stemming from not having been conquered by either the Visigoths or the Arabs. The link between the linguistic argument (preservation of the language) and the political one (preservation of independence and founding laws) is key to Zaldibia's thought: ". . . It is also obvious to all that this nation, alone among all the provinces and kingdoms of the world, conserves its laws as they were conceived by nature . . . and is the only nation to conserve its first language."[211] Referring specifically to the Basque language, he makes a number of observations regarding nouns with a final *a* and those with a final *c*, the declination of nouns and the phonetic system, as well as the geographic dominance of the Basque language. Finally, he mentions the existence of dialectal variations and the relative "correctness" of each, thus becoming the creator of one of the classic myths about Basque and other languages: the linguistic superiority of some varieties over others. As an example of the lack of linguistic interest of some of Zaldibia's etymologies in comparison with their political interest, one would have to quote what he says about Vardulia (the region of the Varduli) and Gipuzkoa: he posits that the former derives from *veardu leya,* meaning "he loves a stubborn fight," and that the latter comes from *Guc pusca* or "we'll chop you to pieces." Thus, the essence of the two names allows Gipuzkoans to warn sailors of two supposed group peculiarities: that they are warlike and given to butchery.[212]

Andrés de Poza both continued and strengthened Garibay's basic ideas. Endowed with greater linguistic knowledge, Poza's opinions enjoyed greater weight among later authors. In fact, by way of Larramendi, a great number of Poza's etymologies have survived in Humboldt's work. His linguistic beliefs were articulated as follows: firstly, he supports Garibay's idea that in antiquity Basque was the language that had been spoken all over the Iberian Peninsula, thereby refuting Morales, who had entertained the belief that several different languages had been spoken in Spain. According to Poza, the language spoken by Adam was Hebrew, which had originally been the world's one language. Then, after the confusion at Babel, the seventy-two languages emerged, one of which—"Babylonian" or Basque—would have been brought to Spain by Tubal. Then came Greek, Phoenician, and the languages of Africa and Rome. To verify any traces of the ancient Peninsular languages, Poza followed the method employed by Garibay, launching himself into the study of toponyms—some of them inaccurate, most of them mistaken, and others occasionally nonsensical, such as his reading of Asturias as *aztu-uri* (region of forgotten towns). Secondly, Poza was a Cantabrianist, but a much more prudent one than Garibay, for he realized that neither the people of Aquitaine nor the Navarrese could be included here. Secondly, he defends the (ethnic and linguistic) link between Western and Eastern (Caucasian) Iberia. Finally, he inaugurates a line of argument that in the long run was to become fruitful, describing Basque as "an essential and philosophical language."[213]

The only book published by Baltasar de Echave is a singular one, devoted as it is to linguistic apologetics. From a theoretical point of view, he merely follows in the footsteps of Garibay and Poza, although he does take them to extremes. His experience in the New World familiarizes him with indigenous Mexican toponymy and convinces him that the most accurate method to follow is in fact the etymological analysis of place names. He is, of course, a Tubalist, Iberianist, Cantabrianist, and compulsive etymologist, basing his arguments on the traditional comparisons between Western Iberian and Caucasian-Iberian names: Armenia, Gordeya, Ararat, Araxes, and so on. However, perhaps the most interesting aspect of his work is his total defense of the Basque language (in which he has it speak in the first person) and in his deeply felt lament over its lack of cultivation and state of abandonment. Echave blames this neglect on the greed that overcame those Basques who, blinded by the advantages that the exploitation of the New World had to offer, changed over to Castilian once they arrived in Potosí or New Spain, forgetting their mother tongue. This author must have known something about this, because he himself had been one of those emigrants and had written his work in Castilian. Also notable is his consideration of Basque as the true language of the Basque people and of Castilian as a foreign language. In fact, basing himself once more on etymology, he defends the fact that the Basques call their language *gueuzera* (that which is ours), while viewing Castilian as a degeneration of the old language of Spain—that is, of Basque—corrupted by contact with Latin. So when Castilians speak "that courtly language of which they think so highly," all they are doing is speaking the old Basque language that had been debased after the Roman invasion and which Basques call *herdera* or "foreign." To prove the prevalence of Basque over Castilian, Echave cites a list of terms shared by both languages, but, of course, without clarifying who had borrowed the terms from whom.[214]

Because we are continuously referring to the abuses of the etymological methods employed by Basque apologists from the sixteenth century practically to the present, let us include here an example to illustrate the massive lack of methodology and critical sense with which etymology was not only practiced but held to be irrefutable, thus laying the foundations for the most complicated and risky theoretical edifices to be later built upon it. Let us take a look at the uneven fate of the key word "*Cantabria*" as assigned by different scholars. Poza posits that "Cantabria, that is to say Cantabriga, is composed of two words, *brigo* and *canto*, of which the first means "shelter" and "company" . . . That is why we say that Cantabria—*Cantabriga*, in the ancient Spanish Basque language—refers to a shelter, refuge, or resting place of the people living among the harsh mountain peaks, stony plateaus, and ranges of this province, as opposed to the other populations situated on the plains of the other provinces of these kingdoms."[215] Echave writes that "they named [it] Canta Uria, which means 'a city or town made of stone,' (*canto*) or *canta*, because as you know, in our language we call a city or town Yria or Uria, pronouncing it both ways."[216] Friar Juan de Luzuriaga related the word to the Ebro River: "Cantabria means 'by Ebro' [*junto à Ebro*], from the word *Cata* that we use in old Castilian to refer to 'something that is next to another thing.' The City of Cantabria, whose remains can be seen to this day, was founded on the banks of this mighty river..."[217] In his chronicle, Ibargüen notes another etymological interpretation of a more political and ethnographic nature: the Cantabrian custom of transmitting their laws and the praise of their heroes in song. "This is how Cantabria came to be called the Home and the Land of Songs, because they would sing out their laws and the brave deeds of their heroes who had died on the battlefield." We will come across a similar etymology at the beginning of the nineteenth century in the writings of D'Iharce de Bidassouet, who maintains a purely Romantic form of etymology: ". . . the Cantabrians, *Khanta ver*, *Cantor* (singer, or peerless singer)... The Romans called them Cantabri because of the excellence of their voices."[218] Moguel emphasizes the Iberianist hypothesis by proposing the following etymology for "Cantabria": ". . . and I continue to believe that the word *Celtiberia* means 'lowland Iberia' or 'the Iberia of the plains,' and Cantabria or Canta-ibria (*Ibero* or *Ebro* are synonymous) is called *Iberia alta* or 'highland Iberia.'"[219] And so on. It has always been the case that the argument that appears to most suit the needs of any given political and social moment is the one that prevails, and several authors saw nothing against adapting their etymologies to the needs of their moment.

After the essentially Tubalist positions set by the first apologists, from Garibay to Agramont by way of Zaldibia and Sada, the seventeenth century saw a new generation of scholars who developed other, more nuanced theories. Arnaud Oihenart (1592–1668) marks a change in the arguments and strategy employed in defense of the Basque language. His position was that, in addition to its literary and communicative value, the language possessed an intrinsic value in and of itself. His position was supported by Scaliger's authoritative argument: *Nihil barbari aut stridoris aut anhelitus habet, lennisima est et suauissima, estque sine dubio uetustissima et ante tempora Romanorum illis finibus in usu erat*

([The Basque language] is not at all Barbarian, nor rough or shrill, it is extremely soft and sweet and undoubtedly very old, being used in this region before the Roman era).[220] He breaks with the Cantabrianist tradition that had taken root among both Basque and Castilian authors (Mariana, Prudencio de Sandoval, and Pedro Mártir de Anglería), but maintained a moderate Iberianism by having the Basque language extend to all the mountain villages of the north and west of the Peninsula: Navarre, Aquitaine, Bizkaia, the upper Ebro Valley, Cantabria, Asturias, Galicia, and Lusitania. To prove this, of course, he turned to the traditional methods of etymological and toponymic analysis. However, in his view, the true, original Basques were the *vascones* (the Navarrese), whereas the Western populations would have been "vasconized" (*vascongados*) by them; the same would have occurred with what were then called *tierras de bascos* or "Basque lands," that is, the lands of the northern Pyrenees, which had also been subject to linguistic colonization by the Navarrese. In any case, in writing his historic work, he was fully aware of the cultural unity brought about by the Basque language in spite of the political diversity of the area, and his work is conceived of as a history of Vasconia, "including both Iberia and Aquitaine." Finally, he wrote a basic grammar of Basque, which was viewed as highly praiseworthy and innovative and which was to constitute the first serious attempt until Larramendi's work.

The Chronicler of the Kingdom of Navarre, José Moret (1615–1687) followed the same line of criticism as Oihenart, albeit in a much more diffident and cautious manner. This Jesuit author did not share the Tubalist theory of the origin of Navarre and the rest of the Basque towns, and in his *Annales del Reyno de Navarra* (Annals of the Kingdom of Navarre) (1766) he is extremely cautious in broaching this matter: "The Navarrese, like their neighbors the people of Gipuzkoa, Araba and Bizkaia, are extremely proud of being descended from the original inhabitants of Spain, and also because this part of the Pyrenees, with its mountains and the banks of the Ebro River, is where Tubal, fifth son of Japhet, began to populate Spain."[221] Although he goes on to quote several authors who share this opinion, he never once indicates that he agrees with it. Conchillos also published a book in which he went into great detail regarding the Tubalist etymology of the city. Moret brought out a pamphlet ridiculing it, but—just in case—he did so under a false name and in a semi-clandestine edition with a false place of publication.[222] He acted with similar prudence and artfulness in establishing the link between the survival of the Basque language and the country's never having succumbed to a foreign yoke.[223]

10. The Basque Language as a Pastoral Tool and as the Subject of Apologistic Frenzy, 1640–1789

Meanwhile, during the seventeenth and eighteenth centuries the need for pastoral activity and the spread of Catholic doctrines spurred certain ecclesiastics to put together a handful of works in the Basque language. These were devotional books, catechisms, writings on mysticism, etc. In some cases, these works contained points of view praising the Basque language. It has been calculated that ninety books were published in Basque in the northern Basque Country, eighty-three of which were on religious subjects,[224] this figure being applicable to the whole of the Basque lands. During this period, José de Ochoa de Arín published a number of catechisms (1713), as did Martín de Arzadun (1731), Eleizalde (1735), and Juan de Irazusta (1742). Three translations of Thomas à Kempis' *The Imitation of Christ* were published by Arambillaga (1684), Miguel Chourio (1720), and Martín Maister (1757).

But it would not be until the end of the 1740s before any firm steps in the use of a superior version of Basque were to be seen in religious oratory, especially encouraged after the creation of the Franciscan College of Missionaries of Zarautz (Gipuzkoa).[225] This institution was renowned both for its work in training preachers and in its gathering of whatever materials, whether published or in manuscript form, might aid in the preparation of sermons. Consequently, the monastery's library housed one of the largest collections of texts in the Basque language. Finally, the College was also known for the preaching duties of the missionary friars themselves. Among these, Francisco de Palacios, Francisco Santos Guerrico, Antonio Añibarro, and Juan Mateo Zabala stood out for their oratory skills in Basque.

During this time, other religious orders also carried out missionary activities in this language, such as the Capuchins of Bera (Navarre) after 1731, and particularly the Jesuits of colleges from Bizkaia and Gipuzkoa: Bilbao, Lekeitio (Lequetio), and especially Loiola. Until they were expelled in 1767, the Company of Jesus employed a two-pronged strategy in regards to the Basque language: on the one hand, the strategy was a practical one consisting of evangelizing Basque-speaking areas in a dialectally appropriate and highly cultured language, and on the other hand, by theorizing, both in Basque and in Castilian, about the Basque language in terms that were mostly passionately apologistic. During the two decades between 1740 and 1760, Sebastián de Mendiburu (1708–1782) stands out above the other Jesuit missionaries preaching in Basque.

Agustín de Cardaberaz (1703–1770) was another of the Jesuit missionaries who traveled all over the Basque Country preaching tirelessly in exceptional Basque. The most notable effort made by a member of the Company of Jesus toward the dignification of the Basque language was the publication in 1761 of *Eusqueraren Berri Onac* (Good News for Basque), a didactic work in defense of that tongue. Cardaberaz composed this short essay in elegant Basque, which thus increased its suitability for both oral and written transmission and for its use as a teaching instrument. Cardaberaz was one of the first to raise his voice from the pedagogical arena in condemnation of the eradication of the Basque language from the educational process and begin promoting bilingual education in such a way as to avoid what he described in realistic terms as "*gaztelania ez ikasi, ta euskera aztu*" (Don't learn Castilian, and forget Basque).

Before we speak of Father Manuel de Larramendi (1690–1766) as the person who brought this process of defense and cultural enrichment of the Basque language to its zenith—a process which also linked the language to the maintenance of the order associated with the *Fueros* and even to the formulation of proto-nationalist proposals, we must mention an author whose work was twenty years in advance of many of these pronouncements: Joannes de Etcheberry, from Lapurdi. This author was unique in that he was not a priest but a physician, at a time when the great majority of writers and scholars came from an ecclesiastic background. But apart from covering the same ground that the Jesuit from Andoain (Gipuzkoa) became involved with years later—the defense of the language, work on a grammar, and a dictionary—Etcheberry accomplished this in Basque, thus simultaneously defending the language and helping to cultivate its literary aspects. However, his work did not make much of an impact, whereas Larramendi's was highly successful in this.

The Jesuit Manuel de Larramendi abandoned the critical and scientific arguments that Oihenart and Moret had delineated and returned to the traditional arguments of the scholars of the sixteenth century. Or rather, like the dyed-in-the-wool polemicist that he was, he used all kinds of arguments to demolish his opponents' opinions, especially Mariana's. He particularly cultivated Tubalism, Cantabrianism, and Basque-Iberianism, employing few nuances but instead used a great accumulation of examples, arguments, and quotations from authoritative figures. The apologists' main concerns, noted in their early studies and becoming more acute as time wore on, centered on the ability of Basque to be reduced to rules and codes and on its superiority over other languages in the quality of its grammatical structures, rich lexicon, and social usage. These concerns became radicalized in the work of Manuel de Larramendi. Bearing in mind his passionate, argumentative nature it is not surprising that he not only published works in defense of Basque, but also religious writings attacking the opinions of Jansenists and Quesnellians, among others. Larramendi's work is valuable for two reasons: in its own right, because, as has already been indicated, it gives the Basque language its first usable grammar and dictionary.[226] But its value also lies in the fact that it constituted a real warning to the consciences of many Basques whose apathy and neglect in linguistic matters was to be shaken by the mordant and impassioned works of the Jesuit from Andoain. He is successful in his goal of gathering as much artillery as possible to fire at the detractors of the Basque language, believing that what other apologists had achieved in the past was all very well but that the enemy had to be administered a final, lethal blow: "Garibay stated that it was a methodical language, and Grammar could be applied to it; Oihenart discovered aspects of its perfection, Moret did the same, castigating Mariana's harsh criticism; but they were content with too little, and left Basque in its old state of neglect."[227]

Larramendi believed that the superiority of Basque over other cultivated languages was not in doubt and that it could even be compared with Hebrew. He exclaims to the Latin language: "Be quiet, dead language, worm-eaten in your old parchments, covered in dust and cobwebs, there is no nation that claims you as its own." To Castilian he says: "You truly are, even more than gibberish, a language of disorder and confusion, admitting all kinds of words from here and there, whether they be noble or base, never putting them to the test regardless of where they come from." And as for French: "What are you but a muddled heap of corrupted, heterogeneous languages, thrown randomly together by hazard with very little connection between them, making your birth no more decorous than that of Romance, your brother?"[228]

Larramendi relates the perfection of a language to its rationality, and looks for the latter in its internal cohesion, regularity, absence of exceptions, etc., without concerning himself overmuch with its degree of cultivation. From this quest for regularity and perfection, he achieves a magnificently constructed grammar. Some authors defended the possibility of reducing the Basque language to rules, whereas others judged the task futile or impossible; Larramendi took on the job and reconstructed the language brilliantly. His grammar is composed of one section devoted to conjugations and declinations, another to syntax, and a third to prosody. The lexography is divided into two distinct parts: the prologue, which constitutes a work in its own right and is one of the most personalized and impassioned defenses of the language, followed by the dictionary itself. The main characteristic of this dictionary is that it is organized as Castilian-Basque, since Larramendi's principal concern was to show that any term in any cultivated language had a Basque equivalent, if the term had not actually been Basque in the first place and hijacked by other languages. The dictionary's prologue was made up of three parts: the first devoted to highlighting the perfection of the Basque language, the second to defending the idea of its having been the original and universal language of Spain, and the third ("A Defense of Basque") to responding to those who had made attacks on the language, especially Mayans y Siscar, Mariana, and Armesto y Ossorio. Larramendi was consumed by etymological fever, bent on proving Basque origins for hundreds of Castilian, Italian, Latin, French, or Greek terms. In view of most of the etymologies he posited, one can only think that Larramendi was poking fun at his opponents, who in general possessed a rudimentary knowledge of Basque—it is impossible to take the majority of these etymologies seriously. The problem is that many of his followers took his proposals literally, which had grave consequences for the later evolution of the cultivated language by afflicting it with an excessive emphasis on purity. In addition to the prologue to his *Diccionario*, Larramendi wrote a very similar work that is exclusively apologetic in tone: *De la antigüedad y universalidad del Bascuence en España* (On the Antiquity and Universality of Basque in Spain), but there is no lack of chapters containing a defense of Basque in works dealing with unrelated subjects, such as his *Corografía*.

But apart from all this, Larramendi was the first to establish clearly and expressly the unity of identity of Euskal Herria (that is, the land of the Basque-speaking people) and the Basques as a political nation. Suitably disguised as a fictional literary character (an "elderly gentleman" and councilor who speaks in his own name and whose speech wavers between senility and reverie), he expounds upon the unity of nation and language, arguing that since the Basques possess a distinct language of their own, they should also belong to a nation independent of all others. In spite of all his precautions and the fact that he then invented another, more realistic and moderate "Deputy" to explain the elderly gentleman's opinions, this work did not go to press in his lifetime and two centuries were to go by before it was published. This was not surprising in view of his message. The Gipuzkoan genius states that he has appeared to the decrepit old gentleman in dreams:

> What reason is there for the Basque nation, the original populator of Spain and even its neighbors—and I make bold to say this because I am the very model of a genius—what reason is there, I repeat, that this privileged nation of such noble origins should not be a nation apart, a nation in itself, free and independent of all oth-

ers? The defunct languages, such as Latin, Greek, Hebrew, Arabic, and others, had separate, self-governing nations, quite independent of others near or far. Living languages today, such as French, Spanish, and others, enjoy the same independence and freedom. Why then should Basque, a living and more lively language than any other, not have all its regions united together in a single independent nation free from any other language or nation? Why should three of Spain's provinces, Gipuzkoa, Araba, and Bizkaia (not to mention the kingdom of Navarre) have to be dependent on Castile, and another three—Lapurdi, Zuberoa, and Lower Navarre—dependent on France?[229]

Larramendi does not proclaim a stance of outright independence for several reasons. First and foremost, this is because of ideological reasons because the basis of his belief is strictly *foralist*: he is looking more toward maintaining the original independence of the Basque provinces, an independence subsumed in the ancient *Fueros*, than in seeking a new autonomy outside of them. Prudence and pragmatism also played a role. If the *foral* system remained intact, it would be better to leave things as they were: "To Castile, Gipuzkoans, to Castile!" This was, when all was said and done, a wink in the direction of the Bourbon monarchy that was placing the *Fuero* in grave danger by surreptitiously including in it a currently unviable project that would later become a desirable alternative: "The Project of the United Provinces of the Pyrenees is no doubt a magnificent and attractive one . . . but if this Republic is still no more than a pipe-dream it needs a great deal more time before it is founded in reality."[230] After Larramendi, there was a proliferation of explicit connections between the preservation of the *Fuero* and that of the Basque language, from Moguel's *Peru Abarca* to Iztueta's *Guipuzcoaco Provinciaren Condaira...* (Account or History of the Province of Gipuzkoa...).

It would be legitimate to wonder why certain eighteenth century religious orders, especially the Franciscans and Jesuits, were to become the defenders of the Basque language, in both theory and practice, at least in regard to its use in the evangelization of the masses. Why did these friars go to the trouble of preaching in the language of the country and publishing apologies, grammars, and dictionaries, while the majority of the parish priests and lay preachers (whether educated or not) with direct responsibility for the "care of souls," adopted an attitude that was at least passive when not belligerently in favor of the spread of Castilian and French? What is more, is it mere coincidence that a Jesuit, who was the only theoretician of the eighteenth century and who was in the center of the crisis, linked the Basque language to the *Fuero* system, and who even dared to come to nationalistic conclusions? At that time, the Jesuits exerted a political influence on the enlightened governments and monarchies of Catholic Western Europe, an influence that eventually ended with their expulsion from Portugal, Spain, and France. Among other more weighty matters, the Jesuits and the governments of these countries differed radically on linguistic policy. Whereas the former were supported by the peasant and tradesmen classes and were in favor of indoctrinating them in their own language, the latter followed a policy of linguistic homogenization that sought to lower the status of the different "patois" and "regional languages" and promote the official court languages. Once again, language has become an instrument of communication as well as a political tool. This is fundamentally a confrontation between two strategies of political and ideological power and control: the Catholic Church turns a mother tongue into an instrument of Christian indoctrination and ideological domination of the masses, and the secular powers attempt to achieve that very same domination via the imposition of the Romance languages.

In the same way that the Jesuits were to clash with the nationalist and royalist plans of the 1760s and 1770s, the Franciscans were to become the natural allies of the popular classes who would attempt to save the *foral* system, from which they benefited as consumers through Carlism a few years later. Both Jesuits and Franciscans were to adopt positions against gentlemen, *andiquis* (local power brokers), traders, and liberals who were undermining the *foral* order either with reforms or, more openly, with revolutionary changes. Already they could see looming on the horizon the beginning of the disentailment of Church property, the forced civil constitution of the clergy, the collapse of an order that placed peasants and regular soldiers on the same side of the barricades; these groups were by then beginning to see the relationship—in theory at least—between the preservation of that (*foral*) order and that of the language of the people. It would be unfair to paint all the friars of this or that order with the same royalist or Carlist brush, but at least we know that those who most distinguished themselves in the use and defense of the Basque language, the Franciscans of Zarautz, being royalists and counterrevolutionary sympathizers, were decidedly in favor of the values of France's *Ancien Régime*. The description of the political events after 1791 that left Father Añibarro in charge of writing a chronicle of the order in its Record Book leaves no doubt on the matter. As we read that the French nation welcomes "heretics, atheists and Jacobins" to her breast; that "one Napoleon Bonaparte manages by deceitful means to make our beloved Catholic King Fernando the Seventh Head and Absolute Sovereign Monarch of the Kingdom of

France"; and that the Cádiz liberals are presented as "atheists, Jansenists, Freemasons, Jacobins, sectarians of every stripe," we note that these are all highly legitimist actors in Father Añibarro's impassioned version of the wars, revolutions, secularizations, disentailments, etc. of the time.[231]

After the boost given by Jesuits and Franciscans to preaching and the general cultivation of Basque for pastoral purposes, and with that language now in possession of a dictionary and grammar, a trend arose regarding its use. Many priests, both attached to orders and working in the parishes, followed the path laid down by Mendiburu or Palacios and, armed with Larramendi's grammar and lexicon, they felt encouraged—with varied literary fortune—to write their sermons, song lyrics, poetry, devotional books and other texts in the Basque language. One example was the parish priest of Elkano (in the Egüés valley, Navarre), Joaquín de Lizarraga (1748–1835), who had been educated at the Loiola convent and who wrote a large number of pious and evangelical texts in Basque. Although the bulk of his work was indeed used in his pastoral duties, most of it has remained unpublished.[232] Other individuals who cultivated the Basque language with ecclesiastical ends in mind were the Franciscans Juan Antonio de Ubillos (1707–1789) and Pedro Antonio de Añibarro (1748–1830). In both the northern and southern territories of the Basque Country, a modest lexicographical fever was unleashed, mostly following in Larramendi's footsteps. As examples of this activity, both Jean Martin Hiribarren (1810–1866) and Maurice Harriet (1814–1904) left behind unpublished dictionaries; in 1856, M. Salaberry d'Ibarrolle brought out a Lower Navarrese–French lexicon, and Pedro Novia de Salcedo (1790–1865) and José Francisco de Azkibel (1798–1865) published an etymological dictionary and a Basque–Spanish dictionary, respectively. For his part, Bilbao native Juan Mateo de Zabala (1777–1840), a Franciscan missionary of the Zarautz establishment, was obliged for the sake of his missionary endeavors to expand his study of the language; this resulted in the posthumous publication in 1848 of his *Verbo Regular del dialecto vizcaíno* (Regular Verb in the Bizkaian Dialect).

Simultaneously, with this Basquist wave among the monasteries in the Basque Country, a powerful movement was taking place toward the values and activities of the Enlightenment. In 1764, the Count of Peñaflorida (Xabier María de Munibe Idiáquez), Manuel Ignacio de Altuna, and Joaquín de Eguía (Marquis of Narros) founded the Real Sociedad Bascongada de los Amigos del País, whose area of interest covered the three western provinces. In 1776, this institution opened a center for higher learning dedicated to teaching and research, the Real Seminario Patriótico de Bergara (Bergara Royal Patriotic Seminary). In

Tudela in 1773, another such group was created with the expressive title of the Sociedad Tudelana de los Deseadores del Bien Público (Tudela Society of People in Favor of the Public Good), sponsored by the Marquis of San Adrián (José María Magallón y Mencos), who gathered around him the cream of the local notables and intellectuals, such as the Marquis of Montesa, Manuel de Cruzat, and Cristóbal María Cortés. But there appear to have been a number of opposing sentiments regarding the Basque language within the heart of the Sociedad Bascongada. There were members who were rather hostile toward it, such as Valentín de Foronda, and others more inclined in its favor, like the Count of Peñaflorida himself, but on the whole, the Society considered Castilian to be the only mode of communication and the sole pedagogical instrument. In 1772, it put forth a plan of incentives for primary schools, and, in parallel fashion, the diffusion among other Basque educational establishments of two works recently published by the Academia Española de la Lengua (Spanish Academy of the Language) on Castilian orthography and grammar. This provoked one member of the Society residing in Armiñón, Araba, to send a written response under the pseudonym "a friend from Araba" criticizing the initiative. He argued that the most famed linguists recommended primary instruction in the mother tongue and that since for Basque children this was Euskara, this language, rather than Castilian, should be the medium of instruction in the Basque Country's schools. The Society's response was unequivocal. There were two arguments in defense of the use of Castilian in the Basque Country's schools. The first was that the government had prohibited the use of Basque as a medium of instruction. The second argument wrongly interprets the concepts of a "native" language, alleging that although Basque is the language "peculiar" to the region, Spanish is its "native" tongue because it is the language of the nation as a whole.[233] There can be no greater dishonesty than defining a language as a mother tongue simply because it is the official language.

In the context of the awakening of Celtic studies in the eighteenth century, we should take a moment to consider some of the movement's most outstanding authors, since their linguistic methodology was, in the middle term, to exert some degree of influence on the Basque linguists of the turn of that century. Antoine Court de Gébelin (1728–1784), an enlightened Calvinist pastor, physiocrat, and Freemason from Geneva, Switzerland, carried out all his pastoral and intellectual work in France. Concerned with esoteric and theosophical doctrines, he published his magnum opus, an encyclopedia[234] that attempted to gather in one place all knowledge regarding a supposed "Primitive World," a single, perfect, golden civilization for all Humanity that had disappeared in the biblical flood. In his view of the course of history, the passage of time was merely a process of decomposition of this primal state, so that—paradoxically—the more history advanced, the more distanced it became from his proposed antediluvian civilization and thus from the primal plan. He saw history as synonymous with decadence and cultural fragmentation. Nevertheless, according to Court de Gébelin, it was possible to discern part of this "Primitive World" through mythical folktales and, above all, through linguistics. Living languages, he believed, retained traces of the original common tongue, and these could be subjected to relevant etymological analyses to provide an idea of the nature of that first language. Of course, he believed that the language least distanced from the original one was Celtic, that is, French. To reconstruct the original language, Court de Gébelin set out to compile a comparative dictionary, to include the roots of every single language, and a comparative grammar as well. His influence on the legitimists and traditionalists, with De Maistre at their head, was notable. In British Celtic circles, each language community tried to benefit from the notion of Celtic purity, and the Welsh, Scots, and Irish vied with the English in a mad race toward perfect Celticness. Among the English, Rowland Jones (*The Circles of Gomer*, 1771) was one of the most influential theorists. He applied a theoretical methodology similar to Court de Gébelin's to prove that the closest language to the original one was—naturally—Celtic, although, of course, the closet and purest of the Celtic languages was English. The flowering of this tendency to search for a single protolanguage on the eve of the nineteenth century is truly paradoxical in view of the fact that a multitude of authors had been proclaiming for decades various polygenic theories of language, rejecting Hebrew as the originator of all languages and intensifying their focus on comparative methods.

According to the top-down method used by Court de Gébelin and, more radically, by Jones for linguistic analysis, each syntagm would link two or more roots in the original language. It appears that he was following the methodology of the sixteenth-century Flemish writer Johannes Goropius Becanus, whose work had already been put into question by Gottfried Wilhelm Leibniz (who coined the term "to Goropicize," meaning to make up wild etymologies) and Justus Lipsius. Jones, instead of relying on the roots of words for his etymologies, relied on significant sounds and letters. These, he believed, were the basic elements of a language, existing within a kind of hieroglyphic matrix in a relationship, as he explained it, like that of atoms to matter. Jones supposed that the original Celts possessed a *claves angelica* (heavenly key) to the original language, contained in letters with ideographic meanings, which were based on significant elements (such as animals and movements) that antediluvian peoples had beheld in Paradise. Each word was composed of combinations of these meanings found in the letters/sounds.[235] These and many other European authors shared similar theories about language and the original world, with the difference that their studies inevitably led to the conclusion that the language most similar to the perfect, paradisiacal one was without fail their own. These theories took root somewhat later in the Basque-speaking world, particularly in the work of Pablo Astarloa and Juan Bautista Erro. Humboldt, and later Sabino Arana, were indirectly influenced by these scholars.

The generation that lived through the beginning of the fall of the *Ancien Régime* and by extension the *foral* order can be represented by two priests who were apologists for Basque: Pablo Pedro de Astarloa (1752–1806) and Juan Antonio de Moguel (1754–1804). Astarloa, as has already been indicated, was an ideological and linguistic follower of Court de Gébelin, except that he applied the methods used for French to Euskara. He believed that there had been a primitive tongue whose letters possessed their own natural properties, and that traces of it could be found in the oldest remaining languages, and most particularly in Basque. It is no coincidence that he titled his main work *Discursos filosóficos sobre la lengua primitiva* (Philosophical Discourses on the Primitive Language), and he would have done better to call it "Mystical Discourses," because his analysis is more philosophical-mystic speculation than a scientific treatise. He fought heatedly with everyone, from Joaquín de Traggia to José Antonio Conde, who opposed his notion of the virtues and the heaven-born antiquity of the Basque language, and he even felt the need to correct other apologists with whom he was not entirely in agreement, such as Tomás de Sorreguieta.

We know that Moguel, apart from his priestly duties, had also sheltered in his home every dissenting Catholic cleric fleeing across the border from the French Revolution. These religious counterrevolutionaries caused an enormous impact on the population with their tales of Jacobin excesses and the Terror, especially in Bizkaia, Gipuzkoa, and Navarre. Moguel's notion was based on a hypothetical crystalline, pure, and perfect Basque matrix language that was still spoken by peasants and artisans and on whose lips it should be sought. The language spoken by cultured types, on the other hand, was corrupted and so full of barbarisms as to be barely recognizable. His theory of language is to be found in an excellent book, a treatise in prose in the manner of *Diálogos de la Lengua* (Dialogues on Language) by Juan de Valdés and which is considered the finest Basque narrative of the nineteenth century: *El doctor Peru Abarca* (Doctor Peru Abarca). Like many other Basque works of the time, it was not published for eighty years, although copies of the manuscript circulated profusely. Although his theories appear throughout the book, they are most systematically stated in the final dialogue in which two men of the cloth, Brother Pedro de Urlía (Brother So-and-So) and a priest, Juan de Sandía (John Doe), representing Pedro de Añibarro and Moguel himself, discuss at length the linguistic matters that concern them. It was a useful means of reaching the congregation, and therefore it had to be a reflection of the language spoken by those same tradesmen and peasants. Precisely because it needed to be intelligible to them, it had to be pure, free of borrowings and corruptions of any sort. The Basque language as such, given its outstanding nature, was quite capable of expressing any kind of thought whatsoever, no matter how elevated or complex; any incapacity was because of a lack of work on the part of the wicked *vascongados* who should have cultivated it and omitted to do so.

Also belonging to this generation was Lorenzo Hervás y Panduro (1735–1809). This highly erudite Jesuit from Cuenca carried out the first serious and systematic study of global comparative linguistics. It is useful to bear in mind that, after his expulsion from his order in Spain, he ended up establishing himself in Rome, where Pope Pius VII named him librarian of the Quirinal Palace. From this privileged position he was able to make use of a large number of grammars and dictionaries of many diverse languages. He wrote a vast book, *Idea dell'universo* (1778–1787), in Italian, of which the third part (in five volumes) he devoted to the languages of the world, but some years later he went back to the subject and wrote the work in Spanish, after which it was published under the title *Catálago de las lenguas de las naciones conocidas* (Catalogue of the Languages of the Known Nations) (1800–1805). Among the other languages, Basque occupied a dignified position as the sole, ancient matrix language of Spain, having given rise, according to Hervás, to a great part of the Peninsula's toponyms and to the majority of Spanish surnames. Regardless of the accuracy of his judgments on the Basque language, the most important point is its inclusion in a vast cataloging plan in a superbly erudite, decidedly scientific work.

Somewhat older than Astarloa's generation, the Carlist minister of government Juan Bautista Erro was a follower of his theories, but he took them to extremes. His work follows the same quest as Astarloa's, searching for the original language through Basque. It is no coincidence that his most mature book is titled *El Mundo primitivo* (The Primitive World).[236] Its originality lay in attempting to find evidence for his arguments not just through the usual etymological studies but also through archaeological artifacts, particularly ancient coins. In any case, his philological speculations were amazing, as he would add and subtract letters as he thought fit—a habit that made him an easy target for more serious, better-informed critics, such as Conde.

11. Nineteenth Century Paradoxes Concerning the Basque Language

The nineteenth century saw two simultaneous and generally contradictory lines of approach to the Basque language and culture. In contrast to a proliferation of scientific studies, there emerged a profusion of falsified legends and apocryphal historical songs. This is not to say that fraud was making its first appearance in Basque letters. The most outstanding case is that of the *Lelo's Song,* which is included in the anthology by Ibargüen and Cachopín. There emerged a real vogue for pieces in the Romantic style of James MacPherson's *Works of Ossian* (1765). Garay de Monglave published the *Song of Altabiscar* in 1835, Chaho published the *Song of Aitor* in 1845; Francisque-Michel brought out the *Song of Abarca* in 1859, and Claudio Otaegui published the *Song of Beotibar* in 1882.[237] Excluding, of course, traditionally esoteric, supernatural, or simply religious explanations, a large number of the scientific studies on the Basque language dating from the beginning of the nineteenth century were based entirely on rationalist analysis and were fully immersed in the current of academic research of the time.

We should pause a moment to consider two figures, both foreigners who nevertheless made decisive contributions to the scientific study of the Basque language. Wilhelm von Humboldt and Louis Lucien Bonaparte contributed greatly to the dissemination of knowledge of the Basque culture internationally and set in motion its process of dignification, as did two others, new arrivals in the country: Francisque-Michel and Antoine d'Abbadie. The fact that these four individuals, who were responsible for the scientific analysis of the Basque language and its introduction into literary and academic circles, were a German, two Frenchmen, and a person of both Irish and Basque descent clearly reflects the cultural situation of the country, particularly its lack of universities but also its lack of interest in the scientific study of Basque subjects among Spanish academic circles.

Wilhelm von Humboldt, founder of the University of Berlin and one of the most respected German and European scientists of his time, became interested in the Basque language because of a decidedly Romantic impulse to find a linguistic connection to his original people and, given the antiquity of Basque, he could link himself to the language. He traveled to Euskal Herria between 1799 and 1801 and made contact with several of the most famed Basque scholars of the time, especially Astarloa and Moguel. He upheld some outdated theories, particularly Basque-Iberianism, but without the religious influence and basing himself exclusively, if mistakenly, on scientific criteria. He made a remarkable contribution to spreading information about the Basque language, and its real and imagined peculiarities, throughout the European scientific community.

Louis Lucien Bonaparte (1813–1891) was the nephew of Emperor Napoleon I, and during his peripatetic life, he managed to achieve a remarkable scientific background in several fields (such as chemistry and mineralogy), especially linguistics. Born in England, he lived in Italy, the United States, and several other places. He had a perfect command of five languages and knew several more, but he devoted himself, in particular, to the study of Basque, and specifically, to its dialectology. His second marriage was to Clemencia Richard, a Basque speaker, and he achieved an extraordinary mastery of Basque and its dialects. He amassed a library that included practically everything that had been published in Basque up to his time. He surrounded himself with a series of exceptional informants and collaborators (Emmanuel Inchauspe, Jean Pierre Duvoisin, José Antonio Uriarte, Claudio Otaegui, Bruno Echenique, Julián Achotegui, and Salaberry d'Ibarrolle) and developed the atlas of Basque dialectology on which later studies have been based. His rather varied works were published between 1860 and 1880.

Beyond the area of research but within the no less important domain of dissemination, one individual—also a foreigner—stands out for his contribution to a less impassioned but academic approach to the Basque language and to Basque cultural studies in general: Francisque-Michel. A member of the Institut de France (French Institute), in 1857 he published a work titled *Le Pays Basque. Sa population, sa langue, ses moeurs, sa literature et sa musique* (The Basque Country: Its Population, Language, Way of Life, Literature and Music), which helped to introduce and spread among the French public, in a rigorous and accurate manner, the most important aspects of what had been discovered about Basque culture at the time. This work can be said to be the beginning in Euskal Herria of a discipline that was taking its first steps at the time: folklore.

Antoine d'Abbadie (or Abbadia) was only partly a stranger in Navarre, because although he was Irish, his father was from Zuberoa. He was a traveler, a student of astronomy, ethnography, and linguistics. He collaborated with the Prince Bonaparte because they met in London in 1855. After 1853, he founded, supported, and financed the *Juegos Florales Bascos* (Basque Poetry Competitions) in which the treatment of the language contributed to its process of dignification, at least in regards to cultured and popular poetry.

Abbadie and Bonaparte carried out much of the work of the diffusion and dignification of the Basque language and of arousing public interest in it, and their work bore fruit immediately. Researchers of different levels devoted themselves to studying the country's heritage of the near-extinct oral literature. Chaho had already gathered together several collections of traditional songs, a part of which he had published in *Ariel* during the 1840s. Then in 1857, as has already been mentioned, Michel published in his *Le Pays Basque* the fist systematic compilation of Basque songs. Two collections of traditional songs were brought out in 1869, one by Julie Adrienne Carricaburu that was included in her book *Souvenirs des Pyrénées* (Memoirs of the Pyrenees) and the other by Pascal Lamazou, titled *Cinquante Chants Pyrénéens* (Fifty Pyrenean Songs). The following year, Jean Dominique Julien Salaberry published his *Chants Populaires du Pays Basque* (Popular Songs of the Basque Country). Then came the compilations of José Manterola, Charles Bordes, Jean de Jaurgain, and finally a work by Father Azkue. Like the songs, collections of legends and proverbs abounded. Outstanding among these were the works by Cerquand, a Frenchman, and the Englishman Wentworth Webster, who published his *Basque Legends* in 1877. Julien Vinson's work was to come later.

Finally, we should mention a matter related to the above that began to take shape in Europe (particularly all of central and eastern Europe) after the Napoleonic wars, a matter that was inevitably to affect Basque linguistic and political stances after the 1830s. I am referring to the relationship between language and nationhood. Of course, we can find positions that closely relate these concepts from the Renaissance. In his *Lexicon polonicum* (Polish Lexicon) of 1564 Jan Maczynski had defined a nation as "a people of a country or a kingdom, especially one that speaks the same language." There was no dearth of "patriotic" exaltation of the cultivation of German at the end of the seventeenth century in the work of Gottfried Wilhelm Leibniz (1646–1716), but it is not until the middle of the eighteenth when analyses connecting the language spoken by a people to its "genius" begin to proliferate. Etienne Bonnot de Condillac (1715–1785) devotes a chapter to "Du genie des langues" (The Nature of Languages) in his *Essai su l'origine des connaisances humaines* (Essay on the Origins of Human Knowledge) (1746). The evidence that French was taking the place of Latin as the international language of culture and diplomacy, and that it was finding its way into the cultured vocabulary of other languages, caused members of linguistic circles who had felt culturally colonized to feel protective toward it and to experience a sense of prestige. This was the case from Russian to Spanish by way (naturally) of German. French began to be considered a legacy to be safeguarded and the preservation of its purity, use, and cultivation a demonstration of patriotism. From Father Isla in Spain to Johann Herder (1744–1803), Golthold Lessing (1729–1781), and Friedrich Klopstock (1724–1803) in Germany, literary figures harangued their compatriots to banish the wave of Gallicisms that was flooding their languages and to maintain the latter in their greater state of purity. But it was not until the 1780s when the idea that a nation is defined by its own language began to take root and become popular among ordinary people, particularly in German and Slavic-speaking areas—the notion that its language is the most refined expression of the genius peculiar to each nation as demonstrated throughout its history. Language was considered simultaneously as an instrument and as memory. It was later, in the traumatic context of the Napoleonic wars, when the process of politicization of linguistic identity began to take place. Czechs, Poles, and Germans all made their respective languages the crux of the right of nations to have their political formulations of statehood coincide with their cultural realities. In this regard, Herder's work was to become a reference-point not just for Germany but also for other peoples of central and eastern Europe. In this stew of nationalism, Romanticism, organicism, and the defense of one's own language, a greater opposition took shape between (French) cosmopolitanism, thought of as a fleeting fad, and (Polish or German) populism, characterized as identity-bearing and concrete. In the case of Basque, we have already seen demonstrations that clearly associated nation and language in authors like Larramendi and Iztueta, but this Romantic-populist movement was most clearly expressed by Chaho. Later, as the *foral* organization came under attack and was gradually dismantled, experiments and projects with language (and its recovery) as their main point of interest began to be formulated. The most highly developed of these would be the Asociación Euskara de Navarra (Euskara Association of Navarre).

12. The Fall of the *Foral* System: Was It Linked to the Eradication of the Basque Language?

In the northern Basque Country, the institutionalized language policy was to undergo a violent change of outlook with the French Revolution. Despite the fact that throughout the eighteenth century the French monarchy intensified its policy of enhancing the prestige of French to the detriment of "dialects" and "regional languages," Basque was hardly affected at all in its French territories.[238] However, the national character of the new regime that emerged after 1789 called for the use of a single language and the rejection and disappearance of all the rest. Linguistic variety was presented as synonymous with tyranny and oscurantism. The vast plan to eradicate what was generally called patois meant a change of language for most French citizens. Reports by Bertrand Barreré and Henri Grégoire presented before the Convention in 1792 leave no doubt whatsoever as to the prevailing determination to "*anéantir les patois*" (obliterate all dialects). The Decree of the Second Thermidor of year two banned the use of all languages except French not just at public events but also in private life, and although this was later repealed, its spirit was preserved in the legislation that was to follow. From a theoretical and symbolic standpoint French was presented as the instrument that could attain universal values, the "general will," and express philosophical and scientific concepts; it was to be a tool of unity and progress. All other languages spoken in the land were the legacy of diversity, of "individual will," of confusion, discord, and the inability to speak in a civilized fashion. Otherwise, as these other languages were presented in profoundly inferior terms, they were rarely, if ever, called languages, rather, in the best of cases, they were referred to as "speech" and most commonly "cant," "dialects," or "manners of speech." It should not be forgotten that among those patois were tongues that in other countries were considered national languages, such as Italian and German. Be that as it may, as the Revolution advanced, the language = unity equation (as opposed to patois = diversity) became deeply entrenched. From a political standpoint, the French language was the expression of all things national and revolutionary, whereas the patois were vehicles for servility, feudalistic thinking, fanaticism, superstition, slavery, barbarity, etc. French was "the language of liberty," whereas mention was made of "servile" or "slave" tongues. In simple terms, the political message of the French Revolution was "one nation, one language."[239] The alternative of German nationalism, with its roots in Romanticism (Herder and Humboldt), would be exactly the reverse: "one language, one nation," or language as the most pristine expression of that imprecise notion, *Volksgeist*, the national genius or spirit. Indeed, the attempt to promote liberty to a universal level, a concept conceived by the Revolution and put into practice by Bonaparte's imperial armies, incited the occupied countries from Spain to Russia by way of Germany to proclaim the right to diversity under various national, political, and cultural formulations.

Nevertheless, the linguistic situation did not undergo a brusque change in the north of the Basque Country. In 1833, when the Guizot Law regarding primary education was passed, a vast survey was carried out to discover the educational and linguistic level of the French population. The results from the Basque Country leave no room for doubt: the majority of the population continued to be monolingual in Basque, and even in the area around Gascony, including Angelu (Anglet), Bokale (Boucou), and Bidaxune (Bidache). According to a note on the subject published in the *Memorial des Pyrénées* that same year, "*un voyaguer qui ne parlerait que français, serait dans l'impossibilité de se faire comprendre, à mois qu'il n'eut recours au curé*" (to a traveler who only spoke French it would be impossible to make himself understood, unless he turned to the priest).[240] It was no easy task to turn the linguistic situation around, but the theoretical framework and the relevant laws were already in place and would begin to bear fruit during the years of the Second Empire.

During these years at the turn of the eighteenth century, the southern Basques were to become the object of a theoretical offensive sponsored by the Madrid government, whose ulterior aim was the abolition (or at least the reform) of the *Fueros*, although the plan centered on undermining the historical and linguistic goals of Basque scholars. At this point educated, early liberal Spaniards perceived attempts at presenting Basque as the ancient language of Spain, at bringing up the fact that the Basque Country had never been conquered, and at the fact that the *Fueros* had been in existence previous to the royal concessions as parts of a single package and as justification for obsolete privileges that ought to be wiped out. Within the Basque Country, on the other hand, any questioning of its presumed cultural excellence was taken as an attack on the *Fueros* and vice versa. The future director of the Academia de la Historia, José de Vargas Ponce (1760–1821), who during his stay in the Basque Country struck up a friendship with Moguel, wrote to the latter in 1802 indicating that ". . . my readings and my dealings with all of you have totally convinced me that it is not humanly possible to disabuse you people one iota of those gigantic pretensions that you have adopted to increase the privileges of your country."[241]

In 1802, the Academia de la Historia began to publish its vast *Diccionario Geográfico-Histórico de España* (Geographical-Historical Dictionary of Spain), which was then suspiciously reduced to the first two volumes, ones that dealt exclusively with Basque Country-Navarre and Rioja. Despite the great historical interest of the work and the modern methodology in which it was conceived, the political intent of the dictionary was undeniably to question the traditionalist positions of the Basque scholars. The task of writing the dictionary was divided up as follows: the liberal partisan of the Spanish Constitution of 1812 and member of the Academia de la Historia, Francisco Martínez Marina

(1754–1833) was responsible for the section on Araba. Other members of the Academy, Joaquín Traggia (1748–1813) and Manuel Abella, took on Navarre; and Vicente González Arnau wrote the part that concerned Bizkaia. The articles on Gipuzkoa were divided among all four authors. The articles titled "Álava" and "Vizcaya" turned out to be a compendium of strictly political *antiforalist* arguments, the gist of which was to deny the possible original independence of those territories from the Kingdom of Castile. Martínez Marina devotes several pages to refuting the existence of the Cofradía de Arriaga (Arriaga Brotherhood) and the pact between Araba and the King of Castile, and attributing the union to simple rights of conquest. He also alleges, controversially, that:

> This event [the conquest of Araba] is so incompatible with the imaginary ideas that the people of Araba held and still hold today regarding their ancient sovereignty and independence (which, according to them, dates back unchanged to 1332), and with their commonly stated belief that they have never been conquered, that it is quite incredible the number of ruminations, subtleties, and ingenious games to which they have resorted, even the most judicious of them, to interpret and concur with this story.[242]

From our point of view, there were greater repercussions from the opinions written by Joaquín Traggia in the article "Navarra," because it was centered particularly on linguistics. In fact, to argue in favor of Navarre's dependence upon the Hispanic institutions, Traggia turns to the "argument" that Euskara was not the original language of this territory, but that it had been introduced in the eighth century "so that its people could believe themselves to be totally independent from the foreigner." Nothing could convince Traggia that the Basque of his day could be the same as that spoken by the Navarrese. To the contrary, he believed that all that remained of the original language was a syntactical reference, whereas the Basque of the present day is a bastardized construction using terminology from all the surrounding languages with the political purpose stated above. However this assertion is no less interesting for being false, for it recognizes the association between the political and the cultural—in this case between the established system and the Basque language. Otherwise Traggia shows himself to be against the idea that Euskara might have been the original, overall language of Spain. What is curious about this case is that the political intention of the article commissioned by the Spanish authorities is totally contrary to the position that Traggia had taken some years previously. Over a span of ten years he went from considering Basque the original language of Spain and the Basques themselves as a people that had never been subjected to a foreign power, to positing the theory that the language was a ploy invented in the late Middle Ages to justify Navarrese aspirations to independence. Let us look at the opinions that Traggia initially expressed:

> The multitude of Basque words spread all over the continent; the ancient character of this extraordinary language and the fact that it has avoided the common fate of Hebrew, Greek, and Latin; the uniqueness of its roots and construction, which are in no way similar in any known language, prove, to my way of thinking, not only that it existed in Spain before recorded history but also that it leads us to conclude that it was very probably universal all over the Peninsula . . . Never having been conquered, not possessing a taste for forming alliances with foreigners and mixing their blood, populating the wilderness first, speaking a language different from any known tongue that exists to this day, and with an origin going back to remotest antiquity, one can hardly doubt that Basque is the original language of the first people to populate Spain.[243]

But the offensive had only just begun. In 1805, Martínez Marina himself brought out an *Ensayo crítico sobre el origen y progreso de las lenguas* (Critical Essay on the Origin and Progress of Languages), which, if possible, was even more disparaging of the presumed excellence of the Basque language than the *Diccionario* of the Real Academia de la Historia. In 1804, the Arabic scholar José Antonio Conde (1765–1820), protected by his pseudonym of *El cura de Mantuenga* (The Priest of Mantuenga), published a work titled *Censura crítica de la pretendida excelencia y antigüedad del vascuence* (A Critical Censure of the Supposed Excellence and Antiquity of Basque), and two weeks later published another: *Censura crítica del Alfabeto primitivo de España y pretendidos monumentos literarios del vascuence* (A Critical Censure of the Primitive Alphabet of Spain and Supposed Literary Monuments of Basque), in both of which he attacked the apologistic works of Astarloa and Erro. To close this offensive within a strictly politico-historiographic domain, Canon José Antonio Llorente (1756–1823) published his *Noticias históricas de las tres Provincias Vascongadas* (Historical Notes on the Three Basque Provinces) between 1806 and 1808. The fundamental thesis was that the Basque *Fueros* had been a royal concession and therefore could be revoked by monarchs, and in the same spirit Tomás González brought out his *Colección de cédulas...* (Collection of Documents...).[244] There is no doubt that the Spanish authorities were directly behind some of these studies, especially the government and the Academia de la Historia; Manuel Godoy himself confesses in his *Memoria del Príncipe de la Paz...* (Biography of the Prince of Peace...) that the publication of Llorente's *Noticias históricas* was a premeditated and calculated blow against the Basque *Fueros*. The Canon began salaried work from the Peace of Basle (1795) onwards, although the extremely learned nature of the task slowed down its publication until 1806.[245] Would it be too suspicious of us to recall that many of these works were being printed in official or at least public presses, like the Imprenta Real (Royal Printing Press)?

The Basque response was remarkable, although several of the works were published late and amid great difficulties and obstacles. In the arena of political linguistics, Astarloa, Moguel, and Erro responded to Traggia, whereas in the political-institutional field, Francisco Aranguren y Sobrado, Juan Antonio Zamácola, and Pedro Novia de Salcedo responded on behalf of the Provinces with José Yanguas y Miranda speaking for Navarre. As to the character and opinions of these destroyers of all things Basque and the tone that the controversy adopted, we should remember that the Spanish polemicists were cultured, erudite, and prestigious academics who must have become very irritated at the politico-linguistic pretensions of the Basque authors, because they were driven to lose their manners and waste their precious time arguing with them. I think that the following quotation from José Antonio Conde sums up the position of the cultured academic scandalized by the errant opinions of Basque supporters who were trying to turn a vernacular into a competitor among the cultivated languages:

> It is not my intention to note and correct all the errors and frivolous claims of these writings, as this would be a very long and exasperating task, and one should not waste precious time on such ineptitude, arbitrary plans, and chimerical descriptions of antiquity founded on the false supposition of the ancient culture of the Basque language and its status as the general language of Spain, when it is a country dialect that at no point and in no nation was ever worth consideration, and which to this day continues in its rustic barbarity like the languages of nomadic and cultureless peoples.[246]

As the aspirations of the Basque apologists increased, progressing from their traditional claim for the language to be recognized as one of the matrix languages of Babel and the ancient universal language of Spain to the claim that it was a language that had existed in pre-Babel times and was therefore the language of Paradise, their opponents' rebuttals became more virulent, belittling, and denigrating—sometimes rudely—against the entire Basque culture. If Mariana raised a huge cloud of dust in his day for having called the Basques uncouth barbarians (to put it in a nutshell), at the dawn of the nineteenth century the tone of the controversy, now imbued with heavy political overtones, could be measured in judgments like the following (also penned by Conde):

> The Basque language, regardless of the delirious praise heaped upon it by its apologists, is a coarse tongue, incapable of elegance, unkempt in its composition, and full of unpleasant sounds and monotonous endings. A vulgar and poor language, it is like a ragged cloak, covered in patches, mixed with strange, poorly pronounced, and even more poorly applied words, without expressiveness or grace. Its verbs are a tangle of particles and auxiliaries, which cause its insufferable sentences to drag along, and it has never contained, nor contains now, nor ever will contain, anything worth reading. No famous language, ancient or modern, owes its origin to it. The words that its impassioned supporters defend do not belong to it nor are similar to it in nature, composition, or sound. If they are to be considered Basque because they are included in catalogues or because they are now being used for communication with other peoples, then whenever any word from any language, no matter how isolated and distant from Basque, is pronounced in the language, it must have originated from this hodgepodge.[247]

As has already been indicated, the controversy surrounding Basque Iberianism and the Basque language in general transcended the interchange of books and essays and appeared for the first time in the press. In 1806, the Madrid newspapers dedicated space to an exchange of opinions that was a mediated extension of the arguments that had been previously presented and that were now being presented in the conventional publishing world. As was to be expected, their tone was even more heated than what had appeared in book form. The arguments being brandished were the usual ones about Basque being a barbaric, uncultivated, unintelligible cant, and to prove this, there was insistence on an argument that was not entirely new: that dialectal fragmentation had made it difficult for the Basques themselves to understand each other. For example, this was how it was explained by one of the most radical polemicists, writing under the initials D. A. C. B. in *El Memorial lite-*

rario: "Spend some time in Bizkaia, wander around the swamplands, then the valleys, and after that the fountains and hills without stopping at any of the larger towns, you will find that they not only have nine main dialects but that the inhabitants of the same place cannot understand each other, and that the Apologists themselves, although one should consider them to be educated men, do not understand each other either."[248] The debate, which was taken up by several Madrid newspapers (*El Mercurio de España*, *La Minerva*, *Diario de Madrid*), involved several authors, most of them protected by pseudonyms. Among those who favored the Basque theories (apart from Astarloa), it is possible to recognize the style of Zamácola and Erro. Indeed, the controversy was organized around the former when he published his *Apología* and diminished immediately after his death in 1806.[249]

After the first half of the nineteenth century, education was considered strategic to the eradication or preservation of Euskara. Of course, the state language policies of France and Spain emphasized the educational monopoly of their respective official languages, leaving a unique niche for the vernacular languages: the teaching of Christian doctrine. The extension of education to layers of society that had previously been totally excluded from it caused a complex set of problems. For some, the medium of primary education had to be exclusively Castilian or French, as a guarantee that all the citizens of every state would learn the language concerned, despite the fact that in Euskal Herria a large number of children were coming to school without a single word of the official languages. The well-known, infamous ring method then became commonplace in classrooms as the culmination of this repressive language policy. Reactions to this in the Basque Country were varied. Educational centers gave in and hired teachers who agreed to prohibit Basque in the classroom, and preference was even accorded to Castilian or French educators with no knowledge of the Basque language, to eliminate the slightest possibility that they might communicate with their pupils in the language. The late establishment of the *Escuelas Normales* (teaching-training schools) in the Basque Country (Gipuzkoa's was only founded in 1865) also explains why there were few educators among natives of the country. As to other matters, violent pedagogical methods were the norm at the time, so Basque students received a double dose of blows from the rod: the usual number for failing in mathematics or history plus an additional set for not expressing themselves correctly in the dominant language.

Despite this situation, there were attempts to guide education along other paths, and a timid pedagogical movement arose in favor of bilingual education; however, its proposals found scant, if any, echoes among the *foral* authorities. Indeed, only a few voices (such as those of Cardaberaz, Larramendi, and Moguel) were raised against the barbaric figure of the schoolteacher armed with his ring and rod. However, it wasn't until the 1820s when initiatives supporting the spread of education in Basque began to be known. Pablo de Ulibarri proposed this idea to the General Assemblies of Bizkaia in Gernika, but had no success. Iztueta was also in favor of Basque as the language of instruction, but it was a friend of both men, Agustín Pascual Iturriaga, who did the lion's share of the work in this field, publishing two manuals in 1841 on the teaching of Castilian to Gipuzkoan children, written at the behest of the liberal Diputación of 1821.[250] In 1830, Iturriaga sent an interesting memoir to the Assemblies of Arrasate-Mondragón, in the hope that the material would be used to increase bilingual education, which would guarantee that both Castilian and Basque would be learned correctly. In 1825, Luis de Astigarraga published a dictionary with the same goal in mind; his pro-bilingual stance was similar to that of Iturriaga.[251] Astigarraga was one of the promotors of mutual education, a method known in the Basque Country as *lancasteriano*. Joseph Lancaster had designed a massive plan to teach the poor children of the outskirts of London how to read and write. Its basis was an emphasis on self-teaching and on economy of effort on the part of teachers. In 1820, Astigarraga taught a course on the method in Bilbao, having failed in his request for support from the General Assemblies of Gipuzkoa to establish it in the province.[252] A different point of view was that of Primary Education Inspector Juan María Eguren, whose position on the language question coincided with that of officialdom: making certain that all Spanish citizens would have sufficient knowledge of Castilian through the school system. The possible fate of the Basque language was irrelevant. To pursue his goal he developed a method intended to teach Castilian to Basque children, which he published in 1867.[253] Practically the same ideas were held by Jean Baptiste Archu (1811–1881), a native of Altzürükü (Aussurucq), as regards the implantation of French in the northern Basque Country. Like Eguren, Archu was also a primary school inspector and his interest in Basque culture (he collaborated with Francisque-Michel and Prince Bonaparte) did not prevent him from directing his greatest efforts to the learning of French by Basque schoolchildren. In 1852, he published a work to that effect: *Uskara eta Franzes Gramatica, Uskalherrietaco haurrentzat eguina* (Basque and French Grammar, written for the Children of the Basque Country). His chief objective is clearly stated in his prologue: "*En composant cette Grammaire bilingue nous avons eu por bout de fournir aux instituteurs du Pays Basque un moyen d'initier leurs eleves à la connaisance de la langue française . . . Et de les familiariser avec le genie de la langue nationale.*" (In publishing this bilingual grammar, we intended to provide the teachers of the Basque Country a means by which to initiate among their pupils an understanding of the French language (...) and familiarize them with the nature of the national language.)[254] In any case, during this period of Basque history, the Basque language never progressed beyond its spoken form, but it was nurtured by practices that were cherished and carried out in isolation and that were limited to contexts that favored its use, such as sermons, poetry competitions, and *bertsolaris* (versifiers or popular improvisational poets). However, these practices were never limited to language instruction and official use in the schoolroom. On the contrary, the efforts undertaken were aimed at the teaching of Castilian to the monolingual Basque-speaking masses, in some cases (but not all) accompanied by the cultivation of Euskara. Symptomatically, this policy began to fall apart in the context of the second Carlist War (1873–76).

In 1875, when the war was about to end, the Carlist authorities were on the verge of proposing for the first time an education system that made a complete break from what had existed previously. Gipuzkoa passed a regulation for primary education in the province stating that learning to read and write had to take place first in Basque and then in Castilian, that is, starting with the mother tongue of the majority of the students. The Carlist *Diputación* (Government) also undertook to provide much-needed learning materials in the Basque language, but political circumstances related to the war did not permit it to carry out this line of action in any significant way. The only tangible result was the publication of a modest primer founded on the original concept, designed for learning to read directly from the Basque language and without the help of any other. Given the circumstances, it should not surprise us that its author, Gerónimo Zalacain, concealed his identity under the initials G. Z., and never made it public.[255] On the one hand, this educational and linguistic policy might be considered the swan song of the *foral* system, which, faced with the disappearance of both the *Fueros* and the language of the people, radically changed its traditional cultural strategies. But on the other hand, it marked the starting point of a new era in which, slowly and laboriously, the Basque language was to begin to enjoy a different status, both socially and institutionally.

In any case, between 1815 and 1876, after the urgency of international conflicts had subsided and internal problems of a social, political, and cultural nature were more pressing, it became clear that sensitivities regarding Euskara had changed. There was less interest in its origin, its antiquity, the perfection of the language, its supposed superiority over other tongues and emphasis was now placed at a much more pedestrian and anguishing level—the possible disappearance of the language itself, a battle that would now be extended to other fields, including teaching, methods of social transmission of the language, prestige, etc. From the most prescient warnings of Pascual Iturriaga to the poignant swan songs of José María Iparraguirre and Felipe Arrese Beitia, these years were fraught with constant concern, and indeed the linguistic collapse of Euskara during this period was too evident to leave any room for optimism.

The death throes of the *foral* system, which was to disintegrate under a series of martial, judicial, and political attacks throughout the nineteenth century, as was the case in 1812, 1820, 1839, 1841, and 1876, coincided with a campaign to tarnish the prestige of Basque institutions and culture, and once again the language was to find itself in the eye of the storm. As the new political and administrative space of the liberal regimes were configured and the capitalist economic and social model was developed, the survival of the Basque language began to be looked upon as an anomaly, endearing in some cases, nostalgic in others, barely tolerable in the majority. The opinions that emerged from diverse ideological positions agreed on one basic point: that the Basque language be denied the ability to serve as a means of communication in the modern industrialized society. We have already noted the revolutionary positions that stated that linguistic diversity clashed with the construction of a nation of citizens who were free and equal before the law. Also behind these positions were the Spanish political classes, fiercely hostile to any kind of cultural diversity that questioned the total and absolute unity of the state under construction.

In some cases, socio-anthropological analyses emerged that posited the total identification of the Basque language with agrarian society and which therefore refused to admit their capacity to adapt themselves to a new, modern status. An example of these studies was published by the anarchist geographer Elisée Reclus in a well-known article in *Revue de deux Mondes*, in which he literally banished not just the Basque language but the entire Basque culture from industrial society and refused it a place in future society as well. Also very interesting was the position of Antonio Cánovas del Castillo, who is well known as the architect of the political system of Restoration Spain after the First Spanish Republic (1873), and who as president of the government abolished the *Fueros* of the Basque provinces. In a work written in 1873, in the midst of the second Carlist War, Cánovas flatly rejected the possibility of doing away with the *Fueros* (an act that he would in fact implement three years later), but prepared political and public opinion to facilitate his doing so. He put together an ostensibly flattering and friendly image of the

Basques ("most noble provinces"), but underneath it was highly destabilizing, refuting Basque-Cantabrianism as well as any suggestion of original Basque independence, describing the Basques as "a people without history" and conservative ("locked in their solitary language, the Basques have so far defied the impetuous current of new ideas"), and bringing up their pro-French stance during the war of the Convention (on the basis of the correspondence between Manuel Godoy and Francisco Zamora).[256]

Even its defenders were convinced of the inability of the Basque language to adapt to modern society. As one of many possible examples, in 1879, the conversation at the Donostia-San Sebastián Ateneo (Cultural Association) turned to whether the disappearance of the Basque language was relevant. Some members believed that the language should be abandoned as soon as possible, whereas others were disgusted by the proposition. Nicolás de Soraluce, a well-known admirer of Euskara, offered to defend the latter position. But in his conclusions, he did not refuse to admit that the steamship, the telegraph, and education would end up causing the disappearance of the Basque language. He merely refused to accelerate the process. For his part, the Lapurdi-born geographer and military officer Victor-Bernard Derrecagaix, responding to some degree to what had been said by Reclus, sounded a discordant note in 1876 with regard to the majority of the analyses of the time, by disassociating the political fate of the Basque Country from that of its culture. He was convinced that political changes would bring about the imminent abolition of the *Fueros*, but, thanks to certain geographic circumstances, this did not necessarily imply the disappearance of the Basque people along with their linguistic characteristics. Inhabitants of mountain areas were, he believed, more apt to maintain their individual and collective signs of identity and personality.

Except for a few rare cases, the extremists among the defenders of the Basque language favored supporting the *Fueros* as well. Larramendi favored this approach during the period of attacks on the *Fueros* by the governments of the Enlightenment. Iztueta and Moguel were also of this persuasion during the fall of the *Fueros* in the northern Basque Country and Navarre, and Iparraguirre and Arrese Beitia, among others, would continue to support the *Fueros* when the threat of their total abolition became evident. Of all the early statements identifying the *Fueros* and the Basque language, Iztueta's was the most unambiguous. In his *Guipuzcoaco provinciaren condaira edo historia...* of 1847, he forcefully expresses the identification of the *Fueros* with the Basque language in the process of their destruction or survival:

> *"Guipuzcoaco biztanle prestu guztiac badaquite arguiroqui, beren zoriona datorquitela jatorriz dituzten Fuero onesquietatic; bañan oec oso ta garbi gordetceco gauzaric bearrena cer dan ezagutcen dutenac, guichi dira chit. Fueroac beren oñean irozoteco quirtenic irme-ena eta euscarriric seguruena da Euscarazco itzcuntzari ondo contu eguitea; cergatic alcarri laztanduric arras itsatsiac arquitcen diran . . . Euscara ill ezquero Fueroac ez dira bicico; bañan Euscara bici bada, Fueroac piztuco dira"* [Every honorable inhabitant of Gipuzkoa knows clearly that their happiness comes directly from benefits furnished by the *Fuero*; but there are few that completely understand the things that must be retained from it in its entirety. In order to maintain the fundamentals of the *Fuero* the firmest grasp and the strongest support is to carefully pay (affectionate) attention to the Basque language; because both embrace one another joining together completely (...) If Euskara dies the *Fuero* will not live, but if Euskara lives, the *Fuero* will be resurrected].[257]

When the *Fueros* were dissolved, the political system of the Basque territories and the survival of the language were therefore seen as linked by detractors of the language and apologists alike. Because of this, it should be no surprise that, coinciding with the suppression of the traditional institutions, there arose a movement devoted to the recuperation of political and (especially) cultural losses. It seemed that the very awareness of the loss of distinguishing institutions sharpened the perception of the corresponding process of linguistic homogeneity that was taking place. Thus, during the period between the wars, with the *Fueros* of Navarre abolished and those of the provinces threatened, a strong *foralist* movement that was institutional, political, and symbolic was formed; it was no accident that Iparraguirre's "Gernikako Arbola" (Tree of Gernika) was such a great success. But it would be between 1876 and 1918 when, in connection with the definitive loss of the *Fueros* and enveloped in a climate of late Romanticism, there emerged among the Basques an intensification of support for their unique culture and language that developed into a modest Renaissance (*Pizkundea*). Abbadie's Juegos Florales was now joined by the Sociedad Euskal-Herria (Euskal-Herria Society) in Bizkaia, founded by Fidel de Sagarmínaga; the Asociación Euskara de Navarra (Euskara Association of Navarre) (1877–1883), sponsored by Arturo Campión and Juan Iturralde y Suit; the Asociación de Artistas Vascos (Basque Artists' Association) (1911) of Bilbao, toghether with Eusko Ikaskuntza (Basque Studies Society) and Euskaltzaindia (Academy of the Basque Language), both appearing in 1918. Partly under the auspices of the above institutions, the Provincial Governments, political parties, and private enterprises, a number of publications emerged that were to some degree pro-Basque and enjoyed relatively long lives: in Vitoria-Gasteiz, Fermin Herran's *Revista de las Provincias Euskaras* (1878–81); *Revista Euskal-Erria*, edited by José Manterola in Donostia-San Sebastián (1880–1918); *Revista Euskara* of Pamplona-Iruña (1878–83); *Escualdun Gaceta* (1885) in Los Angeles, California; *Eskualduna* (1887) in Baiona; *Californiako Escual Herria* (1893), again in Los Angeles; *Euskalduna* (1896–1909) and Bizkaitarra (1893–95), both in Bilbao; *Euskal Esnalea* (1908) in Tolosa, Gipuzkoa; the *Revista Internacional de Estudios Vascos* (1907) and *Euskal Erriaren Alde* (1911), both in Donostia-San Sebastián and *Euskal–Erria* of Uruguay (1912). In 1896, Resurrección María de Azkue founded in Bilbao the first *ikastola* (Basque school) called the Colegio Ikastechea and in 1914, Miguel de Muñoa opened a similar school, Koru'ko Andre Maria'ren Ikastetxea, in Donostia-San Sebastián. These were the first steps toward the institutionalization of education in the Basque language.

Notes

1. *Liber Sancti Jacobi. Codex Calistinus* (c. 1143), ed. Walter Muir Whitehill (Santiago de Compostela, 1944); reprint, in José García Mercadal, *Viajes de extranjeros por España y Portugal*, vol. 1 (Salamanca: Junta de Castilla y León, 1999), 157–59.

2. The difficulties that the Spanish and French experienced with Basque toponymy and anthroponymy are classic. The deformations and distortions of the names of persons and places are continuous and extraordinary. Even Pomponius Mela (*Geography*, L. III) pointed out that "among the Cantabrians [Basques] there are rivers and towns whose strange and inconceivable names exceed the capacity of our ears." For his part, Cristóbal de Villalón, in his *Viaje de Turquía*, refers to Basque names in a most expressive manner: "Machín Artiaga de Mendarózqueta . . . Ochoa de Galarreta, and other names such as these that might well have come from the books of *Amadís*."

3. Norman Cohn, *The Pursuit of the Millennium: Revolutionary Millenarians and Mystical Anarchists of the Middle Ages*, rev. ed. (New York: Oxford University Press, 1970).

4. Mircea Eliade, *Le mythe de l'éternel retour: Archétypes et répétition* (Paris: Gallimard, 1949). Whether or not one is in agreement with Eliade's premise of a "cosmic religion" developed by prehistoric civilizations, connected to the Neolithic revolution based on a continuous and cyclical renovation, what is certain is that these beliefs, whether in a diffuse or organized form, are present in traditional agrarian cultures.

5. For an interesting reflection on the millennium in the Basque case, see Juan Aranzadi, *Milenarismo vasco: Edad de oro, etnia y nativismo* (Madrid: Taurus, 1982). On the historical phenomena of the millennium, see Eric J. Hobsbawm, *Primitive Rebels: Studies in Archaic Forms of Social Movement in the 19th and 20th Centuries* (Manchester: Manchester University Press, 1959) and María Isaura Pereira de Queiroz, *Historia y etnología de los movimientos mesiánicos* (Madrid: Siglo XXI, 1969).

6. Juan Martínez de Zaldibia, *Suma de las cosas cantábricas y guipuzcoanas*, ed. Fausto Arocena (San Sebastián: Oficina tipográfica de la Diputación de Guipúzcoa, 1945), chs. 3 and 10.

7. Alfonso Rodríguez de Guevara, *Fundación y antigüedad de España, y conservación de la nobleza de Cantabria* (Milan: Pablo Gottardo and Leonardo Poncios, 1586).

8. Ibid., ch. 2.

9. Ibid., a4.

10. Francisco de Mendieta y Retes, *Quarta parte de los Anales de Vizcaya que Francisco de Mendieta, vecino de Bilbao, recopiló por mandato del Señorío* (San Sebastián: Juan Carlos Guerra; Hijos de J. Baroja, 1915), 44.

11. Joseph Augustin Chaho, *Paroles d'un Voyant en réponse aux Paroles d'un Croyant* (Paris: Dondey-Dupré, 1834), 5.

12. Joseph Augustin Chaho, *La leyenda de Aitor y otros relatos* (San Sebastián: Orain, 1995), 13.

13. Pedro de Agramont, *Historia de Navarra 1632* (Pamplona: Mintzoa, 1996).

14. Manuel de Larramendi, *Corografía o descripción general de la M.N. y M.L. Provincia de Guipúzcoa* (San Sebastián: Sociedad Guipuzcoana de Ediciones, 1969), 144.

15. Juan Luzuriaga, *Paraninfo celeste. Historia de la mystica zarza, milagrosa imágen y Prodigioso Santuario de Aranzazu,...* (Mexico City: Viuda de Calderón, 1686; Madrid: Juan García Infanzon, 1690), 5.

16. Martínez de Zaldibia, *Suma,* ch. 9.

17. Juan Huarte de San Juan, *Examen de ingenios para las sciencias. Donde se muestra la differencia de habilidades que ay en los hombres, y el genero de letras que a cada uno responde en particular.* (Baeza: Juan Bautista de Montoya, 1575); reprint, ed. Esteban Torre (Barcelona: PPU, 1998), 277–78. In spite of the cleansing suffered by the less euphonic or "incorrect" surnames in the recent past, "Mandojana" and similar names are currently still in use.

18. Martínez de Zaldibia, *Suma*, 84.

19. It goes without saying that one need not look far to find holes in this assertion. To begin with, the theorists themselves (Garibay and Larramendi) changed their surnames, a frequent practice in the sixteenth century and occasionally even in the eighteenth century, leading to the rather frequent circumstance of brothers with different last names. Such was the case in a proceeding regarding the noble lineage of one who had changed his name from Imirizaldu to Fuentes. The deponent testified that "in this kingdom it is not unusual for brothers to take different last names although they have the same parents, as is the case in the town of Falces with three brothers who, despite being [of the same family], have three different surnames: one that of Irumberri, another (the Colonel in the Belgian Regiment), that of Balanza, and the other Monreal." Eufrasio de Munárriz Urtasun, "El cambio de apellidos en la vieja Navarra," *Revista Internacional de los Estudios Vascos* 14 (1923): 401–03.

Other surnames were translated (de Jauregi to Palacio). But most commonly, couples adopted the royal house or surname that would prove most advantageous from the marital union. For the most part, a simplification of the complete medieval forms of designation (First or Christian name; Patronymic—a surname formed from the father's name; Locative) appears in different forms according to the territory: in Bizkaia, Gipuzkoa, and most of Navarre, the patronymic is lost in the seventeenth century (for example Juan Pérez de Echevarria becomes Juan de Echevarria) whereas in Araba the original formulation is used, with cases in which the locative is lost and the patronymic is retained. The conversion of names into surnames should also be noted (as in García). Given the foregoing, the presumed continuity of surnames through time is indeed questionable.

20. Julio Caro Baroja, *Vasconiana* (San Sebastián: Txertoa, 1986), 26ff.; Aranzadi, *Milenarismo vasco*, 302–03.

21. Justo Zaragoza, *Castellanos y vascongados. Tratado breve de una disputa y diferencia entre dos amigos, el uno castellano, de Burgos, y el otro vascongado, en la villa de Potosí, reino del Perú, documento hasta ahora inédito publicado por Z* (Madrid: Víctor Sáinz, 1876), 32, 39–40.

22. *El Tordo vizcaíno* (N.p., [1638?]). The author of this work could have been Father Henao, according to Andrés Mañaricúa, *Polémica sobre Vizcaya en el siglo XVII: El Búho gallego y el Tordo vizcaíno* (Bilbao: La Gran Enciclopedia Vasca, 1976), 153–54

23. *Fueros, privilegios, franquezas y libertades del M. N. y M. L. Señorío de Vizcaya* (Bilbao: Biblioteca Bascongada de Fermín Herran, 1897), Ley 13, Título 1°.

24. Estanislao Jaime de Labayru, "Suma o recopiliación de todo el contenido de las Ordenanzas de Bilbao," in *Historia General del Señorío de Vizcaya*, vol. 4 (Bilbao: Andrés P. Cardenal; Madrid: Víctor Suarez, 1900), 467ff; reprint, in Ángel Rodríguez Herrero, *Ordenanzas de Bilbao. Siglos XV y XVI* (Bilbao: Ayuntamiento de Bilbao, 1948).

25. Martínez de Zaldibia, *Suma*, ch. 20, 78–79.

26. Juan Arce de Otalora, *Summa nobilitatis Hispaniae, ac immunitatis regiorum tributorum, causas, ius, ordinem, iudicium, et exusationem breuiter complectens: nunc postermo recognita, atque infinitis prope locis emendata, nouisque additionibus aucta* (Salamanca: Juan Bautista Terranova, 1570).

27. Francisco Elías de Tejada, *El Señorío de Vizcaya (hasta 1812)* (Madrid: Minotauro, 1963), 86–87.

28. Baltasar de Echave, *Discursos de la lengua Cántabra-Bascongada compuestos por...* (México City: Henrrico Martínez, 1607), ch. 17.

29. Lope Martínez de Isasti, *Compendio historial de la M. N. y M. L. Provincia de Guipúzcoa* (1625) (San Sebastián: Ramón Baroja, 1850); reprint (Bilbao: La Gran Enciclopedia Vasca, 1972), chs. 3 and 7.

30. Huarte de San Juan, *Examen*, 273–74, 278.

31. Martínez de Isasti, *Compendio*, 36–47.

32. *El Tordo vizcaíno*, 168–70.

33. *El Tordo vizcaíno*, 141–42.

34. Echave, *Discursos*, 66–67.

35. Manuel Llano Gorostiza, "Francisco de Mendieta y el cuadro sobre el besamanos de la Jura de Guernica," in Jacinto Gómez Tejedor, Francisco Sesmero Pérez, and Manuel Llano Gorostiza, *Tres estudios sobre Guernica y su comarca* (Bilbao: Diputación Provincial de Vizcaya, 1970).

36. The Tubalist and racial antiquity of the Basques was exemplified by Mendieta in the Leintz Valley shield: "'Armas del Valle de Leniz (Leintz).' The insignia and coat of arms of this Valley depict Noah's Ark on the waves of the sea and an angel with a sword in his hand on top. There is a glow in the sky with a ray of light that surrounds the Ark. This leads to the interpretation that those of this town and this land are the true descendants of the first inhabitants of Spain, who came with the

patriarch Tubal in the Ark, as they were the ones closest to the Flood, and once here, they did not mix with any foreigners; rather, they bore the nobility of the first sons of Noah, without interference from other nations. Thus, the angel that guided them with the furor of God, who is represented in the resplendent sky, and the sword, the wrath of God and the universal punishment of humankind they bore as well." Mendieta, *Quarta parte*, 26.

37. Mendieta, *Quarta parte,* 51, 56–57, 83.

38. Ibid., *Quarta parte,* 71–73.

39. Andrés de Poza, *De la antigua lengua, poblaciones y comarcas de las Españas en que de paso se tocan algunas cosas de la Cantabria* (Bilbao: Matías Mares, 1587), fol. 57v.; reprint, as *Antigua lengua de las Españas*, ed. Ángel Rodríguez Herrero (Madrid: Minotauro, 1959); Poza, *Ad pragmáticas,* fol. 597v.

40. Martínez de Zaldibia, *Suma*, ch. 9.

41. Martín de Aguirre, *Responsum de succesione Regni Portugaliae pro Philippo Hispaniarum Rege Principum omnium potentissimum* (Venice: Franciscum Zilettum, 1581).

42. Esteban de Garibay, *Los XL libros d'el compendio historial de las Chronicas y universal Historia de todos los reynos de España* (Antwerp: Christophoro Plantinro, 1571), vol. 1, 337 and vol. 2, 1179–80.

43. On the historiography relative to the incorporation of Gipuzkoa into Castile, see Xosé Estévez Rodríguez, *La historiografía guipuzcoana, desde Zaldivia a Gorosabel, sobre la adhesión de Gipuzkoa a Castilla,* Koldo Mitxelena Kulturunea; www.gipuzkoakultura.net; Lourdes Soria Sesé, *La historiografía castellana sobre la incorporación de Gipuzkoa a Castilla,* Koldo Mitxelena Kulturunea, http://www.gipuzkoakultura.net/euskera/index.htm (accessed February 8, 2006).

44. Garibay, *Los XL libros d'el compendio historial,* vol. 3, 200; vol. 2, 727–28.

45. *El Tordo vizcaíno,* 182–83.

46. Martínez de Zaldibia, *Suma,* ch. 25, 116.

47. The following citations are taken from Agramont, *Historia de Navarra*, bk. 1, ch. 18.

48. Ibid., bk. 1, ch. 21.

49. Sebastián de Covarrubias, "Cantabria," in *Tesoro de la Lengua Castellana o Española* (Madrid, 1611); reprint (Madrid: Turner, 1977), 228.

50. *El Tordo vizcaíno,* 92, 123.

51. Ibid., 129–30.

52. Silius Italicus, *De bello punico* (Geneva: Haeredes Iacobu Chouët, 1607), bk. 3, verse 320.

53. Martínez de Isasti, *Compendio*, 259–60.

54. Juan Sada y Amézqueta [pseud. García de Góngora y Torreblanca], *Historia apologética y descripción del Reyno de Navarra y de su mucha antigüedad, nobleza, calidades, y Reyes...* (Pamplona: Carlos de Labayen, 1628), bk. 2, fol. 15b.

55. Francisco de Mendoza y Bobadilla, *Tizón de la Nobleza Española, presentada al rey Felipe II el 20 de agosto de 1560* (Madrid: Antonio Luque y Vicens, 1849), 55.

56. Zaragoza, *Castellanos,* 41–42.

57. Ibid., 42–43.

58. Julio Caro Baroja, *La casa en Navarra* (Pamplona: Caja de Ahorros de Navarra, 1982).

59. Juan Madariaga Orbea, "Espacio doméstico y espacio sepultural en Euskal Herria, siglos XVI al XIX," in *Casa, familia y sociedad*, ed. José María Imízcoz (Bilbao: Universidad del País Vasco-Euskal Herriko Unibertsitatea, 2004), 429–87.

60. Martínez de Isasti, *Compendio*, 196–97.

61. Echave, *Discursos*, ch. 17.

62. Agramont, *Historia de Navarra*, fol. 553.

63. *El Tordo vizcaíno*, 183.

64. Luzuriaga, *Paraninfo*, 9–10.

65. Ibid., 14–15.

66. Ibid., 16.

67. Garibay, *Compendio*, vol. II, 1304–12.

68. Garibay, *Las Grandezas de España*, vol. I, fols. 32–33, transcribed by Julio Caro Baroja, *Los vascos y la historia a través de Garibay (Ensayo de biografía antropológica)* (San Sebastián: Txertoa, 1972), 316n53.

69. Echave, "Dedicatoria al Excelentísimo Conde de Lemos…" *Discursos*.

70. On the presumed collective characterization of the people of Spain, see Emilio Temprano, *La selva de los tópicos* (Madrid: Mondadori, 1988).

71. *Claros varones de Castilla* (Toledo, 1486); reprint, ed. J. Domínguez Bordona (Madrid: La Lectura, 1923), 8.

72. Temprano. *La selva*, 207.

73. Pedro Fernández de Castro (Count of Lemos), "Historia del Búho gallego con las demás aves de España" (early seventeenth century), in "Castellanos y Bascongados…", in Estanislao Labayru, *Historia General de Bizcaya*, ed. Andrés Mañaricúa, app. 3 (1895–1903; reprint, Bilbao: La Gran Enciclopedia Vasca, 1976), 233–62.

74. *Floreto de anécdotas y noticias diversas que recopiló un fraile dominico residente en Sevilla mediados del siglo XVI*, ed. Francisco Javier Sánchez Cantón, Memorial Histórico Español series 48 (Madrid: Real Academia de la Historia, 1948), 272–73. The etymology of Bizkaian to Vice-Cain is also a reference to Garibay and the *Crónica* of Ibargüen-Cachopín.

75. Paulus Orosius, a historian of the wars between the Basques and the Romans, wrote at the beginning of the fifth century (circa 417) *Historia adversum paganos libri VII, ex recognitione Caroli Zangemeiter* (Lipsiae [Leipzig]: B.G. Tevbeneri, 1889).

76. *El Tordo vizcaíno*, 170.

77. Miguel Abendaño Eztenaga, Prologue to *De divina scientia et predestinatione. In civitate lassionensi vulgo San Sebastián.* (San Sebastián: Martín de Huarte, 1674).

78. Manuscript dated 10 October 1670, ch. 7, Title 4, 205–06, 208, 210–11.

79. Collection Vargas Ponce, Real Academia de la Historia, Manuscript 41.

80. Miguel de Aramburu, *Nueva recopilación de los Fueros, privilegios, buenos usos y costumbres, leyes y ordenanzas de la Muy Noble y Muy Leal Provincia de Guipúzcoa* (Tolosa: Bernardo de Ugarte, 1696), 76. The manuscript of the new compilation was also found among the papers of Larramendi. See Francisco Elías de Tejada and Gabriella Percopo, *La Provincia de Guipúzcoa.* (Madrid: Minotauro, 1965), 117–18, 125–28.

81. *Población eclesiástica de España, y noticia de sus primeras honras, halladas en los escritos de S. Gregorio obispo de Granada, en el chronicon de Hauberto Monge de S. Benito, ilustradas por el maestro fray Gregorio de Argaiz, Chronista de la misma Religión. Dedicadas a la Majestad Suprema, y Soberana de Dios, Trino y Uno* vol. 1, pt. 1 (Madrid: Melchor Sanchez, 1667). Between the years 1668 and 1669, the Second Part of vol. 1 and Part One and Two of vol. 2 were published. *Corona real de España por España fundada en el crédito de los muertos y vida de San Hyeroteo, obispo de Atenas y Segovia, por el Maestro Fray Gregorio de Argaiz, monge y cronista del Orden de San Benito. Dedicada a la Reyna nuestra señora Doña Mariana de Austria, madre y tutora de Carlos el Deseado, Rey de España y Nuevo Mundo, y única Governadora destos reynos* (Madrid: Melchor Alegre, 1668).

82. See Julio Caro Baroja, *Las falsificaciones en la Historia (en relación con la de España)* (Barcelona: Seix Barral, 1992), 99–103.

83. Annio de Viterbo, *Comentaria super opera diversorum auctorium de antiquitatibus loquentium.* (Rome, 1498).

84. Lucio Marineo Sículo, *De rebus Hispaniae memoriabilibus* (Burgos, 1496). Spanish edition: *De las cosas memorables de España* (Alcalá de Henares, 1539).

85. Florián de Ocampo, *Las quatro partes enteras de la Corónica de España que mandó componer el Serenísimo Rey don Alonso llamado el Sabio* (Zamora, 1541).

86. Pero Antón Beuter, *Primera parte de la Crónica general de toda España y especialmente del Reyno de Valencia* (Valencia, 1548) (1st edition in Catalan, 1538).

87. A critique of Annio's false Hispanic kings is to be found in Juan de Mariana, "Obras," *Historia General de España* (Madrid: Biblioteca de Autores Españoles, XXX, 1854), bk. 1, 7:7–8.

88. Juan Francisco de Masdeu, *Historia crítica de España y de la cultura española*, 20 vols. (Madrid: Sancha, 1783–1805).

89. Other Tubalist writers included Juan de Pineda, *La Monarquía Eclesiástica o Historia Universal del Mundo* (Salamanca, 1588) and Alonso de Maldonado, *Chronica universal de todas las Naciones y Tiempos* (Madrid, 1624).

90. On the false narratives of Berosio, Annio, Ocampo, Lupián, and other Tubalist fabrications, see Julio Caro Baroja, *Las falsificaciones de la Historia,* 45–111, in particular. This subject is also discussed in Jon Juaristi, *El bosque originario. Genealogías míticas de los pueblos de Europa* (Madrid: Santillana, 2000).

91. On the different accounts that various cultures have developed on the regenerative nature of the Flood as well as the confusion of tongues in Babel, see James George Frazer, *Folk-Lore in the Old Testament: Studies in Comparative Religion, Government, and Law,* 3 vols. (London: Macmillan and Co., 1918).

92. *Historia General de España*, bk. I, ch. I, Biblioteca de Autores Españoles, vol. I, 1–2 (Madrid, 1854). See also Pedro de Mantuano, *Advertencias a la Historia del Padre Juan de Mariana* (Madrid, 1613).

93. Garibay, *Los XL libros d'el compendio historial*, bk. IV, chs. 1–5 (fols. 81–93).

94. Florián de Ocampo, *Los cinco libros primeros de la Crónica general de España, que recopila el maestro...* (Medina del Campo: Guillermo de Millis, 1553).

95. María Rosa Lida de Malkiel, "Túbal primer poblador de España," *Ábaco* 3 (1970), 12–13.

96. For example, Barthelemy Jean-Baptiste Sanadon, *Ensayo sobre la nobleza de los bascongados, para que sirve de introducción á la Historia general de aquellos Pueblos, traducido por D. Diego de Lazcano Presbytero* (Tolosa: Francisco de Lama, 1786). Well into the twentieth century, Basque-Iberianism continued to be a literary resource, as for Gabriel Celaya in his *Iberia sumergida* (Madrid: Peralta, 1978), where he exclaims: "We, from Euskera, are the last Iberians." Likewise, Pío Baroja and other twentieth-century literati include Iberianist elements in their works.

97. Marineo Sículo, *De las cosas memorables.*

98. Garibay, *Compendio*, bk. 4, ch. 4.1, 89–93.

99. On Basque-Iberianism, see: Julio Caro Baroja, "Observaciones sobre la hipótesis del vascoiberismo considerada desde el punto de vista histórico," *Boletín Emerita* 10, no. 2 (1942), 236–86 and 11, no. 1 (1943), 1–59, 2nd ed. in *Sobre la lengua vasca* (San Sebastián: Txertoa, 1979), 11–120. See also Antonio Tovar, *La lengua vasca*, 2nd ed. (San Sebastián: Biblioteca Vascongada de los Amigos del País, 1954).

100. Carlota Del Amo, "El debate sobre la lengua vasca en los periódicos madrileños a comienzos del siglo XIX," *Actas del Congreso La Lengua y los Medios de Comunicación*, ed. J. Garrido Medina, vol. 2 (Madrid: Universidad Complutense, 1999), 602–11.

101. Karmele Etxenike, "Apuntes sobre el vascoiberismo actual," *Euskonews & Media* 54 (November 12–19, 1999), http://www.euskonews.com/0054zbk.frgaia.htm (accessed February 8, 2006). The writers behind this new Basque-Iberian offensive are Edelmio Zamanillo, *Lectura y traducción de la lengua de los iberos* (Zaragoza: Ibercaja, 1988); Juan Luis Román del Cerro, *El desciframiento de la lengua ibérica "en ofrenda de los pueblos"* (Alicante: Aguaclara, 1990) and *El origen ibérico de la lengua vasca* (Alicante: Aguaclara, 1993); and Jorge Alonso and Antonio Arnaiz Villena, *El origen de los vascos y otros pueblos mediterráneos* (Madrid: Complutense, 1998).

102. Echave, *Discursos*, ch. 17.

103. Larramendi disagreed with the Peruvian author in this sense. See *Discurso histórico sobre la antigua famosa Cantabria. Questión decidida. Si las provincias de Bizcaya, Guipuzcoa y Alaba, estuvieron comprendidas en la Antigua Cantabria* (Madrid: J. de Zuñiga, 1736).

104. Enrique Flórez, *La Cantabria. Disertación sobre el sitio, y extensión que tuvo en el tiempo de los romanos la región de los cántabros, con noticia de las regiones confinantes, y de varias poblaciones antiguas. Discurso preliminar a la España Sagrada...* (Madrid: Antonio Marín, 1768; San Martín, 1786; J. Rodríguez, 1877).

105. Manuel Risco, *El R. P. M. Fr. Enrique Flórez, vindicado del Vindicador de la Cantabria, don Hipólito de Ozaeta y Gallaiztegui. Por el P. M. Fr. Manuel Risco, del Orden de S. Agustín.* (Madrid: Pedro Marín, 1799). After Flórez other authors, such as Fernández, Guerra, Sánchez Albornoz and Schulten, also began to ignore the delimitation between the ancient Cantabrian and Basque peoples.

106. Martínez de Zaldibia, *Suma,* ch. 3, 9.

107. Juan Iñiguez de Ibargüen and García Fernández de Cachopín, *Crónica General Española y Sumaria de la Casa de Vizcaya y su antigua fundación, y Nobleza* (1588?), ms. in the Biblioteca de la Diputación de Vizcaya, notebook 48, fols. 11–12.

108. Ibid., notebook 64. See Julio de Urquijo, "La Crónica Ibargüen-Cachopín y el Canto de Lelo," *Revista Internacional de los Estudios Vascos* 13 (1992), 97.

109. Ibid., notebook 65, pt. 2, fol. 1.

110. Pierre d'Iharce de Bidassouet, *Histoires des cantabres, ou des premiers colons de tout l'Europe avec celle des basques, leurs descendants direct, qui existent encore, et leur langue asiatique-basque, traduite, et réduite aux principes de la langue française* (Paris: Julie Didot Ainé, 1825), 12.

111. Martínez de Isasti, *Compendio,* 23.

112. Larramendi, *Corografía,* 3.

113. Martínez de Zaldibia, *Suma,* Prologue.

114. *El Tordo vizcaíno,* 177–78.

115. Luzuriaga, *Paraninfo,* 2–3.

116. Martínez de Zaldibia, *Suma,* ch. 13.

117. Ibid., 130.

118. Gabriel de Henao, *Averiguaciones de las antigüedades de Cantabria enderezadas principalmente a descubrir las de Guipúzcoa, Vizcaya y Álava, provincias contenidas en ella, y a honor y gloria de San Ignacio de Loyola…,* 2 vols. (Salamanca: Eugenio Antonio García, 1689–91), bk. 3, chs. 45 and 46, 394–404.

119. Sada, *Historia apologética,* bk. 3, chs. 19–23, fols. 75–82.

120. Ibid., bk. 1, ch. 3, fol. 7.

121. Ibid., bk. 3, chs. 25–26, fols. 84–86.

122. Ibid., bk. 3, ch. 27, fols. 86–87.

123. Agramont, *Historia de Navarra,* ch. 3.

124. Ibid., fol. 555.

125. Ibid., ch. 24, fol. 620.

126. Ibid., bk. 6, ch. 2, 1291.

127. Sanadon, *Ensayo sobre la nobleza,* 5–6.

128. Hiribarren posits an interesting periodization of Basque history, which in part grows out of traditional and mythical historiography and in part assumes a global Basque identity. These phases would be: 1) "Iberia" (protohistory), 2) "Cantabria" (Roman antiquity), 3) "Escal-Herria" (from the High Middle Ages to the conquest of Navarre in 1512), 4) "Escal-Herri bakhotca" (each Basque territory individually), from 1512 on.

129. Other legend writers, like Araquistáin in 1866, also cite in passing "Aitor, the patron spirit of the Euskaro people," in Juan Venancio Araquistáin, *Tradiciones vasco-cántabras* (Tolosa: Imprenta de la Provincia, 1866), 139. Others who appropriated the figure of Aitor included José María de Goizueta and Vicente de Arana. But the dazzling popularity of Aitor reached its zenith when Juan Mañé y Flaquer introduced him in his *El Oasis: Viaje al País de los Fueros* (Barcelona: Jaime Jesús Rovíralta, 1879).

130. See Joseph Zabalo, *Xaho, el genio de Zuberoa* (Tafalla: Txalaparta, 2004).

131. Agustín [Joseph Augustin] Chaho, *Viaje a Navarra durante la insurrección de los vascos* (San Sebastián: Txertoa, 1976), 76–77.

132. Ibid., 221–22.

133. Ibid., 135–36.

134. Agustín Chaho, *Bizkaiko baten eleak. Palabras de un bizkaino a la reina Cristina* (Bilbao: Likiniano elkartea, 1999), 34.

135. Agosti [Joseph Augustin] Chaho, "Azti begia eta beste izkribu zenbait," *Ariel*, July 25, 1848. Reprint, in *Azti begia eta beste izkribu zenbait* (Donostia: Euskal Editoreen Elkartea, 1992), 37.

136. Agustín [Joseph Augustin] Chaho, *Histoire primitive des Euskariens-Basques* (Bayonne: Jaymebon, 1847), 170–71.

137. See an anthology of writers of Basque legends in Jon Juaristi, *La tradición romántica. Leyendas vascas del siglo XIX* (Pamplona: Pamiela, 1986).

138. Araquistáin, *Tradiciones*, 4–16.

139. Araquistáin, for example, counts among his legends many that are related to the theme or to characters of the imaginary construct of the *Fuero*: "Los Cántabros," "Beotibar-co-celaya" or "La Dama de Morumendi."

140. On the ideologies and myths related to these languages, see León Poliakov, *Le mythe aryen. Essai sur les sources du racisme et des nationaismes* (Brussels: Complex, 1987); Arno Borst, *Der Turmbau von Babel. Geschichte der Meinungen über Ursprung und Vielfalt der Sprachen und Völker* (Munich: Deutschen Taschenbuch Verlag, 1995); and Juaristi, *El bosque originario*.

141. Among the authors who attempted to prove the Hebrew derivation of languages through etymologies based on the likeness of words were Etienne Guichard, *L'harmonie étymologique des langues* (Paris, 1606) and Athanasius Kircher, *Turris Babel* (Amsterdam: Janssonio-Waesbergiana, 1679). This method of analysis was used even much later by Antoine Fabre D'Olivet, *La langue hébraïque resituée* (Paris, 1815). See also Humberto [Umberto] Eco, *La búsqueda de la lengua perfecta en la cultura europea* (Barcelona: Crítica, 1994), 76–80 and Maurice Olender, *Las lenguas del Paraíso. Arios y semitas una pareja providencial* (Barcelona: Seix Barral, 2001).

142. Platón [Plato], "Cratilo o el lenguaje," *Diálogos* (Mexico City: Porrua, 1981), 249–94.

143. Rule 5 of the *Index* of Antonio Sotomayor, 1640, cited in Dominique Julia, "Lecturas y Contrarreforma," *Historia de la lectura en el mundo occidental*, 2nd

ed., eds. Guglielmo Caballo and Roger Chartier (Madrid: Taurus, 2001), 426 [First edition, Paris: Latertza y Seuil, 1997].

144. The text titled *Ordonnance genérale sur le fait de la justice, police, et finances*, consists of 192 articles; number 111 states that: "*Nous voulons donc que drénavant tous arrêts, et ensamble toutes autres procédures de nos cours souveraines ou autres subalternes et infériures, soient des registres, enquêtes, contrats, testaments et autres quelconques actes et exploits de justice ou qui en dépendent, soient prononcés, enregistrés et délivrés aus parties en langage maternel françois et non autrement*" (Therefore we wish that henceforth all decrees and, as a whole, all the proceedings of our sovereign courts, as well as secondary and minor ones, whether they be legal records, formalities, contracts, wills or any other act and execution of justice, or anything dependant on this, be delivered, registered and sent to the [relevant] parties in the French mother-tongue and no other).

145. Ceiwen H. Thomas, "The Welsh Language," *Journal of the Faculty of Arts* (Malta University Press) vol 3.2 (1966), 73–101, quoted in Oscar Uribe Villegas, *Situaciones de multilingüismo en el mundo* (Mexico City: Universidad Autónoma de México, 1972), 169.

146. The notion of a link between language and empire (or to put it another way, the political nature of language) was widespread among humanists at the end of the fifteenh century. Lorenzo Valla's position, in *Elegantiae Linguae Latinae* (Venice, 1444), is paradigmatic in this regard: "We lost the empire, we lost dominance . . . nonetheless, with this empire [of language] we are even more magnificent than kings in numerous parts of the world . . . Given that, where the Italian language reigns, the Roman Empire also reigns."

147. Cristóbal de Villalón, *Gramática Castellana. Arte breve y compendiosa para saber hablar y escribir en la lengua Castellana congrua y deçentemente* (Antwerp, Guillermo Simon, 1558).

148. Fernão de Oliveira, *Grammatica da Lingoagem Portuguesa* (Lisbon: Germão Galharde, 1536).

149. Etienne Pasquier, *Recherches de la France* (Paris: Sonnies, 1560), bk. 8, ch. 3.

150. Ibid., vol. 2, letter 1, 213–14.

151. Juan Pérez de Lazárraga, *Dianea & Koplak*, ed. Patri Urkizu (Donostia: Erein, 2004); transcript of an unpublished manuscript, Señor de la Torre de Larrea (1564–67), at http://lazarraga.gipuzkoakultura.net/ (accessed February 8, 2006).

152. Joannes Leiçarraga, *Iesus Christ gure Iaunaren Testamentu Berria. Othoitza ecclesiasticoen forma Catechismea. Kalendera. ABC edo Christinoen instructionea* (La Rochelle: Pierre Hautin, 1571; reprint, Bilbao: Euskaltzaindia, 1990), 250–53.

153. Even well into the eighteenth century, the poet Friedrich Gotthiebb Klopstock (1724–1803) felt pressured to defend the cultural possibilities of German against Latin and French, the dominant languages of the culture at the time.

154. On editions of the Bible in relation to the spread of literacy, see Jean-François Gilmont, "Reformas protestantes y lectura," and Dominique Julia, "Lecturas y Contrarreforma," in *Historia de la lectura*, ed. Caballo and Chartier, 373–414 and 415–68.

155. Adrian Hastings, *The Construction of Nationhood: Ethnicity, Religion and Nationalism* (Cambridge: Cambridge University Press, 1997). Hastings maintains that the language spoken by a community is not the primary factor in nationality; rather it is the written language, and he underscores the importance of the text in processes of establishing identity.

156. Julio de Urquijo, "Cosas de antaño. Las Sinodales de Calahorra (1602 y 1700)," *Revista Internacional de los Estudios Vascos* 14 (1923): 335–52.

157. Juan Pérez de Montalbán, *La toquera vizcaína*, Biblioteca Autores Españoles 45 (Madrid, n.d.), 522, quoted in Anselmo de Legarda, *Lo "vizcaíno" en la literatura castellana* (San Sebastián: Biblioteca Vascongada de los Amigos del País, 1953), 140.

158. *Codex Barberini*, fol. 108 v., a. 11 lat. 5250 (Vatican Library), quoted in *Historia de una ciudad, Vitoria* (Vitoria: Bankoa, 1977), 164.

159. Pablo Gorosabel, *Noticia de las cosas memorables de Guipúzcoa* (Tolosa: E. López, 1899–1901); 2nd ed. (Bilbao: La Gran Enciclopedia Vasca, 1972), vol. 1, 515–18.

160. José María Jimeno Jurío, *Navarra, historia del euskera* (Tafalla: Txalaparta, 1997) and *Navarra, Gipuzkoa y el euskera* (Pamplona: Pamiela, 1999).

161. Larramendi, *Corografía*, 286.

162. "Peregrinación de Anastasio,"dialogue 13, in *Obras*, vol. 3 (Burgos: Ed. Silverio, 1933), 204, quoted in Legarda, *Lo "vizcaíno" en la literatura castellana*, 134–35.

163. Larramendi, *Corografía*, 283–88. Larramendi notes a single exception to this bleak view: the Franciscan preachers of the Zarautz school, who had specialized in preaching in the Basque language.

164. Ibid., 289.

165. José Goñi Gaztambide, *Historia de los Obispos de Pamplona. IX. Siglo XIX* (Pamplona: Universidad de Navarra; Gobierno de Navarra, 1991), 673–77.

166. Darío de Areitio, *El gobierno universal del Señorío de Vizcaya* (Bibao: Junta de Cultura Vizcaína, 1943).

167. Juan Madariaga Orbea, *Historia social de Bergara en su época preindustrial* (Bergara: Ayuntamiento de Bergara, 1991), 71–72.

168. The ring method is not exclusive to the Basque Country, but it was widespread there. It consisted in the teacher giving a ring to a student that he had caught talking in Basque; the student then had to give the ring to a classmate who had committed the same transgression, so that the infamous piece of jewelry was passed around thanks to betrayal and a lack of solidarity. Whoever had the ring at the end of the day was severely punished. There is a wealth of testimony as to the use of this system until recent times in Basque schools.

169. José Miguel de Barandiarán, "El euskera en Álava a fines del siglo XVIII," *Revista Internacional de los Estudios Vascos* 17 (1926), 464–67.

170. Moguel y Urquiza, Juan Antonio, letter to José Vargas Ponce, May 24, 1802, in Esteban de Garibay, *Memorial histórico español: colección de documentos, opúsculos y antigüedades que publica la Real Academia de la Historia*, vol. 7, *Memorias* (Madrid: José Rodríguez, 1854), 703–04, 743–44.

171. For apologists of the Basque Language, see *El libro blanco del Euskara* (Bilbao: Euskaltzaindia, 1977); Joseba Intxausti, "El Euskara: de su mito a la conciencia nacional. Hizkuntzaren kontzienzia eta eskea, historian," *Euskal Herria. Errealitate eta egitasmo. Realidad y proyecto*, vol. I, ed. Joseba Intxausti (San Sebastián: Caja Laboral Popular, 1985), 361–68; Antonio Tovar, *Mitología e ideología sobre la lengua vasca* (Madrid: Alianza, 1980); José Ramón Zubiaur Bilbao, *Las ideas lingüísticas vascas en el siglo XVI (Zaldibia, Garibay, Poza)* (San Sebastián: Universidad de Deusto, 1990); Julio Caro Baroja, *Los vascos y la historia a través de Garibay (Ensayo de biografía antropológica)* (San Sebastián: Txertoa, 1972).

172. Joannes Etcheberry, *Manual Devotionezcoa* (Bordele [Bordeaux]: Guillen Millanges, Erregueren Imprimatçalleareanean, 1627).

173. Joannes Etcheberry, *Eliçara erabiltceco liburua* (Bordele [Bordeaux]: Guillen Millanges, 1636).

174. Axular, Introduction, *Gero. Bi partetan eta berezia...* (Bordele [Bordeaux]: Guillen Millanges, 1643).

175. Juan de Beriayn, Prologue, *Doctrina Christina en Romance y Bascuence, lenguajes de este Obispado de Pamplona* (Pamplona: Carlos de Labayen, 1626).

176. Jean-François Gilmont, *Reformas protestantes y lectura*, 386ff.

177. Luis Desgraves, *Le livre en Aquitanie XV–XVIII siècles* (Biarritz: Atlantica, 1998).

178. *Extractos de las Juntas Generales celebradas por la Real Sociedad Bascongada de los Amigos del País, en la Villa de Bilbao por Septiembre de 1772* (Vitoria: Tomás de Robles 1772), 94–96.

179. Anselmo de Legarda, "Primera frase vasca impresa reconocida, en Torres Naharro, 1513," *Boletín de la Real Sociedad Bascongada de los Amigos del País* 7, (1951), 41–48.

180. Anselmo de Legarda, *Lo "vizcaíno" en la literatura castellana*, 155.

181. Juan de Valdés, *Diálogo de la lengua, (1535–36)*, Clásicos castellanos series 86 (Madrid: "La Lectura", 1928), 19–20, 24–25.

182. Pedro de Madariaga, *Honra de escribanos* (Valencia: Mey, 1565); *Gramática de la lengua vulgar de España* (Louvain-Leuven: B. Gavio, 1559).

183. Tovar, *Mitología e ideología*, 22.

184. Gregorio López Madera, *Historia y discursos* (Granada, 1602). See also Emilio Alarcos Llorach, "Una teoría acerca del castellano," *Boletín de la Real Academia Española* 21 (1934): 202–28.

185. Mariana, *Historia General*, vol. 1, ch. 5.

186. Manuel Larramendi, *De la antigüedad y universalidad del Bascuence en España* (Salamanca: A. J. Villagordo, 1728?), 106–08.

187. Miguel de Cervantes, "La gran sultana," *Obras* (Madrid: Aguilar, n.d) 331 (quoted in Legarda, *Lo vizcaíno*: 131–32).

188. Valdés, *Diálogo de la lengua*, Colección Clásicos Latinos 86, 31.

189. Garibay, *Los XL Libros d'el compendio historial*, vol. 14, ch. 4, 91.

190. Ibid., vol. 4, ch. 4, 92.

191. Ibid., vol. 4, ch. 4, 92.

192. Thus, for example, when Echave refutes those who declare: "My language can be neither written nor explained," he gives the Basque version of the Hail Mary to prove the capabilities of the language. Echave, *Antigüedad,* 58. Later on, to show the versatility of the language, Moguel translated several classical Latin texts (Sallust, Titus, Tacitus, and Cicero) and included them in his *Peru Abarca.*

193. *Plauto Bascongado o el Bascuence de Plauto . . . por D. Juan José Moguel,* (Santander, 1828). In fact Moguel was the editor and Bartolomé de Santa Teresa the author. The translation begins on pages 8ff.

194. Manuel de Larramendi, *Diccionario trilingüe del castellano, bascuence y latín* (San Sebastián: Bartolomé Riesgo, 1745), ch. 21, 38.

195. Mariana, *Historia General,* vol. 1, ch. 5 (30), 6.

196. José Yanguas y Miranda, *Adiciones al Diccionario de Antigüedades de Navarra* (Pamplona: Javier Goyeneche, 1843), 271–72. See under "Vascuence."

197. Francisco de Quevedo, *Premáticas y aranceles,* Clásicos Castellanos series 56 (Madrid: Espasa-Calpe?, n.d.), 59.

198. ". . . and unravel the opinion of Ambrosio de Morales and his followers by saying that many of the [words] that I have explained above are not to be found in my speech." Echave, *Antigüedad,* 59–61.

199. Mateo Alemán, *Ortografía castellana* (Mexico City: Academia Mexicana, 1609), 12–13.

200. Manuel Larramendi, *Diccionario trilingüe,* vol. 1, 14–24.

201. Beuter, *Primera parte de la Crónica,* 174, quoted in Tovar, *Mitología,* 23.

202. Garibay, *Compendio IV,* bk. 36, ch. 15, 960.

203. These texts have been collected and commented upon by Juan Carlos Guerra, *Viejos textos del idioma. Los cantares antiguos del euskera* (San Sebastián: Martín y Mena, 1924); Caro Baroja, *Los vascos y la historia*; Juan Gorostiaga Bilbao, *Épica y lírica vizcaína antigua* (Bilbao: Centro Estudios Vascos de Falange Española, 1952); Luis Michelena, *Textos arcaicos vascos* (Madrid: Minotauro, 1955); and Antonio Zabala, *Euskal erromantzeak* (Oiartzun: Auspoa-Sendoa, 1998).

204. Garibay, *Memorias,* 251, 459.

205. For Garibay's views on language, see Caro Baroja, *Los vascos,* 344ff.

206. For example, in *Grandezas,* III, fol. 277, bk. 36, title 10, he practically includes a dissertation on alternance in toponyms of *r* and *l.* Ayara / Ayala, Gebara / Gabala; *uli / ulli / uri,* etc. Complete text in Caro Baroja, *Los vascos,* 348.

207. Garibay, *Los XL libros d'el compendio historial,* vol. 1, 84.

208. Opinions on this matter were still being included in the Navarrese press at the beginning of the twentieth century, such as the pseudonymous letter in defense of the idea that names like Barrabas, Iscariot, or Pilate are Basque. "Pedro Abuelo" in *El Eco de Navarra* (April 20, 1903).

209. Garibay, *Grandezas,* 1, fol. 50, bk. 2, title 6; *Memorias,* 632, quoted in Caro Baroja, *Los vascos,* 345–46, 350.

210. Garibay, *Memorias,* 631–32.

211. Martínez de Zaldibia, *Suma*, 1–13.

212. Ibid., *Suma*, 130–31.

213. Poza, *Antigua lengua*, fols. 4, 6; chs. 12, 13, and 15.

214. Echave, *Discursos,* fols., 5, 7, 31, 47, and 58.

215. Poza, *Antigua lengua,* fols. 3v, 4r.

216. Echave, *Discursos,* 22.

217. Luzuriaga, *Paraninfo*, 2.

218. D'Iharce de Bidassouet, *Histoire des cantabres.*

219. Moguel, letter to Vargas Ponce in Garibay, *Memorial histórico español,* 746.

220. The following citations are taken from Oihenart, *Notitia Utriusque,* 35–37.

221. José Moret and Franciso de Alesón, *Annales del Reyno de Navarra*, vol. 1, *De la población y lengua primitiva en España* (Pamplona: Pascual Ibáñez, 1766), 1–30.

222. José Conchillos reacted against Moret's opinion on the etymology of Tudela in his *Investigaciones históricas* and published the *Propugnáculo histórico y jurídico, Muro literario, y Tutelar. Tudela ilustrada y defendida . . . Dedicado a la misma Ciudad de Tudela, primera población de España, por el patriarca Tubal* (Zaragoza, 1666). Under the pseudonym "Flavio Silvio y Marcelo," Moret published *El Bodoque contra el propugnáculo histórico y jurídico del licenciado Conchillos* (Cologne [a false place of publication; it was actually Pamplona], 1667). Conchillos countered this by immediately publishing *Desagravios del Propugnáculo de Tudela contra el Trifauce Cervero, Autor del Bodoque* (Antwerp [also false: the piece was published in Zaragoza]: Sebastián Sterlin, 1667).

223. José Moret, *Investigaciones históricas de las Antigüedades del Reyno de Navarra* (Pamplona: Pascual Ibáñez, 1766), bk. 1, ch. 5, 99.

224. Manex Goyhenetche, *Les basques et leur histoire: mythes et réalités* (Baiona: Elkar, 1993), 44–46.

225. Juan Madariaga Orbea, "Predicación y cambios culturales en la Euskal Herria de los siglos XVIII–XIX," in *Euskal Herriko Erlijiosoen Historia. Familia eta Instituzio Erlijiosoen Euskal Herriko Historiaren I. Kongresuko Aktak*, ed. Joseba Intxausti, vol. 1 (Oñati: Arantzazu E.F., 2004), 498–525.

226. Larramendi did not completely start from scratch, but many had been lost and most of those that had been conserved were very incomplete and unpublished works. Without attempting to provide an exhaustive list, one might mention the *Dictionarium Liguae Cantabricae* (1562) by Nicolás Landuchio; the *Modo breve para aprender la lengua vizcaína* (1653) by Rafael de Micoleta; the basic grammar and dictionary by Silvain Pouvreau; the *Dictionarium latino-cantabricum* (1715) by Pierre D'Urte; the *Gramatica escuaraz eta francesez, composatua francez hitzcunça ikhasi dutenen faboretan* (1741) by Martin Harriet, and a few more.

227. Larramendi, *Diccionario trilingüe*, 4.

228. Larramendi, *De la antigüedad*, 128–37.

229. "Conferencia 4ª Junta General de Guipúzcoa, segregada de Castilla, Raros dictámenes de los Caballeros junteros," in Manuel de Larramendi, *Conferencias*

curiosas, políticas, legales y morales sobre los Fueros de la M. N. y M. L. Provincia de Guipúzcoa (San Sebastián: Caja de Ahorros Municipal, 1983), 57–58.

230. Larramendi, *Conferencias curiosas*, 70.

231. Luís Villasante, "El colegio de Misioneros franciscanos de Zarauz (1746–1849)," *Scriptorium Victoriense* 21 (1974), 281–330. See also Madariaga, *Predicación*, 514–17.

232. Lizarraga was able to publish a book of sermons, a slim volume of religious poetry, a translation of the Gospel according to John, and a short work on the life of St. Francis Xavier. See also Luis Vilasante, *Historia de la literatura vasca* (Bilbao: Sendo, 1961), 233–35, and Juan Apesteguía, "Juan de Lizarraga," *Gran Enciclopedia de Navarra*, vol. 7 (1990), 89–90.

233. *Extractos de las Juntas*, 100–01.

234. Antoine Court de Gébelin, *Monde Primitif analysé et comparé avec le monde moderne, consi-dérédans son génie allégorique et dans les allégories auxquelles conduisit ce génie; precedé du plan général des diverses parties qui composeront ce Monde primitif: avec des figures en taille-douce*, 9 vols. (Paris, 1773–1782). Court de Gébelin also had an interesting response in the Slavic world. Catherine II, who knew of his work, conceived the idea of a great comparative vocabulary that would comprise all the languages spoken in the Russian Empire and beyond. The work, undertaken by a group, was led by the German naturalist Peter Simon Pallas (1741–1811), who included the comparison of 285 terms in more than 200 languages. The first edition was entitled *Linguarum totius vocabularia Augustissimae cura collecta* (1787–1789) and the second, revised and expanded, *A Comparative Dictionary of All Languages and All Dialects* (1790–1791).

235. Juaristi, *El bosque originario*, 336–95.

236. Juan Bautista Erro, *El mundo primitivo, ó Exámen filosófico de la antiguedad y cultura de la nación vascongada* (Madrid: Fuentenebro, 1815).

237. Jon Juaristi, *El linaje de Aitor. La invención de la tradición vasca* (Madrid: Taurus, 1998), 56–57, 99. See also Patri Urquizu, ed., *Historia de la literatura vasca* (Madrid: UNED, 2000), 27, 49.

238. The situation of the French language on the eve of the Revolution was paradoxical: although the majority of the King of France's subjects did not speak French, it had become the international language of culture and diplomacy. Several theories have been put forward for this. In 1784, the counterrevolutionary Count Antoine de Rivarol published his theories in his speech *De l'universalité de la langue française* [On the Universality of the French Language], whose title is sufficiently explicative. Thus both revolutionaries and legitimists were persuaded of the superiority of the French language and its capacity to become a national and universal medium.

239. Michel de Certeau, Dominique Julia, and Jacques Revel, eds. *Une politique de la langue. La Révolution française et les patois: l'enquête de Grégoire* (1975; Paris: Gallimard, 2002). See also Brigitte Schlieben-Lange, *Idéologie, révolution et uniformité de la langue* (Liege: Pierre Mardaga, 1996).

240. Pierre Hourmat, *L'enseignment primaire dans les Basses-Pyrénées au temps de la monarchie constitutionelle, 1815–1848* (Anglet: IPSO, 1973).

241. José de Vargas Ponce, "Cartas y disertaciones de don Juan Antonio Moguel sobre la lengua vascongada," in Garibay, *Memorial histórico español*, 665. Ponce

had been commissioned by the government to write a history of the Spanish navy. However, during his stay in Gipuzkoa he devoted himself more to literary and demographic works. Because of this, he wrote an extremely interesting report, which was published rather late: *Estados de vitalidad y mortalidad de Guipúzcoa en el siglo XVIII. Trabajados por el Teniente de Navío don...* (Madrid: Real Academia de la Historia, 1982). Outstanding among his achievements is his service as a Deputy in the Cortes de Cádiz in 1813 and 1820 and as Director of the Academy of History in 1804 and 1814, and that he was interested in the purity of the Castilian language, publishing a *Declaración contra los abusos introducidos en el castellano* [Declaration Against the Abuses Introduced into Castilian].

242. See under "Alava," *Diccionario Geográfico-Histórico de España por la Real Academia de la Historia. Sección I. Comprehende el Reyno de Navarra, Señorío de Vizcaya, y Provincias de Álava y Guipúzcoa* (Madrid: Viuda de don Joaquín Ibarra, 1802), 35.

243. Joaquín Traggia, *Aparato a la Historia Eclesiástica de Aragón,* vol. I (Madrid, 1792), 351–53. This radical change of opinion is doubly interesting if we bear in mind that Traggia was considered one of the first truly critical historians, which he clearly proclaims in the introduction to this same work: "Truth is the soul of History: everyone wishes to find it . . . Even so, truthful histories are extremely rare: there is no historian who does not deviate to some degree from the facts . . . Whoever does not love truth should know that this book is not for him."

244. Tomás González, *Colección de cédulas, cartas-patentes, proviones, reales órdenes y otros documentos conciernientes a las Provincias Vascongadas* . . .; 4 vols. (Madrid: Imprenta Real, 1829–1830).

245. Manuel Godoy, *Memoria del Príncipe de la Paz, o sea cuenta dada de su vida política, para servir a la historia del reinado del Sr. D. Carlos IV de Borbón* (Madrid: Impresa de Sancha, 1836), 66.

246. José Antonio Conde, *Censura crítica del alfabeto primitivo de España y pretendidos monumentos literarios del vascuence* (Madrid: Imprenta Real, 1806), 4–5.

247. Conde, *Censura crítica del alfabeto primitivo*, 45–46.

248. Del Amo, "El debate sobre..."

249. José María Uriarte Astarloa, *Pablo Pedro Astarloa (1752–1806) Biografía* (Durango: Durangoko Arte eta Historia Museoa, 2002), 276–298.

250. Agustín Pascual Iturriaga, *Arte de aprender a hablar la lengua castellana para el uso de las escuelas de primeras letras de Guipúzcoa* (Hernani, 1841) and *Diálogos basco-castellanos para las escuelas de primeras letras de Guipúzcoa* (Hernani, 1842).

251. Luis Astigarraga, *Diccionario manual bascongado y castellano. Elementos de gramática. Para el uso de la juventud...* (San Sebastián: Ramón Baroja, 1825).

252. Jesús de Benito Pascual, *La enseñanza de las primeras letras en Guipúzcoa* (1800–1825) (San Sebastián: Diputación Foral de Gipuzkoa, 1994), 38–40, 187–204.

253. Juan María Eguren, *Método práctico para enseñar el castellano en las escuelas vascongadas* (Vitoria: Semanario Católico Vasco-Navarro, 1867).

254. Jean Baptiste Archu, *Uskara eta Franzes Gramática, Uskalherrietaco haurrentzat eguina* (Bayonne: Fore et Lassarre, 1853), 5–6.

255. *Reglamento provisional de las escuelas de instrucción primaria de la M. N. y M. L. Provincia de Guipúzcoa* (Azpeitia: Imprenta Excelentísima Diputación a cargo de Pablo Martínez, 1875); G. Z. [Gerónimo Zalacain]: *Iracurtzaren asierac edo lenasteac euscalerrico aurrentzat* (Tolosa: P. Gurruchaga, 1875). See also Paulí Dávila Balsera, "Los libros de texto en euskera, siglos XIX y XX," *Enseñanza y educación en el País Vasco contemporáneo,* ed. Paulí Dávila Balsera (Donostia: UPV-Kutxa, 2003), 60–61.

256. Antonio Cánovas del Castillo, Prologue to *Los vascongados*, by Miguel Rodríguez Ferrer (Madrid: J. Noguera, 1873), 25–26, 43–44.

257. Juan Ignacio Iztueta, *Guipuzcoaco provinciaren condaira edo historia* (Donostia: Ramón Baroja, 1847), 6.

Anthology of Apologists and Detractors of the Basque Language

AN ANTHOLOGY OF TEXTS ON THE BASQUE LANGUAGE (FROM THE SIXTEENTH TO THE NINETEENTH CENTURIES)

1. Bernard Dechepare

(c. 1480, Sarrasketa [Sarrasquette], Lower Navarre – ?)

We know almost nothing of the life of Bernard Dechepare except for facts that he himself provides in his only published work. He was an inhabitant of the Garazi (Cize) region in Lower Navarre and a priest of the parish of Eyheralarre (Saint-Michel-le-Vieux). He was possibly the second-born son of the Etxepare family of Sarrasketa (Bussunarits-Sarrasquette), and born in that Navarrese town or perhaps in the same town where he served as rector of the parish for many years, at least from 1518 until his death, which probably occurred after the publication of his book in 1545. Before becoming priest of Eyheralarre, he was general vicar or archpriest of Donibane Garazi (Saint-Jean-Pied-de-Port). A typical exponent of Renaissance culture, he divided his interests into three areas: religion, eroticism, and the vindication of the national language.

Comparison with other authors of the period is inevitable. In Castilian literature with Juan Ruiz, archpriest of Hita (in Guadalajara), and to a lesser degree with Gonzalo de Berceo, and in Basque literature, with the recently discovered manuscript of Joan Pérez de Lazarraga, published some ten years after the publication of Dechepare's work and responding to similar concerns: the use of the vernacular, the exaltation of religion, and the frank presentation of erotic relationships. Foremost among the similarities between Ruiz and Dechepare is that both were ecclesiastics and both were imprisoned. In the case of the Lower Navarrese priest, his imprisonment was apparently for political reasons—his enemies accused him of collaborating with Castile in the dispute for control of the Kingdom of Navarre.

His collection of published poems in *Linguae Vasconum Primitiae* (Primitive Basque Language, 1545), the first work written in the Basque language that was ever consigned to print, is quite brief. It consists of a short introduction in prose and seventeen poems, three relating to religious matters (Christian doctrine, the Ten Commandments, the Judgment), the next eleven amorous in nature, one autobiographical, and the last two in praise of the Basque language.

LINGVAE VASCONVM PRIMItiæ per Dominum Bernardum Dechepare Rectorem sancti michælis veteris.

Selected Text(s):

"Contrapas" and "Sautrela," *Linguae Vasconum Primitiae*, ["Contrapas" and "Saltarello," Novelties of the Basque Language] ed. François Morpain (Burdigalae [Bordeaux]: Franciscum Morpain, 1545).

CONTRAPAS

Basque language, go forth!

May the country of Garazi be blessed for conferring on the Basque language the prestige it deserves.

Basque language, go forth into the public square!

Others think this language can't be written. Look how wrong they were!

Basque language, go forth into the world!

You were considered the least of languages; but now, you will be honored among all others.

Basque language, traverse the globe!

Other languages have reached their apogee. Now she will rise above all others.

Basque language!

All men respect the Basques, although they do not understand their language. Now everyone will know the Basque language.

Basque language!

If until now you have never been seen in print, from this day you will cross the globe.

Basque language!

No language, not French or any other, can be compared to Basque.

Basque language, go forth and dance!

SAUTRELA (Saltarello)

The Basque language came out and let's all go and dance.

Oh, Basque language, sing the praises to the land of Garazi,
for it is there you've won the respect you deserve.
If until now you were the least of languages,
now you will be first.

The Basques were respected throughout the world,
but all others mocked their language
because nowhere did they see her written.
Now they will see how great she is.

If you speak Basque, lift up your head;
your language is about to blossom.
Princes and great lords were fascinated;
they wanted to learn it, wishing it could be written.

Their wishes have been granted by a son of Garazi,
and a friend of his from Bordeaux.
He's the first printer of the Basque language.
We Basques are forever in his debt.

Hooray, hooray, calloo, callay!
The Basque language came out and let's all go and dance!

FROM A HUMBLE BEGINNING, MAY BETTER FORTUNE COME

2. Juan Martínez de Zaldibia Elduayen, known as "Zaldibia, the Graduate"

(Tolosa, Gipuzkoa, first half of sixteenth century – Tolosa?, 1575)

He was a descendant of important members of the Oñacinos, a clannish faction that, from the twelfth or thirteenth century, struggled with its principal rival, the Gamboinos, for control of Bizkaia. He was thus an extremely influential figure, not only in Tolosa, his birthplace, but also throughout Gipuzkoa. Hence, he was elected mayor of Tolosa three times (1544, 1552, and 1574) just as his father and uncle had been. Moreover, he was entrusted with a provincial post that was technical in nature but of great political transcendence. That tells us of the distinction that his contemporaries accorded him: the codification of the ordinances of Gipuzkoa. He also served as attorney representing Gipuzkoa on several occasions. Zaldibia's achievement of such distinction can be attributed to three qualities: as a jurist, as a politician, and as an intellectual. He studied law and earned his degree, perhaps from the University of Alcalá de Henares. He married María Juaniz de Arteaga, and they had a son, who later died. When his will was read, Zaldibia was a widower without heirs, so he resorted to a practice relatively common at the time among pious persons in such circumstances: he declared his soul as his heir. Although close relatives contested this will, his wish finally prevailed and his estate (which was significant) was donated to charitable and pious ends. Among other things, he left endowments for a chair in Latin and for two poor young women. From these gestures, we might perceive other facets of his personality: a concern for the education of his countrymen and his piety, although he was a layperson.

Beyond this, another relatively common political characteristic that Zaldibia shared with the ruling classes of Gipuzkoa at the time was his hostility to Navarre and support of Castile. In this case, Zaldibia became the first proponent of one of the foundational myths of Gipuzkoa, incorporated over centuries into the escutcheon of the province: the myth of the Battle of Beotibar, in which a presumably miniscule group of Gipuzkoans notoriously defeated a far larger Navarrese army. Additionally, Zaldibia was a Gipuzkoan of his time, an avowed supporter of the Spanish monarchy, and harsh critic of the old system of political factions, although he himself belonged to one of the most important feudal lineages. He was one of the first to portray Gipuzkoa historically as an independent political body, superior to and before that of any ruling kings, voluntarily allying herself with Castile,[1] but subsequently exercising her freedom to break that alliance and join Navarre, only to re-ally herself voluntarily with the King of Castile in 1200 over differences with the former. "They returned to their pristine condition of being Castilian, as free, unconquered people." His works were not published during his lifetime but had great impact because they were circulated in manuscript form and known by most of those who studied these matters. His principal, and at the time unpublished, works were *Suma de las cosas cantábricas y guipuzcoanas* (Summary of Events in Cantabria and Gipuzkoa); *Libro Viejo de Guipúzcoa* (Old

1. Martínez de Zaldibia, *Suma*, ch. 11.

Book of Gipuzkoa); *Historia de los Cántabros, Vizcaínos y Guipuzcoanos* (History of the Cantabrians, Bizkaians, and Gipuzkoans), a manuscript contained among the papers of Salazar y Castro in the Real Academia de la Historia in Madrid (9/830, folios 8–17v.); *Hidalguía de los guipuzcoanos* (Nobility of the Gipuzkoans); and the *Cronicón de Fuenterrabia* (Short Chronicle of Hondarribia).

SUMA DE LAS COSAS
CANTABRICAS Y
GUIPUZCOANAS

INTRODUCCION Y NOTAS

SELECTED TEXT(S):

Suma de las cosas cantábricas y guipuzcoanas [Summary of Events in Cantabria and Gipuzkoa]. Edited by Fausto Arocena. San Sebastián: Diputación Foral de Guipúzcoa, 1945. 11–12, 130–131.

Chapter 4
Which Tells of the Basque Language and its Origins

After that so memorable flood described in Sacred Scripture in which the entire human race, except for eight souls, perished for building that tower of Babel, mentioned in the eleventh chapter of Genesis, when the number of languages was increased from one to seventy and scattered across the world, Tubal, son of Japheth, came to the Spains with his people and their language and settled in the Pyrenees mountains. The Archbishop Rodrigo de Toledo, speaking of the languages that Jafet distributed throughout the nations of Europe when he came to Spain, said that the Basques and Navarrese had their language, which is the Basque language brought by Tubal and his companions, and that if it had been Chaldean, as some conjecture and try to affirm, that entire language or at least some remnants of it would have survived, and since the Archbishop does not speak of any other language in Spain, it is clear that Basque was Spain's maternal language until the Romans came there, conquered it, and imposed their language, which is called Romance, except in that region where the original language has always remained, which is further clear evidence that it had never been conquered; almost the same can be deduced from the ninth book of Isidoro's *Etimologías* [Etymologies], second chapter, and perfectly verified in book 20 of Venero's *Enquiridión de los tiempos* [Manual of the Ages] , folio 73, and in the fourth book of the *Cosas Memorables de España* [Memorable Things of Spain] by Lucius Marineus, and by Antón Beuter in his history and by the modern authors Tobio and Valdés. And one thing is certain: that no author speaks of any language in Spain before Basque, of which Strabo says: "which we regard as incompatible with the names, because they cannot be explained." Pomponius Mela says the same thing at the end of chapter one of book three: ". . . whose names cannot be explained in our language." They have those peculiarities in their language: that all nouns, except for a few proper names, end in 'a' in the singular and 'c' in the plural ['k' in modern Basque orthography]; and they use articles to distinguish cases; and they pronounce by putting a stress on the penultimate syllable and sometimes on the last. This language is spoken in Gipuzkoa, Bizkaia, and Encartaciones, Araba, in the center of Navarre, and in Lapurdi and Basques [Lower Navarre], where it is spoken most perfectly and with least mixture of other languages. Titus Livius says that in Hannibal's camp there were some Spaniards whose language could not be understood, against whom Marcus Marcelus initiated a certain tactic: that the members of the cavalry should carry young boys who were skilled dart throwers on the withers of their horses. According to Plutarch in his *Life of Marcus Marcelus*, the ones whose language could not be understood were from this land, because the Romans understood the romance language that they imposed in Spain, but not the Basque language.

. . .

Bardulia has this etymology: *Veardu leya* which in Spanish means: "He loves persistence," alluding to their stubbornness and constancy in war.

Of Gipuzkoa, some say that its etymology is *Guc pusca*, which sounds like a fierce threat to the enemy: "We will tear you to pieces," thus meaning, "one who tears asunder."

3. Esteban de Garibay y Zamalloa

(Arrasate-Mondragón, Gipuzkoa, 1525 – Madrid ?, 1599)

The descendant of a distinguished family from Oñati but of lesser lineage, Esteban de Garibay y Zamalloa's father, whose name should have been Zamalloa Garibay, reversed the order of his parents' surnames, because his mother was of higher lineage and greater social distinction. The mother of this historian was Catalina de Sagurdia, so the chronicler should more appropriately have been named Zamalloa Sagurdia or at best Garibay Sagurdia, but Esteban too decided here to maintain the surnames that presumably conferred on him greater honor, keeping the two names of his father in the order he had chosen. He studied in the newly created University of Oñati and then continued his education in Vitoria (Gasteiz) in Araba y Santo Domingo de la Calzada in La Rioja. He married Catalina de Asurduy in 1556 but she died in 1572, and he immediately married a fifteen-year-old girl from Toledo (although her family was from Araba). As an alderman from Arrasate-Mondragón, he joined the local militia as a lieutenant and took part in the border wars against France in 1558. In 1559, he was appointed an Agent of the Inquisition and from that year forth served as historical consultant to the General Assemblies of Gipuzkoa. From 1568–69, he served as mayor of Arrasate-Mondragón, member of the General Assemblies of Gipuzkoa and director of exports with a residence in Irun. He also took part in the reformation of provincial and magisterial regulations, proposing some sixty articles relative to the planting of trees and naval construction.

A self-taught historian, he traveled tirelessly throughout the Empire, partly to work in archives and gather materials for his historical work and partly to print it in a more professional form (hence his journey to Antwerp). In 1575, he had his first contact with Felipe II, by whom he hoped to be appointed royal chronicler. Despite having powerful supporters at Court, especially the Idiáquez family, and having been personally interviewed by the king on several occasions, he did not attain official appointment as chronicler until 1592, seven years before his death. However, before that he served as salaried (although unofficial) chronicler for several years. With his appointment, Garibay became the genealogical evaluator of royal privileges, those already granted as well as those petitioned, and therefore a pillar of legitimization of the Monarchy and the monarch.

He simultaneously worked, in this case without remuneration, for the institutions of Gipuzkoa. His service in judicial reform and in various other functions has already been mentioned. After establishing his residence in Castile, he functioned as de facto reprsentative or unofficial ambassador of Arrasate-Mondragón and Gipuzkoa at the Court, recommended by Domingo Pérez de Idiáquez for these functions. Juan de Idiáquez, a good friend of his, tried to persuade him to take charge of systematizing *foral* legislation, a task at which Zaldibia, Cruzat, and Zandategui had already tried their hand. However Garibay did not accept, preferring instead to write a history of Gipuzkoa, which he thought more valuable for provincial institutionalization than a simple task of legal compilation. Moreover, he tried to restore the title of Kingdom to Gipuzkoa (which it had supposedly enjoyed at one time); but the rulers of Gipuzkoa themselves rejected this effort, for they believed that an acknowledgement of such a title would signify greater responsibilities and obligations, as well as an even greater integration into Castile at the expense of the nascent *foral* system.

Finally, another aspect of his personality was his fervent Catholicism. This led him, among other things, to interview Francisco de Borja and Teresa de Jesús. He worked for the beatification of Ignacio de Loiola, sought to create Jesuit academies in both Toledo and Arrasate-Mondragón, and when that failed, he managed to build a Franciscan monastery in the place of his birth, where he was finally buried. He also undertook an infinite number of projects until he finally succeeded in moving the remains of Saint Leocadia from Flanders, where they were buried, to Toledo, the birthplace of the saint.

Garibay was, along with father Mariana, one of the founders of Tubalism. "The arrival in Spain of its first King, the Patriarch Tubal" and his "settlement and residence in the region of Cantabria and the lands of Navarre" was put forth with a picturesque argument concerning the appropriateness of the Basque Country for the establishment of Tubal's realm. According to Garibay,[1] the Pyrenees and Cantabria were at that time rich in wild fruits, millet, and mushrooms; that is to say, the type of food that primitives like Tubal and his sons would have liked. With such arguments, he thus rejected the possibility that Tubal would have settled in Catalonia as Master Esquível de Alcalá claimed, because it did not suit his primitive lifestyle. Garibay emphasized the purity and nobility of the Basques, and their having been the first inhabitants of Spain, resorting to the argument of toponymy that subsequent writers, such as Manuel de Larramendi, would expound so thoroughly. As such, place names throughout the peninsula had Basque etymologies ("the names of our rivers, or important sites, common to ancient Armenia and to this part of Spain"), linking the names of Araxes (Aras) River in the Caucasus Mountains with Araixa (Orio, Gipuzkoa), Mount Ararat

1. Garibay, *Los XL libros d'el compendio historial*, 84, 88.

with Aralar, a mountain range between Gipuzkoa and Navarre, and so on. Contradicting those like **Ocampo** who identified Setubal (in present-day Portugal) with Tubal, Garibay also proposed Tudela (Navarre) as deriving from Tubela. As such, "the pure and perfect Basque language" must have been that of Armenia, with no contamination from Latin, or Greek, and even "far less from Hebrew."

As a historian, Garibay was very traditional, with a genealogical and religious idea of history. For him, the genealogical method began with the Bible itself and led him to investigate the genealogies of religious figures, kings, and his own family, which he used, of course, to discover the identity of the Iberian Peninsula's ancient peoples. Politically, he followed the same line as Zaldibia, contributing to the establishment of the basic elements of the *foral* system: universal nobility, loyalty to the Crown and voluntary alliance with Castile. Garibay's historiographic work, consisting of Basque etymologies, an analysis of the language, proverbs and ancient songs (among various other linguistic questions), consisted of the following: *Los XL libros d'el compendio historial de las Chronicas y universal Historia de todos los reynos de España* (The Forty Books of the Historical Compendium of the Chronicles and Universal History of all the Kingdoms of Spain) (1571); *Los siete libros de la progenie y parentela de los hijos de Estevan de Garibay* (The Seven Books of the Heirs and Relatives of the Children of Esteban de Garibay), known popularly as *Memorias* (Memoirs) and later published as volume 7 of the *Memorial Histórico Español* (Spanish Historical Memorial), edited by Pascual de Guayangos, (1854); and *Ilustraciones genealógicas de los linajes bascongados* (Genealogical Portraits of Basque Lineages), published by Juan Carlos Guerra, extracted from *Las Grandezas de España* (The Grandeur of Spain), in *Revista Internacional de los Estudios Vascos* 2 (1908): 535–556 and vols. 3–6, 8, 14 and 15, and subsequently in book form (San Sebastián: Nueva Editorial, 1933).

Selected Text(s):

Los XL libros d'el compendio historial de las Chronicas y universal Historia de todos los reynos de España [The Forty Books of the Historical Compendium of the Chronicles and Universal History of All the Kingdoms of Spain], 3 vols. (Antwerp: Christoforo Plantino, 1571; reprint, Barcelona: Sebastián Cornellas, 1621), bk. 3, ch. 2, 86–87; bk. 4, ch. 4, 90–93.

The Patriarch Tubal and his people, in fond memory of their country of Armenia, named the mountains of Cantabria using the names of the mountains, rivers, and features of Armenia, and it is remarkable that even today we can still see, not just traces of these descriptions and of their feelings after so many centuries but, even more surprising, we find many of these names in their entirety, without any alteration. It can be seen according to Ptolemy and other geographers that the mountain where Noah's Ark came aground in the flood in Armenia was named Gordeya, which is very famous among writers because of this and its great altitude; and if we want to find another by the same name in Cantabria, we will find an extremely high mountain between the province of Araba and that of Bizkaia, called Gordeya, whose height exceeds all those in the region. If we simply change the *D* to *B*, they call it Gorbeya, which is well known by everyone in Cantabria, who when they want to express their love for their country and their pleasure in living there say, "the cow from Gorbeya always loves Gorbeya," which is an old proverb of theirs.

If the river that has its source in greater Armenia is called Araxa, or Araxes, a river that is famous and well-known to cosmographers, there is also, among all the good rivers in Cantabria, another by the same name, called Araxes, which originates in Cantabria and ends in Navarre near the church of San Miguel de Excelsis, not far from Larraun, and flowing from there through the valley of Araiça, originally named Araxa like the river itself. It goes down to the province of Gipuzkoa and, skirting the villages of Tolosa and Usurbil, enters the Cantabrian Sea at Orio, a town in that province two leagues from the town of San Sebastián [Donostia], and five leagues from the well-known promontory Olearso, which is the point and cape of Fuenterrabia [Hondarribia].

If we want to look for further verification of this, for the name of that proud construction of the Tower of Babel, which these same people that the Patriarch Tubal witnessed, we will find, right there in

Cantabria, less than a league away from the village of Mondragon [Arrasate], where this history is being written, a site and section of land where there are some windmills that are now called Babel, without any change or alteration in spelling, and this group of windmills was originally called the Forge of Babel, as can be seen in ancient public inscriptions. This resulted in all probability from its similarity with a lofty peak that, rising up from a place near this site called Babel, seems to reach up to touch the sky like the Tower of Babel. This huge, impressive peak, which derives its name from a small settlement called Udala that consists of just a few small huts, is called Udalaacha, which means Udala peak. It is one of the highest places in all the kingdoms of Spain, and beautiful and rich, especially in metals, and nearby is another lofty peak named Amboto, and the two are like sisters that were born to make each other look even more beautiful, and both of them are near Mount Gordeya, but the latter exceeds them in fertility and in the great abundance of its metals, such as iron, and the steel that is forged from the metal of this peak and is the hardest of all Europe. Between these lofty peaks, there is a valley named Arraçola because of its similarity with Arracillum, a Cantabrian town famous among historians, where the hardest fighting took place in the war that the Emperor Octaviano Cesar Augusto waged in Cantabria. . .

So without dwelling further on the extraordinary features of this mountain peak, let us return to Tubal and his people who, having witnessed that extremely tall Tower of Babel, when they came to Cantabria not surprisingly gave the name Babel to this place because of its similarity in shape and height to the Tower of Babel, and I would have no difficulty believing that this peak would have been given the name Babel at that time because of the many indications and reasons regarding its documentation.

If some scholars, following the Holy Scripture, were to say that the mountain in Armenia where Noah's Ark came aground was called Ararat, I can offer them another mountain in Cantabria that was called by the same name, Ararat, which today is called Aralar, one of the highest mountains and richest pasture lands of all Cantabria, located on the border with Navarre and extending into the jurisdiction and region of Villa Franca, a village located precisely in Gipuzkoa.

If in the first year after the flood Noah built a city in Armenia called Saga Albina, so too in Cantabria, near that same Mount Gordeya, there was a territory called Albina that was covered with large fruit trees that provided abundant food for those living there. So the first inhabited area of Spain, according to such evidence and many facts we will indicate below, was Cantabria, founded by Tubal and his people who came from Armenia, and because with the passage of time they spread across the Pyrenees toward France, they populated many lands where we will find many examples of names from Armenia, according to Bertrando Helia Appamiense in his history of the Counts of Fox, who populated the land of Armenac in France with people who came from Armenia, and today we call that region Armenac, which is one of the good states of France whose Counts have been Princes of great distinction, some of them loyal servants of the Kings of Castile, as we will show below.

. . .

Concerning the language that Tubal brought to Spain there are also differing opinions among our chroniclers, a few of whom claimed it was Chaldean because they found in the lands of Andalusia some Chaldean names whose meanings will be explained in chapter 14 of book 5, where I suggest to the readers, as will be seen there, how those names had their origin during the powerful arrival in Spain of Nebuchadnezzar, Prince of the Babylonian Chaldeans, quite famous in Holy Scripture, who was the one who destroyed the city of Jerusalem and the Temple of Solomon. By the time this Chaldean Prince came to Spain, more than 1,570 years had passed since Tubal's arrival, as the readers will be able to see from the ensuing discussion in this chronicle, especially if they are skilled in computation. Thus when this Prince came to these parts, there were already numerous languages spoken in the regions of Spain from the many nations that came to Spain after him with their different languages.

Most of our authors write that the first language to have been spoken in Spain was the one they call Basque, which is the same language spoken to this day in the regions of the greater part of Cantabria, especially in the provinces of Gipuzkoa, Araba, Bizkaia, in most of the kingdom of Navarre, and in particular throughout the fiefdom of Pamplona, including the city itself, it being the largest of the five divisions into which that kingdom is divided. This language extends even into the regions of France that are contiguous with Navarre and Gipuzkoa, because it is spoken in the city of Bayonne, its bishopric, and on all the slopes of the Pyrenees as far as the realm of Bearne. Where there are different opinions, each person can choose the one that seems most sound and probable, and where no error exists, there can always be different opinions, and in this case people do indeed have different opinions; but it seems to me, and many distinguished men of our time have agreed with me, that the language of Cantabria was the first to be spoken in Spain for the causes and reasons already presented as well as those that will be presented below as evidence of her first inhabitants and that is one of the seventy-two languages created at the time of the dispersion throughout the world because it is a language without any connection with any other. It's obvious that it is the first language of Spain because, as has been shown, the regions of Cantabria and Navarre were the first in Spain to be inhabited following the flood, we can infer and conclude from this that their language is the first, and this argument is persuasive. Although foreigners generally call this language Basque, which means in the language itself, 'the language or speech of the Basques in the land of France that borders on Gipuzkoa and Navarre,' but the native speakers themselves, Spanish as well as French, call it Enusquera [Euskara], and so it is illogical to call it Bascuençe [vascuence], because its original and first name was Enusquera, and they of other countries, especially Castilian, they call Erdeera [erdara].

It's a matter of great importance and mystery regarding this language to see that, at least in Spain, all children from the time of their birth speak this language because the first words they speak are *tayta*, for this is what they call the father, and *mama*, which is what they call the mother: names originating undoubtedly from Cantabrian, in which the father is called *ayta* and the mother *ama*, so whether this is because children in their innocence corrupt it or for whatever other reason, the only difference is a single letter at the beginning which the Cantabrians delete or add: because in the name of *ayta* they add the T, and to *ama* they add M. These same children, when they want to refer to their evacuation, say *caca*, which in this language means "man's manure." If these examples aren't enough, I could write a discourse so long that there would be no room for it in our history, but this seems sufficient to me as documentation of the antiquity of this language, which has been preserved in this land from the time of the Patriarch Tubal until now without any contamination or admixture from any nation foreign to its law, whether this is because of the toughness of the land or the people, or both.

Beuter, in chapter thirty of the first book, [of his Crónica general de toda *España y especialmente del Reyno de Valencia*, 1538 (in Catalan); 1548 (in Castilian)] speaking of this language, offers some unsound arguments, unworthy of such a writer, arguing without any evidence at all that this language is composed of several other languages, and although he admits that this language was the first to be spoken in Spain he feels on the other hand that it is not the pure language brought to Spain by Tubal and his people because, as he says, it isn't Armenian, which he claims is the first language spoken in the world, or Chaldean, as if this were already proven and as if either of these languages were his own. He makes these conclusions without any knowledge of Armenian or Chaldean and even less of Cantabrian. Having arrived in Spain twelve years after the confusion of languages, Tubal would necessarily have had to bring one of them, but his language wouldn't necessarily have been the first in the world; instead, this is evidence of the opposite.

Through diligent examination it can be verified that the Cantabrian language is pure and perfect and that is linked to the language of Armenia, which is called Aramaic, but has no connection with Latin or Greek, and even less with Hebrew, Chaldean, French, Flemish, or the language of Bourgogne, and no connection with English, Tudescan, Hungarian, Turkish, or Arabic, but is in fact a pure language, with no mixture with any other, and if a few words have come into it now and then, it's been from Castilian because of the extensive communication between the two nations; and it is a language that could be easily taught, its grammar having fewer rules than Latin. This makes it easy to learn and master as experience shows day by day. With one example alone we will be able to demonstrate this, because the navigators from the province of Gipuzkoa and the kingdom of Bizkaia and the land of the Basques, sailing out once a year to Terranova [Newfoundland] to fish for codfish and whales, the savages from that region manage to learn this language in less than two months a year with little communication with the people from here, and if these wild people, lacking all reason and all political knowledge, manage to learn it in such a short time, how much easier would the civilized people of our old world do so if it were necessary and they applied themselves?

. . .

Hence, when the Romans conquered Spain they found different languages in the different provinces. This was very much to their advantage, making their conquests less difficult, because all the nations of Spain had different languages so they did not unite against their armies. The Romans introduced their language into the rest of Spain over the course of time, except for Cantabria. It is worth noting that in this language that all nouns, except for proper nouns, end in *a* in the singular and *ac* in the plural, this being such a general rule that there aren't any exceptions.

4. Miguel de Alonsótegui

(?, early sixteenth century – ?, c. 1590)

His place of birth is unknown, but it must not have been far from the town of his surname, in Barakaldo (Bizkaia). He completed his studies for the priesthood, although it is not known where (perhaps Alcalá or Salamanca, in Castile). He took orders as a Mercedarian in the monastery of Burceña (Burzeña) in Barakaldo, and later became abbot; he was given important offices in his order.

He was an ascetic of distinction—*Tratado que muestra la vida miserable que padece el hombre* (Treatise that Demonstrates the Pitiful Life Suffered by Man) (1561)[1]—who was most unlucky as a writer, his entire oeuvre surviving only in manuscript and exploited in part by others. A rigorous contemporary of Alejo de Venegas, Juan de Avila, Luis de Granada, and Diego de Estella, together they all belonged to the same literary and religious movement. In addition to his ascetic writings, he left behind his *Crónicas de Vizcaya* (Chronicles of Bizkaia), published in 1577, which have been lost but from which Juan Ramón de Iturriza borrowed extensively. The latter transcribes some of Alonsótegui's *quintillas* (five-verse stanzas) describing his love of the Basque language. In these *quintillas,* he presents Basque as an ancient language, one of the seventy-two originating in Babel that was kept pure and unmixed ("uncontaminated") in Bizkaia, unchanged by wars or centuries. Miguel de Alonsótegui could serve here as an example of something that was common in his time and in the following centuries: Basque writers who wrote in Castilian, French, or Latin on different topics never missed an opportunity to praise their native land and especially their language, always mentioning its supposed characteristics: antiquity, purity, etc.

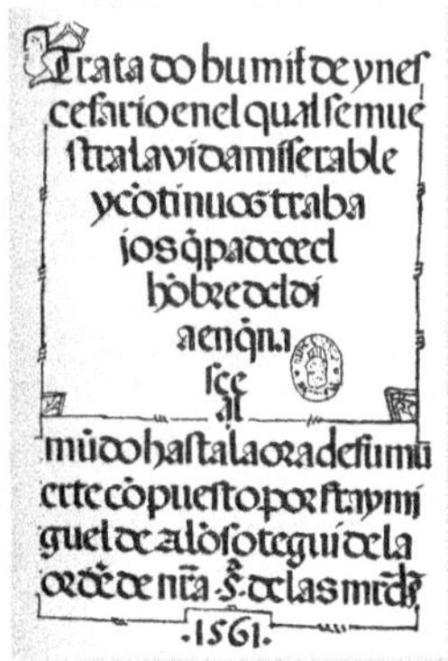
Tratado bumil de y nes
cessario enel qual se mue
stra la vida miserable
y cõtinuos traba
jos q̃ padece el
hõbre del di
a en q̃ na
sce
al
mũdo hasta la ora de su mu
erte cõpuesto por fray mi
guel de alõsotegui de la
ordẽ de nr̃a .S. de las merc
·1561·

1. See Miguel de Alonsótegui, *Tratado que muestra la vida miserable que padece el hombre*, ed. Pedro de Ortúzar (Bilbao: Diputación Foral de Vizcaya, 1970).

Selected Text(s):

Crónicas de Vizcaya [Chronicles of Bizkaia], 1577, in Juan Ramón de Iturriza y Zabala, *Historia General de Vizcaya comprobada con autoridades y copias de escrituras y privilegios fehacientes* [General History of Bizkaia Officially Authorized and Copied with Written, Valid Permissions] (1787); reprint, (Bilbao: Cipriano Lucena, 1885), 60.

That first language
brought from the Confusion
is now the last
still preserved intact
and uncontaminated in Bizkaia.

It is the Basque language
as we see in its purity
unaltered by wars
but preserved here by us
century after century.

5. Pedro de Madariaga

(Arratia, Bizkaia, c. 1537 – ?, 1587)

He may have been born in the town of Zeanuri, but whatever the case, he was from the Arratia valley. Educated in the Humanities, he served as a soldier for the Spanish Empire, especially in Italy, but also in several Spanish cities. He was a friend of Martín de Gaztelu, secretary of Emperor Carlos V and a model for Basque scribes in the service of the Habsburg administration. These "Basque quill-bearers" distinguished themselves not only in keeping accounts and writing agreements but also in the perfect calligraphy of such documents. In Zaragoza, he studied with the Basque calligrapher Joanes de Iciar, becoming his favorite pupil. He invented a new system of calligraphy, and after 1562, gave classes on the subject at the University of Valencia. He published his system in *Honra de escribanos* (Honor of Scribes) (1565).

Although Madariaga lived most of his life outside the Basque Country he nonetheless dedicated a chapter in his work to the Basque language, of which he was proud and displayed good knowledge. He was active in the system of philosophical arguments of his period, arguing that the simpler, older, and more elegant a language is the more it resembles the language Adam must have spoken under God's inspiration. Among all languages, those best fulfilling these characteristics are Chaldean, Hebrew, and Basque, and he tries to demonstrate the similarities and connections between them. In effect, he is positive that Basque derives from Chaldean. One of the arguments for primacy and antiquity in these languages is that some of their letters themselves have significant features, because there is no greater simplicity than for a single letter to have meaning. Thus, for example, *A* means "that," *I* means "you," and *R* means "something burned." Additionally, he railed against his countrymen for not using their language in letters and business matters, leading many to believe that Basque is not appropriate for learned texts, although Madariaga insists that there are books printed in that language. Although by the year 1565, we know of only one published book, that of Dechepare, Madariaga insisted that there were "books." Is this an exaggeration or were there in fact others that have been lost?

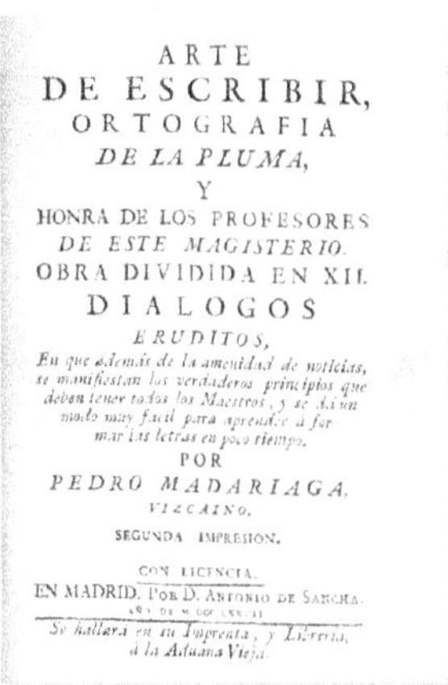

ARTE
DE ESCRIBIR,
ORTOGRAFIA
DE LA PLUMA,
Y
HONRA DE LOS PROFESORES
DE ESTE MAGISTERIO.
OBRA DIVIDIDA EN XII.
DIALOGOS
ERUDITOS,
En que ademàs de la amenidad de noticias, se manifiestan los verdaderos principios que deben tener todos los Maestros, y se dà un modo muy facil para aprender à formar las letras en poco tiempo.
POR
PEDRO MADARIAGA,
VIZCAINO.
SEGUNDA IMPRESION.
CON LICENCIA.
EN MADRID. POR D. ANTONIO DE SANCHA.
Se hallarà en su Imprenta, y Libreria, à la Aduana Vieja.

Selected Text(s):

Honra de escribanos, arte de escrebir bien pronto, ortografía de la pluma [Honor of Scribes, the Art of Writing Quickly, Orthography of the Pen] (Valencia: Pedro Patricio Mey, 1565; reprint, (Madrid: Antonio de Sancha, 1777), 249–254.4 [Note: The use of the word(s) Bizkaian(s) here refers to Basques as a whole].

Plato says that one part of our birth pertains to our friends and the other part to our country. Now that I have fulfilled what I promised to my friends, I want to address my language in greater detail, as well as the inventors of the letters. Plato says that a philosopher named Theuth was the inventor of letters. Pliny and Suidas are of the opinion that Cadmus discovered as many letters as the serpent has teeth, that is, sixteen. Saint Augustine says [it was] Queen Isis. Saint Isidore is of the opinion that [it was] Carmenta, mother of Evander. Josephus attributes them to the sons of Adam. But ultimately, although Latin letters might have been invented by Carmenta, Greek letters by Cadmus, Egyptian letters by Isis, Hebrew letters by Moses, Assyrian letters by Abraham, the fact is that the letters of the Chaldean language (from which our Bizkaian language is derived) [were invented] by Adam, as is apparent in what the apostle Saint Judas tells in his Canon about the prophecy of Enoch, who was the seventh after Adam. And Saint Thomas says that he came upon a book written by Abel, who killed Adam. From this we can infer that the first, most important, and most elegant language was that of Adam, as the necessary consequence of words being made up of letters, which Adam first invented, as well as the fact that the more ancient, simple and elegant a language is the more it will resemble that of Adam.

But in the judgment of all the historians that ever existed, there are no languages less contaminated and more thoroughly preserved in their purity, or less corrupted from their original form than Bizkaian and Hebrew during the Confusion and Differentiation of nations. For in their elegance, succinctness, and etymology, these three languages resemble each other greatly; and thus we have an infinite number of words, as do the Chaldeans and the Hebrews, which end as follows: *Ceruach*, the Heavens; *Guch*, We; *Zuech*, You; and finally all the plurals have the same endings. *Iaicoa* in our language is the holy name of God. *Iehoua* in Hebrew has the same meaning; the Latins do not have the phoneme *Zamach* but must use the *S*, but the Bizkaians have it in the *C* itself, because we say, as do the Hebrews, *Mezea* for Mass, and so it is with other letters and words. Also, this language of ours has many metaphors and figures, which give it great distinction and brevity. *Guztian adin ona* means "moderation is in all things good," expressed by an elegant metaphor, and very few of our words lack brevity and elegance. I cannot help feeling a bit annoyed at my fellow Bizkaians because they do not use the language in letters and business matters; and this makes many people think that it cannot be written, although there are books printed in this language.

A single *R* at the end of a syllable has the force of a double *r*; as in *uguer, nadar* (swim), *eder, hermoso* (beautiful), *laster* (soon), and *presto* (ready). The *S* is frequently pronounced by pressing the tongue tightly against the upper palate in mid-syllable, as in *essea*, house; *ossoa*, wolf; and *assoa*, old woman. Therefore, the *S* is doubled to denote that stress in pronunciation. The *N* is sometimes lost in a nasal sound, as in *oraciô* (sentence, prayer), *Ardaoa;* and to indicate that *n*, it is necessary to write a symbol above the letter in the form of a nose, like this (ˆ). All of our other letters preserve the same order as the ordinary Latin letters.

In its succinctness, as I said, it also has close resemblance to Chaldean and Hebrew; and thus many of the letters of the alphabet are significant in themselves, for instance *A*, which means "that;" the letter *I* means "you;" *R* means "something burned;" and the two vowels *O* and *A* joined together mean "an important Bizkaian town at the foot of Axmutil, where that ancient and famous house of Madariaga is situated and whose ramparts are touched by the very first rays of the Sun entering that Province each day, and from which you can see all of Arratia and Bizkaia as far as the Portugalete estuary.

THE END

6. Juan de Mariana

(Talavera, Toledo, 1536 – Toledo, 1623)

He is considered one of the most distinguished Spanish scholars of the sixteenth century. After studying art and theology in Alcalá, he took orders in the Company of Jesus, completing his novitiate in Simancas under the direction of Francisco de Borja. After teaching in the Jesuitical schools of Rome, Sicily, and Paris, he returned to his homeland because of ill health, residing in Toledo until his death. He was also an advisor to the Inquisitional Court, a specialist in oriental languages and versed in history and several sciences. He did not disdain economic and political analyses, although most of his vast work is religious in nature.

One should emphasize two characteristics in his work: Spanish patriotism and criticism of established power. In the former, he devoted enormous effort to his *Historia general de España* (General History of Spain), published first in Latin (editions in 1592 and 1595) and subsequently in Castilian (1601). In it, he sought to inform Spaniards as well as foreigners about the excellence of the Spanish nation founded by Tubal. With regards to his critical spirit, it led him to publish a work,

De mutatione Monetae (On the Alteration of Money) (1601), in which he censured the monetary policy of Felipe III, who burdened the common people with the loss of monetary value and purchasing power by his practice of making coins of copper alloy of less actual value but with the same face value. Mariana was brought to trial and imprisoned because of this publication. He also aroused animosity, although not as grave, with another of his works, *De Rege et Regis institutione* (About the King and the Instruction of the King) (1599), on the education of princes in which he enunciated principles that some have chosen to regard as proto-liberal, long before their time. Finally, a text was discovered among his papers in which the ills afflicting the Company of Jesus were diagnosed along with their remedies: *Discurso de las cosas de la Compañía* (Discourse on the Company's Matters); this was published posthumously in Bordeaux. His strong critical spirit does not mean that he opposed the institutions that he judged; on the contrary, his interest in the monarchy and the Company of Jesus led him to document and correct their flaws. He does not stand out specifically for his defense of vernacular language; his interest was in cultured and classical languages, and he composed nearly all of his work in Latin. Because it of this, it is inevitable that he would have viewed the Basque language as he did: a barbaric slang unworthy of attention.

Selected Text(s):

Historiae de rebus Hispaniae [History of Things in Spain] (1592, in Latin) (1601, in Castilian); reprint, as *Historia general de España, la compuesta emendada y añadida por el Padre Mariana, con la continuación de Miniana completada por el Conde de Toreno y la de nuestros días por Eduardo Chao* [General History of Spain, Edition Revised and Expanded by Father Mariana, with Additions by Miniana Completed by the Count of Toreno and the Current Edition by Eduardo Chao] (Madrid: Gaspar Roig, 1848–51), vol.1, bk.I, ch. 5, epigraph 30, 6. [Note: The use of the word(s) Bizkaian(s) here refer to Basques as a whole].

Only the Bizkaians continue until this day to speak their crude, barbaric language, unrefined and quite different from all others, it being the oldest of Spain and in ancient times the common language of the entire country, as many believe. And they say that all of Spain used the Bizkaian language before the Roman armies entered these provinces and imposed their language on them. They say too that those people were innately crude, fierce, and wild, and could have been improved and domesticated like trees if planted in good soil, but because the mountains where they lived were inaccessible, they either resisted the yoke of the Roman Empire completely or quickly shook it off. Nor it is improbable that with their ancient freedom they also preserved the ancient and common language of the entire peninsula of Spain. Others feel differently and, to the contrary, say that the Bizkaian language was always peculiar to that region and not common to all of Spain. They are moved to say this by the testimony of ancient writers who say that Bizkaian words, especially those referring to places and towns, were harder and more barbaric than those of the rest of Spain, and that they could not be reduced to Latin declensions. In particular, Strabo certifies that there was no single alphabet or language common to all of Spain. This is confirmed by words like *briga*, meaning "town"; *cetra* (escutcheon); *salarica* (lance); *gurdus* (fat); *cusculia* (kermes oak); *lancia* (lance); *vipio* (demoiselle crane); *buteo* (bird of prey); and *Necy* (the god Mars), along with other words that formerly belonged to the language of the Spaniards, as is proven by the authority and testimony of distinguished authors; and there were even some words that passed from the Spanish language into Latin, but there isn't a trace of any these words in the Bizkaian language. This shows that the Bizkaian language was not the common language of Spain. We do not deny, however, that it was one of the many languages that were used in Spain in ancient times; we only insist that it was not common to all of Spain. We do not wish to argue this opinion at greater length, nor does it fall within the scope of our intent to address it further.

7. Andrés de Poza Yarza, known as "Poza the Graduate"
(Lendoño de Abajo, Orduña, Bizkaia, 1547 – Madrid, 1595)

Son of a wealthy family, nothing was denied him when he was young, enabling him to attain an extraordinary education for his epoch. His father, Pedro, and his uncle, Martín, held high posts in the Habsburg administration in Flanders, where he was raised. Because the possibility of receiving instruction from foreign university–based teachers was not yet forbidden, he was one of the last to benefit from that option, and as a child, studied mathematics and cosmography (among other disciplines) for nine years in Louvain-Leuven, Flanders. Following Felipe II's 1559 decree, however, forbidding Spaniards to study in foreign universities (even Catholic ones), he was obliged to undertake his college education in Spain, transferring to Salamanca, where he studied law for another ten years. In 1570, he returned to Flanders as part of the Spanish army of occupation, which later withdrew in 1579. He was, according to records, "employed by the monarchy in Flanders," under the command of Luis de Requesens. From that point on, his situation became quite uncomfortable, because he was the target of a lawsuit and an assassination attempt. He sought to be transferred to the Indies but was denied permission, so in 1583 he decided to return to Bizkaia and practice law, reorienting his life completely following marriage to Antonia de Otaola, a native of Llodio (Laudio, Araba), with whom he had two sons, Juan (1588) and Pedro (1589), the first of whom was a combative Jesuit polemicist whose writings were placed on the Index.

Poza spoke French, Latin, Flemish, English, and Italian, in addition to Castilian, Albanian, and presumably Euskara. He was educated, as mentioned, in law, mathematics, and cosmography. His knowledge of philology was very solid for his epoch, and he contributed keen observations in the field, among which was the discovery that Romanian was a Romance language. After his return to the Basque Country, he was the rector of several nautical schools in Bilbao and Donostia, and was highly regarded by the local authorities in these cities. During the last years of his life he obtained a post in the Castilian administration, that of Mayor of Illescas (Toledo). He died in Madrid, leaving a young widow and two young sons.

In addition to his fame as a cosmographer and role as apologist of the Basque language, Poza had a political profile of undeniable interest. In 1588, Juan García, Treasurer of the High Court of Valladolid, published a book (*De hispanorum nobilitate*, About the Nobility of Spaniards) in which he refuted the Basque claim to universal nobility. The Assemblies of Bizkaia decided to challenge him because the arguments formulated in the work affected a crucial point of the *foral* system. Among other authors, Poza was selected to reply to García either because of his reputation as a lawyer and intellectual or his *foral* knowledge; what is certain is that he was given the responsibility of writing a reply titled *Ad pragmaticas, sive de nobilitate* (For Non-Royal Proclamations, or About the Nobility) that remains unpublished. Poza's reply, as well as those by others, had the desired effect. In 1590, García's work was expurgated from the proceedings concerning Bizkaian nobility, and in 1591, the author retracted his refutation. Poza thus emerged as an intellectual in the service of the interests of the Seigniory of Bizkaia in the construction of the ideological complex of "universal nobility" that would be of such great benefit to the Basques in the political-administrative system of the Habsburg monarchy. The fundamental thesis defended by Poza was that the nobility of the realm of Bizkaia predated even the existence of the monarchs of Castile and was therefore not subject to Castilian law. This author constitutes an initial and important factor in the linkage between the defense of the language and the defense of specific *foral* privileges.

The work by Poza that is of interest to us here is, of course, *De la antigua lengua, populaciones y comarcas de las Españas* (Concerning the Old Language, Populations and Regions of the Spains) (1587). In addition, he also published his *Hydrografía la mas curiosa que hasta aquí ha salido a la luz, en que de mas de un derrotero general, se enseña la navegación por altura y derrota, y la del Este Oeste: con la Graduación de los puertos, y la navegación de Catayo por cinco vías diferentes* (The Most Curious Hydrography That, Up to This Point, Has Come to Light, In Which, More Than a General Voyage, Navigation is Explained by Height and by Course, and from East to West: With a Ranking of Ports, and the Navigation of Catayo Via Five Different Routes) (1585). He also left several unpublished manuscripts, such as *Ad Pragmaticas de Toro y Tordesillas, sive de nobilitate in proprietate* (For Non-Royal Proclamations by Toro y Tordesillas, or About the Propertied Nobility), in the Codice National Library of Madrid; and *De Prisca Hispanorum lingua in gratiam eorum qui nesciunt Hispaniae* (About the Ancient Spanish Language in Gratitude to Those Who Were Born in Spain) and *Memorial al Rey Felipe II pidiendo la revisión de las leyes que favorecieran la construcción de naos gruesas, por ser contrarias a la navegación en general*[1] (Report to King Felipe II Asking For a Revision of the Laws Favoring the Construction of Bulk Carriers, For Being Contrary to Navigation in General).

1. Reproduced in Estanislao Labayru, *Historia General de Bizcaya*, ed. Andrés Mañaricúa, vol. 4 (1895–1903; reprint, Bilbao: La Gran Enciclopedia Vasca, 1976), vol. 4, 595ff.

DELA ANTIGVA LEN-
GVA, POBLACIONES, Y CO-
marcas de las Españas, en que de paſo ſe tocan
algunas coſas de la Cantabria. Compueſto por
el Licéciado Andres de Poça natural de la ciudad de Orduña, y auogado en el muy
noble y leal Señorio de Vizcaya.
Dirigido a Dõ Diego de Auẽdaño y Gãboa, ſeñor delas
caſas de Vrquiçu, y Olaſſo, y dela villa de VillaReal y ſus
valles, y Balleſtero mayor del Rey nueſtro ſeñor. &c.

Con priuilegio real, Impreſſo en Bilbao por Mathias
Mares, primer impreſſor de Vizcaya. Año de 1587

Selected Text(s):

De la antigua lengua, poblaciones y comarcas de las Españas en que de paso se tocan algunas cosas de la Cantabria [Concerning the Ancient Language, Peoples, and Regions of the Spains in which Certain Matters Pertaining to Cantabria Are Discussed in Passing] (Bilbao: Matías Mares, 1587); reprint, as *Antigua lengua de las Españas* [Ancient Language of the Spains], ed. Ángel Rodríguez Herrero (Madrid: Minotauro, 1959), fols. 1–35.

Concerning the Ancient Language of the Spains

Chapter 1

Wherein it is shown by examples how place names reveal the nation and language of their original founders.

Anyone with knowledge of the Basque, Hebrew, and Greek languages, and also aware of the century in which the rivers, mountains, provinces, and oldest cities of these realms were named, will thereby realize which language predominated in each of the epochs in which these names were imposed. We intend to avail ourselves here of this line of reasoning, as did Flavius Josephus in his *Antiquities of the Jews* and Florián de Ocampo, in chapter 34 of his Book 3, not to mention that ordinary experience demonstrates its validity.

As this is one of the fundamental principles of our endeavor, it seems important to verify it definitively through argument and examples.

Seneca, in the book *Consolatione* (On Consolation), in one of the letters addressed to his mother, whose name was Albina [Helvia], dealing with the original inhabitants of the island of Corsica, where he was living in exile, says that, according to ancient legend, the Spanish populated it before the Gauls or other nations that inhabited it. And to confirm this opinion, he argues that the footwear, headgear, and many words used by those on the island were the same as those used in that time by the nations of Cantabria, in the region of the Ebro River. The reader should note here that our endeavor is partially validated by this observation of Seneca. The first point is that in Seneca's time the people of Cantabria had preserved and continued to use their clothing and original language from the times he calls ancient, which would have been at least a thousand years earlier, assuming that the Spains had not abandoned their native language until after the Greeks, Phoenicians, and Romans occupied their realm, which was in fact more than a thousand years before Seneca. The second conclusion derived from this letter of Seneca is that, although the other Spaniards from Ebro to Castile in that era had already changed or abandoned the clothing and language they used in ancient times, the nations of Cantabria had not yet abandoned either their clothing or their language; because if their language and clothing were the same as those of the Spains in general, Seneca would not have referred to the vocabulary, habits, and customs of the nations of Cantabria. Third, it is important that Seneca does not say that the island of Corsica was populated by the Cantabrians, but rather, somewhat mysteriously, by the ancient Spaniards, meaning, one would assume, that it must have been the Celt-Iberians and people from Tarraconensis along the entire coast from the Cape of Creus to the kingdom of Valencia, or because these were the closest, it certainly wouldn't have been the Cantabrians who populated Corsica (as Seneca testifies, because he would have said so), but rather other Spaniards from within the kingdom who in those ancient times (according to Seneca) used the clothing and language that had been preserved only in the province of Cantabria.

And that the ancient Spanish language was our own language from Bizkaia can be verified on the authority of Pomponius Mela, in the 3rd book, chapter 1 [of *De situ orbis*, "A Description of the World", c. 43–44], presupposing first (as we have said) that, in the time of the Roman emperors, many different nations had already entered these territories, and through their frequency and large numbers had introduced their language, rites, and ceremonies throughout the kingdom, although no further than the border of the province of Cantabria, because neither the Greeks nor the Carthaginians ever penetrated or conquered that province. And the second presupposition is that the names of the villages, provinces, and territories are connected to things that, except on rare occasions, seldom or never change. Proceeding from these two premises, we will discover that the aforementioned Pomponius Mela, in speaking of the cities of Cantabria, mentions two towns named Iturisa and Sauria, which are purely Basque names, as spoken in the Basque language today. Iturisa, or as it is written in Basque, *Ituriça*, means place with many springs. Sauria, or *Zçauria* [sic.] (because the Romans and Latins have no phonetic equivalent of our *ç*), means place of beating, cudgeling, hitting, and that because these two words, like the others of Cantabria, were so hard to write and pronounce in the Latin language, the above-mentioned Pomponius Mela says that, because its pronunciation was so difficult, he does not attempt to refer to the other places in that province. "*Et alia quoedam nomina, que ore nostro concipi nequeunt*" (And any other name that our speech does not understand). In this, he expressed a great truth, because to non-Basques, the pronunciation and writing of Basque is difficult because of the elongation and different pronunciation of the consonants and the way the vowels run together, so that in light of the description of this language, it is clear that this language, discussed by Pomponius Mela, really could not be any language other than contemporary Basque, in which the two words have a clear and simple meaning and significance. Strabo makes an equally curious linguistic observation when he attempts to describe the coast of Bizkaia, saying that it was hard to give names to those places. So the foregoing two examples of the names Iturisa and Sauria, not to mention those to be examined later, combined with the argument of Josephus and the authority of Seneca, will, I believe, provide some satisfaction to those with an average reading ability. For although it might be well known and accepted that those who inhabit and conquer territories impose names from their own language, we still want to have examples of this practice so that it will be more clearly accepted here, inside our kingdoms.

Toledo, in Hebrew, means "mother of people," and Zamora means "congregation of people"; *Zamorathi*, in the modern African language, means "place of white stones," and indeed there are many there and very good ones.

Salamanca, *Salamantica*, a Greek word, called *Elmantice* by Polibius and Stefano, means "prophetic song."

Asturias, from the Basque *astu*, *asturiá*, with a long *a*, means "province or region of forgotten villages," because *astu* means "forgotten," and *uriá* means "village or town." I'm well aware that some will argue that the Asturians derived their name from the Greek *Astur*; but this is more easily and more naturally derived from the language we are discussing, unless we concede what liars the Greeks were.

Emerita, the city we now call Mérida, means "place or dwelling of retired soldiers" in Latin.

Cantabria, as if to say *Cantabriga*, is composed of the two words *brigo* and *canto*, the first meaning "shelter" and "company," and from which the Castilians derive the word *abrigar* [to shelter, keep warm]; and it can be assumed that if the ancients used *brigas* to mean "enclosed cities," this was because of the shelter they provided to those living in them. Whereby we will say that *Cantabria*, *Cantabriga*, means, in the ancient Spanish Basque language, "shelter," "refuge," or "restoration," for those who live in the harshness of crags, cliffs, and mountains of this province, unlike other cities that are situated on the plains of the other provinces of these realms. And that *briga* is the ancient name of *Cantabria*, Florián de Ocampo acknowledges this in book 1, part I of chapter 7, where he writes: "Similarly, we will see in future books that when Emperor Flavius Vespasianus [Vespasian] decided to build a city in Spain beside the shore of the Bay of Biscay, they called it Flabiobriga, combining his name, Flavius, with the language of the region in which they referred to towns as *brigas*." Finally, regarding the fact that the Basque language is the maternal language of Spain, Pero Antón Beuter, Lucio Marineo Sículo, Mario Arecio, and the scholar Esteban de Garibay confirm it in their *Compendio Historial*. All of these, as well as other scholars of antiquities of these realms, agree that Basque was the ancient language of the Spains. But because Florián de Ocampo and Ambrosio de Morales have written in opposition to this, we wish to respond to their objections in the following chapter.

Chapter 2

In refutation of those who claim that the Basque language was not the ancient language of the Spains.

Florián de Ocampo does not indicate the basis of his argument because he did not reach the section he set aside for that purpose, and Ambrosio Morales advances only one argument to demonstrate that the Basque language was not the ancient language of the Spains, arguing that it could not be so because in the time of the Romans, the other Spaniards of these realms had different languages, which he confirms on the authority of Seneca, Cornelius Tacitus, and Strabo who, in regard to the languages of these kingdoms, provided written documentation that not all Spaniards used the same language. He also reports what Seneca writes about the Spanish orator Porcio Latrón, telling how eloquent he was in his own language, implying here how the Spaniards of his day had their native languages.

But this argument is very weak because we have to consider that more than nine hundred years before the era of Seneca, Quintilian, and Cornelius Tacitus (from whom Ambrosio de Morales derives his argument) a great number of different nations, such as the Lydians, Thracians, Rhodians, Phrygians, Phoenicians, Egyptians, Milesians, Carians, Lesbians, Phocians, Nebuchadnezzar the Great, and the Africans had invaded, inhabited, and established themselves as natives of these realms. All of these nations came here by the thousands and populated the villages and cities that have no awareness of either the Hebrew or the Basque languages. And this being so, as is well known, it's quite easy to understand that all these different nations, after almost a thousand years, could and did inhabit these kingdoms, each one with its own maternal language.

This is why in the time of the emperors and the authors mentioned by Ambrosio de Morales there were as many languages in Spain as they claim. Because, who can deny that the new arrivals, being almost infinite in number (as those who came here actually were) after a thousand years, would have established and imposed their own languages? Especially because all of these invading nations were sufficiently superior in number and power as to be able to inhabit as many villages and cities as has been written.

From this it can be inferred that, if in the time of Seneca and Quintilian there were different languages in Spain, as they say, the cause of this is what we have just expressed. But we are not claiming here, nor do we want to imply, that in the time of the Romans the Basque language was the common language of these kingdoms, although all these languages would have undoubtedly been greatly influenced by Basque; what we are trying to demonstrate is that it was the principal language before the aforementioned nations occupied these kingdoms. Thus, Ambrosio de Morales is writing about the time of the Caesars, whereas we are concerned with a period many centuries earlier, from the time of the Patriarch Tubal until the occupation by Greece and Egypt succeeded in obscuring and almost completely suppressing the mother tongue in many parts of these kingdoms so that it was only preserved in the Basque Country; I say almost completely because today in our Romance language we have many Basque words that the common people do not recognize as such, as will be shown below. And if there were any man who doubted this we could ask him if he thinks that the Spaniards of Castile and Andalusia were mute and without a language before the invasion here by the Greeks and others who followed them, or if, by chance, there were no inhabitants in all of Spain other than a few Basques. And because this hypothesis makes no sense and cannot be defended, it can be clearly argued that the mother tongue common to these realms was none other than the Basque language, although subsequently as many languages were introduced into the peninsula as there were nations occupying it. And presumably, this brought about a great admixture of words, some languages persevering, others fading out, and so it would have been especially with Egyptian and African, which became completely naturalized in Betica [Andalusia and southern Extremadura] and parts of Lusitania [most of contemporary Portugal and some parts of western Spain]. This can be demonstrated by an argument that seems quite probable to me. Because although it is indisputable that vast numbers of Greeks invaded these kingdoms and inhabited a great number of villages and cities, there is no trace or memory in Roman history that pure Greek was ever spoken here in all of those two hundred and more years of rivalry between the Romans and Carthaginians before the coming of Our Lord. Because, if during those centuries, any region of these realms had used the Greek language, even in a corrupted form, the Romans would not have refrained from celebrating and writing about it, especially because they had always been so admiring of it that only to Greece had they granted the full and complete freedom and use of their own language (as Quintilian writes) because of its polish and elegance. But because the Greek language was not and could not have been preserved in these kingdoms, this is an indication that it could make no headway against Basque, the earlier mother tongue, or that the Egyptians and Africans imposed their language in some of those regions where, according to Strabo, Seneca, and Quintilian, the language of Cantabria was not spoken, that is, evidently, the region south of the Guadiana from the Strait of Gibraltar as far east as Cartagena and Valencia; this can be verified by what Pliny wrote to Marcus [Terentius] Varro, claiming that the entire region of Betica was controlled by the African nations.

And thus, although in the period of Seneca and Quintilian there may have been two or three different languages other than Basque, what is certain, since none of them was Greek as we have already demonstrated, is that they could have been no other than those introduced by Nebuchadnezzar the Great and those of the Egyptians and Africans; so these could have been established in some regions of these kingdoms, mixing with the native Basque, and everywhere else the aforementioned Basque language survived and was preserved.

. . .

Chapter 5

Concerning the seventy-two languages of the confusion of Babel, and which of them were established in the Spains.

The Holy Scripture is so rich and elegant that it comprises not only the exact truth of history but also everything that can be conceived in the highest deliberations of theology, astrology, and philosophy, natural as well as moral.

In ancient times, the languages that were to span the surface of the earth were seventy-two, just as its entire circumference is surrounded by seventy-two celestial facets: thirty-six in the North and an equal number in the South. This is because six times twelve, a number comprising the elements, equals exactly seventy-two, which is exactly the number of the republic of twelve Tribes with six nations each. The reason for this number of languages, according to the secret theology, was as punishment of that number of major relatives who consented to the audacious Tower of Babel.

From Japheth and its elders two hundred nations emerged, divided into twenty-three different languages.

From Ham 394 peoples emerged, with twenty-two languages.

From Shem came 406 nations with twenty-six languages. Thus the number of languages is seventy-two, and the nations or peoples are one thousand, according to Arnobius in *Psalm* 104; Eucherius, in *Genesis*, book 2, ch. 7; Augustine, *De Civitate Dei*, in book 16, 63 and 21; and from these seventy-two languages the infinite number that we do not know emerged. And considering Europe alone, the languages spoken there are enumerated below, and this was the worst affliction that God visited on the world with the exception of the universal flood. Because men from whichever nation they come do not share a common language through knowledge and use (and it's impossible to learn all languages), they cannot travel even twenty days from their own country without finding themselves mute because they do not understand the language of the adjoining region.

The languages generally used in Italy, Spain, France, and Walachia [Romania] were derived from Latin.

The languages spoken generally in the Attic, Ionian, Aeolian, and Doric regions, as well as the mixed languages currently spoken in Greece, were derived from Greek.

The language used by the Germans, Flemish, Swabians, Danes, Goths, Finnish-Lapps, and Austrians was derived from the Cimbrian language, and although some adhere more closely to it than others, it is still possible for them to understand each other somewhat.

The Poles, Bohemians, and Muscovites derive their languages from Slavic.

The Basque language is spoken in the provinces of Bizkaia, Gipuzkoa, Navarre, the land of Araba, and Gascony.

Breton is spoken in Brittany.

Etruscan was, following Hebrew, the first language of Italy, and with the [rise of the] Latin nations, it was completely lost.

Irish is from Ireland and it extends as far as the Hebridean Islands.

In England, they speak Cornish, Welsh and English, and the latter is made up of the following four languages: Cornish, Welsh, Flemish, and French.

Albanian is the language of Albania, formerly called Epirus, which is that part of Greece bordering on Apulia [Puglia] and Calabria, and this is a language distinct from Slavic, although the Albanians use both, as I was informed by the Albanian cavalrymen who served Our Majesty the King in the states of Flanders in the year 1576.

In France, in addition to the common language, there are four others: Gascon, Auvergnat, Provençal, and Breton.

In Italy, in addition to the general language, there is Piedmontese; the other languages are dialects that are more or less confined to one region, although for the most part, speakers of one dialect can be understood by those who speak another.

In our Spain, in addition to the Hebrew spoken everywhere, there was Basque, one of the pure languages of the Confusion, and the third language was Greek, then Phoenician, African, and Latin, and in the seventh place a few Gothic words found their way into the language; finally, the Arabs naturalized their language as far north as the mountains.

All of these languages were established in these kingdoms, creating a kind of salad in terms of vocabulary, neither pure Basque nor pure Latin. Some of these languages prevailed in one part of the peninsula, others elsewhere. The Greeks and Egyptians imposed their languages on the coasts as well as in the interior, as will be shown below:

The Phoenicians, from the Strait of Gibraltar to the source of the Guadiana River; and the Africans in the provinces bordering their coast, leading Marcus Terentius Varro to write that the Andalusians were descendants of the Africans. The Romans imposed their language on the entire kingdom, except for the province of Cantabria, achieving this through the maintenance of extensive military encampments. And if the Cantabrian nations were occupied by the Roman forces, it was not permanent, because their language was not changed by the language the Romans imposed on the other regions they controlled.

Chapter 6

Regarding the Kings, rivers, regions, and towns with Basque names

As the numbers of the Basque people from Armenia and the plains of Sumer began to multiply, their language gradually began to supplant Hebrew until its use and even its memory vanished completely, all of which could be verified through the names of the Spanish kings who ruled after King Gera, the eighth king of the Spains, as follows:

If Hercules, surname Luabis, was from Cimbric Chersonese [Chersonesus Cimbrica], which is Denmark and the surrounding area, as [Johannes] Goropius Becanus claims in his *Origines* [*Antwerpianae, The Origins of Antwerp*, 1569], Hercules has the same meaning in the northern language as *Luabis* in Basque. Because the word probably referred to that unnatural sexual potency described by Higinius, whereby beyond all credibility he deflowered in one night, not with all fifty virgins as has been written but at least most of them, such excess causing him to be given the name *Hercules*, *Hërencul*, abbreviated *Hërcul*: which in Flemish and German indicates what its corresponding name Luabis means in Basque, *aluabiz*, referring implicitly to the virility and size of his sexual organ. But if this idea seems indecorous and we would prefer a simpler and more honest interpretation, then it could mean "prince," "landowner," or "Lord of a region"; because the name *Lu*, or *Lurra*, means "land," and *abiz* denotes "concession" or "permission for a thing to be." This same Hercules was called Heracles by the Greeks (who have generally claimed him as theirs), making use of a similar word. And thus, *Heracles* in Greek means "a man famous in armed combat."

Some say that King Hesperus was an African. If so, he could have been either a native of the people from the Berber coast who settled there, or he could have been of Spanish descent, because it is quite common for kings who win power in foreign lands through inheritance or election to ascend to power using their ancestral name. And this name Hesperus, although no one has pointed this out, seems to be purely a Basque name, and not Latin or Greek. Because in Basque *Espero* means "lack of excessive heat," which is the late afternoon called *vespers* in Latin, most likely without knowing why, just as in Basque. Hence, the word *bero*, *beroa*, means "heat" in Basque, and if we add *es*, then we understand it to mean "the opposite of heat," or heat which has recently declined. And from this ancient Basque word the people of Italy derived the word vespers, and therefore they named the planet Venus *Hesperus* because it's like a star that resembles a sun, but already low on the horizon. Farmers, shepherds, and sailors call it Hesperus or the planet Venus, or by the name *lucero* [bright star], either because it shines so much that it casts a shadow, unlike any other planet or star except the sun or moon, or because this *lucero*, when it has set in conjunction and then emerges from it after a few days, shines very bright, even before the dawn, before daylight.

Noraco, without any alteration, is a purely Basque word, and it was the name of a nephew of the Geryons who, although he courageously supported his uncles, had to retire finally to Sardinia where he founded the city of this name [medieval Nugoro, modern-day Nuoro]. This word *noraco* represents "person who is confident or determined" when the occasion demands, and to this day, if we ask if someone is very determined, *noraco* is the word we use.

. . .

Chapter 12

Wherein it is demonstrated that the Basque language is no less substantial and philosophical than the most elegant languages of Europe.

A language is regarded as excellent when the nouns themselves reveal their derivation as well as the quality and definition of the thing named, this being the subject of the argument between Plato and Cratylus as to whether names were given by chance or by divine intervention, because in languages that can be called elegant, substantial, and philosophical we will find, not only the indication but also the meaning and definition of the thing being named; but in languages that are not like this, but are mixed and imperfect, we will find nothing but the names alone, with no mystery to resolve except that the thing was so named, in which case, we can say that such a language was and is completely casual.

For because the works of God are always the product of supreme knowledge, it necessarily follows that the seventy-two languages of Babel, having emanated from God, would undoubtedly be profoundly elegant so that, as would be entirely reasonable, there could be no idle word or syllable lacking its mystery. Because who could doubt that a difference so artful as to allow no confusion between one word and another, or one face with another, or between animals of the same species—that such an absolutely remarkable and mysterious creation, the product of divine knowledge, could be anything less than perfect and complete. From this we must draw two conclusions: first, that in each of the languages of Babel, the noun itself reveals to us a cause or hidden property for the thing to be so named; and second, that the noun that lacks such cause or hidden property is accidental, adulterated, casual, and unnatural to that language.

. . .

I believe that through these few examples, out of the many I could provide, I have shown that a language is superior to the extent that its words are mysterious, because it is clear that the language that reveals the definitions and properties of things has spirit, soul, and doctrine, and by a single path teaches the simple man and the wise man the nature of the thing without further mastery or study; but the language that lacks all or part of this is patently imperfect, simply indicating the thing it seeks to name in the driest way, without further substance or information about the thing.

Of these languages that can be called perfect and elegant, Basque is one of the seventy-two languages that were divinely imparted. And it is noteworthy to observe that God made it no less perfect than the others that were brought to Europe. It may well be that God wanted to distribute the languages according to the happiness of the sky and soil of the province for which it was destined and that for this reason he gave Spain one of the best.

If we can demonstrate this, as I hope to do with a few of many words that could be offered, perhaps from this day forth it will be apparent that the Basque language is not barbarous or deficient as some claim but is deep with mystery and no less elegant in form and substance than the others spoken in Europe.

The Basque language refers to almighty God as *Jeaun* [*jaun*], in a syncopated syllable in which each of the vowels is pronounced as if it were but one syllable, the word signifying in Basque "thou who art good in thyself," which is without doubt the most exalted and succinct sentence that could possibly denote the attributes of God, who is three in one. This elegance offers confirmation that, because nothing can be pronounced nor any concept be demonstrated without the five vowels, thus in this name *Jeauna*, which is composed of the five vowels, we have proof that neither form nor matter can exist without that God who created all things.

Greek refers to God as *Theos*, imitated by the Latins, Spanish, Italians and French in the names *Deus, Dios, Idio,* and *Dieu*, and if we ask why he was so named, there are but two possible explanations: either because *theaeín* means "contemplation" in Greek or because *theastai* refers to "the velocity with which the heavens move."

Those in the North call God *Godt*, which is derived from *Guet* or *Goet*, meaning "highest good par excellence."

Only Hebrew even comes close to competing with Basque in this designation, conjoining the singular or plural forms of a word, for at times the Holy Scripture says *el hoim*, meaning "makes" and on other occasions *el hoim*, meaning "make." Here the mystery of the divinity is expressed, the singular form competing equally with the plural; but Basque with no additional diction or supplement clearly and elegantly reveals the Holy Trinity, the tri-syllable pronounced with syncopation denoting the Trinity quintessentially as principle in itself that never fails and can never fail because the *i* denotes that "only God has being," whereas the second vowel shows that this being is self-generated, and the third bountiful diphthong *ú* (*on* – "good" in Basque) manifests "the highest good and highest felicity of the visible and the invisible."

Let us now consider the sun, the most illustrious creation of visibility, and we will find that only in Basque does it reveal its essence, enhanced by a most succinct emphasis: *Eguzguia, Egusgueya* [*eguzkia*], signifies "look, behold the principle, the foundation, the creation, the evocation of beginning of the day;" because all of this is implied in these brief and substantial syllables of the word *Eguzgueia*; for although in Latin, Castilian, Italian, and French the sun is enhanced in the excellence of its unrivalled and unequaled solitude, this is surpassed in Basque by its more philosophical and substantial etymology because in Latin and the languages derived from it, all that is manifested is what everyone can see and know: that there is but one sun, that the sun is unique; but Basque in its admirable complexity demonstrates that it is the source of light and brightness in this universe.

Those in the North call the sun *sonne*, signifying "the health proffered by the warmth and gentleness of its rays." The Greeks call it *Helios* and *oulios*, according to Strabo and Macrobius. And according to Apollodorus, they also call it *Jeios*, with the same meaning as in the North; so clearly, no other language paints it as vividly as the Basque language.

Irarguia [*ilargia*], in Basque, means "moon," the etymology signifying "dead light," "borrowed light and brightness," which is exactly what it is, and here we see the image of a mirror in which the brightness and light it receives from the sun is reflected toward us, as Macrobius describes it in *Scipio's Dream*. The Latins call it *luna*, abbreviating the word *lucina*, which means "something that brightens and illuminates." The Greeks call it *selini*, which indicates the "ordinary newness and renewal of its light." The Northerners call it *Mane*. However, if we look at the Basque word, we will see that it incorporates the astronomical doctrine of a thing that has no light or brightness of its own, but borrows it from the sun, which is the beginning and foundation of the world's light, an elegance lacking in the other languages, which only represent what everyone can see and know of it.

Eriotcea [*heriotza*], in Basque, means "death," and it signifies "blow, wound, or cold accident," encapsulating a succinct philosophical essence. Because coldness is the enemy of generation and life, and old age perishes in this coldness, this word spells out its opposition to the warmth, heat, or prevailing moistness necessary to maintain life so that we understand what death is. *Mors* in Latin, *Thanatos* in Greek, *doot* in the language of the North—these mean "death," plain and simple, with no deeper mystery, except that the Northern word does indicate that "death is a resolution or liquefaction of humors."

By way of these few examples, of the many that could be offered, in demonstration of the highest truths of the universe, the Spanish nations should now be able to appreciate the elegance of their first language, before the Romans, Carthaginians, or Greeks ever entered these kingdoms, and how this language, which has been preserved in Cantabria and survives even today, is based on a most profound philosophy of essential meanings, and that such a language is not and could never be considered barbaric, as some declare simply because they do not know or understand it.

8. Baltasar de Echave Orio, known as "el Viejo"
(the Elder), (Oikina, Gipuzkoa, 1548 – Mexico, ?)

He emigrated to Mexico in the 1570s and there became one of the most prestigious painters of his epoch, being considered the founder of Spanish-Mexican painting. He was known as "el Viejo" (the Elder) to distinguish him from his son, "the Younger." His most famous painting was the altar of the Jesuits in Mexico and especially his "Adoration of the Magi." He also studied law and in 1606 became a judge in the Royal High Court in Mexico. An intellectual interested in a number of topics, concerning the Basque language he wrote the apology titled *Discursos de la lengua Cántabra-Bascongada compuestos por . . .* (Discourses on the Cantabrian-Basque language composed by . . .) (1607). Despite the fact that his contemporaries regarded him primarily as a famous painter, he has gone down in posterity more because of his single literary work. Nonetheless, he seemed to have no doubt about his dual role, because in *Discursos de la lengua* his self-portrait is engraved holding a brush as well as a pen, bordered by an inscription that alludes to this double vocation: "*Patriae et penicillum et calamum utroqueae artifex D.D.*" (The artifice of, or made by, D.D., for the land of penicillin and calamum).

Echave's mode of address in the *Discursos* is original, consisting of a speech spoken in the first person by the Basque language itself; a language that has been marginalized, forgotten, insulted, and who addresses songs of praise describing its excellent qualities both to its own speakers and to the rest of Spain, which bears a certain responsibility for its preservation, it being its first language. As a new emigrant to America, it has the opportunity to come in contact with the indigenous linguistic reality and in particular with the toponymy existing there, which reinforces in Basque the idea that all peoples give names to their rivers, cities, mountains, and so on in their own language and not in some other, and that as these names endure in time they speak to us of the first inhabitants of those places. Echave proceeded, therefore, in the same line of argument and interpretation as Garibay and Poza. An avowed Tubalist, he set out to interpret Babylonian terms, such as *Senaar* (Sumer) (male field), by way of the Basque language, defending of course the connection between Caucasian Iberia and Western Iberia, and illustrated through a series of toponyms that were presumably shared: Ararat = Aralar, Gordeya = Gorbeia, Armenia = Araxes. He argued that the Basque language extended all across the Iberian Peninsula, basing his proof on a series of toponyms: Setubal, Ybarra, and Celtiberia, for example. He regarded the entire region between the Pyrenees and Asturias (including Castile) as Cantabrian, with Bizkaia and Gipuzkoa being the zones that were most specifically Cantabrian, the "armory" of Spain. According to Echave, the Basque language would have been, after the arrival of Tubal, the only language spoken in the peninsula, but after a "long drought" that afflicted Spain, and with it the arrival of Celts and other peoples, Basque receded toward Castile and Cantabria. But the worst was yet to come, for after the war between the Carthaginians and Romans and the defeat of the former, the latter proceeded to extend the language of the Empire by force. Thus, according to Echave, the emperor Octavian issued a decree prohibiting the use of Basque, and this was enforced even more rigorously during the reign of his successor, Hadrian. In this way, part of ancient Cantabria (Asturias, the mountains, and part of Navarre) abandoned the Basque language, leaving its use confined to Bizkaia and Gipuzkoa. Two of Echave's arguments concerning Roman domination in the peninsula seem to contradict one another: on one hand, the obvious policy of Latin linguistic implantation as a vehicle of imperial articulation and on the other, the claim that Cantabria retained its independence from Rome and was in fact an ally. If the second claim was true, how could the policy of linguistic colonization have been derived from the first? For Echave, Castilian was derived from Basque, so that when the Castilians expressed themselves in "that courtly language they admired so greatly" they were merely speaking in the old Basque language that had been corrupted following Latin penetration. He offered a series of related Basque and Castilian terms in support of this, although without proving or even making it clear which borrowed from which. He regarded Castilian as a "foreign" language in Cantabria, but because it was derived from Basque, he did not disapprove of Basques knowing Castilian, because it was a way of better understanding and knowing their own Basque language. This was an ambivalent posture, but in a certain way, consistent with the basic premises of his argument.

Setting aside the inexact conclusions, errors, and myths into which Echave often fell, the vindicating force of his work is undeniable. Pained by the discredit into which the language had fallen, he defended its elegance and capacity for written expression and could not understand the oblivion and marginalization to which it was subjected; not by foreigners, but by its own sons. Echave concluded with a fascinating argument relative to the conservation and cultivation of the Basque language, and largely autobiographical: the fault for the loss and forgetfulness of the language was due to the greed of Basques who, seeking to enrich themselves quickly, emigrated in large numbers to the Indies, where they lost their Basque identity. Few returned, and those who did had lost their language, and their heads were more focused on their American interests than in adjusting to the life and culture of their country. Was Echave speaking from personal experience regarding the difficulties in speaking Basque following a prolonged residence in Mexico? What is certain is that his work was composed and published in beautiful Castilian and that its author was all too familiar with the phenomenon of Basques abandoning their language and shedding their Basque identity once they were in the Indies. Moreover, Echave developed some of the ideas already expressed by Zaldibia and which, by this point at the beginning of the seventeenth century, were commonplace in Gipuzkoa: the secular independence of Cantabria, never conquered by the Romans, Visigoths, or Saracens; a place therefore inhabited by the same progeny since the time of Tubal, maintaining the same language and professing the true religion from that period, without the slightest contamination by heathens. There was no mixing with foreign blood or foreign laws or government. The egalitarian and legal ideology was founded as much on the values of purity of blood as on linguistic purity; both values would travel hand in hand down through the centuries.

SELECTED TEXT(S):

Discursos de la lengua Cántabra-Bascongada compuestos por . . . Introducese la misma lengua, en forma de una Matrona venerable y anciana, que se quexa, de que siendo ella la primera q. se habló en España, y general en toda ella la ayan olvidado sus naturales, y admitido otras Extranjeras. Habla con las Provincias de Gipuzcoa y Bizkaia, que le han sido fieles, y algunas vezes con la misma España [Discourses on the Cantabrian-Basque Language Composed by . . . The Language Herself Appears in the Form of an Ancient and Venerable Matron Who Complains that, although She Was the First Language in Spain and Common to the Entire Peninsula, Her Native Speakers Have Forgotten Her and Accepted Other Foreign Languages. She Speaks to the Provinces of Gipuzkoa and Bizkaia, Who Have Been Faithful to Her, and At Times to Spain Herself] (Mexico: Henrrico Martínez, 1607), Prologue, 5–11, 17–18, 40–42, 56–59, 64–69, 82–85.

Prologue to the Reader

There has never been a historian or chronicler in our Spain unwilling to admit that the Basque language spoken today in Navarre, Bizkaia, and Gipuzkoa was one of the first to be spoken in Spain, and although there is no reason to claim that it was not the universal language of the entire peninsula, few of them are willing to acknowledge that it was. Instead, they have chosen to put together hypotheses implying that it never extended beyond the provinces where it is spoken today, these being utterly unconvincing to anyone with knowledge of the matter; and there are far more substantial and compelling proofs that it was not only the first language but the universal and common language throughout Spain. The reason for these being so hidden and occult to many for so many years was simply that no one even tried to understand it well, regarding it as an inferior, barbaric language, impossible to pronounce, even its native speakers dismissing it, not of course because they didn't understand it, as something abandoned because it was useless and of no value. Basing their conclusions on such evidence, our historians have succumbed to the many myths shrouding the language concerning the names of cities and provinces of our Spain and its origins, attributing everything to foreigners of whom they have always been so fond. This respect and great love I feel for my country and my language—and not any presumption that I am endowed with sufficient knowledge and genius—are what have forced me, curious reader, to take up my pen in defense of the ancient Spanish language, so as to inspire its sons, many far more qualified than I, to undertake a task and matter so urgent, conferring on her the status it deserves before the earth buries it in oblivion, it being the first language, as will be shown in these treatises, and every bit as perfect and elegant as the romance language spoken in Spain, having no need to beg words from any other foreign languages for adornment. This being so, there is no reason for a language that does honor to all of Spain to be cast into oblivion because of the lack of curiosity and awareness by Basques, and because it is natural for all nations to respect their native language, as they do, it is most appropriate that Spain consider herself honored by a language so much her own and having so many specific features useful and honorable to our true Spanish nation. Because if conjectures merit any credit and authority, regarding ancient Spain none are as clear and true for our purpose as those to be found through a clear understanding of the Basque language, reinforced by what we see today in the settling of provinces and founding of cities and in the corruption and alteration of languages and words that took place in the New World of the Indies. All of this provides an example and vivid portrait of what happened long ago in the Old World, and especially in Spain and her provinces. This can be proved by the all-wise King Solomon in the first chapter of *Ecclesiastes* (. . . what has been is what will be, and what has been done is what will be done . . .) and what I want most of all, and with particular affection, and what all Basques should want, is for someone to make an effort to follow this path that has been so hidden and to make it obvious and plain to all those who are curious and would want to go there and see for themselves, for I am quite certain that they would discover very specific things, worthy of remembrance, which I have not personally been able to uncover for reasons that have prevented me from doing so. I have not chosen to cite the sources where the names of rivers, mountains, and cities could be found, which I mention in these Discourses, so as not to confuse the order of the narration I follow in them, and anyone who wishes to find them can do so in Titus Livius, Strabo, Pomponius Mela, Ptolemy, and other ancient and modern authors; and there are two points to consider, the first being that not all of these authors name them with the same pronunciation (as will be discussed in due time), leading to much confusion and obscurity for those who do not know the Basque language, and therefore this point is repeated a number of times; the second point, is that many of the names that are translated into Basque in these *Discourses* might bear great resemblance to Basque except for the extraordinary rigor of their etymology and true denomination which we apply to the names of the towns, houses, mountains, and rivers that we have in our Cantabria, and if it seemed to some curious Basque that in the place where he was born, or in his native province, a different interpretation and meaning could be given to some of the things to be found in these *Discourses*, he should be aware of the variety in pronunciation of many names and words used in the provinces where the Basque language is spoken, whereupon it will be clear that we chose the most appropriate and significant to illustrate our intent.

Chapter 2

Concerning the Origins of the Basque Language and the Earliest Inhabitants of Spain

One hundred and forty-three years after the universal flood, when the arrogance of that first tyrannical king named Nimrod had grown and his accomplices were trying to construct the famous tower named Babel, and at the height of their efforts the Creator of all things, Almighty God, chose and ordained the humbling of their pride with a wondrous artifice: confusing them with many strange languages that all those builders of the proud construction suddenly began to speak to each other without any common language among them. I was born with the rest of my sisters on the plains of Sumer which in my language means "male field," where I was chosen by the Patriarch Tubal and his family who were imprisoned there by the power of the tyrant, and they named me *Guçuzera*, which in vernacular romance means the same as "ours" or "in our manner." At less than fifteen years after my birth, my father and his family ordered the long pilgrimage and journey to these very remote parts of Spain, about which his grandfather Noah had given him a thorough account, so that before and after the flood during a period of more than 141 years that had passed, he knew about its region and its western territory, that being the westernmost end and limit of this part of the known earth, and making his decision to go there because his families were growing larger and because as a good and faithful man he disapproved of the tyrannies and superstitions that were increasing among some of his relatives, abandoning the true way that Saint Noah had taught them. Having ordered the journey and gathered provisions for it, accepting the blessing of the Holy Patriarch Noah, he departed with his entire family and herds of cows and sheep and other domestic animals in numbers he thought were sufficient to start the new population of the region of Spain where they were going, leaving behind their natural and beloved country of Armenia, not without tears among those left behind, because although even with the differences in languages, they were very closely related to each other; where we left, among others, four famous relics of my language, which are Armenia, Gordeya; Arage, and Ararat, or Aralar, similar to another to which we gave the same name in this Cantabria, meaning "pastureland" and "mountain in which cattle are raised," and Gordeya, which is where Noah's ark came aground, meaning "the one who watches" or "the one to whom the watch is entrusted."

Arriving after many days at the coast of the desired Spain, in those parts adjoining France along the eastern sea, and having disembarked we settled there to begin our blessed habitation in the place now called Colibri [Colibre] in Catalonia, to which I gave the name Ulibarri or Erriberri, which means "new land," as it was at that time. And feeling the desire to take respite and rest from the long voyage for which we were not accustomed, although we went from island to island and from coast to coast, finding it quite gentle and pleasant, not worrying about going further for a few days, attracted to it by the fertility and warmth of the land which we found very much to our taste with an abundance of fruits, herbs, and plants that we saw on all the mountains where we passed some time, and we finally arrived in these provinces of Cantabria, where we established our settlement with greater comfort. Here we populated almost all the heights of the mountains, where we found the nourishment we needed without having to exert ourselves. Here in sweet memory and remembrance of our beloved country Armenia, we gave names to some regions which seemed to us to have great similarity and likeness to those we left behind: in particular, the fertile mountains of Gordeya, and that of Aralar, and the river Arage, and Armenia itself which means rocky mountain, with other places and territories whose names are still preserved with little corruption in these provinces of ours, much to my honor. Scattering the herds through all the regions they found most suitable and natural to them, their numbers increased greatly, especially the goats and pigs from which they later began to make dried meat, which was the first agricultural product traded by our people.

In those days, the disposition of this land was very different from what it is now because it was entirely uninhabited by men and wild animals, and because the soil was fertile for the flora growing there naturally with the constant rains brought by the breezes from the northern sea, it was covered with thick forests and groves, which even now are quite abundant, providing the timber needed for all the ships they build each day; and it would be more abundant if they were not cut down to build the ships and the infinite ironworks in the region. The forests were so thick that the valleys were uninhabitable by men, and there were so many birds of every variety that their music gave us great happiness and their flesh was delicious. All the peaks were covered with beech trees, whose fruit, along with hazelnuts, walnuts, and acorns, was an extraordinary gift to us until we began to produce dried meat; and with all the smoke from the herd, as I have said, some of the valleys began to be stripped of trees, opening paths where people could walk down to populate comfortable sites and places, and so it is that they have remained there until this day, as you can see by the names whose etymology and meaning is quite clear for you in my language, and I wish this were apparent to those who write the chronicles so that they would finally realize that I am the first to inhabit these regions and the first whose language Spain knew, as you will see more clearly below. This is what I wish to demonstrate, because it is quite obvious and clear that no nation ever gave names to its towns and places in a foreign language, and as for the things whose purpose and nature are clearly explained by the common name that they have in the language that is used in the same land, there is no reason to look for them in a different and foreign language, causing them to be foreign for all time, and if the thing is not understood or its purpose and nature known in the language that is spoken, it's obvious that the name is corrupt or the thing or its name are not natural to that land, and this is how we can know whether things are natural to the Indies or brought there from Spain, because the latter are referred to by the Indians by the names used by the Spaniards, so that the horse that they did not have was called *cavallo*, and the bull, *toro,* and the ram, *carnero,* and so forth. And it was the same with the Spaniards with the things that were unknown to them even allowing for great corruption, so they could barely understand the names of the things that were native, because the character of a thing is quite obvious from its name, especially regarding the locations of their towns and other territories and mountains; so it seems quite evident that those were named by the original inhabitants of those provinces. And the same is true in our own country, where the primitive names that our ancestors gave things have been preserved with extraordinary integrity and clarity, for if we observe carefully, we find something very important: how very ancient I am, which cannot be denied, no other language in Spain having preference for its antiquity. And additionally, I have been preserved with such singularity and purity that no other language of all the nations that have surrounded me in these mountains have corrupted or affected me in any way, a truth so surprising that some modern historians have refused to accept it.

. . .

Whereby you can and should see that I am not as barbaric and worthless as some writers claim simply because they do not understand me and because they note that there are no written texts in my language, which they attribute entirely to my crudeness and brevity, this being true to a certain extent, as I lack some of the adornment and elegance of others that are bedecked and spoken as if the truth could not be painted naked: by this I mean that I am not inferior to another language simply because I choose to preserve the true meaning of things with less adornment of words, just so what is crucial is clearly and perfectly expressed through the words I do say; and if there are no written texts, this isn't because I should not or could not be written and proclaimed throughout the world, as I once was, nor because I cannot be expressed with all the resources essential to the perfection of rhetoric, but rather because (as I will explain shortly) the Roman emperors tried to banish me from the world as they did with so many other languages of Spain and other countries, their arrogance and hostility toward me being intense although I had done nothing against them but bring glory to their Rome and their Italy with excellent cities and distinguished families that even today still exist there to my great glory and their confusion, and if you doubt this, consider *Urbina* and *Urbieta*, which they call *Urbino* and *Urbieto*, so appropriately named by me that their name clearly declares precisely what they mean, the confluence of two waters, an apt description of their ancient settlements Metola and Mirandula in Italy, and the ancient city of Sarausa, which in Sicily today is today called Çaragoça, whose names, as you know very well, have also been given to some towns and places here in Cantabria. The families too are distinguished and renowned, one in particular, the Colonas, conferring great prestige on Rome, just as those from Oria bring honor to Genoa, and the Gambaras, Savelos, and Arbeztain families whose noble and ancient ancestors were called the Coloneses by our sons, praised and honored even today by acknowledging their origins in the very ancient Villa [municipality] of Hernani, according to information provided by the Bishop Urbieta, a native of the same villa who was raised in Italy.

. . .

Seven hundred and twenty four years passed between the death of Geryon and that of Avidis, during which a great many and diverse things occurred in Spain, which would be impossible for me to recount, nor are they important to me except as sad reminders of malicious and grievous wounds I suffered. Suffice it to say that with the diversity of nations that came to your provinces and with the conflicts that afflicted them, great changes befell the region, in languages as well as customs and other matters, so that I scarcely recognized it or it me. And thus I was besieged, abandoned and persecuted, until another calamity came from the hand of almighty God that made me and everyone else in Spain forget what had happened before: this was a period of years so hot and dry that there was hardly a river or spring that did not dry up or any herds or people who did not die. Only in these mountains of ours and their long cordillera that extends all the way to the end of Spain, which is in Galicia, and all along its steep slopes that fall into the northern sea, were the herds and people saved, the continuous breezes from the sea that runs beside them sending mists over the highest mountains, which seemed like a wall raised up against the water so that it could not reach the land in the interior. An infinite number of people took refuge in the coolness of these mountains of ours that are little known or respected. And thus, beyond this barrier of which I spoke, my ancient language vanished completely from Spain from this moment on, as did that which all those various peoples and nations had brought there from outside Spain. Therefore, I had great hopes that my Glory would be reborn, bringing to mind that ancient proverb or refrain of mine that says: *Bataren gaytçaz, Besteac ona*, which in Romance means: "Something good comes from every evil." But it did not turn out like that for me; quite the contrary, because as the drought extended over a period of years, exactly how long I cannot say because there was no drought in the region where I was spoken, although from what they say it lasted for twenty-five years. And because there was no longer any province anywhere on the globe so remote that did not have complete information about Spain and her fertility and abundance of gold and silver, that even among savages was now esteemed and desired, no sooner did they learn of the fair weather and prosperity than, one after another, so many and such diverse nations came that it made invasions of former times seem insignificant. Thus, within a few years all of Spain was inhabited once again, by new peoples, especially the cities and villages that were well known from before and famous, to which many of those who had first inhabited them returned. I did the same thing with my children, in the places that seemed best to me, although not with the great authority I had once had; because I was not compatible with any of the languages that were spoken or with any of those that came to be spoken afterwards either in Spain or outside. I have no affinity or kinship with any other language, which is astonishing to many. And it's enough to observe that I alone have maintained my purity and ancientness in this corner of Spain, although at the time I am telling you about other provinces that I have mentioned recognized me, Aragón and Old Castile retaining many of my nouns and words as I will demonstrate below, offering evidence that I was spoken throughout Spain if what I've already described has not convinced you.

. . .

And because of the extraordinary reputation of the Cantabrian nation in Rome, many of the senators and the people were friendly with our people although the emperor's guards were almost all Basques as were those of his uncle Julius Caesar, although they had dressed in Roman uniforms, and not like those mentioned previously who went to Rome with their own weapons and ordinary clothing and their own footwear, which they call *abarkas* [a type of low-cut leather shoes], still worn today in our villages and designed originally in the Pyrenees mountains and by some of my very ancient inhabitants in the Basque Country of France where today there are almost no houses, a place writers called Basconcio and the natives called *Bascogne*, which means "people of the mountains or forests," which the people of those regions and all the provinces of Navarre called Basque, and my language Basque. In the same region today they wear another kind of shoe very similar to *abarkas*, except that they are made of wood. The swords that our people used in those days were few and of poor quality because they had not then discovered the way to forge iron as skillfully as in later years, as can be seen from all the places and towns in these provinces that we call Olea, which means "forge," such as *Olaçaval, Olaverria, Çuazola, Gaviola, Mendiola, Egurrola, Balçola, Loyola*, and so many others it would be tiresome to mention them, most of which were places with anvils where iron was forged by hand and not with the novel technique of water power which in our century is used to such advantage and profit. Many of our people moved their farms down to the banks of the rivers by order of the Roman Emperor, so that many families who were very ordinary and common in ancient times ended up being very distinguished and wealthy.

Finally, concluding my sad story, although the bloody war that was being waged against our children ended, there was no let up in my persecution and humiliation; because in the same period when they were beginning to enjoy some relief and rest from their long travails; in Rome, my complete destruction and the final calamity that could have befallen me was ordered by way of an edict the Emperor Octavian ordered to be distributed throughout Spain (although, as was later apparent, it did not take effect until the reign of his successor Hadrian) decreeing that none of the languages that until then had been spoken in general or in any region of Spain were to be spoken; nor was it permitted for anyone to write in any language except Romance, or Latin. This led to my abandonment even by my native speakers, who were the Asturians, and the Aragonese, and the Navarrese from the mountains; and the few who still speak me are fewer every day, and I have lost my former value and worth, all through the fault of my legitimate children who should have preserved me without allowing them to discredit me ignorantly as many, many are doing, affirming that my language is incapable of being written or explained, and that I am incapable of declension or any elegance at all, all of which is utterly false as is proven by clear evidence, because in my language, those who understand me write me as much as they want, and to prove to you that this is so, I want to explain to you the Ave Maria as the Bishop of Pamplona with divine inspiration has ordered that it be taught in these provinces, side by side with the Christian doctrine which always until these times had been taught in Latin and Romance.

—*Ave Maria, Graciaz betea, jauna da çurequin, Vedeicatua cera, Andre guztien artean, Vedeicatua dà, cure Savel Virginaleco fructua, Iesus, sancta Maria, jaun goicaoren amà, erregu eçaçu gugatic, çerrenguera Vecatariac, eguinbidi ala* [The Ave Maria in Basque].

With equal facility, anything else could be written and pronounced in my language, which is a certain argument that my words are capable of being declined and that everything necessary for human life can be written and expressed in me with the same polish and elegance as in all other languages, and even if the Romance speakers they call Castilians want to consider this point they will find that in their courtly language which they so greatly esteem, they speak many of my words with the same letters and significance that I understand, speak, and pronounce them, and to warn my children of the harm that it caused them so that they would refrain from speaking it when it was introduced into Spain they called it *Herdeera*, which means "foreign," as it truly was then for me more than all the others. Hence, it can be inferred that all those who formerly spoke in Spain already had more affinity and kinship with me than with the most ancient and original language, so all that is left to do is to inform you which of my nouns are to be found in Romance, although to avoid tiresomeness and prolixity, I present only these few examples that are undeniably mine and not from any other language, as their etymology, derivation, pronunciation, and meaning demonstrate, these few having been preserved among the infinite others that were formerly mine; and in Spain they have abandoned them in order to use many, many others from the barbaric Arabian language, which they take such pleasure in pronouncing, and whose etymology and meaning certain grave and learned scholars of our day exploit so inordinately, leading many sensible people to believe this is the reason why the Spaniards are so fond of foreign lineages, ceremonies, languages, and clothing.

How do you expect me not to be hurt by this unnatural neglect by the children of my beloved Spain, or to refrain from repeatedly lamenting their ingratitude and villainy, when she surpasses all the known nations of the world in glorious deeds, notable exploits of most distinguished princes and brave captains who are themselves Basques, the exalted genius of wise and heroic men, illustrious ladies who are a rare example to the world with their many graces and qualities, and when they go out seeking languages through many foreign regions resuscitating those which should have been dead and buried forever. Who among those of my blood should not resent such turning away by their own children? My Spain, what does this mean; why do you nourish your children with milk from foreign nursemaids? Beware what you are doing, correct them, and put them on the road that all good men follow. And because they know that I am so useful and advantageous for achieving their honorable ambitions, it is just that they respect and honor me.

Tell me, Mighty Spain, I beg you, and forgive my audacity: if it falls within my jurisdiction to ask you, I who am your mother: Where will you direct the curious man who wants to know of the antiquity of your birth, for which there are so many indications and reasons, except to your Cantabria? Where will you seek your ancient language, if the one you prefer is not your own, as is obvious, except in your Cantabria? Where is your ancient and simple clothing, which is so different from that which so many nations design for you each year as for a young girl? Where are the trophies and glory of your ancient freedom, purity, and high nobility to be found, except in your Cantabria? Where have you always found healing and perpetual defense in your travails and misfortunes, except in your Cantabria? Throughout your empire, who do you think stands up for your causes and suffers for them, as does your Cantabria? Which regions have you acquired through armed combat for your vast dominion for which Cantabria did not shed much blood? Whither did you ever sally forth, by land or sea, which the captains of infantry and lances of sailors from your Cantabria did not go with you? What remote province do you possess anywhere in the world, or what local campaign, in which the sons of your great Cantabria do not serve you? Consider this: Cantabria is the nightmare and fright of your enemies, the shield and horrible escutcheon of your powerful insignia which they fear: generous as kings, impetuous and terrible as the sea, swift and furious as the serpent and sword of battle; green and perpetually cool in virtue as the yew tree; hungry, ravenous wolf against your enemies; strong chains for their imprisonment and opprobrium. And consider that, if your enemies and theirs have not conquered you, it is not because of their savagery and impotence as some ingrates have said and written, seeking to unfairly obscure the truth to the extent possible—because you have other provinces far more impotent and scabrous whom I cannot forgive the tyranny of foreign arms—but because of the invincible courage of my noble sons, your faithful Cantabrians.

Consider then your obligations, and the reverence you owe her, and do not, simply because of your great power, disregard or forget those whom you should always hold dear in your memory. Know that the best and greatest reward for generosity is gratitude; and if you are unaware of this, or knowing it forget it, you have no security in anything, nor do you deserve it; and I do not ask you for anything not mine, but for what is truly mine and what you owe me naturally as your mother, and what I want and ask is that you acknowledge this to be so. Take pride in your Cantabria, much pride, as noble, generous men take pride in the ruined, crumbling walls of their ancient estates, disregarding the dry and craggy site where they had their origin, the destruction caused over centuries by the audacious, twining tendrils of ivy, as testimony of their high nobility; and listen carefully to the rest of what I have to say to you on this same subject so that you will more clearly understand my just complaints and exactly what your obligations are.

Chapter 22

The Basque Language Concludes her Argument Advising Bizkaia and Gipuzkoa what they must do to Preserve Her and the Harm they bring upon themselves through excessive greed

I truly believe, my daughters, that you have understood what I have told you, and this cannot be otherwise because of your attentiveness to my long exhortation; and why should I fail to say everything I am obliged to say that might be important to you in times to come just because they do not seem important to me at the present time? Attend to what I have to say for awhile longer, for it is quite reasonable that, in keeping with our character, I speak to you clearly and truly about a matter that I feel is deleterious to our honor and survival, not to mention that it is to my own disparagement, and as I am your mother, you should watch over me: because I want you to know that this is something I have learned through my great antiquity and long experience: that your honor is entirely dependent on my survival.

I do not want to dwell on how the discovery of the Indies brought about my total destruction and ruin, and that of my sons. How is it that its silver and gold uplift so many others, providing enlightenment and distinction and lineages, while destroying your houses and estates and causing you to forget your ancient memories and names; bringing new life to many who were dead and buried, while degrading, killing, and burying you alone? Would it be useful for me to inform you how covetousness for the riches of the Indies has destroyed the entire world, and how our Spain seems like nothing but a debased army, where no one knows his proper place and role? This is not my purpose, nor do I wish to annoy you by insisting on it. I only want you to know that the irresistible greed for its riches afflicting everyone has managed to exile, disorient and kill those whom neither the cruelty of the Carthaginians, nor the shrewdness of the Greeks, nor the power of the Romans, nor the ferocity of the Goths, nor the savagery of the Moors, nor the constant harassment by the French ever succeeded in subjugating. It was this that made her weep; and your lack of feeling hurts me, and I sigh for the continuous absence of my sons, and it terrifies and consumes me to see that this great calamity has no remedy. Do not be shocked to hear me speak of covetousness as your mortal enemy and mine as well. Oh, cruel, false, effeminate covetousness, root and origin of all evils, stop, hold, slow your pace, for it isn't possible that what you acquire can last for long. Oh, my sons do not trust her, for she leads you into perpetual exile. Oh ravenous thirst, the ancient estates of my sweet sons are abandoned, destroyed, and bereft because of you. You take them from me, weaning them all too soon, before they learn to speak or are old enough to recognize me as their mother; and of all those you take away, very few are those you allow to return, and even fewer those who recognize me when they return: a hundred leave and five return, and only two recognize me, and the three with memory of your nourishment are not content with my style and ancient plainness: they neither recognize me nor understand me, nor do they appreciate it or wish to live with what is sufficient and honest.

Another condition and doctrine of yours they bring with them, totally denaturalizing them from this their country and kinship: and this is that when the few I have mentioned return to it, they come leaving pledges and monies in foreign lands far away from their own; and since the heart of the rich man is where his treasure is, and his soul is more where he loves than where he lives, although they come here, they remain there where they love, and where they live, sleep, and eat is what they care least about, which is this country of theirs; and when she has need of her sons for the common good and survival, these are the ones who sooner or later grow weary and faint because they do not live with me, nor did they suckle at my breast, or so briefly that they are thin and weak and without strength; and instead of helping me and sheltering me and favoring me, they are the first to throw the stone against me.

Infernal covetousness, these are your feats, your triumphs and your grandeur. You are mother of Eolus, who controls the winds. You order the wind to blow and move the weathervanes all over the world; and riches and their daughter pride follow you: with all your other daughters and theirs, who can resist such power? You level the mountains and raise up the valleys, you turn day into night, night into day: you foul what is pure, darken nobility, forget antiquity, despise courage, beat down truth, inspire presumption, and enshroud charity; and finally, you kill virtue and reward vice. What can I say no matter how much I say, of all that can be said about you and your evil deeds, and how you have worked to harm my sons during these last eighty years? And to keep from saying what should be said, but falling short, I prefer not to speak of it.

Now you see your obligations, now you have heard about your birth, and how you were raised, and my antiquity and nobility, my dominion and grandeur, and also about my accomplishments and how difficult it has been for me to survive in these mountains, and the harm some parts of our Cantabria have suffered because they forgot me, let them say whether they have understood: only I protect you; do not make light of it, because I am known all over the world, and because of me they honor you and know you; because of me you are worthy, and if you abandon me you abandon yourselves. At a very grave moment a lord of Spain understood and confessed this, for he said that among my sons, those who were most worthy were those who prized and valued me most, because they were endowed with true fidelity, nobility, and courage, hidden and disguised; and this should not be doubted, for experience proved it to be so on every occasion, as was well documented. That prince was right, and he came to understand, although late, the virtue my sons acquire through me. This is not to say, nor do I wish for you to reject the foreign Castilian language with all its potential eminence: know it, understand it, and acknowledge that it is of great importance in your effort to know me, love me, and respect me. How should you do this? By always giving first priority, as loyal and obedient sons, to your true and legitimate mother. I only want and command that you refrain from embracing or wedding yourselves to her excessively, just because you see the young maiden bejeweled and made lovely with ornaments and make-up, because I want you to know that all her adornment and jewelry is alien and from various nations and peoples with whom she has cohabited and kept company, loving many and lacking purity, firmness, and constancy, because she turns with every breeze and changes in every epoch, each nation alters her, and she rejects no one and each one influences her customs.

I am just the opposite of this, being ancient in age, as you have heard, little adorned or made-up, simple, plain, noble, legitimate, and proper, without admixture from other foreign nations. Constant, steadfast, good, and praiseworthy in customs and appearance; well bred, with good heart and clean blood; and unique in the world, and finally, free, noble, and generous, in debt to no one, and endowed with particular grace among all other languages, which is to be friendly, amorous, and pleasant to all nations, although they are enemies of our sons. These, my daughters, are my virtues—these adorn my sons, for these they are valued, these they have preserved; and these you should preserve, love, and esteem; and you should teach your children, because if you do not, consider me dead and buried and your Glory ended.

PRAISE BE TO GOD

9. Pierre de Lancre

(Bordeaux, 1553 – Sainte-Croix du Mont, Cadillac, 1631)

His grandfather, Bernard de Rosteguy or Arosteguy, was a wealthy vintner from Jutsi (Juxue) in Lower Navarre who moved to the Gironde in 1510. His father, Etienne, became Lord of Lancre in 1554, when he dropped his original name and adopted this new one. Pierre received a Jesuit education and then studied law in the Universities of Bohemia and Turin, obtaining a doctorate of law in 1579. In 1582, he was appointed Representative of the Parliament of Bordeaux, and in 1588, married a second cousin of Michel de Montaigne. In 1609, he was appointed as a magistrate responsible for the suppression of witchcraft in Lapurdi, in the course of which he produced a report that became a book, his famous *Tableau de l'inconstance des mauvais anges et demons* (Register of the Inconsistency of Bad Angels and Demons) (1612).

Linguistics is not the subject of this work, but language seems to be one of the pillars of the argument: the demonization of the people of Lapurdi and, by extension, of all Basques. The assignment that Lancre was appointed to carry out in Lapurdi can be considered one of political-cultural control. This territory maintained its own judicial system at the time, which allowed it an autonomous character in the heart of the French kingdom. The liberal tendencies of the local Basque authorities constituted a focus of tension and a challenge to the increasingly centralized French state. Moreover, this territory that bordered on the enemy Spanish kingdom was generally suspected of connivance or relations with its Basque territories. Finally, the language spoken there and its culture were very different from French.

During that period, the diabolical pact could be used as definitive, irrefutable proof of the evil character of an individual or group, legitimizing any judicial or military intervention against it without need for further proof. At the end of the sixteenth century, those even suspected of being involved with the devil were tarnished much like many today who are accused of being terrorists; it was an ontological argument that sought to offer a simple solution against evil, but resolved nothing. The *Tableau* constitutes a validating ideological construct for the judicial and military actions taken against the people of Lapurdi because of the pact with the devil endemic among them; that is, the presentation of an imaginary ethnography of Lapurdi understood to prove the province's identification with Satan. It is not without interest, since it constitutes an extraordinary sign of the collision between two cultures: the civilized, urban, and cosmopolitan culture of the bourgeoisie in Bordeaux against the rural, popular Basque culture.

Lancre regarded Lapurdi as a veritable breeding ground of witches and warlocks; and further, as the sanctuary for the thousands of diabolical spirits expelled from other places in the world thanks to the evangelical actions of the missionaries. And what were the circumstances that caused this land to be so susceptible to satanic penetration? In the first place, Lapurdi was built on a fickle maritime economy, compared to the solidity that an agrarian culture would have provided. The insecurity and inconstancy thought to be caused by the preference of Neptune over Ceres led to the absurd conclusion that the only substantial agrarian product in this territory was the apple—"an entire country of apples," that is, the fruit bringing about the loss of Paradise. Furthermore, the forced and prolonged absences of sailors from the province encouraged the development of an unacceptable spirit of freedom in their women, emblematized among other details in the phalloform headdress they shamelessly displayed. Here was an entire people, in Lapurdi, addicted to dancing and to the night, like cats, and therefore with an enormous proclivity for witchcraft, lacking patriotic loyalty, indifferent to the interests of France, and addicted to smoking an herb called "nicotine" which they grew in their gardens. Finally, Lancre repeats some of the classical themes of the linguistic debate, always channeling the water through his ideological mill. In the Basque Country, "which was called Cantabria" in ancient times, the people spoke a language completely different from French, and which they used for their dealings with the natives of Canada. But beyond this, because it was a border country situated between several kingdoms and bishoprics, this contact with cultures and languages—a mixture of Basque, Spanish, and French—produced that condition of weakness and fissure that facilitated Satanic penetration.

TABLEAV
DE L'INCONSTANCE
DES MAVVAIS ANGES
ET DEMONS.
OV IL EST AMPLEMENT TRAI-
cté des Sorciers & de la Sorcelerie.
LIVRE TRES-VTILE ET NECES-
saire, non seulement aux Iuges, mais à tous ceux
qui viuent soubs les loix Chrestiennes.
AVEC
Un Discours contenant la Procedure faicte par les Inquisiteurs d'Espagne & de Navarre, à 53. Magiciens, Apostats, Iuifs, & Sorciers, en la ville de Logrogne en Castille, le 9. Novembre 1610. En laquelle on voit, combien l'exercice de la Iustice en France, est plus iuridiquement traicté, & avec de plus belles formes qu'en tous autres Empires, Royaumes, Republiques & Estats.
PAR PIERRE DE LANCRE Conseiller du Roy au
Parlement de Bordeaux.
Maleficos non patieris viuere. Exod. 22.
A PARIS,
Chez NICOLAS BUON, au mont Sainct Hilaire
à l'enseigne Sainct Claude.
M. DC. XII.
AVEC PRIVILEGE DV ROY.

SELECTED TEXT(S):

Tableau de l'inconstance et instabilité de toutes les choses. Où el est montré, qu'en Dieu seul gist la vraye Constance, à laquell l'homme sage doit viser [Portrayal of the Inconstancy and Instability of All Things: Where It is Demonstrated that in God Alone Resides True Constancy, to Which the Wise Man Must Aspire] (Paris: Abel l'Angelier, 1610); reprint, as *Tableau de l'inconstance des mauvais anges et demons oú il est amplement traité des sorciers et de la sorcellerie. Livre tres-utile et necessaire non seulement aux Iuges, mais à touts ceux qui vieuent sous le lois Chrestiennes. Avec un Discurs contenant la Procedure faite par les Inquisiteurs d'Espagne e de Navarre à 53 Magiciens, Apostats, Iuifs et Sorciers, en la ville de Logrogne en Castile, le 9 Novembre 1610. En laquelle on voit combine l'exercise de la Iustice en France, est plus iuridiquement traicté, et avec le plus belles formes qu'en tous autres Empires, Royaumes, Republiques et Etats* [Portrayal of the Inconstancy of Bad Angels and Demons in Which Sorcerers and Sorcery Are Fully Discussed. A Most Useful and Necessary Book, Not Only to Judges but to All Those Who Live Under Christian Laws, with a Report Describing the Trial Conducted by the Inquisitors of Spain and Navarre Against 53 Magicians, Apostates, Jews, and Witches in the Town of Logroño in Castile on November 9, 1610, in which We See How the Exercise of Justice in France is Practiced with Greater Juridical Precision and with More Beautiful Forms than in All Other Empires, Kingdoms, Republics and States] (Paris: Jean Berjon, 1613); reprint, ed. Nicole Jacques-Chaquin (Paris: Aubier, 1982), 71–73, 78–85.

But seeing so many demons and evil spirits, and so many warlocks and witches concentrated in this country of Lapurdi, which is only a tiny section of France, and seeing that this is just the tip of the iceberg and that nowhere else in Europe to our knowledge is there anything approaching the infinite number that we have discovered there, we are astonished. This is what we have to examine, while we consider the remedy so that we can advise the King, because the sovereign authority that he has seen fit to place in our hands is not the highest and only cure for this ulcer since the gangrene is already visible. It would be fair to say that the Supreme Creator has chosen this way to punish these people with demons and witches, but even so, it is possible to offer some moral and personal reasons based on the character of these people and on the situation of their country.

The region of Lapurdi is a district made up of twenty-seven parishes, none of which engage in commerce or trading, and because the country is populous, at the slightest sound of the drum from the border where they are lodged they are responsible for providing up to two thousand men to support the King. Meanwhile and by provision, there is a company of one thousand foot soldiers, like the militias of Italy, commanded by the District Magistrate. They are stationed along the seacoast, or scattered up into the mountains, and in ancient times, they were called Cantabrians. They have a very distinct language, although only among us who are French is this called the Basque Country, although the Basque language extends beyond that. Because the entire country of Lapurdi, Upper and Lower Navarre, and part of Spain speak Basque, and no matter how difficult the language is, in addition to the Basques most of the people of Bayonne [Baiona], Upper and Lower Navarre, and nearby Spain, as least those on the border, know how to speak it. And I have been assured that in the year 1609, when a gentleman named Mons argued before the privy council of the King, alleging against those people of Saint-Jean-de-Luz [Donibane Lohizune] certain damages and interests which they claimed they had performed and suffered for having sent some ships to Canada, he was informed that long before he had any knowledge of the situation the Basques traded there; and that in fact the Canadians never did business among the French in any language except Basque.

And to demonstrate specifically that the environment of this place partially explains why there are so many witches there, it is important to realize that this is a mountainous country bordering on three Kingdoms: France, Navarre, and Spain. Hence, there is a mixture of the three languages—French, Basque, and Spanish—and the overlapping of the two bishoprics, because the Diocese of Dax extends even into Navarre.

Now all of these factors give Satan a marvelous opportunity to convene his assemblies and witches' Sabbaths, this being compounded by the fact that life on the seacoast makes these people crude, ill-mannered, and poorly disciplined; their restless spirit as well as their fortune and property being attached to their sails and rifle slings, inconstant as the wind, having no fields but the mountains and the sea, no food or grains but millet and fish, no shelter for their meals but the sky, no tablecloths but their sails. In short, their land is so infertile that they are forced to risk themselves on that restless environment, having become so accustomed to seeing storms and heavy rains that they hate and fear nothing so much as its peace and calm, basing all their good fortune and progress on the waves that jostle them night and day, so that their commerce, their conversation and their faith is utterly caught up in the sea, treating all things when they set foot on land the same as when they are afloat on the waves, always in a hurry, people who for the slightest rude behavior they happen to observe will attack you, holding a dagger at your throat.

But how is it that this country of Lapurdi is so infertile? Because if they were in God's grace the small amount that they were accustomed to plant would be enough at least to ward off the hunger they suffered in former times because of sowing too little grain or over-harvesting.

Now in this land of Lapurdi they cast their lot almost entirely on the fickleness of the sea, scorning the constant labor and cultivation of the soil. And although nature has given everyone the earth as nourishment, they prefer (fickle and inconstant as they are) that of the stormy sea to the nourishment of that sweet, loving Goddess Ceres.

. . .

In the fourth place the men do not love their country, their wives or their children. They are like double-pile velvet, with different markings on the two borders: nature placed them on the border between France and Spain, partly in the mountains, partly on the sea coast, those on this side speaking Basque and French, on the other side Basque and Spanish. As they conduct business more often in Navarre and Spain than in France, they are indifferent to French customs, way of life and feelings, as least with respect to the common people. The gentlemen who frequent the court are not like that, having been raised in the French manner. Many of them, however, have property and noble estates in France as well as Spain, or in Navarre. The absence and long voyages that they make by sea cause this disaffection, and engender this hatred, indifference in some, coldness in others. Because here only children and old men remain at home, people without guidance or judgment who because of their weakness can be led by the Devil as he pleases.

For if the women desire the return of their husbands for some small commodity that they bring back from the voyage, it is winter when they return, the harshest season of the year, and their lack of industriousness keeps them at home, drinking and eating everything up, leaving no provisions for their family, making the return voyage to Newfoundland as poor as they were when they started. I won't even mention the shipwrecks that must be so distressing to their families and to which they are more subject, as we will explain below, than all other voyagers, in addition to which most of them are warlocks and participate in witches' Sabbaths in Lapurdi even though they are at sea.

They have little love for their wives, and scarcely sleep with them because they are away six months at a time, and as for their children, the liberties the men take with their women during several years before marrying them, trying them out so to speak, prevents them from forming any close attachment to them, leaving them constantly in doubt and dreaming of the way and uncertainty of their arrival and departure from home, though if they become sorcerers and possessed by the devil as well, they too become savage and go to sea.

As for the women, they too suffer similar or worse anxiety, all the more since they can only be with their husbands half the time, and with all their struggles, doubts, uncertainties, and waiting they only have half-husbands, lacking the support they need for their families and for themselves, being treated as only half-wives, and when they return most of them discover that the mothers have chosen and given their children to another father, making a present of them to Satan.

And in the same way that the Indians on the island of Hispaniola, inhaling the smoke of a certain herb called *Cohoba*, have their spirits troubled and keep their hands between their knees and their head lowered, remaining in a state of ecstasy like that for some time, emerging from their spells confused and foolish speaking of the wondrousness of their false gods whom they call Cemis, just so do our warlocks return from the Sabbath. In the same way they use Petun or Nicotine, having a small plot of it of their gardens, inhaling the smoke to unburden their brain, though in no way sustaining them against hunger. Now, I cannot say for certain whether that smoke confuses them as that other herb does the Indians, but I do know, and it is true, that it makes their breath and body so noxious that no one who isn't accustomed to it can stand it, and they use it three or four times a day. So the women regard them as foul-smelling savages, their children deformed, stunted bastards, whom they kill and present to the Devil, most in partial fulfillment of their pact. And since the stench and foul smell of the sea pleases them, they embrace an even more abominable stench, preferring to kiss the Devil in his stinking Male Goat form on that filthy part of his behind where they perform their ritual of adoration, rather than to kiss their husbands on the mouth.

. . .

This leads me to believe that the devoutness and the good teaching of a number of good monks, having chased the demons and bad angels away from India, Japan and other places, multitudes of them have poured into Christendom: and having found fertile ground and susceptible people here in Lapurdi, they've made it their principal dwelling place, and little by little they've become absolute lords of the country, have won over the women, the children and most of the priests and ministers, and found a way to send the fathers and husbands off to Newfoundland and beyond where religion is completely unknown so as to more easily establish their realm. And in fact many English, Scots, and other voyagers, attracted here by the wines of Bordeaux, have assured us that on their voyage they have seen large hordes of demons in the form of horrifying men passing through France. Because of this, there are so many witches in this land of Lapurdi, and so many souls led astray, that it is utterly impossible to imagine that they could be brought back or restored to justice. Devotion and good teaching would be in vain here.

. . .

Furthermore, this nation has a marvelous inclination toward sorcery; the people are slight and swift in body and mind, abrupt and quick-tempered in everything they do, always on the go, as they say, so hot-headed it's hard to understand why they wear hats. They are more inclined to homicide and vengeance than to larceny or forgiveness. They like to go out at night like cats or owls; they love to stay out all night and to dance at night as well as during the day. And their dancing is not reposed and grave, but rather jittery and turbulent. When the body is most agitated, twisted and exhausted, they think it's most noble and fitting.

. . .

Dancing to the same tambourine they use to dance on the Sabbath, a number of people have told us they have seen the blind man from Siboro dancing on the Sabbath. They are always true to their word. When nothing else can move them, glory keeps them true, because they believe that larceny is a corruption of the soul and one who swears falsely that he is in need betrays a debasement of an abject heart incapable of redemption with no consideration of the penalty stipulated by the laws for that crime. I have never seen them convicted in Parliament for having stolen anything of importance. And in my travels through their country I have never seen anyone beg for alms or ask for money from foreigners. Finally, it is the most orderly nation possible, and I can say I have seen children and infants hurrying so fast to do what they're told that they throw themselves head first into doors and windows, injuring themselves, they move so fast.

To this I can add the custom of the women and girls, even the way they wear their hair seems not the least bit immodest. I am speaking of the ordinary women, because the coiffeur of the women of quality in Bayonne and the cloth strips hanging down, with their sculpted headdresses that seem to rest on pleated collars, and the embroidered pieces they wear on their chest, however honest, are time-consuming, hard to make and costly. They have confessed to me that it takes them half the day to bleach them, fit them and adjust them. But among the common girls and women, considering Bayonne as the capital city that serves as an example for all the others, some cut their hair short except for the ends which are long, others piled a bit higher, their hair half way down their cheeks, their hair flying over their shoulders, and framing their eyes that way, they seem far more beautiful in that innocence, and even more attractive than if you could see them openly. They arm themselves to such advantage in that beautiful hair that the sun casting its rays down on that cloud of hair as on a storm-cloud, the thunderclap is so violent and creates flashes of lightning as dazzling as when a rainbow suddenly appears in the sky, adding to the enchantment of their eyes, equally dangerous in love as in sorcery, though among them wearing their hair full signifies virginity. And it being common for the women in certain places to want to be warriors, they wear a kind of indecent phalloform helmet so inappropriate that one could say their weapons are those of Priapus rather than the God Mars, and that their coiffure is witness to their desire, because widows wear the helmet without a crest to show that they are without a man. And in Lapurdi the women display their behind so freely that all the ornamentation of their pleated petticoats is in the back, and in order to display it they pull their robe up over their head and cover their head down to their eyes. Finally, it is a land of apples, and they only eat apples, and only drink apple juice, causing them to bite so freely into that apple of transgression that it violates God's commandment and transcends the prohibition of our first father. They are Eves who freely seduce the sons of Adam, and with their heads in the clouds, living among the mountains as freely and innocently as Eve in the earthly Paradise, they listen to men and demons alike and lend their ears to all the serpents who wish to seduce them, and although they frequent cemeteries day and night, they cover and adorn their tombs with crosses and aromatic herbs, not wanting even the scent of their husbands' bodies to reach their nostrils. It is a charade to see one of them weep or pretend to weep warm tears for a husband who has been dead for twenty years when she did not shed a single tear on the day of the funeral. They sit or lie on the ground in groups, not on their knees, spending most of the time cackling and gossiping about what they have seen the night before and about the pleasure they took on the Sabbath, and about the roughness and height of those mountains, the darkness of the caverns they discovered there, the grottoes and love nests to be found along this seacoast, that sea from whose foam Venus was engendered, Venus who is so frequently reborn among those maritime people at the mere sight of the sperm of the whale they catch each year, from which it is said that Venus was conceived. That embracing of girls and young fishermen seen along the coast of Anglet [Angelu] in their mantillas and completely naked underneath, frolicking in the waves, makes Love bind them close, catch them by a thread, invite them to fish in this troubled water, and fill them with desire equal to their freedom, and the convenience, when they are soaking wet, of going off to dry themselves in the nearby love nest which Venus seems deliberately to have placed beside the seashore just for that purpose.

10. Juan Sada Amézqueta, under the pseudonym of García de Góngora y Torreblanca

(Pamplona-Iruña, Navarre, second half of the sixteenth century – Pamplona-Iruña, mid-seventeenth century)

He was educated in Rome and Salamanca, studying "mathematics and liberal arts." Indeed, his history of Navarre has an appendix on mathematics. He initially worked in Navarre as a schoolteacher, his chosen profession. Yet he also applied his mathematical knowledge to measuring territorial boundaries and topography. The publication of his *Apology* seems to have helped him professionally, because he was named master surveyor in the service of the Pamplona-Iruña City Hall.

Polemical in nature, his work *Historia apologética y descripción del Reyno de Navarra y de su mucha antigüedad, nobleza y calidades . . .* (Apologetic History and Description of the Kingdom of Navarre and of its Extreme Antiquity, Nobility and Qualities . . .) (1628) constitutes a qualitative leap for the historiography of Navarre, building on the Cantabrian theses previously developed by writers from Bizkaia and Gipuzkoa and then applying them to the Kingdom. Being an apology, as is clearly indicated in its title, this work is intended to counter the arguments of anyone who casts aspersions on Navarre. Thus, he sides with other Basque authors about the authentic extent of Cantabria and against Aragón, which is the source of certain ideas that could be taken as disrespectful toward Navarre.

HISTORIA APOLOGETICA,
Y DESCRIPCIÕ
DEL REYNO DE NAVARRA,
Y DE SV MVCHA ANTIGVEDAD, NOBLEZA, Y
DIVIDIDA EN III. LIBROS CON VN TRA-
SACADA A LVZ POR DON GARCIA DE GONGORA
Y TORREBLANCA.
DIRIGIDA AL REYNO DE NAVARRA.
Año 1628.
CON LICENCIA DEL CONSEIO REAL.

Selected Text(s):

Historia apologética y descripción del Reyno de Navarra y de su mucha antigüedad, nobleza, calidades, y Reyes que dieron principio a su Real casa, y procuraron sus acrecentamientos . . . dividida in III libros sacada a luz por García de Góngora y Torreblanca [History and Description of the Kingdom of Navarre, Its Great Antiquity, Nobility, Qualities, and the Kings Who Established Its Royal House and Worked to Expand It . . . Divided into Three Books . . .] (Pamplona: Carlos de Labayen, 1628), bk. 1, ch. 2, fols. 3, 14; ch. 2, fols. 15v, 15b; and ch. 14, fol. 39.

Their customs and clothing are so varied that it is certain that nowhere else in Europe or anywhere in the known world can such variety and difference be found in a single kingdom, some of them so exotic that they clearly indicate that its antiquity and age are as great as the Master Florián de Ocampo claims, having first been worn and spoken by their original inhabitants, the Tubalists, and preserved ever since. Two languages are spoken in Navarre—Basque and Romance—but most appropriately Cantabrian Basque, this being the primitive mother language brought by the founder and Patriarch Tubal and spoken without contamination by any other language in most regions of the Kingdom, where it has always been preserved except on the border and frontier with Castile and Aragon, where only Romance is spoken.

. . .

And because there is some conflict among Historians about whether Tubal made his entrance through the Alfaques, north of the Ebro River, or through Lusitania, or Andalusia or through the Pyrenees, I have attempted to ascertain this, not without a great deal of research, because I did not find written documentation by any author specifying the demarcations and geographical tables of Ptolemy, Abraham Orthelius, and other cosmographers, and I have ascertained that the region through which he could have most quickly and easily entered is through the Pyrenees; first, because during that period of 143 years after the universal flood, or 175 years as others claim, the sea routes were not yet known, necessitating a long detour and approach through the Mediterranean Sea, nor were the compass and astrolabe discovered until three thousand years later (which was 250 years ago when a Neapolitan gentleman named Flavius discovered this secret); and second, because the Region and Province of Greater Armenia, from which Tubal came with his people, is closer to Spain by land than by sea because it was almost at the same degree of longitude to the Northeast. Armenia is an Asiatic Province and is divided into Minor and Major, and from Greater Armenia, which is where he came from. He could have come by four routes, two of them by way of the Ebro River, through the Mediterranean Sea, embarking in Trapizonda, or in Sinope, or near Amasia, which are Ports of the great sea, closer to Armenia than any other, and then sailing through the Strait of Constantinople and going by way of the Mediterranean Sea, he could have entered through the Ebro, but these two routes are the longest.

And by land, first passing from Asia to Europe through the Bosporus or Strait of Constantinople, he could have taken two roads without re-embarking, one through Macedonia, Slovenia, and by land from Venice to Lombardy and France, entering through the Pyrenees. And the other was to embark for a second time in the Ports of Macedonia, or Dalmatia, and to come to Italy and France, and enter Spain through the Pyrenees. According to these and other serious authors, it is likely that because these two land routes are more direct, shorter, and safer he would have come by one of them through the Pyrenees Mountains, where he found plentiful game and wild fruit for his people to eat.

According to ancient Memoirs, the first founders and inhabitants of this land of Baztan [a valley in northern Navarre] were the Armenians who came with Tubal, and this can deduced as well from the clothing they wear, especially the women, denoting great antiquity, and from the Basque language that they speak, which is the common mother tongue they brought to Spain, where it has been preserved in its purity ever since, from which it follows that without any decline from such noble beginnings it has been preserved always in its original perfection and that its progenitors are descendants of the Armenians, as they so proudly claim, and that many of them are also descended from Royal Gothic blood, according to ancient traditions and memoirs that I have seen. This can also be inferred from what Villegas writes in the third part of his *Flos sanctorum* (Saintly Flower), and *Illustrious Noblemen*, based in large part on the book which the wise Simon Magus wrote in Rome about the penitent life and virtues of Doctor Martin de Azpilicueta Navarro, and from a funeral Oration delivered at his burial in the city of Rome itself by the most wise Thomas Correa, a Portuguese gentleman, indicating that three Gothic Kings of Spain—Tulgas, Cindasuyndo, and Recesuyndo—came from the House of Baztan, and that during the reign of the Goths in Spain and France, which they call Gotica, which extends as far as Avignon. In the year 640, King Cintilla of Spain died without leaving any heirs to succeed him, and because he was of Royal Gothic lineage and blood and because of the excellent virtues shining forth from this Tulgas, the Goths accordingly elected him King, and when he died without leaving any sons, Cindasuyndo ascended to the Crown of Spain and Gothic France, being succeeded by his legitimate son Recesuyndo; and subsequently the Crown of Spain was inherited by the grandsons of Recesuyndo, and Acosta and Rodrigo, who lost Spain, bringing an end to the Monarchy of the Goths. Afterwards Pelayo came to be the first King of León by an election held by the Asturians and Leonese, and if Pelayo was the son of the Duke Don Favila, and grandson of Recesuyndo, and Cindasuyndo, and Tulgas, as has been claimed of the House of Baztan—and by the House of Baztan we understand all the villages, settlements, and palaces of the valley with solid foundations—we can affirm that all their sons born of the ancient and true Baztanese are descended not only from the pure lineage and race of the Armenians, but many of them from Royal Gothic blood as well; and that they produced Kings for the Kingdom of León, high in prestige because of its nobility, and even more so through the nobility that they themselves have acquired through their own valor and strength—inherited from their ancestors—and through the great fidelity with which they have always served their Kings. And since following the loss of Spain Baztan was one of the Houses appointed by the nobility of the Realm—before the election of a King—to distribute the lands, which the Navarrese won from the Moors, according to the merits and valor of each man in order to avoid the conflicts arising from this, and because they had also been legislators, men in charge of providing rights and laws to Navarre and Aragon, and took part in the election of their first Kings, resulting in their being named distributors of lands and electors of Kings and defenders of the Faith, and because they had helped extend that Faith throughout these Kingdoms at such great cost of their own blood and tireless efforts, whenever the Kings wrote to them they addressed them by very honorable titles.

. . .

And finally some authors who are exceedingly diligent in describing antiquities say that the clothing they wear today and the Basque language they speak are the same that the Patriarch Tubal and his companions, the Armenians, brought to Spain almost four thousand years ago, but at the very least I can affirm, and especially in regard to the women, that theirs is among the most exotic and most ancient worn anywhere in Spain and France, which they have always preserved just as they were originally in ancient times.

. . .

And seeing that there are no Spanish or foreign memoirs, histories, or authentic instruments that mention or characterize these things, they themselves have introduced some handwritten memoirs, so intertwined with fictional elements and so insistent on the antiquity of their lands, families, and lineages that it seems to them, as we said at the beginning, that they come from the beginning of time and are the most worthy and generous in the world, so that they have all the nobility, honors, crowns, titles, and everything else in the world. If we consider the origin and beginning of our first parents Adam and Eve, we are all one, and we have the same ancestry and quality of blood, there being no difference between the King and the most humble farmer. For in the beginnings of the world, in the first age, all things were common, there being no difference between lineages, estates, or property, but with the passing of time, as malice grew and as sincerity and peace were converted into discord and factions, the most valiant and tyrannical becoming *caudillos* [leaders, chiefs], those who could occupy most usurped what had belonged to everyone.

So that what Nature created equal, malice and tyranny made unequal, dividing men into free servants, noblemen, and commoners, so that the weakest and those with least strength, ended up in servitude, regarded as rustics and subjects, and the others as men of nobility and greater worth. And it happened that following the dispersion of Babylonia, in imitation of Nimrod, who tyrannically made himself leader of a group of people, those who proved to be the bravest and strongest did the same thing in their own language, so that after they had taken possession of the lands and sovereign power, the crowns and monarchies of the kings took their descent from them. And those most favored and closest in love and kinship and who most distinguished themselves in service to the kings were honored and respected most, and this was also the origin of the first noble families and titles, and these are the ones who are so privileged and who in future centuries, through the grandeur and splendor of heroic deeds, virtue, and valor that each one achieved, established the different lineages, although as we have said all are sons of the first parents and created from the same substance by God, raising some to great glory and great heights, leaving others obscure and low, but afterwards with the passage of time many of these commoners virtuously showing themselves to be prudent and valiant, and being fortunate as well, won the Crowns of Emperors and Kings.

. . .

11. Pedro de Aguerre Azpilicueta, known as Pedro de Axular

(Urdazubi [Urdax], Navarre, 1556 – Sara [Sare], Lapurdi, 1644)

He took the surname by which he was known from the house where he was born, "Axular." After studying at the University of Salamanca, he was ordained a priest at the age of forty in Tarbes. He subsequently served as parish priest of Sara until his death at the advanced age of eighty-eight.

He was the author of a single work, *Guero*: *Bi partetan partitua eta berezia* (Later: Distributed and Divided into Two Parts) (1643), which is generally acknowledged to be the masterpiece of classical Basque literature. It was written to fill the need for adequate instruments of Counterreformation catechesis for Basque speakers; a need shared by other priests and colleagues of his from Lapurdi. It is an essentially ascetic text, whose introduction establishes the linguistic premises motivating and inspiring it: first, as already stated, the need for Basque texts to use in spreading the message of the Counterreformation; second, the need for that text to be intelligible to all Basques whatever their dialectic (Axular was the first to recognize the necessity of creating a common instrument for written expression capable of transcending dialectical differences); and finally, the defense of the suitability of the Basque language for any level of cultural transmission.

GVERO
BI PARTETAN
partitua eta berecia,
LEHENBICICOAN
EMAITENDA, ADITCERA,
cenbat calte eguiten duen, luçamendutan ibiltceac, eguitecoen gueroco utzteac.
Bigarrenean quidatcenda, eta aitcinatcen, luçamenduac utciric, bere hala, bere eguin bideari, lothu nahi çaicana.
Escritura saindutic, Eliçaco Doctor etaric eta liburu debocinozco etaric. Axular Saraco errotorac vildua,
Ne tardes conuerti ad Dominum, & ne differas de die in diem, Ecclef. 5.
BORDELEN,
G. MILANGES Erreguerén Imprimaçaillea baithan.
M. DC. XLIII.

SELECTED TEXT(S):

Guero bi partetan partitua eta berezia, lehenbicicoan emaitenda, aditcera, cenbat calte eguiten duen, luçamendutan ibiltceac, eguitecoen gueroco utzteac. Bigarrenean quidatcenda, eta aitcinatcen, luçamenduac utciric, bere hala, bere eguin bideari, lothu nahi çaicana [Later, Distributed and Divided into Two Parts: In the First Part, How Much Harm is Caused as a Result of Procrastinating, Leaving Chores Until Later. The Second is Guided and Directed at Those Who, Not Wasting Time, Immediately Want to Apply Themselves to Their Task] (Bordele [Bordeaux]: Guillen Milanges Impresor Real, 1643); reprint, ed. Fr. Luis Villasante (Oñati: Jakin, 1976), 112–17.

TO THE READER

6. One evening, I was attending a social gathering attended only by Basque priests when the conversation turned to the following topic: that nothing was as bad for the soul, and even for the body, as for our sense of obligation to change from today to tomorrow and from tomorrow until the day after. And that it would be useful for a book to be written about this matter in Basque, especially for those who only know this language, and that in such a book it should be explained that when you say "later" you really mean "never." At this same gathering, the question arose as to who should be assigned to write such a book. And all those present began to hint, first with winks and gestures, and finally clearly and explicitly, that I should be the one to undertake this task. Feeling unqualified to do this, I resisted as much as I could, but to no avail because so earnestly and unanimously did they keep after me that they closed every possible objection. Finally, as a way of satisfying their urging I agreed to write a little book, divided into two parts, about this "later."

And I would have liked to publish both parts together and simultaneously. But seeing how little has been written in Basque, I was afraid and anxious that the roads were not sufficiently safe or passable, or that there would be obstacles or pitfalls along the way. And for that reason I decided to begin by trying out the first part, sending it ahead on a kind of reconnaissance mission to gather information about how it would be regarded and to assess critical opinions and reception. Based on this information I could then make provisions for the future, deciding whether to send the second part out to the public or to go into hiding and reduce myself to silence.

7. I'm quite aware that many will be surprised and astonished that I should undertake this project. Because there have been many before me and there are many now far more capable and qualified than I for such a task, yet who have not been so bold as to attempt it. You would think this would be reason enough to give me pause and make me desist. But this very argument, which would seem to militate against me, is what encourages me, because it seems to me that first works offered tentatively as trials, even if they are riddled with flaws, are forgivable simply because they are first, and everyone is willing to overlook and excuse their defects.

8. I am also aware that I cannot cover all the dialects of Euskara, because it is spoken in a great number and variety of ways in the Basque Country: in Upper Navarre, Lower Navarre, Zuberoa (Soule), Lapurdi,

in Bizkaia, Gipuzkoa, Araba, and in many other places. Here you say *behatzea*, there you say *so egitea*. In one place, you say *haserretzea*, in another *samurtzea*. Here it's *ilkitzea*; there it's *ialgitea*. In one place, *athea*, and in another *bortha*. Here *erraitea*, there *esatea*. Or *irakurtzea*, here, *leitzea* there. Or *liskartzeak* versus *ahakartzea*. Or one says *hauzoa*, the other *barridea*. Here they say *aitonen semea*, there they say *zalduna*. In short, each in his own way and style. Not all Basques follow the same laws and customs, nor is there any single way of speaking Euskara, because politically they form different kingdoms.

9. Nor is the written language unproblematic, there being differences here as well. One writes *chehero*, another *gehero*. One writes *chedea*, another *gedea*. Or *ichilik* as opposed to *igilik*. One *lachoa*, the other *lajoa*. Or *choil* and *joil*. In one, it's *kecho*, in another *kejo*, in one *chuchen*, in another *jugen*. Thus, there are also different words written in different ways depending on the convention in each region or kingdom.

But because there are fewer than a dozen words, more or less, that are written in two different ways, I will also write them in one way in the text of the book and in another way in the margin, *in margine*, in an effort to please everyone.

Finally, with regard to this matter of orthography, I say that, just as Latin compresses one *i* with another, or one *v* with another, regarding them as one—*adjicio, conjicio, vultus, vulnus*—and Spanish also unites *l* with *l*, writing them together as in *llamo, lloro*, Euskara also combines one *t* with another, writing *ttipia, ttipittoa, gizonttoa, haurttoa*, it being unacceptable to those who speak Euskara well to write *txipia, txipitxoa, gizontxoa, haurtxoa*.

10. But because it is natural, in writing as well as in speaking, that each person regards his way as best, and because my way is different from yours, I beg you not to speak ill of it or reject it for that reason. If this way doesn't please you, do it in your own way and as it is done in your region. That won't bother me or make me angry. Quite the contrary, this is something I prefer, that is: that this humble essay of mine should instill in you the desire and willingness to write a better one, and even to correct the faults you find in it. Because then Euskara would not be as limited, poor, or inadequate as the world believes and concludes that it is.

Today, oddly, it seems that Euskara is shy and afraid of appearing in public, as if it were not adequate, splendid, or powerful. Because even among its native speakers, there are some who do not know how to read or write.

If as many books had been written in Euskara as in Latin, French, or other foreign languages, Euskara would also be as rich and perfect as they, and if this has not happened, it is the Basques themselves who are to blame, not Euskara.

11. I am not writing this little book for people who are very sophisticated. Nor for those who know absolutely nothing.

Nor do I always translate the Holy Scripture and the maxims of wise men literally into Basque, because Euskara is different from other languages. But this does not imply that Euskara is inferior. On the contrary, it seems that the other common languages end up being mixed with each other, whereas Euskara has been preserved in its initial and original purity.

But leaving aside the different ways of speaking and writing Euskara (because such things are like bark and flower), take advantage of the fruit inside this little book, of the inner substance: let that be what you taste, what you hold in your hands, not reading quickly or superficially or in anticipation of rejecting it. Rather, read it with good intentions, as if the book were yours, made for you. And if in this way you find some sweetness and flavor in it, as can only be found in each of God's creations, attribute all its faults to me and all its graces to Him. And I also entreat you, please, to pray for me.

Vale [Farewell].

12. Pedro Fernández de Castro (the Count of Lemos)

(Monforte de Lemos, Galicia or Madrid, 1556 - ?, 1622)

This writer belonged to an ancient and noble lineage with roots in Monforte de Lemos (Galicia) and was the seventh person to hold the title of Count. He attained the highest offices at Court as part of the administration of the Duke of Lerma, who in turn dragged Castro down with him when he fell from favor in 1618. Before that, between 1603 and 1609, Castro had been president of the Council of the Indies and, between 1610 and 1616, Viceroy of Naples. With his political fall from fortune, he retired to his possessions in Monforte until his death, devoting himself to letters and especially to the composition of the *Historia del Búho gallego con las demás aves de España* (Fable of the Galician Owl and Other Birds of Spain). According to one of his surviving manuscripts, he wrote *El Búho gallego* in 1620 as vindication of this people who were, apparently, held in low esteem at that time by the other regions that made up the Spanish Kingdom. It is regarded as one of the most perfect models of a genre that developed notably during the seventeenth century: the national controversy over which region was superior. The effort of each national community to be more noble, more Spanish, and more Christian than the others would lead to the development of a complete typology of national characteristics: Basques—stupid and violent, but hard-working; Catalans—equally industrious, but greedy; Andalusians—banal and superficial, but New Christians, and so on. But this text had a far more political and immediate purpose: Galicia had lost the seat in the Cortes (Spanish parliament) that it had held since the fourteenth century, and the leading Galicians of the age were determined to recover their vote.

Castro distinguished himself in this campaign, which eventually culminated successfully in 1623, a year after his death. In this context, one can understand better the metaphor of the owl that tries to become a member of the Manzanares choir. The main error of the Owl was that its quest for national prestige was based on the disparagement of the merits of others, if not sheer calumny and insult. With this, he achieved the opposite result. He did not win higher esteem for Gallegos among other Spaniards, but instead he provoked the publication of responses in defense of those slandered, at the expense of Galicians. The first of the responses came from Alvaro Cubillo de Aragón, from Granada (Andalusia), in his poems *El enano de las Musas* (The Dwarf of the Muses) (1654), in addition to *El pavo andaluz* (The Andalusian Peacock) and, of course, *El tordo vizcaíno* (The Bizkaian Thrush). Apparently, *El pavo andaluz* was never published, but the manuscript was widely circulated and has since been published by Andrés de Mañaricúa, along with *El Búho gallego* and *El tordo vizcaíno.*

This little work presents an assembly of Spanish birds, who "might resemble a meeting of the Cortes," convened in a meadow beside the Manzanares River, presided over by the imperial Eagle who was meant to personify Spain herself, and hosted by the Castilian Goose and the Moorcock of La Mancha. There is a confrontation between the Bizkaian Thrush and the Galician Owl over ownership of the meadow; the former being supported by the other birds of Spain (the Navarrese Kestrel, the Aragonese Cuckoo, the Catalan Kite, the Murcian Swallow, the Andalusian Peacock, and so forth) who try to expel the Galician. The dialectical confrontation, in which the Owl claims to be the most Spanish and most Christian bird, discrediting and bringing all the others under suspicion, is presented in two acts. In the first, all the birds elect the Thrush as their spokesman and representative, he being demolished in the debate, however, by the Owl. In the second, the Thrush does not even show up to the meeting, and the Owl sets about thrashing the other birds, especially the Catalans and Andalusians, while respecting, of course, the Castilian and Manchegan hosts. In effect, the birds (or the peoples they symbolize) end up being hierarchized into different categories: in the first place, of course, the Eagle was above all the others, he being the personification of the Empire. Then came the Owl, as the quintessence of Spain; then the Goose and the Moorcock, in the chorus of birds, in their own house (Spain), followed by the rest (Peacock, Swallow, and so on) as members of the chorus, except for the Bizkaian Thrush and the Navarrese Kestrel. The former, accused simply of not being Spanish (but Jewish), reacts with noisy indignation; as for the Kestrel, he is disparaged for his ambiguity and double condition as French and Spanish and every Navarrese is accused of having "a fleur-de-lis concealed in his heart."

Selected Text(s):

Historia del Búho gallego con las demás aves de España [Fable of the Galician Owl and Other Birds of Spain] (anonymous), in Justo Zaragoza, *Castellanos y vascongados* [Castilians and Basques] (Madrid: Víctor Sáinz, 1876), 233–264; reprint, as app. 3 of Estanislao Labayru, *Historia General de Bizcaya*, ed. Andrés de Mañaricúa (1895–1903; reprint, Bilbao: La Gran Enciclopedia Vasca, 1976), fols. 4–5, 34–39.

With regard to Ioancho's main argument that Owls are unworthy of taking their place beside day birds simply because they are night birds, I say this: that same argument places me in the forefront because time is divided equally between me and all the other birds, my allotment being the most dangerous and difficult, bearing on my own shoulders the burden of cleaning and patrolling and keeping watch during dark nights, without hope of help from any other bird. And I might complain about this to the other birds considering their ignorance in naming Ioancho as their procurer when any other bird native to Spain could have been appointed. When Ioancho heard this, upset and dazed, and forgetting the proper etiquette owed to the person of the King, and without asking permission as was the custom, he interrupted my speech and lifted his little beak and screeching, he said: "So, I'm not Spanish?" Laughing to himself, our Owl said to him angrily: "You still don't know?"

Ioancho became even more flustered, and the Owl said to him: "Don't go thinking this is something I made up, calm down, and I'll lay out the path by which you can accept this truth." And having followed the customary protocol, he started by saying: "Marco Orologius, an ancient Italian author who wrote about the Provinces of Europe, their native peoples, their inhabitants, and their origins, in one of his books dealing with those of Spain, Book 3, chapter 17, says the following: 'When the Goths came to occupy Spain, they brought with them a great number of Jewish slaves, who had been spared from death by the conquering hand of Titus Vespasianus when he destroyed Jerusalem, and this same Titus gave them the name that suited them, which was Vicecaynes, imitators of Cain who killed his brother Abel out of envy, and they killed the true Abel our Lord Christ out of envy as well. These same Goths gave that name to these slaves, using them to fashion and bless weapons and other military equipment needed for war. Because these people were of no merit, the historians of those periods in Spain make no mention of them. After the Goths occupied and peacefully conquered Spain, they found a way to expel these Jews from among themselves. Wanting to spare their lives because they had been well served by them, they assigned them lands to live in apart from them and forbade them under grave penalties from speaking in the language of the noble Goths or any other language except their own, and from leaving this land they had allotted them, which were some extremely rugged mountains on the border separating Spain from Gaul, thinking that the harshness of this mountain would be enough to finish them off, because in that mountain there was not fruit, but only iron and steel. They obliged them to bless all of them, and they sent them food from Spain.

'These Vicecaynes named these mountains Vicecaya [Bizkaia] and they still live there today and speak a language totally different from all the nations of Europe, something that never happened in any other nation; the reason for this was that no other nation allowed them to enter their territory. They followed the law of Moses for many years, with their Mezquita [Mosque] and their Rabbi, as can be demonstrated today by the places where they established themselves, using the word *Amezqueta* instead of Mezquita [Mosque] or Synagogue; and Fuente Rabbi the place of the Rabbi, in imitation of Fuente el Maestre in Extremadura, in the Order and Jurisdiction of Santiago, founded by a Master of that Order and Goths came to occupy Spain, bringing a large number of Jewish slaves with them, who had been rescued by the victorious hand of Titus Vespanius when he destroyed Jerusalem; to whom Titus himself gave the name "Vicecaynes," that suited them as imitators of Cain, who, because of jealousy, killed his brother Abel, and they [Bizkaians] for the same reason [killed] the true Abel, Our Lord Christ. These slaves named with this name other similar ones that I will omit to avoid prolixity. They always continued those trades that they were forced to practice: and today they forge iron, lances, arrows, ships, and all types of weapons and other things that necessity taught them, doing this better, or more abundantly than anywhere else in Spain.'"

The Thrush was stymied by this text and the cited author, and struggling to find a way and time, and babbling in an effort to speak, he pulled forth from his breast, or bird breast, a stillborn (for so it could be called because it was so unenlightened) saying: "How is it possible, invincible Queen, that this account told by the Owl's author could be true. The ancient tradition of Bizkaia maintains it is the opposite, which is regarded as undeniable, that two hundred years before Christ came into the world, and two hundred years afterwards, just as other nations had a Serpent, a Lion, and other emblems on their shields, the Bizkaians carried a Cross."

"With your Majesty's permission," said the Owl. "I don't believe that what Ioancho says contradicts what Marcus Orologius said with his authority, and in fact it disparages even more Ioancho and his country, because if before Christ came into the world, they carried the Cross on their shield, it follows that they were already despised people, because in that time the Cross signified ignominy and insult, as the gallows does today. And neither does it contradict this authority for them to have carried the Cross two hundred years after the coming of Christ; on the contrary, it should be understood that the noble Goths forced all of them to carry it, just as today those of us who take pride in being Christians oblige those tried and convicted by the Inquisition to wear it and this allows them to be recognized. For if the Vicecaynes had worn it willingly or out of devotion, they would still wear it today, as they do in my Province where not just one but six crosses decorate the liturgical vessel of the Holy Sacrament which honored them by its presence always. They never neglected its worship since the first time that it was celebrated, and they never changed their escutcheon, as did the Vicecaynes, who exchanged the Cross for one or two male goats, or female goats tied to a cork tree. And I confess that this is true, that they had the Cross in those days."

"Put an end to this colloquium," said the Eagle, "for it seems too long and the day is coming to an end. Let another be convened in which this dispute can be decided, and no one dare discuss this matter in any other place but this."

13. Anonymous (1624), published by Justo Zaragoza as *Castellanos y Vascongados* (1876)

Castelllanos y vascongados. Tratado breve de una disputa y diferencia entre dos amigos (Castilians and Basques: Brief Treatise on a Dispute between Two Friends) (1876) concerns a manuscript that had remained unpublished since its composition in 1624 until the nineteenth century. In 1876 Justo Zaragoza published it, along with other materials relative to the conflict that took place in Peru between Castilians and Basques in the seventeenth century, as well as those dealing in general with the character of the Basques at the time. Its publication date, 1876, was carefully chosen, because it was the year when the Cánovas administration abolished the Basque *fueros.*

The historical context in which the text was produced is not any less interesting just because it is well known: the so-called Vicuña War waged in Potosí, Upper Peru (modern-day Bolivia) between 1622 and 1625. This city represented the most important silver-mining center in the Spanish empire, whose profits had soared following the imposition of the *mita* (the system of slave labor of native peoples) in 1574. The lure of quick wealth attracted all kinds of people to the region, from those who had a more industrious notion of colonial exploitation, eager to profit from the indigenous labor force in the mines, to simple adventurers, who were soldiers of fortune, and thugs with swords. The first group was composed primarily of Basques, whereas the second was made up of Castilians, Extremadurans, Andalusians, and Portuguese. The Basques exercised economic and administrative control of the city, owning almost two thirds of the mines, provoking the confrontation with the others, and leading to genuine war. The Vicuñas, so named because they wore berets made from the wool of this animal, killed Juan de Urbieta in 1622 and this provoked the revolt. Basques ran through the streets "shouting in their language: 'death to anyone who does not answer in Basque!'" As things became increasingly ugly, the natives of Bizkaia and Gipuzkoa finally asked for help from their colonial authorities, sending a representative to the king in 1624 to ask for a resolution to the conflict. Finally, the monarchy intervened to restore peace to a territory that had such great economic importance. The Basques were few in number but, according to contemporary texts, exhibited such intense solidarity that it endowed them with considerable economic and military power. What most angered the Castilians was their collusion with Basques from France, whom they treated as equals and allowed to share in the exploitation of colonial wealth that had been reserved in principle for the subjects of the Castilian Crown. It is important to emphasize that, next to Basques from Bizkaia, Gipuzkoa, Navarre, Araba, France, and the Creoles (descendants of all of these), were Catalans, who, although in principle excluded from sharing in colonial exploitation because they were members of the Crown of Aragón, were also treated as allies. The seventeenth-century Vicuña War incident was conveniently utilized in the context of the political debate surrounding the Second Carlist War (1873–76) and the abolition of the *fueros*, sharpening the argument of the traditional lack of Basque fidelity to the Crown as an endemic evil.

Justo Zaragoza (Alcalá de Chisvert, Castellón, 1833 – Madrid, 1896) was a civil servant who had studied medicine. In 1864, he was transferred to Cuba as Customs Inspector, and there, contact with day-to-day life in Latin America directed his intellectual curiosity toward historiography. This led him to become a member of Spain's Academy of History, focusing his work especially on the Hispanic expeditions to the Indies. As an expert on Latin American affairs, he published the unedited text of "Castilians and Basques," adding a scholarly appendix related to the conflicts in Potosí.

The text presents two characters who can be considered paradigms of the Castilian and Basque condition, respectively. Both are involved in the colonial exploitation of Peru, specifically in the silver mines of Potosí. Alonso, a native of Burgos, is a beneficiary in the mining process and Martín, from Bilbao, is a miner on the hill, or more accurately a foreman in charge of Indians who work in the mine. What they have in common is that they are subjects of the Spanish Crown who profit from the exploitation of Peruvian natives in the mines. From the tone of the discussion, it appears that they have nothing else in common. It is interesting that the antagonists are two men who are natives of Burgos and Bilbao, because in the previous century these cities had been involved in fierce economic competition through their respective consulates. Moreover, the text is not a debate in which both sides express their data and argue opposite positions but an attack in which Martín sums up his character succinctly: "Well I, as a Basque, am not very good at arguing," whereas Alonso sets about systematically and resoundingly undermining his arguments. It is, then, a Castilian counter-apology.

The arguments of both men, seen from our perspective, could not seem more nonsensical. The Basque makes the claim of the inherent nobility of the Basque people, based purely on the grounds of the authority "as everyone knows." Hence, no proof is necessary. Secondly, he invokes the Tubalist argument, on the authority of Garibay, admitting that Tubal came from the East to the shores of the Mediterranean but then advanced toward the Basque Pyrenees because there he was able to find better fruit trees for nourishment. Third, without any evidence of proof whatsoever, he maintains that the Basque language is a ("corrupt") derivative of the first language ever spoken in the world: Hebrew. His fourth argument is that the noblest lineages of the peninsula are of Basque origin, so that even the names are Basque, offering three examples of names of authentic Basque origin: Mendoza, for which he offers a correct etymology; Velasco, which is somewhat erroneous; and Nájera, for which he does not venture an etymology. The fifth argument is multiple: the lack of bibs in the Basque Country; the abundance of costumes, secretaries, and accountants; and the fact that there are so many Basques in the Indies. One final argument was also considered weighty and frequently evoked: that they constituted a bulwark of defense against France. Almost all these arguments are easily refuted because they are ridiculous and lacking in any proof; however, the Castilian in his zeal to demolish them gets lost in a series of proofs that turn out to be even more absurd in many cases than those proposed by his adversary.

But let us consider the arguments related to language, which are many. In the first place, the term *hijodalgo*, or *hidalgo*, is translated as *hidalgot*, meaning "Son of a Goth." Obviously, the Basques are not Goths. And if this bizarre translation were not enough, it is denied that the names Mendoza, Velas, or Nájera are Basque because of "the simple similarity" in form between Mendoza and *Mendioza* (meaning "cold mountain" in Euskara). However, another quite sensible argument is offered: the number of houses of distinguished Spanish lineage whose names are incapable of being translated into Euskara. The most infuriating salvo of all is the assumption that Basque is a variant of the Hebrew language, the Basques being not only Jews but Jewish slaves brought in Roman times to the most rugged corner of the peninsula to serve the Goths by forging iron weapons for them, because iron was the only resource available there. This would explain the lack of similarity between the language and all those around it and its similarity with Hebrew (!), which would make the Basques the most despicable of all the inhabitants of the peninsula: slaves as well as Jews. The anonymous author of "Castilians and Basques" acknowledges that he read this argument in *El Búho gallego*, published a few years earlier and transcribed as an appendix to this book, although he insists that he is not following the "Owl." His source, however, is the same—the text of Osorius in which this supposed origin of the Basques was developed. Among the differences that the text of *Castellanos y vascongados* introduces into the supposed account by Osorius with respect to that of *El Búho gallego*, one stands out: the demonstration that the Hebrew character of the Basques is based on the existence of *Agotes* (Navarrese heretics) among them, assigning them Jewish character and, hence, making them all indistinguishable: Jews, Agotes, and Basques.

Selected Text(s):

Castellanos y vascongados. Tratado breve de una disputa y diferencia entre dos amigos, el uno castellano, de Burgos, y el otro vascongado, en la villa de Potosí, reino del Perú, documento hasta ahora inédito publicado por Z. [Castilians and Basques: Brief Treatise on a Dispute and Difference between Two Friends, One Castilian, from Burgos, and the Other Basque, in the Town of Potosí, Kingdom of Peru, Document until Now Unpublished by Z.], ed. Justo Zaragoza, (Madrid: Víctor Sáinz, 1876), 32, 48, 51–52.

Martin says the following:

. . .

"The third argument is based on this, that our Basque language is a corrupted form of Hebrew, which was the first language spoken in the world, in the same way that Italian today is a corrupted form of Latin.

. . .

And the most succinct way that I can express this, brother, replied Alonso, is that I have established that your origin is Jewish; for because you are such excellent Christians, it follows as I have said that you are all the more to be esteemed, and it is clearly demonstrated in what we attempt to show in the second chapter of argument, which is undeniable, that you and we agree that your native language is a corrupted form of Hebrew. We have already shown, in the same chapter, that it is not a language inherited by you from the grandchildren of Noah, but from the Rabbis who were banished and exiled to your lands and to their rugged terrain by Titus Vespasianus, as punishment for the death of Christ our Lord . . . These Basques named these mountains of Bizkaia, and today they still live there and still speak in their native language, which is very different from all the nations of Europe in every way, something never seen in any other nation: and the reason was that over the ages no one allowed them to enter their lands because they were generally despised by everyone, fearing they might be infected because most of them had tails just as today the *Agoteros* have who live among them and are one with them . . . I prefer not to offer in proof of the truth of what I say certain bad habits of yours that are common to this nation (of the Jews), but you know all too well that the cider that you drink, which is the *zizera* of the Jews, and that in addition to speaking corrupted Hebrew, as we have said, you place the accents of words all at the end, as in Madariaga, Urrutia, Ibarra, Targovra, and Jurioven. Similarly, the Hebrews do not abbreviate Iaco but say Jacob, Israel abbreviated but Israel elongated, although you often pretend to speak Romance. The truth and intention of what I say in further proof of your Jewishness is that many of your former churches have Hebrew names, even the town of Arrigorriaga, in which you defeated the aforementioned Prince Don Ordoño when you revolted against his father Don Alonso el Magno, third king of León. This place, I say, was called *Betulia*, the name of an important city of the Jews; and you know all too well that when the nation is the same, that in foreign languages they use the names of their own lands. This is proven in what we have seen from experience in the Indies, where we use names from Spain because we are Spanish, such as Trujillo, Córdoba, Jaén, Loja, and many others."

14. Álvaro Cubillo de Aragón

(Granada, late sixteenth century – ?, mid-seventeenth century)

He studied Humanities at the University of Granada and held a number of administrative offices including the Director of the Royal Prison of Calatrava. However, the economic difficulties he suffered to support his large family led him to move to the Court in 1646, where he was successful as the author of laudatory compositions and accounts of royal and courtly events: victory parades, colloquies, and so on. He was also a poet and prolific author of over a hundred plays, a quarter of which have been preserved. The work that is of specific interest here, *El enano de las musas* (The Dwarf of the Muses) (1654), is a collection of what are thought to be his best plays (for example, "Las muñecas de Marcela," "El amor como ha de ser," and "Los desagravios de Cristo"), as well as the title poem. It was more than forty pages in length, and written in response to *El Búho gallego*.

It is important to remember that the author was from Granada and that the Andalusians had not come off particularly well in Castro's little satire. Also, keep in mind that following the uprisings that occurred in 1640 in Portugal, Catalonia, and Andalusia, it did not seem prudent to continue exacerbating the tensions between peoples but on the contrary, to seek some degree of reconciliation and harmony among the political-cultural entities making up the kingdom. Álvaro Cubillo reacted quickly to the publication of *El Búho gallego*, publishing in 1625 (although it had been approved in 1623) "Curia leónica" (Lion's Court) (1625),[1] a poem in which he set about singing the praises of the Count of Olivares and especially the Council for the reform of customs which the latter had created. The work was published after Olivares had replaced the Duke of Lerma as royal favorite, so that anything written in homage to him was to the detriment of his predecessor and coterie, that is, the Count of Lemos himself. The poem, suitably revised, is the one that would a few years later be republished as the "Cortes del León y el Águila" (The Tribunal of the Lion and the Eagle) and would be included in *El enano de las musas*. In the poem, the birds of Spain once again assemble under the presidency of the Eagle and the Lion (Felipe IV) to conclude the controversy begun beside the Manzanares, which had been narrated in *El Búho gallego*. As for allusions to Basque matters, two interesting fragments stand out. One refers to specific policies affecting the *foral* regions, both the Basque Country and Navarre, as well as the constituent parts of the Kingdom of Aragón. Cubillo goes further, stressing the positive characteristics of Basques: nobility, religiosity, and their divine language. Finally, there is a somewhat ambiguous allusion to the Thrush that is open to different interpretations: the animal is caged, but "he isn't a captive, nor is he a fugitive when outside the cage." Is this a political metaphor alluding to the peculiar system of integration of Basques into the structure of the kingdom?

---

1. Álvaro Cubillo de Aragón, *Curia leónica. Compuesta por Álvaro Cubillo de Aragón, vezino de Granada, y Alcayde perpetuo de la cárcel Real de Calatrava* (Granada: Martín Fernández, 1625).

Selected Text(s):

El Enano de las Musas. Comedias y obras diversas, con un poema de las Cortes del León y del Águila Acerca del Búho gallego. Álvaro Cubillo de Aragón. Dedicated to D. Sebastián López Hierro de Castro, Caballero del órden de Calatrava, del Consejo de S. M. En el Tribunal de la Contaduría mayor de Cuentas, y su Secretario de la Junta de Millones, Tesorero general de la Santa Cruzada, etc. [The Dwarf of the Muses: Different Plays and Works, With a Poem from the Parliaments of the Lion and the Eagle About the Galician Owl. Álvaro Cubillo de Aragón. Dedicated to Don Sebastián López Hierro de Castro, Nobleman of the Order of Calatrava, in the Council of H. M. In the Tribunal of the Chief Cashier of Accounts, and His Secretary of the Committee of Debts, General Treasurer of the Holy Crusade, etc.] (Madrid: María de Quiñones, 1654).

To the noble, pious Thrush
whose nobility takes it to the top of the belfry,
and who wants to speak as humans do,
even though he speaks Basque, this we say,
that he may be caged, but he's nobody's
captive,
nor is he a fugitive, when he's outside the cage,
nor a slave, from this to the next century
for his long service, fidelity and functions,
a role repeated in the highest institutions
where the Holy Cross of their flags,
of which the Thrush has always availed,
feels celebrated by his shriek,
and his harp-like tongue,
sweetly aided and venerated,
that devotedly flew
from tower to tower in search of it [the Holy Cross] in Heaven:
Forgive me Owl, if this law offends you,
but thus does the general acclaim understand it.

. . .

The Bizkaian Thrush
and the Catalan Kite
walked out, clutching the *fueros* tightly,
hurriedly refusing

the portion they said was a burden,
because of this their often ammended *fueros*
were let down,
followed by the Navarrese Kestrel,
the Valencian Blackbird,
and the Aragonese Cuckoo, they all
began to demand...

15. Anonymous, *El tordo vizcaíno*

El tordo vizcaíno and *El pavo andaluz* were works whose composition was regarded as necessary in light of the circulation of *El Búho gallego*. There were three editions of *El tordo vizcaíno* in the seventeenth century, one right after the other, which tells us something about the diffusion of the Basque response and of the importance of the debate. Indeed, these editions were as clandestine and anonymous as those of *El Búho gallego* had been. The first edition might have been published in 1638. Unlike the burlesque tone of the Galician text, the Basque response was completely serious and erudite, as if to show that the matter was not some kind of game. A later, condensed and altered edition appeared in *Semanario erudito que comprehende varias obras inéditas, críticas, morales, instructivas, políticas, históricas, satíricas y jocosas de nuestros mejores autores antiguos y modernos* (Erudite Weekly Review that Comprises Several Unpublished, Critical, Moral, Instructional, Political, Historical, Satirical and Humorous Works by Our Best Ancient and Modern Authors), by Antonio de Valladares de Sotomayor (1789).[1] The most complete edition is, however, that of Andrés de Mañaricúa. The authorship of the defense has not been determined, but Mañaricúa offers sound arguments for the possibility that it was the work of Father Henao. What is certain is that among the well-known Basque authors (and defenders of all things Basque) of the period, one of the few who had the vast humanistic, ecclesiastic erudition, and knowledge of Basque culture that pervades *El tordo vizcaíno* was this Jesuit from Valladolid. The work transcends a mere response to *El Búho gallego*, devel-

1. "El tordo vizcaíno," in Antonio de Valladares de Sotomayor, *Semanario erudito que comprehende varias obras inéditas, críticas, morales, instructivas, políticas, históricas, satíricas y jocosas de nuestros mejores autores antiguos y modernos*, vol. 22 (Madrid, 1789), 110–210.

oping three additional extensive chapters: "In Praise of Cantabrians (Bizkaians)," "Nobility of the Bizkaians," and "In Praise of the Lords of Bizkaia," constituting a sophisticated and thorough synthesis of what Basque apologists had been arguing up until that time.

EL TORDO VIZCAYNO.

Grabado 25. Edición original de El Tordo Vizcaíno.

Selected Text(s):

El tordo vizcaíno [The Basque Thrush], Anonymous (n.p., c. 1638); reprint, as "El tordo vizcaíno, contestación al búho gallego" [The Basque Thrush, Reply to the Galician Owl]; reprint as app. 3 of Estanislao Labayru, *Historia de Bizcaya*, ed. Andrés Mañaricúa (1895–1903; reprint, Bilbao: La Gran Enciclopedia Vasca, 1976), fols. 85–88, 178–182.

This city, capital of the entire region, was called Cantabriga or Cantabria; in Basque *Cantauria* (city made of stone or built on a stony site). This city and the entire region as far as Villa Real de Araba were conquered by Augustus, who then entered *Vetulia*, which means "herd of cattle," because the land was flat and moist there was abundant grass for grazing. This was where they confined the Vacceos of *Batcaca*, which means "congregation," because there were already settlements in this region. The people of Zuberoa [Soule] get their name from *Zua*, which means "fire," because they were in a cold place and needed to generate heat to keep warm. The Iberians and Iberia derived their name from *Urberoa* (hot water), because it was a more temperate region. They called Zaragoza *Saldivar* (meadows for grazing horses). Tarragona was formerly *Yturriasco*, or *Turriasco* as a corrupted form, because it had many springs. The Orospedas Mountains were *Vroz Vide*, "road of cold water." The city of Anduxar was *Ylitugut* from *Yli Yturgi* (spring of water). The river Tadero was *Esta Bero* (warm water). Ispartorgui, near Anduxar, comes from *Vbastergo*, "a place beside the water." Eliberri, in Granada, was *Erriberri* (new place); Baza, from which Bastetania gets its name, was *Viecia* (a meeting or congregation of two). Astorga, Aturiza, is from *Aizturisa* (rainy mountain). Braga, in Portugal, is from *Bacarra* (isolated place). The city of Oviedo comes from *Obieta* (burial ground). And almost all the places of Spain, if we consider the primitive source, derive their names from the Basque language, although the words ended up being so corrupted, both by the different people who occupied Spain and by the lack of intelligence in the Greek and Roman authors, that they are almost unrecognizable. In addition, all these nations not only introduced their own language but they named places according to their own language or in their own honor, obliterating our antiquity.

These remnants that I have unearthed are sufficient to verify my claim and bring glory to Bizkaia, proving that their efforts were not sufficient to impose these corrupted forms in Cantabria where the language, clothing, customs, and character were always preserved in their pristine perfection. Moreover, these assertions by Romans and Greeks are logically unsound. The original language they discovered was so obscured by Spanish neglect that their claim seems more dream-like than true, the times being very ancient and lacking in fixed memoirs or any written evidence, nor were the evangelists basing their writing on revelations to verify their opinion. Even in more modern matters, their agenda was evident; so it would be more sensible to base our conclusions on the original names of the towns themselves, which offer clear proof of our thesis. The Romans and Greeks were speaking of Spain as she was after invasion by many nations. We would either have to deny that Tubal came and populated Spain or concede that her origins were in the region mentioned above and that all of Spain had a single origin, author, and language—Bizkaian—which at that time was common to all but is now restricted to that region. Because, is there even a single Greek or Latin author who even mentioned Tubal, his arrival, or his way of populating the Mountain? No one can show me the slightest reference. Therefore, they were speaking of later periods, not of the earliest times we are discussing and on which this discourse is based.

They are called people short in language by Titus Livy, author of this action. One needs patience to tolerate such nonsense. Many have written about the exploits of Titus. He was one of the best Emperors

Rome ever had. No one makes any reference to this event, which should be remembered because it was special . . .

Some call the Bizkaian language deficient. And consequently they regard the Bizkaians as deficient in language; not because they cut short their syllables, as Titus tried to show, but by implying that the language is deficient and lacking in words. It is true that Basque is not as verbose as Greek, but succinct and dignified, full of adages and refrains, and perfectly capable of being written, and if it isn't it's because it's confined to a few small provinces and their authorities, who are Castilians, would need interpreters and the native speakers need practice in other languages.

And this is the most ancient language in Spain, according to many writers, and those who deny this are speaking of later periods after other nations invaded and corrupted the native speech. And even the Romans acknowledge that it was spoken throughout Spain and even in Corsica in later periods, according to the testimony of Seneca, who saw and experienced it: "*Eadem enim tegumenta capitum, idque genus calciamenti, quod Cantabris est, et verba quaedam*" (In effect, [they have] the same head-dresses, the same kind of shoes, as the Cantabrians, and the same language). They wear the same clothing, he says, and speak many Bizkaian words; however, through contact with the Greeks and Genovese, I find that all have been corrupted. And thus, in the rest of Spain, it was extinguished and obliterated; only in Bizkaia was it preserved in its pure form, unaltered by any other language, and there was no change in clothing. This is why the noblemen always preserved words in their true form, without exception.

And it is a very natural language, as can be seen in children; because in it they generally address their parents, as soon as they know them, calling the father *Ayta* and the mother *Mama*. And Castilian shares many words with this language, as those who understand both languages observe. And this is not surprising or debatable, for we see that it shares with Roman, Greek, German, and other languages certain similarities even in the formation of the most political and critical terms.

People in Fuenterrabia [Hondarribia] are very clumsy, and they say the name is derived from Rabbi. What a stupid thing to say! What does one thing have to do with the other? In Basque, Fuenterrabia is *Ondar ybia*, from *Ondar*, which means "fat sand," and *ybia* (ebb tide). And the name Fuenterrabia in Castilian comes about over a certain conflict between Bizkaians and Frenchmen, and from Nuño Rabia, governor of that castle. And other places have different names in Basque from the corresponding name in Castilian: they call San Sebastián *Donostia*, and

Pamplona *Yrum*. Don't you remember the Gallic siege in the year 1638, where without weapons, ammunition, or food a few [Basques] held off hordes of Frenchmen. Even the women practicing the art of Mars with such precision, skill, and spirit that those who had been spinning wool yesterday were fighting more skillfully than Bellona. It was as if there had been a rebirth of those centuries when they had confounded the Romans and been looked on as the example and model of the Globe, exposing their sons in the dawn of their lives to the coldness of Thetis and the rugged peaks of Europe, killing their loved ones courageously on dire occasions to keep them from being enslaved, and afterwards charging out like true Amazons to avenge their deaths and anoint them with enemy blood.

Think of Amezqueta [Amezketa], which sounds like *mezquita*, there being many mosques in Galicia at one time. I'm not surprised: but tell me, savage, what does *mezquita* have to do with *Amezqueta*? Don't you know that Amezqueta and Amesaga take their names from the places where their houses were established, a place where there were *Amesac* (hybrid trees), just as Insaurraga, Insaurreta, and Insausti take theirs from the place where there were many walnut trees, and Arteaga and Arteeta from ash trees and from the place where they grew? And mosque, what does it have to do with synagogue? In Galicia, there were many of these sisters, but they were never found in Bizkaia. In Galicia, you could find Huns, followers of Priscilian, Ocem, Ogul, Jews, and Moors, but no outsiders were ever allowed in this country. The Bizkaians and Gipuzkoans are one people, equal in nobility and equal in valor; their origins the same. Spain had her origins in them, they populated her, created her, gave her their clothing and their language; they have always defended her. These provinces are sisters, equal in origin and beginning.

16. Lope Martínez de Isasti Lezo

(Lezo, Gipuzkoa, c. 1565 – ?, ?)

A priest, he was endowed with a benefice in the parish of Lezo (Gipuzkoa), and subsequently held other ecclesiastical and secular offices: abbot, confessor, Court Treasurer, and supply foreman in the shipyards of Lezo. His father, Onofre, had served the Crown, first as treasurer in Flanders, then as artillery captain, and finally as outfitter of a ship for the Magellan-Elcano expedition in 1581. As for his brothers, they studied to be lawyers or priests in Salamanca, or served as captains of ships or officials in the royal shipyards. Ships or the priesthood were, therefore, the "natural" destinies of the men of the family. His was to study in Salamanca with two of his brothers, although at a certain moment in his life he was unable to overcome the call of the sea; thus, on the death of his brother Onofre, the office of director of the royal shipyards was passed on to him. When he completed his term in 1618, he was transferred to Madrid to render his accounts, remaining in the Court to expedite this process for more than seven years, during which time he availed himself of the opportunity to satisfy his intellectual curiosity and write his works, among them the *Compendio historial de la M. N. y M. L. Provincia de Guipúzcoa* (Historical Compendium of the Most Noble and Most Loyal Province of Gipuzkoa) (1625). He was actively involved in the suppression of witchcraft, belonging to a group of authors who literally believed in the diabolic pact and the capacity of witches to change their physical appearance, fly through the air, and cause harm, among other wiles. Isasti represented the perfect model of the repressive true believer, a disciple of the medieval doctrines of the *Malleus maleficarum* (The Hammer of the Malefactors), the standard handbook on witchcraft at that time.

His historical work, as well as his investigations into witchcraft, although written in the first third of the seventeenth century, remained unpublished during his lifetime, having to wait until 1850 and 1933, respectively, to be available in print. This does not mean, however, that they were not read or failed to exert significant influence. It is important to keep in mind that the original manuscripts of his *Compendio* were lost and that there were several versions in circulation that had been annotated by Rafael Floranes and other authors. They reorganized the materials somewhat; therefore any evaluation of his work must necessarily be based on the text that was finally published in 1850. As a result, it may be the case that the errors and insights found in the text cannot be attributed entirely to the original writing.

Although it was not his only work,[1] here we will examine Isasti's *Compendio*, a manuscript intended to demonstrate the universal and original nobility of Gipuzkoa, where language is one of the pillars of the

1. See, for example, Lope Martínez de Isasti, *Relación que hizo el Doctor don Lope de Ysasti presbytero y beneficiado de Leço que es en Guipuzcoa acerca de las maléficas de Cantabria por mandado del Sr Inquisidor Campofrío en Madrid, 1618*, ed. Julio Caro Baroja, *Anuario de la Sociedad de Eusko-Folklore* 13 (1933).

argument. Although he might seem to be beating a dead horse, Isasti succeeds in reinforcing egalitarian ideology through a thorough accumulation of convincing materials. In his emphasis on secular independence and voluntary surrender, he follows Garibay.[2] Beginning with the mythical arguments relating to Tubal, followed by an ethnographic reconstruction of the province focusing on its ancestral character, and then evoking the services that the people of Gipuzkoa contributed to the Crown historically and the role this territory played as a buffer zone, and culminating in an endless list of the illustrious Gipuzkoan noblemen who have contributed to the construction of the kingdom, starting with Ignatius of Loyola and concluding with the captains of ships in the royal navy; the list includes admirals, bishops, doctors, accountants, treasurers, officials of the Inquisition, and so on. Isasti places special emphasis on the religious argument viewed in political terms: the continuity of faith from Tubal through the preaching of Saint James in the Basque Country.[3]

This linking, or continuity, between Tubal and Saint James had already been posited by Miguel de Zabaleta,[4] who presented Gipuzkoans as being continually at war with Islam or the "wicked Luther." He was probably the first author to make clear the extension of the nobility as far as Gipuzkoa, in the sense that family seats came to signify territorialized nobility. Thus, Isasti stands as a model exponent of the "egalitarian" philosophy, in which the Tubalist origins of the initial inhabitants of the territory would confer nobility implicit in the land, language, clothing, and customs; and which were subsequently assumed to have been maintained pure and unsullied by outside influences. The continuity of the Basque language represented proof of a secular independence, "an argument based on their never having been conquered or mixed with other foreign nations," making Basque the "most ancient language" of Spain.[5]

With regard to the chapter dedicated to the Basque language,[6] Isasti is not particularly original, but he has the merit of accumulating

2. Lope Martínez de Isasti, *Compendio historial de la M. N. y M. L. Provincia de Guipúzcoa* (San Sebastián: Ramón Baroja, 1850), 271–74.

3. Ibid., 196–97.

4. Miguel de Zabaleta, *Relación verdadera de la jornada que su Majestad el Rey don Filipe Tercero de España, hizo a la Provincia de Guipúzcoa* (Logroño: Matías Mares, 1616).

5. Martínez de Isasti, *Compendio*, 261.

6. Ibid., "De la lengua Cantabra bascongada, de su antigüedad y elegancia," bk. 1, ch. 12.

a considerable amount of material and quotations from other authors who had shown themselves to support or reject the capacity of the language to be written, governed by rules, and its barbarity or refinement, for example. These writers include Garibay, Echave, Poza, Marineo Sículo, Mariana, Brother Alonso Venero, Morales, Alderete, and so on. In effect, the chapter constitutes a kind of summation and updating of the arguments presented to that moment in the debate about the language: its antiquity, its importation by Tubal, its extension throughout Spain before Latin and Castilian and hence its Spanish authenticity, whose character allowed it to be used for literature, for example. Of course, Isasti was a proponent of the Cantabrian and Basque-Iberian theory. In proof of the ancient extension of Basque throughout the peninsula, he invokes the standard study of the toponymy of Spanish towns and cities that could be interpreted as Basque as well as the analysis of a collection of Castilian, Latin, Greek, Hebrew, Galician, and Asturian terms that were equally understood to be purely Basque. Additionally, an argument that has special importance in the mental universe of Isasti (the insistence on Basque nobility) is based on the fact that that a large proportion of the most distinguished lineages of Spanish nobility was also Basque in origin. A fair number of the cases that he analyzes are obviously Basque, and he provides valid etymologies for them: Anaia, Mendoza, Velasco, and Artza, for example; others, however, such as Ossorio are somewhat forced. With regard to the capacity of Basque to be a literary instrument, he recalls the example of the "Ave Maria" transcribed by Echave, and in turn he introduces several examples, from a few verses by Dechepare to a long list of proverbs with their corresponding Castilian translation, proceeding to a version of the "Salve Regina" and an octave by Miguel Suescun. Moreover, Isasti, like Poza, employs a philosophical and mystical interpretation of the language, in such a way that the words take on more or less didactic explanations of their capacity for abstraction, intellectual sophistication and Christian character, with interpretations of examples that are for the most part pure fantasy. Particularly delirious is the "philosophical" interpretation that is offered regarding death (*eriotza*), which would mean "cold wound," because "since coldness is the enemy of generation and life, and old age ends in this coldness, in order for us to understand what death is, it is spelled out for us as just the opposite of the predominately temperate or hot, moist warmth that sustains life."

Selected Text(s):

Compendio historial de la M. N. y M. L. Provincia de Guipúzcoa (1625) [Historical Compendium of the Most Noble and Most Loyal Province of Gipuzkoa]; reprint, (San Sebastián: Ramón Baroja, 1850), bk. 1, chs. 3 and 13.

Chapter 3

14. The nobility and valor of the natives and original inhabitants of Gipuzkoa are well-known throughout the world, having survived from ancient times in their ancestral homes with great purity, unmixed with other foreign nations, as is evident in their Basque language, clothing, and style of life; and this is evidenced by the decrees, laws (these being confirmed by the Kings of Castile), privileges, escutcheons, and coats of arms, which the greatest and earliest won by their heroic feats and exploits in battles, so that finally, in recognition of their prosperous and felicitous actions, their heirs and descendants are honored and ennobled in memory of such deeds.

15. Historical accounts verify that they did not mix with the Romans, Moors, or Jews, particularly that of Bishop Sandoval concerning the descendants of the house of Haro, his account being confirmed by Brother Juan de Mariana, that when the Moors entered Spain they did not pass beyond the fortified rock of San Adrian (which overlooks the border of Araba), and this is repeated by Dr. Illescas and Garibay, and confirmed by Brother Juan Benito Guardiola in his *Treatise* [on Can-

tabrian nobility] saying that those who come from the ancestral homes of Gipuzkoa, Araba, and Bizkaia consider themselves noblemen, because in those regions the Christians were as free of Moorish influence as they had been of Roman influence originally, conserving until the present the language that they spoke then, as attested by Per Anton Beuter, a very wise and learned Master of Sacred Theology, among many other authors including Ambrosio de Morales, Lucio Floro, Marineo Sículo, Juan Gutierrez, and Poza. And Dr. Guevara in the *Treatise on the founding of Spain* printed in Milan in the year 1586, in folio 8, says vehemently that neither Gipuzkoa nor Bizkaia was ever conquered.

Chapter 13

Of the Cantabrian/Basque language, its Antiquity and Elegance.

1. Among the other wondrous gifts that mankind received from the hand of God were, first, reason and her interpreter, language. With the former, he made him in his own likeness, and with the latter he allowed him to have company with other men, through communication and interaction. Both were sovereign gifts worthy of all gratitude, which man failed to fulfill, however, rising against his superiors by beginning that proud tower of the first King called Nimrod, later called the tower of Babel, which he and his accomplices tried to build in the plain of Sumer so high that its top would touch the sky in celebration of his name, before they were scattered, as they were completing this, at the very culmination of their efforts, Almighty God, the Creator of all things, decided and proceeded to humble their pride with an admirable device, for suddenly all those people building it began to speak to one another without the common language they had used until then, as the Holy Scripture says in *Genesis*, which was God's just punishment.

2. This diversity of languages divided men, alienating their hearts and minds from those who did not speak as they did; and from this, hatred and wars ensued, men judging those who were different in language as different in nature. Historians say that there were seventy-two languages created in the confusion of the tower, and that one of these was Basque, which is the one Tubal brought, as Esteban de Garibay tries to prove and Marineo Sículo, a serious and objective writer, states clearly, as do others cited below. This happened 1,788 years after the creation of the world according to the calculations of the very erudite Brother Alonso Maldonado and Tubal, son of Japheth, populated Spain, as ordered by his grandfather Noah 1,799 years after the creation of the world, and according to Poza he arrived twelve years after the confusion of languages.

3. In this province, the Basque language, called *Euskara*, has been spoken since the beginning, and its survival over so many centuries is proof that the province was never conquered or invaded by other foreign nations, as Orozco observes in the *Tesoro de la lengua castellana* [Treasury of the Castilian Language] and Dr. Guevara in his *Tratado de la nobleza de Cantabria* [Treatise on the Nobility of Cantabria].

4. This language is spoken in the Basque Country, in most of Navarre, and in French Guinea, called Lapurdi, which is on the border, in Araba and the Kingdom of Bizkaia, except in the city of Orduña; and it differs in certain words. The farther removed it is from Castile the purer it is. They apparently called themselves Basques as a derivation from *Bascos*, but this in no way means that it was not the language brought by Tubal, for he reached Navarre before he came to Gipuzkoa, as has been explained in chapter 2.

5. It is thought to be the oldest language in Spain, and this is proven not only by the native speakers but by writers outside Gipuzkoa. The first of these, perhaps, is the Master Pedro de Medina, who in his *History of the Kingdom of Castile,* affirms that before the Romans imposed their language (Romance) on Castile they spoke a barbaric, or Basque, language. Father Mariana, a native of Talavera, says the same thing in his *History*, but that it was not common throughout Spain. Dr. Bernardo Joseph de Alderete, canon of Cordoba, says that Tubal and Noah brought this language to Spain and that, in the time of the famous cosmographer [Pomponius] Mela, Spanish was spoken, as can be inferred from his words quoted here in the first chapter, and this author flourished in the time of Augusto Costa, although Ambrosio de Morales places him in the time of the Emperor Claudius in the year 42 after the birth of Christ. The legal authority Andrés de Poza, a native of Bilbao, in his book on the original language and inhabitants of Cantabria cites authorities and offers sound arguments against the claims of Ambriosio de Morales and Florian de Ocampo, proving that this language was the oldest and the first to be spoken in Spain: and the first authority he cites is Seneca of Cordoba, tutor of the Emperor Nero, who when living in exile in Corsica wrote a letter to his mother Alvina, saying that according to ancient legend Spaniards inhabited it before the arrival of the Goths or any other nation, because the footwear, headgear, and many words used by the islanders were those used in earlier times by the peoples of Cantabria who lived near the Ebro, the assumption being these islanders had not had occasion to lose their mother tongue until other nations arrived, and that they had preserved it in ancient times. Dr. Alderete mentions this letter of Seneca's and affirms that this language

was one of the 72, and it was maintained in Bizkaia, and he adds: if this is some consolation to them, they will never lose it on my account, for I'm not trying to take it from them. Bishop Sandoval states emphatically, in the catalogue of the bishops of Pamplona, that Basque is the original language of the ancient inhabitants of Spain. Brother Alonso Venero of the Order of Santiago (who wrote the *Enchiridion de los tiempos* in the year 1551) disputes this point bizarrely, concluding that since before the Romans came there was no other foreign language in Spain except Basque (which the natives have always used without surrendering to the Romans, Goths, Vandals, or Suevians), it obviously follows that this was the native language of Castile.

6. Esteban de Garibay, in several places in his *Compendium*, and Baltasar de Echave, a resident of Mexico, in a special book that he wrote in this language, prove our point with many sound reasons and examples of names of mountains and places, which will be cited separately: and further proof is provided by the graduate Zaldibia in his treatise, citing the Archbishop Don Rodrigo and Saint Isidoro. And finally Antonio Navarro de Larreategui, Secretary to His Majesty and to the Most Serene Prince Philiberto, expresses this view in his *Epitome de los Señores de Vizcaya* and cites as sources Marineo Sículo and Father Mariana, as well as Pomponius Mela, saying that Tubal and Noah introduced this Basque language. Per Anton Beuter and Mario Arecio said the same thing; and Don Miguel de Zavaleta sums the matter up succinctly, saying, "It is well known that their Basque language is one of the seventy-two, and the first in Spain, however much envy denies this."

7. Be sure that this is not a barbaric, crude language, lacking in elegance, as Medina and Mariana claimed; rather, it is elegant and well structured, as Joseph Scaliger said elegantly, because it has its meanings and etymologies, is spoken fluently and has its grammar, as some have demonstrated, forming conjugations in Basque . . . It is easy to learn when studied regularly, as experience has shown by the Castilians who have lived near the border of Gipuzkoa and speak Basque reasonably well, and by the savages in the mountains in a region as remote as Newfoundland through their contact with the Basque sailors who go there each year to fish for cod, who on being asked in Basque: *nola zaude* (how are you?) answer wittily: *Apaizac obeto* (Not as well as the Priests!), having no idea what a priest is, but simply because they've heard it. They speak and trade with our people and help them fish on the shore in exchange for some biscuits and cider that they do not have.

8. It is also easy to write, as proven by the Graduate Elso, a Navarrese Basque who one hundred years ago wrote a book on Christian doctrine

in Romance and Basque: and Baltasar de Echave offers as proof of this many things written in Basque, in particular the Ave Maria: and the Bishop of Pamplona, Don Antonio de Venegas ordered a catechism or primer on Christian doctrine to be written in Basque, which is in print, and later others have been written so that the children of Gipuzkoa and Bizkaia can learn the prayers and doctrine in them. Many years ago, Monsieur Echapare from Lower Navarre composed a divine book in this language, and among other curious things, he wrote some notable sentences, which go like this:

Each thing consists
of just two points, to wit:
if we do good, be sure
that Paradise is ours.
And he who dies in sin
forever more is lost;
no other roads exist,
choose wisely then.
Each man, no matter where,
should be aware
how God on high
made him a man,
and how he chose to shape
our soul like his,
endowed with memory,
intelligence and will.
What Lord would hire
a servant steeped in sin,
or pay him if he failed
to serve him well?
Just so it is with us,
the Lord on high
won't share his glory
unless we do his will.
I see great wickedness
among us here:
so many serve
our prideful enemy,
heeding not Christ
our Savior; in this all know
we do great wrong
sans road, sans reason.

9. Although he was a foreigner, Marineo Sículo, because he was informed about the clear system that existed in the Basque language for counting, set it down in his *History* in Basque, saying that, for one we said *bat*; for two (*bi*), for three (*iru*), for four (*lau*), for five (*bost*), for six (*sei*), for seven (*zazpi*), for eight (*zorci*), for nine (*bederatci*), for ten (*amar*), for twenty (*oguei*), for thirty (*ogueita amar*), for forty (*berroguei*), for fifty (*berroguei ta amar*), for sixty (*iruroguei*), for seventy (*iruroguei ta amar*), for eighty (*lauroguei*), for ninety (*lauroguei ta amar*), for one hundred (*eun*), and for a thousand (*milla*).

10. All the singular nouns end in *a*, and the plurals in *ac*. For instance: *cerua* (sky), *ceruac* (skies); we call God, *Jaungoicoa* (Lord on High); our Lady Saint Mary (*Andre done Maria*); Saint Michael (*Jaun done Miquele*), Saint John the Baptist (*Jaun done Juanis Bautista*), Saint Peter (*Jaun done Petri*), Saint Stephen (Jaun done Estebe), Saint Sebastian (*Jaun done Sostie*), Saint Martin (*Jaun done Martie*), and the Feast of all Saints (*Done Sancturu*), because *done* in Basque means "Saint"; and it should be noted that because of the obligation that priests have to be saints, they are given the title of *Don* (which sounds the same as Saint) in the Bishopric of Pamplona, which includes the greater part of Gipuzkoa. Garibay observed this about the village of San Sebastian, saying that it is called *Donostie*, as did Abrahan Ortelio and Friar Gerónimo Roman.

11. We call the Church *Eliza*, derived from the Hebrew word *Eli*, which means God, as if to say, "House of God." Christmas Eve we call *Onenzaro*, "the season of those who are good"; others say *Gavon* (good night); we call the sun *eguzquia*, "guide of the day"; the moon, *illarguia*, "dead light" or "month light"; death we call *eriotza*, meaning "blow," "wound," or "cold accident," which incarnates a brief philosophical discourse since coldness is the enemy of generation and life, and old age ends in this coldness, thus, so that we will understand what death is, it is spelled out for us as the opposite of the predominately temperate or hot, moist warmth that sustains life.

12. These four examples of the names of God, sun, moon, and death are mentioned by Poza in his book, and he defends this language, saying that it is neither barbaric nor inadequate, but elegant and founded on deep philosophical principles, and is one of the seventy-two that were divinely imparted, as has been said; and that a language is superior to the degree that its words are mysterious, because it gives the definitions and properties of things with intelligence and doctrine, revealing the nature of the thing by a single path both to the simple and the wise,

without the need for further teaching or study. We call the eyes *beguiac*, which means "two guides"; we call parents *gurasoac*, "those who are our responsibility, as we were theirs," the word derived from *gure jasoac*, which has the same meaning. The old man we call *agurea*, as if we were saying "our father and good sir," because *agur Jauna*, which is a very common greeting that means "I pay homage to you, Sir, as my elder and an old man," derived from the name *agurea*; we call a gentleman *zalduna* (he who rides a horse); the rich man, *aberatsa* (abundant in cattle) because *aberea* is "'cattle," and *atsez* is "abundance"; and so the Castilian *haber* (have) and *asaz* (enough) is taken from the Basque words for cattle and abundance, because the first wealth the Spanish people ever had was an abundance of cattle; this is also why Latin used the name *pecunia* for coin, as Saint Augustine observes. We call the house, *ichea*, others call it *etsea*, which means "enclosed thing"; and something that is enclosed by a wall we call *ormaichea*; this is why Castilians call walls *ormazos*, as Morales observes, a word derived from Basque; *aramburu* is what we call "the house at the head of the valley," because *aranea* means "valley" and *burua* "head"; we call the castle *Gaztelua*, which means "a place of watching," *gaiztela loa*, and "it's not good to sleep there"; frost we call *izotza* (cold dew); the goat is *aunzumea* (child of the she-goat); curd is *gaztambera* (soft cheese); trout is *amuarraina* (fish caught with a hook) because it is caught without bait with a feather around the hook; we call the frog *iguela* because it walks by swimming, which is *igueri* in Basque; the swing is *zoraburua* because when we're afraid the head swings back and forth as we walk; wicker is *zumea* (slender stick), because that's how it is. There are many other nouns of this sort, which have their intentional derivation and etymology as in a perfect language. And what is most amazing is that pointed objects end in *cia*, which is "the sharpened pole," like *Lancia*, which is "very pointed," and according to Marcus Varro and Aulo Gelio, cited by Alderete and Roman, the word *Lancia* is Spanish, not Latin; *Guecia* is "a small throwing dart held between two fingers bound together with a strap made of boar's bristle which our warriors used in fighting against the Romans"; *burruncia* is "the spit"; *ciria* (the wedge), similar to "the snake," which is narrow and makes the same hissing sound. All of this goes to show how natural this language is, and those who deny it make this mistake because they do not understand it.

13. Emperor Charles V of glorious memory enjoyed speaking Basque, having learned some words simply out of curiosity or because his confessor, priest, and doctor were Basques, as is noted in the appropriate place; and I have learned from trustworthy witnesses that when he met

a muleteer from Navarre on the road he asked him in Basque: *Mandazaia nondic zatoz*? (Muleteer where do you come from?) and he answered *Nafarroatic* (from Navarre); and then he asked another question: *Nafarroan gari asco*? (Is there much wheat in Navarre?) and the man answered, *bat Jauna asco* (Yes, sir, there's a lot!); and the Emperor concluded by saying: *Nafarroan gari asco, batere batere ez neretaco* (Lots of wheat in Navarre, but none for me!).

14. On the day they elected her Abbess of the convent of Santa Maria de la Cruz in the village of Cubas, five leagues from Madrid, the blessed Sor Juana de la Cruz spoke in Basque with a man from the Basque provinces although she had never studied the language. Astonished, the man said: "Lady, it is not I who elects you Abbess but the Holy Spirit, who commands it," and she repeated what he had said, and the nuns were overjoyed to see themselves subjects to such a blessed prelate. Friar Antonio Daza mentions this holy woman in his book.

17. Pedro de Agramont y Zaldibar

(Tudela [Tutera], Navarre, 1567 – Tudela?, 1635)

He is just one among an entire family saga of scribes: his great grandfather Fernando, his grandfather Pedro, his great uncle Lorenzo, his father Gaspar, his uncle Miguel, and his cousin Pedro. Despite the surname, this family did not belong to the nobility but to the urban bourgeoisie. He moved to Madrid where he prospered for a time practicing his knowledge as secretary and scribe. However, it would seem that he was not all that successful, perhaps because of his presumed converted origin. On the death of his father in 1591, he returned to Tudela, taking over his notary's office, where he worked until his own death.

His *Historia de Navarra* (History of Navarre), written in 1632 but not published until 1996, seems to have been prepared at a particularly inopportune moment for its publication, considering the national tensions that would break out in 1640 and that it was a work which, having to take sides in the kingdom or king polemic, favored the former at the expense of the latter. Then, after several tense years, the Navarrese authorities acknowledged the need to create a history of the kingdom, naming José Moret as the official chronicler of the realm in 1654 and assigning the project to him. Agramont's *Historia de Navarra* ended up being set aside and forgotten, so completely that only recently was a copy of his manuscript discovered in the monastery of Santo Domingo de Silos, Burgos. Despite the fact that the work was little known and its influence on later authors is negligible, it takes on significant interest because, on the one hand, it is the continuation to the history by García de Góngora affirming the Cantabrian and Tubalist character of Navarre, and on the other hand, a kind of transition between the thought of Arnaud Oihenart and that of Moret. As for the utilization of Agramont's *Historia de Navarra* by other authors, it seems that Moret (in the seventeenth century) was familiar with it but that Francisco de Alesón (in the eighteenth century) no longer had access to it.

Most of the Tubalist and Cantabrian arguments that he uses had already been expressed by writers from Bizkaia and Gipuzkoa, especially Garibay and Echave, whom he cites and follows, although always placing emphasis on the linkage between the Basque language and Navarre and on this region as a reference point for the entire Tubalist episode. The interpretation as to why Tubal's hosts settle in Vasconia (Cantabria) after disembarking from the Mediterranean is quite an interesting blend of economic and political arguments: "the fruits and herbs that were so abundant there,"[1] and "they found it necessary, in order to avoid being oppressed and conquered by others, and to live according to the laws and freedom they had always enjoyed, to take refuge in the mountains of Navarre, Bizkaia, and Cantabria where they could better defend themselves and preserve their language, clothing, government, and way of life."[2]

SELECTED TEXT(S):

Historia de Navarra 1632 [History of Navarre] (Pamplona: Mintzoa, 1996), 44–45, 53–56, 63–66, 69–72, 85, 184.

Hebrew was the First Language Spoken in the World

Concerning which was the first language that was spoken in the world, a number of different opinions can be found among different authors, but those most probable and true are that it was Hebrew because of the many meanings that the nouns of the world's first parents take from that

1. Pedro de Agramont y Zaldibar, *Historia de Navarra 1632* (Pamplona: Mintzoa, 1996), 47.

2. Ibid., 69.

language that are contained in the Holy Scripture, and for other reasons that their defenders offer on their behalf.

Chapter 4

Concerning the motive and the arrival of Tubal in Hespaña, the origin and choice of the Basque language, describing where he set sail and where he landed. What they ate and how they dressed, how they extended and distributed the land. Their customs and dwellings and family hierarchies, and what they did when someone died. The founding of cities. The doctrine and death of Tubal, and the way they gathered in the mountains for burials.

The Reason for Tubal's Journey to Spain

Before the confusion of languages, Tubal was given the name in the Hebrew language that means "nest" or "thing of the world." He was the son of Japheth and the grandson of Noah. And being caught between Nimrod's forces and the other tyrants who were his own relatives, and not being able to tolerate the yoke of subjection, or give up the doctrine that his grandfather the patriarch Saint Noah had taught him, to stay true to it, asking for his blessing to maintain it in freedom because of what he had told them about Spain when he distributed the provinces among them, he decided to go there with his people, seeing how much his families had increased and grown.

Origin and Choice of the Basque Language

Whereupon, because in the confusion of the languages that befell the proud people building the tower of Babel there were no generals, and the Basque language had sprung up in the plains of Sumer, which in Basque means "battlefield," Tubal and his people chose it and put it *enescura*, which is the same as saying "to take in hand" or "speak in our way." And they had spoken it for less than fifteen years when they set out on their journey, supplied with herds of cattle and other things necessary to sustain and help them until they reached their destination. Spain had been uninhabited after the flood for 143 years according to some authors, and according to others a few more or a few less, when Tubal came to populate it, leaving four famous traces of his language and beloved country there, these being Armenia, Gordeya, Arage, and Ararat or Aralar, provoking deep sentiment and tears in those who remained behind and those who were departing, because although different in their languages, they all recognized each other as relatives.

. . .

Chapter 5

In which Tubal and his descendants proceeded to give these mountains names that were similar to those they left behind in Armenia, and others in their Basque language, such as Amenach, Sangüesa, Aragon, and Sobrarbe, thus proving that they entered Spain by way of these places.

They Give the Mountains of Navarre Names Similar to Those in Armenia

Tubal and his people remembered their country Armenia with great love, and on finding in Spain land similar to the native land they left behind, they began to populate it and give it names similar to those they left there and which were appropriate to the qualities and nature of the land they were inhabiting. And this is evident in the many names preserved even today for places in these mountains of Navarre, for in memory of the famous river born in Greater Armenia and celebrated by cosmographers, called Araxa or Arages [Aras], they gave the same name Arages to the river that has its source in Navarre near the church of San Miguel de Excelsi, from which it runs through the valley that takes its name Araxa from the river, which is now called Araiaza, and flows down to the province of Gipuzkoa, and skirting the villages of Tolosa and Usurbil, it enters the Cantabrian Sea at Orio, two leagues from San Sebastián.

. . .

Cantabria, Where It Got Its Name

Another site near the city of Logroño they named Cantauria, which means "place between cliffs," because settlement or city in Basque is called *uria* or *iria*, and by accentuating the *u* and pronouncing it as *be* they called it Cantabria when they should have said Cantauria. And they called the region Cantabriga, because in Basque Cantauria conveys only the idea of the population of a town, and by adding the syllable –*ga* at the end and saying *Cantauriga*, or *Cantabriga*, you include the entire region, as in Orianiaga, Astigarriaga, or Çuriaga, and others like these. So without the final syllable –*ga* they signify the towns, but with it the entire region and province around them; and just because they have these suffixes –*briga* or –*riaga* it doesn't mean that they were the source of Brigo, for they are proper words and syllables from Basque.

Ebro, Where It Got Its Name

They called the Ebro River *Ubero*, which in Basque means "hot river," because these original inhabitants of Spain had come down from these mountains where the water was harsh and cold, and they found the water in this river turbid and hot, so they called it *Ubero* or *Ibaivero*, which means "hot river." On its shore, near the sea, where Tortosa stands today, a city was founded, which they called *Uberia* or *Iberia*, which means "town of Ubero," or "beside the river Ubero." And because of that, they called the region Iberia and all of Spain by the same name. And another foundation by this same name is still in Navarre, beside the river Arga.

. . .

Chapter 7

On the antiquity of the Basque language and how Tubal used it to allow his people to know the true God. And it is demonstrated with many names of places in Basque, which are preserved even today in Spain, and it was the common language of all Spain.

Antiquity of the Basque Language

Many historians have written that the Basque language was one of those that were spoken in Spain when it was first inhabited. And they have been forced to admit this because it has not been found anywhere else in the world, and because it was always preserved in the mountains of Navarre and Bizkaia, which is undeniable. But they refuse to acknowledge its primacy or to believe that it was the common language; instead, they look for ways around this and for reasons to make it seem that it never extended beyond the provinces in which it is spoken today, as if it were not possible to demonstrate the contrary given the profusion of testimony or evidence left behind all over Spain in the names they gave to different places in this language that are still preserved today, even if the native speakers do not understand the meaning or know their origins or antiquity. It is well known that in this language the ancient idolatry came to worship and adore Noah, second father of the human race, as a god whom the ethnics called Jano as these words imply: "*Noe reparatorem orbis profane mundi genesim ignorantes caelum Janum et partum deorum appellarunt*" [Those that ignored Noah as the repairer of genesis, or the origin of that globe termed the world, called heaven Jano and the product of the gods]. This name Jano sounds like *Joana*, which in Basque means "good lord." This was the name the idolators used when they worshiped Noah. And to show his people that there was another lord whom they should adore and worship—God, creator of all things, even more powerful, supreme and better than his grandfather Noah—

Tubal revealed the name *Jaongaicoa*, which means "good lord on high," because *Joana* means specifically "good lord" and the name *jaongoicoa* "good lord on high" who is the true God. And this word is made up of *Jaun*, which means "master" or "lord," and *ona*, which means "good;" and to this Tubal added *goicoa*, which means "high," so his people would understand that the lord in the sky was the true God and lord, creator of all things, as he had learned from his grandfather Noah.

And afterwards his people called their ancient ruling patriarchs *guarascoac*, which in Basque means "those who ruled over us," deriving this name from *gurejasoac*, referring to those who taught them to worship just one God, creator of all things, as they did, having been taught to do so by their patriarchs. And they used and continue to use as a common greeting among Basques the phrase *agur jauna*, which is the same as "goodbye, good sir" in romance, because *agur jauna* is the same as *agurea*, and *agurea* the same as *ayta agurea*, which is "our father," and *agur jauna* the same as "our father" or "good lord" or "master"; and this signifies what they say respectfully when they greet each other with this word, which was reserved only for their elders.

Basque Was the Common Language of Spain

In order to understand that this language was common in Spain it is important to see that throughout Spain there are many Basque words, and that the first words they teach their children to say are *aita* for father and *mama* for mother, which are purely Basque words without any alteration, just as the woman who raises the child is called *ama*, which means "mother," and the evacuation of children is called *caca*, which in Basque means "manure." *Mozo* (young man) and *moza* (young woman) means "without hair," the way the men and women in these mountains of Navarre and Bizkaia remain even today until they marry; and *motza* means anything "sheared," and *motilar* (to crop) means to "moisten," "shear" and "shave" the hair. *Teta* (teat) is a Basque word, as is *aldea*, which means "female neighbor" or "village woman"; *masmordon* in this language means "weak man," who is called *madeja sin cuerda* (lock of hair without a cord; something abnormal) in Castilian, which is to say *madeja sin centenal* (lock of hair without a tie) or *colchon sin bastas* (mattress without stuffing); *hizquierda* (left) in Basque is *eçker* (to the left or sinister side); *escudo* (escutcheon, shield) is called *escutua* in Basque, which means "something that covers or conceals"; green in Basque is "the color of grass"; ocean waves are "planks" or "boards;" *estrada* is "paved road forming the boundary or limit of an estate," and because ordinarily these do not exist in the countryside, this in my opinion is the derivation of the noun *estrado* because in Basque these limits are called *estratea. Vizarro* and *vizarria*, are words derived from this language, in which they call the virile man *vizarria*, which is the same as "bearded man"; *sarna* (itch) means "heat rash"; *guarda* (guard), "someone responsible for something," hence the word *guardian*; *gañibete* is what they call *cuchillo* (knife), which is the same as *filo cortante*, "sharp edge"; *casco* [cask, helmet] and *cascabel* [bell] are Basque words, derived from *coscolloa*, which is *cascara redonda* (round bell), which explains why the same word is used to refer to the *coscoja*, "husk of grain," which is one on the nouns found in the ancient language of Spain.

And Ambrosio de Morales says this language lacks the word *lanza* (lance), formerly called *lançia*, which is the same as "sharpened pole" and because they were made for different purposes they are different in this language, in which their common name is *çia*, and later *lancia*, which is "pole" with a suffix, and *guecia*, or *ecia*, "one that is thrown with the fingers," which the Basques later used as a weapon. *Burnizia* is a tool made of iron that is used to lift up the hard soil and turn it under, which historians say was called *layas* in Spain in ancient times, and in some places they still use that name, which means "tools for turning up the soil," which is their true function; and in some places they are called *layas* and in others *lias*. *Rivera* means "lowland," *honesto* means "goodness"; *cabo*, which in Romance means "completion or end of a thing," has that same meaning in Basque. In the commonly used proverb, "*pan de mi compadre, gran zatico a mi ahijado*" [my friend's bread, a large portion for my godson], the word *zatico* is Basque for "portion."

All of these words, and many others mentioned below, are spoken and used throughout Castile, being Basque words, and are pronounced in this language, and without knowing it they pronounce them in Castilian, and they are borrowed, and it is true that they were applied with great propriety to things. For instance, "man" is called *Guizona* here, a word composed of *Gaz ona*, which means "one who is both good and bad." In this language, they call the woman *Nescaa*, and the girl *nescamea*, which means "daughter of the woman." The etymology of this noun, *nescaa*, is *Neuzcoa* and *neuscoa*; the first means "that which is made from me," and the second, "one with whom one is joined," and it is absolutely true that afterward, because it seemed that to say *nescaa* was too crude for polite people, that word ended up being used for "those who serve," and they called the others *andrea*, from *anderea*, which means "lady"; therefore, to say *andrea Maria*, or *andrea Juana*, is to say "lady Maria," or "lady Juana," and it still has the meaning of *doña*. In Basque the sea is *echasua* [merging of waters]; the day is *eguna* (work of the sun); the night is *gaun* (absence of day); the sun *eguzquia* (causer of day); the week is *astea*, meaning "space"; the month, *yla*, which means "death," taken from what is caused by the moon who is called *yrarguia*, "one who dies and glows and illuminates the months." The year is called *urtea* (circle).

. . .

And almost all of the mountains of Navarre, Gipuzkoa, and Bizkaia are left with only a few towns, which have been forgotten because of their great antiquity and ruin. And we know that there are many settlements and towns with similar names in different places, which is a sure indication that the original founders, when they came to a place that was similar to another, gave it the same name. And by the names already cited, those who pay attention to etymologies and give them credit if they are sound, will be able to see that the names have great similarity with the lands for whose properties they were given and serve as faithful and trustworthy witnesses beyond any doubt, for there are no other authorities or writings that are more public or authentic than those who have written these etymologies. It is true, however, that if some do preserve their primitive and ancient names, others are so altered in different provinces by the wars they have suffered and the nations that have occupied them that the original names cannot be judged or recognized by the names given them afterwards and by which they are still known. And with this some writers have attempted to claim that the names are from the ancient language of Spain, saying that they are no longer used in the Basque Country. And they argue that if this had been the first and common language, these names would have been found in it. And these arguments are not convincing, for from the time Spain was first inhabited until the time the chroniclers on whom they based their argument in favor of their names wrote, more than 1,500 years had passed, during which time so many and such varied nations invaded Spain, changing and altering everything by their power and force, particularly along the coasts of the Mediterranean, and the coast of Andalusia, and other places that they thought were easier and more suitable for sustenance and trade, so that they took possession of them, annihilating the natives and forcing them to leave. For because of the violence they suffered, and their simplicity and innocence, they found it necessary, to avoid being oppressed or controlled by others and to maintain the government and freedom they had always enjoyed, to take shelter in the mountains and in Navarre, Bizkaia, and Cantabria, where they could defend themselves better and preserve their language, clothing, government, and way of life. Thus, it is not surprising that there would be such great change in the names, although some memory or trace of them remains. And yet, many of the names that their original founders gave to places in Spain in the Basque language are preserved in the Castilian language without any change, or only slight changes, the Romans, Goths, Moors, and other nations being unable to destroy or cast them out.

And it's true that one of the things that Spain has conserved and inherited from her original inhabitants is the Basque language, and all the names that were given to her towns explain the properties and nature of the place itself. And considering that the nature of things is explained by their names, there is no need to look for any rationale or etymology or basis other than those provided by the literal meaning of the names; or to ask from which nation the name originated other than that of the language itself, for it's certain that the names given to cities or things come inevitably from their own language. And the name of a thing will be consonant with what the inhabitants and natives know about the thing, and if they are unaware of this it's certain that the name comes from a foreign language, because in the Indies, one can tell which names come from the native language and which have been brought from Spain, for each nation refers to foreign things by the names given them according to their properties in the place where they originated.

And this explains why historians have not acknowledged Basque as the original and common language of Spain, but have attributed the names and founding of diverse places to foreign nations that were more interested in destroying them than building them; because the scholars of antiquities who wrote about this language did not understand it, they were unable to discern their antiquity and origin of cities by their names; and because of a few syllables which they thought to be consonant with other languages, they wrote, ascribing meanings to the names that were different from their true meaning, thus doing great harm as intermediaries, basing their interpretations on etymologies and languages that outsiders brought to them hundreds of years after the establishment of these cities and their names. Thus, some claim that the first language to be spoken in Spain was Chaldean, led to this conclusion by a few words spoken in Andalusia that had been introduced there on the arrival of Nebuchadnezzar, prince of the Chaldean Babylonians, which was more than 1,570 years after the arrival of Tubal, failing to consider that it may be true that over time the conquering people and their language will end up eradicating the conquered but not the names of towns, provinces, mountains, rivers, and springs, although there may be some slight alteration or change in spelling or pronunciation. This is what happened in Spain, Basque names being left behind in every region, misunderstood by the chroniclers and even by the inhabitants of the towns, since they were not in their language. And this can be seen clearly in the Indies, because although the Spaniards went about renaming the towns, the new names are little used and have been forgotten, and over time the original names given them by the Indians returned, even after they had all been killed, as can be seen on the island of Cuba, which the Spaniards first called Fernandina, and in the names of La Habana, Bacamo, Jamaica, Yucatan, Campeche, Mexico, Michoacan, and many others which the Spaniards gave new names that have now been forgotten and those the Indians had first given them restored. It follows that unless they are Basque, the writers who claim that those names are from the original language of Spain lack the knowledge to ascertain whether they are native or foreign before writing their conclusions, since they do not understand well the language of those names, which could be more than a thousand years old because this language is far more ancient.

And when Strabo and Pomponius Mela described Spain and crossed over these Pyrenees Mountains, they did not find the oral pronunciation of words in the language to be as easy as they found it in what they left written, whereby they inferred and concluded that the Basque language was a dialect and not all one language. And because they did not understand it, they named the towns in the mountains arbitrarily, without giving attention to the true derivation and ethnicity of the names.

And this is evident from the variety of ways the writers spelled the names they wrote, a clear argument that they were not careful about adding, subtracting, or changing one letter for another, because although the names were spoken or written down for them, not understanding the language it was hard for them to pronounce them. And this is undeniable because although communication between the people of these mountains of Navarre, Bizkaia, and those of Castile was so common, when they pronounced a Basque name, they removed, added, or changed letters in such a way that the entire meaning of the word was changed. And this happened frequently, as for instance if a man's name is *Pedro de Vrieta*, which means *Pedro de las Aguas* (Waters), but if they say *Pedro de Vreta*, by this simple removal of the *i* he becomes *Pedro de las Poblaciones* (Towns). And the same change of meaning can happen by switching one letter for another, calling someone named Almendariz, Armendariz or Aguerri for Aguirre, and many others like these, which although they changed the names radically, it's hardly noticeable. And in this way, historians in this and other languages changed and distorted them so that it was impossible to tell what they meant. And eliminating many ancient words from the *Fuero Juzgo* [a juridicial code, based on the ancient Visigothic ordinances and dating from the seventh century] and the *Siete Partidas del derecho* [Seven parts of the law, a version of civil law elaborated in the thirteen century and put into effect a century later], which because they are common words in Spain many do not understand them, and change their meaning, there are other modern words that have been changed in the same way because people are not familiar with their true meaning or have not learned how to read them, because it is difficult to understand what they mean. They changed Rada to Reuda, Mueleon to Manleon, and Mendurria to Medulia. And this is so true that if Abraham Ortelio were alive today, and there's no pilot or sailor who does not have his maps, every day maps by modern writers are published with the names so changed that it would be impossible for him to recognize the places by the names. And thus, those who have written have made so many mistakes because they are following foreign writers and did not know the true names and properties of the languages of the thing they are writing about, failing to inquire about the true properties. And it's almost impossible for one who writes from sources and without very clear and solid information about what he's describing to fail to err in many of the names of places and the things being described, either because of errors in printing or misspelling in the manuscripts, which might well happen to me at some time.

. . .

Throughout their travails and wars, the descendants of Tubal, the original founders, always preserved their way of life, food, language, and clothing in the mountains of Navarre and along the border with parts of France. And if some left for Castile in order to learn about its cities and do business there, acquainting other nations with the primitive names those places had after Spain became repopulated by various and diverse nations of peoples, languages and clothing, and these invaders confiscated their property and they had to return to their mountains and rejoin their own people in their former cities, maintaining their own ancient language, clothing, and nobility, which were preserved in Spain only in these mountains of Navarre and Bizkaia. These Basques—from whom the Basque Country on the other side of France in the Pyrenees Mountains took its name, because of their dealings with one another in those times—never accepted any other language from any of the invading nations but only the one they speak and converse in today, and they recognized it in those times in the diverse provinces and towns of Spain that still go by the names they were given in this language.

. . .

The Basque Language Could Never Be Eradicated from Navarre

If any single thing has led to their language being banished from other parts of Spain, it is that during their constant defense, the Goths and Romans, and other foreign nations have always been hostile to them, seeking to destroy them. And since they were unable to destroy them physically, they avenged themselves by banishing their language. But with all their power, they were never strong enough to eradicate them from these mountains or to keep towns with names derived from the Basque language from surviving throughout Spain, so many indeed that if we had to name them it would be necessary to fill a huge volume to hold them all. Thus, in these mountains of Navarre we saw that from the time Spain was first inhabited there are mountains and towns with the same names, and the people continue to use the same language, clothing, and way of life, which serve as trustworthy witnesses and clear proof of their great antiquity and value, so that throughout Navarre nothing can be found that shows any trace of having been added later, nothing that fails to have its Basque name. And there is no evidence that this language exists in any other nation. And it is clear that names from Castilian and other languages for certain mountains were introduced by those who arrived long after Tubal. And it's obvious that if there were things with names from a foreign language in these mountains of Navarre, they would be preserved with that language, just as in the Indies, all the things brought there by the Spanish, and in Spain, things that have been brought in from the Indies and from other places keep their own names from their native land, such as fruits and vegetables, and other things, such as stones and medicines, that are known by their names from the places from which they came, such as peaches from Persia, damascene plums from Damascus, and many other things that would take too long to list.

18. Juan de Beriayn

(?, late sixteenth century – Uterga, Navarre, 1638)

We know little about him, only that he was first the holder of a benefice and later a priest (he used the title abbot) of Uterga, in Valdizarbe. He published two bilingual works oriented toward pastoral exercises: *Tratado de como se ha de oyr Missa, escrito en Romance, y Bascuence, lenguages de este Obispado de Pamplona. Dirigido al muy ilustre Cabil-*

do de Pamplona en sede vacante. Compuesto por . . . (Treaty on How to Hear Mass, Written in Romance and Basque, Languages of this, the Bishopric of Pamplona. Directed at the Most Illustrious Chapter of Pamplona in its Unoccupied Seat. Composed by . . .) (1621); and *Doctrina Christiana en Romance y Bascuense, lenguajes de este Obispado de Pamplona. Compuesta por el Licenciado Juan de Beriayn Abad de Uterga* . . . (Christian Doctrine in Romance and Basque. Composed by the Licenciate Juan de Beriayn Abbot of Uterga . . .) (1626).

He wrote texts in a dialect, that of the southern part of Upper Navarre, which he presumed to be the one most intelligible not only to the members of his congregation, but also to most Navarrese in general. In the first of these published books, he provides little explanation about what motivated him to write it, except for the obvious intent of writing it in the two languages that are spoken in his bishopric and that, because most of the population was monolingual, speaking either Castilian or Basque, the pastoral mission should be performed in both languages. Beyond that, he reveals the dialectical fragmentation afflicting the Basque language, which lacks a unified, official version, such as Castilian has, leading to the use of that language as a reference when there are problems in understanding a different dialect. But this does not suggest that Juan de Beriayn does not feel the need to dignify this marginalized language. He feels it to be his own and naturally feels that it should be used. In his *Doctrina Christiana,* he provides us with a far more complete explanation to justify the use of both languages: "because there has never been a nation in all the world that has not taken pride in its native language."

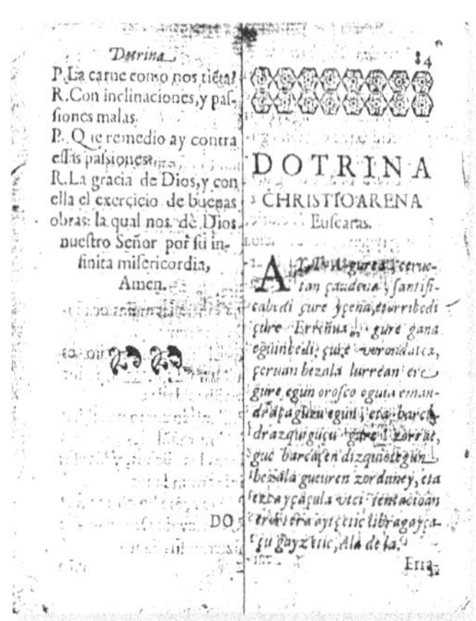

Dotrina

P. La carne como nos tienta?
R. Con inclinaciones, y passiones malas.
P. Que remedio ay contra estas passiones?
R. La gracia de Dios, y con ella el exercicio de buenas obras: la qual nos dè Dios nuestro Señor por su infinita misericordia, Amen.

DO

34

DOTRINA
CHRISTIOARENA
Euscaras.

Selected Text(s):

Doctrina Christiana en Romance y Bascuence, lenguajes de este Obispado de Pamplona. Compuesta por el Licenciado Juan de Beriayn Abad de Uterga [Christian Doctrine in Romance and Basque, Languages of this Bishopric of Pamplona. Written by the Law Graduate Juan de Beriain, Abbot of Uterga] (Pamplona: Carlos de Labayen, 1626).

I write in Romance and Basque, languages of this Bishopric: first, so that each of you can understand it in your own language, because otherwise it is impossible to understand it. This was taught to us by the Holy Spirit through Saint Luke, referring to the coming of the Holy Spirit to the Apostolic College and the marvelous effects it caused. There were (says Saint Luke) in Jerusalem at that time many people who had come from nations from all over the world to participate in that solemn festival, and the Apostles were so enthused and so filled with grace that they could not keep from going out into the public squares to proclaim the greatness and immensity of God's goodness. So they began to speak in several different languages, because having to preach to so many and such diverse nations, in order to be understood, it was very convenient that they had the gift and knew everyone's languages and that they spoke different languages; and so the sacred scripture says: *Audiebat eius quisque lingua sua illos loquentes* (that each one heard them in his own language), because although they were speaking in different languages, each one only understood his language and not the others, and thus, speaking in the other languages, they were not speaking for those who did not understand them.

The same thing happens now, for if those who only know Romance are attending a sermon that is being preached in Basque, or those who only know Basque are attending a sermon in Romance, it is obvious that they won't understand what is being said, and therefore, when questioned about what has been preached, they cannot offer any account. So it's very sad that there are so many people who only speak Basque, or only speak Romance, and they say the prayers and the Credo in Latin: *Pater noster, qui es incoelis, Ave Maria gratia plena, Credo in Deum, etc.* [Our Father, who art in heaven, Hail Mary, full of grace, I believe in God, etc.] but it's certain that they do not understand what they are saying but are speaking like parrots; if you do not believe me, just ask those who are saying the Prayers in a language they do not understand whether they know what they are saying, and you will discover that they do not and that they cannot make any sense out of what they are saying.

Secondly, I write in Basque because there has never been a nation anywhere in the world that has not been proud of its native language and has not wanted to teach its children to read and write it in the schools.

The Romans, as Valerius writes in book 2 of *Institutis antiquis*, took such pride in their language that although they knew the Greek language, which was more highly regarded at the time, they did not respond to the letters or embassies of the Greeks, they did not speak to them, except in Latin. After they came to rule over the other nations, although they spoke Greek quite well, they pretended they did not understand those who spoke to them in Greek, but obliged them to speak through an interpreter who would speak to them in Latin; and they did not do this only in their city of Rome, but also when they were in Greece and Asia, where their own language was Greek, all this to bring honor to their Latin language in every nation. And the Emperor Claudius, as Dión Cassio writes, although he took great pleasure in reciting Greek verses and sayings, severely punished a Roman citizen because he did not know Latin; and because one from Licia, which is a Province of Asia Minor, whom they had made a Roman citizen and who was one of the ambassadors he sent to that Province, when the Emperor spoke to him in Latin, did not understand him clearly, so the Emperor took away his title and privileges as a Roman citizen, saying that anyone who did not know the Latin language, which was the language of Rome, should not be a citizen. And even until today the kings and princes have such high regard for their native language that when they send their ambassadors with some mission, they write the mission in Latin, and not in any other language, even if those to whom the mission is being sent do not understand it and afterward have to have it translated by an interpreter. And Cicero had such high regard for his language that he was insulted by those who prided themselves on being able to speak Greek and refused to speak Latin, when it was their native language: *Ego* (Tullio, *lib* 1. *de finibus, nu.* 8) *Satis mirari non, queo unde hoc sit tam insolens domesticarum rerum fastidium? Ita sentio, et saepè differui* (Cannot I be but quite amazed (says Cicero, book 1, end of section 8) from where such insolent loathing of domestic things comes from? That is how I feel and calm myself).

By this same logic, it is appropriate for us to respect our Basque language, because God wanted many different languages to be distributed throughout the world, as testament to the astonishing beginning and mystery of the Holy Chapel of San Miguel de Excelsis, and in reference to a compendium taken from its archives, writings, and serious authors. Tubal, Son of Japheth, who was the third son of the just and perfect

Noah, spoke and taught the Basque language in this kingdom, and from then until now it has been preserved in the very noble City of Pamplona and in all the Basque Country. And the Catholic Faith, after the glorious bishop and martyr Saint Saturnino, sent by Saint Peter, Prince of the Apostles, to preach the Gospel in this kingdom, established it here, as proven by the lessons of the second night of his festival, which is celebrated in this Bishopric on November 29, has been lost, as it is known to have been lost in other places, as the Illustrious Don Brother Prudencio de Sandoval, former Bishop of this Bishopric, relates in the book he wrote titled *Catalogo de los Obispos que ha tenido la santa Iglesia de Pamplona* [Catalogue of the Bishops who have served in the Holy Church of Pamplona], which is a very great mercy of the Lord, to whom all glory forever and ever, secula seculorum, Amen.

19. Arnaud Oihenart Etchart

(Maule [Mauléon], Zuberoa, 1592 – Donapaleu [Saint-Palais], Lower Navarre, 1667)

He was born of a family of jurists and functionaries on both the paternal and maternal side. His father was a lawyer and royal attorney in Zuberoa and his mother was the daughter of another lawyer and scribe of the court of Lextarre (Licharre) in the same province. As befitted such a family, he studied law in Bordeaux, graduating in 1612 and earning his law degree in 1618. He was elected representative of the Silviet (Assembly) of Zuberoa by the third estate. The position was delicate because it obliged him to oversee the fulfillment of the "*Coutume*" (Customs) of the Country, an endeavor in which Oihenart excelled because of his faithfulness to it. After his marriage to a Lower Navarrese woman, Jeanne de Erdoy, he became executor of a substantial estate, residing in Donapaleu and serving as legal council to the Parliament of Navarre. He became involved in much litigation in which the rights of the people of Zuberoa were increased (especially in the purchase of common lands carried out by the Count of Trois Villes) and in the suits that he had to litigate. On behalf of these, he began to consult a large number of ancient documents, which led him little by little to the practice of history.

Besides being named executor of the house of Gramont, he gained access to some of the most important archives for the reconstruction of Basque history. He conscientiously sought to document his work and consulted all the archives available to him; consequently, his work excels in its rigor and its faithfulness to sources and in the rejection of anything that is based on nothing more than nebulous traditions, speculations, or simple legends. In addition to his published work, he left an enormous quantity of materials (some sixty volumes), including handwritten copies of documents that he had used for his historical expositions. From a methodological point of view, he can be considered the first historian of the Basque Country in modern times; not only, as previously mentioned, for having worked his sources conscientiously and rejecting speculations but because he was the first who conceived it in its totality as the Basque Country that covered both slopes of the Pyrenees.

Among his public activities, there is one that deserves our attention here. In 1639, he urged and was granted royal permission for the establishment in Donapaleu of a court of first appeals, or seneschal; this court allowed locals to be tried in their Basque language without needing to travel to Pau (in Béarn) to make statements through interpreters. Obviously, this measure was of exceptional benefit to the popular classes who did not know any language other than Basque and who found themselves disadvantaged when they were involved in lawsuits against important people who had mastered French and even Latin. His petition reads as follows: "The poor people who do not know or understand any language other than Basque suffer great expense and inconveniences, being obliged to go to Pau accompanied by interpreters in order to instruct their lawyers and procurers and continue their cases against noblemen and other privileged persons." The seneschal was made up of a seneschal, a vice-chancellor, and four advisors, one of whom could be ignorant of the Basque language but the remaining magistrates were required to know it. Oihenart himself became a member of this institution.

His major work is the *Notitia utriusque Vasconiae tum Ibericae tum Aquitanicae* . . . (News of the Two Vasconias, both in Iberia and Aquitaine . . .) (1637), in which, in addition to undertaking the central topic of a history of both the northern and southern Basque Country, he dedicates considerable attention to the language (especially chapters 11 to 14 of book 1) as an important ingredient of that history. Oihenart does not believe that the defense of the language has to be based on its antiquity or on the presumed independence and immemorial purity of its speakers. Consequently, he denies the identification of Basques with Cantabrians, extolled by the Basque authors of the Crown of Castile, including a number of important Spanish authors: Mariana, Prudencio de Sandoval, and Pedro Mártir de Anglería. He opposed this imported interpretation with a good knowledge of Cantabrian and Basque geography in Roman times. Oihenart's interpretation is that the Varduli, Caristi, and Autrigoni tribes could be linked to the Cantabrians in ancient times, but that the Vascones, who were the authentic, original Basques, most likely conquered them and enforced Basque values on them, so that Cantabria, to coin a phrase, ended up being "Basquified." As for the Basque territories to the north of the Pyrenees, he offers an explanation similar to that to the west, claiming in this way that the "Basque Country" was but an expansion, a cultural colonization in the northward expansion of the authentic Basques: the Navarrese.

Establishing boundaries for the Basque people with all the rigor allowed by seventeenth century science, Oihenart then shifts his focus to the language itself, without regard for Tubalist or Cantabrian origins. It goes without saying that he rejects the insulting denigrations of Mariana and marshals the dignifying eulogies of J. J. Scaliger concerning the Basque language: "*nihil barbari aut stridoris aut anhelitus habet, lennisima est et suavissima, estque sine dubio vetustissima et ante tempora Romanorum illis finibus in usu erat*" ([The Basque language] is not at all Barbarian, nor rough or shrill, it is extremely soft and sweet and undoubtedly very old, being used in this region before the Roman era). Despite his generally careful criteria, he partially shared with the other apologists the idea that the Basque language was in ancient times the only language of Spain. According to Oihenart, the Basque language, although it did not extend over the entire peninsula, must have been the language of all of people in the northwestern regions. In other words, in addition to the Basques and "Basquified" peoples, it was probably spoken by the Asturians, Cantabrians, Galicians, and Portuguese. He found it unacceptable that Nature would have created a language for such a limited number of people, concluding that it must have been distributed far more widely in ancient times. To demonstrate his thesis, he resorted to etymologies of words that include a mix of everything: from genuine Basquisms introduced into Castilian to fantasies or nonsense, including Latinisms or Arab imports common to both languages.

To conclude, his knowledge of the Basque language was more than impressive, as demonstrated in three areas: as a poet, as a compiler of popular refrains, and as a grammarian. At the very least, he composed an elegy on the death of his wife, an autobiographical poem, and put together a truly remarkable collection of proverbs that followed the wake of those already compiled by Garibay, but in this case, they achieved printed form. But he stands out especially for his grammatical contributions. Aside from making it clear that the endings "*a*" and "*ac*" corresponded respectively to the singular and plural article, correcting Marineo Sículo and criticizing Garibay for failing as a Basque to notice this suffix, he composed, in chapters 13 and 14 of book 1 of his *Notitia,* an absorbing grammatical outline that is the first ever written, identifying the alphabet, the declension of the nouns, articles, pronouns, simple and compound verbs, their conjugations (correct or incorrect), the incorrect conjugation of neutral verbs, the incorrect conjugation of active verbs, the auxiliary verbs *Adi* and *Ezac*, those that cannot be declined, and the number of syllables. It would be necessary to await Larramendi before we would again encounter an "Art" of this quality.

Oihenart also published *Déclaration historique de l'injuste usurpation et retention de la Navarre par les Espagnols* (Historical Declaration of the Unjust Usurpation and Confiscation of Navarre by the Spaniards) (1625); *Mémoire touchant l'usurpation de la Navarre* (Memoir Concerning the Usurpation of Navarre), Collection Dúchense, vol. 598, fol. 123; and *Atsotizac edo Refraüac. Ohienarten gastaroa neurthizetan* (Proverbs or Refrains: Recounted in Oihenart's Youth) (1657). He also wrote a history of the house of Gramont and a Basque dictionary, both now lost.

NOTITIA
VTRIVSQVE
VASCONIÆ,
TVM IBERICÆ,
TVM AQVITANICÆ,
scitu digna, NAVARRÆ Regum Cæterarumque, in iis, insignium vetustate & dignitate familiarum stemmata ex probatis Authoribus & vetustis monumentis exhibentur.
Accedunt Catalogi Pontificum Vasconiæ Aquitanicæ, hactenus editis pleniores.
Authore ... Mauleosolensi.
Sumptibus SEBASTIANI CRAMOISY Typographi Regij, via Iacobæa, sub Ciconiis.
CVM PRIVILEGIO REGIS.

SELECTED TEXT(S):

Notitia utriusque Vasconiae tum Ibericae tum Aquitanicae, qua praeter situm regionis et alia situ digna, Navarrae Regnum, Gasconiae Principum, Caeterarumque, in iis, insignium vetustate et dignitate familiarum stemmata ex probatis Authoribus et vetustis monumentis exhibentur [News of the Two Vasconias, Both in Iberia and Aquitaine, as Well as of the Situation of That Region That, Like Other Things, Is

Worth Mention, the Kingdom of Navarre, the Principality of Gascony, and Other Things Therein, Through Their Antiquity and Dignity, the Coats of Arms of the Families, Are Described Based on Prestigious Authors and in Ancient Monuments] (Paris: Sebastián Cramoisy, 1638), bk. 1, chs. 11, 12, 13; bk. 2, ch. 1; bk. 3, chs. 1, 4; reprint, trans. Javier Gorosterratzu (Vitoria-Gasteiz: Parlamento Vasco-Eusko Legebiltzarra, 1992), 553–555, 561, 571–573, 590–591, 900–903, and 917–919.

Book 1

Chapter 11

About the Basque language and whether it is true that its nouns end in A in the singular and in AC in the plural.

The Romans routinely imposed the use of the Latin language on the peoples they conquered, as we can see from these words of Saint Augustine in book 19, chapter 19 of *The City of God*: "It was established that the ruling city, under the pretext of an alliance, would impose on the conquered peoples not only their rule but also their language." This is why the native languages of the Gauls as well as the Spaniards have disappeared completely, being replaced by Romance except among the Britons, Armoricans, and Basques, who have preserved their own languages until the present time. The great Scaliger, in the *Treatise on European Languages* and in the *Diatribe on the Modern Dialects of France*, claims Basque is Cantabrian and enumerates it among the mother tongues of Europe, adding his eulogy in these words: "Cantabrianism originates in the towns that are dependents of Bayonne and Lapurdi and extends into the mountains for a distance of a six or seven day journey. The French call those who speak this language Basques or Basculos; the Spanish use the general name Bizkaia for the region in which this dialect is spoken. There is nothing barbaric, harsh, or difficult about it; it is delicate and subtle, and additionally, without any doubt, extremely ancient, and was spoken in those territories prior to the epoch of the Romans." It is now used on this side of the Pyrenees in most of Navarre, all of Gipuzkoa, Araba, and Bizkaia; and on the other side of the Pyrenees in three districts, which are designated by the name of Vasconia, or the Basque Country, that is, Lapurdi, Lower Navarre, and Zuberoa. Marineo Sículo confirmed that it was a characteristic of this language for most of the words to end in *a* in the singular and in *ac* in the plural, (in book 4, final chapter of his *History of Spain*). He was incorrect in this: because the letter *a* in the singular, and the syllable *ac* in the plural, when added to the end of Basque words sometimes serve as articles which are equivalent to Greek words ending in *ο*, *ἡ*, and *το*. For example, the word *Guizon*, in itself, means "man"; but if you wish to make it definite, as the Greeks do, saying *τον ανδρα* the French *l'homme*, and the Spanish *el hombre*, it will be necessary to say *Guizona*, and in the plural *Guizonac*: that is, in Greek *ανδρες*, in French *les hommes*, and in Spanish *los hombres*. Garibay, in book 4, chapter 4, of his *Compendio historial*, and Paulo Merula, in book 2, part II, chapter 8 of the *Cosmografía,* followed Marineo in this error. We have to forgive Marineo and Merula, because they did not know the Basque language and did not have access to good information, because they lived far from the region where it is spoken. But Garibay is guilty of considerable negligence because, Basque being his native language, the error was far more serious in him, for their error was limited to only a few words, whereas he did not hesitate to affirm that it was true of all words.

Chapter 12

About the ancient language of the Spaniards. Whether it was the same as the current Basque language. The arguments of Ambrosio Morales challenging this view are examined.

Both Marineo himself and Garibay believe that no other language was spoken anywhere in Spain in the past other than Basque, or Cantabrian, as they call it, and their authority is greatly strengthened by the opinion of the most distinguished gentleman Joseph Scaliger, who shares their view in his *Diatribe surrounding the Modern Languages of Europe*. The same view was held by Alonso Venero in the *Enchiridión de los tiempos*, Manuel Vasconcello in the *Historia del Municipio de Ebora*, Paulo Mérula in book 2 of the *Cosmogr.*, part I, chapter 8, and Mariana in book 2, chapter 5 of the *History of Spain,* whose words, which are elegant and worthy of such a great writer (except for his remark that it is a barbaric language incapable of cultural expression, the fact being that he did not know the language), will not I believe displease the reader if I translate them here: "Only the Basques continue until this day to speak their crude, barbaric language, unrefined and quite different from all others, it being the oldest of Spain and in ancient times the common language of the entire country, as many believe. And the say that all of Spain used the Basque language before the Roman armies entered these provinces and imposed their language on them. They say too that those people were innately crude, fierce, and wild, and could have been improved and domesticated like trees if planted in good soil, but because the mountains where they lived were inaccessible, they either resisted the yoke of the Roman Empire completely or quickly shook it off. Nor it is improbable that with their ancient freedom they also preserved the ancient and common language of the entire peninsula of Spain."

Morales attempted to destroy this assessment in book 9, chapter 3, gathering from Pliny and others a number of Spanish words that he believed do not exist in the modern language of the Basques. But even if we concede to Morales that all those words are purely Spanish, would this not be sufficient to force us to admit by the same logic that many languages totally different from each other existed in that nation? Does it not happen in other languages that over the long course of time, words and modes of expression change?

. . .

Chapter 13

The author's view concerning the ancient language of the Spaniards.

And so, amid these conflicting opinions, just as I cannot maintain too insistently that all Spaniards spoke a single language in past epochs, especially in light of Strabo's assurance in book 3 that there were several, neither can I admit that the Basque language was enclosed within the same limits as today, for they are very small; and it is for that same reason unlikely that the wise hand of Nature would have given such a small group of people their own language, almost inadequate for conducting trade and inconvenient for interacting and establishing alliances with neighboring peoples. Therefore, I will express my opinion succinctly. I believe that this was the language of all the mountain peoples who lived in the northern part of Spain, that is, of the Basques, Varduli, Autrigoni, Caristi, Asturians, Cantabrians, Galicians, and Portuguese, because since we know on the authority of Strabo that all of these peoples lived with the same customs and that they shared the same way of life, it's reasonable to believe that they also had a common language; and further, that the language of the other Spaniards was not so different that it did not have many features in common with the others. And that these other languages differed more as dialects do than languages (just as now the Castilians, the Portuguese, and the Catalans differ), I am persuaded by finding in the composition of the present-day Spanish language certain vestiges or traces very similar to elements of the Basque language, many purely Basque expressions or derivations thereof, of which I will provide a demonstration based on the first three letters of the alphabet, keeping in mind that the syllable *ze* or *te*, placed at the end of Basque verbs, is the ending of the present participle or verbal noun, as grammarians call it: that the semi-vowel *s*, small case, should be pronounced like *ç*, and that *ts* or *ds* is equivalent to double *zz*.

. . .

I could also review the other letters of the alphabet and observe in each one many Spanish-Basque words; nor would it be difficult to add to these those that I inserted above, taken almost entirely from the language of the Aquitaine Basques, especially those that are common to the Iberian Basques and the Spanish inhabitants; but as I am seeking brevity, I must leave those for others to investigate. Meanwhile, I want to point out that also among the idiomatic expressions that the Spanish use in modern Romance, many are formed in the same way as in Basque or in the ancient Spanish language, among these the expressions *hijo dalgo*, or *hidalgo* in contracted form, are used to designate a nobleman among the Spanish. Well, who could fail to see that this word has been formed in imitation of the Basque idiom or expression, *Aitoren seme* (which denotes the son of a father), as if to say: *Ait joren seme*, who is regarded among Basques as a nobleman as well? The same should be observed in certain adages, which in Basque are formulated in verse with a certain grace and beauty of language, and translated into Spanish into somewhat inelegant prose, of which I will cite a few examples.

	In Basque	**In Spanish**	**In English**
1.	*Erroya has ezac,* *Beguiac dedezac.*	*Cría cuervo,* *sacar te ha el ojo.*	Even a baby crow, can pluck out your eye.
2.	*Maiaz eurite,* *Urte oguite.*	*Agua de mayo,* *pan para todo el año.*	Water in May, bread all year long.
3.	*Edale-huna,* *Chapachar-duna.*	*Debajo de mala capa,* *hay buen bebedor.*	He wears a cheap cloak, but drinks like a duke.
4.	*Usqui maite,* *Higun Elaite.*	*Culos conocidos,* *a cabo de cien años* *son amigos.*	Assholes twenty years, now they're good friends.

Also the syllable *go*, which is sometimes joined to first and second person pronouns with the preposition *con* (with), is a vestige of the ancient language, which used the preposition *cum* instead of *go* at the end of the word in the same way Basque does today, with *ga* or *gas*, as in *niga* (with me), or *higa* (with you); as for the plural, it isn't *go* but *co*, and we say *connusco*, *conbusco*, instead of *connusgo*, *conbusgo*; this should also be pointed out, because in that language the intercalary *g*, omitting the consonant *s*, is transformed into the soft *c*; which is preserved today in the Basque language: for example, the word *gara*, which is the first person plural of the verbal noun. When this is combined with the negative particle *es*, *b* changes to *c* or *k*. Thus, from the simple *gara* (*somos*, we are), we form the compound *escara* (*no somos*, we are not). Ambrosio Morales, archive of all Iberian antiquities, observed long ago that *Ilia* is a Spanish word denoting "city." But this word is still used in Basque with the same meaning, by changing the liquid *l* to *r*, as is common also with many other words, such as *Araba* for *Arava*, *Añgeru* for *Angel*, and *ceru* for *cielo*. The author of the *Epítome of Livio*, book 41, tells how the Proconsul Tiberius Sempronius Graco, in memory of his own exploits after conquering the Celt-Iberians, founded in Spain the town of Gracuris, a word that means City of Graco in Basque; because what the Navarrese and the Aquitaine Basques call *Iri*, the other Basques, who live in Vardulia, cal *Uri*. Finally, Andrés Poza and Baltasar Echave, in the books published about this issue, have already observed that the proper nouns of some cities, towns, men, mountains, and rivers of Spain, that are preserved in ancient writers, contain traces of the Basque language; however, those who are trained in these matters should keep in mind that there are quite a number of things omitted from those books and others written somewhat carelessly.

Finally, the Basque language and Spanish have in common the use of the same letters, most of which are almost identical to Latin, although both exclude some letters from their alphabet, to wit—*k, q, x, y*, and the consonant *v*; on the other hand they have others that never existed in Latin, such as the following five consonants, which the Spanish write as follows: *ll, ñ, z, ch,* and *x*. It seems too that neither accepts the *f* as theirs for it is used in very few words, these mostly foreign or borrowed, in which, however, it is sometimes pronounced with full or half aspiration, being changed to *B*. Finally, *b* has a somewhat different pronunciation among Spaniards than among other peoples, and is pronounced exactly the same by the Basques as by the Spanish.

. . .

Book 2

Chapter 1

Regarding the Navarrese and their territory, called Navarre.

As for the Basques, some live in Iberia, on this side of the Pyrenees, others in Aquitaine, on the other side. On this side live people from Navarre, Jaca [in present-day Huesca], Araba, Gipuzkoa and Bizkaia; on the other side of the Pyrenees, the Gascons and the Basques. In this book, the first will be considered, in the next, the others. Let us begin with the Navarrese, the quintessential Basques from whom the others took this name. Their territory is bordered on the east by the Pyrenees Mountains, to the west by the Ebro River, and in part by the region of Tarazona; to the south, the ancient Kingdom of Aragón, and finally, to the north by the provinces of Araba and Gipuzkoa. The origin of their name must be sought in the language of the Basques, which designates, by the word *Nava* (a plain contiguous to mountains). Hence, among these people, "the palm of the hand," or "the concave part," is called *Escu-nava*. The denominative *Navarr* is formed from *Nava*, and with the addition of the article, *Navarra*, designating "the inhabitant of the flat region." Its opposite is *Menditarra*, a contraction of *Mentarra*, that is, "mountain person," or "inhabitant of the mountains." It seems that the denomination *Navarros* (Navarrese) was introduced into Spain in particular during the period of the Gothic Kings. At that time, then, because the most courageous Basques, unable to resist the armies and power of the Goths, leaving behind the flat plain and retreated to the mountains to preserve their freedom, the others, who remained in their primitive dwellings, after acknowledging the supremacy of the Goths, began to distinguish themselves from them by using the name Navarrese, the mountain people alone preserving the common name of the entire nation along with the glory of having preserved their freedom. But after a few centuries when the Kingdom of the Goths of Spain was destroyed by the Saracens, when the mountain Basques recovered their beloved homes, under the auspices of those sovereigns whom they crowned as their own kings, and occupied the entire region, at the same time Pamplona, their principal city, chose to establish the capital of the kingdom there, and afterward the name of the Kingdom of Pamplona, Navarre, emanated from here and soon extended to the neighboring mountainous region.

. . .

Book 3

Chapter 1

Concerning when the Basques emigrated from Spain to Aquitaine, the many incursions they made to the region of Aquitaine, and their many conflicts with the Franks.

I said in the first book of this work that the Basques inhabited this side of the Pyrenees, in Spain, in ancient times, and scholars are in complete agreement about this. But it is more difficult to say precisely when it was that they emigrated from here to Aquitaine. Joseph Scaliger, in book I, *Auson. Lecti.* ch. 6, says that the Cantabrians and Basques who previously lived in Spain on this side of the Pyrenees, on being defeated by Mesala, crossed the Pyrenees and established themselves in the region now occupied by the Tarbelos [Gascons]. But this renowned authority erred in his conjecture as can be deduced from the fact that Strabo, Ptolemy, and Pliny, who lived after Mesala, place the two nations of Basques and Cantabrians in Spain, not in Aquitaine; moreover, there is no record of any writer making the slightest reference to a war waged by Mesala against that nation. I know that Tibulo, in Elegy 8, book I, celebrated the victories won by Mesala against the defeated people of Aquitaine. But anyone reading that elegy will admit that it makes no reference to Basques or Cantabrians. Nor is there any better reason to rely on the opinion of those who say that after Pompey [the Great] conquered the Basques in Spain, fearing new uprisings by that restless and indomitable people, he forced them to leave the region and settle in that part of Aquitaine now inhabited by the Convenos, for which the city of Convénica was named. This claim is as easily refuted as the former because it is not supported by testimony from any writer before Saint Isidoro of Seville, and ancient geographers also oppose that claim, also placing the Basques in Iberia in the period after Pompey, making no reference to any town by that name in Aquitaine.

But Saint Jerome, in his book against Vigilante, chapter 2, informed us that the Convenos, people from Aquitaine, were not descended from the Basques, as Isidoro believed, but from the Victorinos, Arrebacos, and Celt-Iberians on the Spanish side, as he writes in his chapter about that heresiarch, saying: "True, this is consistent with his lineage, he being born of the seed of thieves and Convenos, whom Pompey, accelerating his victory once Spain had been conquered, exiled from the Pyrenees, confining them to a single city, so that they were subsequently called Convenos. Descendents of the Vectones, Arrebacos, and Celt-Iberians, until this day they plunder the Church of God, making incursions against the Churches of Gaul, marching not under the banner of Christ but the insignia of the Devil." In fact, the Basques remained in their own territory until the reign of the Emperor Gratian, and it can be inferred from the following verses by the poet Ausonius who lived during the reign of Gratian that the region of Aquitaine, which they later occupied, was inhabited by the Tarbelos, the original inhabitants of that region, because in his twenty-third epistle to Paulinus, whom he believed to be a resident of the city of Calahorra near the forest of the Gallic Pyrenees, he writes:

Et quando iste meas impellet nuntius aures,
Ecce tuus Paulinus adest, iam ninguida linquit
Oppida Hiberorum, Tarbellica iam tenet arua,
Ebromagi iam tecta subit.

When that news resonates in my ears,
Hey, you, Paulinus is arriving! He's already left
the snowy cities of the Iberians, he's already on the soil of the Tarbelos,
He's already taken refuge under the roof of Hebromagus.

The same poet, in his twenty-fifth epistle to the same Paulinus, writes in the following verses that the Basques settled in a region very different in situation and customs from that of Aquitaine, that is, in Iberia:

Vertisti, Pauline tuos dulcissime mores
Vasconis hoc saltus et ninguida Pyrenaei
Hospitia et nostri facit hoc oblivio coeli
Imprecer ex merito, quid non tibi Hiberica tellus?

Sweetest Paulinus, have you perhaps changed your customs?
Is it that the forested mountains of Vasconia, the snowy shelters [of the Pyrenees,
and the forgetting of our sky have done this?
What deserved curses will I not hurl at you, land of Iberia?

But in the following verses from Paulinus himself, in response to Ausonius, makes it even clearer that these people lived in Iberia at this time:

Quod tu mihi vastos
Vasconiae saltus et ninguida Pyrenaei
Obicis hospitia? in primo quasi limine fixus
Hispanae regionis agam?

> Do you reproach me for having elected the extensive forests of Vasconia and the snowy shelters of the Pyrenees?
> As if I had lived rooted among the first seeds of the region of Hispania?

After the death of Gratian, Roman domination of Gaul and Spain was in decline and approaching its end, and the region of the Pyrenees being particularly devastated by the Alani [Alans], Vandals, Suebi [Suevi], and other barbaric nations, who two years before the fall of Rome, inspired by Estilicon, had crossed the Rhine and invaded Gaul, and having advanced as far as the Pyrenees, but delayed for some time by that obstacle, had spread out into the neighboring provinces, as Orosius testifies, it was not difficult for the Basques, a bellicose nation eager to expand its borders, to take control of that mountainous country, which is at the foot of the Pyrenees on the Gallic side. How far their impetus took them, it is impossible for anyone to say. Indeed, what could possibly be said or inferred about a matter so obscure and almost obliterated by such great antiquity? However, it is fair to conjecture that in addition to the territory now inhabited by the Basques, the mountains of the principality of Bearne also augmented the area controlled by them.

. . .

Chapter 4

Concerning Vasconia, or the Basque territory of Gaul, and the customs of these people and their ancient sovereigns, dukes, and counts.

Aquitaine Vasconia includes two peoples, the Gascons and the Basques. We can refer to the Basque territory as Vasconia, although it was annexed long ago to Gascony; but because in the past it is identified as distinct from Gascony, and even today they differ from the inhabitants of Gascony and the rest of Aquitaine in their customs, language, and way of life, it may be useful to discuss that region first. It is situated in the furthest extremity of France bordering the northwest corner of Spain, with the ocean to the West, the Bidasoa River and Pyrenees Mountains to the South, to the east the Principality of Béarn, extending North as far as the Adour [Atturi] River and the plains of Bayonne, which are partially contained within that principality and partially within the dominion of Agramont. Its length is approximately fifty thousand yards, its width twenty-four thousand. It is divided into three sections, the first being Lapurdi, and the second Lower Navarre, and the third

Zuberoa. Lapurdi and Zuberoa are under the jurisdiction of the Royal Prefect of all of Aquitaine, Lower Navarre under that of the Viceroy of Béarn: both of those are subject to the Senate of Bordeaux and this, the Parliament of Pau.

It seems that the province of Lapurdi was named after the town of Lapurdum (currently Bayonne), and was subject to her Viscounts in ancient times; today it is under the jurisdiction of the Royal Prefects of Bayonne. Lapurdi is a Basque or Bizkaian word that may have been imposed on that town because in ancient times its inhabitants were pirates by trade, as the author of the life of Saint León, Bishop of Lapurdi, attests. This province has no fortified cities or towns, but is spread out over thirty-two separate towns, the largest and richest being the one called Luizio by the ancients, [Donibane] Lohizune by its native speakers, and commonly *Saint-Jean-de-Luz* [Saint John of Light]. The word *Luizio,* or *Loitzunio,* in that language denotes "a swampy place," and the town lives up to its name, being rich in silt deposited there by the ocean tide pushing up toward the source of the small river flowing down into the town. Almost all of the residents are sailors, a profession in which they are very skilled, and making annual voyages to that part of North America we call Newfoundland, they bring back great quantities of those fish they call *Bacalao* (cod) and the French call *Morua*, reaping great profits. The judge who rules on lawsuits generally serves another town called Ustaritze, in the region of Lapurdi, as well.

Lower Navarre is made up of many villages and provinces because the Viscounts of Bigorra [Baigorri] and Arberoa fall under its jurisdiction; the districts of Garazi [Cize] with the natives of Garazi [Cize], Amixiens [Amikuze, Mixe], and Ostabares [Oztibarre, Ostabarret] under those of Agramont [Agaramont] and Luxe [Lukuze], whose main towns are Saint-Jean-Pied-de-Port [Donibane Garazi], Saint Palais de Garruz [Donapaleu, Garruze/Garris], and La Bastide Clairence [Bastida], founded by the decree and authority of Louis Hutin, King of Navarre. But the name Navarre came from the Navarrese kings who exercised jurisdiction and authority over it for long periods.

The name Zuberoa (Sola) is a contraction of the ancient word Subola, which means "wilderness" in the Basque language. Its only town is Mauléon [Maule], defended by an ancient fortress constructed at the top of a steep cliff. It is bathed by the River Saison, abundant in trout that are extraordinarily delicious. Also, from here and from Lower Navarre the most exquisite hams are distributed throughout France.

20. Gabriel de Henao

(Valladolid, 1611 – Salamanca, 1704)

A Jesuit and teacher of philosophy, theology, and Holy Scripture in several Jesuit schools, especially in Salamanca where he remained for fifty years, Gabriel de Henao was a meticulous and erudite researcher, author of an enormous oeuvre relating to theological, philosophical, historical, and political matters. In his youth, he spent some time at the College of Bilbao, where he founded an Academy of Humanities in which he directed works relating to the history of Bilbao and Bizkaia.

From among his writings, we will cite the books and manuscripts related to the Basque Country: *Vizcaya illustranda ab Academia Humaniorum litteratum Bilbaensis Scholae Societatis Jesu* (Bizkaia Illustrated by the Academy of Humanities of the Bilbao School of the Society of Jesus) (1637); a *Defensa histórica de Guipúzcoa* (Historical Defense of Gipuzkoa) (1702), which he left in manuscript form; and above all, his *Averiguaciones de las antigüedades de Cantabria enderezadas principalmente a descubrir las de Guipúzcoa, Vizcaya y Alava, provincias contenidas en ella, y a honor y Gloria de San Ignacio de Loyola, nacido en la primera y originaro de las otras dos, patriarca y fundador de la Compañía de Jesús* (Investigations into the Antiquities of Cantabria, Aimed Primarily at Discovering Those of Gipuzkoa, Bizkaia, and Araba, Provinces Contained Therein, and in Honor and Glory of Saint Ignatius of Loyola, Born in the First and Founder of the Other Two, Patriarch and Founder of the Company of Jesus) (1689–1691). The fulcrum of the "Basque connection" of his thinking is Ignatius of Loyola. In effect, his dedication to studies on the history of Bizkaia during his residence in Bilbao is understandable, but his project of writing (at the age of 91) a *Defensa de Guipúzcoa* and especially the two thick volumes of his *Averigüaciones* when he lived the rest of his life in his native Castile is only conceivable if there was an extraordinary motivation. And this was the desire to demonstrate the purity and nobility of the Basque homeland of the founder of the Company of Jesus. Beyond this, if it could be proven that he was the author of *El tordo vizcaíno*, we would have before us the embodiment of the perfect spirit of the Basque apologists.

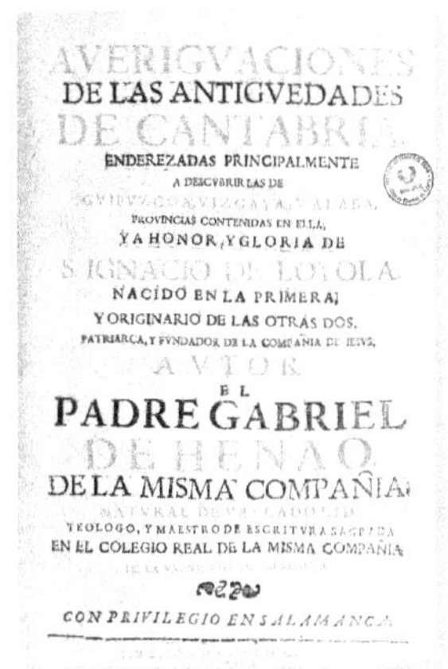

AVERIGVACIONES
DE LAS ANTIGVEDADES
ENDEREZADAS PRINCIPALMENTE
A DESCVBRIR LAS DE
PROVINCIAS CONTENIDAS EN ELLA,
Y A HONOR, Y GLORIA DE
NACIDO EN LA PRIMERA;
Y ORIGINARIO DE LAS OTRAS DOS,
PATRIARCA, Y FVNDADOR DE LA COMPAÑIA DE IESVS,
AVTOR
EL
PADRE GABRIEL
DE HENAO
DE LA MISMA COMPAÑIA;
TEOLOGO, Y MAESTRO DE ESCRITVRA SAGRADA
EN EL COLEGIO REAL DE LA MISMA COMPAÑIA
CON PRIVILEGIO EN SALAMANCA.

SELECTED TEXT(S):

Averiguaciones de las antigüedades de Cantabria enderezadas principalmente a descubrir las de Guipúzcoa, Vizcaya y Alava, provincias contenidas en ella, y a honor y Gloria de San Ignacio de Loyola, nacido en la primera y originaro de las otras dos, patriarca y fundador de la Compañía de Jesús [Investigations into the Antiquities of Cantabria Aimed Primarily at Discovering Those of Gipuzkoa, Bizkaia, and Araba, Provinces Contained Therein, and in Honor and Glory of Saint Ignatius of Loyola, Born in the First and Founder of the Other Two, Patriarch and Founder of the Company of Jesus], 2 vols. (Salamanca: Eugenio Antonio García, 1689–1691), bk. 1, chs. 2 and 3, 14–22.

Remarks to the Reader

As it has been my longstanding intention to write about the three Cantabrian provinces, Gipuzkoa, Bizkaia, and Araba because our most Glorious Patriarch and Founder of the Company of Jesus, Saint Ignatius of Loyola, had his origins there. I now embark on the first Book of Investigations of their Antiquities from the moment of the arrival of the first inhabitants of Spain through the entire period of the Roman Empire on the peninsula. I conceived this Work because it seemed to me that greater extrinsic glory would redound to the Saint if information were provided about the glorious events in the lands of his birth and origin, for it's true that the excellence of one's country and origins brings honor to its inhabitants and founders. Although the three provinces are honored by such a son and founder by blood, it seemed appropriate that one who could be regarded as a spiritual son of the Saint by virtue of his religious estate should dedicate his studies to an inquiry into the illustrious antiquities of these provinces blessed by being the place of his birth and origin. In truth, what little information has been gathered about these three nations, because their inhabitants have been more interested in winning praise through action than by writing, and outsiders have been afraid to explore unknown aspects of their history. I became persuaded that the task of contributing to make them known would be worthwhile, especially because the three provinces are extremely important parts of our Spain, as famous in peace as in war, boasting distinguished and noble families within their borders and all across Spain and the Indies. They deserved a better pen, but at least I can say that I have spared no effort since I set down the first lines of these books so long ago.

. . .

6. The name of Ireland offers another curious example of Cantabrian origin because it can be presumed that *Iria* is Basque, and *Uria* means "small town." This root is conserved in many places where Basque is spoken. Because in Navarre they call the village *Iria*; and in Araba, Bizkaia, and in much of Gipuzkoa, corrupting the noun somewhat, they say *Vria*, and in the native language of the country the Navarrese generally call *Pamplona Iriona*, which means *Villabuena* [good town], and now, corrupting the old noun, they say *Iruña*, according to Garibay. And concerning *Iria Flavia*, which is the *Padrón* [leader, head] in Galicia, Andres de Poza noted that it meant 'Villa de Flavio' in Basque. And Oihenart derives from the root *Iria*, or *Vria*, the suffix of many names of towns in Spain, such as *Gracuris, Calaguris, Ilarduris*. Also in Basque, *Landa* means *llanura verde* [green plain], *praderia* [meadow], and [fertile fields]. Quite a few Bizkaian surnames are composed of this word, such as Landaeche, Landaverde, etc., which is a perfect etymology for *Irlanda*, [a region abundant in grassland]. And perhaps in the language of Ireland they called their land *Erin* based on the Basque prefix *Iria*, as Ortelius observed. I see that Ortelius himself, Geronimo Rusceli and Covarrubias explain that just as in Spain the word *Briga* signified city, or land, so did *Land* in other nations, from which the names Olanda, Celanda, etc, are formed. All of this is conjecture, and it should be considered such, for the river Ierno that Ptolemy places in Ireland, would be given the same name as another which Pomponius Mela describes in Galicia. And Ireland is still called *Ierna*, according to Orpheus and Aristotle, quoted by *Uvalfinghamo* [Walfingham] and also

Claudian, as some interpret one of his verses. The title *Onel*, which some of the principal lords of Ireland put in front of their names and signatures, was thought by some to be derived from *Oneen*, which in Basque means "the best." The most distinguished men of Ireland use the prefix O, which could be an abbreviation of *Onel*, or *Odonel*. *Osulevano* [O'Sullivan] speaks of these titles.

. . .

8. There remains one other indication that some might take to mean that the Spaniards inhabited Great Britain. Cornelius Tacitus in two places mentions some British towns called *Brigantes*. Others speak of them as well, including Seneca, Ptolemy, Martìn del Rio, and Scaliger. Some will say they were named by vassals of Brigo, the fourth King of Spain, and according to the *Beroso* of Joan Anio, who claims that they later inhabited Ireland and named a river Brigo and some towns Brigantes. And there will be others who say that without any need for King Brigo, those who inhabited Ireland were Basque Cantabrians because they gave Basque names to towns. Ocampo and other writers base this on the word Briga, the former writing: "We will also observe in the following books that when the Emperor Flavius Vespasianus ordered a city to be built in Spain beside the coast of the sea of Bizkaia, he ordered them to name it Flaviobriga, a combination of his name Flavius and the word Brigas which meant towns in the Basque language." And later he repeats this: "For the name Briga meant city, or large town in the old language of the Spains."

9. I neither challenge nor affirm the derivation *Rey Brigo*, because I recognize what Francisco Cascales and others observe regarding it: "This opinion is so widely implanted in the minds of the Spanish people by the Chroniclers and so rooted in many and diverse books that I believe everyone would rise up against me with lance in hand if I said now that this is all a fable and that these founders and almost all the others woven through the Chronology never existed. So says Cascales. And whether a Prince Brigo ever existed or not, it could be a coincidence that in England and other neighboring Islands certain towns were named Brigantes, and a river or two might have been named Brigo. The suffix *Briga* added to the names of cities was not limited to the territory of Cantabria, but extended to many others throughout Spain where Basque was not spoken, such as Caliobriga, Varobriga, Mirobriga, etc."

10. In light of such a variety of opinions regarding the word *Briga*, I will not insist in expressing my own, leaving it up to the Reader to

accept whichever he wishes, it can be inferred that there is insufficient reason to argue definitively that the Basque Cantabrians inhabited Great Britain, although as has been demonstrated previously there is reason to so argue with regard to the Cantabrians in general. And Gregorio Lopez Madera and Brother Juan de la Puente consider the Scots to be descendants of Spain. And Hector Boethius, a Scot, writes at great length in support of this theses, which I have a hard time accepting totally, because although I do believe they are descended from Spain, I have to reject in large part the series of epochs, places, events, and personages, as it is quite common in the investigation of antiquities and origins of nations to mix false things with true. But if the English and Scots boast of having their origins in Spain, I add that they should indeed be proud to have such illustrious lineages, and even prouder if in addition to the kinship in blood they also acquired their kinship to Spain from those two noble Kingdoms through their public profession of faith in the Roman Catholic religion. Pray God it be so!

21. José Moret y Mendi

(Pamplona-Iruña, 1615 – Pamplona-Iruña, 1687)

He took orders in the Company of Jesus in 1629 and was professor of philosophy and theology in the Jesuit schools of Pamplona-Iruña, Oviedo, and Segovia. He also served as Rector of the schools of Pamplona-Iruña and Palencia.

In 1654, the Parliament of Navarre found it necessary to institutionalize the office of chronicler of the kingdom, and Moret was the first to be appointed to this post. His primary mission was to write a general history of the territory. As a historian, Moret proved to be not only prolific but rigorous and critical, calling into question some of the commonly held assumptions, or at least, presenting them in a prudent form with all due qualifications.

This occasioned him no few polemics and hostilities. Thus, he debated with the lawyer from Tudela, José Conchillos, who maintained the traditional view that his city had been founded by Tubal, because Moret did not accept this view. On the other hand, when he disagreed with the claims of the Benedictine Domingo Larripa regarding the antiquity of the Kingdom of Sobrarbe, finding them exaggerated, Larripa responded by writing a work about the matter, in response to which the Navarrese historian took the trouble to refute.

His greatest work, the *Annales del Reyno de Navarra* (Annals of the Kingdom of Navarre) (1766), was updated and expanded by the second chronicler of the kingdom, Francisco de Alesón. Although his primary objective in this work was historiographic, some of its passages contain interesting aspects related to the Basque language, as is the case with his *Investigaciones históricas de las antigüedades del Reino de Navarra* (Historical Investigations on the Antiquities of the Kingdom of Navarre) (1766).

INVESTIGACIONES
HISTORICAS
DE LAS
ANTIGUEDADES DEL REYNO
DE
NAVARRA
POR EL P. JOSEPH DE MORET

CON LICENCIA

SELECTED TEXT(S):

Investigaciones históricas de las Antigüedades del Reyno de Navarra, por el p. . . [Historical Investigations on the Antiquities of the Kingdom of Navarre, by the . . .] (Pamplona: Pascual Ibañez, 1766), bk. 1, ch. 5, 96–117; *Annales del Reyno de Navarra*, vol. 1 (Pamplona: Pascual Ibáñez, 1766), 3–6.

Historical Investigations on the Antiquities of the Kingdom of Navarre

2. That the Basque language still spoken in the northern mountains of Spain—Navarre, Gipuzkoa, Bizkaia, and Araba—is ancient, primitive, and original to these regions since the time of the first inhabitants in Spain seems to be proven, not only by probable, prudent conjecture, but also by even greater evidence. It is called the language of Navarre in a

text written almost five hundred years ago, in the year 1167 after the Incarnation, which can be found in the Round Book of the Church of Pamplona, in which King Don Sancho the Wise, the Bishop of Pamplona Don Pedro de Paris, and Count Don Vela offer to defend the crematorium and the herds of cattle belonging to the Church of San Miguel de Escelsis. And because there were two individuals interested in this crematorium, the text continues: "And in this dispute between Ortiz Lehoarriz and Aznar Umea, it is determined that Ortiz Lehoarriz will appoint, as they say in the Language of the Navarrese, a *Maizter* (which in Basque means a foreman of shepherds) and Aznar Umea will appoint whoever he wants as Buruzagui (which is a foreman of workers)." And if being the original inhabitants of a region is accepted as legitimate proof of the nobility of one's lineage, demonstrating illustrious antiquity in that region with the necessary qualities, there being no evidence of outside origin at some later time, even more proof of originality and antiquity will accrue to the language in those regions by demonstrating not only its illustrious antiquity, without any imputation of outside origin, but through positive argument, proving that any outside origin is utterly inconceivable. The cited passage provides such proof.

3. If the language of the Basques were not the original, earliest language of its region, it would have been followed inevitably by a grand influx of foreign people who would have subjugated it and introduced their own, banishing the primitive language from the region. And it is inconceivable that this should have happened because we know the peoples who invaded Spain in great multitudes sufficient to conquer her. And Basque hasn't the slightest kinship with any of their languages—no affinity of simple words, no inflexion, and no interaction with them or with their dialects.

. . .

25. And if some of the nouns clearly demonstrated to have been from the ancient primitive language of the Spaniards had been missing, which Morales did not succeed in demonstrating among those he did gather, there's a great difference, as is clear; because from those that have been preserved it is possible to prove the identity of the language, and from those that are missing, it is not possible to disprove identity. But how can we expect that time acting on the language of the Basques over so many centuries would not have done what it does on the hardest metals of its mines, wearing down the iron, changing this language as it does all languages, for time both wears them down and builds them up. In the common language of Spain that we speak today, what changes will

time not have imposed in the five hundred years (demonstrably fewer) since the Kings of Spain began to use it in their Royal Charters, abandoning Latin? Who can run through the lesson without stumbling and without looking for the meaning of many words in the context? The ancient writers offer ample evidence of the changes that occurred in Latin in even less time. Arnaud Oihenart collected some of these. And he himself is a witness to the changes in French and German. Time does to languages what it does to clothing and customs. Only gold is immune to time.

26. Not only in the words that have survived from the ancient language of the Spaniards is it obvious that it was Basque, but also in the many that have remained in the common language of today, which we call Romance. Arnaud Oihenart compiled many of these with great erudition, running through the first three letters of the alphabet, and if he had had the time it would have been a simple matter, and most helpful, for him to examine the rest, thus discouraging the habit some writers have, when they are unable to find a Latin derivation for Spanish nouns, of assuming an Arabic or Hebrew origin. This came about through ignorance of the Basque language, which more often than not will provide the least violent, least strained, and most probable derivation; for who can doubt that it's more probable that the Spanish language would have borrowed words from friends whose blood they share than from enemies they hate? And in case of doubt, the presumption favors the domestic, more ancient language rather than some upstart language that came into Spain from outside at a later period, such as Arabic. Even the name we use for the common language of Spain today, is the Basque name *Romance*, formed from *ance* or *ence*, which is Basque for "in the style of," so *Romance* is equivalent to "in the Roman style, or form," just as *Vascuence* is a compound of *Vasco* and *ence*, which means "in the Basque style, or form."

27. A person exploring the origins of nouns carefully will recognize these derivations even in the most ancient adages of the Romance language, as the following examples will show. The word *Zatico* appears in three adages in the Spanish language: 1) *Del pan de mi compadre buen zatìco à mi ahijado* [From my friend's bread, a good portion for my godson]; 2) *Romeno hito (vale fixo) saca zatìco*, meaning "the poor man who stays beside the door and asks persistently will get some bread"; and 3) *Mas vale migaja de Rey, que zatìco de hombre rico* [A crumb from the King is better than a portion from the rich man]. And this is the source of the word *Zatiquèros*, officials who served bread at the table in the ancient Royal House, as is indicated in the Registry of

Seville. And Zatico is the name of a noble family whose coat of arms had small pieces of bread around the edge, mentioned by Argòte de Molina, bk. 2, ch. 146. *Zatìco* is obviously a Basque word, and it means "small piece" and is derived from *Zati* (piece), and *Zatìco* is the diminutive, so in Basque it means "small piece." And this being so, and so widely known, that even the children who ask for bread know it in the Basque Country, it's quite odd to see the disjuncture in the way even Father Guadix confuses it, and even Don Sebastián de Covarrubias y Orozco gives it an Arabic origin with a Hebrew root.

28. It's the same with the word *Zubìa,* which in some regions of Spain means "congregation," or "confluence of waters," whereas in Basque, without adding or taking away a single letter, *Zubìa* means "bridge, where waters flow." And it is the same with the word *Zanca*, and others that derive from it, which is so smoothly and naturally derived from the Basque *Zango*, which is "the leg." And they derive the word *Otear*, and *Otero* from the Greek *Optemo*, "to look at," when it is so natural to derive it from the Basque word *Otèa*, meaning "height" or "eminence." And some derive the name of the river *Betis* from the fabled King Betis of Beroso, whom the Ancients never heard of, simply because he was close at hand. Others, like Garibay, derive it from the Chaldean language, in which they say it sounds like the word for "house," because many rivers come to an end by houses: a totally nonsensical metaphor. Others say it is from Hebrew, meaning "deep" in that language, as if the Hebrews had come to Spain in a period when they had the good fortune to be able to name the most important rivers, when the Basque derivation I have already suggested is so smooth and natural: *Beti* [in Basque means] "always" because it was said to have always flowed during the general drought, or from *Bete* meaning "full," because it was known to be deep even along the shores, and also because of its size, so that it was later called *Guadalquivir* in Arabic, meaning *agua grande*, "big water, big river." In the Land of Plasencia [Extremadura] there is another derivation that is obviously Basque, because the natives and villagers call their town *Vera*, which is famous for its abundance of fruits, *Vera de Plasencia* [shores of Plasencia], and *Tierra baxa de Plasencia* [lowlands of Plasencia]. And *Vera* in the Basque language is *Baxa* [low]. And from this we have *Erri-vera* the Low Land of Navarre, which with a slight corruption they call *Ribera* [shore]. And the people of Plasencia, unaware of its derivation, continue to use the Basque word. But that should be enough for now, although I'm not sure if this will even begin to satisfy certain Geniuses of Spain addicted to pilgrimages, who place great value on what came from far

away, scoring what was born at home to such a degree that they would rather find kinship of their language with Moors or Hebrews than with the Basque language that was born at home.

29. Father Juan de Mariana, acknowledging Basque as the primitive and common language of all Spain in ancient times, and that the provinces of Spain preserve it with their ancient liberty, never having admitted a foreign yoke, or if they did, they quickly threw it off, writes: "Only the Cantabrians (which is what he calls the Basques) have preserved until today their crude, barbarous language, unfit for elegant expression, and which differs greatly from all the others." If it is primitive and common to all of Spain, and preserved as testimony of their freedom, why mock them for preserving it? Tiny pieces of copper or bronze, simply because they bear the faded image of an ancient king or emperor; old ramparts, broken walls, destroyed by force or by the ravages of time—these are preserved with respect, in memory of what they were, and for a certain natural respect in men for antiquity; venerable memories of the original inhabitants of Spain, illustrious monuments of her liberty despite so many and such barbaric foreign peoples who have invaded her, are these to be condemned to oblivion and desolation? The very conception of such an insult seems unfair.

30. It does not even seem like a condemnation to call the language barbaric and original, the strange thing being that the one who condemns it has no knowledge of it. In languages, one focuses on the materiality of their pronunciation, which is like the body, or on the vitality of their signifiers, especially the compound words, which is like the soul. If we know nothing about the former, why call the language of the Basques barbaric unless of course we're speaking as the common people do, who regard any language they don't understand as barbaric. The European ear, accustomed everywhere to the sound of Latin or their own language or others that are derived from it, is perplexed by one like Basque that sounds totally different. But this is not a defect in the language but in the ear. Saint Isidoro, speaking of the pronunciation of languages, said: "All Oriental people, like the Hebrew and Syrian people, articulate words and speech in the throat. The Mediterranean people articulate the words on the palate, like the Greeks and Asians. All western people articulate speech against the teeth, like the Italians and Spaniards." There is no guttural quality in the Basque language, and although in some regions they have picked this up a bit, influenced by what the Romance language has taken from Arabic, he argues that this is not a native vice of the language but an infection spread by commerce, seeing that the regions closest to both sides of the Pyrenees have not been

affected, nor do they pronounce the *jota* with guttural quality the Arabs introduced into Spain, but smoothly as in Latin. Neither do we note any sharp articulation of the tongue against the palate. It does share the last property of articulating words against the teeth, as the Italians and Spaniards do, although with moderation, and without the hardness of the northern languages, which because of the combination of many consonants without the interpolation of vowels make the pronunciation difficult and harsh. Joseph Scaliger, who knew Basque and was well versed in languages, in his treatise on the languages of Europe and modern French speaks as follows about the Basque language: "The Spaniards in that region in which this language is used refer to it generally as Basque. There is nothing barbaric about it, no gnashing of teeth, no guttural quality. It is smooth and gentle and without any doubt very ancient and spoken in those Provinces before the time of the Romans."

31. If we focus on the vitality of signification in the derivation of compound nouns, for in simple nouns made up of basic elements there is no room to manifest such vitality, we find in the Basque language an extraordinary and rare vitality. Of the many nouns that could be offered as examples, let us make do with just a few to avoid prolixity. They call God *Jaungoycoa*, which means "Lord on High." The sun is *Eguzquia* (day-maker). The moon is *Ilarguìa* (month-light), as if we might say in Latin "menstrual light." Death is *Eriotza*, meaning "cold sickness." "Man" is *Guizon*, a corruption of *Gauzòn*, meaning "good thing," which is a vivid and elegant antonomasia, and in all of these, we can see the energy of ingenious philosophers, and with its superb concision, each word is practically a definition. This being so, we cannot understand why this writer condemns it as barbaric and crude, and incapable of elegance. If he had said spare and unsophisticated, we would have concurred with his criticism. But one does not condemn a wilderness just because it is not cultivated; men's lack of industry, yes. But the Basques can certainly not be accused of that. But one can attribute the condition to bad fortune, for Spain was so often overrun by foreign nations that they had to retreat into the mountains, and live sparely and tend to their weapons. War has its effect on languages just as it does on the fields, which lie fallow; and due to the demands of commerce, this wandering language of rare perfection that was once common to all of Spain, does what the great river does, swallowing others and washing away the shores. If one does not condemn other nations for having lost their language entirely through the ravages of fortune, why condemn these people for retaining theirs, even if in somewhat diminished, uncultivated condition?

32. Whether these reasons and arguments prove that the language of the Basques was common to all of Spain, as the authors we have cited believe, or prove only that it was common, if not to all, at least to several provinces—in particular to Asturias, Galicia, and Portugal—as demonstrated by the uniformity of rites, customs, and laws that Strabo claims these peoples had in common with the Basques and Cantabrians, an opinion Oihenart apparently came to accept, although tending to argue for a wider expansion, the reader, unmoved by passion, can judge for himself. In our opinion, these arguments hold more weight than conjecture and probability, leading us to believe that it was the general language common throughout Spain before the subsequent invasion by latecomers.

Annals of the Kingdom of Navarre

Chapter 1

1. The Names Basques and Navarrese. 2. Their Situation. 3. Their Origin. 4. First Memories of the Time when the Carthaginians and Romans Conquered Spain.

1. The Names Basques and Navarrese

(i) In ancient times the Navarrese were referred to by the name *Vascones*, which in their native language means "People of the Mountains" because their territory was frequently mountainous. And the word *Vaso*, which means "mountain," followed by the case of the noun, gave us *Vasocò*, which means "of the Mountain," and by contraction, *Vascò*. The name Navarre seems to have been introduced in the last years of the Gothic kingdom in Spain, when the Basques, forced to take up arms and confined to the harshest part of the Pyrenees, began to make a distinction between the mountainous region and the region spread out more gently in wide valleys. And the latter, from the word *Nava*, which means "plain surrounded by mountains," combined with the word *Erri*, which means "Land," or "Region," gave us the contraction *Navarra* [Navarre]. And with the extension of this name across the more level regions through victories against the Arabs and Africans, as the larger cities, which they recovered became repopulated, and because of the greater fertility of the land, the new name gradually made inroads against the older one, until it absorbed it completely. But until the earliest days after the invasion of the Arabs and Africans into Spain, we find no evidence that the name Navarre had ever been used.

. . .

3. *Their Origin.*

(iii) The Navarrese pride themselves, as do their neighbors in Gipuzkoa, Araba, and Bizkaia, on claiming descent from the primitive, original Spaniards and on having been the first to populate this region of the Pyrenees and their slopes and the shores of the Ebro through Tubal, fifth son of Japheth, son of Noah; their persistent belief in this being reinforced by the testimony of distinguished authors who affirm it, many of them specifying the cities of Tudela and Tafalla as places inhabited by them. This was also notoriously affirmed with regard to Pamplona by Fernan Perez Mexia of Ávila in his *Nobiliario* [Peerage], citing ancient writers; and with less authority by the Archbishop of Toledo, Don Rodrigo, who indicated the Pyrenees as the first place populated by Tubal and his sons, who spread out from there to the shores of the Ebro.

(iv) They also put forth as evidence their native Basque language, which is distinct from and totally unrelated to the language of any other peoples who invaded Spain in large numbers and who might have been expected to alter the native language. In ancient times, this language was common to all the Basque people, as the name itself, *Vascuence*, implies. And the King, Don Sancho the Wise, called it the language of the Navarrese. But in our times, some of the people, after long contact with countries bordering them, have forgotten it. Others speak a mixture of Basque and the common language of Spain; all the mountainous regions retain it as their unique language. And from time immemorial in texts by ancient writers, we see cities, mountains, and rivers with Basque names throughout Spain, serving as evidence that it was the original language and that it was the common language of all Spain before the arrival of later invaders, as Doctor Navarro and many serious writers argued.

(v) And this is reinforced by a powerful and very natural conjecture, this being the multitude of towns that the Romans found in Spain with names formed with the suffix *Iria*, or *Uria*, which are identical because of the frequent transmutation of *i* and *u* in the Basque language, *Iria* being equivalent to "town," as is well known. From the time of King Don Pedro who conquered Huesca, we have evidence of this in a gift that he made to [the Church of?] Saint Marìa of Pamplona and Don Pedro, Bishop of Pamplona, consisting of his village of Zubiri, and noting that it was called this because it was a town situated beside a bridge, as the town of Zubiri is indeed situated beside the bridge of the Arga River, three leagues north of Pamplona. "*Unam Villam meam,*" he writes, "*que vocatur Zubiria, scilicet iuxta pontem sita*" [One of my villages named Zubiria that is situated beside the bridge]. In this way, the King, as one who knew the meaning of the Basque name, verified that it was a compound of the root *Zubi*, meaning "bridge," and the suffix *Iria*, meaning "town."

(vi) And Ambrosio de Morales and a number of the most precise writers having acknowledged that this word existed in Spain in ancient times, and that it was a compound in the names of many cities, and affirmed with great certainty that it was Basque and that it means "town," and observed that it is retained not only in Navarre and the Basque Country but also that the Romans had already observed it as a component of the names of many towns spread widely throughout several regions of Spain and in the most remote places in the Basque Country. It seems necessary to acknowledge that long before the arrival of the Romans the Basque language was universally dominant throughout Spain; for it is utterly inconceivable that they would use proper nouns from a language that was not currently used in the country at the time, and which were not family names, to name their cities, just as it would be inconceivable that the names of towns known to be Roman that were composed of the words *city* or *village*, such as Ciudad Rodrigo, Ciudad-Real, Villamayor, Villamediana, and countless others like them would be used as names, either in pure or corrupted form, before the Roman language was common there. And similarly, in Navarre and its surrounding mountains, we frequently see towns, mountains, and rivers with the same names that were used in ancient times in the province of Armenia, the first birthplace of the human race after the universal flood.

(vii) It is well known that the Basques today still use the same language that is common in Spain today, although for the most part derived from the Latin language introduced during the long occupation by the Romans, although those who do not know this language continue to seek and claim remote origins. The name of the Ebro River, which was the source of Spain's ancient name *Iberia*, and its natives *Iberians*, seems to be of Basque origin, signifying "hot water," because those who come down from the mountains and miss the greater coolness of the streams try to walk in the shade and stay close to its springs.

22. Marie Catherine le Jumel de Barneville (Countess d'Aulnoy), known as Madame d'Aulnoy

(Barneville-le-Bertan, Normandy, c. 1650 – Paris, 1705)

Madame d'Aulnoy is an interesting character because of her adventurous life and her literary talent. She serves as a rather ideal model of the cultured and cosmopolitan courtly nobility of the epoch of Louis XIV. Born of a noble family, at the age of fifteen she married the Baron d'Aulnoy, who was thrice her age and from whom she tried to separate by means of an accusation of high treason, which turned out to be unfounded, whereupon she had to flee from France. She combined her activities as a spy in the service of the French crown with her work as mother to five sons (some of whom were not recognized by her husband), promoter of literary salons, and successful writer. Cultured and fluent in several languages, she represented the culture of the dominant social order, providing models of behavior and conduct to the lower classes, taking popular topics, and converting them into toys for the consumption of the elite society. She cultivated the genre of the travelogue, and in fact, published two books of voyages through Spain and a book of fairy tales, a genre in which she competed with her contemporary Charles Perrault and achieved exceptional fame. Worth citing are her *Histoire d'Hippolyte comte de Douglas* (History of Hippolytus, Count of Douglas) (1690); *Contes des fées* (Fairy Tales) (1697); *Nouveaux contes de fées ou Les Fées a la mode* (New Fairy Tales or Fashionable Tales) (1698); and the *Relation du voyage d'Espagne* (Account of a Journey through Spain) (1691).

With regard to language, and the Basque language in particular, Madame D'Aulnoy represents a good example of those cultivated travelers aloof to the reality of the country that they must cross on their journey toward the Court and of which they offer a superficial panorama, excessively flattering, resoundingly disparaging, and emphatically romantic. The countess, who spoke perfect Castilian and was able to communicate in French with the notable Europeans of her time (most of whom knew the language), found herself in an anomalous situation in the Basque Country, where the people in both the north and south turned out to be strangely attached to their language; or better, their jargon, as the good lady puts it. Her description of the language, although interesting, could not be more astonishing. She characterizes the language as difficult and so barbaric that its lexicon suffers from inevitable polysemy. But the best part is that the Basques themselves impose, according to d'Aulnoy, the exclusive use of their language and try to prevent others from learning it, and to that end, they only use it orally and deliberately refrain from writing it.

As it happens, these opinions were based more on books than on direct knowledge of reality or on a reliable source of direct information. In effect, Madame d'Aulnoy limits herself to reproducing almost literally what had been written almost twenty years earlier by another French traveler who had passed through the Basque Country: Antoinne Brunel. In 1655, he had observed that, "They speak a language here that can only be understood by those who live in this country; it is so poor that a single word has to mean several things. And to keep it from being used for general communication it isn't written, and the children in the school learn to read in Castilian or French, depending on the king under whose authority they live."[1] This is how, through sheer repetition, prejudices and distorted information end up acquiring credibility and being generally accepted. Apparently, Juan Antonio Moguel responded to this verdict by Brunel and d'Aulnoy in his work.[2]

Selected Text(s):

Relation du voyage d'Espagne [Travels in Spain] (1691), translated as "Relación del viaje de España, 1679," in Mercadal, ed. *Viajes de extranjeros por España y Portugal*, vol. 4, 10–281, 11–14.

I have described for you in my last letter everything that has happened to me since Bayonne.

. . .

1. Quoted in Justo Garate, *Viajeros extranjeros en Vasconia* (1942) 2nd. ed. (Buenos Aires: Ekin, 1989).

2. See Miguel Rodríguez Ferrer, *Los Vascongados. Su país, su lengua, y el príncipe L. L. Bonaparte* (Madrid: M. Martínez, 1873); reprint, (Bilbao: La Gran Enciclopedia Vasca, 1976), 124.

Immediately on arriving, I begged the Baron of Castelnáu, who had accompanied me from Dax, to introduce me to some attractive ladies with whom I might await without impatience the litters they were to send to fetch me from San Sebastián.

He managed to do this effortlessly because, being a man of quality and character, he was held in high regard in Bayonne; from the following day forward, he sent a steady string of ladies to visit me, as it is the custom in this country to pay a visit to newly-arrived ladies once they have been identified.

They are beginning to be annoyed here by the heat of the sun; their complexion is a bit dark; they have bright eyes; they are friendly and affectionate; their spirits are happy. I would be able to give you a better explanation for their gaiety if I had been able to understand what they were saying; it isn't that they do not know how to speak in French, every one of them, but they are so accustomed to the dialect of their province, that they cannot stop using it, and because I do not know it, they held long conversations among themselves that I could not understand at all.

. . .

The war does not prevent trade on this border; in truth, it is a necessity, because their lives depend on it; they would die of starvation if they did not help one another. This country is called Bizkaia; it is full of high mountains in which there are many iron mines. The Basques climb up these rocks as fast and with all the agility of a deer. There language (if you can call their jargon a language) is so poor that a single word has several meanings. Only the natives are capable of understanding it; and they told me that to keep it exclusively their own, they do not use it to write and they make their children read and write in French or Spanish, depending on which king they live under. It is true that as soon as I had crossed the little Bidasoa River, they did not understand me unless I spoke to them in Castilian; and what is strange is that only a quarter of an hour earlier they would not have understood me unless I had spoken in French.

23. Manuel de Larramendi Garagorri

(Andoain, Gipuzkoa, 1690 – Loiola [Loyola], Gipuzkoa, 1766)

Larramendi placed his maternal surname before the paternal one, which was not uncommon at the time. He took orders in the Company of Jesus in 1707 and did his novitiate in Villagarcía de Campos (Valladolid), then transferred to the Colleges of Valladolid and Salamanca, in the latter of which where he also taught in the university. In 1730, he was appointed confessor to the widow of Carlos II, María Ana de Newburg, which obliged him to abandon his university career and reside in Baiona (Bayonne), in Lapurdi. In 1733, he left this office to move to the College of Loiola where he remained until his death.

The polemical nature of his writing, and the clearly anti-Jesuit political environment in which it was his misfortune to live, prevented many of his works from being published during his lifetime. "I leave other writings that are ready for publication but which have, however, been put on hold for political reasons," he wrote in his autobiography. Larramendi died only a few months before the 1766 *Matxinada* or popular revolt, which had its epicenter in Azpeitia (Gipuzkoa), and which was partially blamed on the Jesuits one year before their expulsion from the kingdoms of Spain. This explains why those responsible for the Order sequestered Larramendi's writings at the time of his death and kept them safe. In effect, as soon as his death was announced, the Provincial of the Order, Father Idiáquez, forbade the Abbot of Loiola, Juan Bautista Mendizábal, "from removing any papers from the quarters of the deceased . . . [as] I have extremely serious reasons that involve the welfare of the Order . . . I find myself forced to proceed in this manner, and I know that the papers of the deceased have already been a topic of discussion at Court by the Secretary of State," who had ordered him in no uncertain terms to send his papers immediately to Valladolid.

Despite the fact that his most controversial writings were not published, the influence of Larramendi was not only philological, but political as well. Although his texts were not widely circulated, his ideas were, and they affected a generation of legal scholars immediately following him. Juan Ignacio de Iztueta dedicated a poem to him in which he speaks of "the truths sung" by the Jesuit before his death: "*Ay, nere biotzeko / Aita Larramendi! / Bost egiya esanda / joan ciñan emendik* (Oh, my dear father Larramendi! / Uttering five truths / you left from here."[1]

1. On Larramendi's life, see his autobiography, in José Ignacio Tellechea Idígoras, ed. *Autobiografía y otros escritos* (San Sebastián: Sociedad General de Ediciones y Publicaciones, 1973), and Patxi Altuna, "Aita Larramendiren bizitza," in *Manuel Larramendi. Hirugarren mendeurrena, 1690–1990*, ed. Joseba Andoni Lakarra (Andoain. Andoaingo Udala; Euskaltzaindia; Gipuzkoako Foru Aldundia; Eusko Jaurlaritza, 1991), 3–26.

It can be said that almost all the intellectual projects undertaken by Manuel Larramendi involved the Basque language and the *fueros*. Confirming the repeated attacks against the *foral* system unleashed following the advent of the Bourbons, Larramendi gathered together all of the traditional theories of the original pact, the voluntary surrender, and the limited use of monarchical power permissible in Gipuzkoa (and the other *foral* territories). Incensed by the possibility that the Castilian Monarchs might try to exercise those powers in violation of the *fueros*, Larramendi proposed the right to resistance and went so far as to suggest a hypothetical, although not desirable, separation from Castile. Moreover, the Basque language constituted for him one of the essential elements of the true meaning of the *foral* system. Therefore, it is impossible to understand his passionate defense of the language, unless we keep in mind the political context of the *foral* crisis, because the two elements are inseparably united in Larramendi's thinking.

In his life, Larramendi published four major works. The first, *De la antigüedad y universalidad del bascuence en España: de sus perfecciones y ventajas sobre otras muchas lenguas, demonstración previa al arte que se dará a luz desta lengua* (Of the Antiquity and Universality of the Basque Language in Spain: Its Perfections and Advantages over Many Other Languages, and a Forecast of the Art That Will Be Born of This Language) (1728), was an apologetic for the Basque language, many of whose arguments would later be reproduced in the prologue to the dictionary. The second was the Basque grammar, *El imposible vencido: arte de la lengua bascongada* (Achieving the Impossible: Art of the Basque Language) (1729). The third was a work debating the inclusion of the Basque territories in ancient Cantabria: *Discurso histórico sobre la Antigua famosa Cantabria: question decidida si las provincias de Bizcaya, Guipuzcoa, y Alaba, estuvieron comprehendidas en la Antigua Cantabria* (Historic Debate about Famous Old Cantabria: As to Whether the Provinces of Bizkaia, Gipuzkoa and Araba Were Included in Ancient Cantabria) (1736). And finally, he published his *Diccionario trilingüe del castellano, bascuence y latín* (Trilingual Dictionary of Castilian, Basque, and Latin), in 1745. The *Corografía o Descripción general de la Muy Noble y Muy Leal provincia de Guipúzcoa* (Geography or General Description of the Most Noble and Most Loyal Province of Gipuzkoa), was not published until 1882, and the rest of his writings in the second half of the twentieth century.

According to Larramendi, language was like man himself, being composed of body and soul. Words represented the body, whereas the grammatical structure was the soul. The body in turn mutated, growing or shrinking, but the essence of a language remained unchanged as long as it remained true to its grammatical soul. And so, Larramendi devoted his life to providing an orderly revelation of the body and soul of the Basque language. First, he declared that Basque could, in fact, be shown to have a grammar; what many had regarded as an impossible undertaking, he called "Achieving the Impossible." Considering the level of knowledge at the time, and how little had been done in that field, Larramendi produced an excellent grammar. In the body of his work, he proceeded from a premise that would condition the entire results. In the first place, he conceived his work from an essentially apologetic spirit, aiming to prove the virtues and richness of the language; and for this reason, he produced a Castilian-Basque dictionary and not the inverse, seeking to prove that all Castilian words had their Basque equivalents, and therefore he included a prologue that constitutes an entire apologetic in itself.

He also embraced the concept of matrix languages, Basque of course being one of the seventy-two languages originating in the confusion of Babel. Therefore, in cases where terms were assimilated from one language to another, it was always necessary to give prevalence to the matrix language and to assume that the others had borrowed the term from it. Moreover, from the very first page of his dictionary, Larramendi adhered to the thesis of the natural meaning of words, explicitly citing Plato's *Cratilus,* which lead to the realization of mimogenetic etymologies. Finally, Larramendi argued (in opposition to Gregorio Mayans) that Euskara had remained unchanged over the millennia, and that in essence the language that was spoken during his time was the same as that of the ancient Cantabrians, which made it possible for him to establish linguistic connections down through the ages. All of this led him to affirm the inner perfection of the language, its distinction and elegance, its harmony, the abundance and wealth of its terms, and its identity as a major matrix language from which others that had borrowed words were derived, including Greek, Latin, French, Castilian, and Italian. The Basque language was of course erudite, facile, eloquent, and methodical. Being a matrix language, and therefore perfect, it should not accept foreign words into its lexicon, and if it became necessary to create neologisms to adapt to technological and social developments, it should be done by using roots authentic to the language and not by importing others from outside. And above all other considerations, the Basque, or Cantabrian language had to be acknowledged as the ancient language extending throughout Spain. According to Larramendi, after an exhaustive analysis of the 5,385 root terms of the Castilian language, 1,951 were derived from Euskara, 2,786 had no obvious origin, and the remainder came from Latin, Arabic, Greek, Hebrew, and other languages.

The apologetic and etymological excesses of Father Larramendi were aimed more at confusing and bewildering his polemicist adversaries than at using them as authentic instruments for the literary cultivation of the language. There are all too many indications that the author himself did not believe much of what he had argued, especially with regard to neologisms or rhetorical terms of forced construction, because in the few texts that he wrote in the Basque language, he used almost none of the words he created, using instead a cleaned-up Euskara of popular origin. The problem is that some of his successors did take some of his purist suggestions seriously, provoking in later times an effect that was surely not desired and definitely pernicious.

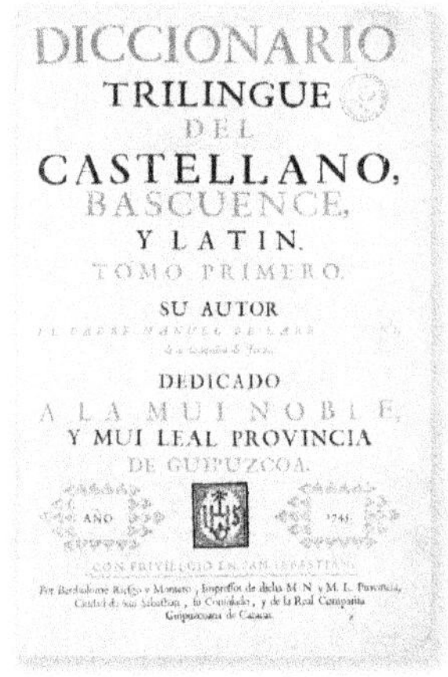

DICCIONARIO
TRILINGUE
DEL
CASTELLANO,
BASCUENCE,
Y LATIN.
TOMO PRIMERO.
SU AUTOR
DEDICADO
A LA MUI NOBLE,
Y MUI LEAL PROVINCIA
DE GUIPUZCOA.
AÑO

Selected Text(s):

Diccionario trilingüe del castellano, bascuence y latín [Trilingual Dictionary of Castilian, Basque and Latin] (San Sebastián: Bartolomé Riesgo, 1745), i-ii, ix-xiv, xxxiii-xxxiv, xxxviii-xxxix, xli-xliii, xlviii-xlix, lxxxi-lxxxiii.

PROLOGUE

I have for years been promising the public the Basque Dictionary, but have not been able until now to make my work available, among other reasons, because of the almost insuperable difficulties standing in the way against all expectations. Now at last I am keeping the promise I made and will publish my Dictionary. But first I want to speak with some deliberation about the Basque language, demonstrating its advantages and perfections and the current state of its dialects: I want to vindicate her of the objections and calumnies leveled against her by ignorance and passion; I want to affirm the glory to which she is entitled for having been the original and universal language of Spain; and I want finally to write on her behalf the apologetic against those who have decided so unreasonably to deny her this valuable prerogative. And because there is so much I want to do, and it cannot be done in abbreviated form, I have chosen to consign this apology to an extensive prologue, which is divided into three parts. The first will focus on the perfections of the Basque language: the state of her dialects, her art, and her Dictionary. The second will assure the Basque language of the glory of having been the original and universal language of Spain. The third will consist of an Apology on her behalf.

First Part

Revealing the Perfections of the Basque Language

The previous work demonstrating the art and grammar of the Basque language offers a compilation of the numerous perfections and specific advantages of Basque over other languages; and because they represent a great homage to our language, and have not been impugned in the slightest to this day, I want to include them here, so that the bulk of them will be more widely distributed and others added later.

I
Basque Is the Most Perfect Language, In The Propriety of Its Words

I am well aware that some believe all languages are equal in the propriety of their words, because all of them are *ad placitum* of the Inventors and do not have any "natural meaning"; and therefore they say that there is no reason to claim that one word is more suitable than another. But those who believe this are egregiously deceived. First, because although it is true that all of the words might have any arbitrary meaning the Inventors chose to give them, it is also true that they could well accommodate the meaning to the qualities of the objects. Words that acquire their meaning by onomatopoeia do so quite rationally and naturally through correspondence with their objects, as in the case of the *rugitus* (of the lion), or *tinnitus* for "buzz," or in that verse "*At tuba terribili sonitu taratantara dixit*" (And then the Bugle with a Fearful Cry

Blew "Tarantara"); and many others. And in the same way could inventors of a language accommodate word to meaning so that soft objects, for example, are associated with the smoothness of the words themselves, and the harsh ones with harshness; which is exactly what Quintilian observed: *nam rebus atrocibus verba etiam ipso auditu aspera magis convenient* [To subjects of a repulsive character words that are harsh in sound are the most suitable]. And just as following the invention of a language, a rhetorician or a poet who practices this precept of Quintilian claims that he can understand more naturally and appropriately the materials he is presenting, so too in the very process of inventing languages, the inventor would probably shape the words appropriately to make them match their meanings. Undoubtedly, then, the appropriateness of the words is what makes a language perfect, and this is not the same in all languages, as is obvious.

The second and main reason is that a language has simple as well as compound words, native as well as borrowed, as Cicero says. Let us listen to this distinction in the eloquent words of Quintilian: *nam cum sint eorum alia ut dicit Cicero, nativa, id est, quae significata sunt primo sensu; alia reperta, quae ex his facta sunt: ut jam nobis potere aliqua, quae illi rudes homines, primique fecerunt, fas non sit; at derivare, flectere, conjungere, quod natis postea concessum est, quando desiit licere?* [Since, when some words—as Cicero says, are primitive, that is, used in their original sense, and others derived, or formed from the primitive—though it may not be allowable for us to coin new words, different from those which the first men, however barbarous, invented, yet at what time did it cease to be allowable to derive, vary, and compound words, a privilege which was surely granted to the immediate successors of the first men?] Very well, although we might agree that in simple, native words, which are like the roots of others, one language is no more appropriate than another, in compound and derived words, this is patently false. This is because, although simple words might have a completely arbitrary meaning, without any accommodation to the objects (although this is not always the case), with compound words, their meaning already established in native languages, does not have a purely arbitrary significance, but one that is natural and precisely appropriate. Let me explain what I mean. It is *ad placitum* and arbitrary that this word *lux* signifies "that beautiful quality that illuminates us"; it is also *ad placitum* that *fero* signifies "the action of carrying." Despite all this, the word *Lucifer*, a combination of both of these, is not purely *ad placitum*. Why not? Because once the meaning of the word *lux* and the word *fero* are established, it would be ludicrous to apply the word *Lucifer*, say, to the night, to shadows, or to a cave. And this was the topic of Plato's *Cratilus,* when he said that words acquired their meanings naturally, and not what those who have only read him in the forum believe he said, making a big show of charging after straw men. In this he also follows what Plato himself establishes in that same dialogue, that this practice of picking appropriate names for objects is an undertaking that demands great genius: *Nominum igitur impositio, Hermogenes, haud quaquam levis, aut exigua res esse videtur, quemadmodum tu arbitraris, neque humilium, vulgariumque hominum opus. Ac proindé verum dicit Cratylus, cum affirmat, naturá rebus nomina existere, nec quemlibet hominem nominum esse artificem; sed illum demùm, qui ad illud nomen respicit, quod rerum naturæ exprimendæ, at que repræsentandæ peculiaritèr quadrat.* [Thus, Hermogenes, imposing names seems to be in no way trivial or of little importance, as you think, nor a practice of humble or uneducated men, and therefore Cratilus is right when he affirms that things, naturally, have names, and not any man can devise such names, but only he who is capable of coming up with an appropriate name to express and represent the natural quality of things].

These principles established, it follows that Basque is a more perfect language in the appropriateness of its words than many others, even excluding onomatopoeia, which is more frequent in Basque than in other languages. Nor do I include words that are simple or native, but only compound and derived words. The appropriateness of words, which is so important in the Hebrew language, consists in their significance being explained by some attribute, condition, or property, because we do not recognize the essences as they are in themselves; and this is called signifying objects philosophically. For in this virtue Basque exceeds other languages, not even ceding to Hebrew.

. . .

Basque Is a Richer, More Copious Language Than Many Others

I will need much doctrine to demonstrate this point. Let us imagine first, that Basque is a poor language. Decorous, decent poverty is no shame, and is in fact more admirable than indecent, dirty wealth. And the cleanliness and decency of the Basque language is manifested far more clearly than in other languages, for she has her jewels so well ordered, so well placed, so beautifully set, that one can see nothing but harmony, good taste, imagination, and genius in any aspect of her construction; whereas in the others, we see only *naste barraste,* [or] "confusion" and shapeless heaps of what they call wealth. Let us imagine that Basque is poor. With all her poverty, she dresses with such spirit, such elegance, that human speech can do no more, making other languages look shabby by comparison. Each one enters the dressing room, Italians into the Cruica, the French into the Paris Academy, the Spanish into the Academy in Madrid, some here, others there, to dress their languages, and all these many dressers succeed in doing after so many years is dishevel the bride. Let us imagine that Basque is poor. Good, graceful men garbed in sackcloth are worth more than wicked, graceless men bedecked in gold. What do we make of a language that has pieces of very precious cloth sewn on, but we recognize the original cloth from which it was made? In Romance, we call that having at best some very expensive patches.

But I emphatically deny that Basque is a language poorer than others. In regard to this, let us consider what exactly is the wealth and copy we prize most in a language. There are two levels of richness in languages, and I want to explain myself here didactically: one is formal richness, which is inherent; the other is material, which is circumstantial. Formal richness consists in the variety of precepts, the certainty of the rules, the beauty, and harmony of the Syntax, and in other attributes that are effects of the idea, of the imagination, of the understanding of the Inventor of languages. Then, there is material wealth. Well, tell me, then—in these attributes are not other languages impoverished in comparison with Basque? Where is there a language with three such distinct dialects so well structured, and by this I mean structured to include even the dialects of the Greek language, because the dialects of other languages are footless, headless, lacking rules, or common or even private roots, each one on its own, mindless, ungoverned? Where is there a language in the world with twenty-three regular modes of conjugating an active verb, corresponding to the twenty-three combinative modes of which verbal action is capable? Consequently, in the three dialects combined there are sixty-nine different modes of conjugation, but all with true, infallible roots with a single way of shaping tenses. What language has seven, or actually eight, modes of verbal action (because even if the verb is regarded as neutral, it always involves some action)? Where is there a language with such great congruence of rules, such consistency, and such harmony? Thus, Basque is a more worthy language in terms of crucial attributes, which is an indication of formal wealth in a language.

Material wealth, circumstantial in a language, consists in the multitude of separate words, synonymous or not. And I say, that in this, the Basque language is richer than many others. To prove this assertion I consider Basque from two points of view: the first, its origins, and antiquity; the second, its present state. And I assume that Basque, as it was in the beginning, was second to no other language in the world in the opulence of its words. Some will argue that this is conjecture without any basis; because my supposition cannot be substantiated by historical record, by inscriptions, by hieroglyphic evidence, or by tradition. I reply, that this is a totally superficial objection, lacking the solid inductive force needed to comprehend the ancient richness of Basque on available evidence; and regarding these points I anticipate their arguments. One does not need histories, books, inscriptions, lapidaries, or tradition to know that a city was great and densely populated in the past; it is enough to witness with our eyes the ruins of ancient buildings, here a section of broken wall, there the foundation of some temple, vestiges of a palace in one place, in another relics of some fortress. In the same way, we can easily ascertain that Basque was a language extremely rich in vocabulary simply by examining the ruins and vestiges that have been left to us. I will offer only two examples in proof of this.

The first indication of this ancient richness of Basque is what we have so recently learned about—its formal richness; because in this regard at least it seems that there is not now, nor has there ever been, a more copious and abundant language in the world; and this is a convincing argument of a miraculous fecundity in its inventors and original founders: additionally, it was the richest language in the materiality of its words. I can demonstrate this, because it cannot be rationally claimed that the inventors of Basque were sterile or impoverished in what is easy, if they were productive and felicitous in inventing and discovering what is difficult in the construction of a language. For who can be unaware that the easiest part of building a language is finding loose words, new or ancient, and that the hard part is the systematic act of combining them and organizing them according to rules?

The second indication is that the Basque language spoken today in Gipuzkoa, Bizkaia, Araba, Upper and Lower Navarre, Lapurdi, and other provinces of France has preserved such a multitude of words that even in its material aspect it equals any language in the world, as will be seen in the Dictionary that will soon be published, God willing. For what greater proof can there be of its ancient richness than that Basque has preserved such a multitude of words in spite of the voraciousness of the centuries that obliterates not only words and letters, but even events and heroic actions? So how could all these words have survived the ravages of time without books in which to inscribe them, or any other remedies? For it cannot be said that time has treated Basque more gently than other languages; consequently, it must have erased many words from the memory of the Basques as it did with other peoples. Then they will tell me perhaps what many historians have noted, and which academics repeat, and that is that only the Basques have preserved their language tenaciously, noting how they have been exceptions to that shameful servitude to which other nations surrendered, abandoning their own languages in order to speak the foreign languages of their conquerors. But I reply, that this tenacity only proves the Basques to be more punctilious, more honorable, caring, and true to their language; it does not prove that time has not inflicted the same ravages on the memory of the Basques, than on other nations. Why? Because time has no jurisdiction over the freedom of affection, but it does have jurisdiction over the fragility of a necessary faculty, memory. So, for Basque to find itself now in possession of such a rich vocabulary, despite the ravages of time, is clear proof of its initial abundance and wealth.

. . .

Basque Is a Matrix Language

I have little to do to prove this. It is a truth supported by common belief; learned men acknowledge it, and even those with little schooling believe it to be so, as we see when they include among their ordinary vexations their passionate complaint that other languages can be partially understood, but not Basque; which means that it is a language apart, and of itself, no less than the other matrix languages.

In its soul or essence, that is, in the harmony of its rules and syntax, Basque has no common origin, affinity, or similarity with any other language, either in part or completely. To demonstrate this, it might seem that it would be necessary to know the other Matrix languages and compare them with Basque to discover if any aspect of its art or grammar and syntax was derived from these other languages. However, this is unnecessary for a number of reasons: first, because other Matrix languages are no more ancient than Basque, as will be shown later; and for this language to have its origin in one or more of the other Matrix languages, it would be necessary for them to be more ancient than Basque.

The second reason is that grammars of other Matrix languages have been published with explanations of their rules in Latin, and it is clear from them that they have no affinity with Basque and that in fact it has many advantages over them, especially in the precise fecundity of its conjugations. The third, is that learned men, fluent in other Matrix languages and having knowledge of Basque or the language of the Cantabrians, admit that it has no connection with them and that it is a Matrix language. The fourth, is that I have investigated thoroughly all possible contingencies to assure myself of this truth, including the following.

I spoke on numerous occasions in Seville, with a Prelate who was a member of the Pope's entourage, adept in Hebrew and in some Eastern languages, and who sought me out because he was curious about the harmony and art or grammar of the Basque language. He told me he was impressed by the advantage it has in forming compound words, and signifying objects in a way that defines them. And what he admired most was that there were so many modes for conjugating an active verb, all of them so orderly, coherent, opportune, and free of confusion, and that they had been preserved over so many centuries without a grammar and without books. And he was unaware of anything comparable or similar to the Basque language, not even Hebrew, or the Eastern languages with which he was familiar.

When during these past years some Maronites came to Spain, who said they were princes from Lebanon, my curiosity about Palencia caused me to make another effort. I begged them through the interpreter to speak to me slowly in their language about the description of the Maronites and their country, customs, State and Religion, which Father Maimbourg had written in his book, which I had in my hand. I explained my purpose, which was to ascertain whether my Cantabrian language was in any way similar to theirs. They spoke to me for a long time in their Syrian language, repeating the words as slowly as I wanted, the interpreter pointing out to me their meaning in the French words in the Book. They would pronounce a word, and I would try to repeat it, correctly pronouncing some, mispronouncing most, making them too guttural. Afterwards I spoke Basque to them slowly, and about the same material; but they could not understand a single word of my language, nor could I understand theirs. And I concluded that they were totally different, not only in pronunciation, but in everything else as well.

Another experiment: They informed me in Saint-Jean-de-Luz [Donibane Lohizune, Lapurdi] that on hearing some Armenians speak it had seemed to them that their language had some words that were similar to those in Basque; and I was inclined to think this might be so, because in the rivers and mountains of this country of Cantabria, there are many words and names that some mountains and rivers in Armenia have. But it didn't take me long to see my error. Four or five years ago, I brought an Armenian cleric here to Loiola, who said he understood Castilian fairly well. I explained my curiosity to him, and he began to speak to me slowly in his language, translating what he said into Romance afterward. He also read to me slowly from a book that he had with him; but it did not contain any word that resembled those in

Basque, except in the way some were pronounced. Through these experiments, I confirmed for myself the common opinion that Basque has no kinship with other languages, and that it is a Matrix language.

. . .

This reminds me of a certain person's opinion that the language of Adam and of the others up until the Flood and the Confusion of Babel there was a language so abundant in synonyms that it had seventy-two to refer to the same object: and that the Confusion that God caused consisted in restricting those synonyms, leaving each family with just one of those that there had been before, and thus they were divided into seventy-two languages. And so, they generally believed that this was the number into which they were divided, although others think there were fewer. From this, it follows that all the languages have their origin, and are still part of that first language of the world, which was Hebrew.

But this opinion is unsound; and even if it were based on fact, it is enough for us to know that the other languages, Basque among them, were not derived from Hebrew as it existed after the Confusion of Babel, in the family of Heber. And there is even less reason to believe that opinion, if we are speaking of the formal aspect of languages, which are quite different in their syntax. I ask, was the language before the Flood equally rich in the harmony of its syntax, or wasn't it? If it was not, then the others were Matrix languages too, independent of that original language in terms of structure and rules. If it was, then we have to say that men did not speak just one language before the Flood, but that each one knew as many languages as there were synonyms for loose words and as there were different Syntaxes.

It is demonstrably true, then, that Basque is a matrix language, with no origin except divine inspiration during the confusion of Babel, and one which God imprinted in a certain family of those who were building the Tower, and different from those he imprinted in the others, and also distinct and independent of all of them, so that they could not understand each other at all. And this is confirmed by the singular advantages of Basque, and the perfections of its structure in which if she does not surpass all others, it seems at least that she is surpassed by none; for it is true that no man could have been the Author of such admirable harmony.

Basque Is One of the Major Matrix Languages

Some scholars divide the Matrix languages into greater and lesser, and like Scaliger and Mayans, count Basque among the lesser. But deriving the name *matrix* from the origin and beginning they had, all the Matrix languages are equal because they acknowledge an identical sovereign Author who inspired them at a single moment in the Confusion of Babel. If the denomination *matrix* is taken to mean that some enter to a lesser degree, others to a greater degree in the body of the other languages, then there can be greater and lesser. And I say that even in this sense the Basque language, at least by comparison with Castilian, is one of the major matrix languages, and that those who deny this have reached this conclusion without adequate reflection.

. . .

Basque Is a Living, Erudite Language

Hebrew, Greek, and Latin, among many other languages, had the misfortune of dying, and they were left buried in books. There is no nation that uses them as their own vernacular, maternal languages, and this is what we mean when we say they are dead languages. They died, not because the bulk of their body, that is, their words, do not have lives in what we refer to today as living languages, but because even that portion of their words, utterly lost their soul and their harmony, which are their rules and syntax, and now have a different harmony and soul, so that they become integrated into very different languages. They died, and therefore they cannot acquire and assimilate new words needed to describe new objects and new inventions. When they were alive, they had power and the freedom to create new words and to adopt those of different languages, enriching themselves with them and transcend their poverty and wretchedness. They died, and by their death, they lost that virtue and freedom, and they can no longer create a word or adopt one from other languages, unless it is some barbarism.

Basque has avoided and is free of this misfortune, because from the moment of her origin in the Confusion of Babel, she has been, and is alive, without all those centuries, wars, disasters, upheavals of empires, and religions that destroyed other languages and having the power to take her precious life, much less bury her in oblivion. She has lived from the beginning as the vernacular mother tongue of the Spaniards, in the beginning universal and spread all across Spain, later more constricted, and finally limited to the sacred precincts of these mountains, where she still enjoys a life and robust health, suffering none of the caducity of the other languages. Neither Moors, nor Goths, nor Vandals, Swedes [Suebi?], Romans, Carthaginians, Greeks, Phoenicians, or any other nation were able to extinguish her, succeeding only in banishing her from the rest of Spain, but dug in among these crags, in spite of time and its ravages, she has known how to keep her soul and body alive in a state so vigorous and strong that she stands now on the verge of rejuvenation, with aspirations to immortality. By this, I mean that Basque has preserved the power to create new words, composed of her most fecund roots, and the freedom to appropriate and adopt many others from different languages to name new objects and grow rich among all languages.

Many will laugh, and all will be surprised, when I say that Basque is an erudite language; but laughter and surprise are not arguments. For a language to be erudite its words and structure are rich in teaching and doctrine so that those who speak and understand it become erudite and learned. In this, Basque is more vigorous than other erudite languages. In her words, Basque is a philosophic language because she explains objects by their attributes and properties, and each word is a definition or description of its significance, so that not a single one (I am speaking of compound words) lacks this power. So that if we knew the composition of all Basque words, as we do for many of them, a person who spoke Basque with intelligence would understand and teach the attributes and properties of all the objects, whose science is contained in her words. Nor can it be denied that in this sense that Basque is a language more erudite than many others.

For a language to be erudite means that it has the power to make those who speak and understand it learned and erudite in the arts and sciences and other disciplines; and indeed Basque is a language capable and suited to this end because she can speak fluently in all the arts and sciences without difficulty or embarrassment, and if there is any embarrassment, it's because they know so little about how widespread Basque was once, and how perfect she is, and about her best qualities; and in regard to this lack of knowledge, even by native speakers, I will complain below.

But they will tell me that today the languages that are considered to be erudite are those in which the Sacred Scriptures and the Arts and Sciences are written, for example, Hebrew, Greek and Latin, because they are all indispensable for the attainment of a solid erudition, although they are dead languages. This is true, and I say that in this sense Basque cannot be called an erudite language, except with qualification; because except for the few books, which I will mention, she has no others in which the arts and sciences have been taught or written. This is not the fault of the language but of those who have been unwilling to speak her, and even these can be excused, because Basque is confined to these mountains, her written texts would be of no use to the rest of Spain or

Europe, no matter how erudite they were. But this is a well-known illusion. If there were, for example, some authentic history written in this language a thousand years ago describing events in Spain, I believe there would not be any curious, erudite Spaniard who would not value it and who would not take the trouble to learn Basque just to be able to read it in the original. I say the same of other ancient writings that might exist in this language.

. . .

Basque Is an Easy Language

Basque is burdened by none of the difficulties afflicting many other languages; it is written just as it is spoken, and everything spoken can be written easily without any need for usage or tacit intelligence to add or subtract a single sound from the pronunciation established by the letters. There are three or four sounds that make pronunciation difficult for those who do not know Basque, but who want to learn it, and here I am speaking about the Spanish, for as I have demonstrated by experiment they are not difficult for those from other nations. The first of these are words that are written with *tza*, for example, *otzá, atzó, latzá*, which mean "cold," "yesterday," "rough," or *eguitzic* (make them), *ematzic* (give them), which they find it hard to say, and changed to *ozá, azó, lazá, eguizic, emazic*, or *ot-zá* and *at-zó*, separating the *t* from the *z*. But this pronunciation is easy. The *t* and the *z* are always placed in the syllable with the vowel that follows, if there is one, and never with the preceding vowel, and if we hurry and make the *t* collide with the *z*, we produce a very funny pronunciation. The second, involves words that are written with *tsa*, for example *otsá*, "noise" or "sound," *matsá* (grape), *patsá* (the remains of grapes or apples after being pressed), *bagatsá* (dirty), *liquitsá* (hog), *emoten deutsat* (I give them to you), etc., and here the same effects are produced as with the cluster *tza*. The third involves words that have an *x* sound and its Latin pronunciation, for example, *auxe* [this very one], *orixe* [that very one], *guexeago* [a little more], *goxo* [sweet, pleasant], which are pronounced approximately *ausye, orisye, gueisyeago, gosyo*. The fourth is the pronunciation of the weak *t*, sliding into the semi-consonant *y*, as in *ematen ditut* [I give you], which in addition to the strong pronunciation has the [*t-y* sound] of *ematen dityut*.

Basque has none of those sounds that Quintilian calls unpronounceable, nor any that are heard far back in the throat and on the palate. Ordinarily it is a very deliberate, gentle language, as Scaliger said its normal pronunciation is very melodious and graceful, with a naturally sibilant *th* sound, lacking both the harshness and the effeminate effect of Castilian. The guttural pronunciation of *j* spoken in some places does not appear in Basque, which closely imitates the Castilian *j* in *jauna* [lord, sir, mister], *jan* [eat], *joan* [go], *jo* [hit, strike], although sliding toward *yauna, yan*, etc. In Lapurdi, Lower Navarre and Zuberoa, it is very common to aspirate the written letter *h* in speech, but not in the dialects of Spain, as I said earlier; and although the *h* is not aspirated, I am inclined to believe that many words are written using it the way it is used in France, to distinguish between different meanings. For example, *ori ori ori* looks like one word but actually they are three different words, meaning "take that yellow one" and they should be distinguished in this manner: *óri, orí, hori,* because *óri* (take) has the accent on the *o* and we also say *orizu* [take it]; [whereas] *orí* (yellow) has the accent on the *i;* and *horí* also on the *i* but it is differentiated by the *h* with which they write and pronounce that word in Lapurdi, although this aspiration is never guttural as it is in Andalusia. I can say the same about *hurá* (that) and *urá* (water); *haria* (ram) and *aria* (thread), *haur* (this), which we pronounce *au*, and *aur*, *aurra* (child); and so it is with many words. But in this I am not bothered if the distinctions are lost, and so sometimes I will write words one way, on other occasions the other way.

With these exceptions, which might be called embarrassments, the Basque language is easy and modern, so easy that a person, who would need two years to learn any other language, could learn Basque in four months. And this can be demonstrated by reason and by experience. The reason is based on the fact that Basque is a language so methodical, and with rules so regular and unvarying that they are continuously imprinted in the memory of the one learning it, without the need to learn the irregularities or exceptions to rules so common in all the other languages. What does it matter, for example, if it has twenty-three ways to conjugate an active verb, if by memorizing one we know how to conjugate all the others? What does it matter if the different dialects have different ways of ending the verb, if they are completely regular and consistent? I say the same about the dialects with respect to the articles of the nouns and the entire syntax.

But experience is the best and most convincing proof. Many Castilian men, and even more Castilian women, who have settled in the Basque Country have learned to speak Basque perfectly, and this in a short time simply by hearing it spoken, without a grammar or a teacher, and this comes from the regularity and uniformity of Basque speech in such and such a way of using the verbs, and in such and such a way of using the nouns, which we call conjugations, declensions, and so forth, without the need for a grammar or a teacher. For example, I need only mention two Jesuits who had never learned a word of Basque before coming to this country, and nevertheless in no time at all they ended up being Basques themselves. One is Father Bernardo Recio, who in just eighty days of studying the grammar was able to go to confession in Basque even before taking the exam in the language, mainly in the dialect of Gipuzkoa; and here in Loiola and Azpeitia I had the great pleasure of hearing him speak our language in a lengthy conversation with great precision and reflection, and he even corrected those who were speaking it improperly; and not even eight months had passed since he had begun to learn it. The other is Father Manuel Porta, who in almost the exact same time learned the language in the dialect of Bizkaia, which he now uses when he preaches on missions. And they tell me that a number of members of other religious orders have learned it equally well with only the aid of the Grammar and its questions for learning verses and the names of things. And it is quite sure that they could not learn another language as easily, even it they set about studying and practicing it with even more care.

. . .

About the Words of the Common Language Contained In the Dictionary

The Basque language is spoken throughout the provinces mentioned above. I do not mean the soul of the language, which is entirely in Gipuzkoa, entirely in Bizkaia, entirely in each one of the dialects; nor is there any more soul and harmony in all of them together than in one alone. I am speaking of the body, which is the multitude of Basque words informed by this soul. Not all of them are in Gipuzkoa, not all are in Bizkaia, etc., and one part is in Bizkaia, another in Gipuzkoa, another in Navarre, another in Lapurdi, another in Araba. In Gipuzkoa, many words needed to explain many objects are lacking, and for that reason Castilian is used, which has more at hand; but this is not because the Basque language is lacking in words but because it has them elsewhere, outside of Gipuzkoa, and if it needs to call them forth it will find them in Bizkaia, Lapurdi, or Navarre. In the same way, there are not enough words in Bizkaia to name everything, but there are enough in Gipuzkoa and in other countries and they are Basque words, legitimate words. This distribution of the body of the Basque language is the reason why Basque has been thought to be poor. The Basque from

Gipuzkoa is only aware of that portion of Basque words that exist in Gipuzkoa, or if he is aware of others he refuses to make use of those that exist in Bizkaia, and the same is true for the Bizkaian with his portion of words with respect to those of Gipuzkoa; and because each one of these portions is insufficient to span the universality of ordinary objects, the Basque language is unfairly judged to be poor.

To do away with this embarrassment to the extent possible, I have made an effort to include in the Dictionary without any distinction as to dialect, all the words I was able to think of in the Basque language so that they will all become common to all the provinces and to all the different dialects of the language in the same way that a large portion of words that are used in all the dialects are common to them all. Thus, for example, under the word *Amar* [to love], I enter *amatu*, *onetsi*, *oneritzi*, *maitatu*, *maite izan*: under *poner* [to put, place], *ipiñi*, *ibeni*, *ereñi*, *ezarri*, *paratu*: under *cansar* [to tire], *cansatu*, *necatu*, *aricatu*, *unatu*, etc. without specifying that *aricatu* is used in Bizkaia, *unatu* in Lapurdi, *necatu* in Gipuzkoa, [and] *cansatu* everywhere. In this way the dialects are mutually enriched, picking up words from one another, and become more understandable and ordinary, but without ceasing to be different dialects. The word *aricatu* is common to them all and used by each dialect in combination with a different ending, for example, *aricatu jataz, aricatu zaizt, aricatu zaizquit* (I have tired). The common word *ereñi* is common to them all, with all of its different endings, for example, *ereñi diozcat, ereñi dizquiot, ereñi deutsadaz, ereñi darotzat, ereñi derautzat* (I have placed them on it).

No doubt they will tell me that this is like introducing into each country and dialect a new kind of gibberish, totally unintelligible because the words that are not in use in Gipuzkoa will be as strange and poorly understood as if they were from Greek or Latin, and it will be the same in Bizkaia and in other provinces. But they will be wrong. A person who speaks in Gipuzkoa will be happy to use the words that are current and understood there, but if it turns out that a few or many Basque words are lacking to refer to things, do not use Castilian or Latin words, use Basque words from Bizkaia or Navarre or Lapurdi, if you find them in those dialects; because by using Castilian words you are using words that are not yours, and that will not be understood; whereas by using words from Bizkaia you will be using your own treasure, words that belong to you and that will be more understandable because they will bring their own Basque flavor. Besides, the sense of strangeness a word arouses at first will fade after you hear it two or three times, as can be seen in all languages when new words are introduced. And although the Gipuzkoan ordinarily uses *necatu* [to tire], once he learns the word *aricatu* he will be able to use it, either when talking to a Bizkaian or when it happens to suit the rhythm of a verse, or simply because he wants to vary the sentence for the sake of variety and beauty; and in this way each dialect will be enriched.

. . .

When Basques see such an enormous quantity of their common language in the Dictionary, some will ask if all the words are really Basque words. Others will insist that they are not, but are words I made up and invented. To those who ask calmly and without passion I say that they are all Basque words and that I have not included any words that I have not read in a printed book, or heard spoken frequently, writing down as many as I can as I hear them to keep from forgetting them. Only three words are of my own invention, words that I have been using for many years: *sutumpa*, for "artillery cannon," *godaria,* for "chocolate," and *surrautsa,* for "tobacco ash." And then I will confess the one license that I've allowed myself. If you are amazed by the multitude of words that are included, be even more amazed to hear me repeat that I have not included them all, and that there are innumerable still undisclosed and commonly used ordinary words scattered throughout the Basque provinces. To those who arrogantly maintain that they are not Basque words (a truly intolerable impertinence) I will respond that they do not get to vote in this matter, so what they need to do is stay out of it. These people, where do you suppose they are from, somewhere outside the Basque Country, like Madrid, Seville, or other places, or are they from within these provinces? If they are from outside, they hardly know any Basque, having forgotten even the words they learned when they were children, so the words of their own dialect are as new to them as those from others. The second, no matter how good they are, only know their own dialect and are totally ignorant of the others: and furthermore, without the least doubt, they are even unaware of an infinite number of ordinary and currently used words in their own dialect. So it would be absurd for them to say that these are not Basque words, because they have either forgotten them or they have never heard them before, and so it would be equally absurd for them to say that about the words they are going to read in the Dictionary.

This discourse would be superfluous and unnecessary if the judges and critics of the Basque language were even slightly informed and reasonable about the matter; but it is a disaster for this language that even the ignorant think they have a right to criticize her. It is quite laughable—after all my years of reflection, research, observation, study, journeys, and interviews to create an art and grammar of the Basque language and to observe her perfections, the differences between her dialects, the multitudes of her words and their regularity and correspondence to Castilian words—that without any work or study or even an ounce of talent in these matters a few ignorant Basques, who have no Latin, speak Romance badly and Basque even worse, would all of a sudden turn into experts about all this. Sit down and try to write a letter in your language; you cannot. Open your Axular and try to read it; you will be stymied. Everything he writes will be like Greek to you. And these are the ones who want to exercise their right to vote regarding the Grammar and Dictionary of the Basque language, men who can only tell one word from another by the way they smell, so much for these arrogant ignoramuses.

. . .

Concerning Academic Terms and the License I've Taken in Forming Certain Words

In addition to the words from everyday language, I also include in this Dictionary those that pertain to the academic disciplines, the arts, and the sciences. In one sense, it can be said that Basque is weak, lacking such terms; but in another sense it can and should be said that she has all the necessary components in her roots or origins. In the first sense, Basque has had no need for words of her own, or for borrowed words because no one has written about the disciplines and sciences in Basque, nor has it been thought that Basque is a language suitable for speaking about them. But Basque has now entered a new phase and is ready to speak about any science and discipline; and now is the time to seek out appropriate terms that she has lacked up until now, either borrowing them from other languages or inventing and forming them from her fertile roots, as Cicero puts it [in Book I of *Academica*]. At the time of this Prince of Eloquence, Latin had fallen into a similar state; it had no academic terms, and was quite poor; it had the right and the need to seek them out, whether they were foreign or proper Latin words. Cicero invented some, as did others; but intimidated by the enormity of the project, they made use of Greek words and left Latin in her native poverty.

I do not want the Basque language to suffer this same misfortune; and because in all other aspects, she is a language of such harmony and beauty, and the opportunity now presents itself, I want to enrich her, not with foreign words, but with her own, not letting myself be overcome by the painful work that awaits me. Basque needs academic terms and does not have them fully formed, but she has riches of her own from which to create them and add to them without borrowing them from other languages; and this is the other sense in which I have said that she has all the words needed, even to express herself in the arts and sciences. The Greek language, from which Latin routinely borrows them, has words of this kind through the combination of two or more simple words, having the inherent capacity to form them and the ability to form them with great ease, something Latin and the Romance languages lack. Take for example *Theologia, Astrologia, Uranologia, Chronologia*, and other pompous words she uses to name the various sciences, and then the adjectives *Theologos*, *Astrologos*, etc. In these, as is obvious, the common component is the word *logia*, *logos*, from which they are formed, which means "a basic word," and the difference is in the prefixes *Theos*, *Astros*, *Uranos*, *Chronos*, which are also simple and lose one or more letters in the combination, signifying respectively, "the science that deals with God," "with the Stars in the Sky," "with the weather," [and] "with time." What they do with the stems *logia* and *logos*, they also do with other words making up the names of the other arts and sciences, for example, *graphia* [the art or method of writing] and *graphos* [something written], *metria* [the science or process of measuring] and *metras* [something measured].

In this way, Basque has the method for creating her own words to express herself in the disciplines and sciences. She has simple words that are quite suitable and abundant for the particular objects in the sciences and arts. It is her nature and habit to form compound words from simple words. It is so common that even ordinary Basques invent them and understand them effortlessly as they go along, and this can be observed by anyone in the ordinary words I include in the Dictionary, and they are for the most part compound words. Science is expressed as *jaquindea, jaguiundea, jaquiñera, jaquiera, jaquintasuna* [knowledge]. "God," "Stars," "Sky," [and] "time," we call *Jaincoa, Izarrac, Cerua*, and *era*. In the same way that Greek composes the names of the sciences *Theologia, Astrologia, Uranologia, Chronologia* and others from the word *logia*, so does Basque, following that method and character, create from the contracted form of *jaquindea* the corresponding names *Jaincoquindea, Izarquindea, Ceruquindea, eraquindea*, which mean "Science of God," "of the Stars," "of the Sky," [and] "of the weather and time"; and like the adjectives *Theologos, Astrologos*, etc., so in Basque there are, *Jaincoquindea, Izarquindarra*, etc. What I do with these general names of the sciences, I do with their particular objects, and the same in the other sciences and arts.

Here are some Basque words that are suitable for explaining the arts and sciences: they are new in terms of their combination, but ancient in terms of their roots; and without having recourse to outside help, Basque discovers within herself the abundance sufficient for everything. They are new, as the Greek words were, when they were first invented; and like them, they became old as time passed, just as these Basque words will become old as time passes. They are new but opportune in the way they show the rationale and significance of their object, which is an enormous advantage. They are new but not *ad placitum* or made up just to please and flatter me, but totally natural to the meaning of the simple words from which they are composed, the analysis of which reveals their appropriateness. They are new, not for the Basque language, but for the Basque, who has not attempted or been able to discover or record the treasures their most fecund language contains. And, if as Cicero said the Greeks are permitted, not only at the beginning but also after centuries to form compound words, why are we not even more entitled to do so now, as we begin to deal with these objects? It is undoubtedly permissible and even necessary, provided that in the invention of the words the appropriateness prescribed by Plato is maintained, keeping in mind the quality and character of the Basque language and the appropriate meaning of the simple words. It is already clear to me that the Castilian I speak is Greek to the ignorant, who although they speak Basque, do not have the slightest understanding of these principles; but "that matters very little to us," as Don Quixote said to Sancho.

They will say that these words are incomprehensible. In the first place, they are not ordinary words but academic words, and it is enough if the professors of science understand them, as in the case of the corresponding Greek and Latin words. Secondly, it does not matter if they are not understandable at first, because with time and repetition they will be easily understood. Third, even for the ordinary Basque these Basque words *Jaincoquindea, Izarquindea, Ceruquindeea, eraquindea,* and more intelligible than the corresponding *Theologia, Astrologia, Uranologia, Chronologia*, because the latter sound nothing like Basque, but the former do. Fourth, there is no one who, once the Basque word is explained, will not make it and its meaning his own.

. . .

I Refute the Criticisms against the Basque Language

The first allegation was that Basque is a barbaric language, incapable of culture, grammatically inconsistent, crude, and tasteless. This is a charge made in the past, for now, no one would dare repeat it. Those who made such charges on the authority of a serious writer, as blind men attempting to identify colors, are now deservedly humiliated and publicly refuted following the demonstration that the opposite is true. It is a perfect language with many advantages over those regarded as civilized, elegant languages; it is so highly sophisticated that I doubt there is a language capable of greater culture; it is methodical and grammatically consistent, as its Grammar makes evident; it is melodic and smooth, as Scaliger said, without harshness or tastelessness, and all those who have studied and examined it carefully acknowledge this to be the plain truth. There are still others, I am told, who without having learned or studied it deny this language the perfections with which I endow it or show it to be endowed, because they do not know if what I say is true. They deserve even more opprobrium than those who until now have treated Basque as a barbaric, unsophisticated language; because the ancients had no way to enlighten themselves, but the moderns today do have and can learn for themselves the truth of my assertions, if they know Castilian, which the ancients of course did not; yet they have the gall to coolly and blindly reject what is proven. Let us disregard them, for the plain concision of one wise man, even if he is all alone, is worth more than the clattering condemnation of a thousand fools.

Their second charge is that if Basque is a language so melodic and harmonious in its perfections, why have its native speakers so completely forgotten and abandoned it? And why have they not defended it against so much mockery, opprobrium, and slander? And if the abandonment and silence of the Basques is true, then it must also be true that the Basque language is not as I have depicted it. I confess that this is a circumstance that might partially exonerate those who in ancient times claimed that our language was barbaric. The Basques have apparently acquired no appreciation for their language, or if they have, they do not express it. They leave their country and then make a point of forgetting it: they do not write nor do they show any desire of writing even a letter in their language. Inside the Basque Country, they block every avenue that might lead to her preservation and the discovery of her splendor. Nothing is read to, written to, or taught to children in Basque: you cannot find a teacher who wishes, or knows how to spell, in his language. Neither inside nor outside the Basque Country has anyone published anything useful to these provinces in the Basque language, with the exception of a few books from Lapurdi that are almost impossible to locate. They see and hear the jokes people tell about their language, and their only response is and has always been anger and fury. Garibay said long ago that she was a methodical language with rules capable of being synthesized into a grammar; Oihenart discovered some of her perfections, as did Moret, lambasting Mariana's tasteless assault; but they made few demands, leaving the Basque language in her former state of abandonment. What conclusion could foreigners deduce from this, except that she was indeed a barbaric and primitive language? But such conclusions are no longer accepted, finally, and the continuing neglect now had other causes, which can be seen in Moret. And it is clear that for modern writers, all rescue efforts have been closed down and without any apparent rationale they have gone on treating her as a barbaric language despite all evidence to the contrary.

. . .

Fourth, they argue, and it is the Basques themselves who make this argument, that the Basque language is an obstacle to learning and speaking Castilian well, so it would be better to forget or banish the Basque language from the world to gain the advantage of mastering the dominant language. According to such thinking, even today it is laughable to see in these provinces, many people whose speech is as bewigged as their heads, and who are so puffed up with "Language" and so berouged in Castilian that they regard any Basque word as a blotch or a pimple. They arch their brows, scrunch up their noses in a precious little frown, listening with disdain and distaste, acting as if they do not understand it, saying "could you please say it in Castilian?," proud as peacocks to have forgotten their mother tongue. The ladies of this country, although they speak Castilian reasonably well, always prefer to speak Basque. Behold one of these Romancified nits walking in to the parlor to pay a visit to one of these ladies and initiate a dialogue or a heterogeneous conversation under the natural courtesy of acceding to the wishes of the lady, but he will answer in Castilian to what she is saying in Basque: *Ongui etorriadala urlia Jauna* [Welcome, Mr. So and So]. And his hands, feet and neck all aquiver and affected with gesture, he'll reply [in Castilian]: "Milady, allow me to kiss your feet." *At seguin det berori orrelaxe icustea: onic dago, eta ederric, dirudienez beintzat* [I am pleased to see you. You appear well and in good health]. "I am most grateful, Milady, for your concern, and I am feeling better now, and always at your service." *Jarri bedí, ta esan beguit, cer dacarren, ain goiztar dabillenean: lo gozoric ez bide deu eguin, edo loguiró gaistoren bat izan al deu?* [Please sit down, and pray tell me, what do you bring, coming here so early: have you not slept at all, or had a bad night's sleep?] "Milady, correspondence and vexing concerns are bad friends for a soothing night's sleep." *Eztet aditzen* [I don't understand] *orrec cer esan nai devan, ote dira loeraguille iñudcenac?* [what that means. Perhaps, that they are sleepy wet-nurses for a good night's sleep?] "That is true, Milady." And he goes on and on, without lapsing into a single Basque word. And the ladies who have to put up with this are far too polite to tell him: *zoaz ordu gaistoan emendican, eta urrengoan jaquin ezazu nere eusquera, ta nere erara hitzeguin beardidazula, eta ez nic zuri erdera erbesteco, arrotz ori* [Get out of here at this bad time, and the next time let it be known that you should know my Basque and my ways, and that I should not have to speak to you in that foreign Castilian, you foreigner].

It is true that Basque is something of an obstacle to learning Castilian, but only in the sense that Castilian is an obstacle to learning Basque or any other language that is unrelated to Castilian, and any language can be learned more easily when one is a child, because it is the only language, and no other stands in the way. But who, except for a few fools, would deliberately try to lose their mother tongue for that reason? Saint Jerome pulled out or filed down his teeth because they made it difficult for him to speak Hebrew, but he did not cut off his Latin tongue and throw it away just to learn Hebrew. Once the barbarism of the previous centuries had been overcome, and the Greek and Latin languages began to flourish in Europe, there were indeed a number of wise men in the fifteenth and sixteenth centuries, but so ridiculous that with incredible affectation they chose not only to forget their mother tongue, but to appear to be Roman in all things and utterly Latin, they ended up changing the names and surnames of their House and Family. There were others equally Roman, but also Gentile, who did not want to read the Latin text of the Holy Scripture in order not to lose the pure Latin quality, or even pray the Breviary in Latin. These impertinent fools are surely the model for these affected Castilians, who in order to speak Romance more correctly forget Basque or choose not to speak it, and all that is lacking is that when they sign their Basque names, they translate them into Castilian, as they can easily do, so that they don't retain even a trace of the Basque language, although this is their best and most valuable characteristic.

It should also be admitted that the Basque language presents a special obstacle to speaking Castilian well, and the Basques are oblivious to the existence of this obstacle, and therefore they never, or only with great difficulty, learn Romance well just by using it and practicing it without reflecting or comparing the two languages. And thus in long conversations in Castilian, rarely does the Basque fail to show himself for what he is. And this, which provokes insipid laughter in the Castilians and causes the Basques to blush for no reason, actually makes me very happy because even without trying I discover by mistake that I am a Cantabrian and a Basque. If they knew the reason for this embarrassment, they would overcome it easily and acquire a greater mastery of Castilian. The difficulty consists in the fact that the structure of Basque in comparison with Castilian is postpositive: Basque does not differentiate between the masculine and feminine gender of articles; the verb endings absorb the article, either singular or plural, and its relation with first, second or third person, none of which occurs in Castilian.

Because they are unaware of this in the elementary schools, from the very beginning they start out speaking Romance incorrectly. Being unaware of the postpositive construction and using it in Castilian the children end up producing a thousand precious effects. *Escuetan muñeguiten diola*, means "is honored to kiss your hands," but imitating the Basque construction they say "the hands that kiss your worship." For *etortecoadala*, which means "is coming," they say "from coming which is," because they do not know the difference between the infinitive and the participle, and there is no one to teach them, they translate this Basque sentence, *gosaldu ta joango guerala*, as "to eat lunch and that we will go," when it really means "we will go once we eat or after having eaten." Because they do not know that in Basque the articles are unvarying but in Castilian they are differentiated by gender, and that they are not used excessively in Castilian, they say "*del mano*" instead of "*de la mano*" [of the hand] and "*de las hombres*" [of the men] using the feminine article instead of "*de los hombres*," and although they're referring to *noticias* [news, a feminine noun], they say, for example, *ya los he traído* [I have already brought them, using the masculine pronoun *los* instead of feminine pronoun *las*]. Because they do not know that the Basque ending swallows the distinction between singular and plural, or the corresponding article as well as the transition or relation to person, they leave out the articles from the Romance. *Ecarri ditut, ecarri det, ecarri dizut*, means "I have brought them," "I have brought it," "I have brought it to you," and because they do not distinguish mood and difference in the simplicity of the endings, they only translate "I have brought" in the three cases. "Have you brought the horses?" / "I've brought" / "Have I brought you bad news?" / "You have brought" / "Have you brought him money?" / "I have brought" [are] always in the same form, which is indistinguishable, for in Basque they correspond to three different endings: *ecarri ditut, ecarri diot, ecarri didazu* [I have brought them, I have brought it to him, you have brought it to me]. The special difficulty imposed by the Basque language for learning Romance correctly can be reduced to these three features; yet they are so far from being an obstacle, once the differences are learned, that they might even be very helpful, and if they are not helpful, it is because they are not known, or differentiated, or is not something easy for all Basques.

. . .

It Is Proven By [The Actual Existence of an] Ancient Monument That Basque Is the Original Language of Spain

On reading this title, modern readers will smile and say, "Here we have someone accepting at face value some supposed Chronicle from those times that even today continues arousing zeal and devotion to the antiquities of Spain." But it is not that. The monument is a lamina or metal tablet, previously unknown, that was found on the coast they call Buena Vista, above the Port of Santa Maria. It is two yards long and somewhat less than two thirds of a yard wide. It was ascertained by the weight and sound that it was made of metal, even before the rust was scraped away so it could be seen. They began to peel away the layers of dirt and rust, and in the places uncovered by the scraper they recognized that the tablet had writing on it, and this is how it looked after it was clean and smooth. The characters are large and stand out in relief, although some are worn away. A multitude of scholars and antiquarians attended and made lengthy presentations about the discovery at the unveiling. The characters were unrecognizable and unrelated to those from other languages that were made available for comparison; and after lengthy conferences they concluded that that lamina as well as the language in which those words and characters were written was from a period in Spain that predated the Romans, Carthaginians, Greeks and Phoenicians by several centuries.

But fate had it that one more curious scholar, after repeated observation of those unknown characters, noticed that all of them had some mathematical form, neatly inscribed, and by making a thousand combinations he managed to decipher the alphabet that corresponded to those characters and their language, which cannot be printed here for lack of molds in the press. When the alphabet was finally deciphered, what was written on that tablet is the following in our letters:

GUR. EGUILL. AND.
BER. MEN. ESCAL. MNAST. OL
SEN. AU. JAS. D. GU. ERDALD.
LENB. SART. Z. NEAN. OND. AD.
ARAZ. BAT. ETA. BEN. GUR. LA.
EC. EZ. ARR. BEC. AMB. JAIN.
GUEZ. TA IRR. RRI.

As soon as this text was deciphered and published among these learned Antiquarians, an investigation was made to ascertain in which language it was written, and it became demonstrably clear that it had no relation to any other language and that it was in fact precisely the language we call Basque today; and when the abbreviations were read, this is what it said: *Gure eguille andiari, bere meneco Escaldunac menast-ol sendo au jasotzen diogu Erdaldunac lembician sartu zaizcunean; ondocoai adiarazteco, bati, eta benaz gurtzen gatzaiz-cala, ecen ez arrotzoc becala, ambeste Jainco guezurrezco, ta irri garriri.* Translated into Castilian, this means: "To our great creator, the Basques of his hand and subjection erect this tablet of solid metal at the time when outsiders speaking another language have entered our land for the first time, to make it known to our visitors that we truly worship one God only and not a legion of false and ridiculous gods as these visitors do."

At this point you should have heard the learned and ingenious commentary of all and sundry, for example, one scholar said, in Buena Vista and beside the Port of Santa Maria a prodigious metal tablet [has been discovered], which he calls the Muasta Tablet, or [was it] Menasta? This is the true origin and cause of having named that city *Puerto de Muesteo* in ancient times and not what has been hitherto believed; because from such a famous trophy of the Cult and Religion of the true God, which was erected by the primitive Spaniards for the instruction of the new arrivals, it is not surprising that the city in which it was erected should be famous. And this was confirmed when they told him that *menasta* in Basque means "metal," a most suitable meaning, and that it meant "vein," or "mineral alloy," from *mea* (vein or mineral), and from *nasta*, *nastua* (mixed): and that famous tablet would have far more than this.

There was no Martis, no Mayanses, no Diaristas, who on seeing the lamina with its signs of antiquity, and its unknown characters, did not cry out that all of it—lamina, language, characters—belonged to the primitive Spaniards. The fact that it was discovered only in Spain and nowhere else, despite the fact that all the learned scholars from other kingdoms had searched for some sign of it. That it revealed no sign of invention or fraud. That the characters did not belong to the Romans,

Goths, Arabs, Greeks, Phoenicians, or other nations, not only from among those that invaded Spain but also not even from those that had never invaded. That such a famous lamina had not been created by the magic arts or by miracle in Buena Vista. All of these circumstances brought all of the sages and learned men into perfect agreement, causing them to believe and publish without the least scruple that the letters, language, and tablet belonged to the primitive Spaniards, even before they saw half the alphabet of the text deciphered into Basque. But when with barely half of the alphabet established they could see that the text was deciphered in Basque, some in semi-astonishment presented their first opinion, others condemned their opinion as frivolous, others denied the correspondence of the text, taking it all for a dream or a fable, stripping away the mask from their subtle passion and agenda.

The description of this monument is purely parabolic, as everyone was aware from the time it was first discovered; but it's a dynamic parable that places right before our eyes the truth we seek and affirm, and the injustice and excessive passion with which our adversaries deny us that truth. To persuade them that Basque is the original language of Spain, we placed before their eyes an ancient monument with the identical signs, but even more convincing, contained in the Menasta or Lamina of the parable. Here before us, an entire nation that we call Basque, was undeniably the ancient language of Spain. Search wherever you will, you won't find such a nation in any corner of the world. This monument could not possibly have been counterfeited or fraudulently produced. Neither its language nor words come from the Romans, Goths, Arabs, Greeks, Phoenicians, or other nations that have occupied Spain, as I have proven by comparison. This nation was not created by magic or by miracle in Spain. Is there any evidence or reason not to acclaim it as the original nation of Spain, and its language Spain's original language?

A tablet buried for many centuries, not just in the ground but in the depths of oblivion, dug up by chance in our time, is by its inscription a convincing monument originating, like its characters and language, from ancient Spain; and an entire nation, ever vital and flourishing in Spain for all to see, with the same inscriptions, but even better and stronger—is this monument not a sufficient proof to persuade us that this is the nation and language of primitive Spain? Here I invoke fair rules of argument, and men who will abide by them; and without exception all respond to me that one monument and another argue in favor of the antiquity of the Basque language in Spain, and only a few, who follow other interests, answer that they conclude that these signs speak of another nation; but no, they speak of the Basque nation, and its language. But these people deserve no reply.

24. Juan de Perochegui

(?, end of seventeenth century – ?, ?)

Little is known about his life. Ainhoa (Lapurdi) or Puente la Reina (Gares, Navarre) are considered possible birthplaces. In his book, he claims to be a speaker of Basque, rendering the second possible birthplace, although still possible, less probable. Whatever the case, he is undeniably of Navarrese origin and sensitive to events on both sides of the Pyrenees. What we do know is that he was a soldier; however, his military career is hard to reconcile with his having been born in France. It seems that he was a colonel, a provincial artillery officer, and artillery commander of the Kingdom of Navarre.

He is known for a single small book, *Origen de la nación vascongada y de su lengua* (Origin of the Basque Nation and Its Language), that was widely distributed. Corrected and published under two different titles, it had at least one edition in 1731, another in 1738, two more in 1760, and another in 1877. In the most widely distributed edition, that of 1760, he alludes to "Larramendi's Dictionary" that appeared in 1745 and to the work by Francisco Javier de Garma: *Origen y antigüedad de la lengua bascongada y de la Nobleza de Cantabria* (Origin and Antiquity of the Basque Language and Nobility of Cantabria) (1738).

To prove his linguistic theories, he pushed to the limit and beyond all sorts of etymologies that, although meant to praise the Basque language, did it small service because they have been reproduced thousands of times by detractors of Euskara as evidence of the nonsensical and baseless pretensions of Basque apologists. Perochegui's fundamental thesis is that the Basque language was universal not only in Spain, as other apologists before him had maintained, but also in France and that there was evidence of its use even in Italy and many other places in Europe. Additionally, he claims that this language was the one spoken by Noah before the Flood and therefore the primitive language inspired by God, placing it ahead of Hebrew, as had been previously argued in rather general terms. The proof that he adduces could not be more improbable. Take, for example, his use of the word *ur*, which in Basque means "water" and in Hebrew "fire." Perochegui speculates that if the builders of the Tower of Babel had asked for *ur*, it must have been water needed for the mortar and not fire, and thus it could be deduced that the Hebrews mistakenly copied this term from the primitive language, that is, Basque. Certain political details that Perochegui introduces into his text are of interest. For one, he attempts to prove that the name *Borbón* [Bourbon], "that most heroic house, which has provided royal members of both monarchies," is of Basque origin; according to him, it should be written *Buru-on*, which means "good head." Secondly, he does not neglect to recall the "pact-like" character of the bonds that unite the Basques with the two monarchies, emphasizing, finally, the zealous loyalty and sacrifice of the Basques in the service of the two Bourbon crowns.

ORIGEN
DE LA NACION
BASCONGADA,
Y
DE SU LENGUA,
DE QUE HAN DIMANADO LAS
Monarquias [illegible]ñola, y Francia, y la
Republica de Venecia, que existen
al presente.
COMPUESTO
POR EL CORONEL DON JUAN DE
Perochegui, Theniente-Provincial de Artilleria, y Comandante de la de este
Reyno de Navarra.
Segunda impresion
CON LICENCIA DE LOS SUPERIORES:
En [illegible], en la Imprenta de los *Herederos* de
Martinez, Año 1760.

SELECTED TEXT(S):

Origen y antigüedad de la lengua bascongada y de la Nobleza de Cantabria [Origin and Antiquity of the Basque language and the Nobility of Cantabria] (Barcelona, 1731). Alternate title: *Origen de la nación vascongada y de su lengua, de que han dimanado las monarquías francesa y española, y la República de Venecia, que existen al presente, lo que se hace demonstrable por su propia narrativa y encadenamiento* [Origin of the Basque Nation and Its Language, from Which the French and Spanish Monarchies and the Republic of Venice Now in Existence Were Derived, as Can Be Proven by Their Own Narrative and Interconnection] (Pamplona: Herederos de Martínez, 1760); reprint, (San Sebastián: Roger, 2000), 162–64, 170–72, 184–85.

That everything in existence had an origin is undeniable, and because the people and the Basque language have existed in France and in Spain for over four thousand years, it is necessary to acknowledge that this primitive language was common in both kingdoms, as is infallibly verified by the ancient and immemorial monuments of mountains, rivers, entire provinces, and houses of the original greatness visible in both realms, the rationale for the significance of the names of almost all the objects corresponding to that language to be made abundantly clear for Spain in the course of this narrative, no single letter of any single word or name being open to the slightest question, particularly when its application to its object literally proclaims the force of logic that I will be explaining. For example, there is a village or town on the border between Gipuzkoa and Bizkaia called Hermua [Ermua], whose name means nothing because a letter (the letter *e*) is missing, the addition of which will change the name to *Heremua*, which means "boundary," "limit," or "border." Similarly, consider the syncopation of the name Fuenterrabía, which the Basques call *Hondarrabia*, or *Hondarribia*, meaning "the ends of the two," or "the limit of the two," alluding to the ancient limits of the Gauls and the Spaniards, because the sea enters there and the lands of both nations end.

Unarguable proof of this sort would be even more infallibly corroborated by the territorial expansion of the Gauls who, running out of room in the Pyrenees and foothills and adjoining regions, began to spread out and populate the country known today as France, which in ancient times was called the Land of the Gaubes (Gauls). These people initially settled in the regions of Languedoc, Béarn, Guiena, Gascony, and Vigor, which are the countries closest to those mountains; and it should be noted that the five provinces mentioned are in fact Basque, or more accurately provinces whose names are derived from the Basque language: for example, *Languedoc*, or *Langueroc*, which means "to do the work ourselves," differing only in the change of the *d* to *r*. *Gascon* is the same as *gauscón*, meaning "good at night." *Biarnes*, or *Biarnoes*, means "of two wines." *Guiena*, which should be *Eguiena*, means "the most authentic." *Vigor* means "two deaf men."

I will leave these border regions now and go deeper into the provinces of France, all of them populated not only by our Gauls, but whose colonies also spread out and inundated half of Europe, many of them journeying to other areas, as history proves by tangible evidence that still exists today, some of which will be cited below. Most of the provinces mentioned, and even those beyond their borders, are patently names made up of words from the Basque language, and to show that my argument is beyond question let me point out from the start that the

Basque letter *v* is equivalent to the two letters *o v* in French, and the French word *bon* is simply *on* in Basque; thus, the most august name Bourbon would be written *Buruon* in Basque, which means "good head," and the *Bourbonois* [Bourbon] Province would be *Buruones*, meaning "good heads."

I will turn now to the province or kingdom of *Bourgoña* [Bourgogne], derived from *Burugoña*, which in Basque means "high" or "elevated head." The province of *Normandía* [Normandy] is a contraction of *Horma-andia*, meaning "big frost." *Picardía* [Picardy] is nothing but *Pica erdia*, which means "half bite." *Hulandia* [Holland] comes from *Holanda*, meaning "wetland," which was originally called *Batavia*, a name derived from the Basque language and which, if what some believe is true, means "two things that have become one," which is what we frequently see in Holland when the waters flood the land and the two elements are thus reduced to one. *Lorena* in Basque means "without removing or adding to the flowers," and *Lore-ene* "my flower." *Alsacia* [Alsace] is a contraction of *Alza-azia*, which means to "raise up" or "save the seed" (*Ala-eman* in Basque). *Franco* [Frank] means "abundance," and *Franconia* means "good abundance" [bounty], a name given to it by the Gauls who penetrated far into *Germania* [*Alemania*, Germany], led by Segovese in the year 3434 following the creation of the world, or 566 years before the coming of the Savior; and the descendants of those same *Francones* [Franks], later called the French, led by Faramón [Pharamond], or Mérrua, came in the year 420 of the decline of the Roman Empire to initiate the French monarchy, and having little currency the name Gaul was buried in oblivion. In England, *Cantorberri* is a Basque word, and *Irlanda*, or *Irrilanda*, means "field of laughter." *Dinamarca, Suecia*, and *Noruega* (Denmark, Sweden, and Norway) are Basque names and were spread by sea and by land to North America, which is where they [also] exist.

. . .

What is left for us to discuss is whether the Basque language or the Hebrew language was the first ever spoken in the world; that is very difficult to determine and given the weight of the authorities who give priority to Hebrew it will be necessary to conduct an investigation based on reason to find the most appropriate and consistent evidence to overcome this difficulty. No one can dispute the fact that the name *Jaungoycoa* in Basque, or *Escuàra* [Euskara], is the God known by the Basques, and that it means "Lord on High," an attribute that Basque, among all the other languages, identifies as the sole characteristic imprinted on the soul as God's sovereignty and power over all creatures, there being no more effective antidote to hold man within the limits of subjection and obedience to the Creator than the glorious revelation of the name *Jaungoycoa*, Lord on High, and this was the mission to which Noah adhered before and after the Flood. Jonah, in the preaching and conversion of Nineveh, whose sudden transformation from vice to virtue, and the penitence experienced in the person of the king himself and in that entire great nation, indicates that the tradition of the tragedies of the Universal Flood, which is the mission Jonah would explain in his preaching, was vigorous and alive in that city whose name is part of a Basque prayer whose conclusion should be pronounced *Ninive-a-nago*, which means "I am watching and keeping accounts," which is the language Noah would have used to repress the bad behavior and vices he saw in his descendants, whose excesses he would naturally reprimand, being the legitimate legislator of the natural Law dictated to him by God himself. Thus, as the population of the human race began to grow, he must have ordered the creation of *Ninive-a-nago*, which after many years was adorned and made beautiful by Nino, son of Bel, or Belus: it was in that famous city where Noah took pains to introduce the Holy name of *Jaungoycoa*, that "Lord on High," or "Lord of the Heights," from which the rains fell to inundate the world and submerge those who were disobedient and who persisted in doing evil; and truly, what more effective remedy could Noah have preached than the tragedy they saw inflicted as punishment for their sin and the offenses committed against God on High?

To this preponderance of facts, another can be added, and that involves nothing less than the immortality of the soul. The gentleman Bosuet, Bishop of Maux, in his brilliant book on *Universal History*, folio 278, says that the ancient Gauls (who were Basques as well, as I have proven) used to kill some of their slaves so that their souls could go to serve the souls of their ancestors in the other world; and even if we regard this action or custom as inherently evil, nonetheless, given the immateriality of the soul, they could not have learned to do this except through the teaching and instruction of Noah, who undoubtedly received these from God himself speaking in his own voice to Noah himself; from which it can be deduced that the Basque language was the first in the world, an opinion also corroborated through certain pairs of opposite nouns that exist in the two languages, that is, Basque and Hebrew, and one of these is the noun *Ur*, which in the former, means "water" and, in the latter, "fire." I can already anticipate that some will argue that the Basque language derived this word from Hebrew, and I will respond that the Hebrew language derived it from Basque, where it already existed; and it was when the Confusion began to reach its climax and the Tower its summit that they began to experience total confusion, which goes without saying. And it is obvious that when they called down from the top of the Tower for the materials they needed to continue, there would have been no reason for them to ask for fire, but they would indeed have needed water to moisten the mortar to hold together the materials for the bricks and stones; from which it clearly follows that in the Hebrew language the name of that substance was confused, and the Basque language preserved and kept it in its ancient and original integrity with the word *Ur*, or *Ura*.

. . .

If the Basque language deserves to be respected and venerated inherently, the Basques themselves deserve the highest admiration, both in Spain and in France, where the most heroic houses of both monarchies, including even the distinguished House of Bourbon, a contraction of *Buruon* as has been observed earlier, were descended from the Basque nation, which in many respects surpasses the Greek as well as the Roman, of whom not a trace or a shadow can be found in a region where the Basques keep pace with the centuries winning eternal fame through glorious service to their sovereigns, especially during the reign of Felipe V when illustrious families, such as the Idiáquez, Amezagas, Arizagas, Armendarices, Eslavas, Antillones, Ripaldas, Aramburus, Argaines, Guendicas, Zuluagas, Muniaines, and others so distinguished themselves that even the echoes of cannons announce their fame, seeing which Greece and Rome would blush with amazement and shame if they returned to the world to accept homage for their own heroes. The singular battles in which these illustrious Basque families won glory were followed by seventy or eighty others who displayed their courage and heroism on February 8, 1743 in the glorious battle of Campo Santo in which, as officers of the Spanish Royal Guard, most of them sacrificed their lives, bringing new luster to the weapons of the sovereign; their honorable actions are recorded not only in the annals of this kingdom in the Basque nation, but in the history of all time, as in the history of the period by the Silius Italicus and Horaces, and especially in the words of the great lawgiver Gutiérrez, who says that the Basques were the people who won back Spain, noble of blood; and in praise of the entire region of Cantaberria he affirms that it is of the highest nobility, warlike, strong, distinguished by nature, a veritable river of nobility, a lineage of proven nobility, and the ancient seed bed of the nobility of all Spain.

Many Basques, who are proud of having learned a few rudiments of the Latin language, and even prouder of their Castilian and French, criticize their own language with great scorn, saying that it lacks words and expressions both for writing and for speaking well, hearing which I cannot refrain from saying to them that although they have learned these languages that were foreign to them, they have forgotten the original language or that the little they knew of it was most superficial; but to make such slurs against a peerless language that has the glory of having survived for over five thousand years in this part of the world without academies or institutions to preserve its beauty, let these new doctors of philosophy tell us: Where is there a language anywhere else in the world that packs as much energy and soul into three quatrains and a ten-verse stanza as all those that come after ours?

25. Gregorio Mayans y Siscar

(Oliva, Valencia, 1699 – ?, 1781)

He began his grammatical studies in Barcelona, and then transferred to Valencia to study philosophy and law, completing his education at the University of Salamanca. He earned his doctorate there in 1722 and a year later had already been appointed professor at the same institution. His specialty was the analysis and publication of ancient texts, which led to his appointment as royal librarian for Felipe V. He finally retired to the town where he was born so that he could conduct his research in peace and quiet. He was a model of the polymath and prolific author, with an extensive and weighty oeuvre that was quite representative of his epoch. He won numerous enemies with his disdainful dismissal of the works of others, and it goes without saying that he emerged as the adversary par excellence of the Basque apologists of his time for his opinion about the Basque language.

Setting aside his vast work as a jurist, literary critic, and publisher of ancient texts, his work on the subject of philology is what interests us here. Mayans' greatest endeavor was to purify and restore dignity to the Castilian language. With regard to the first of these, he railed against the penetration of barbarisms (especially Gallicisms) that compromise the purity of the language; for example, in *Oración sobre la Elocuencia española* (Oration on Spanish Eloquence) (1727). As for the second, he worked on his *Orígenes de la lengua española* (Origins of the Spanish Language) (1737), a work that earned him great posthumous fame. In it are contained his ideas about the Basque language, which can be summed up basically in two aspects: the first, his emphatic denial that it was the ancient and original language of Spain; and second, his assertion that Basque hardly possesses a lexicon of its own because all the terms related to religion, technology, and civilization were borrowed from other languages.

Selected Text(s):

Orígenes de la lengua española: compuesta por varios autores, recogidos por . . . [Origins of the Spanish Language, Composed by Numerous Authors and Compiled by . . .] (Madrid: Librería Victoriano Suárez, 1737); reprint, (Madrid: Rivadeneira, 1873), 308, 329–34.

33. It has been established, then, that several languages were spoken in Spain, even after the Romans took control of the entire peninsula, which can be confirmed by a most illustrious testimony and made public, for we see on the one hand many medallions inscribed with Roman characters and on the other with totally unrecognizable Spanish characters, which by the variety of their letters seem to be from different alphabets and, consequently, from different languages.

34. But because the Roman occupation lasted so long and they attempted to introduce their language wherever they ruled (S. August. de Civit. dei. lib. 19; Ch. 7), the Latin language was spoken in Spain, so that the old languages were gradually forgotten and completely disappeared.

. . .

58. But Cantabria as well as the neighboring peoples always tried to preserve their language, when permitted by Roman rule and those that followed. And what contributed most to the preservation of the language was that it had regressed to its ancient crudeness and lack of contact with more cultured nations, it being true that where there is little communication with outsiders, the ancient language is preserved intact; and more so if there is no effort to acquire knowledge through study, because by study many new words are learned and a large portion of them stay in the minds of the readers. It is true that where there is little study there is little knowledge and where there is little knowledge the language is very limited, and as the centuries go by it cannot fail to be corrupted.

59. After the Romans, the Goths and other northern peoples came to Spain and, depending on the extension and duration of their occupation, introduced their languages; although not to the extent that they abolished the Roman language which by then was in use generally across Spain, except in the rugged mountains in the north, many words still used today in Spain were introduced by the Goths, Vandals (also called *Silingos*: see Isidorus in *Hist. Wand* [History of the Vandals], 449), Alans, and Suebi.

60. The last to invade were the Africans who conquered all of Spain except for part of the mountain regions of Asturias, León Cantabria, and some strongholds in Aragón and Catalonia. And because the occupation by the Africans, as punishment for the sins of this nation and, in particular, for disobeying the Pope, lasted for many centuries, the language they brought (Arabic) became universal throughout Spain, except for small pockets where the few Christians who did not want to be subject to domination by barbarians took refuge in fortified positions, thus gloriously maintaining their religion, freedom, and language. It is true that, as always happens, the language underwent many changes, depending on the peoples with whom they were in contact.

61. For this very reason, the Cantabrians who were in contact with the Spaniards who had taken refuge there and who spoke the Latin language, although quite corrupted—these Cantabrians, I say, in addition to the Latin words they had already received directly from the Romans themselves, adopted many more from the Spaniards, accommodating them to their endings and their pronunciation, and at the same time they communicated to the Spaniards other words of their own that still survive in the Spanish language. This becomes obvious if we compare the two languages, Spanish and Basque, discovering through close observa-

tion of the roots of words that most of the Basque language has its origin in Latin, as I observed in the hand-written vocabulary, composed in the year 1532, located in this Royal Library. And although it is true that the author of said vocabulary does not always use purely Basque words that correspond to the Spanish words, it is also the case that the Basque language has received from other languages the words related to the arts, their tools and creations, and to the sciences and related objects, (which are innumerable), to religion, professions, and exotic objects of the country, such as trees, herbs, animals, stones, clothing; vanity items foreign to the cleanliness and poverty of the country, and those related to the artful gluttony of the times, which has reached such extremes that in regard to drinks alone more than two hundred different kinds can be listed, for just five years ago a curious Spaniard managed to count one hundred and eighteen. This means that if one looks through the most complete dictionaries of the languages of today, you will not find words in Basque corresponding to many others, and of those you do find, if you look at their roots, some will be Latin, others Spanish, others French, others from other languages, and few that are purely Basque. If this language had a dictionary in print, and I wish it had, it seems to me that if it were expanded and combined with others, what I am saying would become clear. And it could not be otherwise because the Basque language is not known to have produced any books, which are truly the only preservers of most of a language.

For this reason they do not use today many words they used in ancient times, and thus Pliny says (Nat. Hist., bk. 36, ch. 41) that they used the word *bubbatio* to refer to the "vein of the lodestone or magnet," a word they no longer use. Pliny's statement that this word was Cantabrian indicates that these people had their own language, so different now from what it was then that it no longer retains the names, not just of ancient cities, because there is no trace of them, but I am almost prepared to say of the rivers and mountains, which have not changed at all. And this is why it is so difficult to trace the ancient boundaries of Cantabria, a matter that the most diligent of the Spanish historians, Jerónimo Zurita, investigated thoroughly, and which needs to be taken up again, without judging the efforts of previous historians. But even more important, we are unable to ascertain the antiquity of this language because each language is determined by the words contained in its lexicon and their definitions and the particular way they were pronounced, we do not even know if the words used today are the same ones that existed a thousand years ago, or if the ancient meanings are preserved today, or if the way it was spoken centuries ago is the same. With good reason, then, the wise archbishop of Tarragona, Don

Antonio Agustín, speaking of the Basque language, said: "Since there are no books or other written materials in that language, it's hard to know the truth about its origin" (*Dial.* 6, p. 237).

62. I will always grant this language great antiquity, and I will say that that antiquity survives today in the general characteristics of the Basque language, but not in the specialized aspects of that language. I mean that the multitude of conjugations, the postposition of articles, and other features of Basque are very ancient, but I am not convinced that even those words that are considered to be purely Basque are the same as they were in ancient times, because if we note that to say *poco* [little] the Basques [in this case, meaning Gipuzkoans] say *guchi*, the Navarrese *guti,* and the Bizkaians *guichi*, and in this way there are many words that are very different from each other and form very different dialects, why then should we believe what they claim, that only this nation in all the world has the special privilege of preserving its words uncorrupted, with no change in its pronunciation over thousands of years? Especially because Cantabria was invaded and ruined numerous times. Let each one of the conquering and neighboring nations claim the words that are theirs, and then let us examine what is left, distinguishing which is a dialect of Basque and which is not, and we may be left with a reservoir of the relics of many ancient languages.*

* Based on what we know today, and to establish operating principles, some more and some less hypothetical, we can divide these languages into three classes. The first consists of those that maintain without variation the monosyllabic root of signification, as well as the monosyllabic root of relation, which is also invariable and separate from the former: for example the root *am* means in general *amor* [love], and to express the first person singular of the present indicative they use other monosyllabic roots that, without constituting a body, express separately the verb or action, the time, number and person; and Chinese and many other languages belong to this group. The second consists of those that combine the root with other roots of relation, and form a single word, whose parts are however distinguished clearly from each other and have not been confused and amalgamated to the extent that they form a single body; Basque and many Tartar languages belong to this group. And finally, the third consists of languages, and this includes all Indo-European languages, in which signification and relation form perfect, complete words that become meaningless if the components are separated from each other.

.../...

26. José Francisco de Isla, known as "el padre Isla" (Father Isla)

(Vidanes, León, 1703 – Bologna, 1781)

Endowed with a precocious intelligence, he was already a graduate in civil law at the age of eleven and then took orders as a Jesuit, studying philosophy and theology at the University of Salamanca. Educated in the brilliant ambience and style of Feijoo, he emerged as one of the most distinguished critical minds of the Spanish eighteenth century. He was especially critical of the inertia, superstitions, jingoism, and other similar defects so common in his time. His writings provoked no little scandal, for his fiercely mordant and sarcastic character raised blisters on everything it touched. Naturally, his criticism of incompetent preachers, which by extension referred to the ineptitude of the entire clergy, provoked an immediate reaction from the Inquisition who responded by

---

.../...

Additionally, there is no doubt that Basque is the most ancient language of Spain and that, unlike all other European languages, it bears no resemblance to other languages except for those that are spoken in the extreme Far East of Asia. Beyond that, we have no idea where these people with their unique language came from when they immigrated to Spain, nor why they preserve their language today, just as they preserve their simple and patriarchal customs and their passion for dances, etc. Because of these characteristics, it might be speculated that they are an Asiatic people, but this is mere conjecture, based on analogies, which in themselves are so often misleading. Concerning the language and literature (if you can call the few books printed in this language literature) you can consult Oihenart's *Notitia utriusque Vasconiae* [News of the Two Vasconias]; *El impossible vencido* [Achieving the Impossible], the *Arte de la lengua vascongada* [Grammar of the Basque Language] and the *Diccionario espanol, vasco y latino* [Spanish, Basque and Latin Dictionary] by Larramendi; the *Grammaire vasque et française* [Basque and French Grammar], by [Martin] Harriet; the *Antiquités de Navarre* [Antiquities of Navarre], by Moret; *L'Essai français sur la Noblesse des Basques* [French Essay on the Nobility of the Basques], the *Constitutions du monastère de Roncesvaux* [Constitutions of the Monastery of Roncesvaux], the *Diccionario de los fueros de Navarra* [Dictionary of the Fueros of Navarre], the *Historia de Navarra* [History of Navarre], by Yanguas; the research conducted by Adelung and Vater, which can be read in Volume 2 of the *Mitridates* [*oder allgemeine Sprachenkunde*] [Mithridates, or General Linguistics], the works of Wilhelm von Humboldt, those of the Hellenist Lucheso and the Abbot Dorrigol, the *History of Spain* by Marineo Sículo, the Basque proverbs and poetry by Oihenart, his translation of the *Catilinarias*, the *Historia de las danzas, fiestas y juegos de Guipúzcoa* [History of the Dances, Festivals, and Games of Gipuzkoa], the *Alfabeto primitivo* [Primitive Alphabet], by Astarloa, and the *Guerico* [sic] *güero*, by Achular [sic].

banning his book (the second volume had to be published clandestinely). Navarre was the target of his pen in *Día grande de Navarra* (A Great Day in Navarre), a fierce attack on the excessive vanity, provincialism, and patriotism of the Navarrese people, disguised as homage so dithyrambic that by contrast it made those praised seem ludicrous. Of course, it's clear that for an intellect like Father Isla's, the Navarrese myth (as well as its Basque counterpart) of original nobility, purity of blood, and so on, were nothing but provincial, jingoistic vanity so abhorrent to Spanish and, in his case, cosmic intelligence.

He did not participate wholeheartedly in the controversial debate over languages, but in his most famous work, *Historia del famoso predicador Fray Gerundio de Campazas* (History of the Famous Preacher Brother Gerundio de Campazas), he touches on linguistic theory in an interesting way. The topic he addresses is that of the petulance and affectation that had spread through Spanish society and that saw distinction in everything French, leading to the Frenchification of style, manners, cuisine, and of course language. Thus, Isla includes some interesting verses in which we see women from La Mancha and Castile bastardizing their language to appear more fashionable (in the French style, of course), but he includes Basque women as well who not only introduce Gallicisms into their speech, but also Basque expressions, and he concludes "quite pleased with themselves for speaking in a foreign style, ignorant of their own language." Applied to women from Extremadura or La Mancha, the poetry leaves no doubt: they are ignorant of their own language, Castilian, and that they boast about this in French; but applied to Basque women, it is important to understand that for Isla "their true language" is also Castilian, for the word *monsieur* sounds as foreign as *echeco andrea* (housewife). Expressed this way, his Jacobinism keeps him from conceiving that the "true" language of Basque women is Basque and not necessarily Castilian. It might seem overly meticulous, but I believe that this is an eloquent manifestation of a certain type of stubbornly Spanish mentality that by the middle of the eighteenth century was already working to marginalize non-official languages and to impose a certain political-linguistic unification around Castilian as the only official language.

Selected Text(s):

Historia del famoso predicador Fray Gerundio de Campazas, alias Zotes [History of the Famous Preacher Brother Gerundio de Campazas, Alias Zotes], vol. 2 (1768; Madrid: Editora Nacional, 1978), 627–28.

They've got some other minor flaws,
but their husbands will be idiots,
if they just put up with them and keep quiet.
For just when they think they've found
a Castilian or Andalusian girl,
without realizing it, overnight,
she's become French,
because they say that's the fashion.
She woke up happy enough with her title *Doña*
and went to bed the *Madame* of Begoña;
although her surname is Velasco
it started to disgust her,
When she realized that in France the married ladies
are used to
giving up their surnames for ever,
on marrying their husbands.
And those that are usually most faithful to the name,
are the least faithful to the man.
The girl born in Castile,
even though she might be the ninth wonder
does not regard herself as pretty
if she doesn't speak as they do in Marseille.
Girls from La Mancha, Extremadura, or Tierra Campos,

pretend they're from Orleans; the girl from Bizkaia,
between [saying] her *Jaincoa* [God] and *Echeco Andrea* [housewife],
throws in a *monsieur de Goicoechea*
Thrilled to be speaking in a foreign tongue,
and they don't know their true language.

27. Agustín Cardaberaz

(Hernani, Gipuzkoa, 1703 – Bologna, 1770)

He belonged to a family involved in cultural matters, because his father was a scribe in Hernani. He studied grammar with the Jesuits of Donostia-San Sebastián and later philosophy and law in Palencia, as well as theology in Valladolid. He then took orders as a Jesuit in 1721. He was a professor of grammar in the College of Bilbao (Bizkaia) and of ethics and theology at the University of Oñati (Gipuzkoa). His spiritual mentor was Pedro de Calatayud from Tafalla (Navarre), one of the most outstanding apostolic missionaries of his time, both for his theoretical writings and for his practical work on this topic. Moreover, Calatayud received the Mission of Devotion to the Sacred Heart from France, and was one of the pioneers of its diffusion south of the Pyrenees. Cardaberaz defended his doctorate in Theology under the direction of Larramendi. As recipient of all these influences, Cardaberaz became a tireless missionary and proselytizer of the Cult of the Heart of Jesus and a defender of the Basque language. It is estimated that he carried out more than 150 missions, both in the Bizkaian, as well as Gipuzkoan, dialect, and in Castilian.

Larramendi's influence was decisive in shaping his views on the language. Cardaberaz became his most brilliant follower in the work of dignifying and facilitating the use of the Basque language, and the difference between Larramendi and Cardaberaz is not one of purpose. Both tried to make Euskara an instrument capable of cultural communication qualified for the function to which they were devoted: the evangelization of the masses. The difference was that if Larramendi chose to undertake the apology for the language in Castilian, through his grammar and dictionary as indispensable tools for correct written expression, Cardaberaz wrote and preached in Basque, achieving in a practical way the cultivation of the language—in other words, demonstrating its viability by using it. Cardaberaz became an involuntary protagonist at an interesting moment in the history of the Basque language; namely, when one of his books was banned specifically because it had been written in that language. Cardaberaz had written a *Life of St. Ignatius,* which failed to receive the necessary permissions for its publication in 1766. Because of the context of the *Matxinada* (a popular Basque revolt against central authority) and the book's completion on the eve of the expulsion of the Jesuits from the Kingdoms of Spain, the publication of a work on this topic was not particularly propitious. Yet apart from this, in the decree by the Count of Aranda banning its publication, there was an explicit stipulation against the printing of books in languages other than Castilian, as well as an express prohibition of publishing writings in Basque without explicit permission. This restrictive policy was maintained for several years, until the intervention of Mariano Luis de Urquijo, Minister of Bilbao, in 1798 seems to have relaxed it.

Without a doubt, the most interesting work for our purposes here is his *Eusqueraren berri onac* (Good News for Basque) (1761); a short treatise offering the basics for correct linguistic expression, addressed to parish priests and teachers who were carrying out their mission in Basque-speaking areas but who had difficultly expressing themselves orally or in writing. Of course, the author was thinking of ways to maintain the privileged relationship the Church had been working to establish with the peasants, *gure pobrecho* (our little poor ones), over the centuries. For this, and because the majority of ordinary Basques were still speakers of the language, Euskara proved to be an indispensable instrument and its correct usage a matter of urgency. How did the Basque language compare to the other languages of high culture? There were only two problems: its lack of literary development and its dialectical fragmentation. With those exceptions, it was as capable of expressing as much abstract knowledge and sophisticated cultural content as any other language.

EUSQUERAREN

BERRI ONAC:

ETA ONDO ESCRIBITCECO, ondo iracurteco, ta ondo itzeguiteco Erreglac

CURA JAUN,

TA ESCOLA MAISU CELOSOAI Jesus-en Compañiaco Aita Agustin Cardaberaz ec esqueñitcen, ta dedicatcen dieztenac.

1761. Urtean.

BEAR DAN BEZALA.

Iruñean Liburuguile ANTONIO CASTILLA-ren echean.

Selected Text(s):

Eusqueraren berri onac: eta ondo escribitceco, ondo iracurtceco, ta ondo itzegiteco Erreglac: cura jaun, ta escola maisu celosoai Jesusen Compañiaco Aita Agustín Cardaberaz-ec-esqueñtcen ta dedicatcen dieztenac [Good News for Basque: Rules to Write Well, Read Well and Speak Well, Written and Offered by the Priest and Fervent Teacher of the Company of Jesus, Father Agustín Cardaberaz] (Pamplona: Antonio Castilla, 1761), 7–10.

Who knows when, whence and how the Basque language reached this place? From Heaven, from God, without the interference of human beings—in other words, it was a superhuman event.

. . .

The Basques say jokingly that in paradise, God asked Adam in Basque: "Adam, where are you?" as though the Basque language were divine.

. . .

Today, as in the past, Greek and Latin are the most highly esteemed languages. Although both Latin and Greek have borrowed many words and terms from Basque, Father Larramendi established clearly that Basque, together with these two [languages] or even before them, was one of the ancestral languages. In any case, it is true that Latin and Greek have linked hands and pulled each other to the forefront of all languages. They have been treasured by wise men and have benefited from this, because everywhere in the world people have written in Greek and Latin—and good rules have been established for writing and reading all these books.

. . .

Our Basque language has not had as much help from such wise men anywhere in the world. Because Latin and Greek have been so blessed and glorified, it is miraculous that Basque, alone and without any help, has survived for such a long time in so many places, in such a clear manner and spoken in such a way as to make its detractors blush. But in any case, it is true that Basque is disappearing. This, however, is not the fault of the tongue, but of its speakers: instead of using it, instead of adorning and embellishing it, they shamelessly torture and destroy it out of laziness.

. . .

But God wants Basque to survive to save the souls of our purest and yet neediest. While there are honest farmers in our farmhouses, Basque will survive. Basque cannot disappear unless all who speak it are decapitated.

28. Real Sociedad Bascongada de los Amigos del País (Royal Basque Society of Friends of the Country)

The importance of the Real Sociedad Bascongada de los Amigos del País for the social and especially the cultural future of the Basque Country was indisputable. A pioneer in the founding of many brilliant associations south of the Pyrenees, this organization became an indispensable reference for the other economic associations that proliferated throughout the Spanish Kingdom after 1764. Moreover, this group made education one of the fundamental axes of its reformist thought and practice. In keeping with this purpose, it made a great effort to establish the exemplary Seminary of Bergara, initiated the teaching of women, raised funds for the instruction of the lower classes, and to whatever extent possible, promoted the spread of primary education to the general public.

Of course, the dominant legal and ideological parameters of the time drastically limited its linguistic policy. For the Real Sociedad Bascongada, Euskara was reserved for oral use within the family and local community, and to some extent for the cultivation of certain genres of literature, for example, fables, religious texts, poetry. However, it is also true that some of its members sought to encourage more in-depth study and knowledge. For example, Count Peñaflorida commissioned the scholar José María Azpitarte (Elgoibar, Gipuzkoa, 1751 – Vitoria-Gasteiz, Araba, 1809) to edit a Basque-Castilian dictionary, a work in which he invested considerable effort, but which remained unpublished (consisting of a manuscript of more than forty thousand words).

However, for the most part, these brilliant men considered the Basque language incompatible with the cultivation of the sciences and use in education. These sectors were reserved for Castilian, French and, occasionally, Latin. Moreover, the Real Sociedad Bascongada understood that knowledge of other languages was beneficial for the education of future businessmen or first sons and included in their programs of study, the teaching of French, English, or Italian, but nothing related to the country's own language. This attitude was clearly reflected in the accord signed in the organization's 1772 annual general meeting, whereby it was agreed that the language to be used for primary education was none other than Castilian. This provoked complaints from a member from Araba, and the official reply leaves no room for doubt as to the Real Sociedad Bascongada's attitude: "The only authority for linguistic education is that emanating from the government of Madrid and the *Academia Española de la Lengua* [the Spanish academy of the language]." This accord was published, as was customary, in the *Extractos de las Juntas Generales . . . de 1772* (Proceedings of the General Meetings . . . of 1772) (1772).

EXTRACTOS
DE LAS
JUNTAS GENERALES
CELEBRADAS
POR LA
REAL SOCIEDAD BASCONGADA
DE LOS
AMIGOS DEL PAIS
EN LA CIUDAD DE VITORIA
POR SEPTIEMBRE DE 1771.
CON LICENCIA.
MADRID. Por Don Antonio de Sancha.
Año de MDCCLXXII.

Selected Text(s):

Extractos de las Juntas generales celebradas por la Real Sociedad Bascongada de los Amigos del País en la Villa de Bilbao por setiembre de 1772 [Proceedings of the General Meetings held by the Royal Basque Society of Friends of the Country in the Town of Bilbao during September of 1772] (Vitoria: Tomás de Robles, 1772), 97–101.

At the same time the Council members acknowledge receipt of a letter dated this last July 24 in Armiñon, signed by *el Amigo Alabés* [the friend from Araba] and written in a disguised hand and in a style that is more satirical than genuinely critical. Because of these circumstances, it should be understood to be subject to the general by-law, which the Society has imposed against this kind of communication. The Council members believe that it might be important to make an exception for the paragraph relating to this matter of public schools. The erudition and authority he evokes to impugn the system might be of concern to some people, who have not been made aware of the error on which it is based.

There are two provisions that the anonymous author seeks to ridicule in his letter: first, the idea of introducing the use of Castilian grammar into Basque schools, and second, the plan to prepare extracts for this purpose. Regarding the first, he cites authorities such as Mayans, Barbadiño, Rolando Marsio, the Abbot Fleuri, Lami, and Lancelot, to establish that the first grammar that should be taught to children is that of their native language. Concluding from this, that in the case of these provinces, because the language is Basque, not Castilian, the intent of the Society is diametrically opposed to the doctrine of these wise men and to that recommended by the Greeks and Romans. The second part is based on the fact that because the Grammar of the Royal Spanish Academy is a work written too succinctly for the instruction of young people, a summary of it will be so abbreviated that it will bewilder and confuse the boys.

The anonymous author implies that it would be truly reprehensible if in a matter so essential to this institution, the Society were to deviate from the path laid out by the great masters; but this is far from the case. It has followed the most classical authorities on this topic, in particular that of the famous Spaniard, Pedro Simon de Abril, whose opinion should provide the basis for the law of the nation without the need to beg others from foreign authorities. Entrusting its administration to the guidance of such a wise director, the Society has not been content with a merely theoretical approval of his maxims, but has put them into practice with all due dispatch. This is clear in the change made in the teaching of Latin grammar in the Royal High School of Bergara, which is under his direction. There, in place of the *Mascula sunt maribus* criticized by the anonymous author, an extremely simple system for determining gender has been adopted. Conceived by Don Ignacio Xavier de Balzola, teacher of grammar in the aforementioned Royal High School, the Latin course has been structured in a way that adheres most closely to the ideas developed by the wise Spaniard in his *Apuntamientos de como se deben reformar las doctrinas y la manera de enseñarlas para reducillas a su antigua entereza y perficion* [Notes on How the Rules Should Be Reformed and the Method for Teaching Them in Order to Restore Them to their Ancient Integrity and Perfection], etc. This is verified as well in the idea of introducing the use of the Castilian grammar in the public schools recommended in this same precious little book: "because the first error in the teaching of grammar is the failure to begin by teaching children the grammar of their own language in the schools where they are teaching them to read and write in it, as we know the Latins and Greeks did in theirs." From this it can be inferred how far the Society is from incurring the error that has been imputed to it.

Then (the anonymous will reply), it contradicts its own recommendation by teaching Castilian grammar in Basque schools. Here we see his mistake: first, because although the particular language of the country is Basque, the language of the nation is Castilian, which is, therefore, the native language of all Spaniards; second, because by government decree, no other language except Castilian can be used in the schools of the country. It is this decree that is the reason all the notebooks, books, manuscripts, and materials that are given to the children are in Castilian, prohibiting the use of the Basque language to such a degree that a ring has been established and passes from hand to hand among those who are careless in this regard. At the end of the week the one in possession of the ring suffers his specific punishment. His third mistake is in not recognizing that by instilling a knowledge of the Castilian language into the Basque schools and adhering to the goal discussed here of teaching grammar in the language known beforehand, this is achieved perfectly by the method proposed by the Society.

As for the concerns of the anonymous author concerning the extracts, nothing need be said, except that because the Society has agreed to make use of them to the satisfaction of the Royal Spanish Academy, they will be above criticism.

29. Barthelemy Jean Baptiste Sanadon

(St. Nicolas de Neuamésnil, Evre, 1729 – Oloron, 1796)

A Benedictine monk, and teacher of Rhetoric, History and Literature in the High School of Pau (Béarn) when the French Revolution broke out, he was ordained Bishop of the Diocese of the Lower Pyrenees and was a member of the National Convention (the legislative body of the early revolutionary years); imprisoned for awhile during the Reign of Terror in reprisal.

His work, *Essai sur la noblesse des Basque . . . por un ami de la Nation* (Essay on the Nobility of the Basques . . . by a Friend of the Nation) (1785), was immediately translated into Castilian by Diego de Lazcano and published the following year in Tolosa. In this work, he expands and systematizes the manuscript that had been left unpublished by Jean-Philippe Bela (1709–96), from Zuberoa; an interesting synthesis of Cantabrianism and universal nobility (as posited by Garibay, Henao, and Larramendi) with Oihenart's focus on the concept of Vasconia and historical constitutionalism. Sanadon persuaded Dominique Joseph Garat to request, within the context of the French Revolution, the construction of a separate Basque state known as New Phoenicia. Bela and Sanadon constitute a late, northern-Pyrenees manifestation of egalitarian expression and the universal nobility of the Basques in resistance to Bourbon absolutism and its centralizing offensive in the northern Basque Country.

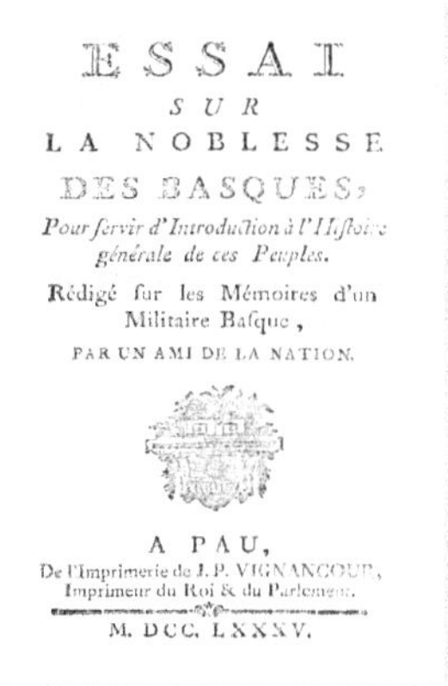

ESSAI
SUR
LA NOBLESSE
DES BASQUES,
Pour ſervir d'Introduction à l'Hiſtoire générale de ces Peuples.
Rédigé ſur les Mémoires d'un Militaire Baſque,
PAR UN AMI DE LA NATION.

A PAU,
De l'Imprimerie de J. P. VIGNANCOUR, Imprimeur du Roi & du Parlement.
M. DCC. LXXXV.

Selected Text(s):

Essai sur la noblesse des Basques, pour servir d'Introduction à l'Histoire générale de ces Peuples. Rédigé sur les Mémoires d'un Militaire Basque, par un ami de la Nation [Essay on the Nobility of the Basques, to Be Used as the Introduction to the General History of These People: Extracted from the Memoirs of a Basque Soldier by a Friend of the Nation] (Pau: J. P. Vignancour, 1785) 24–30, 250–54; reprint, (Tolosa: Francisco Lama, 1786), 15–22.

Beyond this, it differs so essentially from all other dead or living languages that, just as the Greek and Latin authors complained that they could not adapt Basque nouns into Greek or Latin, we can again today justifiably lament that we cannot adapt them into French, Spanish, etc. From this difference and these qualities that have been acknowledged and confirmed by the most ancient authors, it follows: first, Basque was by no means the language of an isolated tribe in the Cantabrian mountains (caught between two countries as powerful and densely populated as Spain and the Gauls), but the language of a sizeable continent separated from all others and inhabited only by indigenous peoples. [According to Mariana] *Cantabri linguam retinuerunt multùm à reliquis omnibus discrepantem, & totius olim Hispaniæ communem* [The Cantabrians Maintain a Language That Is Very Different from All the Rest and That Formerly Was Found throughout Hispania].

Second, because this language, before all the settlements founded in Spain by foreign nations, was preserved only among the Basques, this people are right to regard themselves as the most ancient inhabitants of Spain; even more so because the qualities characterizing this primitive nation—freedom, customs, and the language—are nowhere to be found, except among them: [According to Mariana] *Cum antiquâ libertate, veterem gentis atque communem Provinciæ sermonem conservatum fuisse fide non caret* [He who, with its ancient liberties, maintains the old language of the people found in this province, is not without credit].

Third, only by refusing to interact or merge with the foreign peoples who successively invaded their peninsula did the Basques succeed in preserving their original language in its ancient purity.

Fourth, they have only been able to resist merging with foreign people by retreating little by little toward the eastern and northern provinces of their peninsula. There, it seems, the sterility of the soil and the ruggedness of the mountains must have sheltered them from the avarice and cupidity of foreign nations.

They were so successful in preserving their country from the civil and religious customs of foreign peoples that you will find not a single monument in their territory that bears any resemblance to those that the Phoenicians, Carthaginians, etc. built in other countries they inhabited. In every land they occupied, there are ruins of temples dedicated to Diana, Hercules, and other divinities. But there was no cult of these divinities anywhere in the Basque Country. According to Strabo, they had no temples or public cult, and they were so resistant to any innovation that they did not tolerate or allow any foreigners to live among them.

When the thirst for the gold, so abundant in the southern region of the peninsula, or the desire for conquest began to attract foreign peoples to Spain, most of the Basques living there did what Pelayo and his followers would do in subsequent centuries after the invasion of the Moors. The Basques abandoned the flat country and withdrew into the mountains rather than subject themselves to the yoke and accept foreign ways. Only a small part of the nation was able to remain among the conquering peoples and make alliances with them. This explains the variety of languages that Strabo found in Spain. But the true patriots preferred to leave, to preserve the language and customs of their ancestors in the land where they took refuge.

The number of emigrants was so large that according to Polybius, because Gracchus conquered more than three hundred cities (a gross exaggeration) in Celt-Iberia alone, which was only a small part of the Basque Country.

It could be argued that because the origin of all nations is the same, none can claim greater antiquity than the Basques.

Such an argument would be reasonable if it could be proven that there never existed a people who underwent a revolution, after their initial establishment, that forced them out of the land they had originally occupied, or a people who had preserved their customs and primitive language despite such a revolution; or finally, that a large segment of such a people had never formed a separate nation that was distinguished by an inviolable adherence to the customs and language of their founding fathers.

But the opposite is true, and all the people of Europe are living proof of the hordes of foreigners and barbarians, who swept through in succession and ravaged every nation, changing the way of life, customs, and language of the lands they conquered and forced them to forget even the names of the original people who had inhabited them. In almost every case, the natives of the invaded countries have gradually been assimilated and merged with those from outside, unconsciously adopting the way of life, customs, and language of the invaders, or at least the combination of the two have formed a new language that borrows elements from both, thus betraying origin and its transformation.

It is in this way that Spanish, French, and other languages have been gradually formed, and although they have attained a degree of perfection today that leaves nothing to be desired, they are nonetheless no more than an amalgam of a number of older and different languages, whose combination has no connection with the language of the original people who inhabited those lands.

The Basques and the Welsh in England are perhaps the only people in Europe who have preserved the purity of the language of their initial founders. There is, however, this difference between the two: it is not yet certain whether the Welsh are descendants of the original inhabitants of England, or of the Picts, the original nation of Scythia, or Scandinavia. Whereas the Basques can trace an uninterrupted affiliation back to their original inhabitants, who have always inhabited the country that they still occupy in that portion of Europe.

We conclude then that their privileges, which are merely the practice and use of liberty accorded to all men by nature, have no other source or origin than that boundless passion for independence and freedom that has characterized the Basque people throughout the centuries, and consequently, that these privileges are as ancient among them as their freedom.

. . .

As we have proven, the Basques, despite the innumerable revolutions that have swept through Spain, have preserved their freedom throughout the ages. It follows then, that through the ages, they have demonstrated their respect and admiration to those among them, who for their exploits and bravery have contributed most to the preservation of public freedom; hence, the distinctions, or different degrees of nobility that have always existed among them, which are consequently as ancient as their freedom.

That their nobility, inseparable from their freedom, and equally ancient, has been preserved pure from the time they settled in Spain, is no more open to question than the fact that the Basques have always resisted the presence of outsiders among them. They are reluctant to make alliances with their neighbors, who never approached them except to wage war against them or pillage them. The ruggedness of their land is inaccessible and impassable except to those who were born there; and their way of life and their customs are totally different from those of all other people. Finally, their language is totally unrelated to any other ancient or modern language.

Nor can there be discovered a single instant in all the course of their history, when the people of this nation have bowed to the yoke of any foreign power or given up self-government by their ancient laws. Quite the contrary, it is clear as we have demonstrated that along with their liberty, they have preserved throughout time the purity of blood that was transmitted to them by the ancient Cantabrians, which they received from the original inhabitants of Spain.

30. Lorenzo Hervás y Panduro

(Horcajo de Santiago, Cuenca, 1735 – Rome, 1809)

He exchanged his first surname, García, for his maternal grandfather's, Hervás. The son of farm laborers, he became a Jesuit in 1749, studying in Madrid and Alcalá. He was director of the College of Nobles in Madrid, a teacher in several centers, and a member of several academies and scientific organizations, among them the Real Sociedad Bascongada de los

Amigos del País. He wrote more than ninety volumes on different topics, for his areas of knowledge included mathematics, astronomy, ethnography, paleography, the art of writing, and his specialty, languages. His work has a distinct encyclopedic flavor, very appropriate to his period.

He is considered one of the founders of comparative linguistics. At the very least, if he was not the inventor of the comparative method, he was the first to devote rigorous and voluminous works to it. In part, he was able to work on a very diverse number of linguistic materials (dictionaries, grammars, and so on) thanks to his position as librarian to Pope Pius VII in Rome, and his research was based on the comparison of some 350 different languages. Hervás discounted the idea that all languages were derived from a matrix, and he rejected the traditional interpretation of identifying Hebrew as a presumed original language. The languages that emerged from Babel would have gradually undergone transformations over the centuries, and the transformations would be those that had survived until our times. Moreover, he was one of the first to determine that the kinship between languages had to be sought in the similarities of their grammatical structure (their "artifice" as he called it) and not in their lexical resemblance. To the two classical dimensions—syntax and lexicon—that had already been defined as the basic components of a language, he included a third: phonetics. He rejected the identification between the degree of civilization of a people and the corresponding perfection of their language. He proclaimed the similarity of the intrinsic level of the language of a barbaric people compared with that of nations that were highly civilized. Additionally, he established the ethnographic base for languages by seeking correlations between language and people.

In his *Catálogo de las lenguas de las naciones conocidas* (Catalogue of the Languages of the Known Nations) (1800–05), he displayed a quite substantial, and even almost preferential, interest in Basque. Hervás accepted most of the arguments of his religious brother Larramendi, by whom he was strongly influenced. Specifically, he insisted on the inherent perfections of the Basque language, superior to those of other civilized languages, and praised the tenacity of the Basques in the preservation of their tongue, seeing this as part and parcel of the secular preservation of their political independence. He also criticized Spanish lexicographers for failing to consider Euskara when it came to seeking the origin of Castilian words. He was convinced that he could demonstrate the extension of Basque throughout the peninsula in ancient times by the etymological demonstration of Basque toponyms and Basque origins of most Spanish surnames. Finally, he denied what had become a commonplace assumption among European authors, the kinship between Basques and Celts.

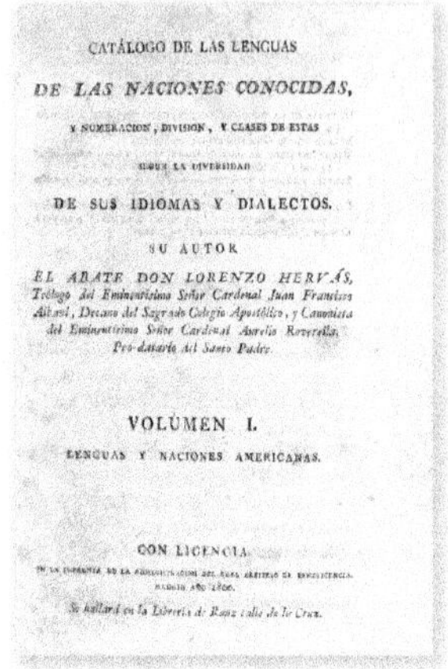
CATÁLOGO DE LAS LENGUAS
DE LAS NACIONES CONOCIDAS,
Y NUMERACION, DIVISION, Y CLASES DE ESTAS
SEGUN LA DIVERSIDAD
DE SUS IDIOMAS Y DIALECTOS.
SU AUTOR
EL ABATE DON LORENZO HERVÁS,
Teólogo del Eminentísimo Señor Cardenal Juan Francisco Albani, Decano del Sagrado Colegio Apostólico, y Canonista del Eminentísimo Señor Cardenal Aurelio Roverella, Pro-datario del Santo Padre.
VOLUMEN I.
LENGUAS Y NACIONES AMERICANAS.
CON LICENCIA.
Se hallará en la Librería de Ranz calle de la Cruz.

Selected Text(s):

Catálogo de las lenguas de las naciones conocidas, y numeración, division, y clases de estas, según la diversidad de sus idiomas y dialectos. Su autor el abate Don Lorenzo Hervás, bibliotecario de NN. SS. P. Pío VII, Volumen V. Continuación del tratado III. Lenguas y naciones europeas: y de la parte II. Naciones primitivas: sus lenguas matrices, y dialectos de estas [Catalogue of the Languages of the Known Nations, and the Numbers, Divisions, and Classes of These, According to the Differences in Their Languages and Dialects. By the Abbot Don Lorenzo Hervás, Librarian of Our Supreme Pontiff Pius VII, Vol. 5. Continuation of Treatise III: European Languages and Nations, and Part II: Primitive Nations: Their Matrix Languages and Their Dialects], (Madrid: Imprenta Real Arbitrio de Beneficencia, 1804), 205–06, 217–22, 239–41, 244–47, 254–55, 259, 261–62, 270.

Mayans himself in the work dealing with the different languages from which Spanish has borrowed words [Origins of the Spanish Language], gives first place to Latin, and then, in succession, says: "Arabic is the language from which, after Latin, we have the most words . . . after the Arabic language, we have more from Greek than from any other . . . and after this, I estimate that we have more from Hebrew than from any other, including Phoenician . . . and in my opinion, adds Mayans, Celtic is next . . . after which there is good reason to give next priority to Gothic; and finally comes Basque."

This classification of the languages to which Spanish owes its words would be tolerable if it had been done by a person who did not have the least knowledge of Spanish or Basque; but it is hard to accept that a Spaniard would make such a statement. The Spanish language, as an obvious dialect of Latin, has borrowed its grammar and countless words; after Latin, the next in order of words contributed are Basque, Celtic and Arabic; Phoenician, Hebrew, Greek and Gothic should be excluded altogether.

. . .

704. In the year 1784, I wrote in the Romanian language and published in Italian the tome titled *Catálogo de las lenguas* [Catalogue of the Languages], which is the seventeenth volume of my Italian work; and because I lacked the books and documents necessary to learn the nature of the Basque language, and having decided not to rely on the authority of any other writer in matters of language, when I could consult their grammars and dictionaries myself, I put no trust in the texts cited by Martiniere and the English writers (who could confuse the most critical intelligence) and wrote to Don Josef Beovide, a Jesuit fluent in the Basque language, asking him to look through the Celtic dictionary of [Gottfried] Leibniz and tell me if he found any Basque words. This gentleman Beovide quickly sent me the following reply that I published in the cited tome [Catalogue of the Languages], and this is the gist of it: "Bologne, April 28, 1784: I have found only two Basque words in Leibniz's dictionary, and these are *arth*, which in Celtic means "bear," and *trippa*, which in Celtic means "entrails" [tripe] or "intestines": in the Basque language bear is called *arzà*, and the intestines are called *tripea*." Behold, I added in that book, after receiving the reply from Beovide, incontestable proof, the difference between the Cantabrian (or Basque) languages and Celtic, which according to Martiniere is so similar that he went so far as to say in the article "Celts," that a Basque would be able to understand the languages of the Bretons and the Cornish, which are Celtic dialects, without much difficulty. It is obvious then, that knowledge of languages is necessary to correct no few errors filling the books of history. And it can be shown immediately that the knowledge of the Basque language is most necessary to writers in order to untangle the many events that have become confused in the ancient history of Europe. Thus, James MacPherson, who in 1771 published in London the introduction to his history of England and Ireland, confesses that he discovered by comparing the Celtic and Basque languages how different they were, and that any conclusions based on the supposed kinship between these two languages were false.

In truth, the study of the similarity or difference between languages is the only way to cast the light needed to eliminate the confusion and darkness that has shrouded many events described or implied in the ancient history of nations. This leads to continuous abuse concerning the national names of Celts, Dacians, Getae, Huns, etc., and it is almost impossible to correct the errors of this abuse without knowing and determining the respective languages of the nations that are misidentified by these names. The names of countries, cities, inlets, promontories, islands, etc., identified by the respective languages of their origin allow us to understand the transmigrations, navigations, conquests of the nations, and the qualities of the founders of the cities. The Iberian, or Spanish nation from time immemorial, and before that of the first epochs of secular history, was established in the western European countries where it is still situated. This has always formed a large national area of Europe, and the land has always been, since the most remote antiquity, a common dwelling place of the nations that have settled there, and with whom the Iberians and Spaniards have had continuous relationships; and having preserved among them their primitive language, which is Basque. It deserves the utmost attention from Spanish scholars in order to illustrate through it, her ancient history.

. . .

III

Persistence and tenacity of the Basques to preserve the native Basque language of the ancient Spaniards.

705. The admirable tenacity of the Basques to preserve the language they inherited from their progenitors during the confusion of languages in Babel can be seen in the preservation of that same language with extraordinary purity in Spain, despite the fact that this country has adopted the foreign language of her conquerors, the Romans, and has been the European country invaded by the greatest number of foreign nations. The Basques have preserved their language with the same care and tenacity corresponding to the determination they have always shown in resisting the foreign domination they observed in the languages these invaders introduced into Spain. Larramendi includes in his dictionary of the Basque language a great number of Spanish words that had been introduced into the Spanish Basque language, which he should have omitted; however, this does not mean that the Basque language has lost its purity, for I have observed that almost all of these Spanish words are redundant and totally useless, because Basque has its own equivalents. Such Spanish words should not be put in Basque dictionaries except to signify those things whose names are lacking in the language

of the Spanish and French Basques. These people, who have preserved their language with such admirable tenacity, saving it from the common calamity that befalls so many languages of conquered peoples, should make every effort to banish all useless foreign words in order to prevent its corruption.

...

V
The Character of the Basque Language

710. Manuel Larramendi, in his prologue to the Basque dictionary cited earlier, discusses at great length the character and perfection of this language, in order to praise it and respond to certain objections made against it by critics, who have absolutely no knowledge of the diverse and admirable artifice of all languages, and of the intrinsic difference of the so-called matrix languages. Truly, the creation of the most barbaric language ever known surpasses the limits of human ingenuity, as I will demonstrate practically in the first volume of my work on the Spanish school of deaf-mutes; and the difference in intrinsic perfection between greater or lesser languages in no way depends on human industry, which is not capable of inventing any language at all, but only of adding exterior perfection to those already created. Barbarous nations, which lack all evidence of ever having been civilized, use languages that are comparable to the most perfect languages of nations, which have always been civilized. The Araucanians, commonly called Chileans, use one of the most perfect languages known to man, yet no evidence has been discovered of their ever having been civilized in the least. Anyone with a practical knowledge of ancient and modern languages, civilized or savage, will stand amazed at the astonishing variety of critical conclusions used to characterize languages as perfect or imperfect, or as greater or lesser matrix languages. Larramendi, in the seventh section of the first part of his abovementioned prologue, sets out to prove that the Basque language is one of the greater matrix languages because Scaliger and Mayans place it among the lesser ones. Mayans adopted this term, merely repeating the conclusion of Scaliger, who for no apparent reason had divided the matrix languages into greater and lesser. All languages are matrixes, or dialects of matrix languages: a language that is not the dialect of another. Even if it is spoken only in a single village, their language can be as much a matrix as a language which, not being a dialect of any other, is spoken in the grandest empire. As I have observed continuously in my discussions on language that can be found in my Italian

books, languages (all of which are matrixes) are distinguished by their words, their syntax or grammatical artifice, and by the accent or pronunciation of their primitive speakers. Nations, with their greater or lesser civilization, endow their languages with greater or lesser perfection, which we should refer to as extrinsic, and in this I include their different ways of deriving words; for as will be explained in the practical essay on languages, from the earliest times, derivation has been brought about in some languages by differentiating between the pronunciation or accent of the same letter, as is still the case in some American nations and in many Asian nations from the Ganges to the most remote corner of China, whereas in others it was done by adding different radical endings to words.

. . .

711. The perfect artifice of languages can be reduced to the difference between substantive and adjectival nouns, the difference in the number and case of the nouns, and the variety of conjugations of the verbs, with their respective difference between modes, and between time within each mode. Basque has all of these features with utmost perfection, as Manuel Larramendi demonstrates in his published grammar. The Basque language distinguishes number in nouns by adding *a* or *ác* for singular, *ac* for plural. For example: *iauná* and *iaunác* mean "gentleman," and *iaúnac* means "gentlemen," the difference in accent between the singular *iaunác* and the plural *iaúnac* being quite distinct. The cases of each number are distinguished by the addition of postpositive particles: thus, the genitive singular is *iaúnaren*, and the plural is *iaunen*; and so on. Basque nouns have no gender at all and thus are lacking in this imperfection rendering the study of the Greek, Latin and Romance languages intolerable. The invention of gender in things that have no sex at all is ridiculous, as I have demonstrated at length in the first volume of my "Spanish School for Deaf-Mutes." *Boca* [mouth] is feminine, *labio* [lip] is masculine, *lengua* [tongue] is feminine and *diente* [tooth] is masculine: this invention of gender is improper, ridiculous and burdensome for anyone studying languages. Italian and Spanish are dialects of Latin; in the latter, the word *caput* [person] is neuter in gender; from *caput* come *capo* (masculine gender) in Italian, and *cabeza* (feminine gender) in Spanish. The use, then, of genders in things that have no sex is pure gibberish in Latin, more so in its dialects; because in their origin, such genders are used improperly in the matrix language, and capriciously or arbitrarily in its dialects.

The system of conjugations in the Basque language clearly lacks the imperfections I find in Latin and its dialects, Italian, French, Spanish, as well as possessing a number of perfections lacking in these dialects. They say that there are several conjugations in Latin and its dialects, but this diversity, far from constituting a perfection, is obviously an imperfection, because it adds nothing in the way of quality, but simply causes simple verbs that ought to be conjugated in one way to be conjugated with different endings, whose difference, adding no perfection, is merely a function of the material ending of the verbs.

. . .

In the Basque language, there are twenty-three conjugations, or to put it more clearly, a verb is conjugated in twenty-three different ways with as many different meanings. For example: *iatendec* [you eat it]; *iatendizquidat* [you eat them]; *iatendidac* [you eat it but it is mine]; *iatendituc* [you eat them but they are mine], and so forth. It gives four conjugations for the verb *iaten*, and in each one, it expresses a different meaning. These examples should demonstrate the perfection of the Basque language, and the imperfection of several languages, which have been regarded as perfect, simply because they have not been given sufficient reflection. In the following essay, the pronunciation of the Basque language will be discussed.

Vocal accentuation in the Basque language. In this language, there are no guttural sounds and the letters *b, v,* and *f* are silent. I propose that the first and most effective proof that Basque was the primitive and universal language in Spain is based on the vocal accent used by Basques in their speech.

. . .

Because Latin, or Romance, has been the language of Spain for almost eighteen centuries, and is so today, it would seem that in Spain, except for the Basque provinces, there should hardly be any Basque surnames and that almost all of them should be Latin, and only a few would be from Arabic and other European languages; but if we look closely, we will see that today there are still almost as many that are derived from Basque, as from Latin.

The Spanish surnames derived from Arabic and the living languages of Europe are few and easily recognized. Those from the Latin language are many; and in my opinion, it is commonly believed that a good number are derived from Basque. As a general rule, the many Spanish surnames that have no meaning in Latin, Arabic and the living languages of Europe are most certainly from the Basque language.

. . .

As it is obvious that the formation of Spanish patronymics has been influenced by the Basque language, and because many of these were formed several centuries after the Christian religion was established in Spain, it should be said that during this period in Spain, the Basque language was still commonly used by the common people; for it is inconceivable that they would have continued to form their patronymics from the Basque language, if they had completely abandoned it.

. . .

5. From the preponderance of evidence that I have elaborated, we can clearly infer the universality of the Basque language in Spain before people began to speak the language of the Romans (Latin) or the present language we know to be a dialect of Latin. If the uniformity of family surnames in a nation can be considered to be an argument, or proof to infer that these families belong to a single tribe, should it not be inferred that the Spanish families with surnames derived from Basque, or formed under its influence, are descendants of progenitors who spoke the Basque language? These families still constitute a near majority of Spanish citizens scattered across Europe, America and Asia; few of them have immigrated from the Spanish Basque provinces, where Basque is still spoken, but have remained in Spain, far away from those countries; wherefore, they must have spoken Basque and used Basque surnames, before arriving in those countries.

. . .

The etymologists of the Spanish language (among whose works the *Tesoro de la lengua castellana* [Treasury of the Castilian Language] by Sebastián de Covarrubias is famous) had before them the Greek, Latin, Hebrew, Arabic, and Gothic languages in their search for the derivations of Spanish words, failed even to mention the Basque language, from which the Spanish language has borrowed so many words, and to which innumerable geographic names in Spain belong, and by extension, Spanish surnames—because as in all nations, the majority of these allude to the names of cities.

31. Juan Manuel Martín Ugarte, known as Manuel Risco

(Haro, La Rioja, 1735 – Madrid, 1801)

This historian from La Rioja was, on his mother's side, a native of Lezama (Araba). The religious name by which he was known derived from having been ordained in the Augustinian Order of the Monastery of Our Lady of Risco. He expanded upon and defended the work of Enrique Flórez de Setién, another Augustinian historian who was a follower of the school of historical criticism founded by Feijoo. He wrote Volume 32 of the *España Sagrada* (Sacred Spain) (begun by Flórez) under the title: *La Vasconia. Tradado preliminar a las santas iglesias de Calahorra y de Pamplona* (Vasconia. Preliminary Treatise for the Holy Churches of Calahorra and Pamplona) (1799). Additionally, Flórez had dismantled the traditional Basque-Cantabrian theories, but as some authors (in particular, Josè Hipólito de Ozaeta) persisted in defending them by attacking the Augustinian, Risco published his: *El R. P. M. Fray Enrique Florez, vindicado del Vindicador de la Cantabria, Don Hipólito de Ozaeta y Gallaiztegui. Por el P. M. Fray Manuel Risco, del Orden de S. Agustín* (The Reverend Monastic Father Brother Enrique Florez, Defended from the Defender of Cantabria Don Hipólito. By the Monastic Father, Brother Manuel Risco of the Order of Saint Augustine) (1799). Similarly, Landázuri wrote an Appendix to his *Historia del Ilustre País Bascongado* (History of the Illustrious Basque Country), defending the Basque-Cantabrian theories in identical terms against Flórez, which was never published and has disappeared. Risco was one of the defenders of the theory that the language that in ancient times extended from Lusitania to Aquitaine, throughout the northern region of the Iberian Peninsula, had been the Basque language, which he identified with Celtic.

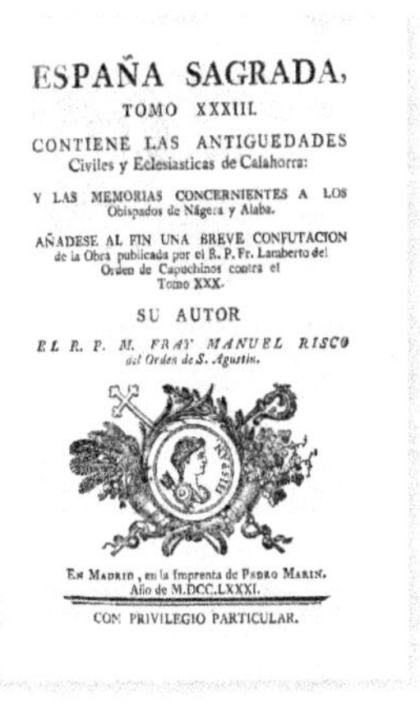

ESPAÑA SAGRADA,
TOMO XXXIII.
CONTIENE LAS ANTIGUEDADES
Civiles y Eclesiasticas de Calahorra:
Y LAS MEMORIAS CONCERNIENTES A LOS
Obispados de Nágera y Alaba.
AÑADESE AL FIN UNA BREVE CONFUTACION
de la Obra publicada por el R. P. Fr. Lamberto del
Orden de Capuchinos contra el
Tomo XXX.
SU AUTOR
EL R. P. M. FRAY MANUEL RISCO
del Orden de S. Agustin.

En Madrid, en la Imprenta de Pedro Marin.
Año de M.DCC.LXXXI.
CON PRIVILEGIO PARTICULAR.

Selected Text(s):

España Sagrada. Tomo XXXII. La Vasconia: Tratado preliminar a las santas iglesias de Calahorra y de Pamplona. En que se establecen todas las antigüedades concernientes a la región de los vascones desde los tiempos primitivos hasta los reyes primeros de Navarra [Sacred Spain. Volume 32. Vasconia. Preliminary Treatise for the Holy Churches of Calahorra and Pamplona. In Which All of the Antiquities Related to the Region of the Basques from Primitive Times until the First Kings of Navarre are Established] (Madrid, 1799); reprint, by the Real Academia de la Historia [Royal Academy of History] (Madrid: Imprenta José Rodríguez, 1878), 2nd ed., treatise 68, ch. 1, pp. 11–13.

---

16. In my opinion, the establishment of the Lusitanian Celts and Artabrians throughout all the northern coastal regions including Vasconia is irrefutably proven by Strabo's clear and unambiguous assertion that the way of life of Galicians, Asturians, Cantabrians, and even Basques in the Pyrenees was in every way modeled on the Lusitanians, who were the most ancient Celts known to history, and whose population extended from the westernmost region of Spain all the way to the eastern lands of those provinces. It would be easy enough to compare each of the customs of all of these regions, proving that they are identical and demonstrating by the testimony of a number of other authors that they are Celtic, but I consider that superfluous because Strabo's evidence demonstrated the total equivalence of every feature and aspect of style of the people, who lived in the territory between Lusitania and the Pyrenees.

17. The power of my argument will be apparent to anyone who reflects that the writers of greatest authority used this very method to investigate the origins of the people. Pliny, speaking of the Celts of the Betica region south of the Guadalquivir [River, in contemporary Andalusia], says it is obvious that they descended from the Celt-Iberians of Lusitania, as proven by the similarity of the two peoples in religion, language, and the names of cities. Basing his conclusions of the use of headgear and certain words that were similar to those used by the Cantabrians, Seneca speculated that some Spaniards must have migrated to Corsica. Given this uniformity in all the customs of the people of the northern coast with those of the Lusitanians, the original Celts of Spain, is there any doubt that these people at one time dominated those regions?

18. It can be inferred from what has been said that it is not improbable but quite likely, based on the conclusion of scholars, that the language of the Lusitanians was the same as that spoken by the people in the northern regions as far as Aquitaine, and that this language was the one we call Basque today. Such general and perfect uniformity does not seem possible unless the people are identical or maintain frequent contact with each other, which would be impossible if their languages were different. Additionally, it is clear that the Roman conquest could not have introduced a different language to the people of the Basque Country [*Vasconia*], or the neighboring regions along the coast, nor did other foreign nations after them succeed in changing their ancient ways, as will be demonstrated throughout this volume. Thus the use of the Basque language in ancient times, in all of the regions we have mentioned, is quite verisimilar; although we can be sure that in its present form it will be quite different, as has been the case with other most noble and widely spoken languages.

32. José Ramón de Iturriza y Zabala

(Berriz, Bizkaia, 1741 – Munitibar, Bizkaia, 1812)

He was the son of a schoolteacher. His first job was as a scribe. In 1760, he migrated to Mexico, sponsored by his maternal uncle Gabriel de Zabala, who owned a bakery in the capital. His uncle died after a few years, but the only thing Iturriza inherited from him was a cheap jacket. He had left everything of value to the friars of the Mercedarian order of Mexico, who had convinced him to do so during spiritual exercises. A failure, he thus had to return to Bizkaia in 1768. Despite this disappointment involving the friars, Iturriza was a fervent believer and supporter of the religious orders. He enjoyed writing and published, in Mexico, a treatise written in mystical style entitled *Lucero espiritual* (Spiritual Guide Star) in 1768. When he returned to Europe, he went on several pilgrimages (to Rome and Santiago de Compostela, for example) and tried in vain to take orders in several monasteries. He worked as a researcher, and went through almost all the archives of the Seigniory of Bizkaia in search of documents, becoming a historian and unofficial chronicler of the province. The Provincial Government of Bizkaia remunerated his work, and he dedicated himself to traveling tirelessly through the territory in search of information.

The proper title of his most important work, *Historia general de Vizcaya, comprobada con autoridades y copias de escrituras y privilegios fehacientes, en la cual se relaciona su población y posesión perpetua por sus naturales, conservando su primitiva lengua, fueros, franquezas y libertades . . .* (General History of Bizkaia: Based on Authorities and Copies of Writings and Reliable Permissions, in Which Is Described Her Population and Perpetual Ownership by Her Native People, Preserving Their Primitive Language, Charters, Privileges and Liberties . . .) (1884) gives a rather clear expression of the ideological spirit behind it, and the role that language plays in his conception of history. Iturriza's work is weakened by his lack of genuine criteria and training as a historian, and his inability to synthesize; he became the prototype of the learned accumulator of facts. In large part, his work is a gigantic index file of data from every possible source, from the most reliable to the most transparent misrepresentations and falsifications. Thus, he reproduces the classical topics of sixteenth and seventeenth century historiography: Tubal, the identity of Basque / Armenian toponymy, the sermons of St. Paul and St. James, and so on, following the lead of Pedro de Fontecha y Salazar, in *Escudo de la más constante fee y lealtad* (Shield of the Most Steadfast Faith and Loyalty), written around the decade of 1750 and published in the 1760s.[1]

Nonetheless, some linguistic elements in his historical work are not entirely lacking in interest. Iturriza defended the idea that there existed early versions of the *Fuero* written in Basque; the first in the days of the Agarene [Moorish] invasion, another during the election of Jaun Zuria, and the third from the year 931 in the time of Sancho López, great grandson of the former.[2] He also relies on the chronicle of Ibargüen-Cachopin to affirm that in ancient times there were written documents in the Basque language that were subsequently lost. Unfortunately, the sources cited to prove these assertions are so weak that Iturriza's credibility in this respect is seriously compromised.

---

1. For example, the text in José Ramón Iturriza y Zabala, *Historia general de Vizcaya, comprobada con autoridades y copias de escrituras y privilegios fehacientes, en la cual se relaciona su población y posesión perpetua por sus naturales, conservando su primitiva lengua, fueros, franquezas y libertades . . .* (Barcelona: Viuda e hijos de J. Subirana, 1884), 30–31, 54, reproduces the ideas of Pedro de Fontecha y Salazar, *Escudo de la más constante fee y lealtad* (Bilbao: Diputación de Vizcaya; Antonio de Egusquiza, 1762), reprint (Bilbao: Juan E. Delmas, 1866; La Gran Enciclopedia Vasca, 1976), 8–11, 24–26.

2. Iturriza y Zabala, *Historia general de Vizcaya*, 87–88 and ch. 17 of pt. 1.

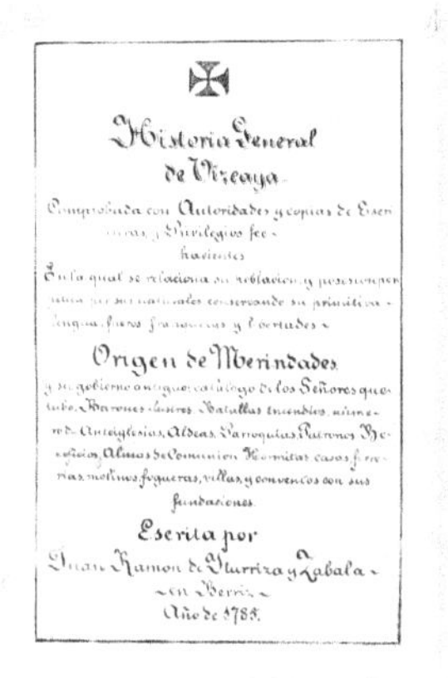

Historia General
de Vizcaya
Comprobada con Autoridades y copias de Escrituras, y Privilegios fe-
hacientes
En la qual se relaciona su poblacion y posesion perpetua por sus naturales conservando su primitiva
lengua, fueros franquezas y libertades
Origen de Merindades
y su gobierno antiguo, catalogo de los Señores que
tubo, Barones ilustres, Batallas, incendios, nume-
ro de Anteiglesias, Aldeas, Parroquias, Patronos, Beneficios, Almas de Comunion, Hermitas, casas ferre-
rias, molinos, fogueras, villas, y conventos con sus
fundaciones
Escrita por
Juan Ramon de Iturriza y Zabala
en Berriz
Año de 1785.

SELECTED TEXT(S):

Historia General de Vizcaya. Comprobada con Autoridades y copias de Escrituras, y Privilegios fehacientes. En la qual se relaciona su población y posesión perpetua por sus naturales, conservando su primitiva lengua, fueros, franquezas y libertades . . . [General History of Bizkaia: Based on Authorities and Copies of Writings and Reliable Permissions, in Which Is Described Her Population and Perpetual Ownership by Her Native People, Preserving Their Primitive Language, Charters, Privileges and Liberties . . .] (Bolibar-Berriz, 1782–1785); reprint, (Barcelona; Viuda e hijos de J. Subirana, 1884), ch. 16, 87–88 and ch. 17, 94.

Chapter 16

Of the Fueros and Brotherhood of Bizkaia in the Times of Their Founding

131. Juan Iñiguez de Ibarguen, whom I repeatedly identify in this History as the writer who, of all the authors I mentioned at the beginning of this work, provided the most details and facts about Bizkaia, because he had educated himself more than others about the antiquities of this realm. In the sixteenth century, he had been responsible for collection from the Archives of Simancas, Valladolid and other places of information and battle gear from the Noble Houses of Bizkaia, as Brother Martin de Coscojales mentions in his fragments. Juan Iñiguez de Ibarguen writes in reference to the free *fueros* of Bizkaia, that the first ones grant-

ed to her natives were discussed and negotiated and written down in Basque in *Forua*, as I noted in chapter 15. I am convinced the first *fueros* were probably granted for the purpose of electing officers and judges to govern and defend the country against the African enemies, who conquered almost all of Spain, and against the English and French pirates, who threatened an imminent attack in these territories, landing on the coast to steal cattle, and who were unable to force the Asturians and Navarrese to ally with them as they wished, because they were free. The Asturians and Navarrese were not subject in that period to any Prince, because they had destroyed the Royal Kingdom of the Goths and brought an end to their power, confirming the rights of the people they regarded and treated as free. The Doctor Don Pedro Salazar de Mendoza writes in folio 208 of the first volume of the *Monarquía de España* [Spanish Monarchy], they were allowed to ally themselves with whomever they chose because of their *fuero*. Finally, the Basques allied themselves with the Castilians and together they joined the Kings of Asturias in mutual alliance to conquer and expel the Moors.

132. The second time the articles of the *fuero* of Bizkaia were expanded in the Basque language was at the time of the election of Don Lope Fortun, alias *Jaunzuria*, as their first Prince with certain pacts and conditions that will be included in chapter 19 of book 1 of this History.

133. The third time they were expanded and also written in Basque was during the time of Don Sancho Lopez, great grandson of Prince *Jaunzuria*, who entered the realm in the year 931 for the purpose of negotiating a pact with the farmers, who were occupying his houses. They agreed on the schedules and kinds of cattle and grains for bread and apples, etc. They would pay for rent, and negotiated other matters for their governance and relations with the Nobles [*Infanzones*] and Senior Lineage Heads [*Parientes Mayores*]. These *fueros*, even if they had been written as claimed by the aforementioned Ibarguen, had not been preserved on parchments in the time of the Prince Don Juan Nuñez de Lara, but many chapters of the charter were preserved in the memory of the Bizkaians, and especially by the mayors of the *fuero* and the lawyers in whose interest it would have been important to remember them. The most ancient *fueros* that were written and whose original copies still exist are those which the aforementioned Don Juan Nuñez de Lara and his wife Doña Maria Diaz de Haro, presented to Bizkaia before the general council of Gernika in the era of 1380, which is in the year 1342.

. . .

Note—Garibay mentions these charters in chapter 8 of book 24 of the *Compendio Historial* [Historical Compendium], and he says that King Don Sancho VII of Navarre gave them to the town of Durango in the year 1150; but as can be ascertained from them he gave them to the farmers of the region [*merindad*] and not [specifically] to the town. Brother Miguel de Alonsótegui copied them in chapter 20 of book 1 of the *Crónica de Vizcaya* [Chronicle of Bizkaia], and they say that they were written in the middle of an illuminated manuscript of a Missal of the Church of San Agustin in Elorrio. But, because two pages had been cut out, it was not possible to ascertain the year in which the aforementioned King Don Sancho had granted them. Brother Martin de Coscojales also copies them on the back of folio 261 and 262 of Volume 6 of his *Recopilaciones* [Compilations], as well as the general *fueros* of the region [*merindad*] of Durango. Father Henao also mentions these *fueros* in book I, chapter 7, of the *Averiguaciones de las antigüedades de la Cantabria* [Verification of the Antiquities of Cantabria], [but is] uncertain as to whether they were granted by the aforementioned King Don Sancho, or his son, also called Sancho, who began his reign in 1194, promising that he would copy them in chapter 16 of book 4, which was never published and its whereabouts are unknown.

33. Juan Antonio Moguel Urquiza

(Eibar, Gipuzkoa, 1745 – Markina, Bizkaia, 1804)

Moguel came from a family of doctors with an estate in Markina. He happened to be born in Eibar because his father had taken a faculty appointment there at the time. But his father, Juan Ignacio Moguel Almazán, was not only a doctor, but a devout practitioner of Enlightenment principles. He worked in the center of the Real Sociedad Bascongada on a number of experiments related to plagues and contagious diseases, published a small book on medicine and was the personal physician of Count Peñaflorida. Another son, Juan Ignacio Moguel Urquiza, continued his father's experiments in the inoculation of vaccines. But the progressive character of the Moguel family and its orientation toward the Enlightenment did not prevent him from professing simultaneously a deep religious devotion. As was the custom in such families, one or more younger sons were always destined for that profession, and this fell to Juan Antonio. He was educated in philosophy and Latin at the Royal Jesuit School for Nobles in Calatayud (Aragón) and after taking other courses in theology he returned to Markina in 1770, where he lived for the rest of his life dedicated to practicing the priesthood and writing a series of literary works and essays, both in Basque and Castilian.

The choice of languages for the composition of Moguel's work was completely symptomatic, as he used Basque for his literary work *El doctor Peru Abarca* (Doctor Peru Abarca) (1881) as well as books of religious indoctrination addressed to his parishioners, such as *Confesio ta Comunioco Sacramentuen gañean Eracasteac* (Teaching about Holy Confession and Communion) (1800), *Confesio Ona* (Good Confession) (1803), and *Cristinauaren jaquinvidea* (Christian Learning Method) (1805), whereas the works written as apologies for the language itself, and addressed to his Castilian adversaries, were written in Castilian: *Cartas y disertaciones de don Juan Antonio Moguel sobre la lengua vascongada* (Letters and Dissertations by Don Juan Antonio Moguel on the Basque Language) (Lepizig: 1847; Madrid, 1854); *La Historia y Geografía de España ilustradas por el idioma vascuence* (Illustrated History and Geography of Spain for the Basque Language) (1925–1937); and *Apología de la lengua bascuence contra las erradas ideas y conjeturas de D. Joaquín Traggia* (Apology for the Basque Language Against the Mistaken Ideas and Conjectures of D. Joaquín Traggia) (1881). It is also quite symptomatic of the political and editorial situation of the time that he was able to publish his religious works during his lifetime, whereas his literary and apologetic works had to be published eighty or a hundred years after having been written.

It is important to recall here once again that Moguel, with his *Peru Abarca*, proved to be the most interesting Basque writer of the eighteenth century. This work, which is not easily categorized, is part ethnographic essay, part narrative, part linguistic theory and apology, and part ethical treatise, in the style of the classical "dialogues." Therefore, if *Peru Abarca* has Juan de Valdés as a distant source in terms of format, its intrinsic content is more reminiscent of Jean Jacques Rousseau.

The Basque language was, along with religion, the fundamental preoccupation of the life and work of Juan Antonio Moguel. He held the position as book censor and tried (unsuccessfully) to be appointed a Minister of the Inquisition. He did, however, become involved in one inquisitorial trial, because of a supposed apparition of the Virgin to one of his parishioners. It should be said that his moderate, enlightened and sensible disposition constitutes an exception within the exaggerated and perfervid panorama that surrounded the controversy regarding the Basque language and its polemicists during his lifetime. In other words, he occupied the prudent center, far removed from the extreme positions of Larramendi, Astarloa, Erro or Sorreguieta on the one hand, and those of Traggia or Conde on the other. Therefore, it should come as no surprise to find out that he maintained good relations with other scholars, who were at least as prudent as he, such as Vargas Ponce or Humboldt. He was an avid supporter of Larramendi's passionate Basque-Iberian theory, and maintained in his writings a fundamental thesis: that the true and pure Basque language resided in the popular language preserved in the rural settlements and peasant workplaces, whereas the inhabitants of the towns spoke a totally corrupted form of Basque and the things they discussed were barely spoken about in their own language. The vindication of purism in rural areas carried connotations that were partially related to the Enlightenment, partially romantic, and partially conservative with respect to the socio-political changes occurring in the urban environment.

Selected Text(s):

a) *Cartas y disertaciones de don Juan Antonio Moguel sobre la lengua vascongada* [Letters and Dissertations by Don Juan Antonio Moguel on the Basque Language], in *Memorial histórico español: colección de documentos, opúsculos y antigüedades que publica la Real Academia de la Historia* [Spanish Historical Memoir: A Collection of Documents, Pamphlets and Antiquities Published by the Royal Academy of History], vol. 7 (Madrid: José Rodríguez, 1854), 713–719.

b) *El doctor Peru Abarca, catedrático de la lengua bascongada en la Universidad de Basarte o Diálogos entre un rústico solitario bascongado y un barbero callejero llamado Maisu Juan* [Doctor Peru Abarca, Professor of the Basque Language at the University of Basarte, or Dialogues Between a Lone Basque Peasant and an Itinerant Barber Named Maisu Juan] (Durango: Julián Elizalde, 1881), app.; reprint, as "Separatas de la Gran Enciclopedia Vasca" 4 (Bilbao: La Gran Enciclopedia Vasca, 1970), 403–410.

---

a)

Markina, March 30, 1802

Dear Sir and friend:

This afternoon I received through the good graces of the Count of Peñaflorida the very elegant literary epistle from your worship, and before addressing other points I have to tell you that a certain Don Pablo de Astarloa, a resident of this town, but holding a benefice in the town of Durango, has compiled a new dictionary that, if it fulfills its promise, will satisfy your desires. He came to Madrid with all of his materials: he will collaborate with the Academy, etc.

He has written works [mostly unpublished]: a dictionary of the language, a geographical dictionary, a dictionary of surnames, and extensive artwork that leaves nothing to be desired. I know much about this person; he is competent and has done extensive research on the language. I do not wish to cast aspersions on his talent and gifts; but neither do I wish to conceal from Your Worship that his methodological genius and fiery temperament, that put even Larramendi's to shame, will not be pleasing to critics of good taste. He is too metaphysical, and much of what he has written is pure gibberish. I have spoken with him on several occasions; he has spoken to me of his works and offered to lend them to me so I can read them. But the occasion never came up, and I cannot offer an opinion about his manuscripts, in which there are sure to be some good things. I have read only the prospectus. In order to make comparisons between as many languages as he cites, it is necessary to know them, and not superficially: he only knows Latin, Castilian, and Basque, and can translate from French. Although he has probably read some instructional materials concerning the multitude of languages he writes about, and perhaps a grammar for the others, this is not enough to make valid comparisons and all of his ability is insufficient to allow him to carry out his project. A particular language may possess some extraordinary and excellent grammatical feature, but others may also have interesting qualities lacking to the former.

I am going to offer your worship an example from the Basque language that you will find instructive. Basque forms verbs from all adjectives without exception, as does Castilian on occasion: for example, *enterar* [to complete, finish off, acquaint oneself with everything] from *entero* [complete]; from *hermoso* [beautiful], *hermosear* [to beautify]; from *malo* [evil, bad], *malear* [to do evil, bad]; from *feo* [ugly], *afear* [to make ugly]. But Castilian is no more consistent in this than Latin. From *bueno* [good], *recto* [straight, upright], *prudente* [prudent, sensible] and countless other adjectives, no verbs are formed, and it has to borrow a foreign word for the adjective to make a sentence. Is it not far better to say *este muchacho se ha maleado* [this boy has worsened] than *se ha convertido en malo* [he has become bad]?" Well, the Basque invariably observes this rule, making a verb from all adjectives. The Castilian says this: "*Este hombre, antes tan liberal, se ha hecho ó convertido en ruin y codicioso*" [This man, previously so generous, has become stingy and covetous]. The Basque says it this way: *Len ain escuzabala zan guizon au, citaldu ta cequendu da*, forming verbs from the adjectives "stingy" and "covetous." This seems to have the advantage of greater eloquence. Another example, very delicate in its artfulness: The Basque even derives verbs from the possessive pronouns "mine," [the familiar singular] "yours," "hers," "his," "ours," and [the familiar plural] "yours."

CASTILIAN	BASQUE
Yo he hecho mía la casa [I have made the house mine]	Neuretu det echea
Tú la has hecho tuya [You have made it yours]	Zeuretu dezu
Aquel la ha hecho suya [He has made it his]	Beretu du
Nosotros la hemos hecho nuestra [We have made it ours]	Gueuretu degu
Vosotros la habéis hecho vuestra [You (plural) have made it yours]	Zeuendu dezute
Aquellos la han hecho suya [They have made it theirs]	Berendu dute

Basque saves many words with this structure, fitting them succinctly into the pronoun from which the verb is derived. There is another curious artifice in the verbs we call irregular:

CASTILIAN	BASQUE
Yo te los traia [I brought them to you]	Necarzuzan
Tú me los traias [You brought them to me]	Cencardazan
Aquel me los traia [He brought them to me]	Ecardazan
Nosotros te los traiamos [We brought them to you]	Guencarzuzan
Vosotros nos los traiais [You (plural) brought them to us]	Cegarguzan
Aquellos nos los traian [They brought them to us]	Ecargubezan

Thus, the Basque speaker includes the person doing or suffering the action or event in the verb itself. Let us analyze separately the word *necarzuzan*, which is divided as follows: *n-ecar-zu-zan*. The *n* is the "me" or "I" in Castilian; *ecar* is "the thing brought"; *zu* is "to you"; *zan* is the "it" or "the things." The analysis of the other words can be done in the same way.

It cannot be denied that the inflections in Basque are extremely well organized and refined, and that inflexions like these are innumerable, especially considering four different modes of address and four different genders and persons: reverential address, plain and courteous for lower class males and lower class females, all without offense, distinguishing male from female by the verb, for there is no distinction between male and female in this, and there is no difference of gender in the nouns, all of them common to both. The Castilian says *prudente* [prudent, sensible] for man and *prudente* for woman, but there is no consistency in this. Latin makes *janua* [door, entrance] feminine and *ostium* [doorway, entrance] neutral, signifying the same object.

Latin says *me-cum* [with me], *se-cum* [singular, with him/her/it/oneself], *te-cum* [singular, with you], *se-cum* [plural, with them/each other/one another], *nobis-cum* [with us], *vobis-cum* [plural, with you], avoiding the postposition of the articles, which is consistently used in Basque, and anyone who says *cum me* [me with], *cum te* [you with], *cum se* [him/her/it/oneself with] is regarded as illiterate in Latin. But Latin also makes eloquent use of postposition in the relative pronoun *quis* [who, that, which, what], saying *quocumque, quibuscumque* [both meaning: whatever, no matter who, in any time/way, however small]. Basque consistently observes a fixed rule in all this, postponing adjectives to noun as well. Latin is just as likely to say *formosus puer* as *puer formosus* [a handsome boy]: the same is true in Castilian, in which *hermoso muchacho* is indistinguishable from *muchacho hermoso* [a handsome boy]. Finally, I will not take the time now to point out all the beauties and curious features of this language of ours. I only say, without insulting other languages or giving preference to mine, that it is very well organized, sound in its grammar, and that it has certain advantages over other languages I know. But I would be arrogant if I said that it is the best language in the world and that it is superior to Latin and Castilian in every way.

What I do say is that neither Latin, nor French, nor Italian, nor Castilian are original languages; that Greek has borrowed much from other languages, because of its great and widespread contact with other languages; that Hebrew as it is spoken today is far from being the original language; and that the Basque language that is traditionally spoken by our people has borrowed nothing from Phoenician, Punic, Arabic, and Gothic; that it has no need of any Roman or Castilian word for ordinary conversations or common matters or things that are not newly invented or related to religious matters.

I venture further: that the lack of scientific terms is not a defect exclusive to Basque, or an innate weakness. Our theologians, philosophers, chemists, and physicists writing today, or our astrologers, mathematicians, and doctors, who have written prolifically in Latin, French, Italian, English, etc.—have they enriched or explained their knowledge in their own language? Haven't they introduced a lot of clutter? They all go running to Greek to beg for words. The Aristotelian, when he wants to speak concisely, muddies and corrupts the language with a *per se* here, or an *in se* there, etc. Logic or dialectics, physics or physiology, pneumatics, ontology—these are all cluttered with an endless number of Greek words in books about arts and sciences, and I pity the poor students, who wear themselves out trying to learn the words, or understand their meaning, especially when the teachers themselves have to define the Greek words, often without being able to make sense of them, because they do not know Greek. Poor young men, trying to learn a bit of anatomy, overwhelmed by so many Greek words that their exhaustion makes us grieve for them.

I do have to admit, however, that all of the words proliferating in books of science are *in se* poor, infertile, and that they do indeed have to beg for a multitude of words from foreign languages. Perhaps this is a defect in the teachers and writers, and not in the languages *per se*. Solomon was truly a very wise man, if we are to believe what Holy Scripture tells us. When he engaged in arguments about plants and trees, from the magnificent cedars of Lebanon to the miserable hyssop, he only used ordinary Hebrew words and the same in all the sciences. Thus, if the Basque wants to make use of the same approach, he can write as the speaker of Latinate French does on any subject, and especially if he has a taste for Greek and Hebrew compound words, he can form descriptive words in his own language, although it is certain that he has not done so, nor are there any scientific books, nor to our knowledge has it ever been attempted; in light of this, because our language still preserves its excellent grammar and a multitude of words for things related to everyday activities, and because it has undoubtedly forgotten countless words, it has to be inferred that it is very ancient, predating the arrival of the Phoenicians, and is quite probably the language of the original inhabitants, whoever they were.

In regard to the language of the first man, this is not something that can be discussed among Catholics, who honor the sacred scriptures, nor debated as to whether it was or was not infused. In the book of Wisdom, chapter 18, we read about our first parents: *Deus creavit illis scientiam spiritus, sensu implevit cor illorum, et disciplina intellectus replevit illos* [God created in them the science of the spirit, He filled their heart with wisdom, and with the discipline of understanding He filled them full]; and there is no doubt that at this point they began to speak, and that Adam gave names to all the animals, etc. according to their own properties. This happened in the state of innocence. Whether Adam did or did not lose all natural science or a large portion of it at the same time he lost the gift of grace, we cannot know.

Nor can we doubt, without distorting the words and natural meaning of the Holy Scripture that until the construction of the Tower of Babel there was only one language in the world: *terra autem erat labii unius; eòrumdem sermonum* [and the whole earth was of one tongue, and the same speech], and that God infused many languages during the Confusion. Which ones they were, no one knows, nor whether they were all original or different dialects, but we do know that they did not understand each other, except within the families among whom each language was distributed or mixed.

I have not claimed nor do I say that Tubal came here in person. Not even Masdeu claims that it was he who came, but his descendants and those of Tarsis. Where they came from, where they settled, who can say? What science they possessed, what arts they brought with them? We cannot even speak of this with any certainty.

b)

Appendix to Peru Abarka

Dialogue

Between Two Friends in the Clergy,
Brother Pedro de Urlia and Don Juan de Sandia

Brother Pedro: My friend, I have had good reason to visit you here on previous occasions. The two of us have often talked about the weakness and neglect of many Bizkaian gentlemen, priests, and men of the cloth like me, who are too lazy to learn from books written in Basque without giving themselves a headache because they have no books to teach them Bizkaian Basque. And whose fault is this? It is their own fault. I go from here to there, village to village, through most of the towns and municipalities of Bizkaia. Many priests know me, and I have met only a very few who love the Basque language. They would like to know it, but without effort, like the lazy fieldworker whose fields are full of nettles, thistles, darnel, grass, weeds, and vetch.

Don Juan: My dear Father Pedro. You can go on talking as much as you please, but I at least have to interrupt you in what you were about to say. You probably speak Bizkaian Basque the way it is pronounced in and around your town, and I speak it as I have learned it in mine.

No matter how we pronounce it we must try to speak it correctly, eliminating all traces of Castilian, the way the pure Basque peasants have taught us, and we have to make them see that our ironworkers, carpenters, stoneworkers, blacksmiths, and villagers will understand us better when we present ourselves at the Church to teach them what they need to learn. Then they will understand all those bad speakers of Basque, when they begin to shout half in Basque, half in Castilian. It is fine for us to preserve the words that the Church has adopted, and introduced into all foreign languages; but we have to stop using foreign cognates when pure Basque nouns with the same meanings are used and spoken among the peasants. We have to weed out the thistles, nettles, and harmful grasses from the wheat field; otherwise they will take over and crush and drown out the clean wheat and prevent it from producing the needed grain. But, what happens among us? They have planted great quantities of bad seed, darnel, oats, and vetch, or in other words, foreign nouns stolen from Castilian. They have left the poor Basque language mixed and impure. Those who should be keeping vigil so the bad seed will not be planted are sleeping. If the time has now come to clear the field and produce clean grain, we have to work hard to eliminate the words that have been borrowed from Castilian unnecessarily; we have to gather up the Basque nouns that have been dumped in corners, and abandoned, and try to purify it as it was in ancient times, when there was no contact with those who spoke languages other than Euskara. Don't you agree, Father Pedro?

Brother Pedro: That is true, but who puts this into the heads of those bad Basque speakers? I have worked hard, to the point of making my throat dry and harsh trying to make many people see this. But it does no good to beat María with a stick. It is the people of our class, who have to gather up the discarded Basque words. We spend time with the peasants and we have to listen carefully to the way they speak and remember it carefully so we can dig up many beautiful nouns, and little by little we will bring lovely garments to the naked Basque language and then she will be elegantly dressed, casting off those foreign dresses. What was this foreign Castilian language a thousand years ago? It was a mixed language that would be impossible to understand today. By hard work and the desire to become elegant, although the clothes belonged to another, she has learned to dress in beautiful clothes although it is hard to know who her true father was. From the Romans, Basques, Arabs, Goths and other foreign nations, she has borrowed so many feathers they cannot be counted, and if each one demanded the return of the one belonging to it, what would be left?

The Basque language has no need of anyone to say whatever it wants to say. Have you not heard the way our villagers and many other peasants are speaking without slipping or stumbling on anything? But just go listen to many monks, priests and other gentlemen. How they strain and fret, if they have to tell a story that is a bit long!

. . .

Don Juan: Would you like me to respond to them now refuting the second criticism or accusation?

Brother Pedro: Yes, please, and for that purpose, show how things from the most elevated and elegant language, which the Romans bequeathed to us, can be expressed in Basque, so that everyone will know that the Basque language can be used for any topic.

Don Juan: I will get right to it; let us make Quintus Curcius, Sallust, Titus, Tacitus, and Cicero speak. They were the most famous historians, and in this way it will be clear that Basque has living, elegant, sonorous, and adequate words for expressing even the most elevated things.

[This is followed by translations from Latin into Basque]

. . .

Brother Pedro: I have heard with the greatest pleasure elegant passages in the language of the Romans translated into Basque. The Bizkaians would never have believed that their Basque language was so rich and elegant. That gentleman who sat down to translate the sermon of St. Peter into the Basque language, what will he say when he sees these discussions of words?

Will this embarrass him? Too bad! He will say he does not understand even half the words; that they have written down any words that suited their fancy, making them up. And who will be able to convince such a stubborn fellow?

Don Juan: It does not matter. Bad Basques like him never listen to reason. If they cannot do anything good in Basque, let them beat their heads against a wall. They are aware of their own ignorance, but they will never admit that it is their own fault, but [instead] will insist it is [so] because the Basque language is inadequate. If they had their way, they would forget the language they learned before they learned the foreign language.

When they went to school, although they were threatened and scolded a thousand times, they could not stop speaking in Basque. Getting a foreign language into their heads was like sweating blood. And just when their need of the Basque language is more urgent than ever, they start cursing and swearing, saying: "I wish the Basque language had never been created; I wish it would go off to the ends of the earth where there are no people; I wish that language were stricken with the plague, it is so damn difficult to learn."

Brother Pedro: May God bring the light of understanding to such men! They do not know how much harm they cause by being too weak and lazy to learn the beautiful language given us at our mother's breast. Many of them would rather be hanged than lose even a single comma from the laws of the *Fuero*, but they are happy to lose the Basque language that comes to us from antiquity.

34. Joaquín Traggia de Santo Domingo

(Zaragoza, 1748 – 1813)

He studied and was ordained a brother in the Schools of Piety of Barbastro, Huesca (Aragón). He studied philosophy in Daroca, Zaragoza and theology in Manila, in the Philippines. He became a lay brother in 1793, and taught in Valencia, Zaragoza, and Madrid. After 1791, he was elected to the Academy of History. From 1793 to 1802, he served on the Council of Antiquities as Antiquarian and Librarian. The Council had been founded in the mid-eighteenth century to oversee materials pertaining to "antiquities" or "ancient artifacts," in other words, the physical or archeological patrimony. He was especially interested in numismatic resources. Traggia was the fourth corresponding antiquarian on the Council, and José Antonio Conde succeeded him. Traggia was also an associate member of the Real Sociedad Bascongada. His erudition was proverbial, his knowledge of languages extensive (Tagalog, Greek, Latin, Coptic, Hebrew, and Ethiopian), and the scope of his areas of interest was also enormous: mathematics, theology, history, linguistics, and natural history. In the area of history, his main interests were Aragón and Navarre, and his most outstanding work was the *Aparato a la Historia Eclesiástica de Aragón* (A Device for the Ecclesiastic History of Aragón). Given his knowledge of the history of Navarre and his membership in the Royal Academy of History, he was assigned to write the entry for "Navarre" in the *Diccionario Geográfico-Histórico de España . . .* (Geographical-Historical Dictionary of Spain . . .), which had a powerful political resonance in his lifetime.

Beneath a general tone of apparent sympathy, Traggia never missed an opportunity to reveal the general lines of his thought, which is contrary to the pro-Navarrese-Basque hypotheses. In the case of Navarre, because the historically distinct character of the kingdom was undeniable, the burden of political invalidation had to rest precisely on language. As the Basque apologists had based their notions of *foral* uniqueness and supposed identity on the antiquity, extension, and distinct nature of the language, Traggia went about undermining these bases, in order to indirectly weaken the political arguments that tended to establish the shared peculiarity of Navarrese and Basques. From a rationalist and scientific perspective, it was not difficult for him to undermine the Tubalist, Iberianist, paradisiacal pretensions, and the etymological proof of the Basque apologists, but Traggia went much further than this. Indeed, he went to the extreme of trying to deny any Basque etymology and even rejected the supposed antiquity of the Basque language. As for the first point, in his zeal to eliminate entirely any Basque linguistic legitimatization of the political origins of Navarre, he sought to reject any etymology, including those that were the most obvious, and committed lamentable errors, even denying indirectly that the province had a distinct language of its own in that period. One example stands out: a reference to Iñigo (or *Eneko* in Basque) Arista. He contends that: "Modern people, who look for Basque etymologies everywhere, claim that the words for oak [tree] and ash [tree] come from that language. But the only basis for this is the conclusion of a modern writer, whose papers are in the archives of San Juan de la Peña and who, in his effort to reconcile opposing opinions claiming that it was Iñigo [Arista], or that it was García Ximénez, who was the first king. [The writer] imagined that both were names of a single person, and that the true king was García and that the other was a corruption of *Ennoikos Aristos*, which in Greek means 'first prince.' The idea is ingenious; but [it] presumes the use of Greek in a country where at the time no language at all was spoken well; the imperfectly learned ancient Latin language used in public functions having been forgotten."[1] In light of this, Traggia ventures the idea that the Basque language was introduced in the eighth century and became common during the twelfth century "to allow the natives to claim total independence from foreign powers." The political agenda of the argument, insinuated after long pages of philological analysis, could not be more obvious. The Basques, or Navarrese in this instance, in order to legitimize their distinct identity, had invented a language distinct from Spanish, which they then claimed to be the oldest, the most correct, and the universal language of the peninsula. Further, what astonished and annoyed Traggia was the very survival of the language in a sparsely populated rural area, whose inhabitants stubbornly insisted on preserving it. This called for an explanation that Traggia based on the fact that they "had a different system of law or *fuero*, which combined with the unpleasantness and poverty of the region, kept foreigners at a distance." That is, the survival of Basque was inseparable from the existence of the *foral* system, with the natives controlling the majority of public jobs, and the consequent isolation and lack of appeal to outsiders living there. The conclusion, finally, is devastating. Despite the efforts of Basques to keep their language alive, the reality is that it is gradually losing ground and "if its extinction can be nudged along, in less than two centuries it would be a dead language like others from whose ruins it was formed in the dark ages." Again, the disappearance of the *foral* system and the disappearance of the Basque language went hand in hand in nineteenth century Spanish liberal thought.

As was to be expected, the reaction to the piece was emphatic. The immediate meetings convened by the General Assemblies of Araba and Bizkaia to deal with its dangerous content, with respect to the *foral* system, are indicative of the alarm it created. Indeed, a large part of the work of Pablo Astarloa was motivated and aimed at responding to Traggia, especially in regard to the antiquity of the language. Equally, many other authors devoted their attention to it and formulated their objections.

---

1. Joaquín Traggia de Santo Domingo, "Del orígen de la lengua vascongada," in *Diccionario Geográfico-Histórico de España por la Real Academia de la Historia. Sección I. Comprehende el Reyno de Navarra, Señorío de Vizcaya, y Provincias de Álava y Guipúzcoa*, s.v. "Navarra," vol. 2 (Madrid: Viuda de Joaquín Ibarra, 1802), 77.

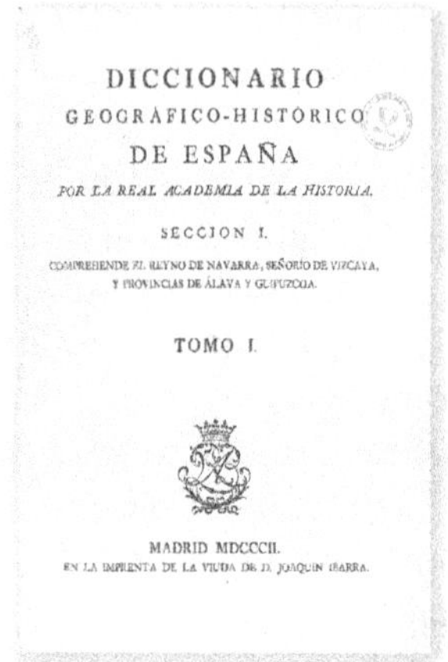
DICCIONARIO
GEOGRÁFICO-HISTÓRICO
DE ESPAÑA
POR LA REAL ACADEMIA DE LA HISTORIA.
SECCION I.
COMPREHENDE EL REYNO DE NAVARRA, SEÑORÍO DE VIZCAYA,
Y PROVINCIAS DE ÁLAVA Y GUIPUZCOA.
TOMO I.
MADRID MDCCCII.
EN LA IMPRENTA DE LA VIUDA DE D. JOAQUIN IBARRA.

Selected Text(s):

"Del orígen de la lengua vascongada" [On the Origin of the Basque Language], in *Diccionario Geográfico-Histórico de España por la Real Academia de la Historia. Sección I. Comprehende el Reyno de Navarra, Señorío de Vizcaya, y Provincias de Álava y Guipúzcoa* [Geographical-Historical Dictionary of Spain by the Royal Academy of History, Section I, Including the Kingdom of Navarre, the Seigniory of Bizkaia, and the Provinces of Araba and Gipuzkoa], s.v. "Navarra," vol. 2 (Madrid: Viuda de Joaquín Ibarra, 1802), 151–66.

Article XIII

On the Origin of the Basque Language

One of the most amazing phenomena of the Basque Country [Vasconia] has to do with the specific language spoken in many towns in Navarre and in the Basque provinces, and in the land of Lapurdi in France. There is no grammar for this language other than that of Father Manuel Larramendi, published in Salamanca in the year 1729. Even if Arnaud Oihenart, in his note on the two Basque Countries [Vasconias], gave some details of its grammar, and Brother Melchor Oyanguren, in his work on the Japanese language, printed in Mexico in the year 1738, implies that he had written a grammar of his native language, we do not know whether this [latter] work was ever made public; while that of Oihenart is insufficient to learn the Basque language. This language bears no resemblance to Castilian, or French, nor does it have any similarity to any known language. It is hard to understand how a handful of men subject (willingly or unwillingly) to other languages from the time of Augustus Caesar, and with additional contact with other peoples from the time of Wamba [King of the Visigoths in the Iberian Peninsula, 627–80] until the invasion of the Arabs [711], managed to either preserve or create a language so different from that of their conquerors or allies. Our astonishment grows even greater, for two reasons: one, that the Basques lacked, or chose not to use, a written language; second, that its language, far from being barbaric, inchoate and unstructured, is second to no other known language in its culture, richness, vitality, and fluency.

In light of this, I am not surprised by the efforts of Oihenart, Garma, and Larramendi, particularly the latter, who tries to demonstrate that Basque is one of the primitive languages created by God in the Confusion of languages of which Moses speaks, and the universal language of Spain before it was reduced to the confines of the area it now occupies by commerce and foreign invasions. The novelty of these ideas, if indeed they were opposed at first (as all new ideas are once the initial impetus and heat of the debate subsides), has been embraced by wise men. Nonetheless, I do not consider the point to have been as clearly proven, as is believed. Therefore, I am obliged to make clear the reasons for my doubt, leaving the way open to those more fortunate than I to investigate and discover the truth. I do not aspire to do that, but will be content if I can make it possible for someone else to clarify and cast greater light on this matter. First, it seems to me to be a vain endeavor to try to prove that the Basque language was born on the plains of Sumer [Senaar]. This effort is based on the common opinion that the diversity of languages was brought about in order to punish mankind for its arrogance in constructing the Tower. But, not even the Patriarchs or theologians are in agreement about this, nor are the words of Moses so conclusive that they do not allow any other interpretation. On the other hand, we see that when Abraham left Chaldea, he had no trouble understanding the Canaanites, and that his grandson Jacob did not need an interpreter to communicate with his uncle Laban, nor did Moses need one to communicate with the daughters of Jethro. As there is some doubt then, about the Confusion of languages in Sumer [Senaar], it cannot be confirmed definitively that the Basque language had its origin in that country. And because it cannot be proven whether Tubal came to Spain in person or may have been represented by his descendants, the bases for attributing to the Basque language an antiquity concurrent with the population of the world following the Flood are somewhat weakened. Let us see if the second claim—that the Basque language was universal and the oldest in Spain—can be asserted with any greater probability. To prove this convincingly, it would be necessary to know who the first inhabitant was and to assume that his colonies spread across the peninsula before any other nations with different languages arrived by land or by sea. But because the memory of the first inhabitants is shrouded in deepest darkness, there being only conjectures based on incoherent and dubious information concerning that remote antiquity, and because history offers clearer evidence that there were many languages and alphabets, and no credible monument of the Basque language from those times or from much later centuries, it would be irresponsible to say that the Basque language was the universal language of Spain in most ancient times.

I am well aware that defenders of the antiquity of the Basque language do not base their claim only on the portent that occurred in Sumer [Senaar], or on the voyage made by Tubal, Tarsis, or his sons. The crucial proof of their assertion lies in the multitude of Basque words scattered throughout the provinces of Spain in the proper names of rivers, mountains and towns which have survived the passage of time, supposedly demonstrating that they were imposed when the language was common to the entire peninsula. Under this assumption, if it were as certain as the lovers of the Basque language believe, it could be concluded logically that it was the primitive language of the first inhabitants, extending across the peninsula, long before the presence of the Phoenicians, Greeks, Carthaginians, and other peoples, who began to corrupt the primitive language in the provinces. And because common opinion places the origin and proliferation of languages in Sumer [Senaar], and brings Tubal to Spain, it is deduced that Tubal brought with him the language that was given to him, and that this was the Basque language. But this argument is unsatisfactory after some reflection. Because, not only before these names that are thought to be Basque were imposed, there could have been thousands of changes in the nation. But because for lack of more solid proof, etymologies can be used to support anything at all, even something diametrically opposed. It is well known that Goropius Becanus, seeking to prove the antiquity of the Cimbric or Belgian language, made use of that area of etymology, and easily discovered the origin of the names of Adam, Eve, and their children in his language. By this, I mean that through etymologies it is possible to find in every language almost all the unknown names of antiquity, as well as those newly created. It would be a tedious task to make a study of all the words of antiquity; it's sufficient to study a few. I will choose the Spanish words that are thought to be most ancient, i.e., Basque words.

. . .

We could go on at great length extending this nomenclature, but the examples we have provided are sufficient to prove that if we wanted, we could prove that any language is related to any other. If we accumulated enough data, we could even prove that one was the child of the other, even more so given the indulgence that etymologists allow themselves, changing a letter or a syllable, disfiguring the words. Besides which, given the easy combinations of syllables or sounds made up of just a few letters, it is impossible to imagine that the same combinations will not be found in almost all languages, either with the same or with a different meaning. So it is, that lacking sure information about the contact between peoples, all the work done regarding etymologies is difficult and potentially harmful. The word *Roma* [Rome] is Castilian, Greek, and Hebrew, and exists in almost all languages, but they do not all have the right to claim as their own the name of the capital of the world. Many ancient names of peoples and nations can have meaning in a modern language, though its original meaning may have been quite different. The words Rome, Latium, Sabine, Ostia, Alba, and thousands of others, with only slight alterations or none at all, have meaning in current Castilian, even though their meanings in their original language may have been different. Finally, lacking any information about when Basque was first spoken, and whether it was used before the time of the Goths, it is more likely that the Basque language has been enriched from the ruins and debris of the languages spoken earlier in Spain, than to posit its existence and preservation for twenty or more centuries without any substantial change. These reflections are more than enough to undermine the Achilles of Basque lovers. But there is other proof of its novelty provided by its own structure. Nothing certain can be inferred from the Holy Scriptures about the origin of the known languages. It can only be affirmed that God infused some language in Adam and Eve to spare them the long and fastidious work of inventing it. It is clear from the testimony of Moses that the first humans used language from the beginning to communicate with each other, with God, and with the Serpent. But it does not follow from this fact, and from Adam having given names to the animals, either that his language is the most perfect possible, or that it was the one Moses used, or that it was Chaldean, or any other of those in human memory. It is not known whether before the Mosaic Flood there was a multitude of languages, or whether there was just a single language spoken in the world. After the flood that destroyed mankind, except for Noah and his sons, only one language was known in those times, because the population had been reduced to a single family. Nor is it known for certain which language Noah and his sons spoke; but it is quite likely that it was Chaldean or Hebrew, and even more likely that it was the language that Abraham connected with his house and used for keeping the world's promises. At the very least, the Hebrew language of the Pentateuch is known to be more than three thousand years old; and because there is no previous or more illustrious monument for any other language, it has an undeniable right to be considered the language of Noah and his children and most likely the language of Adam and Eve. I am quite aware that not everyone believes this. Some even believe that Hebrew was a language miraculously infused by God in Moses and his people when he went out of Egypt. But even if we accept this unbelievable miracle, Hebrew is more than three thousand years old, and we have no evidence of any older languages. Thus, for lack of other proof, it should be considered one of the most ancient languages, and the only one predating the multiplication of languages after the dispersion of the peoples.

This language consists of roots that generally have two syllables, and there is little flexibility for nouns and verbs. Its grammatical rules are few, and irregularities and anomalies abound. The further back we look, the more impoverished it is in words, less abundant in inflexions and more confined to what is strictly indispensable for the faithful expression of the ideas of the intelligence. Such is the nature of Hebrew, except for the wealth of words; the same is true for Chaldean and Arabic, which can be regarded as dialects of a single language. Hebrew, being confined to a less numerous people, isolated, separated, and having had less contact with others, was preserved without great change until the captivity in Babylon. Because it was a language without contact with others, it remained largely unchanged for a long time, adding few words. Unless it is stabilized by the taste of its writers, not an easy thing to accomplish, no language that is in contact with others can maintain itself over long periods of time without corruption. Forgetfulness of its own words, whimsy, the love of novelty and exoticism, and a thousand chance events make languages change and degenerate. From these reflections, we can deduce from the evidence regarding this matter the utter impossibility that present-day Basque is still approximately the same as the language spoken by its natives two thousand, or even one thousand years ago. From the time of Augustus, and even since the time of Wamba, the Basques have been in forced or voluntary contact with other peoples who spoke differently. They lacked a written language, or at least they have not left us written memoirs in their language, nor is there any reason to believe that they made any special effort to stabilize their language. It is impossible, then, that the Basque language spoken today is not different from that spoken in the country a thousand or two thousand years ago, a difference far greater than the difference between the Latin of the column of Duilius, and the martial verses of Cicero and Caesar. The same lists of words compiled by Father Larramendi to prove what Latin, Spanish, and French borrowed from the Basque language can be used contradictorily to infer that the Basques borrowed them, during their contact with these peoples. In fact, nowadays, and in recent centuries, the Basques, far from lending words to the Castilians, have borrowed many words from them. And that it was the same in more remote centuries is supported by the nature of things, for what is large usually drags along behind it what is small. This is caused too by the greater perfection of the arts and sciences in neighboring populations, from whom the Basques acquired much knowledge and with it the names of the new things. Finally, because Basque is a rich language, full of artifice and very exact rules, fecund in altering nouns and verbs, smooth and in no way barbaric, energetic, and many faceted, it is unbelievable that it is one of the primitive languages, those we know being so poor and deficient in all these features. Two things are never lacking in crude languages: first, words and movement needed to express ideas and to organize and connect them; and second, certain characteristics and contexts of their own for expressing their concepts, which are like the materials and physical properties of architecture that result from their greater unity. But adornment, taste and elegance are only found in cultured languages that are perfected by writers of great skill, or are produced by the slow hand of time through a felicitous conjunction of circumstances. As the Basque language had no ancient writers, its disposition and structure are the daughters of happy circumstance, and the accumulation of words and rules from different languages, combined with love for the country's ancient language. How this came about it is impossible to say with certainty, though the result has all the certainty required. It is quite natural that Basques in the most remote times would have experienced more or less the same political revolutions as other peoples. The history of the Basque Country does not begin until the times of the Seigniory, that is, approximately a century before the Christian era. As the Basques have had contact with the Romans from that time, fought against them, and resisted more than other Spanish provinces the domination of the barbarians of the north until the reign of Wamba, it is utterly unbelievable that the language the Romans encountered there did not suffer considerable change. This continuous contact between Romans and Basques for more than six centuries, and the contact with Spaniards, who spoke a different language, was in our opinion the first cause of the corruption of the ancient Basque language. Hence, contrary to the derivation of Latin words that Father Larramendi believes took place, we believe that it was the Basques who borrowed from Latin. We do not doubt that many words among these were preserved from the ancient language of the country, and that others were derived from the neighboring languages of Spain and France. The Gothic domination, and contact with Aquitaine must have played an important part in the corruption of the language. The Goths established their colonies of Victoriacum [Vitoria-Gasteiz, Araba] and Ologitum [Olite, Navarre] in the conquered country in order to maintain control of the natives. The domination of our Basque people in Aquitaine, combined with the Gothic colonies, must have necessarily caused considerable changes in the customs and language of the country. At the beginning of the twelfth century, a foreign people known by the name "Navarrese" apparently still inhabited the Basque Country, and there are memories of these people as far back as the eighth century. We spoke of them earlier, and expressed our suspicion of their Spanish Gothic origin. Ancient monuments tell us nothing about their language. It is likely that they did not use the language of the country until they intermingled with the native speakers, and that the latter contributed substantially to the formation of present-day Basque. If the western Basques of the province and Seigniory were merged with the Kingdom of Asturias, though this has not been proven, then from the time of the invasion by the Arabs, and the western provinces with the sovereignties of the Pyrenees, the contact with the Asturians, Galicians, and Aragonese, who did not speak Basque, must have changed the language of the country. I do not want to go all the way back to the Dark Ages, and to the Celtic era, whether these were Spanish, or Gauls. What we do know about the history of the last nineteen centuries is sufficient to prove that present-day Basque is not the language the Romans encountered in Spain, nor can the mutability of human experience be denied, as Horace said very well: *Mortalia facta peribunt: Necdum sermonum stat honos, et gratia vivax* [Mortal achievements will be destroyed, and not even the perennial honor and grace of words will be preserved].

With this, we have indicated with sufficient clarity that the sources of the present-day Basque language were the ancient languages of the country, the languages of the neighboring Spanish peoples, whose speech was different according to Strabo, the conquering languages of Romans and Goths with their colonies, the defeated languages of Aquitaine, and those of the Asturians, Galicians, and Aragonese with whom the Basques maintained willing or forced contact from the eighth century until the present time. That vestiges of the ancient language are preserved in the present Basque language is as natural as it is difficult to believe that the native speakers of a province can forget and totally change their pronunciation. That they have borrowed a few, or even many, words from the languages of their Spanish neighbors, which happens on all borders with a different language, is proven sufficiently by the word *Briga* [a common toponymy in the Iberian Peninsula meaning "fortified town" or "burgh"], which is barely encountered three times in all the towns of the Basques, Autrigoni, Varduli, Caristi, and Cantabrians, whereas Lusitania alone offers nine such combinations, according to Ptolemy. So that if *Uriga* or *Uriaga* [town] is the same as *Briga*, by all evidence the Basques must have taken it from the western Celts, and most likely from the Celtic *Broga* [enclosure], no matter what the origin of that country may be. To imagine that the Roman and Gothic domination, and the colonies of these peoples, and the contact with the people of Aquitaine did not change the language in its vocabulary and structure, would be as strange a notion as to say that our conquest of the Americas, where there are Spanish colonies, has not corrupted the language of the Indians, and that the latter have not affected the purity of Castilian. The ancients changed them so much that we are not sure whether the Varduli [people] should be called that, or if they should be called Bardyetas, or Bardyales, or the Autrigoni Alotrigi, or the Conisci, Coniaci, or Concani; and the same with other nations. So the ancient words that the geographers and writers have preserved for us are probably so corrupted that it is very risky to make conjectures about their etymology, for it is obvious that the alteration, or addition or distortion of a letter can alter the meaning considerably.

In light of these reflections and others we could make, there should be little doubt about the corruption and obliteration of the ancient language of the Basques; even less when Strabo, speaking of the Asturians, Galicians, Cantabrians, and Basques, says expressly that in the time of Augustus, those who had previously defeated the Romans in battle, now took up arms in their defense, and that Tiberius, commissioning three cohorts into those countries on direction of Augustus, not only pacified them, but civilized many of the inhabitants. Time must have completed the destruction.

It only remains to ascertain, if possible, how the present language of the Basques was formed. The task is arduous, and it will only be possible to offer some conjectures, which given the lack of certain information may partially satisfy scholarly curiosity. In order to speak with certainty it would have been necessary to know which language the first inhabitants of the Basque Country brought with them, to understand that language and the languages of all the peoples, whose linguistic structure was related to the Basque language. Then it would be possible to make a comparison of the ancient with the present-day language and the stages by which the primitive speech came to be altered. Lacking this information, or any hope of attaining it, it is better to say nothing or to resort to probable conjectures.

. . .

The foregoing discussion should suffice to give some idea of the Basque language, which can be considered basically as a language made up of roots capable of being transformed into nouns or verbs, depending on the particles added to them. In this, it differs remarkably from all the other European languages and this singularity has caused it to be accorded extraordinary antiquity. But because there is no monumental evidence of this language, not only during the past two thousand years but even over the past five hundred, it is impossible to come to a conclusion. One of the modern writers, who has studied languages with a clear appearance of erudition, and who believes that the Basque or Cantabrian language is the ancient language of Iberia, contradicts the claims of those who seek in ancient names the proof of the antiquity of this language, when he reduces to Celtic the origin of the words that end in *-tania*, such as *Lusitania, Oretania, Carpentania, Edertania,* as well as those that begin with *il,* such as *Iliturgi, Ilurci, Iliberis*, etc., which Larramendi and others have regarded as legitimate Basque words. It is customary to follow three rules to examine the kinship between languages: these are words in isolation, grammatical structure, and pronunciation. The first corrupting influence on a language is the adoption of foreign words. When the nomenclature of two nations that are in contact ends up being almost the same, reciprocal usage causes men to adapt themselves to a way of speaking that facilitates their interaction, and grammatical differences begin to be bothersome, embarrassing their intelligence. This annoyance obliges a mutual adaptation of their structure, and in this way the structure of the two languages is corrupted until it degenerates into a third structure that takes from both. In this case, the pronunciation of the two nations, having come to regard themselves as a single people united by blood through marriage, becomes uniform. In this event, because all through recorded history the Basque Country has been limited in size in comparison with Spain and France, and because we know that their language has been more and more confined over the past three hundred years, we have to conclude that in the previous eighteen centuries, during which the Basques were forced into contact with other peoples by non-violent means, they must have borrowed from them, and not contributed substantially to their nomenclature. What is happening now is probably what happened then, that is, that nobody took the trouble to learn the Basque language as the Catalonians and Valencians learn theirs. This practice of learning a foreign language contributes substantially to the corruption of the native language of the country. Seeing then that the ancient inscriptions granting the Basque Country [Vasconia] the privileges and national charters are not in their language, it is clear that the Basques, from our first knowledge of them, must have learned the neighboring languages without the latter having to learn theirs.

During the passing of so many centuries, the first thing to be corrupted was its nomenclature, resulting in the inclusion in its dictionary of a multitude of words derived from Latin, Arabic, French, and Castilian. The Basques have wanted to present themselves as having been alone since the invasion of the Arabs. The incursions of the kings of Asturias into Araba, and the rebellions of the Basques and neighboring peoples against the kings of France and Spain, lead us to suspect that in that period they sought to establish their own language on the ruins of their ancient language, of a Latin that was already corrupted, and of the neighboring languages. The country was inhabited by scattered settlements, and its isolation must have produced a multitude of dialects or accidental variations in declination or conjugation. By gathering in towns and valleys, they must have created a language that was complex in its structure. And finding it easy to speak, they did not hesitate to adopt words from Castile and Aragón, to whom they were subject on several occasions, confident that by adding syllables and disfiguring the words, their neighbors would not understand them. And because they were accustomed to dealing with Castilians and Aragonese since such remote antiquity, it is not surprising that their pronunciation does not have a foreign accent when they learn another language. Meanwhile the Andalusians, who from the time they first learned Castilian have spoken and written it elegantly and properly, disliked the guttural accent of the Arabs, who ruled over them for many centuries; they did not preserve many words from that people in their nomenclature, no more words of Arabic origin than the provinces of Castile. I say that they dislike the guttural accent of the Arabs, following common opinion. But no one has taken the trouble to prove that before the Arabs, there might have already been a guttural pronunciation in Betica, the region south of the Guadalquivir [River]. How many peoples of this region, where the *jota* [guttural letter *j*] is constantly gargled (forgive the expression), were free of contact with Arabs earlier than other cities of the peninsula, where that guttural *j* sound is not known? If the Arabs had conquered the Malayans we would say it was they who imposed that guttural pronunciation, because they pronounce *hari* (king), the way the Andalusian says *jombre* for *hombre* (man). But this is to stray too far into a matter that, in my judgment, is impossible to clarify for lack of monumental evidence. In the meantime, the nomenclature of the Basque language will be for me a collection of words borrowed with more or less alteration from the ancient languages of the country; from neighboring Spain and France, from Celtic, Greek, Breton, Gothic, Norman, Latin, Arabic, and Spanish. As for its structure, more tenacious in ancient usage because it is more difficult to learn grammar than the words of a language, it preserved the radical and primitive simplicity of its declination and conjugation. But because the Basques scarcely had formal towns until the twelfth century, and lived in isolated settlements, it was inevitable that the endings or auxiliaries they used to give movement to their language varied in each settlement, and that when they came together they enriched the common language with their multiplicity. So, in the twelfth century, the language that was introduced in the middle of the eighth century, so that the natives could feign total independence from outsiders, must have begun to take on form and coherence. And because the Basques of this, shall we say, federation were subject in part to Castile, in part to the kings of the Pyrenees, and in part to France, three dialects emerged: those of Gipuzkoa, Bizkaia, and Lapurdi. Nor is the insistence of the Basques on preserving their language without precedent in the nation. The same thing has happened in Catalonia and Valencia with the Limousin dialect, which despite their union with Aragón and Castile, has and continues to survive. In the Basque Country, there is another reason for its survival, and that is so they can have a separate legislation or special *fuero* which, combined with the ruggedness and poverty of the country, keeps outsiders away, for because Basques are given priority for the best civil and ecclesiastical positions, outsiders do not feel welcome in those privileged mountains. This prevents the majority of the Basque people from corrupting their ancient language even further, and even more because very few of those who leave their homes ever come back. Despite these reasons, which ought to stabilize and preserve the Basque language, every day fewer and fewer people speak it, and if its extinction were helped along, in less than two centuries it would be a dead language, like others from whose ruins it was formed in the dark ages.

I understand that my way of thinking will not please everyone, because wonders are naturally pleasing. And for me it would be one of the greatest wonders to prove that Basque or any other language, whose people (few in number) have undeniably lived in contact and dependent on nations that were far more densely populated for almost twenty centuries, was preserved without substantial change, when the peoples living around this region have changed their way of speaking to the point of forgetting what their primitive language was. Nor does the example of China prove anything. This singular nation, although dominated by the Tartars, forced their conqueror to adopt their language and their laws, simply because their population was incomparably greater. The conquered country was a wise people whose language had attained stability through a multitude of writings and their arts had achieved a state of extraordinary perfection. Nor could the conqueror have occupied China without the support and aid of many of the country's inhabitants. For each Tartar there were eleven Chinese, and it was necessary, in order to make themselves understood, for a minority of the conquerors to learn the language of the conquered. Something similar happened to the Goths in Spain, who despite their armed conquest, ceded to the greater number of the native people in terms of language, and forgetting their own, adopted Latin in order to dictate their laws. But nothing like this occurred among the Basques. The Basque population is much smaller than that of the neighboring countries that were forced to interact with them; without having conquered the nearby provinces, only the ruggedness of the mountains and their severe unsociability resulting from living scattered about here and there in settlements in those mountains could have made it possible to gradually form a language that was private and different from those of their neighbors. To pretend that it was the primitive Iberian or Spanish, only slightly changed, seems to me a vanity that has no support except ignorance of the beginnings and development of Basque, and of the etymologies that could just as well allow Hebrew, Celtic, Greek, Latin, and any another language to make such a claim. Time, the great discoverer of things hidden, may perhaps produce more certain data to resolve this question with full knowledge. So far, what has been alleged concerning the extraordinary antiquity of the Basque language does not seem sufficient to remove all doubt, nor to endow with verisimilitude the miracle that this language from the most remote times has been a language rich and organized in its inflections and as cultured and fecund as people claim, positing a certain eternal character to the most decrepit and corruptible object. But let us conclude this article, satisfied to have presented our way of thinking. T.

35. Dominique Joseph Garat Hiriarte

(Baiona [Bayonne], Lapurdi, 1749 – Basusarri, Lapurdi, 1833)

A native of Ustaritze, he was born in Baiona, where his father practiced medicine. A member of the bourgeoisie of Lapurdi, in addition to his medical practice, his father owned a share in a business in Arruntz (Ustaritze) and was beneficiary of a tithe, allowing him to finance his sons' studies comfortably. Consequently, Dominique Joseph studied law and had a law practice in Bordeaux. Then he moved to Paris, where he came in contact with most of the liberal intellectuals of the Enlightenment—such as Rousseau, D'Alembert, Buffon, Condillac—becoming a follower of the linguistic philosophy of the latter, identifying the "genius" of a people with their language. A journalist, philosopher and theorist of natural law, Garat was repeatedly honored by the French Academy, but he is best known as a politician. Elected together with his brother Joseph (with whom he is often confused) as delegate to the General Estates of 1789 by the magisterial district of Lapurdi, he would have to be categorized politically as sympathizing with Girondist, rather than Jacobin, ideology; while always trying to occupy the middle ground between the two. He held the position of Minister of Justice in 1792, and Minister of the Interior in 1793. By virtue of his position, it was his duty to carry out the communication of the death sentence of Louis XVI, even though he opposed it. Arrested on two occasions in August 1793, after Robespierre's rise to power, he was never brought to trial. After the coup d'état of the Ninth Thermidor (in the summer of 1794) that brought to an end Robespierre's reign, he was named professor of philosophy at the Paris normal (teacher-training) school. In Year Seven of the revolutionary calendar (1798–99), he was elected a member of the Council of Five Hundred (the lower house of the legislature established by the 1795 Constitution), rising to the presidency. Close to Abbé Sieyès, he supported Napoleon in his rise to power, was elected senator, and in 1808, Count of the Empire. He retired from political life after the Restoration of 1814–15, moving to Basusarri, and was later appointed to the Academy of Moral and Political Sciences in 1832, following the restoration of that body.

His relationship with the Empire kept changing. Initially he enjoyed the trust of Napoleon, being commissioned to Holland to look for a way to annex this territory into the Empire. However, the conclusions of his report, advocating freedoms for Holland, were not what Bonaparte wanted, leading subsequently to a significant decline in his political influence. It may have been for this reason that when Garat submitted some recommendations related to his native Basque Country, they were received so coldly by the Emperor. The first of these recommendations was submitted in 1808 to the Duke of Rovigo, commandant at the time of the French troops occupying Spain. When Garat saw that his recommendation was not only being ignored, but that the strategy of the French Empire regarding the occupied regions north of the Ebro was to organize them differently, with the creation of distinct military commands in Navarre, the Basque provinces, and Catalonia, in 1811 he sent another memorandum. This time, he directed his concerns to Marat, Duke of Bassano, the French Minister of Foreign Affairs at the time. There is no evidence that Napoleon directly evaluated Garat's proposals. In substance, what he proposed was the creation of a buffer state between Spain and France, dependent, of course, on the latter and made up of all the Basque provinces on both sides of the Pyrenees; and whose potential maritime power might serve as a counterweight to the British navy. The proposal combined French interests with Garat's ideas of nationhood for the Basque Country. He identified the Basque nation with Basque culture, and in particular with the Basque language, so that the seven provinces where Basque was spoken constituted a nation that should aspire to become a state. The administration of this Basque state proposed by Garat was, of course, modeled on the French Republic, with subdivisions into two or three departments, for which he even suggested possible names: New Phoenicia, New Tyre, and New Sidon; names derived from Garat's belief in the linguistic connections between the Basques and the Phoenicians. The 1811 memorandum was an extensive treatise of 126 folios in which many observations of a political, strategic, anthropological, and ethnographic nature were made. The title under which the unpublished manuscript is preserved is *Recherches sur le peuple Primitif de l'Espagne, sur les révolutions de cette peninsule, sur les basques espagnols et français* (Studies of the Primitive People of Spain, the Revolutions in That Peninsula, and the Spanish and French Basques).

Given these assumptions, it should be no surprise that, in his proposals, Garat gave particular emphasis to the linguistic aspects of this Basque state. With regard to Euskara, which he characterized as the "sacred fire of these people," he proposed that it be the official language, that education be conducted in it, especially the maritime studies it would have to encourage, and finally that efforts should be made to unify the language in order to overcome the difficulties produced by division into dialects. In his own words,

> It is strongly recommended that no one should be employed in these departments except true Basques fluent in the language spoken in Tyre and on Tyrian ships. It would seem best to me that teaching in the public schools be conducted in the same language, but any effort to restore the language to its ancient purity would be a vain illusion bordering on madness . . . Prior to the revolution on both

> sides of the Pyrenees, almost all Basques, no matter how uneducated, knew how to read and write; if they lost this basic ability they would soon be able to recover it, and all hydrographic knowledge crucial to the art of navigation, which is of general use to sailors, would have to be taught to them in Basque . . . The Basque language should be encouraged, studied systematically, and differences between dialects eliminated, bringing them all under a common umbrella.

Among the papers that Garat wrote but did not publish are several reflections on the Basque language. Specifically, in some notes titled *Sur l'usage et l'emploi de la langue basque* (On the Use and Usage of the Basque Language) he insists on a point that was of particular concern to him: namely, that the survival of the language depended on the establishment of its written form. For Garat, the maintenance of the language at a level that was almost exclusively oral and fragmented dialectically would open the way to penetration by loan words from Castilian and French, and therefore to its definitive decline and disappearance. Consequently, the way to guarantee its survival was through stabilization. As he understood it,

> languages, before being written, are not maintained pure of all contamination until the people live separated from each other; the Basques today have much contact with the French and the Spaniards, and their language will be lost if it is not stabilized in good written works. Some contamination has already appeared, announcing more to come.[1]

As indicated, his main theoretical effort in relation to the Basque language was the demonstration that it descended from Phoenician. For this reason, he rejected the Iberianst theories of Humboldt and, of course, the paradisiacal and Tubalist pretensions of a religious nature of the "Spanish" apologists, reaffirming that the Basque language belonged to the Semitic stem and had been imported from Asia. Nonetheless, among the authors he refutes, he includes "Spanish" (Sorreguieta, Astarloa, Erro, and Larramendi, "the old man from Bergara") as well as "French" (Iharce de Bidassouet, Chaho) writers.

---

1. Dominique Joseph Garat, "Sur l'usage et l'emploi de la langue basque," *Gure Herria* 4 (1924), 704–06.

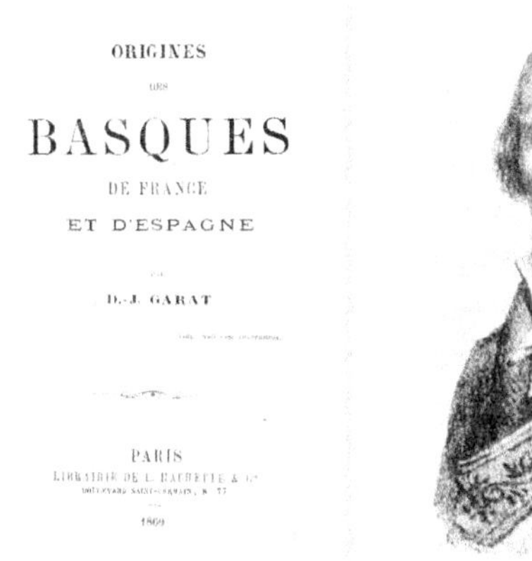

ORIGINES

BASQUES

DE FRANCE

ET D'ESPAGNE

D.-J. GARAT

PARIS

Selected Text(s):

Origines des basques de France et d'Espagne [Origins of the Basques of France and Spain] (Paris: Hachette, 1869), 207–11, 221–23, 239–40, 251–54, 260–61.

Until the recent era, it was less than a century ago that Mr. de Mazade claimed that the academicians of Marseille thought in Provençal before writing in French: after Louis XIV demanded that the language of Roussillon no longer be used in that province for the conduct of civil ceremonies, the French language has subsequently been imposed on all French cities.

This has not been the case in the countryside, where the ancient languages have not been banished; and if you could not locate the borders of Provençe, Languedoc, Gascoigne, Limousin, Saintonge, Poitou, Alsace, and Brittany, all you would have to do to locate them would be to listen to the people who live in them.

For the Basque Country, there would be no need to wonder: the Basques only speak and understand Euskara; religious sermons are still addressed to them in that language.

. . .

The pride the Basques feel for their language is somewhat surprising, because on first sight one might say of it what Molière said about the integrity of the beggar: "Where does he keep it? Is it real?" Is it true, as certain authors have claimed, that the Basque language is the most authentic evidence of the antiquity of these people?

Only trite commonplaces about the origins and kinship of the Basques would allow us to give an affirmative response to this question. The Basque people being the authentic descendants of the Cantabrians, it was necessary for them to believe that the Basque language was as free of change as were their ancestors; it had to be derived from the language of the Cantabrians just as the latter had to be the descendants of the founders of Basque nationality; in other words, the Basque language is derived from the language of the Phoenicians, and the languages of its Semitic descendants.

The conclusion is inevitable; they could not allow it to be invalidated by the duality or plurality of the founders of Basque nationality.

The history of a language is always linked to the social history of the people who speak it. If the founders of the Basque nationality were of Semitic origin, their languages being necessarily united among themselves by family kinships comparable to the analogies existing among Indo-European languages, those language would merge effortlessly with the Basque language, just as, following the collapse of the Roman empire and the invasions of the German people from central Europe, the recasting of Latin merged with the Romance languages, and ultimately with Spanish and French.

Despite the changes caused by contact with neighboring countries, despite the adoption of foreign words required for the expression of new ideas and needs, the Basque language has not lost its personality; it has maintained it all the more because it has not been spoken by learned men, but has been restricted to peasants in rural areas, so that its domain has never been invaded, except during brief periods, by peoples of Indo-European race. Thus, having attributed the preservation of the Basques to their unenviable poverty and customs that kept them aloof from bordering populations, Mr. de Chausenque, in the study of the Pyrenees that he published in 1823, claimed that the Basques gave birth to the language of their founders, and that Basque is a "matrix language." Senator Joseph Garat and Mr. Arbanère, cited elsewhere, have come to the same conclusion; because the Basques, according to them, are descendants of the Phoenicians, they are persuaded that the Basques preserved the language of the Phoenicians.

It would seem that both the learned Klaproth, who discovered in the Basque language a large number of forms proper to the languages of Asia, and Scaliger, who considers this language contemporary with Hebrew, would have had no difficulty supporting these conclusions, even though they were not formulated according to the scientific method.

Basque, then, is not some crude dialect. If some writers have condemned it as such, it is because they failed to learn and study it; it is because, as M. E. Renan has said, we are inclined to regard languages we do not know, as mere jargons.

To judge the Basque language in this way would be frivolous and ignorant.

. . .

Why have Spanish historiographers, who attributed the origins of the Basques to Noah only because the Basque language was different from all the ancient and modern languages they had compared it to—why would they have hesitated to believe that Basque was the language of Noah, and consequently the language of Adam? They were entitled to do so; they granted themselves the freedom they denied others.

I will begin therefore with details that do not, I believe, detract in any way from the serious character I am accustomed to confer on my work. Later on, additionally, I will reveal their importance. At this juncture, as will be seen, they are but an hors-d'oeuvre.

According to don Pablo de Astarloa, the language, which the Eternal deity taught to Adam and Eve, and which the children of our first parents passed on to Noah, was given by that patriarch to Japheth, who in turn transmitted it to Tubal.

Tubal took his Asian family away when there was but one language and one way of speaking on the entire earth. In this way, he and the people who followed him escaped the punishment inflicted on the pride of his brothers, who said to each other: "Let us build a tower, whose top may reach unto heaven" [Genesis, II: 4] and he took to the western Pyrenees that Adamic language which, according to a Spanish historiographer, was none other than "the language of the gods spoken of in Homer."

Superior to all languages because of its priority, the Basque language also had to be thought superior to them for its perfection: thus, all of its Spanish glorifiers have affirmed its universality, its dominance, its naturalism, the wealth of its inflexions, nuances and allusions; they insist that it has more roots than any of the other seventy-two languages that were spontaneously infused "when the Lord came down to see the tower of Babel that the children of Adam were building as so completely confused their language that they could not understand each other." They say too that it is as natural to man as cooing is to pigeons, barking to dogs, and bellowing to bulls. They say that the words *papa*, *mama*, *titi*, etc., which mean "eat," "breast" and "suckle" in Basque, prove that all babies, in all countries, speak Basque to their parents initially; that its roots are so deeply embedded in the nature of things that they lead us to the origin of all the arts and sciences, that its nouns for enumeration sum up in thirteen words the principles of natural philosophy, and that the numerical mysteries of Plato and Pythagoras are based on the Basque number system.

. . .

It is clear that Mr. Humboldt could not be defended.

In conclusion then, I have earned the right to say, not like M. A. Montel, that Monsieur de Humboldt "has identified Basque with the Iberian language, with no other evidence than some absurd etymologies"; but that this language which "more than the physical character of the Basques, reveals their singular originality as a people and their isolation as a race" was not the language of the Iberian peninsula; that "philology does not oblige us to acknowledge the Basques as Iberians," so that the language of the Basques is the product of the fusion of Semitic-Phoenician languages.

A profound study of the Basque language through the comparison of its vocabulary with all other vocabularies, ancient and modern; through the examination of its grammatical forms, its laws, its derivations; through the distinction of elements of the same family that went into its formation; through the demonstration of its influence on the Iberian languages, Celtic, Latin-Spanish, and French spoken around it; and finally the study of the phenomena that, like all languages, Basque reproduced, did not weaken my theory in any way.

Primitive languages have come forth with the psychological state they represent, and one can doubt, despite Mr. Jacob Grimm's assertion in a Memorandum to the Academy of Berlin, that the problem of the origin of languages can ever be resolved in a scientific manner.

Were it not so, the debris of the primitive languages would contain, as has been said, "the archives of humanity," and it would be possible to interpret and decipher the archives of the Basque language, and make a scientific proof of the origin I have attributed to it, which my inability, I regret to admit, kept me from going in pursuit of an event that the wisest and most authoritative scholars have not attempted to discover.

The obstacles that existed at the very beginning of these investigations through pre-historic periods will become apparent if we recall that Basque is divided into seven dialects; that the experts have most often undertaken a superficial study of only one of these, and that more frequently they have claimed as a common characteristic of the language some feature specific to just the one of these dialects on which they have focused their investigation.

But if it seems impossible to write the history of the mental work that governs the formation of Basque, to follow its periods of change, growth, and decline, at least it is not forbidden to acknowledge that it has preserved the signs of its original type and its primitive procedures; to verify that it should be granted the most remote antiquity, that its intimate character should cause it to be placed among the family of Semitic languages.

The proof is to be found in the conclusions of the writers I have already analyzed.

. . .

The justification of the antiquity of the origin of the Basques can also be derived from the negative conclusions that have been formulated with regard to the antiquity of their language. The proposition is not paradoxical, as one might think: I will explain what I mean in the course of demonstrating it.

The refusal of some writers to admit that Basque has a quality of its own; their characterization they have formed of it as a patois, an obscure, formless language, made up of bits and pieces; the astonishment of some and the negligence of others; the enthusiasm of the Spanish glorifiers, who have claimed that its paternity can be traced back to Noah; the surprise it produces to the ear of tourists not involved in linguistic preoccupations, but attentive and intelligent—all these manifestations are essentially the same.

Or at least they all proceed from the same cause: the incapacity of each of these groups to recognize or imagine that Basque did not belong to the family of Indo-European languages.

. . .

The survival of a language is a phenomenon similar to the survival of a race. If the conquering peoples do not totally destroy the conquered, the language of the conquered fuses with the language of the conquerors and preserves it in recognizable form.

I will say then in conclusion, because I have every right to do so: Because history obliges us to believe that the Basques replaced the Cantabrians, it is obligatory to believe that the Basques speak the language of the Cantabrians, and that the latter spoke the language of the Semitic-Phoenician peoples, their ancestors.

With the Spanish historiographers, I have not had to avoid assuming that the Basque language was connected with the period when the mystery of the appearance of speech took place; but without leaving the realm of speculative erudition, basing my study on the scholarship I have accumulated, on the conclusions that flow from them, guided by the evaluations of the most highly regarded authorities, I have posed in principle, and have reason to believe, that the Basque language dates from those epochs when, as Mr. Littré has asserted, the ascent of humanity has no proportion with historical development; that the claim to antiquity, if we want to grant it to Hebrew, can only be traced that far back because there are books in Hebrew and there are no surviving books from Sidon or Tyre; that if the Basque language does not predate the theocratic language, it is at least contemporary with it; that, like the language of Israel, it has preserved the physiognomy of the Semitic languages; that it is one of the varieties of that family of languages; the language of the Phoenicians, combined with the languages of their allies in Asia being the most essential characteristic of the origin and antiquity of the French and Spanish Basque languages.

36. Henri Grégoire, known as "the Abbé Grégoire"

(Gregory the Abbot) (Vého, 1759 – Paris, 1831)

The son of a tailor, he received a Jesuit education in Nancy, later becoming a teacher and an ordained priest. A representative for the clergy in the Estates General in 1789, he swore an oath of allegiance to the Civil Constitution of the Clergy in 1790 and was later appointed the constitutional Bishop of Loir-et-Cher and Blois. He tried to construct a kind of "republican Christianity," organizing the National Council of 1797. Motivated by a strong spirit of idealism and Enlightenment principles, he actively participated in political activities during the early years of the French Revolution, seeking through his projects and memoranda to provide an ethical orientation to some of the areas of action that concerned him; and of course, he was one of those who voted against the execution of the king. Beyond the linguistic question, our principal focus here, there were two other important aspects of Grégoire's political and cultural activity: During the Convention (1792–95), he forced the vote for the abolition of slavery. He was a member of the *Société des Amis des Noirs* (Society of Friends of Black People) and struggled to make real the Declaration of the Rights of Man and the Citizen with all its consequences. He also wrote a blueprint for the formation of a *Conservatoire des Arts et Métiers* (Conservatory of Arts and Crafts) in Paris. This was to be "a repository of machines, models, tools, designs, and bibliography for all genres of arts and crafts"; that is, a kind of encyclopedic accumulation of knowledge of technology, but in practical fashion and not restricted to book-bound theoretical knowledge. In 1802, the *Galeries d'Arts et Métiers* (Arts and Crafts Galleries)—which today is a museum by the same name—opened its doors, in the former priory of Saint-Martin-des-Champs. Thus, the Abbé Grégoire became the first defender of industrial and technological patrimony.

His report submitted to the Convention about the method for destroying non-French languages and dialects spoken in France constitutes (together with that of Bertrand Barére de Vieuzac) the key theoretical work for the creation of the revolutionary linguistic policy. The report is based on a large ethnographic survey, the *Questionnaire relative aux patois et aux moeurs des gens des campagnes* (Questionnaire About the Dialects and Customs of People in Rural Areas), which Grégoire carried out in most of France. In addition to a providing a photograph of the linguistic situation in France at that time, it also offered a vast amount of information on the cultural situation in general. *Rapport sur la nécesité et les moyens d'anéantir les patois et d'universaliser l'usage de la langue française* (Report on the Necessity and the Means for Obliterating Dialects and Generalizing Use of the French Language) (1794). Consistent with his thinking, he conceived the substitution of Latin by French in the liturgy, and a plan for public education that would facilitate the spread of French to the large numbers of speakers of other languages in the Republic. He was an advocate of extending primary education to girls as well, of encouraging technical studies, and promoting normal (teacher-training) schools.

Selected Text(s):

"Rapport sur la nécesité et les moyens d'anéantir les patois et d'universaliser l'usage de la langue française, 16 Prairial, an II" (Report on the Necessity and Means for Obliterating Dialects and Generalizing Use of the French Language, 16 Prairial [Pasture month], year II) (1794). In *Une politique de la langue. La Revolution française et les patois: l'enquéte de Grégoire* [A Politics of Language: The French Revolution and Dialects: Grégoire's Investigation], ed. Michel de Certeau, Dominique Julia, and Jacques Revel (Paris: Gallimard, 2002), 331–51.

National Convention
Public Education
Report

ON THE NECESSITY AND MEANS FOR OBLITERATING DIALECTS AND UNIVERSALIZING THE USE OF THE FRENCH LANGUAGE

By Grégoire

Meeting of the 16th Prairial, year II of the Republic, One and Indivisible; followed by the decree of the National Convention, published by order of the National Convention, and distributed to the constituted authorities, popular societies, and to all the communities of the Republic.

The French language has earned the respect of Europe, and after a century is now regarded as a classic. My intent is not to address the causes that have won it this prerogative. Ten years ago in Germany, in the city of Berlin, there was an enlightened discussion of this matter, which, according to one writer, may have flattered the pride of Rome, eager to consecrate it within its history as one of the *belle époques*. We are aware of the efforts of Roman politics to universalize its language, refraining from using any other in addressing or negotiating with foreign ambassadors; and despite its efforts, it only partially attained the free approval accorded to the French language. It is well known that in 1774, French was used to draft the treaty between the Turks and the Russians. After the peace of Nimègue, it was prostituted, so to speak, by governmental conspiracies in Europe. In its clear, methodical movement, thought unfolds easily, giving it a character of reason and probity that even liars find most useful for protecting themselves against Russian diplomats.

If our language has received such homage from tyrants and courts, where the French monarchy gave its theatres, its pompoms, customs, and manners, should not it receive an even warmer welcome from the people to whom Republican France reveals their rights by setting them on the course toward freedom?

But what fatality has caused this language, accepted for political transactions, spoken in a number of cities in Germany, Italy, the Netherlands, in parts of the country of Liège, Luxembourg, Switzerland, even in Canada, and south of the Mississippi Delta, to be largely unknown, even now, to the French people?

Through all the revolutions, Celtic, which was the first language of Europe, is still spoken in one province of France and in some of the cantons of the British Isles. We know that the Welsh, the Cornish, and the Bretons understand it; this indigenous language went through successive changes. Twenty-four centuries ago, the Phocaeans founded brilliant colonies along the coasts of the Mediterranean; and in a song from the region of Marseille, Greek fragments of an ode to the wine harvest by Pindar have been recently discovered. The Carthaginians crossed the Pyrenees, and Polybius tells us that many Gauls learned the Punic language in order to converse with the soldiers of Hannibal.

Throwing off the Roman yoke, Gaul fell under the domination of the Franks. The Vandals, Goths, Arabs, and English, after having invaded in turn, were all driven out. And our language and the various dialects spoken in France still bear traces of the passage or occupation by these peoples.

Feudalism then came in to parcel up this beautiful country, and to carefully preserve this disparity of languages as a way of recognizing and controlling the fugitive serfs and forging their chains. Even today, the territorial extension where certain dialects are spoken is determined by the boundaries of ancient feudal domination. This explains the great similarity between the dialects of Bouillon and Nancy, which are forty leagues apart and were formerly ruled by the same tyrants; whereas the dialect of Metz, situated not far from Nancy, is quite different from it, because for several centuries the country of Messin, organized as a republic, was in constant war with Lorraine.

There are only fifteen departments in the interior where the French language is exclusively spoken; it is still undergoing perceptible changes, either in pronunciation, or in the usage of improper or outdated terms, especially toward Sancerre, where you can hear fragments of expressions of Rabelais, Amyot, and Montaigne.

We have no other provinces, and we still have some thirty dialects in which to remember their names.

It may be of some use to enumerate them: the dialects of Brittany, Normandy, Picardy, Wallonia, Flanders, Champagne, Metz, Lorraine, Franche-Comté, Burgundy, Bresse, Lyon, the Dauphiné, the Auvergne, Poitiers, Limousin, Picardy, Provence, the Languedoc, Velay, Catalonia, Béarn, the Basque Country, Rouergue and Gascony; the latter [Gascon] alone is spoken in an area of sixty square leagues.

The name "dialect" should be given also to the Italian spoken in Corsica, the Maritime Alps, and the German spoken in the Upper and Lower Rhine, because those two languages are seriously corrupted.

Finally, the blacks in our colonies, whom you have turned into men, have a kind of poor language like that of the Hottentots, or the Frankish language, which only uses the infinitive for all its verbs.

In truth, a number of these dialects are the same generically; they have a similar physiognomy, with only a few traits with differences in accentuation no greater than that between the suburbs of the same town, such as Salins and the Free Commune.

This disparity is conserved in a more striking manner in the villages situated along the opposite banks of a river, where, for lack of a bridge, communications were very rare in the past. The journey from Strasbourg to Brest is easier today than it was formerly. Over a course of twenty leagues, and near Saint-Claude today, in the department of Jura, you still hear people making reference (so they say) to "the eve of a long journey," because you had to go by way of Besançon, which was the capital of the province.

It can be stated without exaggeration that at least six million French citizens, especially in the countryside, cannot speak the national language; that an equal number can barely carry on a dialogue; that as a last result, the number of those who speak it is under three million, and the number of those who write it correctly probably even less,

Thus, with thirty different dialects, we are still, in terms of language, at the Tower of Babel, while, because of our freedom, we form the avant-garde of nations.

Whatever the possibility of reducing the number of received languages in Europe, the political state of the globe banishes the hope of gathering the peoples under a common language. This concept, formed by some writers, is as bold as it is chimerical. A universal language is, linguistically, what the philosopher's stone is chemically.

But at least it is possible to make the language of a great nation uniform so that all the citizens, who constitute it, can feel unhindered in expressing their thoughts. This enterprise, which has never been executed by any people, is worthy of the French people, who are centralizing all the branches of society, and who should be even more eager to consecrate, within a single and indivisible Republic, the sole and invariable use of the language of freedom.

In the report of its Committee of Public Safety, the National Convention decreed, on 8th Pluviôse, that institutions should be established to teach our language in the departments where it is least known. This measure, most salutary, but which does not extend to all those who speak a dialect, should be supported by the enthusiasm of the citizens. The sweet voice of persuasion can accelerate the epoch when those feudal languages will have disappeared. Perhaps one of the most effective means for energizing the citizens is to prove to them that the knowledge and use of the national language are crucial to the preservation of freedom. True republicans need only be shown the benefit; they need not be commanded to attain it.

The two most useful and most neglected sciences are the culture of man and the culture of the land: no one has better understood the value of these than our brothers the Americans, in whose land everyone knows how to read, write, and speak the national language.

The barbaric man, so to speak, is merely unlearned; in Europe, the civilized man is worse: he is degraded.

The resurrection of France is being achieved in an impressive manner. It sustains itself with dignity; but the restoration of a people to freedom cannot consolidate their existence except by customs and understanding. Let us acknowledge that we have much to do in that regard.

All the members of the realm are free to hold jobs anywhere; it is to be desired that they can all take turns occupying them, and then return to their agricultural or mechanical professions. That state of things offers us the following dilemma: if jobs are held by men who cannot speak or write in the national language, can the rights of the citizens be properly guaranteed by acts whose composition will present mistaken terms, imprecise ideas, and, in a word, all the symptoms of ignorance? If, on the contrary, this ignorance excludes people from positions, soon we will see a rebirth of that aristocracy that formerly made use of dialect to demonstrate their patronizing affability to those they insolently referred to as "the little people." Soon society will be reinfected by "the right kind of people." Freedom to vote will be restrained, the cabals will be easier to nourish, more difficult to break, and, by that very fact, among two separate classes a kind of hierarchy will be established. Thus, ignorance of the language would compromise the social wellbeing or destroy equality.

The people have to know the laws in order to sanction them and obey them; and so great was the ignorance of some communities during the initial stages of the Revolution that, confusing all concepts, connecting incoherent and absurd ideas, they were convinced that the word decree meant a warrant for the arrest, and that consequently a decree should be issued to kill all those who were formerly privileged; and one man wrote an anecdote to me about this matter that would be funny if it were not deplorable: In one community the citizens said: "It would be a hard thing to have to kill Mr. Geffry, but at least he would not have to suffer." Through the curtain of ignorance, this anecdote punctures the naiveté of men, who try to calculate in advance ways, to reconcile humanity with obedience.

Are you suggesting that such ignorance can be overcome with translations? You would simply multiply the costs by complicating the political gears; you would slow things down. Let us add that most of the common dialects resist translation or allow only unfaithful ones. If the political party can hardly be believed in our own language, how unreliable will it be in languages abounding in sentimental expressions for painting the sweet effusions of the heart, but utterly lacking in terms related to politics; other dialects are crude, clumsy jargons, without a definite syntax because the language is always the measure of the genius of a people. Words do not grow, except through the advance in ideas and needs. Leibniz was right. Words are letters for changing understanding; so, if new ideas are acquired, new terms will be needed lest the equilibrium be broken. Rather than abandon this enterprise to the caprices of ignorance, it is better to offer our language. Besides, men in the countryside, little accustomed to generalizing their ideas, will always lack abstract terms; and this inevitable poverty of language that narrows the spirit will mutilate your discourses and your decrees, or at the very least render them untranslatable.

This disparity of dialects has frequently blocked the operations of your officers in their departments. Those who found themselves in the Eastern Pyrenees [department] in 1792 will write to you saying that among the Basques, a gentle, brave people, many are subject to fanaticism because the language is an obstacle to the spread of knowledge. The same thing has happened in other departments, where bandits base the success of their counter-revolutionary machinations on the ignorance of our language.

Near the borders in particular the dialects, common to the people on both sides, establish dangerous relations with their enemies to such an extent that within the territory of the Republic all those jargons function as so many barriers breeding commercial activities at the expense of social relations. Through the respective influence of customs on language, and language on customs, the political amalgam is undermined and a single people turned into thirty different peoples. This observation takes on great weight if we consider that, for lack of mutual understanding, many men are murdered and that often the bloody quarrels between nations, like the silly quarrels between schoolboys, were nothing but veritable word-fights. So, it is necessary for the unity of language among the children of the same family to extinguish the vestiges of hostilities resulting from ancient provincial divisions and tighten the bonds of friendship that should bring brothers together.

37. Pablo Pedro de Astarloa y Aguirre

(Durango, Bizkaia, 1752 – Madrid, 1806)

His grandfather, Francisco, was a local dignitary who held a number of posts in the Durango City Hall. His father, Juan Bautista, was a lawyer for the Royal Councils, delegate and attorney general of the Seigniory of Bizkaia, and mayor of Durango. His older brother, José Antonio, was attorney for the Royal Chancery of Valladolid and, as primogenitor, executor of the family estate, so that Pablo Pedro, being the second-born son, was given an education to prepare him for a comfortable ecclesiastical career. He studied Latin, arts, and letters in the town of his birth. He then took courses in philosophy at the University of Oñati (Gipuzkoa) and ecclesiastical studies in the seminary of Vitoria (Gasteiz), Araba. In 1782, he was ordained priest and attained a parochial benefice and chaplaincy of the *Cofradía del Rosario* (Rosary Guild) in his home town of Durango. But his life there was always complicated, embroiled in endless lawsuits, and a depressing economic situation. His problems with the law ran the spectrum from debt, to pressures from the mother of his illegitimate son. Astarloa was even jailed in Logroño, La Rioja, in 1797. In 1802, his economic circumstances worsened together with those of his birthplace, Durango. Specifically, its coffers had been exhausted following the War of the Convention between Spain and France, and this lead Astarloa to go to Madrid in search of better fortune, accepting a number of parochial offices. Additionally, his friends had been encouraging him for some time to leave the limited horizons of Durango and broaden his linguistic investigations. Undoubtedly, his contact with Wilhelm von Humboldt was decisive in that regard. The same year the dictionary of the Academy of History was published (1802), Astarloa began a debate with Joaquín Traggia over his negative treatment of the Basque language in terms of its antiquity, perfection, and excellence. José Antonio Conde sided with Traggia, and Astarloa continued his opposition to both of them until his death in 1806. In effect, we can say that Astarloa's life and work were devoted to this debate, and his apologetic efforts articulated this. In his will, he entrusted the publication of his unpublished work to his friends Juan Bautista Erro and Juan Antonio Zamácola.

He was possessed of vast knowledge, especially of languages, apparently learning as many as sixty according to the testimonies of his contemporaries. Of course, his primary interest was to prove the superiority of Euskara, accumulating for that purpose as many grammars of other languages as he could find, in order to make all possible comparisons. To this end, he only learned what he needed to prove his points, without acquiring any profound or complete knowledge of such languages. In effect, according to Moguel, Astarloa only knew Basque, Castilian, and Latin, and could translate from French. The worst part was that Astarloa only knew Bizkaian Basque perfectly, and had no more than a modest knowledge of other dialectical variations of Euskara. This led him to base all of his speculations on the dialects he knew and to make audacious comparisons between the three of Bizkaia, Gipuzkoa, and Lapurdi with the Holy Trinity, having no idea that Euskara had twice that number with a literary status. Apart from his polemical efforts, he did extensive research, although most of his works were published belatedly, left unpublished, or disappeared. His concerns spanned the gamut from the need for an "Art," or grammar, to a dictionary, leading him to compile collections of adages, surnames, and geographical terms. He belongs to what we can refer to as the "paradisiacal" school of Euskara, which includes Moguel and later writers like Julio Cejador. For Astarloa the Basque language, given its intrinsic perfection, had to be the language spoken in Paradise by Adam and Eve, and therefore directly inspired by God. In this notion, Astarloa was merely continuing a process begun by Andrés de Poza and Baltasar de Echave, and completed by Juan de Perochegui and Manuel de Larramendi to its logical conclusion, bolstered by further erudition and brought up to date.

Astarloa, working from a naturalistic premise key to the Enlightenment, thought that "language should be a mirror or sign of nature," and thus he persisted in trying to discover the entire array of natural elements in the Basque language. The sounds of nature would have their own meaning, and be proof of the character of humanity's primitive language that he attributed to Basque. In other words, phoneme and morpheme would be unified by giving the former its appropriate meaning.

Astarloa established the paradigm of this signifying characteristic of sounds in connection with gender, which, according to him, was carried by the "e" (feminine) and the "a" (masculine). The well-known anecdote as to how this came to be ascertained is worth recounting here. A child was brought to be baptized in Durango, and he cried in the vowel "a"; Astarloa remarked to the nurse how precocious he was to have learned the alphabet, and she replied: "*Ezta bada, jauna, aarra?*" (Sir, is he not, after all, a boy?), because in her mind boys always cried in the vowel "a" and girls in "e." Astarloa set about confirming this fact and used it as the basis of his linguistic theories. Subsequently, Sabino Arana and Koldo Eleizalde made use of this idea to elaborate their *Izendegi* (Catalogue of Names), and it has been perpetuated to this day in Basque names such as *Koldobika/Koldobike*, *Iokin/Iokiñe*, *Iulen/Iulene*, *Joseba/Josebe*, etc.

Probably, Astarloa's most serious error, and one common to earlier as well as contemporary writers, was the assumption that the Basque language was afflicted by (or better, enjoyed) a kind of paralysis that prevented it from evolving, remaining exactly as it had been formed in ancient times, whereas all other languages evolved with the passing of time. This fixed linguistic quality opened the way to every comparative conjecture without any awareness that medieval dirges had little connection with the language of Axular, which in turn had little to do with the language used by Astarloa. Nonetheless, Astarloa deserves credit for having been the first to analyze the Basque verb in depth and to unearth its basic principles, which was no small accomplishment. In pioneering fashion, he both defended the idea that every verb implies movement and rejected the idea of the verb in isolation, arguing that in Basque any noun could be converted into a verb by adding the suffix *–tu*. Of course, his analyses were always passed through a metaphysical sieve that was his trademark. In his own words,

> in its verb, the Basque language is a living portrait of nature. If nature has two different ways of acting, our language finds analogies for them by dividing its verb: namely, with the double verb it describes those actions carried out in conjunction with another agent; and with the simple verb it characterizes those enacted by lone entities, without the help of another subject.[1]

---

1. Pablo Pedro Astarloa, *Apología de la lengua Bascongada o ensayo crítico-filosófico de su perfección y antigüedad sobre todas las que se conocen: en respuesta a los reparos propuestos en el Diccionario geográfico histórico de España, tomo segundo, palabra Navarra, por . . .* (Madrid: Jerónimo Ortega, 1803), 28.

The most serious and prestigious scholars of his day appreciated Astarloa for his great capacity for study and dedication, and his erudition, but they pointed out how his naiveté and excessive passion largely discredited his investigations. Moguel, for example, said of Astarloa: "he is skilled, has done extensive study in language. I do not wish to cast aspersions on his talent and gifts; but neither do I wish to conceal from Your Worship that his methodological naiveté and fiery temperament, putting even Larramendi's to shame, will not be pleasing to critics of good taste. He is too metaphysical, and much of what he has written is pure gibberish." Moguel was even afraid that Astarloa's exaggerations might undermine his own efforts to defend Euskara: "Astarloa's Asiatic boasting in the work he published in the *Gaceta* is going to discredit our language and give ammunition to its enemies, even to Traggia." Humboldt, for his part, although he respected Astarloa's work, did not hide his feeling that "he has girded himself, unfortunately, with all the national prejudices of his race and considers his own language to be the only one so complete, wondrous, and perfect that nothing that does not originate directly from God can even be compared with it. Hence, his most judicious and interesting observations are always mixed with a rash of totally erroneous opinions, baseless assertions, and etymologies impossible to support." As for Gaspar Melchor de Jovellanos, one of the most important men of letters in Spain at this time, he mistrusted Astarloa's etymologies, and in his system in general "which seems very speculative to me, particularly difficult, not to mention that his principles have still not been accepted and proven."

Astarloa is the perfect embodiment of the apologist of the language, who writes for outsiders, so that it is all done in Castilian. There are only two (anonymously published) Basque texts that he might have penned. The first is a leaflet with Latin verses related to the coronation of Carlos, with versions in Castilian and Basque, signed D. P. P. A.,[2] and which was by all appearances written by Astarloa. The second is a panegyric poem dedicated to the Count of Peñaflorida, hand-written and signed "a Friend of the Basques" in Durango in 1782.[3] Apparently, he did not consider these works in verse sufficiently serious and left them unsigned, whereas the authorship of his apologetic works in Castilian was not in doubt.

---

2. D. P. P. A., *Versos a la proclamación de nuestro augusto monarca Don Carlos IV (que Dios guarde) ejecutada so el árbol de Guernica el día 18 de febrero de este presente año de 1789* (Madrid: Aznar, 1789).

3. Joaquín de Yrizar, "Peñaflorida, Crillón y Astarloa," *Boletín de la Real Sociedad Bascongada de los Amigos del País* (San Sebastián) 1 (1949), 11–114.

Astarloa's fundamental work on the Basque language is contained in the *Apología de la lengua Bascongada . . .* (Apology for the Basque Language . . .) (1803) and the *Discursos filosóficos sobre la lengua primitiva . . .* (Philosophical Essays on the Primitive Language . . .) (1883). Additionally, however, he published others within the context of the linguistic debate itself: *Reflexiones filosóficas en defensa de la Apología de la lengua bascongada o Respuesta a la Censura del Cura de Montuenga* (Philosophical Reflections in Defense of the Apology for the Basque Language, or Reply to the Attack by the Priest of Montuenga) (1804) and *Carta de un vascongado al señor don Tomás de Sorreguieta, advirtiéndole varias equivocaciones que ha padecido en su obra titulada Semana Hispano-Bascongada* (Letter from a Basque to the Gentleman Don Tomás de Sorreguieta, Pointing Out to Him Several Mistakes He Has Committed in His Work Titled *Semana Hispano-Bascongada*) (1804). Conscious of the political dimension of his works, when Astarloa published his *Apología*, he sent copies to each member of the Provincial Governments of Araba, Bizkaia, Gipuzkoa and Navarre, which, except for the first, thanked him for his gesture and noted that it was a welcome response to the article by Traggia that had upset them so greatly.

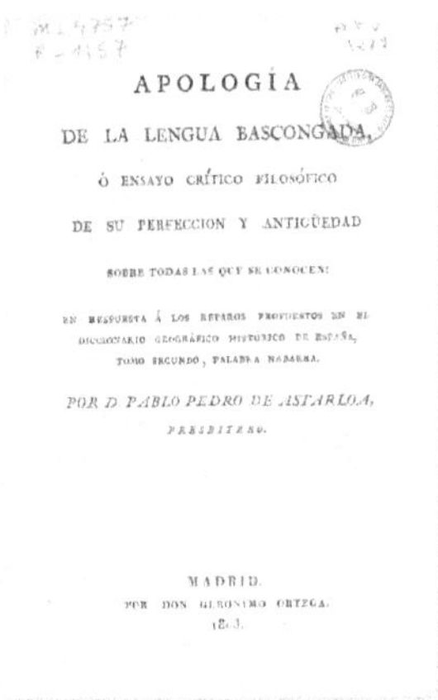

APOLOGÍA

DE LA LENGUA BASCONGADA,

Ó ENSAYO CRÍTICO FILOSÓFICO

DE SU PERFECCION Y ANTIGÜEDAD

SOBRE TODAS LAS QUE SE CONOCEN:

EN RESPUESTA Á LOS REPAROS PROPUESTOS EN EL DICCIONARIO GEOGRÁFICO HISTÓRICO DE ESPAÑA, TOMO SEGUNDO, PALABRA NABARRA.

POR D. PABLO PEDRO DE ASTARLOA,

PRESBITERO.

MADRID.

POR DON GERONIMO ORTEGA.

1803.

DISCURSOS FILOSÓFICOS

LENGUA PRIMITIVA

GRAMÁTICA Y ANÁLISIS RAZONADA

D. PABLO PEDRO DE ASTARLOA.

BILBAO

Selected Text(s):

a) *Apología de la lengua Bascongada o ensayo crítico-filosófico de su perfección y antigüedad sobre todas las que se conocen en respuesta a los reparos propuestos en el Diccionario geográfico histórico de España, tomo Segundo palabra Nabarra, por . . .* [Apology for the Basque Language or Critical-Philosophical Essay about Its Perfection and Antiquity Greater Than All Known Languages, in Response to the Criticisms Proposed in the Geographical-Historical Dictionary of Spain, Volume Two, under *Nabarra*, by . . .] (Madrid: Gerónimo Ortega, 1803); 2nd ed. (Bilbao: Pedro Velasco, 1883), v, xii-xiii, xx-xxi, 128–132, 384.

b) *Discursos filosóficos sobre la lengua primitiva o Gramática y análisis razonada de la Euskara o Bascuence* [Philosophical Essays on the Primitive Language, or Grammar and Reasoned Analysis of Euskara or the Basque language] (Madrid: Gerónimo Ortega, 1803); 2nd ed. (Bilbao: Pedro Velasco, 1883), 43–47.

a)

To the Basques

Some twenty years ago, my beloved fellow countrymen, I discovered in our native language, a certain grandeur and sublimity that captured my full attention. Even before then, Oi[h]enart, Arriet, Moret, Echave, and particularly Larramendi had pointed out the many rare perfections so abundant in the Basque language; but as this did not satisfy my desire, I sought a language that was perfect in all its aspects with the idea of presenting it to all cultured nations so that each of them might elevate their own to the degree of perfection and magnificence, of which it was capable.

The protracted study of more than four years, spent in the contemplation of a language that must have been primitive, led me to what I believed were very precise ideas on how to avoid errors in the selection of the desired language. Using these concepts, I put together a language by my method to serve as judge and arbiter of all the other languages, and with it I began the comparative evaluation of as many living and dead languages as my sleepless nights allowed me to learn.

. . .

To satisfy myself about the perfections of our language, I needed only to assure myself that its syntax was ordered according to the precepts dictated by a sound philosophy. For this it was necessary that the language observe great precision in arranging its words into concepts, as demanded by the three noble qualities I had discovered in nature for organizing the construction. I spoke to myself in my language about every possible combination of words dictated by reason, and in so doing, I discovered all the perfections demanded by its own nature and by the intentionality conferred by correct and appropriate signification. I found that its *nobility of origin* guaranteed to our expression, all the care needed for its *governance* and *fluency or movement*; that nobility of *governance* held priority over nobility of *origin*, but happily deferred to nobility of *fluency*; and finally that the latter, taking highest priority, inspired the vitality that so beautifies the concepts, and causes it to be loved by everyone without distinction. Basque concepts find their way into social communication in such an orderly, balanced, and characteristically distinct manner that they banish with amazement the endless verbosity made necessary in other languages by a flawed syntax. We understand effortlessly the first, second, third . . . cause, which our partner in thought intended to convey to us; and unlike other languages, we have no need to ask all those tedious questions in order to unearth the essence of the concepts being expressed.

I felt no hesitancy in presenting our native language to cultured nations, as the only one that could be used to help each one of them elevate their own language to that high level of perfection and sublimity of which they were innately capable.

. . .

This was the point I had reached in my investigations at the moment of publication of the Geographical-Historical Dictionary of our nation, which for now comprises only the Kingdom of Navarre and the three Provinces of Bizkaia, Gipuzkoa, and Araba. The topic under discussion in this work demanded a consideration of the Basque language—its perfection or imperfection, as well as its origin, and antiquity. As for the first, the author confesses that our language does not defer in culture, wealth, energy, and fluency to any of the known languages; but regarding the second, an endless number of objections and problems are presented.

This event, beloved countrymen, was disturbing, at least to those of you who live here at court, because you were sure that the antiquity of the Basque language was already regarded as dogma among linguists, especially those writing in recent years. Aware of the investigations I have been engaged in over these many years, you urged me to reply in writing to these criticisms. I offered to do so, promising you that my small book would silence for all time any objections raised against our native language.

. . .

The Admirable Philosophy of the Basque Language; Consideration of the Way Its Verb Is Divided . . .

If our language has, to this point, demonstrated unequivocally that there is nothing it can learn from the languages that Don Joaquín de Traggia uses as his models, we will see that this is especially true in its verb.

In its verb, the Basque language is a living portrait of nature. If nature has two different ways of acting, our language finds analogies for them by dividing its verb: with the double verb it describes those actions carried out in conjunction with another agent; with the simple verb it characterizes those enacted by lone entities, without the help of another subject.

There are entities in nature that activate their qualities without the need of any foreign subject; there are others that, although their constitution conceded them faculties, cannot put them in motion without the aid of another entity. Uncreated nature acts without recourse to any agent; created nature must have recourse to uncreated nature to act. Man walks, runs, speaks, perceives, without any other created entity acting as agent in these operations, because he exercises them all merely by the virtue conferred on him by nature. Fire, on the other hand, although it was endowed with the power to burn, cannot activate that virtue unless another outside agent applies the combustible material. The herb that received its healing virtue from nature cannot activate it without another agent applying it to pain. Fire will be consumed without activating its power to burn; the herb will wither without ever healing if the co-agent is missing.

To make an analogy with nature in these two distinct modes of acting, Basque divides its verb into double and simple; it uses the simple verb when the entities exercise their faculties on their own; and the double when another agent is involved.

If our verbs lack the characteristic of double action, they are simple. But if following the first letter of these verbs, we see the syllable *ra*, then it is double. The verb *icassi* [*ikasi*, to study] is simple, because we do not see the characteristic *ra* following the initial *i*, and it means "to learn by itself," but if we say *i-ra-catz-zi*, we imply that the entity has learned through the agency of a teacher, and by this verb we signify what Castilian signifies by the verb *enseñar* [to teach]. *Eguin* [*egin*] is a simple verb, meaning "to do." *E-ra-guin* [*eragin*] is double, and it means "to make another do." With *ebili*, also pronounced *ibili*, we understand the action of "walking by oneself"; with *e-ra-bili,* we signify "to make another walk." In simple verbs, there is only one agent; in double verbs, there are two, one primary and one co-agent.

Is there any other language that has this beautiful analogy with nature in its verbs? Yes. I know two such languages: The Quechua have both simple and double verbs, as do the Hebrews. Traggia tells us nothing about Quechua. He analyzes Hebrew in connection with the verb; he considers the double and simple verbs of the Hebrews, but he does not discuss their functions; he does not use them as teachers for our own verbs. However, we will do so here, in order to show that Basque has nothing to learn from Hebrew in this regard; but first let us consider the Basque verb in all its functions.

In some cases the subjects perform the action represented by the verbs, in which case another entity suffers; on other occasions they suffer, and others act and suffer simultaneously. For languages to analogize these three different states in which actions can be conveyed, there must be three different inflexions or verbs, in simple as well as double; for this reason, Basque has divided its simple and double verb into active, passive, or mixed. All languages have active and passive verbs; many have mixed or semi-mixed; among the languages that Don Joaquín de Traggia converts into teachers of the Basque language, we find the mixed or semi-mixed verb in Greek, but the learned Academician tells us nothing about it. Hebrew too has this kind of verb: its *hiphael* [the causative form] is mixed, or midway between active and passive; Traggia calls it reciprocal. In what follows we will say that neither the Greek language nor the Hebrew language could teach ours anything about the mixed or semi-mixed verb.

We observe too that subjects not only do the action signified by the verb; they do not only suffer it; they do not only do, and suffer simultaneously without the need for any other subject to receive this action, this passion, or this action and passion simultaneously, but also, do so with the concurrence of a receptor subject. And for this reason, the Basque chose to distinguish these two differences, dividing the active, passive, and mixed verb into pure and receptors. *Ilten-dot* is a pure active verb because there is no recipient of the action and it means "I kill it." *Ilten-deutsat* is an active, receptor verb because a third person singular is there to receive it, and three different persons take part in the action; the *yo* [I], an agent characterized in the final *t* of the auxiliary *d-eu-ts-a-t*; a third person recipient or dative characterized in the *a*; another third person of the same number singular patient, characterized in the initial *d* of said auxiliary.

The Basque language was also careful in its observation of the two unambiguous precepts nature demands of us, that is, respect for superiors and compassion for the weaker sex leading us to treat her gently and respectfully; and seeing that the verb was the only part of speech that brought us into close proximity with superiors and inferiors, it chose to divide its verbs into formal and familiar, in order to comply with the first precept and the familiar into masculine and feminine, in order not to violate the second.

So the Basque verb is divided into simple and double, these into active, passive and mixed; these three into pure and receptive; and all six into courteous and familiar; and the familiar are divided into masculine and feminine, as will be made clear in the following table:

		Active		Formal	
	Simple		Pure		
Verb		Passive			
	Double		Receptor		Masculine
		Mixed		Familiar	
					Feminine

. . .

Basque friends: I have done what I promised; may God look kindly on this Apology; should that happen, I know that you will persist in the patriotism you have demonstrated henceforth, and that I will be prevented from revealing your modesty. You know well to whom I speak. You are friends; go on being true Basques, so that your example, by uniting the whole body of whom we are members, will revive the most perfect of languages, lifting it from the obscurity in which it lies buried in the confines of a small, rugged, dark region, awaiting the moment when its perfection can serve as model for all the literature of the cultured nations.

***

b)

The Way Our Newborns Learn to Speak Does Not Mean That the Original Language Was Not Natural.

The first objection leveled against the naturalness of the human language is the way our newborns acquire speech. Those who deny that the primitive language was natural argue that a phenomenon that has persisted down through the ages proves that all men are born mute; that in them gestures or physical actions are the first attempts to communicate their needs; that these gestures or movements are soon accompanied by certain sounds or articulations; that these sounds are not understood by adults except by virtue of the gesture indicating the objects; and that, finally, by hearing or imitating the voice of the adults, they become familiar with the meanings of the words and begin to acquire the language of their parents.

Because of this process, whereby newborns begin to speak, our adversaries infer that the same process must have occurred with the first humans; that these, mute initially, then making gestures or movements, soon thereafter uttering articulated sounds, and applying them by gesture to objects, ended up creating a primitive language, based on convention, a language that was not infused or natural but acquired and formed arbitrarily by man himself through chance; so that the word *dog* pronounced together with a gesture pointing toward, for instance, a bull, ended up signifying that animal; that the same thing must have happened with any other word that we wish to imagine accompanied by a gesture to indicate the object signified by the word articulated.

Before attempting to reply to this objection, the least we can do is point out that the history of the man-child, which the philosophers using this induction wish to make us accept as a premise, is totally erroneous. In the first place, men are not born mute. From the moment they come into the world they give unequivocal indications of their capacity for speech. The sensation caused in their weak limbs by transition they have just undergone from the womb of their mothers to the harsh environment of living creatures makes their weeping inform us of the unhappiness afflicting them. In this weeping we hear clearly the first elements of language. The letters "a" and "e," articulated quite distinctly, leaves us no doubt that those uttering them are destined by nature to speak. This fact is a known principle of speech. Through it, we find ourselves obliged to admit that our newborns use natural language from the very instant in which they find themselves in the world. They speak this language with all the facility allowed them by the weakness of the vocal organ, and from this the philosopher should infer that if these newborns had received by nature a greater robustness in the oral muscles destined for speech, this would have been verified in them with greater extension, reaching its full potential in the situation allowed them by this robustness.

Many philosophers, especially modern ones, are unable to admit that newborn males articulate the letter *a* in their first plaintive cry, females the letter *e*. However, it is a fact that has been accepted in literature from the most remote times. The poet Cato proved it in the following verses,

Clamabant A *et* E, *quotquot nascuntar ab Eva*
Omnis masculus A *nascens,* E *femenina profert,*

[All of them said *a* and *e*; however, every male from
Eve is born *a*, while females are *e*]

that so many other writers have repeated that I will not quote them lest I bore the reader. I myself have witnessed this phenomenon, by sheer chance, during the same period in which the contemplation of languages began to interest me, awakening in me the desire to verify their perfection by any means possible. In my apology, I offered to speak of this, and I will do so with greatest simplicity. Even as I keep my promise, my account will support what Cato and infinite others have observed about the articulation of these letters in the weeping of our newborns.

I was strolling past the large portal of the principal church of the town of Durango, my birthplace, just as a child was being presented there for baptism by the godparents and the church officials. The child was weeping constantly, and you could hear the letter *a* uttered with great clarity all through the portico. I was not aware at the time that that this letter was pronounced by the male child in his first weeping; I was surprised by the fact, and going over to the woman who was acting as nurse, I said to her in our common language: "This must be a very intelligent child, for he is practicing the alphabet at a very tender age." No sooner had I said this than she replied to me emphatically with the following Basque phrase: *"Esta bada jauna aarra?"* [Well, is not this child a boy? So why are you surprised if he says the letter *a* when he cries?] I do not know if I have managed to do justice to the vividness of her Basque expression in my Castilian translation.

I spent considerable time contemplating her reply, and she, who had volunteered her services as nurse, went on to explain that all male children articulate the letter "a," when they first begin to cry, and all females the letter "e." Not satisfied that this pronunciation of the *a* and *e* was common to all newborns, as she told me, although I had personally heard the clear articulation of the *a* in the weeping of the child that led to this conversation, I brought up the matter with Don Juan de Amezua and Don Patricio de Arrugaeta, surgeons from my town, whom I believed to be knowledgeable about this, because they were present for all the births of the town and for many from neighboring villages. The two replied unanimously that on many occasions they had noticed that the first letter the male pronounced was the "a," and that the female uttered the "e," but that they had not taken time to verify this phenomenon with particular attention, and they agreed to make it a point to observe the first cry of all newborns in the future.

Both Amezua and Arrugaeta kept their promise and both verified that this was true by their own experience in more that a hundred babies, whose birth they attended, the only exception being that in those who were weak at birth, the pronunciation of the *a* in males was somewhat unclear, making them wonder on occasion, if the sound was closer to *e*. I tried to conduct the experiment on my own, despite the obvious sincerity that was natural to the two doctors, and I found it to be just as they had described it in the case of five boys and three girls, whose first cries Amezua and Arrugaeta arranged for me to hear.

These facts led me to believe that in our constitution there must be certain principles or traits conferred by the Supreme Being, leading to the construction of the grand edifice of language. I was confirmed in this way of thinking on seeing the analogy between the words used in Basque to refer to masculine and feminine: *Aarra* in this language means the same as "the one of *a*," or "the one who says *a*" in Castilian, and that is the noun that means "male" among us. The word *emla,* which we use for female, means "delicate *e*" or "delicate weeping." This analogy is very beautiful, and it is undeniable that the Basque language meant for the *a* and *e* of the words *aarra* and *emla* to refer to the subject. The *ar* of *aarra* is a meaningful ending, like the ablative *de* used by the Castilians, and the final *a* is a sign or well-known character for the appellative noun. Similarly, the word *me* or the article *mia* is a known epithet that means something "slender" or "delicate," and the subject to whom this quality is applied is the one indicated by the letter *e*.

. . .

From the above it can be inferred that man is not mute at birth; quite the contrary, he begins to speak from the very instant in which he sees the world, and if his language is still wearing diapers, that does not mean that it is not natural to him; but rather that it is because that organ, which the first men received in its total robustness, appears in the man-child, as a known disposition conferred in a weakened state by the Supreme Being.

38. Francisco Xavier Martínez Marina

(Oviedo, 1754 – Zaragoza, 1833)

He took his Bachelor of Arts, as well as his first year of Theology at the University of Oviedo, finishing these studies at the University of Toledo, where he completed his doctorate in 1778. He earned a scholarship to the University of Alcalá de Henares, where he served subsequently as librarian and Rector. In 1781, he obtained, through a public examination, the position of Canon of San Isidro in Madrid. He dedicated himself mainly to historical research, although his vast education allowed him to undertake projects related to juridical, linguistic, moral, and political-institutional subjects. A member of the Academy of the Language, in 1801, he became its director and the director of the Academy of History, serving as president of the latter after 1816. A liberal, he favored the policy of selling off church lands. His political positions earned him many problems during the periods of monarchical restoration, in which counter-revolutionary ideas triumphed. His most interesting political works, *Ensayo histórico-crítico sobre la antigua legislación de los Reinos de León y Castilla* (Historical-Critical Essay on the Ancient Legislation of the Kingdoms of Léon and Castile) (1808) and *Teoría de las Cortes* (Theory of Parliaments) (1813), were banned by the Inquisition in 1817, and all copies withdrawn. During the revolutionary Triennial period (1820–23), he once again held posts: member of the Spanish parliament for Asturias between 1820 and 1822, Canon of San Isidro, and honorary Doctor of the University of Oviedo in 1822, and member of its department of Moral and Political Sciences (1822–23). However, with the Counter-revolution of 1823, he was exiled to Zaragoza and stripped of all emoluments, having to survive on pensions granted him by the Bishop of Lérida (Lleida) and the Academy of History. In addition to the works cited, his *Discurso sobre el origen de la Monarquía y sobre la naturaleza del gobierno español* (Discourse on the Origin of the Monarchy and the Nature of the Spanish Government) (1813), is also interesting politically.

Regarding his relations with the Basque Country, he was assigned to compose the entry "*Álava*" (Araba) for the 1802 *Diccionario de la Academia de Historia* (Dictionary of the Academy of History), participating in the institutional offensive against the Basque *foral* movement and its emphasis on the special historical identity of the Basque Country. As for his linguistic positions, he glorified Spain's national language and was a detractor of the other vernacular tongues spoken in the peninsula. In these views, he was particularly hostile to the Basque language, whose apologists were beginning to cast the linguistic debate in increasingly political terms. Specifically, in 1805 he wrote his *Ensayo histórico-crítico sobre el origen y progresos de las lenguas: señaladamente del romance castellano* (Historical-Critical Essay on the Origin and Progress of Languages: In Particular, the Castilian Romance Language), in which he defended positions diametrically opposed to those held by Larramendi and the other Basque apologists. Specifically, Martínez Marina denied that Basque had been the primitive Spanish language, and argued that it was impossible to know anything about which language this might have been until the arrival of Carthaginians and Romans. In his opinion, it was only necessary to seek two paternities for Castilian Romance: Latin and, to a lesser degree, Arabic. Any other potential contributions (from Celtic, Greek, Gothic, Basque, and so on) were thus irrelevant. Furthermore, he emphatically rejected the Basque apologists' characterization of Euskara as original and wise, doing so without even bothering to name it, and in the most scornful terms.

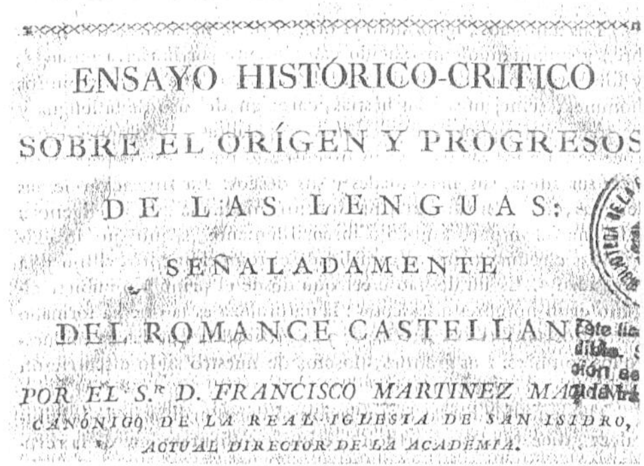
ENSAYO HISTÓRICO-CRÍTICO
SOBRE EL ORÍGEN Y PROGRESOS
DE LAS LENGUAS:
SEÑALADAMENTE
DEL ROMANCE CASTELLAN
POR EL S.r D. FRANCISCO MARTINEZ MA
CANÓNIGO DE LA REAL IGLESIA DE SAN ISIDRO,
ACTUAL DIRECTOR DE LA ACADEMIA.

Selected Text(s):

Ensayo histórico-crítico sobre el origen y progresos de las lenguas: señaladamente del romance castellano [Historical-Critical Essay on the Origin and Progress of Languages: In Particular, the Castilian Romance Language] (Madrid: Joaquín Ibarra, 1805), 10–12, 20, 38, 45–48, 61, 63, i–v.

In most remote times, men were little inclined to form into social groups and were divided into small families, nor did they cultivate their language or use it except to express ideas and feelings relative to things physical and to a small number of necessities. On the other hand, man was free, varied, inconstant, imitative, capable of receiving new impressions, different ideas; of correcting them, modifying them, and forgetting them: the principal instrument of speech was changeable and subject to innumerable inflexions and movements. These are the main causes of the alteration and multiplication of languages, to which we can add education, example, errors in pronunciation authorized by custom; the more or less delicate conformation of the organs of speech, caprice, imagination, circumstances, or changes in climate or country; love and provincial zeal, mutual emulation of neighboring countries, ignorance of the marvelous, and the extremely useful invention of the art of writing, the depiction of languages, sureness of the representative signs for the concepts of the soul, and the most opportune means for spreading them, duration, and stability. Thus, primitive language changed, and dialects were formed; so it is that the ancient Arabs, Egyptians, Assyrians, Canaanites, and Phoenicians, although originating from the same region, sons of the same father, and educated in the same school, altered their native language to such an extent soon after their dispersion that they could no longer understand each other except through an interpreter, as can be deduced from Sacred History.

. . .

When, and why, did the unsophisticated, savage Greeks, ignorant of the bare rudiments of language, emerge from their barbarism? When did foreign colonies show them the essential principles of sociability? It was when Cecrops, Cadmic and Danaus taught them the art of reading and writing; when through the merging of its small cantons into a national body a common language was formed; when the Muses, Orpheus, and Melpomene, and later Homer, Plato, Herodotus, and Pythagoras, after traveling through Egypt, and Asia, through the Orient, and the West, and then returned to their country, enriched it, not with gold and silver but with the invaluable treasures of languages, arts, and sciences stolen from foreigners. Thus the Roman language grew with the addition of Greek words; so did Arabic grow with Greek, Latin, Hindu, and Persian; and so our Castilian with all of them.

We have no idea which language the ancient Spaniards spoke in the fabled times of our history, which encompasses everything that occurred between their establishment in this region until the arrival of the Carthaginians and the Romans. Much has been said, written and researched about this by our scholars, whose zeal and good intentions are certainly worthy of praise; but unfortunately all of their investigations are only good for passing time pleasantly, as when one reads a fable, but not for increasing our knowledge.

Following the principles of sound philosophy, which concur with the few historical fragments remaining to us from such remote times, we can be sure that the language of the Spaniards would not have been rich or abundant then, but wretched, poor and very limited.

. . .

The monuments of our history show clearly that Castilian Romance owes its origin to the ignorance, negligence, and failure of the Spaniards to cultivate their ancient Latin language, and that this was a necessary effect of the confusion they experienced in ideas, concepts, and opinions after the Arabs invaded Spain. Threatened by a bellicose nation, whose only goal was to destroy them, their only concern was to find a refuge for their religion and their lives. With no other education than their ability to wield a sword, with no other passion than the love of the noise and clatter of weapons, with no other science and expertise than military science, with no other desire than to drive the enemy out of the patriotic soil, they were unaware even of the rudiments of grammar, which was only cultivated, and done so very badly, by a few monks buried in the obscurity of the cloisters. As their ideas were limited to such narrow horizons, they necessarily forgot all those unrelated to such an important object, because it is a proven fact that ideas are erased from things when others more urgent and interesting seize the entire attention of the mind: memories that are not cultivated are erased, the strength of the soul, like that of the body, grows weak for lack of exercise. Consequently, because there is a mutual interaction between opinions and languages, between ideas and the signs that represent them, it was inevitable that the language and ideas of the Spaniards would become extremely spare and wretched; this was compounded by the negligence of our people, or more accurately, their inability to cultivate the arts and sciences; their failure to study their own language, which is extremely complex and artificial, the scarcity of books, and perhaps even the inability to write: all of these being the most opportune measures for preserving and perpetuating language.

. . .

But the language that substantially augmented and enriched the Castilian language, so that within a brief period it became superior to those of Europe, was undeniably Arabic, a language common to Spaniards and Moors throughout the southern region of Spain, a wise, rich and abundant language. The Muslims, the most learned and cultured nation in the world in the twelfth and thirteenth centuries, had elevated Spain to the highest degree of honor, bequeathing to posterity innumerable works, eternal monuments of their culture in every written genre: grammar, poetry, philosophy, history, agriculture, astronomy, natural history, arts, and professions.

. . .

Here then, gentlemen, are the sources and true origins of Castilian Romance, as it stood at the beginning of the thirteenth century: a magnificent constructed edifice with loan words and prolific gifts from the rich Arabic language; a summit of precious qualities borrowed from two languages, which conjoining all the advantages, graces and best qualities of those of the known world succeeded, independently and without assistance from any other language, in instilling form and consistency into the rich, sonorous and harmonious Spanish language. And what would we say if to such a treasure, we add that it was loaned to her by the Phoenician, Punic, Celtic, Hebrew, Greek, Gothic, and Basque languages? For so many other languages contributed to the construction of the Castilian language, if we are to believe what we are told by the learned investigators of the origins of our Romance, who were echoed religiously by the anonymous orator, who said: "Wise Greek and Holy Hebrew competed in offering her all the nouns of their belief systems and the cults of their mysteries and ceremonies, as well as others for relating to the faculties, arts, and commerce. Gracious and sophisticated Hellenisms, and expressive Jewish phrases, and they even passed on certain structural aspects of their own to the nascent dialect . . . The courageous Goth bestowed nouns relating to war and military action, and even the decrepit Punic and Phoenician languages, and the primitive Celtic and Basque languages made contributions in those days to Castilian."

We, however, who do not believe that Romance is indebted at all to such a grand concourse of creditors, would like for the anonymous, as well as the authors whom he used in support of this argument, to tell us: How, or in which epoch did the Greeks, Goths, and Hebrews contribute to the formation of Castilian?

. . .

Hence, the Spanish language owes all of its qualities, its nature, genius, constitution, grammar, syntax, elements, and words to Latin and Arabic, and if we divide into four parts, the words of our language, we can calculate with some certainty that three parts come originally from Latin, one part from Arabic.

. . .

The decadence of languages is a necessary consequence of the neglect and decline of the arts and sciences, just as the decadence of these is necessarily followed by the decline of monarchies, and empires. The connection between the prosperity of states and that of the arts, sciences, and languages is crucial and inviolable. This is a truth demonstrated by the experience of all the centuries.

. . .

Because extraordinary efforts were required to uproot all the brambles and harmful plants produced in the vast field of the Spanish language, very aggressive measures were necessary to cure a sickness that had become chronic and an affliction so ingrained; many wise men authorized by the government were needed to restrain the impetuous torrent of bad taste that was inundating the kingdom; it was necessary to banish or burn, if possible, the infinite multitude of unworthy translations with which our peninsula was inundated; to promote talented men and help them publish original works in every branch of science and in a national language accommodated to our best models; it was necessary to compile collections of fixed rules, precepts, and orderly observations, some to avoid errors in writing, and to stabilize and make uniform the pronunciation of words; others to establish and guarantee the just and proper placement and order of the parts of discourse; it was necessary to determine the property and true significance of the words by means of a grand dictionary that would include them all, and to authorize them through examples of our classic authors. All of this was done by the Royal Spanish Academy, which is the body of selected scholars appointed by the great King Felipe to carry out such a serious enterprise. With its grammar and orthography, it forever stabilized the written language, pronunciation, word order, and syntax, and with its grand dictionary, it erected an eternal monument to the Spanish language.

Catalogue of Certain Castilian Words

of pure Arabic origin, or derived from the Greek language, and from the oriental languages, but introduced into Spain by the Arabs

If in order to ascertain the origins of the Castilian language, determine exactly the primitive roots of its words, weave the genealogy of its words, and stabilize its true written and spoken form, we were to loosen the reins of our ingenious and fecund imagination, allowing it to run free and rampant through the vast space covered by etymological science, it would be quite easy and cost very little to fill thick volumes, to win the high regard of the common people as men, who are wise, intelligent, and experienced in the most exotic and strange languages. Even if we were unaware of their basic elements and alphabets, even more, if by catering to national pride we went out of our way to exalt our language to the highest realms of honor, showing it to be one of the original languages of the universe, one of the wisest, richest, sweetest, and most harmonious, a font and fecund spring of almost all those known on the globe; and it would not be a very arduous task to make this paradox believable, because when dealing with honor and glory, and with everything in men's own interest, illusory arguments and words flung together haphazardly suffice to persuade them, especially when they are uttered with a certain tone of authority and expertise.

But because we are not attempting here to publish a work of that nature, and also because we are convinced that our language is quite recent, more modern than all the learned languages, and a product of the Latin and Arabic languages, which were the only ones spoken and known in Spain after the establishment here of the Gothic empire until the eleventh and twelfth centuries, the true epoch of the various dialects that we know were formed then, and whose existence is confirmed beyond doubt by historical monuments; therefore, after having established in our essay the origin of the romance language, the principles from which it develops, the causes and circumstances of its formation, we conclude that in the Latin and Arabic language we would find its true origins, without having to turn to other foreign languages.

It is quite true that in some sections of the northern part of our peninsula, in the valleys and mountains, some people, especially those living away from towns, speak a kind of gibberish, to which they have attempted to call the original language, and even a wise language, and there are even some who have considered it to be in large part, the mother of our own. But, since the Middle Ages in which the known dialects of Spain were born and developed, this language of which we are speaking either did not exist or failed to win any respect among cultured, civilized people, because it has never been written, nor has any public function ever been conducted in such a language. It ought to be considered in its origin as a confused mixture of the common dialect with many other words from all over the map added on, but so altered, changed, and corrupted because of the ignorance of the people, and because it was never used for writing over a period of several centuries, and for the other reasons, which as we have already demonstrated in the essay, naturally influence the corruption of languages, that if it turns out that in most of the elements of that language, the sources from which they emanate are discovered, with respect to others, it is impossible to speak sensibly or come to any clear conclusion. The same thing would have happened to our Romance language, if as soon as a different dialect came to be formed, it had not been preserved in many books and writings of all kinds that were published in Castilian from that time until our days. Even with this, our language has changed remarkably, some of its words have been corrupted and altered so greatly that they resemble very little or not at all the origin from which they were derived: for if nothing had been written in Romance since the thirteenth century, would the language we speak today have any resemblance or connection at all with the language of that century? And in this case, would we be able to speak with any certainty about its true origins?

The first step for discovering them is the history and genealogy of the words, and a thorough examination of the variety with which these have been written in the ages preceding us; but neither of these is possible with respect to those dialects of which antiquity has made no use at all, or bothered to preserve until our days in any public monuments. A language that has left no trace or vestige of its ancient existence is like a family thought to be noble and of ancient lineage that had lost all its titles and genealogical records; their pretensions would be vain and ignored until such time as they could show authentic testimonies concerning their ancestry. In the same way we should distrust all the multiple conjectures they make concerning the origin of an obscure language that is totally unknown in the documents of our history.

39. Bertrand Barère de Vieuzac

(Tarbes, Béarn, 1755 – Tarbes, 1841)

He studied law in Toulouse, earning his degree in 1775 and becoming a brilliant intellectual, frequenting academies and literary circles, first in Toulouse and later in Paris. He was elected a member of the Estates-General in 1789 for the third state of Bigorre, and participated in all the debates of the Assembly. As a member of the Convention, he situated himself in a prudent equilibrium between Girondins and Jacobins, without adopting a precise position and frequently acting as mediator between political extremes. He was elected president of the Convention in 1792, and also served on the Committee of Public Safety in 1793. After the Thermidorian Reaction against Robespierre's regime in 1794, he was arrested and nearly exiled to Madagascar, but he managed to escape. In 1798, he was once again elected deputy for the department of the Upper Pyrenees but after his collaboration with the Empire, when the Restoration occurred, he was one of the twenty-three revolutionaries condemned by the then Minister of Police, Joseph Fouché, forcing him into exile in Brussels. He returned to France after the revolution of 1830, and he was once again elected as deputy in 1834.

In the course of his political activities, he frequently dealt with matters relating to culture and the arts. Of interest to us here is his work on revolutionary linguistic politics, in particular his *Rapport du Comité de Salut Publique sur les idioms* (Report of the Committee of Public Safety on Languages) (1794), in which he defended the necessity of extending the French language to all the citizens of the Republic and of liquidating the "*patois*" (dialects) which incarnated fanaticism and tyranny.

Selected Text(s):

"Rapport du Comité de Salut Publique sur les idiomes, 8 Pluviôse, an II," [Report of the Committee of Public Safety on Languages, 8 Pluviose, Year 2] (1794). In *Une politique de la langue. La Revolution française et les patois: l'enquéte de Grégoire* [A Politics of Language: The French Revolution and Dialects: Grégoire's Investigation], ed., Michel de Certeau, Dominique Julia, and Jacques Revel (Paris: Gallimard, 2002), 321–331.

The Barère Report

Report of the Committee of Public Safety on Languages*

Barère, in the name of the Committee of Public Safety: Citizens, listen to the words of the coalition of tyrants: ignorance has always been our most important ally; let us maintain ignorance; it creates fanatics, it multiplies counter-revolutionaries; let us cause the French to regress into barbarism; let us exploit the poorly educated people or those who speak a different language from that used in public education.

The committee has come to understand the conspiracy between ignorance and despotism.

I come today to call your attention to the most beautiful language of Europe; the first to openly embrace the rights of man and of the citizen, the language chosen to transmit to the world the most sublime concepts of liberty, and the grandest speculations of politics.

She was a slave for many years, she flattered kings, corrupted the courts, and reduced the people to servitude; she was for many years dishonored in the schools and misrepresented in books on public education; shrewd in courtrooms, fanatic in temples, barbaric on diplomas, made soft by poets, corrupt in theaters, she seemed to be awaiting, or rather longing for, a more beautiful destiny.

Purified at last, made sweet by certain dramatists, ennobled and made brilliant in the speeches of certain orators, her power was restored by reason and liberty in the pens of certain philosophers who had won honor by being persecuted before the Revolution of 1789.

But she still seemed to be the exclusive property of certain classes of society; she had adopted the mien of aristocratic distinction; and the courtier, not content with being distinguished by his vices and depravities, sought then to distinguish himself within his own country by speaking a different language. One might have said that there were several nations within a single nation.

That was bound to be the case under a monarchical government, where it was necessary to take a test to be admitted into a school, in a country where it was necessary to belong to a certain lineage to be considered what is called "good company," and to mince the language in a special way to be regarded as a person "of the right sort."

These puerile distinctions have disappeared along with the absurd and supercilious facial expressions and subtly coded gestures of a per-

---

* Archives parlementaires, 1re série, t. LXXXIII, séance du 8 pluviôse an II, n° 18, 713–17 (Paris: C. N. R. S., 1961).

verse court. The very pride of accent more or less pure or sonorous no longer exists, after the citizens, who had come together from all parts of the Republic, expressed in the national assemblies their dedication to freedom and their thoughts concerning common legislation. Previously they had been brilliant slaves of various degrees; they contended for primacy of style and language. Free men are all alike; and the vigorous accent of liberty and equality is the same, whether it comes from the mouth of an inhabitant of the Alps or the Vosges, of the Pyrenees or the Cantal, of Mont-Blanc or Mont-Terrible, whether it becomes the expression of men from the central regions, from the coastal provinces, or from the border.

Four points of the territory of the Republic in particular, require the attention of the revolutionary legislator, under the report on the languages that seem most contrary to the propagation of public spirit, and which present obstacles to the knowledge of the laws of the Republic and their execution.

Among the ancient languages—Welsh, Gascon, Celtic, Visigothic, Phocaean, or Asian—that form certain variations in the communications of different citizens and regions making up the territory of the Republic, we have observed (and the reports of the representatives agree on this point with those of the agents sent into their departments) that the language called Breton, the Basque language, the German languages, and Italian have perpetuated the reign of fanaticism and superstition, assured the domination of the priests, nobles, and doctors, prevented the revolution from extending into important new departments, and may favor the enemies of France.

. . .

At the other end of the Republic live a new people, although ancient, a land of shepherds and sailors, who have never been slaves or masters, whom Caesar was unable to conquer during his triumphant campaign against the Gauls, whom Spain never occupied during her revolutions, and whom the despotism of our despots never subjected to the yoke of overseers: I speak of the Basque people. They occupy the extreme end of the Western Pyrenees [department] that juts out into the ocean. A sonorous and colorful language is regarded as the seal of their origin and the legacy bequeathed by their ancestors. Yet they are priests, and priests make use of their language to fanaticize; but they do not know the French language, and the language of the laws of the Republic. It is, then, necessary for them to learn it, because despite the difference of the language, and despite their priests, they are devoted to the

Republic, which they have already defended with valor along the [river] Bidasoa border and in our armies.

. . .

Citizens, it is in this way that the Vendée was born; its cradle, ignorance of the laws; its growth came from the means employed to undermine the revolution and infiltrate it, and then the gods of ignorance, the reactionary priests, the conspiratorial nobles, greedy doctors, and incompetent or complicit administrators opened an ugly wound in the bosom of France: so let us crush ignorance by establishing institutes of the French language in the countryside!

For three years the national assemblies have been speaking and discussing public education; the need for primary schools has been felt for a long time; these are moral issues of highest priority needed in the rural areas; but we may still be too academic and too far removed from the people to give them the institutions best suited to their urgent needs.

The laws of education prepare children to be craftsmen, artists, scholars, writers, legislators, and public functionaries; but the first laws of education should be preparing children to be citizens; now, to be a citizen one must obey the laws, and to obey them, one must know them. You, therefore, owe the people the early education that puts them within reach of understanding the voice of the legislator. What contradictions are presented by the departments of the Upper and Lower Rhine, or of Morbihan, or Finistere, of Ille-et-Vilaine, of the Lower Loire, of the North Coasts, of the Lower Pyrenees, and of Corsica? The lawmaker speaks a language, which those who are supposed to carry them out and obey them do not understand. The ancients never experienced such shocking and dangerous paradoxes.

It is necessary to popularize the language, to destroy that aristocracy of language that seems to establish a polished nation in the middle of a barbarous nation.

We have revolutionized the government, laws, activities, manners, customs, commerce, and even thought itself; let us, then, revolutionize language as well, which is their daily instrument.

You have decreed the issuance of the laws to all the communities of the Republic; but this benefit is lost for those in the departments that I have already indicated. The lights carried to every corner of France are extinguished as soon as they arrive, because the laws are not understood there.

Federalism and superstition speak Breton; emigration and hatred for the Revolution speak German; the counter revolution speaks Italian, and fanaticism speaks Basque. Let us cast out the instruments of shame and error.

The committee has decided that it should propose to you, as an urgent and revolutionary measure, to give each rural community of the designated departments a teacher of the French language, responsible for teaching the young people of both sexes, and to read, each decade, to all the other citizens of the community, the laws, decrees, and instructions sent from the Convention. It will be the responsibility of these teachers to translate orally the laws to make them easier to understand at first. Rome instructed young people by teaching them to read the law of the twelve tables. France will teach some citizens the French language in the book of the Declaration of Rights.

This does not mean that there are not other languages as inferior, or worse, in other departments; but they are not exclusive; they have not been an obstacle to learning the national language. If it is not spoken equally well throughout, at least it is easily understood. The clubs, the patriotic societies, are primary schools for language and freedom; they will suffice to spread knowledge of the language in departments, where there are still too many vestiges of these dialects and jargons maintained by habit and propagated by an inferior education or none at all. The legislator should see from above, and not just observe the more obvious nuances but also the enormous differences; language instructors should only be sent to provinces which, exclusively accustomed to one language, are, so to speak, isolated and separated from the larger family.

These instructors should have no connection to any cult at all; no priests in public teaching; good patriots, enlightened men; such are the first requisites for involvement in education.

The popular Societies will choose the candidates: these instructors should be men of like hearts, men from their villages; they will be chosen by the representatives of the people, who have been sent to establish the revolutionary government.

Their salary will be paid by the public treasury. The Republic owes free elementary instruction to all citizens; their salary will not arouse greed; it should satisfy the needs of a man living in the countryside; it will be one hundred francs per month. Assiduity proven by the constituted authorities will be the caution of the Republic in the payment it will make to the instructors, who will be performing a mission that is more important than it seems at first. They are going to create men for freedom, bind the citizens to the *patrie* [homeland], and prepare the execution of the laws by giving them knowledge of them.

This proposition of the committee may seem frivolous to ordinary men, but I am addressing the popular legislators, charged with presiding over the most beautiful revolutions, which the politics of the human spirit have ever experienced.

If I spoke to a despot, he would condemn me; even under the monarchy each house, each community, each province existed in a kind of empire separated by manners, practices, laws, customs, and language. The despot had the need to isolate people, to separate the country, to divide interests, to prevent communications, to block simultaneity of thoughts, and the identification of movements. Despotism perpetuated the multiplicity of languages; a monarchy must resemble the tower of Babel; there is but one universal language for the tyrant; that of force to compel obedience, and taxation to collect money.

In a democracy, to the contrary, government surveillance is entrusted to each citizen; surveillance requires knowledge of the person; it especially requires knowledge of the language.

The laws of a Republic suppose singular attention of all the citizens to each other, and constant surveillance regarding the observance of the laws, and the conduct of public functionaries. Is there any way to guarantee this amid the confusion of languages, neglect of primary education, ignorance of the citizens?

Moreover, how costly has it been for us to translate the laws from the first two national assemblies into the different languages spoken in France? As if it were up to us to maintain the barbaric jargons and crude languages that no longer serve anyone, but fanatics and counter-revolutionaries!

To leave the citizens in ignorance of the national language is to betray the country; it is to allow the flood of poisoned or perverted ideas to run their course; it is to misunderstand the benefits of the printing press, because each printer is a public institution of language and legislation.

Will you allow that beautiful invention to bear no fruit in some parts of the territory, when it can multiply thoughts and propagate ideas, reproduce laws and decrees, and extend them all across the Republic in a week, and make the national Constitution available to every community? When it is the only way to assure the enlightenment, education, public spirit, and democratic government of a great nation?

Citizens, the language of a free people should be one and the same for all.

From the moment men begin to think, from the moment they learn to think as one, the empire of priests, and despots, and conspirators begins to collapse.

Then let us give the citizens the instrument of public thought, the surest agent of the revolution: the same language.

What? While foreigners all over the globe are learning the French language; while our public papers are in circulation everywhere; whereas [newspapers like] the *Journal Universel* and the *Journal des Hommes Libres* are being read in every nation from pole to pole, are we to tell them that there are six-hundred thousand Frenchmen, who are totally ignorant of the language of their nation, and who do not know the laws, or the revolution being created among them!

Let us feel the pride that the preeminence of the French language should bring us from the moment it became Republican, and let us fulfill our obligation.

Let us forget the Italian language, consecrated to the delights of harmony and the gushing of soft, corrupting poetry.

Let us forget the German language, hardly fit for free people until such time as the feudal, military government for which it is the most appropriate organ is finally obliterated.

Let us forget the Spanish language, because of its Inquisition and universities until it finally casts out the Bourbons, who have dethroned the peoples of all the Spains.

As for the English language, which became great and free on the day it was enriched with those words, "the majesty of the people," it is now only the language of a tyrannical and execrable government, and of the bank for commercial letters of exchange

Our enemies had made the French language the language of royal courts; they had corrupted it. It is our task to make it the language of the people; then it will be honored.

It was the destiny of but one language that gave its accents to liberty and equality; one language with a legislative tribunal of two thousand popular delegates, with the great potential to move vast assemblies, and theatres to celebrate patriotism; it was the destiny of the French language alone, which after four years made all the people read it, which depicted to all of Europe the valor of fourteen armies that served as the instrument of the glory and of the recovery of Toulon, Landau, and Fort Vauban and of the collapse of the royal armies; it was her destiny alone to become the universal language.

Yet this ambition is that of the genius of liberty; it will keep its promise. As for us, we owe to our fellow citizens; we owe to the consolidation of the Republic; the obligation to make the language in which the Declaration of the Rights of Man is written be spoken all across its territory.

40. Tomás de Sorreguieta Arribillaga

(Tolosa, Gipuzkoa, mid-18th century – ?)

Little is known of his life. What is essential is that he was ordained in 1781 and that he served as a priest in several Navarrese and Gipuzkoan towns: Acedo, Asteasu, and Albistur, for example. He was representative of the priests of his day, interested in literary matters and profoundly preoccupied with the question of Basque pride of identity, although he articulated his arguments on somewhat original terrain. Of course, he made use of the language and of its etymologies to prove his points, but in this case, instead of basing his reasoning exclusively on toponymy, he focused on the names of the temporal cycles: weeks, months, and years. In the frenzied competition of the eighteenth century in which Basque authors competed to come up with convincing etymologies for every presumably historical event, Sorreguieta took the main prize. Unlike Larramendi, however, he did not give the impression that his etymologies might be intended as games destined to mock his rivals. On the contrary, he seemed to take his own arguments seriously, and thus, he went to the trouble of writing a second book to respond to his detractors when the first was universally and immediately criticized.

The fundamental thesis of his work is the claim that the Basques are the most Christian people on earth, monotheistic, even before Christ, in a context of polytheistic gentiles. Once again, the proof would come from language, although in this case, through the names of the days of the week, the word "week" itself, and equally in the names of the months and years. Etymologically, then, *astea* (week) came from *(h)asi* (beginning), that is, in naming the week, Basques would be alluding to the Creation. In the same way, *Urte* (year) would be translated as *aguada or* "flood." As for the word "month," it translates to *illa*, and would be equivalent to "death," linking it to the most remarkable of all "new" things. Creation, Flood, and Death would thus refer to a similar number of the pillars of the Christian message. The Basque week would thus predate the pagan Greco-Roman and the Egyptian astronomical weeks. On occasions, his message is not all that different from certain ideas associated with Larramendi: national antiquity, purity, and linguistic dignity going hand in hand: "why be amazed that the Basques are, among all people, the ones who can prove the perpetual changelessness of their true religion, and the antiquity of more that four thousand years of their national origin with arguments taken from their Basque word for Week?" Sorreguieta's work is limited to the *Semana Hispano-Bascongada . . .* (The Spanish-Basque week . . .) (1804) and *Triunfo de la*

Semana Hispano-Bascongada y del Bascuence (Triumph of the Spanish-Basque Week and Basque) (1805).

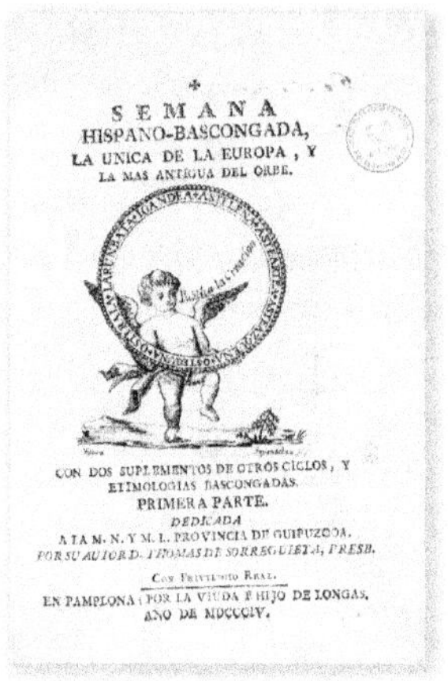

SEMANA
HISPANO-BASCONGADA,
LA UNICA DE LA EUROPA, Y
LA MAS ANTIGUA DEL ORBE.

CON DOS SUPLEMENTOS DE OTROS CICLOS, Y
ETIMOLOGIAS BASCONGADAS.
PRIMERA PARTE.
DEDICADA
A LA M. N. Y M. L. PROVINCIA DE GUIPUZCOA.
POR SU AUTOR D. THOMAS DE SORREGUIETA, PRESB.

CON PRIVILEGIO REAL.

EN PAMPLONA: POR LA VIUDA E HIJO DE LONGAS,
AÑO DE MDCCCIV.

Selected Text(s):

Semana Hispano-Bascongada, la única de la Europa, y la más antigua del Orbe. Con dos suplementos de otros ciclos, y etimologías bascongadas [The Spanish-Basque Week, Unique in Europe and the Oldest on Earth. With Two Supplements on Other Cycles and Basque Etymologies] (Pamplona: Viuda e hijo de Longas, 1804), 4–7, 100–04, 153–61, 176–78.

This being indisputable, it is equally beyond doubt that the Egyptians, Hebrews and other eastern nations had their weekly cycle, their Hebdomad, Week, or space of seven days for a number of uses; so too did the Basques have their *Asteá* for their own purposes.

But what is extraordinary is that whereas those people always used a word with the root "seven" to refer to the seven-day cycle—*Semana, Septimana, Hebdomad*—the Basques called it *Asteá*, which has no relation with the number seven. Why this difference? There seems to be no reason, except the precious nature of the Basque language, which always maintains the greatest propriety between words and the terms of which they are composed.

Whether they are simple or compound, whether their dictions are root-based or derived, they all contain the most perfect idea and concept of what they signify: whether they are referring to spiritual entities, or beings, or to corporal beings: whether abstract or concrete, whether particular or generalized. This is true to such a degree that in many of its terms, especially those that are compound, the words not only describe the objects signified, but they define them according to their nature and inner essence.

This marvelous perfection of the Basque language, absolutely similar to that of the Hebrew, or Holy, language, is obvious to the Basques, who know their Basque language and observe it carefully. And because these are the people to whom this treatise is mainly addressed, they will take for granted everything said or still to be said in this regard.

The word *Asteá*, which if translated into Castilian means *comienzo* or *principio* [beginning] belongs to this genre of utterly appropriate nouns. And, what more appropriate expression could be given for the creation of things which the Creator produced in the nothingness in the space of only six days, resting on the seventh, than the word *Asteá*, or "beginning"? Are not, perchance, all the things that were created in the Week of creation, which only and uniquely and properly experience their absolute beginning, visible?—(leaving aside, of course, those that are purely invisible[1]). Can the other visible productions that have come, or do come, or will ever come into being subsequent to that first Week, compete in any way or as appropriately with the significance of that word? Certainly not, because the works of the six days, and the hush consecrating the seventh, were produced from nothingness; but those that followed from those, created in the beginning.

It is, then, obvious that the word *Asteá* is synonymous with Creation, and that there is no other word, nor can there be another, as sufficient, proper and natural as that for denominating the Week, both that first week in which the Creator produced everything visible out of the nothingness as well as any other week, which having no similarity at all with the primordial week, is destined according to the common understanding of the enlightened nations of the Revelation, for the memory and recollection of that portentous, famous, and admirable initial week.

And because this and the achievement of bestowing on each thing its corresponding name are operations that demand much knowledge, who will deny that the first cultivators of the Basque language were men endowed with singular wisdom and discernment?

. . .

1. "Taking as a given the creation of everything, both the visible and the invisible, by the Omnipotent," we say this without bothering to indicate the instant of angelic creation, whether it was earlier or during the precise interval of the first Week of the world.

But is there any way to imagine that at the end of this chapter, we find ourselves in the enviable position of being able to present an irrefutable monument[2] that expressly guarantees and affirms everything we have just said about the antiquity of the Basques? I believe that everyone, on hearing this, will be aflame and burn in anxiety and desire to taste such a delicious, new, and unexpected food. So then, let us reveal it as soon as possible, so that it can serve as the seal of the truth that we have just proven in this chapter.

Proof of this undeniable antiquity is to be found, of all places, in the very name of the Basque nation and people, preserved in the bosom of their original, native, and true language, which remains uncorrupted and unchanged as in the Basque word for Week, already proven by the Hebdomadal cycle as the most ancient on earth, with monuments from other languages and civic institutions of ancient peoples that have been recognized and accepted as true, generally.

This proper and private name of the Basque people is *Guipuzcoac*,[3] which is the plural of the singular *Guipuzcoa,* which refers to the central territory where they live. But what is the miraculous quality of this name that astonishes us so much, that it is almost unimaginable? Because this name tells us expressly, and by antonomasia, inspired by the genius of the Basque language, the place, time, and cause of the national existence of those, who speak the language in which it is conceived. *Guipuzcoac*, it so happens, is an aggregate of five parts of speech: *Gu iz pusc o ac*: in Castilian: *Nosotros los del habla dividida* [We, of the divided language]. In light of this, without further interpretation, any Castilian knows that in these words lies the meaning "We, who speak the divided language," in other words, of Babel: because the antonomasia *iz pusc* (divided language) cannot mean anything but divided speech or language, and this par excellence is the language that was divided into many, when there was only one language on earth, *erat terra labii unius* [now the whole earth had one language and the same words, *Genesis* 2.1], the miraculous event that could only mean Babel. And I do not have to apologize if one or two letters are missing, because in the structure of a long word like this, it is humanly impossible to pre-

2. The authority of the monument that we are about to announce, and that of many others similar to it by antonomasia, will be recognized in its totality in the second part of this work, in which after analyzing the Basque word *Astéa*, we show the contemporary Basque language to be essentially of the same antiquity as the language of the word *Asteá.*

3. The Bizkaians pronounce it *Guiputzac*, syncopating the syllable *co* to abbreviate it.

serve with absolute integrity the many simple elements of which it is composed.

. . .

The word *Urteá*, signifying "year" in Basque, literally means *aguada* in Castilian, "a place flooded," or "flood." It seems impossible, the first time we hear the word *Urteá*, or *aguada*, that this can in any way signify "the space or interval of a year"; but our surprise will cease when we observe the following doctrine carefully.

We have already stated the word *Urteá* literally means *aguada* or "flooded" in Castilian, which is the same as "flood." This formidable event resembles the year because of the duration of time in which it occurred. This period of time, in addition to the traditional interpretation that it was a complete year, is stated in chapters seven and eight of the holy book of Genesis. Because it says there in verse 2.9 that the flood began on the sixteenth day of the second month of the year 600 of the life of Noah: and this is confirmed in verse 14, that the earth dried out on the twenty-seventh day of the second month of the year 601 of the life of that same Noah. It is in this way, according to these dates, that from the beginning of the flood until its end, 365 days passed, or a lunar year, and ten additional days. So, the flood lasted exactly the length of time as a complete solar year. So, the flood is exactly the same as our civil year in its duration. Therefore, to say *Urteá*, or "flooded," on this side of the border is equivalent to saying "year" in Castilian.

But someone might ask: because there have been so many floods over time, do we have to assume that whenever the word flood is mentioned that it necessarily has to be the one that happened in the time of Noah? How do we know it has to be the one that happened in the days of Noah? Are not there others worth considering, like the one that happened in Attica when Ogyges was king in the epoch of the famous Phoroneus? Or the one that happened in Thessaly, in the days of Deucalion, or all the others the world has experienced down through time? Well, how can there be any comparison or similarity between those partial floods covering only one territory or country with the universal one that flooded the entire earth? So, the general flood that occurred in the days of Noah is precisely the flood or deluge par excellence or antonomasia. So, every time a flood is mentioned without qualification, we understand the universal flood that lasted for the space of an entire year in the life of the patriarch Noah.

Hence, the Basque word *Urteá* or "flood," signifies most appropriately by antonomasia with the annual length of time of 365 days of the duration of the universal flood; and not any other partial flood that happened in a limited interval of time of one or several days. Consequently, the founders and teachers of the Basque language could not have chosen any other name more appropriate or energetic to designate the annual circle represented by the term *Urteá* or "flood": for the occurrence of the flood par excellence consisted of a period of 365 days, which is the exact number of days of all past and present annual solar cycles used by the Basques, achieving additionally with the happy choice of such a word the necessary remembrance of the memorable event of the universal destruction of the earthly globe by waters, for the purpose of imprinting vividly in the minds of his countrymen the idea of the righteous justice of the true and omnipotent Lord of all creation, who is punisher and avenger of those who are evil, but who simultaneously rewards the good.

Having thus demonstrated the mystery or mysteries incarnated in the powerful word *Urteá* or "flood," let us now consider and examine the names, which the founders of the Basque language gave to the parts making up the *Urteá,* for clearly they will be the twelve months comprising the Basque year. In Basque, [in chronological order from January to December] they are called *Illbeltzá*, *Otsárallá* (or *Otsailla*), *Marzoá*, *Aprillá*, *Mayatzá*, *Garagarrilla*, *Uztá* (or *Uztailla*), *Abuztuá*, *Agorrá*, *Urriá*, *Azaroá*, and *Abenduá*. In these names, we see clearly that, with the exception of five, that is, *Marzoá, Aprillá, Mayatzá, Abuztuá,* and *Abenduá,* which are not Basque, all the others are, and they have no other meaning except to express the qualities of the months with respect to the season, "animal fetuses," and "rural labors," as is obvious and clear to anyone knowing the basics of the Basque language.

I have noticed that five of the above-mentioned names of months are not part of the enumeration of the Basque months. And the reason for this is that they were introduced during the past centuries of the common Calendar (which are now observed by all the nations that accepted Christianity) after the Basques came under the domination of the Catholic Monarchs with the condition that their *fueros* and privileges would be preserved. But this intrusion or insertion of such barbaric words is not nor will it ever be to the pleasure of the pure Basques, who desire with greatest ardor the preservation of the primitive, pure and clear civil institution of the annual Basque period, and of the others they hold as precious vestiges of venerable Basque antiquity, simply because they regard them as such.

And the knowledge that there is no longer any danger of idolatry (after the total destruction and universal denigration now being heaped upon it) is not a convincing reason to allow or even tolerate the intrusion of any idolatrous terms from the pagan Calendar into our Basque almanacs and prayer books; because if this can be eliminated it would be most useful as a way of preserving the nomenclature of such civil and religious institutions, as these are fragments from very remote centuries that shed much light and instruction for important discoveries, as we are witnessing in these Basque words *Asteá* and *Urteá*.

Despite this carelessness committed in troubled times by our Basque ancestors, I believe that this can be remedied if some wise patrician will devote himself to replacing the five inappropriate foreign names we have mentioned with five genuine, legitimate Basque names. There exist in the series, or names of months that we Gipuzkoans and Bizkaians are accustomed to use, twelve perfectly good Basque names of months, totally different from each other, which I believe are the same, with minor alterations, as those used originally for the twelve Basque months; because the skies, seasons, and measurements of time allow for no synonyms or variety of words, not only among those who speak only one language, but even among people and nations of different countries because of the universality of the use that is made of them: to wit, following the same cyclical systems, not different ones. I offer them here without precise regard for the order in which they should be placed [namely, January to December]: *Urtarilla*, *Cataillla*, *Otsaralla* (or *Otsailla*), *Ceceilla*, *Baguilla*, *Garagarrilla*, *Uzta* (or *Uztailla*), *Agorra*, *Irailla*, *Urria*, *Azaroa*, and *Illbeltza*.

These are the twelve distinct names of months, completely eliminating others no longer used by the Bizkaians and Gipuzkoans, the latter being generally more obscure. Here are most of them: *Epailla*, *Jorrailla*, *Opailla*, *Aberilla*, *Orrilla*, *Ostaroa*, *Erearoa*, *Garilla*, *Bildilla*, *Acilla*, *Lotasilla*, and *Cemendia*, which is an obvious corruption of *Sementera* (sowing season), a Castilian word. With infinite pleasure, we would adopt or include among our Gipuzkoan names of months the ones we need, no matter that our Bizkaian friends would like to lend us some of theirs, provided that they would also be so kind as to reform their disorganized week, part of which is not even Bizkaian, taking on loan almost entirely our Gipuzkoan system, which is theirs too, and the legitimate, true system of the entire Basque language

But returning to our examination and consideration of the literal meaning of the twelve Basque names of months we possess, we see quite clearly that among them there are no other distinct meanings except for those for the attributes of months referring to seasons, fruits, and farm work; without accepting among them any original or derived name that has ever been used in the calendars of other nations.

. . .

Month in Basque is called *illá*, whose literal meaning is "something dead." This comes from the name of the moon, which in the same language is called *Illarguiá*, which in Castilian means literally "dead light." This is a word composed of two simple words, *Illá* (dead), an adjective, and *arguia* (light), a noun, as everyone knows. So that *Illá* (dead), being an adjective, implies a necessary relation to *arguiá:* and therefore, it is always understood as *Illarguiá*, or "dead light." And it should come as no surprise that because the word *Illarguiá* has the same meaning, whether only half of its letters are pronounced, or all of them, there are times when the two names have two pronunciations, because there is a good reason for this, and a specific purpose, as will be explained.

But someone will say: How can it be appropriate and accurate to indicate "month" with the word *Illá* expressed and the unspoken *arguia*, which together denote "the dead light," taking them literally? We respond that with the greatest one, it can be done. Because, first of all, which of all the dead lights in the universe is the one that literally and properly deserves that name? None other than the moon among the heavenly lights and earthly fires. Because the celestial lights, except for the moon, all have their own, live lights, not borrowed, dead lights. I say except for the moon alone, without considering the other planets, which because of their remoteness or great distance from the earth present themselves to the eye with a magnitude almost equal to that of the stars, and they are commonly mistaken for stars by the people. And speaking of earthly lights, there are no dead ones, but they are all live, as cannot be denied. So "the dead light" par excellence is none other than the lunar light: and consequently, there cannot be in the Basque language any name more appropriate than *Illarguiá,* or *Illá*, for naming the lunar light.

Besides, what is the duration of the dead light, or lunar light? It is twenty-nine or thirty days, which is exactly the number of days in the month. So whether we say *Illarguiá* or *Illá* (dead light), I understand it literally to mean, as I should, the event, phenomenon, or occurrence of the dead light, which lasts for a space of twenty-nine or thirty days, and not the opaque body of the moon (which is neither dead light nor live light); I also understand at the same time the monthly space or the month, which is identical with the abovementioned twenty-nine or thirty days. So the word *Illarguia* or *Illá* (dead light) is the most appropriated word existing in the Basque language for denoting the month, because it is the one, who by antonomasia and par excellence signifies the fact or phenomenon of "dead light," which happens in the space of twenty-nine or thirty days.

. . .

And what can be said about the terms *Urteá* and *Illá,* considering them from the point of view of the philosophical quality they possess? Can there be any doubt that they resemble *Asteá* in their perfection? Indeed not. Rather, the mere thought of the equality between the Basque words for year and month, and the word for the Basque week will amaze us. The ideas of true philosophy contained in *Urteá* and *Illá*, then, are those of the universal flood and the newness of death, as has been demonstrated. The first with the purpose, not only of providing a lesson about true religion, manifesting in such a marvelous event the omnipotence of God in performing such a great and incomprehensible catastrophe, but also with the intent of causing a wholesome fear by declaring with the same event the resulting doctrine of the Lord being a terrible judge, avenger and punisher of evil, impious, and perverted people, and the second with the intention of moderating the actions of human life in a praiseworthy and virtuous way through the memory and recollection of death.

And so, does the word *Asteá* perchance surpass the Basque words *Urteá* and *Illá* with respect to religion and true philosophy? Certainly not; because just as *Asteá* signifies the beginning or creation of all things, with the primary purpose of maintaining the dogma of the unity of God in all times, so that we can live without the danger of falling into superstition or idolatry; so also do *Urteá* and *Illá* represent vividly other different and important dogmas through which to achieve greater knowledge of God and rectitude of customs. So, in this aspect the Basque words *Urteá* and *Illá* equal and complement the word *Asteá* beautifully.

It is true that the enormous idea of the creation, which inspires *Asteá*, is of greater importance than the dogmas represented by *Urteá* and *Illá*, as is clear from the preceding treatise on the Basque week. But this matter of having more, or less, extension in terms of dogma is not important, if all three are equally true, precise and necessary to true Religion.

41. Juan Antonio Zamácola Ocerin

(Dima, Bizkaia, 1758 – 1819)

Renouncing his father's surname (Iza), Zamácola belonged to an educated family, many of whose members were notaries. One of his brothers was the famous Simón Bernardo Zamácola, a notary whose political activities associated with the building of the Puerto de la Paz (Port of Peace) near Bilbao set off the popular uprising known as the "*Zamacolada.*" Another sibling was Juan Domingo de Zamácola, a well-known historian of the Spanish empire. Juan Antonio began his studies in Zigoitia (Araba), continuing in Madrid, where he became a notary to the king in 1783. At the outbreak of the War of the Convention with France, he had married and was living once again in his birthplace, when he was named alderman of the Seigniory of Bizkaia and captain of the Dima regiment. As he was suspected of having collaborated with the French, life in the Basque Country became uncomfortable for him after the war and he moved back to Madrid, where he worked once again as a notary to the king. His intellectual contributions were varied and significant; he was a journalist, jurist, folklorist, and the author of works on local customs. He was even a good guitar player and singer, publishing (under the pseudonym "*Don Preciso*") his *Elementos de la ciencia contradanzaria, Para que los Currutacos, Pirracas, y Madamitas del Nuevo Cuño puedan aprender por los principios á baylar las Contradanzas por sí solos, ó con las sillas de su casa* (Elements of the Science of Country Dancing: So that Newly-Coined Dandies, Fops and Little Madams Might Learn Through Principle to Country Dance by Themselves, or With the Chairs of their Houses) (1796) and the *Colección de las mejores coplas de seguidillas, tiranas y polos que se han compuesto para cantar a la guitarra* (Collection of the Best *Seguidilla, Tirana* and *Polo* Songs That Have Been Composed to Sing to with the Guitar) (1799).

After the French invasion of 1808 and the beginning of the reign of Joseph Bonaparte, Zamácola collaborated with the regime, occupying the positions of Chief Notary of the Civil Tribunal of the Spanish High Court, Secretary General of the Seal, Notary of the Realms of Spain, and Police Commissioner. When the war ended, he fled to France, going into exile in Auch, where he lived in some poverty. There, he devoted himself to the study of history, and in 1818 he published his *Historia de las naciones bascas de una y otra parte del Pireneo septentrional y costas del mar Cantábrico, desde sus primeros pobladores hasta nuestros días. Con la descripción, carácter, fueros, usos, costumbres y leyes de cada uno de los estados Bascos que hoy existen* (History of the Basque Nations on One and the Other Side of the Northern Pyrenees and the Coast of the Cantabrian Sea, from its First Inhabitants to the Present: With a Description, Nature, *Fueros*, Habits, Customs and Laws of Each One of the Basque States That Exists Today). The work was of little historiographical interest, because Zamácola was not a professional in the field, and furthermore, he wrote it in circumstances that made any bibliographic consultation extremely difficult. Its main interest is political, as it follows in the northern Basque tradition of Oihenart, Hiribarren, Chaho, and so on, in considering the group of "states" that constituted the Basque-speaking territories as a single historiographic subject. His subject matter, however, consisted merely of a belated reproduction all the mythological elements that had been developed since Garibay: Cantabrianism, Basque-Iberianism, egalitarianism, primitive Christianity, and so forth. With the implementation of the Spanish Liberal regime in 1820, he crossed the French-Spanish border once again, and, it appears, returned to his home in Dima.

As for Zamácola's work in Euskara, it should be remembered that he was a close friend of Astarloa (it is even said that the latter died in Zamácola's arms), who bequeathed all his writings to him at his death. Not being a professional linguist, Zamácola limited himself to continuing and even extending Astarloa's message, especially regarding the "paradisiacal" aspect of the Basque language. Indeed, on this subject he published the work that is of most interest to us here: *Perfecciones analíticas de la lengua bascongada* (Analytical Perfections of the Basque Language) (1822). In fact, this text was published posthumously by his son, Antonio Iza Zamácola, and was considered an advance summary of Astarloa's work, which had still not been published. At no time did Zamácola ever conceal the fact that he was following the theories of Astarloa and of Court de Gébelin, whom he quotes expressly. Otherwise, in the aforementioned *Historia de las Naciones* he shows concern about the fate of Euskara, and broaches two of the essential elements that contributed to its decline. Firstly, there is his proscription of the educational arena: "Unfortunately, because of one of those twists of fate that weigh upon nations, the school teachers of the Basque Country have been forbidden to teach Basque for four centuries." Then, there is the fact that the low prestige in which the language was held caused some parents to prefer to have their children taught another language: "Some ignorant parents are opposed to having their children learn the language of their elders, and send them away when they are very young to other schools outside the Country."[1]

1. Juan Antonio Zamácola, *Historia de las naciones bascas de una y otra parte del Pireneo septentrional y costas del mar Cantábrico, desde sus primeros pobladores hasta nuestros días. Con la descripción, carácter, fueros, usos, costumbres y leyes de cada uno de los estados Bascos que hoy existen* (Auch: Viuda de Dupret, 1818), 213, 174.

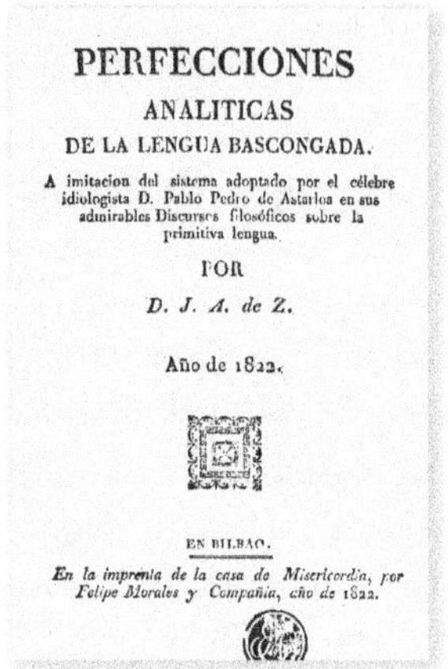

PERFECCIONES
ANALITICAS
DE LA LENGUA BASCONGADA.
A imitacion del sistema adoptado por el célebre idiologista D. Pablo Pedro de Astarloa en sus admirables Discursos filosóficos sobre la primitiva lengua.
POR
D. J. A. de Z.
Año de 1822.
EN BILBAO.
En la imprenta de la casa de Misericordia, por Felipe Morales y Compañia, año de 1822.

SELECTED TEXT(S):

Perfecciones analíticas de la lengua vascongada e imitación del sistema adoptado por el célebre ideologista don Pablo Astarloa en sus admirables "Discursos filosóficos sobre la primitiva lengua" [Analytical Perfections of the Basque Language and a Reproduction of the System Adopted by the Celebrated Ideologist Don Pablo Astarloa in his Admirable "Philosophical Essays on the Primitive Language") (Bilbao: Casa de Misericordia, 1822), 3–14.

Almost all philosophers are convinced by now that primitive man must have possessed a single, reasoned language to teach them mutual and social communication of thought, both by means of its letters, syllables, and meaningful words, and through the action and movement of the tongue and the lips, thus preserving among themselves a perfect analogy with the things that they wished to represent, and Court de Gébelin in his etymological dictionary of the Latin language has deduced from this principle, as have various other scholars, that the many languages that are spread all over the face of the world today descend from the same one, and that according to their structure and analogy are none other than the same primitive language, varied and augmented with words that man has since invented.

In recent years, great debates have taken place to verify which language must have been the world's first tongue, and although literary scholars have tried to establish different opinions, some in favor of the Hebrew language, others of Arabic, Greek, Chinese, Teutonic, or Flemish, and yet others in favor of the languages that they themselves speak, the truth is that they have still not been able to agree on one solid thing, because the primitive language that they were seeking was hidden in the mists of other, much more ancient and distant centuries than those known to the history of nations, of which the world has no memory; and this was the reason why the respectable Basque philosopher Don Pablo Pedro de Astarloa was moved to immerse himself in the great debate over the antiquity of different languages.

With what has so far been written and proven on the subject by certain impartial sages, there exists sufficient data to be assured that the Basques are ahead of the other known nations as to the antiquity, perfection, richness, and excellence of their language, but as there are still stubborn men who have formed a low opinion of Basque from what they have heard from uneducated persons, and who insist upon maintaining that a language that has no illustrious writers cannot possibly be judicious or philosophical, we will make a succinct enumeration of the perfections that make up its mechanism to convince them of their error.

The Perfections of the Basque Language

The Basque language is so perfectly reasoned in all its parts that there is no other known language in the whole world that might be compared to it in good judgment, wisdom, and the excellent union of the words of which it is composed. It shows no anomalies, exceptions, or defects of any kind in its mechanism and composition, and not a single word that might appear ambiguous or incomprehensible to its speakers, because all its letters, syllables, words, and sentences carry [their own] meaning.

. . .

The Basques have never needed writing to communicate their ideas and thoughts: they have a judicious language with the most complete alphabet, but they wrote only what was absolutely necessary to present before their general assemblies for approval. All other writings, such as annals, matters concerning the *fueros*, usages, customs, rituals, religious subjects, history, jurisprudence, politics, medicine, astronomy, and anything else that was presented for the censure of those founding fathers of the homeland, were all burned and torn up on the spot unless the proposal was adopted, so that it would never disturb the peace and quiet of the inhabitants; and this is how their various republics and federations enjoyed long, peaceful governments, that did not fall into the delirium of keeping great warehouses or archives of books like other countries, where men, imbued with the extraordinary ideas that they have read therein, have become converts, taken command, and as conquerors, enthusiasts, or religious men have helped to civilize mankind.

The Basque language consists of 4,146 syllables, from which nearly five million words can be composed, not counting those that are made up of a greater number of syllables: this is such a prodigious number that it seems impossible to employ them all in one language.

The meanings of Basque words are taken from the first utterances of mankind in its infancy: from the exclamations or other recourses of the adult in expressing what he means; in the modulation of the voice; in the noises made by animated objects; and in those noises, made by inanimate objects when they are shaken, which are called onomatopoeic. And the property of these words consists in their having exact and true analogies with the things that they are meant to represent.

. . .

The construction of Basque makes it different in nature from the other European languages, but not from those of the Americas, nor the African interior, which have the same construction as Basque, and this is because they all descend from one unknown primitive language, as is demonstrated by the fact that its antiquity is unknown to history. Meaning in Basque is explained at the rate at which ideas are presented, that is, it forms its sentences by indicating the object first; the use, quality, or shape second; and in third place, the action or movement that is necessary for the thing to be executed. For example, the Basque says *dempora ederra eguiten dago*, which, translated literally into Castilian, is the approximate equivalent of "weather beautiful being it is," and this order cannot be broken unless one wishes to talk nonsense, because the weather is the first idea, its beauty or excellence the second, and the third idea is the execution of the thing. Speakers of Romance languages, like Castilians, Frenchmen, Italians, and others, do without these rules because they say they limit understanding, and it is all the same to them to say the weather is good, good weather we are having, or we are having good weather, etc.; but the point is that with all this freedom they have given rise to that confused muddle called *writing style*, that hodgepodge we observe in the way the different languages arrange their words to explain their ideas. And another thing that is confusing is the strange way the Basques speak. When they begin to speak Castilian, causing many people to laugh at what they think is error, when in fact it is a property of language.

The Basque language is not only distinguished from the other European languages in the harmonious and philosophical formation of its words, which are composed of letters and syllables that each convey meaning, but in the fact that it goes back in antiquity to the dawn of time, allowing us to see in those words, the needs of the first human beings to withstand intemperate climates, and facilitate subsistence. The word *albarquia* or *albarca* [in Castilian], originally referred to a type of footwear made from twigs, according to the meaning of this word, and there is no doubt that this footwear must certainly have been mankind's first invention, to protect himself from the rocks and thorns that would hurt the soles of his feet. *Zubia*, or "bridge," which means two pieces of wood, must also have been the first means found by men to cross rivers and streams. *Chabolia* [Castilian *chabola*], is a "hut or low, round place" in which, no doubt, people took refuge from bad weather. An *echia* is a "house or resting-place that is not small." A *picharra* is the "stone part of a pick," and is "a pitcher" today. An *edarria* is "a rock used for drinking," which later on, when houses began to be constructed, became "the wooden vessel for carrying water" that is still used in the Basque provinces to this day. All these words, and many others that I have omitted in order not to tire the reader, must have belonged to the original language, or must at least be closely analogous to it.

. . .

The Basques write their language in the same way that they speak it, giving each letter the true meaning that it has in the alphabet. The irregularity of giving these letters a sound different from their pronunciation is unknown. It was from them that the Castilians took the valuable circumstance of writing as one speaks, in spite of the fact that they still preserve some slight defects left behind by the Romans. "Literature," as a respectable contemporary philosopher has said, "is the image of the voice, and the more similar it is to the latter, the better it is."

The Basque language has the outstanding ability to distinguish, by means of its syllables and words, between virtuous actions and sinful ones, applying at the same time a reward or a punishment according to the merit of each person. Its word for "intentionally crazed behavior" is *zoraqueria*, whereas it refers to "the illness of true insanity" as *zoratazuna*. *Ordiqueria* is what it calls "the vice of drunkenness," whereas *orditasuna* refers to the "inebriation caused by aromas, bad smells, etc."; thus, a distinction is created between the two types of persons in the endings of the words.

Therefore, one can almost be assured that in other times the Basque language in itself must have been a religious and civil code by which men must have learned the obligations that allowed them to live in communities.

There is no reason to tire oneself out, said the same philosopher. If we want our children to be happy, we need to find the language of nature, and banish all other tongues, because vice and virtue alike are bound up in them. Let us seek those patriarchs of primitive times, if we still know anything about them, and follow them in every way. Away with that appalling education that has filled the world with chains: away with those shackles, those vices that are the work of men, and everything will then be a blessing for us.

. . .

Finally, in support of the primacy of their language, Basques should know that in every single country in the entire world, and in all known languages without exception, when children start to speak they utter their first syllables in Basque, for example *aita* for "father," *ama* for "mother," *papa* for "to eat," *titi* for "breast," *lo* for "to sleep," *aup* for "to sit up," *cac* for "to dirty," etc.

The other perfections of the Basque language, with the proof of its antiquity that place it first among the known languages of the world, can be seen in *Discursos filosóficos sobre la primitiva lengua* [Philosophical Essays on the Primitive Language], by my untimely-departed friend Don Pablo Pedro de Astarloa, a work that will be the admiration of centuries to come, if it should ever be published.

Meanwhile, I hope that this outline will meet with the indulgence of those fond of reading about their country.

42. José Antonio Conde

(Perpleja, Cuenca, 1765 – Madrid, 1820)

He studied both civil and canon law at the University of Salamanca before going on to specialize in languages and numismatics. He taught Greek and Hebrew at the same university, although his first love was the Arabic language, and he had a particular interest in Arab coins minted in Spain. He was Curator of the Escorial Palace Library, a member of the Real Academia de la Lengua, and directed the Bureau of Antiquities. Like Joaquín Traggia, he was both an "antiquarian," and a secular priest. He was persecuted and exiled for his support of French rule in Spain and for collaborating with the government of Joseph Bonaparte. The fact that he used the pseudonym, "The priest from Montuenga," in his epistolary debates with Astarloa and Erro was because he had received (at some point in his life) minor orders and worked in a parish in Montuenga (Soria). However, not only was he never actually ordained a priest, but he left the priesthood during the Napoleonic Wars, and in 1816 married a niece of Leandro Fernández de Moratín, a woman almost thirty years his junior.

Conde wrote two works on the controversies over the Basque language: *Censura crítica de la pretendida excelencia y antigüedad del vascuence* (A Critical Judgment of the Supposed Excellence and Antiquity of Basque) (1804), and *Censura crítica del alfabeto primitivo de España y pretendidos monumentos literarios del vascuence* (A Critical Judgment of the Primitive Alphabet of Spain and the Supposed Literary Monuments of Basque) (1806). Independently of the accuracy of his opinions and judgments, the tone of his polemical style personifies the spirit of the emblematic Jacobin centralist Spanish liberal, persuaded of the superiority and perfection of the classical languages and disdainful of dialects and "patois." From this standpoint he was greatly irritated by the positions of the "paradisiacal" Basques and their claims of the excellence for an uncultivated language spoken by the masses, and although he was shielded by a false name, he nevertheless invested a great deal of energy in combating these positions. He employed a scornful tone and many epithets toward the Basque language and its supporters, often disguised behind Latin or Greek texts; his favorite words for the language were "babble" or "gibberish," and its defenders would be described, in the best of cases, as ignoramuses. One priceless example of many: "[the word] *averatseac* [wealthy] belongs both to primitive Basque and to French and Castilian, because it is composed of [the Spanish] *haber*, "to have," and *asaz*, *asez* [a great deal]; it originates from the two Latin words *habere-sat* or *satis*; but the Basques will say that Latin got it from them; so that form of gibberish has not presented its certificates of ownership and ancient original possession, and therefore is not to be believed."[1]

The list of Basque authors whom Conde contradicted contains the names (apart from the most notable ones) of other, more ingenuous individuals that are easy targets. These were Luis Carlos y Zúñiga, the priest from Escalonilla, a Navarrese whose long absence from the country had caused his Basque to become rusty.[2] He was a well meaning but

1. José Antonio Conde, *Censura crítica del alfabeto primitivo de España y pretendidos monumentos literarios del vascuence* (Madrid: Imprenta Real, 1806), 24.

2. See Luis Carlos y Zúñiga, *Plan de antigüedades españolas, reducido a dos artículos y ochenta proposiciones* (Madrid: Villapando, 1801).

somewhat naive writer who had taken Larramendi's parable to heart, to the exasperation of much more highly critical authors such as Moguel; and Conde was to have a field day with material from this gullible author. Conde criticized Erro, Astarloa, Zúñiga, Hervas, and Larramendi on several fronts, but in essence he refuted the claims that Basque had been the language of paradise, that it was spoken all over the Iberian Peninsula, that it was a perfect language, and in particular Astarloa's method of conferring meaningful ideas upon sounds, and alleging that these ideas were emitted by the vocal organs. To the contrary, Conde upheld the idea that words depended on the will of human beings who arbitrarily assign different meanings to words and to combinations of words.

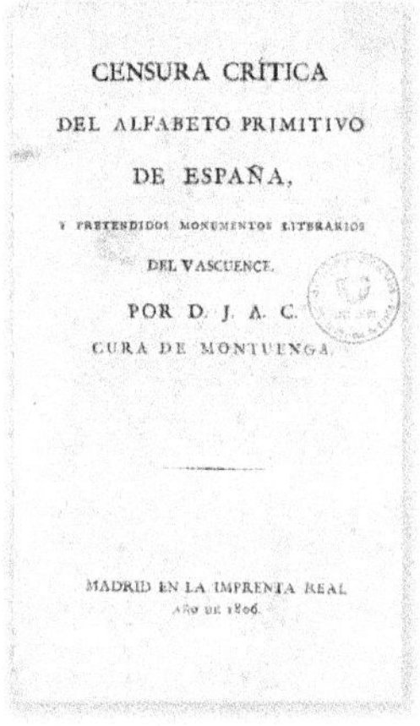
CENSURA CRÍTICA
DEL ALFABETO PRIMITIVO
DE ESPAÑA,
Y PRETENDIDOS MONUMENTOS LITERARIOS
DEL VASCUENCE.
POR D. J. A. C.
CURA DE MONTUENGA.

MADRID EN LA IMPRENTA REAL
AÑO DE 1806.

SELECTED TEXT(S):

Censura crítica del alfabeto primitivo de España y pretendidos monumentos literarios del vascuence [A Critical Judgment of the Primitive Alphabet of Spain and the Supposed Literary Monuments of Basque] (Madrid: Imprenta Real, 1806), 5–8, 32–37.

Mister Zúñiga, parish priest of Escalonilla, dazzled by the coincidental similarity of certain names of towns to Basque words, and without having examined this similarity to see whether it occurs in the roots and original words, and who has at the same time gone astray among the reckless, unscholarly, and futile paradoxes of Larramendi (upon whom Spain should heap opprobrium and shame [for meddling with] its most precious antiquities), wrote his plan in eighty bizarre propositions, all founded on the frivolous and unstable grounds of a supposed ancient culture and the notion that Basque was once spoken all over Spain, which leads Mister Zúñiga to find everything in the Basque language; and Mister Zúñiga will interpret every word that historians and geographers mention, whether these terms be from Spain, Africa, England, or Norway, as being Basque. He has stated with the greatest of confidence that *Escocia* [Scotland] is so named from *escu-ocia* or "cold hand"; *Irlanda* [Ireland] from *ira-landa* or "fern meadow"; *Holanda* [Holland] from *ola-andia* or "great wave of water"; *Suecia* [Sweden] from *sue-cia* or "fire he-lights"; and declares that this mellifluous name fits perfectly within his method. *Dinamarca* [Denmark] refers to whatever you will, and he takes no consideration of the fact that these names were not originally spoken the way we pronounce them, and that they have their own etymology and meaning in their own languages. This author was preceded in this scholarly insanity by Mister Hervas with his catalogue of all languages, a work that deals with the dialects of nations, whose existence has not been conclusively proven, and their affinities, origins, and associations are distinguished in each case by comparison with a few barbaric and poorly copied words, and he weighs their culture and elegance, or rusticity and impoverishment as if he were highly versed in the orators and poets of each one of them. Mister Zúñiga is no less erudite than Mister Hervas, and follows the same criteria, beginning with the name of *España* [Spain], which he says is from *ichs-pa-nia*, "sea under region," as if this were peculiar and unique to Spain, never doubting that the ancient names of its provinces and cities are all from the most beauteous Basque language: many [place-names] have been elucidated with his help, among them the *Cilbicenos* [an ancient people who inhabited the present-day area around Cádiz in Andalusia] who Avienus mentions but which Mister Zúñiga interprets as "those where that which flows arrives." What miraculous concepts this language contains! What delightful ideas are enclosed in so few syllables! If I were not afraid of making myself appear as ridiculous as these etymologists, I would find for the old names of provinces and cities of Spain the most thoroughly researched, cultured, and properly fitting etymologies and meanings. Thus, Bastitania would not be a land of packsaddles, as these gentlemen say *ἀπϱεως* is, but proceeding from the Phoenician and Punic ושיטניה *wasitania*, "intermediate land," "land between two others," and instead of *Turdetania*, which they mistakenly interpret as "region of pigs," that is, Cerdistan [from *cerdo* or "pig"] in the Persian manner, conferring this bespattered name in the place of such a charming one belonging to the most cultured and pleasing region in ancient Spain, having deduced it from תרשיתניה, Tarsitania, the region of Tarsis [Tartessus]. And Tarsis, תרשיש, has two meanings: if the word is a simple one, it means "sea," and if it is compound, as seems to be the case with *tar-sis*, תר שיש it means "beautiful view" or "delightful, peaceful, blissful view"; and when the word is taken to mean "sea," it is not a word from the original language, for in that language sea is ים *(iam),* but instead it is a metaphor taken from the hyacinth or cerulean color of the sea; and so Editania would be צרותניה, *Edytania*, "a region of peaceful and gentle climes." Without forcing the issue, these names seem to be of Eastern origin, and the same procedure might be applied to others of Greek and Celtic origin, without the necessity of turning to Basque, which was not spoken in Spain during those centuries, and which in all probability came to us from northern Europe with the waves of Barbarians that during the time of Probus invaded the provinces of the Roman Empire, or else [the names] belonged to those Barbarians that Paulus Diaconus speaks of, who, during the time of Honorius were permitted, more from necessity than good will, to enter through the Pyrenees, and all those ferocious nations who were laying waste to France were permitted to enter Spain. *Quibus Barbaris dum claustra Pyrenæi montis commissa fuissent, ab eis tota, quæ per Gallias bacchabatur, ferocitas gentium, Hispanarum provinciis intromissa est: itaque post multas strages incendia et rapinas, tandem divisis sedibus, barbari ad aratra conversi, Romanorum residuos cæperunt ut socios amicosque fovere* [While the defense of the Pyrenean mountain passes had been confined to these Barbarians, these same people introduced all their ferocity into all the provinces of the Spains, which was only undone by the violence of the Gauls; thus, after much destruction, fires and violent theft, their townships divided at last, the Barbarians were converted into farmers and began to help the remaining Romans, as allies and friends]. From that time on they continued to inhabit the mountains of the Basque Country, because they were not bothering anyone there, and they encountered a climate that they have never since abandoned, nor has anyone attempted to take it from them.

. . .

The letter, as grammarians tell us, is an arbitrary and conventional character or sign that we might call the image of a simple and indivisible sound in a word. Some people, mistaking letters for what they represent, call them simple or indivisible sounds within a word: a combination of sounds results in syllables, and the union of syllables results in words; from a combination of words come sentences or concepts. The Greeks wisely called them ςοιχεῖα or "elements," for they were the simple, indivisible beginnings of words; therefore, letters that are made of more than one sound should be called ciphers of letters, as happens in the Greek compounds χ, ξ, ψ; and the simple sound, although represented by two or more signs, merits only the name of the letter, as occurs with our Spanish *ch* (previously considered a single letter), and in Latin with its *ph* and *th*.

The speech mechanism is not in the least philosophical, and neither are languages philosophical, as the flunkies of Mister Astarloa deliriously believe, as they follow in his eccentric footsteps: it is a purely natural, simple, and straightforward thing whose operations are never swayed by the vain speeches and musings of philosophers: in sum, languages are not philosophical, but the speeches that philosophers compose in them are, and languages, in and of themselves, are no more than instruments of philosophy or barbarity.

Instead of the riddles that these Basques propose, when they say that "The speakers of Basque, with their philosophical language, found in the modulation of the voice the value and function exercised by the smallest components within [the language], and that to perpetuate these solid observations that lead to the perfect understanding of Basque, they established their alphabet . . ." Therefore, in their philosophical language they had to find the value and function exercised by its smallest components to understand the language itself. This is something best left to the Basques. Instead of this, they would have done better to have said that the main instruments of speech are the lungs and the larynx together with the trachea, the tongue, the teeth, the lips, and other parts of the mouth; and that inhaled air, which is the physical material of words, leaves the lungs through the trachea; the variety of sounds and their tone and articulation result from the action of this exhaled air upon the speech organs; this variety does not proceed from the lungs themselves, whose function is limited to rendering the voice louder or softer, more sonorous or less so, according to the degree of force with which inhalation takes place, so that the lungs are to speech as the bellows are to an organ. Variety in tone, as regards whether the words sound low or high, proceeds mainly from the trachea; one with a longer, narrower tube produces a higher sound, and a trachea with a shorter, wider tube makes a lower sound; and so the trachea and the larynx, according to whether the opening of the Adam's apple is larger or smaller, produce a deeper or higher tone. The two parts generally undergo alteration at different ages, and in different persons and sexes; this, therefore, gives rise to what we call sounds and tones. The articulation of words, or the formation of letters, begins when inhaled air leaves the larynx, touches and is modified by the speech organs; these are the palate, tongue, teeth, and lips: this is where the difference and division between letters appear as guttural, palatal, dental and labial vowels; this is how we obtain different and discrete letters. The vowels and their number differ according to the nature of the languages and nations, possessing nuances that are more apparent or less so according to the greater or lesser intensity of pronunciation and the greater, median, or lesser opening and capacity of the organs. We can say, although there are notable exceptions to this, that there are three types of guttural, palatal, and labial vowels, according to where they are formed, and to these correspond the three Hebrew vowels אוי and the Arab *fatha*, *kesra*, *damma*, which are the equivalent of all the vowel sounds of the human race; but both these and the consonants, so called because they are sounded in conjunction with vowels, have arbitrary characters, and do not present in their written forms any ideas related to their meanings themselves. This is a dream, made up by Mister Astarloa and carried on by Mister Erro with some additional nonsense that shows itself to be patently unfounded and ridiculous. If knowledge of their letters and meanings, that is to say of their pronounceable value, were not communicated, no one would understand them; and if letters were not simple sounds insignificant in and of themselves, it would not be possible to produce the variety of words composed from them.

Ideas are not born by words that never leave their sounds nor the configuration and functions of the speech organs, as Astarloa's minions would have us believe, but from the will of men, who linked ideas to words to understand each other, and, according to their various thoughts, differentiated and established the words that would express them. This gave rise to the difference between using *nouns* when they attempted to express various substances, as opposed to *verbs*. Employed when expressing different actions, and when they wished to reason and join a third idea to two others, they invented the words we call conjunctions, connecting words or particles. So an idea indicated by a word does not come from its sound, nor from the modifications of the speech organs, but arbitrarily from human will; and as Democritus would say, if the word through its very nature could explain any given idea, a single sound or a single word could not indicate several ideas, as has been observed in every language, and neither could a single item have two names; from whence he wisely inferred that this has come rather *ἔϑει ὁμολίᾳ συνθήκῃ νόμῳ*, through use or custom, consent, convention, and the law of men; and certainly, if the sounds of the human voice of itself and by its very nature expressed ideas, there would only be one language for the whole of mankind.

Nevertheless, I do believe that letters have names taken from their pronunciations and conventional characters, and that, although they are an admirable and almost divine invention, they manifest in their characters and in their names a great number of vestiges of the history of humanity, and that all this is *θέσει οὐ φύσει*, I have never doubted that in Phoenician, Hebrew, Syro-Chaldean, or Arabic they have meanings that are to some degree suitable to their most immediate and evident form, nature, or idea.

If letters, as the pseudo-philosophers claim, were expressive signs derived from nature, their characters would be few, uniform, and almost the same among all men, like simple signs and short expressions of natural necessities, and we would be able to read them all without being taught; but as they are arbitrary and established by convention, there are so many of them and they are so different that they cannot all be known or studied, and they have such a poor relationship to natural expressions that the possessor of the most penetrating and subtle mind cannot read a text in Kufic, Georgian, Armenian, or Hindustani, if he has not first learned its characters.

Therefore, as it is likely that the names of letters have meanings in the language that invented them, or adopted and modified them, the Greek letters could not escape this testimony to their Eastern origin: Saint Hieronymus interpreted the names of the Hebrew letters. Eusebius, and later on Cornelius Bertramus, and Bellarminus; and anyone who was at all versed in the Eastern languages, could interpret the names of Jonic-Kadmean, Phoenician, Syro-Chaldean, and Ethiopian letters, all of which share the same origin, the same literal and numerical power or value, and the same names with slight modifications, according to the spirit of each language.

Because Basque scholars know nothing of this, they will not take anyone's word for anything.

43. Pierre d'Iharce de Bidassouet

(Hazparne [Hasparren], Lapurdi, 1765 – 1843)

He began his studies with the Prior of the Elizaberry Hermitage, to whom he was related, and later studied humanities in Suhuskune (Suhescun) (Lower Navarre), philosophy in Pau (Béarn), and theology in the Seminary of Larresoro (Larressore) in Lapurdi. In 1790, he left the Seminary and returned to his native town where he developed an accelerated reading method (four months) for learning Latin and Euskara. He was ordained as a priest in 1792, adding his name to the list of hundreds of ecclesiastics who were forced to cross the border and flee from the

French Revolution, and he subsequently resided in Oronoz and Puente la Reina (Gares, Navarre), as well as El Ferrol (Galicia).

Back in the northern Basque Country, he had a number of problematic encounters with the Bishop of Baiona, resulting in the publication of some of his works. Of interest to us here are those related to the origins of the Basques (and their language): *Recherches sur l'origine veritable et réelle des Escu-alde-duns, par syncope Escualduns: anciennement Guiçons (hommes) cantabres; et aujourd'hui généralement Basque français, espagnoles . . .* (Research into the True and Actual Origin of the *Escu-alde-duns*, by Syncopation *Escualduns*: Called Cantabrians in Ancient Times, and Today Generally French and Spanish Basques . . .]; and especially the *Histoire des Cantabres . . .* (History of the Cantabrians . . .) (1825). A belated Cantabrianist, he carried the linguistic theories of the apologists of his day to the most adventurous extremes, using a picturesque mathematical system to "prove" that the Basque language was the one spoken by Adam in Paradise.

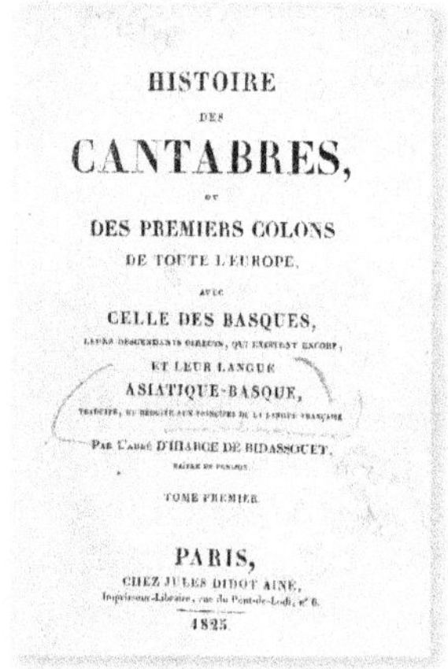

HISTOIRE

DES

CANTABRES,

DES PREMIERS COLONS

DE TOUTE L'EUROPE,

CELLE DES BASQUES,

ET LEUR LANGUE

ASIATIQUE-BASQUE,

PAR L'ABBÉ D'IHARCE DE BIDASSOUET,

TOME PREMIER.

PARIS,

CHEZ JULES DIDOT AINÉ,

Imprimeur-Libraire, rue du Pont-de-Lodi, n° 6.

1825.

SELECTED TEXT(S):

Histoire des cantabres, ou des premiers colons de toute l'Europe avec celle des basques, leurs descendants directs, qui existent encore, et leur langue asiatique-basque, traduite, et réduite aux principes de la langue française [History of the Cantabrians, or the First Inhabitants of All of Europe, with That of the Basques, Their Direct Descendants, Who Still Exist, and Their Asiatic-Basque Language, Translated and Governed by the Principles of the French Language] (Paris: Julie Didot Ainé, 1825), xiv–xv, xvii–xviii, 249–51, 395–396, 401–403.

Preface

To evaluate a people, it is not enough to know about a few wars they have had with their neighbors, how large their population is, and what the soil where they live produces; beyond that, it is necessary to know their institutions, their customs, and their language. It is through these that we can judge the state of their civilization. The Basques, little known until now, are however worthy of taking their place in the history of nations. Their antiquity, their courage, and their noble character have won them a role in the destinies of the world. Carthage and even Rome numbered them among their citizens and their allies.

The Basques, whose mysterious origin I have sought to resolve in my published works, are perhaps the only people whose language has remained unchanged except for the Chinese. In a historical-critical dissertation examining the attributes that constitute the primordial quality of any language, and in which I have tried to prove the antiquity of that of the Basques, I have had to investigate its universality, its naturalness, that is, its conformity to the instinct of each stage of its life in the expression of needs, sentiments and ideas: in short, the advantage it offers over all other languages in the ease with which it is learned because of its sympathy with nature.

Before my efforts, perhaps, no one had ever subjected a language to mathematical analysis. This method might seem peculiar: it is not my intent to defend it from any criticism; but if it is not the best method, it is at least the one I have had to follow to reach the goal that I set for myself. Therefore, I have compiled, under the title of grammatical problems or theorems, a series of questions whose solutions I approach mathematically, thus establishing a logical grammar in which I explain the principles of the Basque language analyzed and compared to that of the French.

. . .

Isolated until now from other peoples living around them and strangers to anything taking place beyond their borders, and with the help of this grammar and dictionary I am publishing,* the Basques will from this day forth gain re-entry into the grand family of the French people from whom only their language seemed to have separated them. Closer and more frequent relations will be established, and once again,

* This is a bilingual dictionary, i.e. French to Basque and vice versa, and presents, in addition to the standard features of French academic dictionaries, the etymological meaning and characteristic significance of each word in small print.

this vast country will take wing. Ports will be opened to commerce; bridges and roads will be built; vital industries will gain access to our towns; at last, agriculture and the arts will flourish in the country of Sartorius and Henri IV; and the ashes of these Cantabrians, proud to have conquered in succession the Phoenicians, the Carthaginians, the Romans, the Goths, the Visigoths, the Ostrogoths, the French themselves, and finally the Saracens, will seem to rise up again to merge their former glory with that of the beautiful and luxuriant France, proud and glorious to be governed by Charles X, worthy scion of Charles VII the Victorious, whose protection the Cantabrians will spontaneously acknowledge.

Finally, this work, being elementary, scientific, and historical, and conjoining the sacred and the profane, will belong to all lovers of literature without distinction.

. . .

Let us admit then that the author of natural language is God, and that the history recounted by Moses is true.

Then, I ask, why should the human race not have its own language as the other species do? Why should man, the most perfect of all beings; man, the only one formed in the image of God, be a mute creature? But if he is the only one created in the image of the Creator, is his Creator then a mute Being? If He is not, why would He have deprived man of a sublime attribute that should necessarily constitute his perfectibility over all the other creatures?

God cannot be pleased that I place man, that noble type of the Divinity, below the wild beasts as the frenzied students of an insane revolution have done; rather, acknowledging the superiority of man, one must at least grant that his language is natural, general, common, flawless, indestructible, and that it will only come to an end with the disappearance of the species with which it has been created. But, what is that natural language?

1. It is the language in which children, at birth, designate in their animate condition, through an initial impulse and through their first cries, their difference in gender: thus, in the Basque Country, we can tell immediately if a child is male or female even before we see it, because a baby boy utters his first cries by forming the letter *a*, which in Basque means *ar-arra*, *Adam*, "male," "masculine"; and a girl by forming the letter *e*, *émé-émea*, *eba*, "feminine," "female."

2. The natural language is the one that most closely resembles its creating force, and that begins its first words by stammering out the

names related to that force. In effect, the first words that infants pronounce in all four corners of the earth when they can barely form sounds, no matter what their parents' language is, are Basque, i.e.: *all-alla* (father); *am-ama* (mother); *tti-tti-tti* (breast); *pa pa pa* (eat); *man-maman* (suckle); *lo-lo* (sleep); *aup, aupa* (wake up); *phu-caca* (dirty). However, we still need to determine whether the Basque language, as the primitive language, and consequently natural, conforms in its locutions to the different ages of life. First, being naturally infantile, that is, small and diminutive with infants, adult with adults, mature with elders, so that we can reasonably infer that it grows progressively the way nature grows. To demonstrate this truth, let us take for example a Basque nurse, who represents all Basque women, and we will observe the different sounds which that woman would use to speak to her infant, until he attains majority.

. . .

Thirteenth Problem or Theorem Resolved

Among all of the more or less cultured languages, and consequently known universally, it is the Basque language that most closely approximates the language that God inspired in Adam, either for its perfectibility or for its inexhaustibility.

I have already demonstrated in my dissertation on the primordial and universal quality of the Basque language that this language embodies all the attributes constituting the primordial quality of any language.

To resolve this problem, I now need to demonstrate that the Basque language is the only one that most closely resembles the language that God inspired in Adam, or created with him.

This task is grand and difficult; my demonstration will no doubt be challenged; but I will at least have made an effort to throw light on a matter that seems to me to be completely resolved in favor of the Basque language.

One might, perhaps, accuse me of having loved my country to excess, of having carried my love of my language too far; I am not the one to judge such a reproach; but at the very least, it is my fervent hope that no one will think that I have deliberately abused the indulgence of the reader by presenting to him these problems which I offer with simplicity.

. . .

But let us return to what we have proposed: that the Basque language is the one that most closely resembles the one God inspired in Adam.

In my dissertation, I have already spoken about the primacy and the antiquity of the Basque language, that the number of languages that were formed at the time of the Confusion of Babel had to be equal to the number of the families who tried to build that tower, that is, seventy-two (at least this is the most likely opinion); today, now that every part of the world is inhabited, it would be difficult to count them all unless we subdivided them.

But although many languages might have been formed by imitation, and they might not be as rich as their paradigms, they should at least have basic elements that I estimate at the number 754, and I assume an equality of inflections, an equality of richness in their radical capacity.

Here is my calculation:

Granting each language its maximum extent, that is, assuming that each has four million syllables, and that number multiplied by seventy-two equals 288,000,000 syllables or elementary particles.

The product of the Basque verbal system is 72,384,000 syllables; the product of the nouns and verbal adjectives is 796,224,000 paired or unpaired syllables, without even counting the declensional product or the adverbial product.

Therefore it is true, assuming the exactness of the mathematical calculation, that the Basque language would have the capacity to furnish the elements for all of the languages in the world, even if we assumed that instead of seventy-two there might even have been 160 and allowing each of them more than four million elemental particles, without even bothering to count the actual syllabic product of the diminutive verbs, or that of the substantive nouns and diminutive verbal adjectives which, being equal to the ordinary nouns, would equal 1,592,448,000 paired and unpaired syllables.

It is clear, then, that there is no other language in the universe that more closely approaches the language which the eternal Father inspired in Adam, either for its priority, its universality, its inexhaustibility, its naturalness, its nuances, its inflections, its allusions, or for its verb system, or, finally, for its perfectibility, than the Basque language; hence, my thirteenth and final problem or theorem is hereby resolved.

44. Dominique Lahetjuzan Etcheto

(Sara [Sare], Lapurdi, 1766 – Sara, 1818)

He was born and died in his family home of Argainea, spending most of his life in his birthplace. As a second son, he was provided with an education oriented toward an ecclesiastical career. He studied theology in Toulouse and was ordained a priest in 1790, returning to Sara where he was appointed parish priest and immediately faced with the choice of accepting or rejecting the Civil Constitution for the Clergy. He rejected it, but instead of taking the path of exile like hundreds of other clergymen who were unwilling to accept the terms of the French Revolution, he remained in the country, practicing his priestly duties clandestinely. He busied himself non-stop throughout his parish, baptizing, marrying, or conducting mass, constantly moving from one place to another. Denounced, he managed to escape his pursuers and hide in a small room in his house, where he was finally arrested, but when he was taken before his captors he escaped and was finally forced to cross the border and go into exile. Lahetjuzan's counterrevolutionary activity has to be considered in the context of the region formed by the towns of Itsasu (Itxassou), Biriatu (Biriatou), Azkaine (Ascain), Ezpeleta (Espelette), Kanbo (Cambo-les-Bains), Larresoro (Larressore), and Sara, which were all located near the Franco-Spanish border on the left bank of the Urdazuri (Nivelle) River. This area was renowned for its anti-Republican resistance, especially in religious matters, and the authorities of the French Republic suspected it of complicity with the Spaniards in the context of the War of the Convention, leading them to deport all its inhabitants en masse in the spring of 1793.

Lahetjuzan was a typical rural priest, attached to the land and to the most traditional ideas. His intellectual interests were quite provincial: thus, for example, between 1810 and 1815, he wrote a text on the peculiar system used in Sara for hunting homing pigeons. Although he wrote most of his works in French, he also left a few unpublished pages in Basque, and of course, the Basque language was one of his primary concerns. He anonymously published a small book titled: *Essai de quelques notes sur la langue basque, par un vicaire de campagne, sauvage d'origine* (Essay of Some Notes on the Basque Language, by a Primitive Country Priest) (1808), which was initially attributed to D'Iharce de Bidassouet. Two of the concepts that appear in the title are quite revealing of his personality and ideology. In effect, he was, and considered himself to be, a country priest, claiming that his maternal language was Euskara and that he had not mastered French. There was, moreover, an interesting allusion to a kind of Rousseauian primitivism, of which he boasted. He maintained some epistolary contact with Humboldt, who in 1802 contacted him for information about Axular, Lahetjuzan's compatriot. Lahetjuzan subsequently sent Humboldt a number of facts, among them, that Axular's real name was Daguerre and that "Axular" was the name of his farmstead, by which he was commonly known. Lahetjuzan apparently had a reputation in his region as a man of letters; and Jean Martin Hiribarren, in his 1853 poem *Eskualdunac* (The Basques), characterizes him as a "*guizon aiphatua*" (a respected man).

His ideas about Euskara were those of the Astarloa school, although carried to ridiculous extremes. Convinced of the paradisiacal character of the language, he ranted in picturesque etymologies about the symbolic meaning of biblical characters and concepts (Adam, Eve, and wine), which ultimately only undermined his theories.

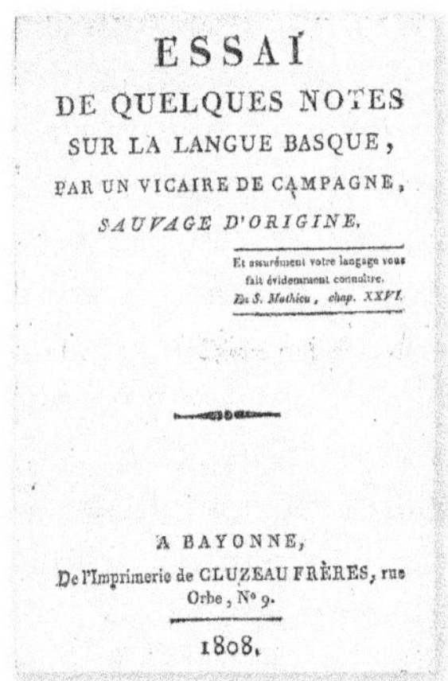

ESSAI
DE QUELQUES NOTES
SUR LA LANGUE BASQUE,
PAR UN VICAIRE DE CAMPAGNE,
SAUVAGE D'ORIGINE.

Et assurément votre langage vous
fait évidemment connoître.
Ev. S. Mathieu, chap. XXVI.

A BAYONNE,
De l'Imprimerie de CLUZEAU FRÈRES, rue
Orbe, N° 9.

1808.

SELECTED TEXT(S):

Essai de quelques notes sur la langue basque, par un vicaire de campagne, sauvage d'origine [Essay of Some Notes on the Basque Language by a Primitive Country Priest] (Bayonne: Cluzeau frères, 1808), 3–5, 9–14.

First Note

Those who have only a modest knowledge of Basque consider it a jargon or an obscure, barbaric, inelegant language. It is a somewhat pleasant surprise to learn that those who have studied it seriously believe they have discovered in this language, spoken by a people who have no apparent interest in literature, a degree of perfection to which modern languages can only attain by virtue of literary practice; they have spoken it with enthusiasm, and they have been condemned for admiring it without due reflection. D. J. A. C., the priest from Montuega, has gone too far, accusing them of ignorance, insensitivity, and insulting them without restraint.

The frivolity with which this gentleman ridicules the Basque writers does not diminish the high regard I have for their talents, and in my role as brother in the priesthood, I believe I have earned the right to offer them my good counsel, hoping that it will not be forgotten in due course.

. . .

To be sure, the task that I take upon myself, insignificant as it is, requires the knowledge of ancient languages both dead and living; it has been my intention to offer it for the purpose of facilitating a deep analysis of the Basque language, and I hope that my efforts will not be misunderstood. French is not my language, so I ask indulgence for my lack of style and grammar. Far from wishing to avoid criticism, I submit all of my reflections to scrutiny; my worst fear is that my weak effort will be found unworthy of such scrutiny; criticism is motivated by love of letters; I love them equally; I am no writer, but I love teaching, and teaching is the primary goal of rational condemnation. Critics are not unaware that in every nation a baggage carrier is needed. This is precisely the role I choose. This choice should bring them a bit of cheer; haste is of the essence; I counsel patience! A poor country priest can endure anything, even the mockery of so-called cultured companions.

. . .

The first language was irremediably crippled in Babel; but there is no proof that it was totally extinguished: Moses says nothing in this regard. The character of primitive languages proves that many beautiful vestiges escaped that catastrophe: the Basque language is one of those vestiges.

Fourth Note

Three years ago a French journal, in an article on the Basques or *Escualduns*, claimed that their language was created mainly for the expression of the basic necessities of life or for matters related to agriculture and the herding of flocks, and that it was almost completely lacking in metaphysical terms and did not have a suitable word for referring to the body in general and to the soul. From that, the author of those remarks concluded that the Basque language is original.

I beg the gentleman who wrote that observation to judge for himself if, given the character that he attributes to the Basque language, he might not draw the opposite or contradictory conclusion. Whatever the case, I see that he is convinced of the originality of the Basque language; and I am presumptuous enough to claim that it will be easy to see that this language is perhaps even more original than he first imagined: it does not lack metaphysical terms; it has as many as any other language in the world.

I will demonstrate that this is so by listing those he refuses to acknowledge. There is a word for expressing the body in general, and that is *gorphutz*, and another for referring to the soul, *arima*. These words do not come from any foreign language, although it might be possible that several of them have borrowed them from Basque; the reason for this is that in other languages these words are devoid of meaning and that in Basque, they are symbolic, and the expression of what they represent is connected to their very origin.

Gorphutz is composed of the three words *go-or-phutz*; *go* means "that which is above, superior"; *or, orra, orratce*, means "petrify"; *phutz* is "an exhalation" or "a way of breathing." This term, then, gives us to understand that it is a breathing organism that is hard on the top; this is the only meaning possible in Basque: it is obvious that it represents the creation of the body of Man.

Arima, *aria*, is "resemblance, rapport, image"; *ma*, is "multitude, center, abyss, peak, abundance, source, plenitude, intimate affection"; it is in this sense, that *ma*, as well as *am,* is always used in the Basque language: we can see from this that *arima* means "a being that has an infinite number of connections, images, and resemblances." Let us consider these etymologies and the manner in which Moses depicts the creation of man; it will be obvious that the term *arima* expresses the text *faciamus hominem ad imaginem et similitudinem nostram* [let us make man in our image and our likeness, Genesis 1.26], and that the term *gorphutz* expresses, by analogy, *fecit hominem ex humo terræ* [made man from the dust of the ground, Genesis 2.7].

The Basque language, then, does have terms for referring to the body and the soul, and they admirably encapsulate what Moses says about the creation of the first body and the first soul. Basque, then, is living proof of the veracity of Genesis; Basque has many similar terms for expressing the origin of things, always in accordance with Genesis.

Fifth Note

In a manuscript that I have seen pass from hand to hand and which I read with interest, we find the following phrase: *Arno est un terme générique qui signifie boisson; c'est pourquoi on dit* mahaxarno, *pour du vin, sagarno, pour du cidre* [*Arno* is a generic term that means "beverage"; because of this, one says *mahaxarno* for "wine," *sagarno*, for "cider"]: this is incorrect; the generic Basque word meaning *boisson* [beverage], is *edaria*, and not *arnoa*; *edari* includes all kinds of beverages, and the denomination *arno* means wine and nothing more; we do not say *mahaxarno* for wine, but simply *arno*. *Mahaxarno* means "wine from raisins," which is a pleonasm.

Arno is an original and expressive Basque word; its etymology is "Invention of Noah"; in effect, the word *ar* in Basque has just one meaning, "creation, invention, formation, extension, original production"; there is an analogy of resemblance among all these words; *no* is the root of the name of Noah. That patriarch, a farmer by profession, said Moses, began to till the land, to plant vines for the purpose of making wine. Consider here the remarkable harmony between Genesis and Basque; the Basque word for wine, *arno*, literally, "invention of Noah," is therefore a perpetual monument to the origin of wine. It is, however, likely that wine was known before Noah; Moses does not contradict this, and the scripture says elsewhere that, from the beginning, wine had been created for merriment. Moses simply gives us to understand that Noah was the first to grow grapevines, to make a wine press, and to decide, apparently, to make wine an ordinary beverage to fortify the stomach and make people happier.

The Basques call cider *sagarno*, which means, literally, "Noah's creation from apples"; this tells us either that it was Noah, again, who planted the first orchard, or else that the orchard was planted in the same place as the vine that Noah had planted. We are inclined to believe, based on this name *sagarno*, that of all the fruit trees, after the planting of the vine, the apple trees were the first to be grown to full size: Moses does not speak of it; let us go on then to the facts mentioned by Moses and remembered by the Basques, so that what is implicit in the first might merit some belief when it is reinforced by the second.

Sixth Note

The names of the first patriarchs mentioned by Moses have, in Basque, a significance that conforms to the ideas that he gives us for them; the first of the series is Adam, which "signifies plenitude of intelligence."

The Holy Scripture teaches us that that our first parents were endowed with intellect and knowledge: *sciencia et intelletu replevit eos* [with the science of the spirit and the discipline of understanding He filled them full]. Adam was a common name for man and woman: *et appellarit nos Adam in die quo creati sunt* [and called their name Adam, on the day they were created, Genesis 5.2].

In the Basque language, Adam means what I said it means, and it could not be otherwise: I have already pointed out in the Fourth Note that the meaning of *am* is "plenitude," "fullness," etc.; now, pure Basque has no word other than *ad* to express intelligence. Thus, "understand" is expressed by *aditcea*, literally, "to have intelligence."

It goes without saying that the names of all the patriarchs are inherently characteristic. From this, because in Hebrew the name of Adam signifies the earth and that his body was formed from it, there are those who think that the Hebrew language was the first in the world. Because it might be unacceptable to give Basque priority over the other primitive languages, it is equally reasonable to deny Hebrew anteriority over them, especially as its interpretation is no more inherently characteristic. It should be enough, then, if the experts do not consider it to have been derived from three others.

Intelligence was the primary characteristic of the first man. God himself decided that he should be appropriately given the beautiful name Adam to make this apparent to heaven and earth. He brought all the animals before him so that he could name them according to the character of each one.

45. Wilhelm Freicher von Humboldt

(Postdam, 1767 – Tegel, 1835)

He studied law, economics, and archeology in Frankfurt an der Oder (in Brandenburg) and in Göttingen. Throughout his life, he reconciled involvement in certain political positions with research in a number of scientific fields, especially philology. As a personal friend of Schiller and Goethe, he maintained contact with the Romantic-Nationalist movement. In Berlin, he was advisor to the Supreme Court in 1790; in 1801, he was sent to Rome as Minister in Residence; and in 1809, he was appointed Minister of Worship and Public Instruction. While occupying this office, he initiated the founding of the University of Berlin. In 1810, he was appointed Minister of State. He participated in the Congress of

Vienna (1814–15) and was named a member of the Council of State in 1817. Due in part to his public responsibilities and his scientific and cultural interests, he resided temporarily in a number of European cities such as London, Paris, and Rome. In Rome, he became acquainted with Lorenzo Hervás y Panduro. This peripatetic existence gave him both a broader perspective on the problems he undertook and an extraordinary international reputation, becoming one of the most respected and well-known scientists of his time. The Introduction to his work *Ueber die Kawisprache auf der Insel Java* (On the Kavi Language on the Island of Java) (1836) is credited with inaugurating new methods of modern philology.[1]

Humboldt first came to know the Basque language in Paris, and he went on to consult some of the ancient and modern works written about or touching on it, by authors such as Landazuri, Axular, Moret, and Oihenart. In 1799, and accompanied by his family, he made a brief journey to the Basque Country, which allowed him to establish his first contacts, and he was determined to return, which he did in 1801. It is thought that the Basque language and culture constituted for Humboldt the perfect revelation, confirming his earlier intuitions about primitive languages and linguistic expression as the manifestation of the popular spirit or genius of each people. The Basque Country thus offered him the opportunity to analyze an exotic and unique linguistic case without having to leave Europe. In a way, the Basques represented for Humboldt the confirmation that the essence of nationality lay fundamentally in language. He never learned to speak Euskara, but he surrounded himself with the people who had the greatest knowledge of it at the time, in particular Astarloa and Moguel. In this way, Humboldt was aware that he was both the only foreign cultured European in the Basque Country who had acquired a certain knowledge of their language and that he was the depository of the legacy of Astarloa and his circle. For all of these reasons, he felt obligated to diffuse the message of the antiquity, originality, and perfection of the Basque language in the European academic media.

Of course, although Humboldt maintained the general interpretative lines of Astarloa and Moguel, particularly with respect to Basque-Iberianism, his exposition was not burdened with all the mystical-religious dogma that until then had been inseparable from Basqueness, and he sought to formulate strictly scientific concepts. Humboldt highlight-

---

1. See Ole Hansen-Love, *La révolution copernicienne du langage dans l'œuvre de Wilhelm von Humboldt* (Paris: J. Vrin, 1972).

ed, therefore, the unusual and interesting aspects of the Basque language without getting into philosophical or abstract evaluations about it. Thus, he emphasized, for example, the ergative construction by which the nominative, by means of the suffix –*k*, appears to be active, or the so-called proximate article (-*ok*, in front of the standard article –*ak*).

Humboldt's texts concerning the Basque language, and the Basque Country in general, included the diaries of the journeys he made there in 1799 and 1801 that were translated and published by Justo Garate in the *Revista Internacional de Estudios Vascos* (International Journal of Basque Studies) in 1923 and 1924, under the title, "Los vascos. Aportaciones sobre un viaje por el País vasco en la primavera de 1801" (The Basques. Notes about a Journey through the Basque Country in the Spring of 1801); his *Prüfung der Untersuchungen über die Urbewohner Spaniens vermittelst der Vaskischen Sprache* (Revision of the Research on the Primitive Inhabitants of Spain Through the Basque Language) (1821); and finally, *Berichtigungen und Zusätze zum ersten Abschnitte des zweyten Bandes des Mithridates über die Cantabrische oder Baskische Sprache* (Corrections and Additions to the First Chapter of the Second Volume of Mithridates on the Cantabrian or Basque Language) (1817).

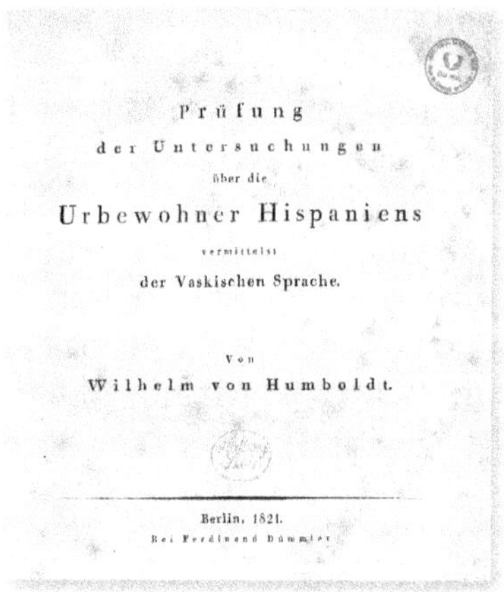
Prüfung
der Untersuchungen
über die
Urbewohner Hispaniens
vermittelst
der Vaskischen Sprache.

Von
Wilhelm von Humboldt.

Berlin, 1821.
Bei Ferdinand Dümmler

Selected Text(s):

a) *Prüfung der Untersuchungen über die Urbewohner Spaniens vermittelst der Vaskischen Sprache* [Revision of the Research on the Primitive Inhabitants of Spain Through the Basque Language] (Berlin: Dümmler, 1821), trans. into Spanish by Francisco Echebarria, prologue by Arnald Steiger, as *Primitivos pobladores de España y*

Lengua Vasca [Primitive Inhabitants of Spain and the Basque Language] (Madrid: Minotauro, 1959), 19–27, 145–147, 197–199.

b) "Diario del viaje vasco 1801" [Journal of the Basque Journey 1801], *Revista Internacional de Estudios Vascos* 13 (1922), 614–658; "Los vascos. Aportaciones sobre un viaje por el País Vasco en la primavera de 1801" [The Basques: Notes about a Journey through the Basque Country in the Spring of 1801], *Revista Internacional de Estudios Vascos* 14 (1923), 205–250, 373–400, 380–385 and 15 (1924), 83–137, 262–305, 391–466; reprint, as *Los vascos* [The Basques] (San Sebastián: Ediciones Vascas, 1975), 119–120.

a)

2

The Principles From Which I Work

It is extremely important to lay out the etymological principles that guide our investigation. In my opinion, those followed by Astarloa and Erro are truly based on certain correct opinions concerning the nature of primitive languages, and of the Basque language in particular, although they are subsequently extended and used in such a way that they do not produce any persuasive argument and are unable to lead to any sure conclusion. The system accepted by them proceeds from Astarloa's study of the Basque language. According to him, each letter, each syllable of this language embodies its own meaning, which is preserved in written composition as well. Therefore one can take each word apart in its elements so precisely that, for example, in one made up of two letters, the first always expresses the gender; the second, the specific difference of the object, or also, the first indicates the owner, the possessor; the second the content, what is possessed. Furthermore, the meaning is not arbitrary, but extracted from the impression the sounds leave on the soul of the primitive man, copied from the articulations of living nature, imitated from the sounds of dead nature. Or it indicates roundness, or something sharply penetrating, or concave, and so on successively.

It is worth noting too that what Astarloa says here about the Basque language, [Edward] Davies [in *Celtic Researches on the Origin, Traditions and Language of the Ancient Britons*, 1804, second edition, 1807] makes the same argument in almost the same terms about Celtic. The roots, says the latter, are very simple. A single vowel or diphthong forms not only a particle, but often a noun or a verb. There is hardly any combination of a single primitive consonant with a vowel before or after it that does not have its own meaning or even head a numerous family of derived words. The longest words of pure Celtic origin, however, cannot be regarded as names of real objects: earth, water, tree, etc; they indicate the different modes of being and acting. A writer who, like Davies in his work, allows his imagination to stray or digress in many truly nonsensical compositions would perhaps deserve little credit. Only [William] Owen, whose dictionary and grammar are of acknowledged merit, although one would like to see the second part amplified, follows the same system and expands it. He says . . . that each derived word can be restored regularly and without any auxiliary other than the system of the alteration of letters, to one or more elemental words, so that nothing is left to the mercy of the imagination of the etymologist. In his dictionary, the elements in all the words that are not themselves elemental are annotated in parentheses and, if we leaf through several of them, we are convinced that their meanings are the ones designated by Davies.

It will be useful, now, to follow these linguists in the use of these principles in a few examples. Astarloa derives *ule* (wool) from *u* (concave, hollow), and *le* (promoter, cause of many concavities); *axe* (air), from extended *a* and *xe*, a syllable of diminution (like a modest extent); *itz* (the word), from *i* (penetrating), and *tz* (the sign of abundance), as for instance, "abundance of penetrating subtlety." Davies says: the Irish particle *ur* signifies "to cover, extend over something," and from this comes the name of a multitude of objects, such as earth, fire, water, misfortune, assassination, etc.; in the Welsh language *a* signifies "to have to proceed or advance," and thus in a related dialect it means "an eminence or promontory, a cart," etc. Owen notes for the word *tan* (fire), the roots *ta* (what extends above something, over it, superimposed on it), and *an* (beginning, element). This use of the meanings of general words, such as vowels for determined objects, in particular, in the examples taken from Astarloa, demonstrates just how vacillating, arbitrary, and even risky such a procedure is, if not based on the discovery of effective relationships of sounds according to a fixed system of derivation. It is almost incomprehensible that a linguist would not notice, on his own, that without such a system it is futile to attempt to ascertain the road formed by the designation of ideas from the general to the particular, and vice versa, except in a few especially appropriate cases, and that even with such a conducting thread the obstacles often remain insuperable. With such an abstract theory, as systematically strained and narrow as the one employed by Astarloa, even real (not purely fantastic) relationships between sound and meaning that are still recognizable in some words, such as the German *Wolle* and the Basque *ule* [both meaning "wool"], become dim and obscure.

5

These Principles Lead to More Exact Judgments

It is in any case true that the words that designate objects are applications of general concepts to specific cases, designations of things by their properties, and that many that seem simple were complex in ancient times. It has also been noted, fairly and shrewdly, that the traces of the composition are much more visible in primitive languages, that is, those that have suffered few alterations, and that the independent capacity of the elements to have significance constitutes the principal characteristic of these languages. The explanation of a language by its roots presupposes, however, a linguistic theory that is far more defined and stable, and other languages will not be as susceptible to it. It can be safely acknowledged that in the base of a language there are a number of simple sounds from which a much larger number of derivative words proceed in ulterior development through external additions or changes brought about from inside.

The first, which we call roots, forms a double link with the others: first, in the material relation of the letters and the analogy of the derivation, and second, in the ideational relation of the meaning. The last is, by its nature, indeterminate and has to be deduced at each step by the first; without the help of the first, there is no guarantee that the meaning has been understood precisely. It is natural that the significance of the roots, as such, has to be extremely general and therefore imprecise, because they have to comprise in themselves all possible derived words. All languages present this character to greater or lesser extent because it lies at the root of the natural process of all linguistic formation. However, not all languages, but only certain ones, allow the search for the majority of the roots and the regular derivation of the remaining words through them. Each one of these derivations can also provoke mistrust, as it can seem to be the arbitrary work of grammarians and not something inherent in the nation, that is to say, not rooted in the language but only transferred to it. Withal, maintaining in this way a certain lack of confidence in what has been said earlier about the Celtic language, it cannot be forgotten, however, that there are also other languages in which a system such as this rules even more visibly and demonstrably through its grammatical construction. This is the case with Sanskrit, which is even closer than other Oriental languages to the nature of

Celtic, which we have described above, because its roots of signification are very general. For the most part they perform no other function than to serve as roots; they cannot be used in speech . . . before undergoing alteration, and they are, because of this, completely separate from the aspect of the language that is elaborated grammatically in nouns, verbs, etc. How it is that this phenomenon, which is frequently repeated in other languages as well, can be possible, whether the roots are merely ideal sounds perceived through analysis or true words that were formerly active in the speech of the people, so that the language is a carrier of relics from an earlier state, is a matter for another study.

The meaning of Sanskrit roots is, as we noted above, indeterminate to an extreme degree [described by Sir Charles Wilkins, in his *Radicals of the Sanskrit Language* as "vague and unsatisfactory"] and it would be a huge mistake to try to put together an inventory of radical words simply by amassing a collection of roots, as in the *Jardin des Racines Grecques* [Garden of Greek Roots]. Although the Sanskrit language is so complete in this aspect, it does not allow the sure reduction of all of its roots, and we know from an entire genre of words that form so-called *unadi* by adding prefixes and suffixes . . . that their reduction to specific roots is often completely insufficient, for neither the meanings nor the analogy of letters correspond, and the rules created for them alone are arbitrary efforts to unify contradictions. Also, Sanskrit demonstrates in this way that the derivation of each and every word with a specific root is, in reality, the work of grammarians, but the derivation of a certain number is surely based on the language itself ([Franz] Bopp, *Analytical Comparison of the Sanskrit, Greek, and other languages* in the *Annals of Oriental Literature*, Vol. 1, art. 1, p. 8). Something similar can probably be said about Celtic, although perhaps only regarding a different matter. Judging Astarloa's method in light of these premises, we see at once how incomplete and unreliable it is.

The comparison of Basque words does, no doubt, guarantee a series of radical syllables, each producing a large number of words; an easily recognizable analogy also governs the origin of the species of different primitive languages (see my additions to [Adelung's] *Mithridates* [*or General linguistics*], pp. 38 and 43). This does not, however, prove that the language allows such an exposition of roots and such a regular derivation from them as Sanskrit and Celtic. Astarloa has, however, undertaken the analysis of each word and carefully separates those radical letters that are merely euphonic or the result of dialectical differences; but he has not established a complete or even partial system of derivation of words from their roots. The Basque language, moreover, is completely different from Sanskrit and Celtic in its formation of literal meaning, insofar as the systematic reciprocal transfer of different kinds of sounds is completely foreign to it. Of the two possible ways of moving from the word to the root, Astarloa is far from choosing the safest, but instead focuses on meaning, looking for words of similar sound that are similar in meaning. There is no need for us to prove how fallacious such a quest is, especially if metaphysical ideas are included in the process. The true linguist will take the opposite course, not worrying about meaning if the path of the appropriate analogy leads him to a specific root. For over time, meanings can end up being quite different, even in sounds that are closely related. Astarloa gives too much value to the supposed significance of each letter instead of focusing on combinations of those letters in the roots, and in this way, he leaps over a stage of linguistic analysis, under the assumption that it could never have gone so far. His method can still be used for the roots, which are usually considered to be elements that cannot be broken down further. Finally, not even the meanings of the sounds themselves can be derived exclusively from sober comparison, but only from general ideas and observations, some of which are shocking for their extravagance. Thus, he interprets the *a* in *aarra* as masculine, and the *e* in *emea* as feminine, in total seriousness (Astarloa, *Apol*[*ogía de la lengua Bascongada*], 35) because he hears an *a* sound in the first cry of the newborn male, and the *e* sound in that of the female. It is obvious that the tendency of both Astarloa and his successor Erro to insist on identifying their language with the original language of the human race has been prejudicial to them. Until Basque linguists make the decision to completely renounce such a vain endeavor, whose uselessness other nations have realized long ago, and limit themselves to sharing their discoveries about their language, their work will offer no genuine benefits either to their own countrymen or to foreigners. These observations, which had to be presented here where it is appropriate to judge the principles used up until now, are in no way intended, nor should they be, to take away from the contributions of these men to their language. Obviously, Astarloa was the first to work on the Basque language with a truly investigative spirit and to seek to break it down into its elements. His contribution to the study of the Basque language has been extremely important, especially in terms of its grammar. And because he has scoured every nook and cranny of his small country with tireless enthusiasm looking for the purest dialect, we can do no less than follow in his footsteps, even where he goes astray, to gather the abundant harvest of his keen and interesting annotations.

37

The Basque Language Throughout the Peninsula

If we look carefully at these series of lists, we cannot avoid the conviction that there is no extensive region of the Peninsula where towns or places are not named by tribes who spoke a language identical to present-day Basque in its phonetic system, roots words, endings, and mode of composition. These are found in all the great tribes, and if they are lacking in the Autrigoni, Lobetani, Oleados, Cerretanos, Ausetani, and Indigetes, it is because they are minor tribes from which fewer nouns have customarily come down to us. Chance might frequently have prevented legitimately Iberian names from being used by writers, and the cause might partially consist in the strangeness of the sounds, partially in the insignificance of the towns and villages. The most important cities frequently took their names from foreigners. It should also be noted that many other place names that we can no longer etymologize with certainty might be Basque. What is certain is that Basque names are distributed unequally across the Peninsula. In terms of area, most of them are found in the Basque Country, and following those, among the Turdetani (Tartessians) and Turduli [from southern Lusitania, mostly corresponding to modern-day Portugal] in Betica [in the southern part of the Iberian Peninsula, mostly corresponding to modern-day Andalusia]. The frequency of the most authentic and primitive sounds in the names of this province leaves almost no doubt that the Turdetan dialect was the same, or at least very similar, to contemporary Basque.* Considering the

* In [Barthold Georg] Niebuhr, *Römische Geschichte* [Roman History] (I, 111) [1812], the exact opposite is argued, as a matter universally resolved; but, he says, even if this investigation (of the words of the Sardinians living in the mountains being conducted by a speaker of Basque) should lead to the opposite result, the hypothesis would not be invalidated because the language of the Turdetani is completely different from the one to which Basque belongs as a dialect, and is now completely lost to us. It is a pity that this sentence is not accompanied by any proof. My investigations lead me to the opposite conclusion. I see no reason at all why the Turdetani language should be considered different; in the place names, I find a completely adequate proof of its identity with Basque, and without acknowledging it, I would not know how to find any way to explain the large number of authentically Basque names in the province of Betica, names which could in no way be imputed to the Celts, either geographically or linguistically, and the Turduli, who might come to mind, were, according to Strabo (III, 1, p. 139), so intimately related to the Turdetani that it is inconceivable that they spoke two different languages. [Francis] Carter (*Journey from Gibraltar to Malaga* [1777], I, 83) says that, according to Pliny, the Turdetani language was a dialect of Celt-Iberian. It is unclear to which passage of Pliny he refers.

size of the country, there are almost no Basque names in Lusitania, although a few are evident. The reason for this might be that it is precisely in Lusitania that the ending *-briga* is the dominant form of the names of the larges cities, and these are the only ones ordinarily mentioned by geographers and historians. Because of this there was almost no reason to transmit genuinely indigenous names to us. In that entire territory, Basque names are scarcely represented among those that seem to be foreign, not Iberian. Even if they had been completely isolated so that in Betica there would only be *Astapa, Iliberis,* and *Urgao*, and in Lusitania, *Mendiculea*, *Iria*, and *Flavionavia* on the northern coast, *Oria*, *Orospeda,* and *Idubeda* in the interior, and *S. Lucentum*, *Iluro*, etc. on the coast, these isolated names would still prove that Iberians who spoke Basque or who had been driven out from [the Basque Country] had penetrated there, and that they would necessarily have had to pass through those intermediate countries to reach those places. I believe, then, that I have proven beyond all doubt the opinion already expressed earlier that the ancient Iberians were Basques, their language being the same or similar to that spoken by Basques today, and that these Iberians occupied all the regions of Spain without being limited to a single section of the country.

An important proof of their ancient expansion, and which we have in the same living language today, is its immense wealth of lexical and grammatical forms, which I have examined extensively in another of my books [*Additions to the Mithridates*, p. 38]. It would be monstrous to believe that such an abundance of forms could have originated in sparsely populated territories and in just one or a very few tribes. On the other hand, all of this is comprehensible if it is acknowledged that a widely extended multitude found themselves forced through time and circumstances to live in a few valleys in mountainous regions.

. . .

49

Results of the Investigations Completed to Date

1. The comparison of ancient place names of the Iberian Peninsula with Basque demonstrates that this was the language of the Iberians and that, because these people appear to have spoken only one language, the terms Iberian and Basque are synonymous.

2. Basque place names are found, without exception, throughout the Peninsula, and consequently, the Iberians lived in every region.

3. But among the names of the Peninsula, there are others that, compared to the place names of lands inhabited by Celts, prove that they are of Celtic origin, and in these, we also find the Celts mixed with the Iberians, and here historical evidence leaves us abandoned.

4. According to this, it was only near the Pyrenees and the southern coast that the Iberians did not live among the Celts. In the interior of the country, Lusitania, and most of the northern coast, the two nations were intermingled.

5. The Celt-Iberians were identical in language to the Celts, from whom the ancient place names of Gauls and Britons are derived, as were the current languages [Welsh and Breton] spoken in Great Britain and France; they were probably not, however, mere colonies of Gaulish tribes (of men who emigrated in isolation from their ancestors and then remained behind), as we can see by the difference in character and institutions. They could have been those who inhabited Gaul from time immemorial, or who had immigrated there previously en masse. In any case, their mixture with the Iberians did not have a Gaulish characteristic, which the Romans introduced to us, but was entirely Iberian.

6. Outside of Spain, toward the north, there is no trace of the Iberians, if we make an exception of Iberian Aquitaine and part of the Mediterranean coast. Quite clearly, the Caledonians did not belong to the Iberian trunk, but to the Celtic one.

7. But toward the south, the Iberians inhabited the three large islands of the Mediterranean, as proven by both historical monuments and Basque place names. However, it is unlikely that they were immigrants from Iberia or Gaul, but that they had occupied these lands from time immemorial, or that they came from the Orient.

8. It is doubtful that they also belonged to the primitive peoples of the Italian peninsula. Nonetheless, a number of Basque place names might give grounds for such a hypothesis.

9. The Iberians were different in character and language from the Celts as we know them through the Greeks and Romans and through vestiges of the language. Even so, there is no basis for denying any kinship between the two nations; the Iberians might well be of Celtic lineage, but torn loose earlier.

My investigations have managed to establish these nine conclusions merely through the comparison of place names, used as a series of reliable historical documents, with the Basque language. I have purposefully limited myself to this as a way of assessing, confirming, and broadening the investigations undertaken until now, investigations which, almost in their totality, avoided the epic language of Iberia. But to complete exhaustively the investigations on the primitive inhabitants of the Peninsula, it will still be necessary to compare Basque as a language with the other languages of Western Europe independent of historical testimony and relations of place, this being the only reliable way to clarify the last of the conclusions presented above. But this is a far more difficult undertaking, requiring other calculations.

. . .

b)

Persecution of the Basque Language in the Schools

At the beginning of the week, the teacher gives a ring to a child, who is designated as "the king." He listens to hear if anyone speaks a word of Basque to another student, outside or inside the school, and passes the ring on to him. In turn, this second child listens for the same thing and passes the ring on successively. At the end of the week, the teacher asks about the ring and inquires in sequence to all the children who have received it one from another. These are then required to hold their arms high in the form of a cross and lift up their shirts, and he punishes them. In this way, he turns his anger against nature. But the schoolboys (Don Pablo Astarloa told me this about his childhood) enjoy this childish game so much that they avoid the prohibition. If one of them wants to say something to another, he says it to the tree, to the star, and the other answers in this way, or to a passerby, but never to each other. The best part is that they are really forced to do this because they do not know Castilian expressions. Many farmers do not send their children to school.

There are few who know how to write in the Basque language. Letters are not written in Basque. They are forced to write the name of the people itself in Castilian.

. . .

The surprising thing is that this local rivalry, as it could be called, also has a great influence on the language. It is quite natural that the Basque holds on to his language in inverse proportion to the unfairness of the persecution, that he is happy when the foreigner shows an interest and takes the trouble to garble a few phrases, that he tries to explain all the details and characteristics of that language to him, and in particular, that he attempts to clarify etymologically the secret of the meanings included in the majority of the Basque words. But more shocking is the stubborn dispute about where the Basque language is spoken better and with greatest purity. Without a doubt, Markina in Gipuzkoa [sic] and Durango in Bizkaia hold primacy in this. Both towns in the middle of the country, close to each other, separated only by the Oiz mountain, both heavily populated, more suited for agriculture and industry than for commerce, and because of this less frequented by foreigners, and finally, both surrounded by mountain people who in their scattered, separated dwellings have preserved, pure and unaltered, the oldest form of Basque, often barely comprehensible today to the urban Basque, and which has remained an exception to the mixture of their dialect with Castilian words and phrases. Both enjoy the preeminence today of possessing in Markina, Don Juan de Moguel, and in Durango, Don Pablo de Astarloa, two linguists so learned and sound that, although the latter has investigated the structure and nature of his language with greater profundity, still even an expert will not willingly offer a definite conclusion about it. What is in question, even now, is to decide which of these two towns surpasses the other, and concerning this, I frequently heard heated and tenacious arguments.

Even more remarkable and difficult for the study of the language is the following phenomenon. The Basque language has, as does every primitive language, an abundance of words with the same meaning, and which, in earlier times, were spoken over an incomparably wider geographical extension. They call the horse *zaldia* as well as *zamaria*, the finger *erhia* and *atza*, the great grandfather *goraçoa* and *arbasoa*, etc. The dialects of different regions have chosen one or another of these words, so that the one not chosen is unknown, or at least less familiar. The rivalry between small communities is such that, as keen observers have assured me, in one of them, they will refuse to use these expressions that are peculiar to the neighboring community, although the proper names show that in a different era they were in general use. In Durango, for example, they say *batu* to express the idea of harvest, but in Gipuzkoa they use *bildu*, this despite the fact that the names of several estates in the latter are composed of the first word. It is not rare to find, therefore, such isolated local expressions, more often in isolated communities than in those less remote. This behavior cannot be of harm to the general intelligibility of the language because it is always simply a matter of only a few expressions. But it makes the search for the complete linguistic richness more difficult, and it denotes the general tendency totally popular in nature to always and first separate into smaller groups rather than unite into larger ones.

. . .

Today it is no longer likely that violent disputes will occur; on the contrary, the Basque provinces in Spain and France can expect increasing growth in their population and well being. But gradual influences throughout Europe during our epoch are bringing about ever more certainly the decline of national peculiarity by forcing smaller groups to renounce their exclusive character through reciprocal contact. The Basque language is gradually receding into narrower use, leading inevitably and simultaneously to the gradual loss of the exclusive character of those who speak it. Even now, it is being forced to retreat further and further into the mountains each decade, under pressure on all sides, treated as a bad mother precisely because of the most illustrious aspect of the nation, and it is predicted that its decadence will, from this point on, be increasingly precipitous. The swift decline suffered by the dialects of Provençe and Toulouse in the south of France from the beginning of the Revolution provides a prophetic and instructive example of this phenomenon. In less than a century, the Basque language might have disappeared from the number of living languages and, even in recent times, similar phenomena have occurred. For in the same way at the beginning of the eighteenth century, the Old Prussian spoken by a few old people in a corner of Sambia [a peninsula on the southeastern shore of the Baltic Sea] died out, and in our days, we have seen the disappearance of a dialect of Welsh [Cornish] in Cornwall.

It seems irrevocably determined, in the course of human culture, that to a certain extent the differences separating smaller peoples from one another must disappear, and that only larger masses can undertake common activities. To induce entire nations toward important intellectual advances and especially to protect them against any possible return to barbarism and ignorance, extraordinary political measures are required; the diversity of new relationships so originated produce diversity and novelty in opinions and ideas; and the human spirit might never have achieved some of its most sublime discoveries without the enticing spectacle of an intense and almost general stimulation of human energy. But is there not a limit to this phenomenon? Will not civilization once again reach a point where it will be just as necessary to confine imagination and feeling into a narrow circle, as to lead understanding into a wider sphere, in order to preserve its character of warmth and strength, without which nothing can be created? This is another question and certainly not without importance.

Even without entering into this question, the decline of a people always arouses a sorrowful feeling, even if it was inevitable for it to fall as a sacrificial offering for the benefit of all humanity; and this is even truer regarding the complete disappearance of a language. We men are accustomed to think of them as permanent; so, if it also silences forever the sound in which people live in a different manner, if the mold in which a human species, master of itself, founded its thoughts and feelings is broken then its disappearance seems doubly sad to us because all communication between it and the future is destroyed. Even when a language, not refined enough to produce a literature, is only used as the pure expression of the way of thought of a primitive people, not even then will its loss be regarded with indifference. It is true also that in the most advanced culture, a moment inevitably comes in which the most delicate emotions of refined sensibility return of their own will to the simple outpouring of natural feeling, and in a truly cultured nation, the most highly educated individuals are in constant and mutual contact with the simplest, healthiest segment of the population.

It is precisely because the Basque language is a popular language and because we should expect of the Basque people greater soundness of judgment than scientific ability, a more naturally warm and vivid sentiment than refinement of sensibility, this language and this nation inspire an even keener interest. Once a language achieves scientific and literary dimension, it is taken from the hands of the people and rarely does it gain in energy and richness after that. For it always takes on a more sensible and varied character in its use by the people than in that of the writer; it had to be used first in the mouth of a strong and widely extended people (of whom it is the primitive property) for the expression of the most immediate needs, the most natural sensations, the most infantile fantasy, and even of the rudest passions, before it can become capable, through its vivacity, vigor, and depth in subsequent more refined generations for the most elevated spiritual use. Man is destined to perfect himself socially: each one must always integrate himself into the mass, and everything human is grounded simultaneously in the simplicity of nature and in the highest flowering of educational perfectibility. Therefore, without a determined, firm, and vigorous character, it will be useless to expect truth, strength, and the fulfillment of obligation even in the finest education of a nation. But the greater the distance between the people and the enlightened classes of the nation, all the more rare will be the appearance of popular characters. So if we want to see them still active and alive today, we have to turn precisely away from the culture to regions in which it has not yet penetrated to any degree. But with the Basques, a number of other circumstances converge to make the phenomenon even more surprising and instructive.

The Basques, especially those on the Spanish side, are not just poor mountain shepherds or absolutely oppressed serfs. They are a people dedicated to farm work, navigation, and commerce, and they do not lack in bodily health, without which moral prosperity is impossible. They have a freely organized society, public deliberations usually in the language of the country, and therefore a common interest that involves each individual and toward which he can act. Inspired by enthusiasm for their country and their nation, which might be surprising to more than one foreigner, they remain true to their country of their own good will, even the rich landowners, even those who receive honorary titles in Castile, or who have held distinguished posts, and in their country, they necessarily live in a large community with the lower classes, because they cannot exempt themselves from the customs and the language. Thus, a certain portion of the most recent advances and education are passed into the popular language and traditional ideas, and there is a less visible separation of classes, whose difference vanishes completely in the eyes of the genuine Bizkaian. Also, it must be visible already to every traveler, in the physiognomy of the country and of the people that in the Basque provinces the people possess a more natural education, and the persons of distinction have a more popular aspect than in the neighboring Spain and France. In this regard, only the small cantons of Switzerland are comparable, in which, however, their political independence conferred a different external attitude and their lesser separateness a different internal one.

The Basque language, organization, customs, physiognomy, and everything around them, without exception, is shaped by the aspect of their country, like a pure and separate species. Their peculiarity, profoundly interwoven in the landscape, is completely independent of exterior and accidental causes; the Basque does not know, close at hand or far away, a species akin to him; rather, he lives in his small territory, between the mountain and the ocean, as solitary as an island. What is called a people's pure character and how it originates cannot be examined anywhere else more effectively than in him. In the progress of education, sharp contrasts between national characters were inevitably established, and consequently, this examination might seem to be a topic of idle curiosity. But to carefully preserve and nourish one part of those characters, and to procure for them as well validity through the finest education incorporating this validation through it is certainly appropriate to the means, not yet prepared, of preserving the strength and character of a nation whose great poverty has been the object of justifiable complaints. For every attempt to educate that fails to keep alive the influence of the child's own basic nature, to the extent possible, is poorly conceived.

The ethnic peculiarity of the Basques takes us back to remote centuries, to the epoch before the Roman and Carthaginian conquest and to the original inhabitants of Spain. It diminishes naturally little by little because there is more frequent contact between them and their neighbors, but even if it is true that they might consequently intermingle and adapt in other ways, there will still remain for a long time a certain part of that ethnic character. Two important questions arise from this, one historical and the other political: Where did the prototype and language of the Basques originate, and with what other peoples and languages are they related? And, how should the Spanish Kingdom treat the Basque nation (because, for the French Republic, its Basque districts can only have a very minor importance) to make their strength and activity as advantageous to Spain as possible?

The first question has been frequently posed, but it has not yet been answered satisfactorily. Almost all the answers that have been given until now are less the result of a solid and pertinent investigation than of arbitrary decisions of systematic obsession and partisan spirit. In truth, none of the foreigners who have written about this subject (because native writers are suspect on other grounds) has started out with an adequate knowledge of the language.

The second question is far more interesting practically and all the more so because now it is common for different peoples to come together in the same state. But it has to be freely acknowledged that until now, more thought has gone into removing difficulties that oppose disparity than in using what is good about the national peculiarity.

From the moment I decided to make a journey to Spain, these and analogous considerations made the investigation of the Basque nation and language an appealing project to me.

46. Juan Ignacio de Iztueta Echeberria

(Zaldibia, Gipuzkoa, 1767 – Zaldibia, 1845)

Among the bibliographies of the other authors reviewed in this anthology—monks, priests, academics, and judicious scholars—that of Iztueta seems strikingly discordant. In the course of his life, in his ideology, and in his political activity, he differs notably from the prototype of conservative, religious, pro-Basque researcher. His was a family of prototypical craftsmen, specifically cape-makers, consisting of the parents and twelve children, of whom Juan Antonio was the fifth. Hence, one of the nicknames by which he was known was "*kapagin-txikia*" (the little wool preparer). His education was, in keeping with the social and economic situation of his family, rudimentary, but his great desire for knowledge and his intellectual curiosity pushed him to undertake a project of self-teaching that bore bountiful fruit, leading to his reading of everything he could about history, linguistics and other subjects.

One of the characteristics of his personality was that he remained distant from the dominant religious and ethical norms of his era. His agnosticism and irrepressible fondness for women and dances kept him constantly under the scrutiny of his neighbors and, naturally, of the most self-righteous and intransigent ecclesiastics. He had five children with his first wife, but the couple's liberal lifestyle meant that Iztueta was not sure that they were all his. In fact, in the trial to which he was subjected by the Inquisition of Logroño, he declared that he slept in the attic of the house and she slept downstairs: "so she could do freely whatever she wanted with any other man who made her happy, because he would do the same anywhere he wanted with any woman who let him because that is why he was a free man and it was nobody's business if he had sexual relations with anyone he chose." Imprisoned for robbery, and a widower after the death of his first wife, he married Conchesi Bengoechea, who was also in jail for having killed the child born of her relationship with a priest, and had three more children with her. After her death, he married for a third time, this time a young girl forty years his junior with whom he had two more children. Neither was his working life conventional or dull. He worked as a mattress maker, vendor of olive oil, miller, shepherd, watchman, dance instructor, and *bertsolari* (versifier), and it was also rumored that he sometimes went out on jobs with a brother of his who was a highwayman. On one occasion, he was described as an elementary school teacher, and although he never held that title, it would not be at all surprising if he had sporadically practiced this profession, given his great concern for the education of the young; an interest that grew through his friendship with the pedagogue, priest, and liberal, Agustín Pascual Iturriaga. Iztueta spent a good part of his life in jail, and was tried before the Inquisition as a result of being denounced by his parish that considered him its bête-noir. Specifically, his ideas were declared heretical, blasphemous, and materialistic.

Given these precedents, it is hardly surprising that Iztueta left Zaldibia, went to live in Donostia-San Sebastián, and that in that city he collaborated with the pro-French authorities after the Napoleonic invasion of 1808, obtaining a position in the Treasury Department. But after the defeat of Napoleon, Iztueta was brought to trial, like many others, for being a Francophile. He was imprisoned for a time, fined, and exiled from Azpeitia and Donostia. This was a difficult time, for it coincided with the death of his second wife, and, being now responsible for five children, he had to survive on a prisoner's income (he was in Tolosa jail at the time) that could not have been large. Thereafter, however, after release from jail, his life became more stable. He married a third time, as previously mentioned, held several posts in Donostia and began his literary career.

His fundamental preoccupation centered on the decadence of traditional dances, because new musicians were influenced by foreign sounds and rhythms and the Basque Country's own themes were danced badly and less and less frequently. In 1819, he was commissioned by the Donostia City Hall, first, to teach the official drummer of the city all the Basque dances he knew so that the man could record and thus preserve them; and second, to instruct the children of the municipal orphanage those same Basque dances. Iztueta systematized his empirical knowledge of dances, and in 1824, published his *Guipuzcoaco dantza gogoangarrien condaira edo historia* (An Account or History of the Most Celebrated Dances of Gipuzkoa). This work was more than a mere compilation of music and dances. In fact, it was in many respects the first treatise on folklore, making Iztueta the first Basque folklorist. Inevitably, he found himself embroiled in a debate about the moral propriety of these dances, in which his opponents were other Basque scholars of his era, such as the Jesuit Mendiburu and the Carmelite friar Bartolomé de Santa Teresa.

His entire work is written in the Basque language. Although his style was accused by Larramendi of being a bit purist and affected, Iztueta nonetheless held to a fundamental premise: that whatever the topic you were discussing, be it history or dances, it had to written in Basque. For him, those Basques who studied abroad and then sought to disrespect the language of their parents, to abandon it, and hide it, were worthy of the most intense scorn. Finally, although he was closer to the Enlightenment and Liberalism than to any traditional absolutist positions, Iztueta still defended, in his *Guipuzcoaco provinziaren condaira edo historia . . .* (Account or History of the Province of Gipuzkoa . . .) (1847), the link between the situation of the Basque language and the *Fueros*, relating the after survival of the former to the maintenance of the latter.

GUIPUZCOACO PROVINCIAREN
CONDAIRA EDO HISTORIA
CEÑETAN JARRITZEN DIRADEN ARGUIRO
BERAREN ASIERATIC ORAIN-ARTE DAGOZQUION
BARRI GOGOANGARRIAC.
EGUIN ETA ZUCENDU CEBANA
D. Juan Ygnacio de Yztueta

DONOSTIAN
Ignacio Ramon Baroja-ren moldizteguian
1847 garren urtean eguiña.

SELECTED TEXT(S):

Guipuzkoa Provinciaren Condaira edo Historia ceñetan jarritzen diraden arguiro beraren asieratic orain-arte dagozquion barri gogoangarriac [Account or History of the Province of Gipuzkoa, in Which Are Recorded the Most Celebrated Events from Its Beginnings to the Present Day] (Donostia: Ignacio Ramón Baroja, 1847), v–vii, 8–10.

There are about a hundred and twenty thousand inhabitants in this little province. Of these, about one hundred thousand speak no other tongue than Basque. Of the remaining twenty thousand, I would say, with a generous estimate, that more than half are stepchildren of the Basque tongue, foreign in origin, ignorant of their own provenance and bloodline, and that of the other ten thousand, at least six thousand speak Basque as badly as they speak Spanish, thinking that this adds glory and shine to their illustrious personalities.

We can therefore clearly see that the natives of this province are all pure Basque speakers and that few of them are acquainted with Castilian. For this reason, our thoughtful ancestors established a most reasonable rule, which was that only priests who spoke Basque fluently should be entitled to shepherd souls in the churches of Gipuzkoa. This sound law, laid down so wisely for the betterment of souls, now tells us loudly that matters concerning the people of Gipuzkoa should be conveyed to them in the Basque language.

Because this is such a clamoring truth, is it not both shameful and painful that the loyal towns of Gipuzkoa, when they set out to educate their young, settle on teachers who cannot speak one word of Basque?

And is it not even more atrocious that when these poor children let one single Basque word slip out at school, these foreign men, their enemies in fact, violently punish them, and that this is considered fair? Why! Is it such a sin that Basque speakers should speak Basque words? Oh, our dear, everlasting, unfortunate Basque tongue! It is not just foreigners who cannot abide to hear you; no, there are many standing near you who, although they owe their whole being to you, will not take the trouble to serve you. And why is this? Simply because they do not recognize the source of their riches.

All the honest inhabitants of Gipuzkoa know that they owe their well-being to our honorable *Fueros*, to which they are entitled by birth; but few are aware of what is required to safeguard the *Fueros'* purity and integrity. The soundest base and the safest foundation for properly serving the *Fueros* is the careful tending of the Basque language: they are linked in a tight embrace and cannot survive without each other. If the Basque language dies, the *Fueros* will not survive. But if Basque lives, the *Fueros* will rise again. Those who love the *Fueros* must love Basque; and those who love Basque must speak and express themselves in Basque with all Basque speakers and in all matters that concern them. Otherwise, Basque will wither, there will be fewer Basque speakers, and the *Fueros* will be lost.

. . .

Although it is true that for many years now our wise Basque language, sweet as honey to us, has been cornered among these crags as if suspended in a dream, it has at last awoken, left its mountainous caves, and shown itself to the whole world with a clear, cheerful countenance. It has gone in search of its priceless relics and it shall discover them with ease, for they are bountiful and can be found here, there, and everywhere; it can loudly proclaim to its beloved mother: "we are still alive," "we are yours," "here you shall find us," "come quick as you can and embrace us," and "at this blessed hour and forever guard us within your generous, revered, and capable bosom."

Although our beloved parents have for a long time now witnessed how the powerful enemies of their beautiful language try to destroy it by pushing it underground, today on this day it reveals itself to us after winning this feud thanks to its loyal and illustrious children: full of beauty, glorious and brimming with health, and alive—and against all the expectations of barbed and arrogant foreign languages.

As if the wise, kind Basque language was damaging or shameful to Spain! Can anyone appraise the struggle and the headaches many men who would call themselves great have endured to scandalously dishonor the Basque language and banish it to a place where it can never show its face again?

Some of the many fierce enemies whose attacks the Basque tongue has survived are Mariana, Mayans, Armesto y Ossorio, Nicolás Antonio, Martí, Belázquez, Ledesma, and Don Joaquín Traggia. All of them were renowned personages, yet none of them knew Basque even superficially. Totally unaware of the gravity of their ignorance, they started pummeling the peerless, upright Basque language, writing with their thick, blunt pens whatever came to their minds, heedless of the consequences. Finally, they had the splendid idea of affirming in their coarse lines, as if it were a great, proven truth, that Basque was a laughable language, roughly constructed from a few lists of words extracted from Eastern languages; a language without its own grammar or vocabulary—characteristics it would never be able to possess anyway, as it had no means of establishing or developing them correctly. Honest Basques were wounded to the quick by such scandalous and damning absurdities (and many others I leave unmentioned), and immediately started to proclaim, for all the world to know, the beauty and riches of the pure and illustrious Basque language. Our dearly remembered Father Larramendi, with a sense of justice and righteousness, published a dictionary of the Basque language as well as a Basque grammar, which he entitled *El Imposible Vencido* [The Impossible Defeated]. In this volume, he clearly established that all detractors of Basque are a gang of weak, ignorant charlatans.

After the sublime Larramendi, the erudite Astarloa, and the intelligent Erro also put their irons in the fire, armed with the honest, kind, and immortal Basque language, to place the following evidence before the eyes of the whole world: that among all the known languages, only Basque was born at the beginning of the world. For this reason and no other, Basque is blessed with the duty of carefully nurturing in its generous bosom the invaluable gifts bequeathed on it simultaneously with the very birth of man. Like a blind man's guide, who will accompany him wherever he goes, with the same or superior diligence, and with greater ease, Basque guides its true children with a tender, friendly hand, while remaining always present in the background.

In this way, under the guidance of Basque, the Astarloas and the Erros reached, without once losing their way, the first age of the world. There they became acquainted with the irrefutable documents about the birth of Basque and thus they voiced them to the world in their pure, honorable names, in such a manner that no one could deny their exclusive kinship to Basque.

47. Bartolomé de Madariaga Garate, known as Friar Bartolomé de Santa Teresa

(San Andrés de Etxebarria, Markina, Bizkaia, 1768 – Lazkao, Gipuzkoa, 1835)

He was ordained as a Carmelite friar, taking orders in Corella (Navarre) and adopting the religious name Bartolomé de Santa Teresa, by which he was subsequently known. He studied philosophy in Logroño between 1790 and 1793, theology in Pamplona-Iruña between 1793 and 1796, and ethics in Burgos between 1796 and 1799. He was known as a tireless preacher and missionary (especially in the Basque language) in Bizkaia, Gipuzkoa, and Navarre. During the Napoleonic occupation of 1808, the Carmelites (and of course, Brother Bartolomé) stood out for their decidedly anti-French opinions. In fact, he was even arrested on one occasion after having gone too far in a sermon. He was later named Prior of the Carmelite Monastery in Markina (1817–20) and Sestao (Bizkaia) (1820–24), and subsequently held other positions in monasteries in Burgos (1824–6), Santander (1826–29), and Lazkao, Gipuzkoa (1832–35). He was a close friend of Moguel, and he knew and worked with members of the generation of great Basque-language preachers that included Mendiburu, Palacios, and Cardaberaz.

He was a notorious polemicist, and found himself involved first in the bitter and prolific debate about the dances, in which he took hard-line positions, being an advocate of the prohibition of any dance that required physical contact between dancers of opposite sexes. These ideas were published in *Euscal-errijateco olgueeta, ta danzeen neurrizco-gatz-ozpinduba Aita Prai Bartolome* . . . (Amusements of the Basque Country, and Moderate Dances, Prepared by the Reverend Father Bartolomé . . .) (1816). On the opposing side, among others, he faced Juan Ignacio de Iztueta and Gaspar Melchor de Jovellanos, who advocated more tolerance regarding dances. Subsequently, he took part in another debate that affected the characteristics of the Basque language. In 1828, he published, in the edition by Juan José Moguel, *Plauto bascongado o el bascuence de Plauto en su comedia Poenulo* . . . (The Basque Plautus, or the Basque Language of Plautus in his comedy Poenulus . . .). Here, among other things, he included an interpretation of a passage by Plautus into Euskara and quite an acerbic critique of Fleury Lécluse's work. This little book also contains a translation of the verses and four long letters that Madariaga sent to Moguel about the matter. Originally, he had no intention of publishing these, but Moguel insisted on bringing them out, and in fact, did so under his own name. Lécluse subsequently responded with his *Plauto Polígloto* (The Polyglot Plautus), bringing

Iztueta into the fray, who disagreed with almost everything Madariaga wrote, criticizing his every position. However, Madariaga did not back down and wrote a work responding to his detractors titled *Anti-Plauto polígloto* (The Polyglot Anti-Plautus).

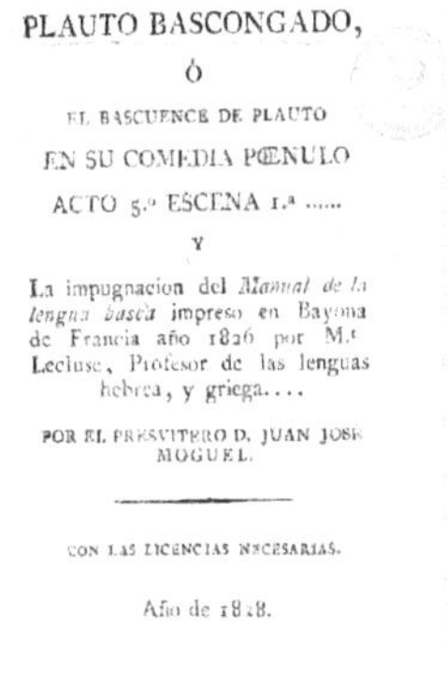
PLAUTO BASCONGADO,

Ó

EL BASCUENCE DE PLAUTO

EN SU COMEDIA PŒNULO

ACTO 5.º ESCENA 1.ª ......

Y

La impugnacion del *Manual de la lengua basca* impreso en Bayona de Francia año 1826 por M.r Lecluse, Profesor de las lenguas hebrea, y griega....

POR EL PRESVITERO D. JUAN JOSE MOGUEL.

CON LAS LICENCIAS NECESARIAS.

Año de 1828.

Selected Text(s):

Plauto Bascongado o El Bascuence de Plauto en su comedia Poenulo, y la impugnación del Manual de la lengua basca impreso en Bayona de Francia, año 1826, por Mr. Lécluse, profesor de las lenguas hebrea y griega [The Basque Plautus or the Basque Language of Plautus in his comedy Poenulus, and the Refutation of the Manual on the Basque Language Published in Baiona, France in the Year 1826 by Mr. Lécluse, Professor of Hebrew and Greek] (Santander, 1828), 7–14, 43–46, 74–76, 111–16.

THE TEXT OF PLAUTUS'S COMEDY *PŒNULO*, ACT 5, SCENE 1

1. Ny thalonim valon uth si corathisima consith
2. Chym lach chunyth mumis tyal myctibari, imischi
3. Lipho canet hyth bymithij ad ædin bynuthij
4. Birnarob syllo homalonin uby misyrtoho.
5. Bythlym mothyn noctothij nelechantidasmachon

6. Yssidele brin tyfel yth chy-
lyschon tem liphul
7. Vth binim ysdibur thinno
euth nu Agorastocles.
8. Ythe manet ihy chyrsae ly-
coch sith naso
9. Bynni id chil luhili gubylim
lasibit thym
10. Body alyt herain nyn nuys
Lym moncot lusim.

DIVISION OF THE TERMS
into ordinary words.

1. Nyth Al oni mv.* Al on
Uths! Icorathisim. Ac on sith.
Basq. Nic Al oni mun. Al on ut-
sa! Ic oratuijon. Ac on zic.
Cast. I adore this power. Power of pure
goodness! Place yourself,
woman, in its care.
For that it is good!

2. Chyn lachchu nyth mum istyal mijctibarij mischi!
Basq. Cein latzchu nic men istia mirabari mizqui!
Cast. How painful it is to me, to
leave so little here for the maid
or manservant.
3. Lipho canethi ith bym itchij;
â dædin bein utztu.
Basq. Lepo ganeti ic bein itehij;
â dedin bein utztu.
Cast. Take the load from his
shoulders, so that he
can rest.
4. Bir narob syll ohom Al oni,
Nu bym isirtoho.

---

* *Al* means "Power"; *Alzuba*, "Powerful"; and by antonomasia, *God*; applied also to the *Judge* or to one's *superior*.

Basq. Bic naroc isill oam Al oni.
Neu bein itzartu.

Cast. Now I am led by two in
silence toward this Power. I
will awake.

5. Byth lym mothyn, noc tot-
hijene lechantid asmachon?

Basq. Bic leien motia, noc toqui-
en letzantic asmauchon?

Cast. Who has revealed,
(woman) the hiding place of
the scene of the crime, that was
committed between the two?

6. Yssi dele brin. Tifel ythchy
Lisch onten liphul.

Basq. Yssi deila brin (Zaata).
Epel ichi leicoc ontzen le-
pua.

Cast. Silence them; let all noise
cease. I'd be a coward
if I did not warm his ribs.

7. Vth bin im ysdi burthin.
Noc utnu* Agorastocles?

Basq. Euc bein an itchi burtian
(or burdian). Noc ostu Agorastocles?

Cast. You leave here in the
cart. Who has robbed
Agorastocles?

8. Ith emanetih yehyr-saelij-
coch. Sith naso?

Basq. Ic emanetic, ichi-zaleicoc.
Zuc nazu?

Cast. From what you have given,
some can be left to him. Do you want it?

9. Byn ni idchi llu. Hil i. Gu
bylim lasi bitthym.

Basq. Bein ni itchi lo. Il i. Gu
ibili lazqui-baten.

* *Vtnu* is unknown. Perhaps it means *gather up*; or *steal*, or *know*, or *discharge, unload* . . .

Cast. Let me sleep a little.
I hope you die. Go away
in a bad hour. Then we
can have some fun.
10. Body alyt? Herain, nyn
nuys lym moncot lusim.
Basq. Badu alic? Erain, nic naiz
leien mocots lucia.
Cast. Does he then have power?
To make, to make the generous
gift, this he can do, if I wish.

The loose words that Pœno or Hano spoke in the following scene, speaking to Milpho, are subject to the same purpose as the previous verses. To understand and examine them more clearly I call to the spectators' attention, since they have the text conveniently open before them, that Pœno said those words with the meaning that I give them in Basque. I feel it unnecessary to translate the entire Scene into a language that I know, which would make my idea even clearer. I have two editions of the Scene before me, both substantially different: that of Milan from the year 1500 and that of Antwerp from the year 1721. I present both editions of the text, except for *Palum* [stick], *erga* [towards], *dectha* [sayings or roofs] [fighting words directed at a post or a stake; a wooden effigy of an enemy that served as a target for soldiers to practice on], which is not Basque, but almost completely Latin.

	Milan Edition		*Antwerp Edition*
No. 1.	Anno muthum balle bacca edre anech.	No. 1.	Hanno Muthum balle bechœ dreanech.
No. 2	vo.	No. 2.	Havo.
No. 3.	Domni.	No. 3.	Donni.
No. 4.	Me bar bocca.	No. 4.	Mebar bocca.
No. 5.	Murphursa.	No. 5.	Murphursa.
No. 6.	Moinlec hianna.	No. 6.	Mivulechinna.
No. 7.	Lalechlabehanani liminichot.	No. 7.	Lalech lachananin liminichot.
No. 8.	Ysan.	No. 8.	Ysan arvinam.
No. 9.	Muphonnium sucoram.	No. 9.	Muphonnium succorahin.
No. 10.	Gunebei balsamenera san.	No. 10.	Gunebel balsamenierasan.

Maintaining the order of the words of the text, I will take them from one edition, and then from the other, in order to translate them into Basque, not knowing which of the two texts is closer to his original.

No. 1. *Han nom uthum balle bech edrea nec*
Basc: An num hutme Baleen belch errea nec
Cast: There where I am son of Balle, black from sun.
No. 2. *Havo. Basq:* Aua. *Cast:* Mouth.
No. 3. *Domni. Basq:* dot min. *Cast:* I'm in pain.
No. 4. *Me barb occa.*
Basq: Ni bart oeca.
Cast: I was tossing and turning all night.
No. 5. *Muphursa* (compound word, or corrupted). This could mean animal, or wild animals, because of what Milpho and the Commentators say, and because of the words in the following number; *Artza . . . Catamotza*—which means wild, mountain animals.
No. 6. *Moin lechianna.*
Basq: Min leiquiana.
Cast: The one who can cause pain.
No. 7. *Lalech labehan anin liminicoth.*
Basq: Alea salchen arin iminicot.
Cast: Then I'll go ahead and sell the grain.
No. 8. *Ysam. Basq*: Izan. *Cast*: Be him, or I am He.*
No. 9. *Muphonnium*; *succorahim.*
Basq: Milphon, ni on. Zuc erain.
Cast: Milphon, I am good. You tempt me to evil.
No. 10. *Gunebel balsameniera san.*
Basq: Guibel bals amaen erara izan.
Cast: You're the son of some mother of a black liver.

. . .

You tell me that in Toulouse, France, a number of French Basques have assembled to examine the Basque translation I have done of the verses of Plautus, and that they have rejected my work. According to the account I have heard concerning the conference in Toulouse, France, my work has not been completely rejected, as you assure me. The Basques from Donibane Lohizune [Saint-Jean-de-Luz] and from Donibane Garazi [Saint-Jean-Pied-de-Port] who met in that city have said that my work, as it has been presented, does not seem to present an intelligible text; but the Commission states that [the problem] may be the Bizkaian dialect. That is not the same as rejecting it completely. I have not

* *Arvina* is a Basque word.

wished, nor did I have to indicate specifically the Basque dialect of the verses, but to put them in proper Basque. Because I do not know from which Basque province it was, nor which dialect was used by the person who suggested it to the author of the comedy *Pœnulo*. If the wise Basques of the Toulouse conference had understood the provincial and municipal Basque words and terms from the entire Basque Country, and had examined them in the ten verses with the plot of the comedy *Pœnulo* open in front of them, they would surely have rendered a more favorable and more extensive critique of my work.

. . .

I say to you that neither in the Grammar nor in the bilingual Vocabulary of Mr. Lécluse do I find anything of use for the purpose which the author has proposed, or for the instructors, or for the students of the Basque language. To the contrary, if the teachers make use of this Grammar and Vocabulary, they will end up knowing less and worse about the Basque language; and the students won't even know how to conjugate a Basque verb halfway through. Instead, the teachers and the students who use the Basque text of Mr. Lécluse will end up being eternal speakers of the Basque language without understanding a word of what they are saying. This is the conclusion I have reached about said Grammar and said bilingual Vocabulary. In order to prove this completely, all I would have to do is cross out every page in the book. For there are very few that do not contain classic errors in the content. But you are quite aware that two or three absurdities can be marked in just one corner, as Mr. Lécluse does in some of his, and in order to refute one of them, it might take twenty or thirty lines or more.

. . .

I would prefer that you not burden me with another letter informing me of the eulogies that Mr. Iztueta has lavished on the Basque work of Mr. Lécluse. It is true, according to what Mr. Lécluse tells us on pages six, seven and twenty-three of his Grammar, that his Basque handbook has earned distinguished praise and repeated applause from Mr. Iztueta, the author of an eight-volume work about dances, songs, festivities . . . in the Gipuzkoan dialect, printed in Donostia [San Sebastián] in the year 1824, titled *Guipuzcoaco dantza gogoangarrien condaira edo historia, beren soñu zar, et itz neurtu, edo versoaquin* [An Account or History of the Most Celebrated Dances of Gipuzkoa, With Their Old Tunes and Words or Verses]. Mr. Lécluse on two occasions praises the work of Mr. Iztueta, announcing to the public that it includes the ancient customs of dances, songs, games, and other original amusements of the very noble and very loyal Province of Gipuzkoa. And two or three more times he informs us of how Mr. Iztueta has praised and honored his Basque Handbook, citing the eulogies, saying "how he and [fellow] enthusiasts . . . have been overjoyed to see that a Frenchman, who until now has had no knowledge of the language (Basque) has praised it so much, and honored it with so many eulogies. And elsewhere . . . Mr. Lécluse says: "Dr. Iztueta has written to me from Donostia [San Sebastián] saying that 'I have read almost everything of interest that has been written about the Basque language.'" So Mr. Lécluse, in gratitude for this kind favor, calls Mr. Iztueta, a "respected scholar."

Undoubtedly, the definitive opinion of a "respected scholar" and Basque writer who has repeatedly praised the Basque work of Mr. Lécluse carries enormous weight. And I have to tell you what I think about this. I agree that those people who have a vocation for distinguished careers as dancers, clowns and mimes will hold Mr. Iztueta in high regard for his work on *dances*, *games*, etc. But the author should not anticipate any further respect from the religious and honest Basque Country. Ask your countrymen what opinion the public has formed about said work on "dances" and you will see that I am not mistaken in my judgment.

Try to find some wisdom in it. I cannot find it. If you consider this work in terms of style and purity of the Basque language, you will have to correct it and expurgate it in many passages and points, starting with its title, from which the words *history* [and] *verses* should be stricken. Or try examining it for its knowledge of the art or modes of entertainment and songs, etc. that it presents to the country; you will find more customs, and more delightful and enchanting entertainments in the girls from remote farmsteads in the mountains of Gipuzkoa, Bizkaia and Navarre than in this author who writes about dances. These girls, without knowing how to write, and despite the strictness of their parents and evangelical ministers, could teach Mr. Iztueta plenty about the imagination and grace of the amusements of their country.

So there is nothing at all in the aforementioned work to cause anyone to call him "respected" or "scholarly." And it won't be surprising if the lovers of literature and fine arts apply to Mr. Lécluse that third fable of Yriarte:

Let an Author accept
this refrain for his gift:
If the wise man doesn't like it, too bad;
If the fool applauds it, far worse.

Enough, friend. I'm off to celebrate mass. Stay well, and be equally free and easy with your affectionate Chaplain.

Santander, August 10, 1827.

F. B. S. T.

48. Juan Bautista Erro Azpiroz

(Andoain, Gipuzkoa, 1773 – Baiona [Bayonne], Lapurdi, 1854)

The son of a famous pedagogue who was a professor at the Royal Seminary of Bergara and who taught rhetoric and poetry in Pamplona-Iruña, Juan Bautista was educated under his father's tutelage in Bergara. Before the Napoleonic Wars, he held the position of quartermaster-general at Almaden, Soria, and Ciudad Real. His clearly royalist political sympathies also enabled him to be appointed quartermaster-general of Madrid and Barcelona in 1820. Following the Riego Manifesto that same year, which ushered in a new Liberal regime, he found it necessary to flee to Spain, returning three years later thanks to the legitimizing intervention of the "Hundred Thousand Sons of Saint Louis," the French armed forces sent into Spain to restore the old regime by King Louis XVIII. As a result, Fernando VII immediately appointed Erro Minister of the Treasury, although a number of political problems again drove him into exile. In London, he made contact with Don Carlos, pretender to the Spanish throne, who supported him so ardently that he was appointed Universal Minister of the Carlist government in 1836, in the midst of the first Carlist War (1833–39). Erro's fundamental mission was to set the Treasury in order, a task that he was ultimately unable to accomplish. In 1839, he was driven into exile once again by the Bergara Agreement that settled the first Carlist War in favor of the triumphant Liberal side. He then took up residence in Bourges, Montpelier, and, finally, Baiona.

His background in literature, philology, and archaeology was by no means thorough, but his enthusiasm and dedication to these subjects was great. His interest in the Basque language was essentially practical and curatorial; he endeavored to explain ancient numismatics through the Basque language and thus prove the Basque-Iberianist thesis. As his theories were scientifically feeble and affected in good measure by metaphysics, he became an easy target for opposing polemicists, such as

Conde. During his exile, he maintained a relationship with Abbot Duvoisin, and his works on the subject of the Basque language were: *Alfabeto de la lengua primitiva de España y explicación de sus más antiguos monumentos, inscripciones y medallas* (Alphabet of the Primitive Langauge of Spain and an Explanation of Its Most Ancient Monuments, Inscriptions and Medals) (1806); *Observaciones filosóficas . . .* (Philosophical Observations . . .) (1807); and *El Mundo Primitivo* (The Primitive World) (1815). In any case, he left behind an abundance of unpublished manuscripts.

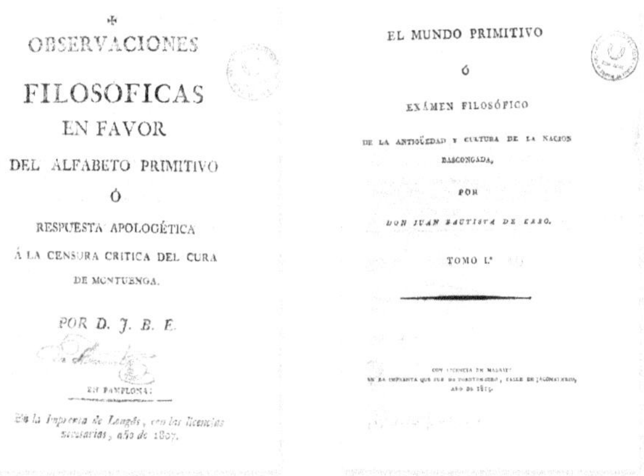

OBSERVACIONES
FILOSOFICAS
EN FAVOR
DEL ALFABETO PRIMITIVO
Ó
RESPUESTA APOLOGÉTICA
Á LA CENSURA CRITICA DEL CURA
DE MONTUENGA.
POR D. J. B. E.
EN PAMPLONA:
En la Imprenta de Longás, con las licencias necesarias, año de 1807.

EL MUNDO PRIMITIVO
Ó
EXÁMEN FILOSÓFICO
DE LA ANTIGÜEDAD Y CULTURA DE LA NACION
BASCONGADA,
POR
DON JUAN BAUTISTA DE ERRO.
TOMO I.°

Selected Text(s):

a) *Observaciones filosóficas a favor del Alfabeto Primitivo o Respuesta apologética a la Censura crítica del Cura de Montuenga* [Philosophical Observations in Favor of the Primitive Alphabet or Apologetic Response to the Negative Critique by the Priest from Montuenga] (Pamplona: Longas, 1807), 8–11.

b) *El Mundo Primitivo o Examen Filosófico de la Antigüedad y Cultura de la Nación Bascongada* [The Primitive World or Philosophical Examination of the Antiquity and Culture of the Basque Nation] (Madrid: Fuentenebro, 1815), 21–23, 27–29, 31–36, 41–43, 48–49, 247–248, 261–264.

a)

Philosophical Observations

Who has told Mister C. that it is necessary to be endowed with *the spirit of prophecy* to refer to things that are unknown, because they are considered impenetrable? How many unknown things that are not found in history books and which seemed unknowable have been made known to us by the learned without these supernatural aids? Who in this day and age would think of stating that to speak of ages predating history is to speak about what is not known, unless he means by this that it is unknowable? Does Mister C. perhaps not know that Man possessed speech for many centuries before the time of the histories that have been handed down to us? And that it is generally accepted by philosophers, who have scrutinized the question very closely, that the examination of language can lead us to knowledge of the most remote past? Is he not aware of the opinions of the noted Court, Des-Broses, Condillac, and others on this particular? And, if according to a well-known author of the day, "the construction of a language is in itself a history of each nation," why should it then be strange that the Basques should seek the history of their own people in their language, whose existence is hidden in the most distant past? If those learned Philosophers, even amid imperfect speculations, believed in these truths and presented them to the public, how much more energy would they have invested in sustaining their opinions had they found a language, perfect and complete in all of its parts, whose words led them to the examination of a mass of interesting ideas and exquisite knowledge predating the time of all histories, and in whose mechanisms they would have found the confirmation of the great plan they had set before themselves?

Yes, Mister Priest, a perfect language that arranges its words according to the precepts of nature is worthy of the highest attention, owing to the knowledge that a study of its words may shed upon mankind, and is a living witness to the laws, customs and progress made by the human spirit in the age during which it was spoken, and upon which a very true history may be formed, although it may be older than the age of Varro, which Erro knows very well.

Basque authors, wielding powerful arguments rather than denials like the absolutely ridiculous ones you have posited, have largely made known, and are on the verge of completing, the plan they have undertaken to show that their language is the primitive tongue of mankind, that it is the most perfect of languages, that it is a faithful copy of nature, an irrefutable eyewitness to the world's most ancient deeds, and an archive of the most precious knowledge of that primeval age. This conviction arose not after the course of an hour, but over the course of many years of arduous tasks, profound meditation, and unshakeable persistence. It has given these learned men, who think as highly of their opinions as Mister C. does of his own, an opportunity to present the fruits of their labors to the public and to lay the foundations for the great work of correcting history, thus clearing the way for the examination of the most distant events, but without opposing in any manner whatsoever the doctrine of the holy books of Moses, as Mister C. would suggest.

b)

The Primitive World

Chapter 1

ON THE ENDEAVORS OF SOME LEARNED MEN TO FIND THE ORIGINAL LANGUAGE—ITS PERFECTION AND SINGULAR NATURE.

Section I

I am undertaking a work whose argument, by traversing the obscurity of centuries unknown, fixes at a certain point the origin of religion, language, and the scientific opinions of the men who lived in the first centuries of creation. A task that is no less impossible in the common opinion, than it is replete with hazards as to the accuracy and execution of the subject. The scant antiquity of the texts, the fables of each nation, the brief lifespan of mankind, and the shadows that envelop the origins of peoples, who are scattered throughout the world, would seem to be insurmountable obstacles that no human ingenuity is able to overcome. The works of Zoroaster, of Berosus, of Enoch, of Sanchoniathon, and others cited for their antiquity, show such powerful arguments against their sincerity that there is no critic who can base his arguments upon them without the danger of being challenged. The chronicles of the sacred historian Moses, inextricably linked to the main goal of his mission, leave great voids open to curiosity, and therefore do not contribute that assistance to the argument that is supported only by faith and the authority of such a qualified author.

However, these obstacles that loom large because of the lack of philosophical analysis are small vapors that are easily dispelled by the shining light of criticism. There is perhaps no easier argument, nor one more authorized by irrefutable documents, than this one, which has taken many learned men so forcefully by surprise that they have described it as impossible. Almost all the sciences, whose ancient history has been hitherto unknown, provide us with a ladder that allows us to take our investigations to the causes of their coming into being. Legislation, Physics, Astronomy, Agriculture, Geography, and various other advances of the human spirit, taken as a whole as well as each one individually, provide extensive material for the purpose of our task.

It is true that amid these general opinions the natural curiosity of mankind, with the support of philosophy, has led some learned men to set aside these difficulties and to consider the possibility of establishing facts and opinions that have come down to us from prehistory. For many years, they have desired to ascertain what transpired during primitive times and to go beyond the discoveries of history and the origins of peoples, languages, and sciences back to the first centuries of creation. Owing to the errors and monstrous fables through which truth has been disfigured thanks to the propensity toward fantasy that is inherent in Greeks, Egyptians, and others; scholars have become convinced of the futility of their efforts in consulting the ancient writings of the most ancient peoples, and have turned to the examination of languages, which as living archives of the times in which they existed, offer in the examination of their words many important landmarks in the progress of the human spirit in ages, which would otherwise be impossible for us to reach.

. . .

Judiciously observing that the construction of the languages of mankind is not the result of whim and caprice but of the organic disposition of the vocal instrument and the mechanism of the human voice, which is set in motion by the irresistible power of nature, which loves order in all its representations; other sages, at whose head we find the great Plato, have adopted for this speculation a more general and philosophical principle for the representation of the quality of objects. By devoting themselves to the discovery in every language of what they consider to be general, common, and original principles, either by fixing their speculations upon a given language, or by seeking the original language in the modulations of voice and in a multitude of general and primitive roots, they have discovered the existence of daughter and mother languages.

These scholars were already very close to the truth, and if they had limited themselves solely to the examination of nature to determine the true value and characteristic of each modulation of the speech organs, they would doubtless have hit upon the solid principle that would have necessarily led them to the end of their quest. The language of nature, if it ever existed on earth, must have been based upon these principles. Everything in the Universe is linked, and the primeval language could have done no less than to bear the seal of its immediate affiliation to and dependency upon it.

This great step toward the discovery of the Primitive World and its language had already been taken, and it appeared that the veil that enshrouded this great secret was about to be rent. But the meager, not to say inexistent, progress made by philosophy toward consolidating and perfecting these ideas from the time in which Plato [in *Cratilus*], albeit imperfectly, advised us of these important notions, convinces us that not even the ancient grammarians like Pubilus Nigidius, nor our modern philosophers, have limited themselves to adopting Plato's principles, applying them in a general way to certain languages, and perceiving the ring of truth in the resulting speculations without ever rising from that point to acknowledge them as part of nature itself. We may therefore state that over the long course of centuries, the progress made toward perfecting the grammatical aspect of the study of language has been of little account.

Plato himself, who although a philosopher was also Greek, left us in this and other treatises, certain statements that testify to his lack of sincerity. Much like the moderns, Plato felt that his declarations were true, and he also sensed the necessity for the modulations of the voice to have their own meanings and attitude to represent signifiers that linked language to nature in their most minimal elements. But that opinion was not his own, and he probably brought it back from the travels he undertook, or else he must have adopted it from those, who introduced it from the East, where this tradition of a primeval language was still maintained, along with the principles of numeral philosophy which both he and Pythagoras held in such high esteem, employing (as we shall later see), the same trick of concealing its origin to attribute to themselves a glory that was not their due.

If philosophical reflection had led the great Plato to the discovery of the plan he published and to the conviction that, among the modulations of the human voice, the "r" (as he says) entered into the formation of words as a note of *movement*, and that the "i" meant a subtle and penetrating thing; that the "d" and the "t" meant detention, that the "l" was the note of torpidity, he would have seen through all these undeniable truths by the very same principle of observing verbal pantomime into the meaning of the other modulations, he would have thought otherwise, and the arguments of his *Cratilus* would have become less metaphysical and much more felicitous. He would have corrected and simplified his Greek alphabet, reducing its elements to sixteen, and would have presented us in the table of their meanings with a small group of signifiers that were nonetheless capable of representing in combination all the objects in nature characterized by the attributes that [human] understanding might wish to endow them. His treatise, *Cratilus*, is the most authentic demonstration that the plan he was announcing had met with strong support in his philosophy, but that it was not an original product of his mind. Thus, unconvinced that his native language lacked the perfection of one that had been part of this great plan, he unhappily insisted on seeking in it the confirmation of his opinions, thereby destroying the exactness of his own principles. Vestiges of the scientific opinions of the Primitive World captured his vast understanding. He learned of the considerable role that nature played in them, but because he had not received them with the purity of their original state, his treatise *Cratilus* suffers from the same confusion of ideas as his *Timeas*.

. . .

The primeval language can be none other than the one that justifies its immediate affiliation to nature. The power of speech contains its elements, just as all living things have their principles; and these had no more become fortuitously linked in the Universal Plan as had the modulations in the words of language, until mankind in his capriciousness began to ignore and violate nature.

Primeval language, as infused by God in the first man in His creation,* was to have been equal in perfection to all of the Creator's other works, and would therefore have been linked to the other harmonies of nature. Anyone who examines in detail the mechanical construction of the vocal instrument in mankind, and the exercise and action of its parts in the various modulations of the voice, cannot help but notice and admire a musical game or pantomime which imparts a particular significance to each sound. That these sounds exist, so long as the action is not violated, in a given number, and by their being neither more nor less than what is necessary to fulfill all the functions to which the jurisdiction of language may be extended, they likewise present, with admirable convenience, the number of signifiers needed to express all of the ideas of understanding with the greatest distinction and clarity. Could such marvelous harmonies be the effect of chance? Can anyone be capable of persuading himself that, having imprinted these qualities in Man since his creation, God would not have given him a language suited to such wise arrangements? This cannot be sustained without a manifest contradiction of the laws of nature.

It is very possible that this infused language would not merely be tied to the specific needs of a rustic man, but would encompass all the knowledge that seems to have ennobled the Universal Sovereign of the Earth. But, even if this premise will not be conceded, the observations made by the first man, on the language that his Creator had bestowed

---

* I am well aware that not all philosophers agree with this opinion, but I will later describe my reasons for supporting it.

upon him, would have made him aware of the existence of elements of speech that allowed him to assign names to things according to the nature and uniqueness of his native language. He could do no less than observe that upon pronouncing the letter "l," for example, his tongue adhered to his palate, and upon consulting the usage and representation of this letter in the spoken language, he would have noticed that it constantly signified "attachment," "obstruction," and other qualities analogous to the latter, and would not doubt that this was its natural meaning. He would note that when pronouncing "k," the root of the tongue would block the main channel of respiration, hindering the operation of the vocal instrument, and he would rightly suppose that this modulation was a sign of "privation," of "sterility," and all similar qualities. He would notice, upon pronouncing the "r," a violent vibration and roughness of the tongue, making him aware that the usage and meaning of this modulation within the composition of words must refer to "roughness" and "movement." He would notice upon pronouncing the [Castilian] "c" or "z" that the tongue was blocked or cut off by the teeth, and this action would inform him that this modulation meant a "cutting," and therefore the "end" or "edge" of something. These truths would achieve a new level of evidence upon his seeing these observations confirmed through the examination of his tongue.

The language of man is little more than musical pantomime, and if the sages who insisted upon the anti-philosophical question of determining whether the language of actions or that of articulated words is older would have stopped to reflect and consult nature, they would have realized that the language of action is not limited, as has been commonly held, to the movements of the hands and face, but also exists in the delicate parts of the mouth: that action and language are simultaneous productions, and that by not being aware of this fact, they became lost among matters that were little better than useless.

. . .

Having been instructed in the ways referred to above in the meanings of the articulations of the voice (if such knowledge was not already infused in him, as one might well believe), Man would proceed to the forming of names in the same manner that a painter, applying a variety of colors to the palette, paints and determines the object by using all of the features and hues that make it recognizable at first sight. In the same way, Man bearing in mind the various modulations and their respective meanings, would take from them the ones he needed to refer to the object he wished to represent. Thus, for example, if he wished to give a stone a name, he would reach for the best suited modulations to represent the qualities of this signifier, and these being those of strength and roughness, would use the "a" to indicate the initial modulations, and for the second the "rr" which is a sign of roughness, and would call the stone "a-rr," and thus, together with the Basque characteristic feature of names, the word would become *a-rr-a* or *arria*. To indicate the leaves of a tree, he would endeavor to bestow upon them a name that would depict and represent in detail all the qualities that an examination of leaves offered him. The circular shape of the leaf would cause him to choose "o" as suitable for representing this characteristic; and the roughness or unevenness of its segmented edges would lead him to avail himself of "rr," a sign of roughness . . . and if the leaf's incisions were also sharp, he would choose "i." The linking of these ideas would result in naming a leaf *o-rr-i*, which becomes *orria* with the Basque appellative feature. And if he should desire to add to these attributes others even better suited to his meaning, and by observing that the lower part of the leaf adheres to the branch from which it is born, he would make sure to denote this lower part with the letter "b," and with the "l" to refer to the union that is its true signifier, he would then call the leaf *o-rr-be-l*, which with the Basque appellative feature becomes *orbela* [the words *orria* and *orbela* are both used to refer to leaves in the Basque language]. In order for man to make a height known, he would choose an "o," but as this is an indefinite signifier that may relate to any type of height and so become incomprehensible to those being addressed, he would make sure to add attributes that would classify it and set it apart from other heights. Thus, if he wished to indicate a rough elevation, he would add "rr" to the "o." Conversely, if the elevation were also sharp, he would note that quality by adding an "i," which characterizes this property. And if this high land could still be mistaken for another such formation nearby, he would add another quality that would clearly distinguish it from the others. If, for example, he wished to refer to a round promontory, he would add an "o" and would call this complete group of attributes *o-r-i-o* [This is the name of a mountain in the Pyrenees called Pico de Orio or Orio Peak, which displays all the features that its combined modulations indicate].

Chapter 2

The primeval language was infused into man at his creation, and not formed by him.

Some polite authors, wishing to say something about the creation of Man, ascribed the execution of this sublime and marvelous work to chance, saying that we owe the origin of our propagation to a multitude of men, who suddenly appeared all over the Earth owing to *some modification* caused by an *unknown influx* of nature. It can already be seen that if such a way of thinking could be accepted in the explanation of different phenomena, there exists no absurdity that could not be proven, nor any difficulty that could not be immediately solved. These are delirious fantasies that weigh down and cloud even the good use of reason . . .

But, as we must deviate from such barely philosophical principles, so contrary to the plan of Creation and nature, we should continue in our research and consider Man as having emerged from the hands of his Creator as an adult, endowed with all the qualities needed to fulfill the purposes of his creation. This principle is consistent not only with the spirit of Scripture, but with that of reason as well. The works of creation were all made perfect and complete, and Man, included among them, could be no less so. To depict him as a savage, nearly devoid of rationality, is an insult to the noblest creature in the Universe, and to the Creator Himself. The ideas suggested to us by the examination of a rough, unkempt man without any education whatsoever are not those of Natural Man. It is a state of degradation that cannot be reconciled in any way with the perfection of the Creator's works. The extent of our understanding, the liberty of our free will, the sublime nature of our ideas, the perspicacity of our senses, tell us that there is a state of natural perfection in Man, as well as in all other works of creation, and it cannot be imagined that God, having created Man as the principle and origin of his species, would have created him imperfect, and deprive this particular piece of His handiwork of the perfections that he so abundantly shed upon others. Let us place the first man at least at the level of all other works of nature and not allow ourselves be carried away by the absurd opinions of a philosophy that cannot be reconciled with its own principles, and let us not deny in Man's creation the perfection of the natural gifts that ennoble him, when we freely grant primitive beasts the gifts of their exquisite instinct.

. . .

A language, like that of the first society, must have been one the definitive feature of all of whose words, minimal although they may have been, was aimed at providing an exact idea of the qualities and attributes of the entity being represented, permitting us to see that, aside from the knowledge and meaning of the roots, profound philosophical examination and acuity are required to properly join one sound to another, syllables to syllables, as well as a very broad knowledge of nature; to provide definitions of all of its products with the perfection and admirable care that is provided by the Basque language. How can we not see in the beautiful mechanism of this language (in which nature is painted with the most brilliant and exquisite colors that such a precise copy of it is not within the reach of Man), that he did not give us at some point an idea of the liberty with which he was endowed at his creation, and which would enable him to depart now and then from its precepts? All the products of nature are in a finished and perfect state, and the divine origin of this law, that formed them independently, and without freedom, has ever been refuted. But at the same time, constant experience is always showing us the most convincing proof that there is no single product of Man that does not carry upon it, the mark of that innate desire of his to improve upon the works of nature. The multiplicity of the languages known to us today gives us a good idea of this truth. Man can be seen in all of them; his caprice is evident in all of them, divorced from the laws of nature; did Man amend his natural proclivity only in the one language we propose as primeval?

Chapter 12

The subject of the previous section continues, and an account is given of the state of Paradise or Man's first abode.

Section 1

We shall finish this subject with an examination of the names of the two rivers: Gihon and Pison, these being the two that bathed and irrigated the Garden of Eden, and whose definition, added to that of the countries that determine its course in the history of Moses, will make evident and without any doubt the true location of this agreeable place about which so much has been written by Ecclesiastical Authors and many others motivated by the desire to discover where it lies. This examination will allow us to see, unlike many other examples we could present, how useful the principles of primeval Geography are in ascertaining the true position of countries, and how valuable today is a knowledge of the Basque language in getting to the bottom of countless truths that are cited only with great mistrust, or are enveloped among fable-based opinions within history. The nature with which the primeval language determines all of the geographical features in Chapter Two of *Genesis* are such, and are presented with such clarity and distinction to understanding, that there can be no doubt whatsoever as to the location of Paradise, no less than in the chronicles of the Sacred Historian.

. . .

The first individuals of the human species could not help but to impose a suitable name upon a place whose pleasant soil and climate brought back the memory of the blessed peace that they had enjoyed there, and which formed, according to the nature of their language, an image of its delightfulness. This must certainly have been the case, because since that distant age Euskara has bestowed the name *Mesenia* upon the entire garden or terrain crossed and watered by the Gihon from the point where it branches out from the Euphrates to the point at which, joined to the western branch of that river, it turns south, bordering the land of Kuth until it flows into the Gulf. Until now, no one has reported the assigning of a name to that location, but the Basque language gives us the name *Me-ez-enia*, a definition of that place, and information about the people, who brought it into being and inhabited it. This name is tantamount to saying in Castilian "place of delicate pleasantness," as a compound of *me*, *me-a*, delicate thing, the patronymic syllable *ez*, equivalent to the possessive "de" in Castilian, and the syllable *en*, with which the marker of an appellative name becomes *ena* or *enia*, and means "a pleasant, voluptuous, fleshy, delicious, and any other analogous quality," which is included in the value of the soft and delicate "*e*" and "*n*" modulations that make up this word.

The name Mesenia, conceived in the language we propose as primeval, and applied to a location where very powerful evidence suggests that the Garden of Eden existed, could only have been conferred by the Basque peoples who lived there, and at a time when the delights of that land presented images to its smiling inhabitants to be conveyed into the language, images that correspond very closely to those that the Sacred Historian gives us of that region. Such a multiplicity of coincidences are never the daughters of blind chance, and if any evidence could still be furnished in support of such a manifest truth, it is the confirmation, given to us by nature itself, of the definition of the word Mesenia in the countries that bear that name.

Conclusion

What has been said hitherto about primeval Geography will give credit to the other documents we have produced and will produce in [the] future in support and justification of our argument, that Euskara, fully preserved in Basque [*Bascuence*], was the universal language, and therefore, the primeval speech of the human species, which has existed uninterrupted in our country of Spain since the time of the Diaspora. In fact, during what time could names have been imposed in the same language on all of the provinces, towns, mountains, and rivers of the entire world, but in the era that preceded the Flood, a time universal to all the human species? During what time could men form names, all of them measured by a single principle, without ever deviating from it, unless it was during an age in which they had accepted a common system of Geography based on nature, and on the character of their language, which is the one we have made known in this treatise? We have shown here the principles that have comprised this knowledge within the Basque language to this very day, and an examination of the oldest names on Earth has clearly revealed to us, with an abundance of proof that we could increase to infinity, that the primeval Geography that imposed these names is not, nor ever could be, anything but that which the Basque language preserves in the incorruptible archive of its admirable antiquity.

Sages may examine the question and opine on whether there could have been a time to which these observations might be adapted, apart from what came before the Flood, which is the epoch of the first centuries of Creation. [The Sages could tell us] if there is a language in the world that could show within itself such a wise Geographical system, as well as evidence such as has been provided concerning its primacy. All new discoveries are shocking, and their novelty increases proportionally to the degree to which the truth that one wishes to make known contrasts with existing ideas and injures the imagination. However, among the Sages, the weight of an opinion must yield before the strength of reason, when the opinion is presented with proof that causes its foundations to disappear. How could Euskara, that language considered by the caprice and detestation of scholars, who never understood it, to be a rude and untutored tongue, not be shocked, if it were presented now in the republic of letters as nothing less than the primeval language of mankind? In spite of this warning, there is nothing more just, than to strive for it. This is the language that will some day delight scholars, and in whose examination history will find much to correct and to learn, the mind will find advances it could not have promised; and languages will find many improvements to aspire to, and, in a word, literature will find an abundance of lights with which to educate, enliven, and adorn human understanding.

49. Fleury Lécluse, known as Lor Urhersigarria

(Paris, 1774 – Auteuil, 1845)

A famous Hellenist in his epoch, Lécluse was a professor of Greek literature at the University of Toulouse. He took an interest in the Basque language and published a *Manuel de la langue basque* (Handbook of the Basque Language) (1826) that included a grammar and a vocabulary, all of this after having made a brief visit to the Basque Country and studying a few of the classic works on the topic. That same year he had to publish an *Examen critique du Manuel de la langue basque* (Critical Analysis of the Handbook of the Basque Language) under the pseudonym Lor Urhersigarria (a picturesque translation into Basque of his name and surname) in which he ruminated on the brilliance of his handbook as if it were the opinion of another critic. He maintained contact with a number of Bascophiles, among them Mateo Zabala and Juan Ignacio de Iztueta.

In 1829, he engaged in one of the strangest debates on the Basque language of this period with Friar Bartolomé de Santa Teresa. The latter had published *Plauto Bascongado* (Basque Plautus) in 1829, a Basque translation of the "Punic" verses contained in Plautus's comedy *Poenulus.* A conference of linguists was held in Toulouse, presided over by Lécluse, to analyze this theory. They rejected it, and Lécluse published their findings in his *Plauto polígloto* (The Polyglot Plautus), (1829), provoking a counterattack from Santa Teresa in another small book, *Anti-Plauto polígloto* (The Polyglot Anti-Plautus), in which he not only defended his positions on the translation of the verses of Plautus, but severely attacked Lécluse's handbook and called into question his qualifications for rendering opinions of the Basque language. Further, because Iztueta supported Lécluse, and the latter had characterized him as a "respected scholar," Santa Teresa extended his attacks to include the dance instructor, whom he placed in the category of "dancers, clowns, and mimes." In this, as in no other polemic, we see the depth of hostility, personal interests, and ideological prejudices that frequently overshadowed the real essence of what was being debated.

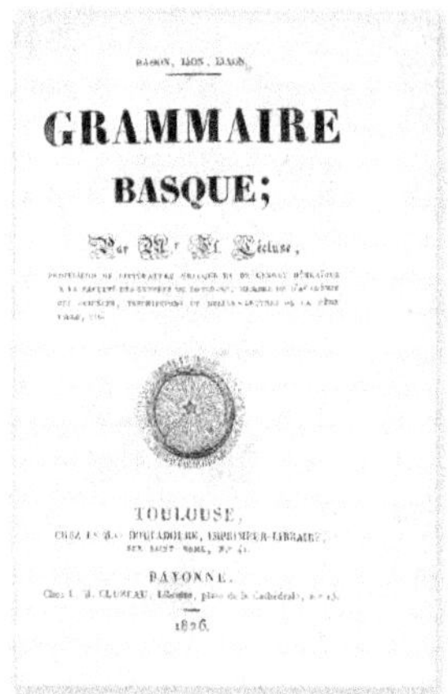

Selected Text(s):

Grammaire basque [Basque grammar] (Toulouse: Jean Douladoure; Bayonne: L. M. Cluzeau, 1826), 2–3, 6–12.

If we can establish, as an absolute fact, the kinship of the Basque language with Carthaginian, will this not force us to acknowledge a definite antiquity of twenty-seven centuries? And because Phoenician itself was a dialect of Hebrew, can we then grant Basque an even more noble origin?

A Latin writer of comedies, who lived two centuries before Christ and died in the year 570 of the foundation of Rome, M. A. Plautus, has left us a comedy titled *Poenulus*, or *The Tiny Carthaginian*, that was performed in Rome around the beginning of the Second Punic War. In the fifth act of this play, Hannon, a Carthaginian, comes to Calydon, a village in Etolia, in the house of Antidamas, with whom it was associated by bonds of hospitality. The purpose of his journey is to search for his two daughters and his nephew Agorastocles, whom Sicilian pirates have kidnapped from Carthage and taken to a foreign land. The old Carthaginian man, followed by slaves carrying heavy loads, opens the first scene of the fifth act with a monologue in the Punic language.

This scene contains twenty-seven verses, of which the last eleven are in Latin. Samuel Bochart, having observed that the proper nouns *Antidamas* and *Agorastocles* are located, in the Punic verses, in almost the same place as in the Latin verses, concluded that they could not be anything other than the translation of the first; and, because there is a great similarity between Punic and Hebrew, he has transcribed the first ten verses in Hebrew characters; then, by situating the words differently and modifying certain syllables, he has discovered the same thoughts that were presented in the Latin verses.

. . .

During my journey to Donostia [San Sebastián], the main city of Gipuzkoa, I consulted a Spanish Basque scholar, Don Iztueta,* about these ten Punic verses; and he tried to explain them easily with the aid of his maternal language. Like Bochart, he has broken down different words, adding or omitting letters as necessary; but the result of his interpretation, that these ten verses have no relationship with the eleven Latin verses, the last of which Bochart had assumed were pure and simple translations of the first. This difference has not surprised me in the least; I was even thrilled to see Plautus spared the reproach of monotonous repetition. However, what has even more urgently convinced me, despite my reluctance, to accept Bochart's opinion, is that Don Iztueta's explanation, in the Spanish language, was pure nonsense. This is his version of the first part:

* In 1824, Don Juan Ignacio de Iztueta published in Donostia-San Sebastián (Baroja Press) an eight-volume work which presents the ancient customs of dance, music, games, and other original amusements of the most noble and loyal Province of Gipuzkoa. This work, written in the Gipuzkoan dialect of Basque, is titled *Guipuzcoaco dantza gogoangarrien condaira, edo istoria beren soñu zar, eta itz neurtu edo versoaquin.* This famous scholar, after having read my dissertation on the Basque language, of which I have had the honor to present him a copy, acknowledges receipt of it in the following terms: "I received the Memorandum which you have written on the Basque language, which has been greatly enjoyed and praised by all lovers of literature and fine arts. These, as well as all of those who love their country and who are interested in its glories, are overcome with joy to see that a Frenchman, who until now has had no acquaintance with this language, has praised it so much and conferred so many eulogies on it!" Someone else has written to me from Tolosa [Gipuzkoa], saying: "I have seen the Dissertation on the Basque language, which has greatly pleased me, and even more to see the work that you are doing to exalt this language of our country." I do not wish to prolong this note with excessive quotations; but I cannot resist recalling a few lines from a letter with which a French Basque scholar, a man as admirable for his intelligence as for his virtues, has honored me: "Every Basque who is even slightly patriotic, and you know that we are all very much so, should be infinitely flattered to see a man with such extraordinary knowledge of languages take so much interest in ours. As for me in particular, I find it difficult to express the enormous pleasure it gives me."

> *Ni hal oni nua onutsi gorat hisi macon, sith*
> *Chimel, lach, chumith mamieti, al mintibari imischi,*
> *Lepho gañethi tha biz mithi ja dedin min urthija.*

[The] literal translation, according to Don Iztueta [is]:

> I see this power clearly poised over the downtrodden, weary scepter or shepherd's crook—the finest and most subtle intelligence permanently entwined or held in the grasp of the painful power—by the back of the neck and binding the tongue doubly to prevent it from speaking about the coming evil.

I was ready to give up all hope of proving the identity of the Basque and the Punic languages, when the Viscount of Panat, sub-prefect of Baiona [Bayonne], honored me with a letter (dated April 26, 1826), in which he spoke to me of a work he had just been told about by the French Consul to Santander. Mr. L. F. Graslin inquires whether, by a new distribution of letters in the Punic text of Bochart, or in a completely different text of an edition of Plautus, it would be possible to find a meaning that is more accurate (than the interpretation that he proposes) concerning the entrance of Hannon onto the stage; particularly if one does not lose light of the fact that he arrives accompanied by several slaves or domestic porters. He also wonders whether the restoration of the text, presented in the ancient Basque language, might actually be considered as an attempt to represent ancient Basque, and whether it might be even more intelligible today to men who are well versed in that language.

To reply to the noble views of the distinguished Consul and his sub-prefect, I have called together a number of bright officials, able ecclesiastics, and other Basque scholars, some from Donibane Garazi [Saint-Jean-Pied-de-Port, Lower Navarre], others from either Maule [Mauléon, Zuberoa] or Donapaleu [Saint-Palais, Lower Navarre]; thus, all three of the dialects of French Basque, that is, the one from Lapurdi [sic], the one from Lower Navarre, and the one from Zuberoa and Amikuze [Mixe, Lower Navarre], are represented in Toulouse.

After having made a few remarks on the subject of Plautus's play *Pœnulus*, and having placed before them the first scene of the fifth act, I explained to them Bochart's opinion and his efforts to explain, with the aid of Hebrew, the Punic verses *Ny thalonium valon uth . . .*, which he thought were faithfully translated by the Latin verses *Deos deasque veneror . . .*, which end that same scene. I then told them of Don Iztueta's essay, *Ni hal oni . . .* [I See this Power . . .]; and, after a number of preambles, I called their attention to the reestablishment of the text of ten Punic verses and their interpretation with the help of the Basque language as it now exists in the Basque, French, and Spanish countries—a project carried out by the Reverend Father Bartolomé de Santa Teresa of the Order of Barefoot Carmelites at the request and following the indications of Mr. L. F. Graslin, French Consul to Santander.

Let us cite here the first three verses, as a sample of the work of the Reverend Father Bartolomé.

Ancient Text:
Ny thalonim valon uth si corathisima consith
Chym lach chunyth mumis tyalmyctibari imischi
Lipho canet hyth bymithii ad ædin binuthii.

Corrected Text
Nyth al oni mu: al on uths! Ic orathisim: ac on sith.
Chym lachchu, nyth mum istyal myctibari imischi!
Liphoca net: hyth bym ithii; a dedin, byn uthii.

Modern Basque
Nic al oni mun: o al on utsa! Ic oratijon: ac on zic.
Cein latzchu, nic emen istia mirabari mizqui!
Lepoca nic: ic bein itchi; a dedin, bein utzi.

Literal Translation
I embrace this power: oh, excellent power!
Be assured
Of its help: for that, it is quite good.—For
I am sorry to leave the slave girl for a while! She
Looks at me: leave her for a while;
for she is resting.

Here is the summary of the Cantabrian Commission, which has wished to make their ideas clear to me:

1. The text of ten Punic verses of the comedy *Pœnulus* (act five, first scene), as printed by Bochart in his Sacred Geography (page 800), or as it is found in all of the editions of Plautus, does not seem to present a Basque text.
2. This same text corrected by the Reverend Father Bartolomé in an effort to offer in the ancient Basque language a text that is even today extremely intelligible, without any change except for a new

way of dividing the words, did not seem to present an intelligible text.

3. The free translation or paraphrase in Modern Basque of Plautus's text reestablished in the ancient Basque language has produced a few isolated Basque words; however, the Commission has declared that the modern Basque of the Reverend Father Bartolomé might well be from Basque, but that a French Basque speaker would only understand the Basque of Don Iztueta, which was undoubtedly written in the dialect of Gipuzkoa.

4. As for the literal French translation, it seemed to offer only disconnected phrases all of which would be rendered into modern French Basque in a way totally different from that in which they are expressed.

This, then, is my personal conclusion: First, that it is not necessary to continue to reject Bochart's explanation, and that we should accept it until such time as someone provides us with a meaning as accurate as his and which is expressed in truly intelligible Basque; second, that because Bizkaian is the most difficult of all dialects for French Basques to understand, for that very reason it might be less remote from Punic, if indeed it was not, as the Reverend Father Bartolomé seeks to prove, pure Carthaginian.

50. José Paulo de Ulibarri Galindez

(Okondo, Araba, 1775 – Abando, Bizkaia, 1847)

He lived most of his life in Bizkaia, his family having moved there from Araba when he was young. He was a professional blacksmith, although he identified himself somewhat hyperbolically as a "veterinary officer" on his trilingual (Basque, Spanish, and French) calling card. He carried out public functions in Abando as alderman, archivist, and accountant of the municipality, and as its representative in the *foral* Assemblies of Gernika.

Most of his literary and public activity was aimed at the promotion and enhancement of the dignity of the Basque language. He published a series of short works between 1814 and 1835 that included songs, Christmas carols, and Basque poems of a religious and patriotic nature, the purpose of which was always the exaltation of the Basque language. He also cultivated a genre that was much in vogue at the time—the compiling of almanacs. His, for the year 1815, was titled: *Egunari eusquerascoa erderazcotic itzuliya Vizcai, Guipuzcoa eta Arabaco Provinciarentzat 1815'garren urteraco* (A Basque-Language Almanac Translated from Castilian for the Provinces of Bizkaia, Gipuzkoa and Araba, for the Year 1815). He also communicated by letter with all the outstanding Bascophiles of his time, as revealed by his epistolary, published in 1975 under the title *Gutunliburua* (A Book of Letters). It includes his correspondence with, among others, Juan Bautista Erro, Juan Ignacio de Iztueta, Pedro de Altube, Julián de Argaiz, the Marquis of Valdespina, Diego Antonio de Basaguren, Novia Salcedo, Juan Ignacio Mendizábal, the missionaries of Zarautz Francisco de Estarta and Mateo Zabala, and so on. In his lesser works—carols, songs, and notes of appreciation to acquaintances—he always expressed his concerns about the maintenance of the *Fuero* and the development of the Basque language. He was especially concerned about the use of Castilian to teach Basque-speaking children, for example commenting: "*Esaizu: ¿zelan da au / zetara adi gara? ¿Euskera berba eginda / eskolia erdera? / Ori da asmo gaiztoak / egitia gu galtzera*" (Tell me: what is it / we're doing? / Speaking Basque / but teaching in schools in Castilian? / That is a trick / to ruin us).

Another matter that raised his ire was the progressive Castilianization of Bilbao. The contrast between rural municipalities (including Abando, where he lived), which were at the time fully Basque-speaking, and the urban nucleus that was becoming more and more Castilian-speaking also carried implications for the traditional country/city dichotomy that had characterized relations between Bilbao and the Seigniory of Bizkaia. Furthermore, this social and linguistic opposition had been deeply politicized in the context of the events surrounding the previously mentioned *Zamacolada* uprising. It goes without saying that Ulibarri did not mince words when it came to seeing Bilbao as the focus of linguistic and social destabilization: "*Dago zer garbitu asko / emengo lekuetan; / uri au da geure galtzaille / gauza guztietan; / egin dan legues pozua / erdera loiekaz / mota gustiko suge . . . / ta ganeko pestiekaz*" (There's a lot of cleaning-up to do around these places; / it's this city that's ruining us / in every possible way; / the way it's been transformed / by this filthy foreign language / into a pit of all kinds of vipers / and other plagues).

In 1829, in his role as representative for Abando, he prepared a motion to present before the General Assemblies of Bizkaia in Gernika, requiring the use of the Basque language in the schools of Bizkaia. However, in the initial attempt he was unable to present it in printed form, and then, after falling down the stairs of his house and being injured, was again unable to introduce it. Between the years 1834 and 1836, he undertook an important campaign in favor of Euskara in the Carlist-dominated General Assemblies of Bizkaia in Gernika. He proposed plans to encourage the use of the Basque language and for the redaction, in Basque as well as Castilian, for activities of the institution, urging especially that the Assemblies themselves establish an Academy of the Basque language. He saw the successful conclusion of some of his efforts after the end of the first Carlist War, in 1841, with the establishment of a chair in the Basque language in the Institute of Bilbao.

Ulibarri was a classic representative of Carlist ideology; a traditionalist supporter of the *fueros* and a strong advocate first of Fernando VII and later of Carlos, a fervent Catholic, and a worthy opponent of the Constitution (which he labeled *"deabruziñoa"* or deviltry), a champion of presumed ethnic virtues, and an avowed enemy of upstarts and outsiders. We have a verbal portrait of Ulibarri in a memorandum he presented in May of 1834 to the Assemblies of Gernika in which he describes an imaginary ancient Basque society that was respectful of religion, church figures, with festivals to maintain, and the importance of property and the Bourbon monarchy (it is important to remember that for him the Bourbons were of Basque origin, *Borbón* being derived from *Buru-on*); all of this in contrast to the contemporary society in which the constitution, liberalism, and urban merchants, all of them *erdeldunes* (Castilian-speakers) hiding behind the walls of Bilbao, a modern Sodom and Gomorra, and corrupting the Basque soul. He considered the introduction of the Castilian language an ideological Trojan horse contributing definitively to the destruction of the idyllic agrarian, religious, and moral society he imagined. There are a number of obvious similarities between his ideology and that of another illustrious citizen of Abando who would come into his own a few decades later: Sabino de Arana y Goiri, the founder of modern Basque nationalism.

DON JOSE PABLO ULIBARRI, MARISCAL VETERINARIO conocido por sus talentos y acierto en la facultad, vive en Vizcaya en la Ante-Iglesia de San Vicente de Abando, pegaute a la villa de Bilbao.

YOSE PAULO ULIBARRI-CO, ABERE SENDATZALLEEN yakinena orain munduan ezagutzen dana, bicida Vizcaiyan Yaun-done Vicente Abando-co Eleix-atétan, Bilbo Uriyaren alboan.

MONSIEUR JOSEF PABLO ULIBARRI, RECONU PAR ses talens et sa maniere de travailler, etre Vetrinère et marechal ferren. Son domisille est en Vizcaya dans le viloge Abando, touchan la ville de Bilbao.

Selected Text(s):

"Peru Novia Salcedori," *Gutun Liburua,* facsimile (Vitoria: Diputación Foral de Álava, 1975), selections.

In these new songs
I again give
my regards to Don Peru Novia Salcedo
translated into Spanish:
our father learned
Basque well
so clearly and correctly
he left erudite Spanish speakers
speechless.

Llorente's lies
Have not yet been dismantled
because a man hasn't been born
like Don Paulo de Astarloa.
While he lived in Madrid
Llorente still lived on his farm
he stumbled to and fro
till the day Astarloa died
awaiting his chance
with malice and hatred.

After Paulo Astarloa died
they paraded Llorente the canon;
haughty and irate,
dressed up in lies,
he made the world crazy
with his evil books
against the three provinces;
he accused them of involvement
in the social riots.

Under the orders of Godoy
Llorente undertook
to pervert many people
in exchange for the three-hundred *reales*
Godoy gave him.

Was Llorente happy?
Being as he is
an abominable charlatan
surely he wanted to be part of this.

Without knowledge of Basque,
without knowledge of its roots,
without help from its light,
the provenance of the ancestral names
cannot be deduced
so there cannot be wise men;
sad but true;
not even when caught at the start,
can the liar be straightened
even if he is altered
from head to foot.

. . .

Our beloved Basque tongue
honey of wisdom
is the divine word
sent straight from Heaven.
Let the influence of Castilian
not pollute it
let us not lose it
this is our greatest responsibility.

. . .

In all the villages of the Basque Country
under the guidance of a priest
there was a school
in which our beloved Basque was taught.
By the time they were six
they had learnt the teachings
of Christ our Lord in Basque.
And after learning them in Basque
they learned them in Latin.
Thus, by the time they were eight
they spoke both languages correctly.
There was a school
in each church

that is how teaching was done
in all the villages of the Basque Country.

. . .

There is much that needs
purifying in these parts.
This city [Bilbao] drives us
to perdition in all senses:
influenced by the dirty Spanish tongue
it has become a well
full of toads, serpents,
and other beastly beings.

51. Agustín Pascual Ugalde Iturriaga, known as Agustín Pascual Iturriaga and Agustín Iturriaga

(Hernani, Gipuzkoa, 1778 – Hernani, 1851)

His paternal family was from Autol (La Rioja) and involved in education and letters. His grandfather, as well as his father and one of his brothers, were scriveners, whereas he and another brother were teachers. His father preceded him at the University of Oñati, where he would later study Philosophy and Theology. In 1804, he was ordained as a priest, spending the rest of his life as holder of a benefice in the parish of his native town.

But his religious career was compatible with what inspired and stimulated him even more: his teaching vocation. In 1817, he requested the permission of the Provincial Government of Gipuzkoa to open an educational institution in Hernani, together with his brother and other professors. The school subsequently operated between 1818 and 1823 and acquired great fame in the region, attracting many students from Gipuzkoa and Navarre. The methods advocated by Iturriaga were very advanced for his era. For example, four languages were used—Basque, Castilian, French and Latin—and all physical or humiliating punishments were banned. In the 1817 proposal for the school it reads literally, "All corporal punishment is forbidden. As a consequence, no teacher or inspector will be allowed to lay hands on the students for any reason or pretext. Punishments will be limited to withholding of desserts and recreation and similar means." Despite his position as priest he actively participated in proto-liberal and enlightened discussion groups in both

Hernani and Donostia-San Sebastián, among others that of the Duke of Mandas. And his political posture was clearly oriented toward constitutionalist liberalism. This being the case, in 1821, Gipuzkoa's Liberal Provincial Government authorized him to compose bilingual educational texts to be used in the province's schools, but the traditionalist return to power in Spain in 1823 scuttled not only the publication of these materials but the school itself. It was closed down, and although his brother, Cayetano, asked permission in 1825 to reopen it, this was denied. In addition, Iturriaga was denounced as a follower of Voltaire and a corruptor of youth, which resulted in his being tried by the Inquisition. He had enemies among the most conservative sectors, which forced him into exile on more than one occasion.

In 1830, the General Assemblies of Gipuzkoa convened in Arrasate-Mondragón and agreed on an accord for "the preservation and prestige of the Basque language," which motivated Iturriaga to send a Memorandum supporting the move in which he offered his educational system and texts as ideal instruments for that purpose. The sociolinguistic and pedagogical considerations of this memorandum were not wasted. For the first time, a voice seriously proclaimed that the internal excellence of a language and other presumed additional values (antiquity, universality, and so on) would not save it from disappearing; in other words, that the debate should not focus on whether it was brought by Tubal, whether it was spoken in Paradise, or whether it was the only language in ancient Spain, but on which methods would guarantee its survival as a living language. Iturriaga's answer to this problem was bilingual education. In his opinion, given the circumstances at that time, the only way to save the Basque language was through its simultaneous study together with Castilian. However, the outbreak of the first Carlist War in 1833 once again scuttled his proposals and efforts to extend bilingual education to the children of Gipuzkoa.

During the war, Iturriaga participated in one of the most curious political-military incidents of that conflict: Muñagorri's revolt. The two were close friends, their families being related and sharing a common profession, because Muñagorri was a scrivener as well in his native town of Berastegi (Gipuzkoa). Like Iturriaga, Muñagorri was a moderate liberal (therefore opposed to Carlism) yet defended the *foral* system, one of the principal demands of the Carlist cause. In the spring of 1838 he led a revolt, organizing a party in which he succeeded in enrolling some two thousand men, financed by the governments of Madrid and London, with the hope of attracting most of the Carlist troops to the party slogan: "Peace and *Fueros*." Muñagorri's proclamation was addressed to the ordinary Carlists, seeking to separate them from the dynastic conflicts of Spain and advocating a surprisingly independent Basque *foral* system:

> Why are you fighting? For whom? PEACE AND *FUEROS*! Such should be our goal. If ambitious men aspire to the throne, let them! Navarre and the Basque provinces, united by so many bonds of friendship, blood, customs, freedoms, are from this day independent. From this day, we are no longer the slaves of those wretches accustomed to ruling as lords and growing wealthy at the expense of the poor. To arms! Long live Independence! Peace and Freedom! Obedience to new authorities! Berastegi, 1838. The commander-in-chief of Independence, GENERAL MUÑAGORRI.

To achieve his objectives, Muñagorri used an effective propaganda system that was obviously appealing in popular Basque circles: *bertso-paperak*, or written compositions of simple verses; a previously composed and written-down version of the oral and extemporaneous Basque art form known as *bertsolaritza*, or versifying. These *bertso-paperak* basically expressed the political concepts stated in the manifesto, for example: "*Pakea ta Fueroak / da gure bandera / gure anai maiteak / atozte onera / Nafarrak, alabesak, / giputz, bizkaitarrak, / atozte guregana / gazte eta zaarrak* (Peace and the Fueros / are our flag / our beloved brothers / come here / from Navarre, Araba / Gipuzkoa, Bizkaia / come to us / old and young)." It turns out that Pascual Iturriaga, who at the time was living in exile in the northern Basque Country, specifically in Arrangoitze (Arcangues), Lapurdi, may have been acting as the intellectual impulse behind Muñagorri's armies, and he may even have penned the verses, which were extremely successful.

After the first Carlist War ended, both Iturriaga and Muñagorri settled once again in Gipuzkoa, but in 1841, the latter participated in the moderate uprising against the more radical liberal leader, Baldomero Espartero. On this occasion, he was not so lucky and was captured and shot by liberal volunteer troops. After that, Iturriaga withdrew more and more from public life. In refuge in Hernani, he dedicated himself to publishing didactic and literary works, until his death in 1851. The aforementioned works were, *Arte de aprender a hablar la lengua castellana para el uso de las escuelas de primeras letras de Guipúzcoa* (Art of Learning to Speak the Castilian Language for Use in the Primary Schools of Gipuzkoa) (1841); *Diálogos basco-castellanos para las escuelas de primeras letras de Guipúzcoa* (Basque-Castilian Dialogues for the Primary Schools of Gipuzkoa) (1842)—which had many subsequent editions under the title *Solasak* (Words)—and *Fábulas y otras composi-*

ciones en verso bascongado, dialecto guipuzcoano con un diccionario vasco-castellano de las voces que son diferentes en los diversos dialectos (Fables and Other Compositions in Verse Written in the Gipuzkoan Dialect of the Basque Language) (1842).

SELECTED TEXT(S):

"Memoria presentada a las Juntas Generales de Gipuzkoa reunidas en Mondragón en 1830, relativa a la conservación de la lengua vascongada" [Memorandum Presented to the General Assemblies of Gipuzkoa Assembled in Mondragón in 1830, Regarding the Preservation of the Basque Language]. General Archive of Gipuzkoa, sec. 1, neg. 21, leg. 133. Cited in Joxemanuel Bujanda, *Euskara eskolan eraiki nahi zuen Euskal pedagogo aurrerakoia: Agustin Pascual Iturriaga, Hernani, 1778–1851* (Bilbao: Udako Euskal Unibertsitatea, 1991), 178–190.

Memorandum

Concerning the decree of the latest General Assembly meetings in Mondragón regarding the preservation of the Basque language

Salutem ex inimicis nostris, Zacarías
[Zacharias, I salute you on behalf of our enemies]

The anonymous author of the critical or apologetic dissertation on the Basque language complains that few people have studied this language, and that even fewer have studied it to any advantage. I will not go into the question of whether the complaint is well-founded or whether, as I believe, there is still work to be done, or little to be done to fathom the mechanism of our native language and discover its perfections, but what I do see is that while our philologists are studying the anatomy of this language, it is slipping out of our hands, shall we say, and that if we are not careful, we are going to end up like the crow in the fable, all swollen up with vanity but with no cheese. What does it matter if Basque is the most precise language in the meaning of its words, very polite in its formulas and expressions, extremely orderly in its rules, coherent and logical in its construction, and harmonious like no other; rich and abundant in words, the most ancient language of Spain, universal for a period in the primitive Peninsula, if you will, and given to our first parents through God's inspiration? What does all this matter, I say, if every day it is heading faster toward its ruin and is going to end up disappearing completely. If the intrinsic merit of a language were enough to save it, the beautiful languages spoken by Demosthenes and Cicero would still be alive with all their finery, but domination is the arbiter of all languages, and sooner or later they have to surrender to its irresistible rule; so it is that the Basque language is experiencing the fate common to all the others. A language preserves its primitive purity, and remains unchanged, as long as it is isolated. From the moment in which, emerging from its isolation, it comes into contact with others, the process of corruption and decay begins. If countries or provinces that speak different languages come to integral parts of a state or nation, the language which the government adopts officially will be the dominant one, because all the interests and advantages will merge to cultivate it and make it general. It will then prevail over all the others, growing richer every day and, perhaps in many cases, at the expense of the others, and it will end up eclipsing them until it makes them disappear completely. Such, over several centuries through to the present day, is the state of the Basque language with respect to Castilian, and such is the ultimate fate which will irremediably befall it. The constant and intimate contact which we maintain with Castilian, and the necessity we have to master it if we are to preserve our political relations with the government and practice different professions, and find our place in the peninsula, and abroad, have caused our native language to experience the effects of the action that Castilian exercises over it, encroaching on it constantly and pulling it toward its total disappearance. And, how could this not be so, if, consulting our own advantage, we ourselves persistently seek to exterminate it from its native soil as they advise us to do. And if you doubt this, just take a look at our primary schools, and there the sad truth will be obvious. There you will see assembled a permanent and systematic conspiracy against the Basque language; the establishment of offices where weapons are constantly being forged to destroy it, turning the children into so many titans pledged to overthrow their mother. These are not just figures of speech; this is not hyperbole; these are not scarecrows; they are the pure and unadulterated truth, and we will feel it viscerally if we stop to examine the practice introduced into these schools from time immemorial for the purpose of teaching the children through the age of puberty, which is the period of time that they attend school, from the age of five or six. For as soon as they walk into the school, the Castilian primer is shoved into their hands. Once they have learned to read from it, they are given, in succession, the [catechism by Father] Astete, the Cato, and other books, all in Castilian, and if they are required to read and learn the Christian doctrine in Basque, it is only because most of the parishioners are used to asking for it publicly in the parish for the instruction of the faithful.

Scarcely have they learned a few loose words in Castilian, [than] they are required to speak that language and, consequently, to begin to forget their modest store of Basque words. Later, when they feel an even greater need to master Castilian, they begin to notice how their knowledge of Basque makes it harder to learn Castilian, and this awareness, along with the memory of the notorious rings and the punishments that went along with them, makes them start hating their native language. In light of such powerful forces and the many and continuous tactics used to undermine our unhappy language, I can almost hear the reader say: why, it is impossible to save it from the claws of such mortal enemies! And then to add: even if it were possible, why bother saving and preserving a language limited to a tiny corner of the Peninsula and which, for that very reason, is of no use.

. . .

We have already shown how dominant languages prevail over those that are neglected to give them priority. So let us give priority to the Basque language and we will see how the same cause produces the same effect.

But, how can we give it priority if we have seen that all our interests and advantages work against it? We can do so by converting those interests and advantages to favor it. But that is impossible, you will say. But I will reply that this impossibility is neither absolute nor complete, but to some extent possible, and that this partial possibility is enough to save our native language, to make it understood throughout the Basque Country, and to reverse its decline, which is the object of this decree that I am addressing.

To this end, let us begin dividing the enemy by getting rid of the offices where he forges his weapons. The reader already knows I am talking about the primary schools. But let us first consider their pernicious effects in those towns of Bizkaia, Araba, and Navarre that adjoin others where the Castilian language is already enthroned and in full and peaceful possession of the terrain. In those towns today, the children of parents who learned to speak Basque, and would still be able to speak it, do not understand this language, and the parish priests are the ones who have initiated the introduction of Castilian into the temples. By teaching the children to read and speak that language, and to detest and forget the Basque language, and being in constant and continuous contact with the neighboring towns where no other language is spoken except the one they are seeking to teach them, they do indeed end up detesting and forgetting it. Thus, the parish priests, pressured to speak to them and teach them in Castilian, do so all the more willingly because, among other reasons, they themselves speak their native language badly and it is easier for them to express themselves in Castilian.

So let us immediately put an end to this practice, so pernicious to the Basque language, and replace it with another that will wed it to the Castilian language by making them mutually reinforcing, turning what once were enemies into intimate friends and companions from this day forward. What is it that we want or need to accomplish with the Castilian language from our present position? Learn it and master it as perfectly as possible.

And, what have they done to teach it to us, and how have we gone about teaching it to our young people? We have hedged it with difficulties, forcing it into direct conflict with our native language, fighting against it, but in a conflict as bloody and as bitter as it is harmful to our own language and as it is to the introduction of another that would be in our interest to learn. Because, by the very nature of things, the struggle is unfair and the victory will inevitably go to the Castilian language, let us embrace the encounter, and do so peacefully, accepting it into our house as a friend, and after we have shown ourselves to be civil and courteous, let us offer it permanent lodging as befits the generosity of which we are so proud.

Let us imagine that, just as we pride ourselves on our affability and courteousness, Castilian prides itself on being French, munificent and generous, and that it will know how to respond to our obsequious welcome, not stingily and selfishly but with nobility and generous gratitude.

Turning our primary schools into something quite the opposite of what they have been, we will have achieved the dual purpose, which we have proposed, that is, the elimination of a practice pernicious to our language, and the introduction of another that will be to our advantage. Let us teach them to read Basque. Have they been forced to speak Castilian with no prior preparation? Let us not oblige them to speak it until enough Castilian words and phrases have been translated into it.

. . .

The current method, obliging children to speak Castilian by imitation without any prior preparation, forces them to have to choose between being mute at their most loquacious age, or to speak a language they do not know, have not heard spoken, with the result that to emerge from the classroom each day without incurring the punishment that accompanies the fatal ring, they create among themselves, by means of a few loose words, a kind of slang or mongrel language that is all the more ridiculous and extravagant because the two languages are diametrically opposed in their structure, and this jargon leaves such an unpleasant aftertaste that never goes away even after they have graduated and begun their university studies. By skirting around this enormous obstacle, this new method of reading dialogues in both languages will allow the children to learn gradually, effortlessly and almost unconsciously, pleasurably and without violence. I am not saying that Basques will not encounter any difficulties at all in learning to speak Castilian in the future. The native language, which has shaped our ideas according to its nature and structure, will always be an obstacle for expressing ourselves properly, correctly, and fluently in any other language, especially those so different in quality and syntax. What I am saying is that, through the new method, children will learn to speak a far more standard Castilian and to do so far more expeditiously. This will result in another extremely important advantage: our native language will thereby be improved and enriched with new words and phrases, as well as with words which, created through analogy by Father Larramendi, have never before emerged from the dictionary except to be used as examples in a few works in a way that has caused them to be unintelligible and annoying, and consequently to be marginalized forever. Once our language has been stabilized to some extent through the aforementioned dialogues, it will become used and made comprehensible generally throughout the country, because the only difference will be that caused irremediably and specifically by the various dialects, which should only affect the way words are declined or conjugated. It is true that to achieve this result it will be necessary to successively increase the number of short works of Basque-Castilian dialogues; but starting with the distribution of two that I have mentioned, it is to be desired and expected that the publication of others of invaluable benefit for the instruction of the young people of the country will be assured, without the obstacle that embarrassed Father Larramendi when he said: "I'll write more books in Basque if you come up with the money to publish them."

Father Larramendi would surely have written them if this idea had occurred to him, because it would have guaranteed their publication. If this had happened, the Basque language would even today have been in the position of many other people that have come under the domination of Castilian, and all the trouble my fellow countryman went through to get his grammar and dictionary published would have borne far more fruit. But because, unfortunately for our language, it has not turned out that way, let us waste no more time in adopting this idea, which is going to save it. The new method of teaching the new generation the language of their parents from their earliest years will prevent any further destruction by the Castilian language, because it will no longer advance sword in hand as in the past, building its fortunes on the ruins of our native language; on the contrary, it will come into our land as a brother, to live alongside it in total harmony and the most intimate friendship. Should anyone say that the idea I am proposing is nothing new and is obvious to everyone, I will reply first of all in the happy phrase of Larramendi: "*Ikusi ta urrisa*" [Look and Learn], and second, that it would never have occurred to me, or probably to anyone else, had it not been for the excitement over the Basque alphabet and the primitive world motivated by the decree emanating from the Assembly Meetings in Mondragón. Without his ardent love for the country where he was born and for the language in which he spoke his first words and which he champions, the indifference, or even aversion, with which we regard the language, for the reasons enumerated earlier, might have continued to grow. But now that it is within our power to cast those feelings out with all their lamentable effects, let us not allow them to survive for another moment, but immediately inaugurate a method that, as we have seen, will be fertile with promising results.

Who knows whether this spirit of brotherhood, good relations, and harmony in which we would place the two languages, which until now have been irreconcilable enemies, will facilitate the unimpeded entry of Castilian all across this country without problems of any kind, bringing with it many advantages for the Basque language, which will in turn begin to win new victories in those towns where it is in serious decline today and on the verge of dying? To achieve this, it would be necessary to invite the Provincial Governments to communicate with those towns and to adopt the method under discussion, adapting the Basque language in the short books we spoke of to their respective dialects and taking care to conserve the same terminology in order to standardize its use in the different provinces, thus making our language better understood in all of them. If, as we hope, the experiment has the desired result, it would be possible to begin multiplying the dialogues successively, and making them focus on matters of agriculture, domestic economy, etc., and in this way the language would be enriched, instruction would be extended to young adults, and primary teaching in our schools would be perfected. This would also greatly facilitate the study of Latin grammar, which is generally very difficult for the natives of this country because they do not know Castilian. And, how many Basques who know how to read in their native language, but do not understand Castilian, would be unable to learn through the dialogues or take advantage of the instruction they contain? Their number is considerable if we include the girls who currently attend the schools taught by women, and it would be unforgivable to deny them the benefit they would gain by the adoption of the new method, which would inevitably be to their advantage.

I believe I have proven, as the epigraph to this text suggests, that the reefs on which the Basque language would otherwise be scuttled can turn out to be the anchors for her salvation. And that sailing her into a safe port can turn her into an excellent means of instruction for our country. And finally, that by preserving and fortifying this link binding our companionship and admirable brotherhood, we may be able to claim one further victory to make us proud to belong to this privileged and enviable land.

52. José Yanguas y Miranda

(Tudela [Tutera], Navarre, 1782 – Pamplona-Iruña, 1863)

His family's lack of economic resources kept him from undertaking any advanced studies, but his inclination for letters endowed him with a remarkable education in juridical and historical subjects, which he pursued on his own. He practiced as a clerk and scrivener in the city of his birth. In 1823, he was arrested as a constitutionalist pro-liberal, and after being released, he sought refuge across the border. He worked as a watchmaker, first in Baiona and later in Donostia-San Sebastián. After his return to Navarre in 1830, he was appointed archivist of the Provincial Government, and on the death of Fernando VII, his obviously liberal political sympathies led to his being appointed secretary of this same institution, a position he held until his own death. He was a corresponding member of the Spanish Academy of History. Politically, he combined his liberal constitutionalist sympathies to a Spanish patriotism. His position with respect to the Navarrese *foral* system was ambiguous. Although he demonstrated a keen archeological and emotional interest in the *foral* patrimony, his ideological sympathies favored the conversion of the Kingdom of Navarre into a Spanish province like any other. Indeed, he experienced this very transformation, as secretary of the Provincial Government, when legislation in 1841 removed the former status of Navarre.

His publications were literary, such as *Vida del capitán D. Juan Lanas* (Life of Captain Don Juan Lanas) (1845); historical, such as *Historia de la conquista del Reino de Navarra por el Duque de Alba* (History of the Conquest of the Kingdom of Navarre by the Duke of Alba) (1842) and *Crónica de los reyes de Navarra, escrita por D. Carlos Príncipe de Viana* (Chronicle of the Kings of Navarre, Written by Don Carlos, Prince of Viana) (1842); and juridical, such as *Análisis histórico-crítico de los Fueros de Navarra* (Historical-Critical Analysis of the *Fueros* of Navarre) (1838) and *Diccionario de los Fueros y leyes de Navarra* (Dictionary of the *Fueros* and laws of Navarre) (1828). In the legal field, he entered into a debate with the magistrate, José María Zuaznavar, who had published an *Ensayo histórico crítico de la legislación de Navarra* (Historical-Critical Essay on the Legislation of Navarre) (1821; second edition, 1829), to which Yanguas responded with his *Contragerigonza* (Counter-Gibberish), in 1833.

Regarding any thoughts he might have had about the Basque language, his posture is interesting. In his work, there is hardly any reference to it, for certainly he had no problem with the exclusive official use of the Castilian language for the entire nation. However, he did have two rather interesting ideas. In 1843, Yanguas added some supplements to his *Diccionario de Antigüedades del Reino de Navarra* (Dictionary of Antiquities of the Kingdom of Navarre) (1840), and in them, the word *vascuence* (Basque language) appears. However, he says only one thing about this language: how difficult it is to pronounce, especially because of the length of its compound terms. To demonstrate, this he offers a list of toponyms from the Aldude (Les Aldudes) region on the border between Navarre and Lower Navarre, the most complicated ones he can find. It is interesting that this combinative character of the language is used by some Basque apologists, such as Larramendi and Moguel, as a sign of its superiority over other languages, because it presents in a more abbreviated and synthetic form concepts that would otherwise have to be expressed by more extensive formulations, whereas its detractors, more or less indirectly, spread the idea of its lack of intelligibility for that precise reason. Moreover, in his *Historia compendiada de Navarra* (Brief History of the Kingdom of Navarre) he discretely introduces some opinions about the Basque language. Of course, he doesn't bother addressing the Tubalist polemic because the mythic character of that history is considered to be scientifically proven. Furthermore, he considers that most of what has been written about this language lacks a clear foundation and is based on mere speculations, and he only bothers to offer a few of his own etymologies, such as *vasco* = *vasoco* (*basoko*) meaning *montaraz* (wild, rustic).

HISTORIA
COMPENDIADA
DEL
Reino de Navarra.
Por
D. José Yanguas y Miranda.

CON LICENCIA.
EN SAN SEBASTIAN,
En la imprenta de Ignacio Ramon Baroja.
Setiembre de 1832.

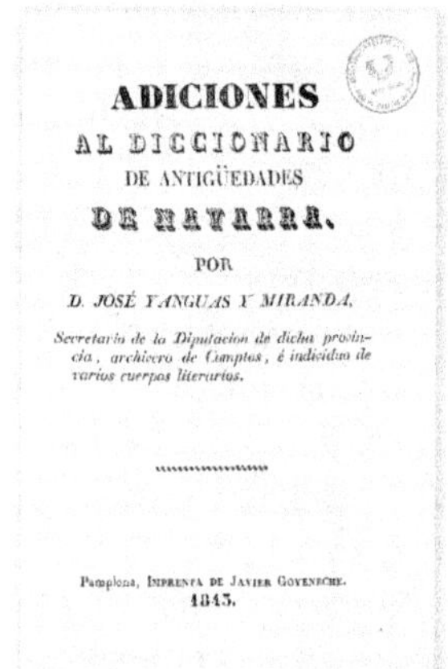

ADICIONES
AL DICCIONARIO
DE ANTIGÜEDADES
DE NAVARRA.
POR
D. JOSÉ YANGUAS Y MIRANDA,
Secretario de la Diputacion de dicha provincia, archivero de Camptos, é individuo de varios cuerpos literarios.

Pamplona, Imprenta de Javier Goyeneche.
1843.

Selected Text(s):

a) *Historia Compendiada del Reino de Navarra* [Brief History of the Kingdom of Navarre] (San Sebastián: Ignacio Ramón Baroja, 1832), 2, 1–3.

b) *Adiciones al Diccionario de Antigüedades de Navarra por* . . . [Additions to the Dictionary of Antiquities of Navarre by . . .] (Pamplona: José Imaz y Galdea, 1840), s.v. "Vascuence" [Basque Language], 1420–21.

a)

In considering the origin of the ancient Basques, concerning which more than a hundred different opinions had been expressed by the beginning of the past century, I have had no difficulty in choosing the one that was regarded at that time as the most outrageous, that is, the opinion of Genebrardo who believes that Spain was not even inhabited in the two thousand years following the flood. Other modern critics have already wisely refuted the notion that Tubal came to Spain, and this is sufficiently discredited so that we do not need to waste time considering it.

. . .

Of the Situation of Navarre and the Origin of Its Name and of Its Inhabitants.

Navarre was called *Vasconia* in ancient times and its inhabitants *Vascones* [Basques], which in the language of the Basque Country means *Montañeses*, from the word *vaso* which means "mountain," *vasoco*, "of the mountain," and, by contraction, *vascó*.

The name Navarre was first used in the later period of the Kingdom of the Goths in Spain, during which [time] Basques, confined by force to the most rugged part of the Pyrenees, began to distinguish the mountainous region from the plains, calling them *Nava*, which means "plains surrounded by mountains," and, from the word *erri*, which means "land or region." The word *Navaerri* was formed and later *Navarra*. Some people believe that this word comes from the *Navaros*, the people mentioned by Ptolemy, a northern nation that must have formed part of the federation of Barbarians from the north who inundated Spain at the end of the fourth century. They believe that these people established themselves primarily in Pamplona, and that it was called "city of the Navarros"; in support of this opinion, they point out the name of the neighborhood called *Navarrería* that was named for some time for its inhabitants, who lived separate from the original Basques of the country.

. . .

Most likely, Navarrese Basques were descended from the inhabitants of the other side of the Pyrenees, who, after having settled the rest of Europe over the centuries, increased in population and spread out in search of more pastures for their herds and lands for farming, which was the only occupation of the original inhabitants; and they introduced those crude customs which Basques complained about in the time of the Arabs.

If we only look at the ancient and singular language of this nation, so different from the others that surround it, we might think that the Basques are unrelated to any of them, but this is because they have not been conquered as others have, and because their independence and their customs have been spared in the rugged mountains from the general calamity and foreign invasions that have inundated all the other countries of Europe.*

b)

VASCUENCE [The Basque Language]: There are words in this language that are remarkable for their prodigious length and difficulty of pronunciation. In and around the mountains of the Aldude, there are places whose names, composed of several others in order to distinguish their origins from others that sound the same, form a combination of words put together in a single word, like the following:

Adarrecolepoa: in Castilian, *collado de cuerno* [hill of the horn].

Ardanzesaroyarenburua: in Castilian, *cabezo* [small hill] or *parte superior del sel*** *de la viña* [upper part of the hill where the grapevine is planted].

Ardanzesaroyareniturricoburua: in Castilian, *cabezo* or *parte superior de la fuente del sel de la viña* [small hill or upper part of the fountain of the hill where the grapevine is planted].

Arizmeacaburua: in Castilian, *parte superior de la colina del roble* [top of the hill of the oak].

Azpilcuetaberecolarrea: in Castilian, *campo bajo de Azpilcueta* [field below Azpilcueta].

Azpilcuetagaraycosaroyarenberecolarrea: in Castilian, *campo bajo del sel alto de Azpilcueta* [field below the hilltop of Azpilcueta].

Elormeacareneguiarenburua: in Castilian, *parte superior de la loma de la colina de espino* [upper part of the hillside of the hill of hawthorns].

Izarysaroyarenlarrearenbarena: in Castilian, *centro del campo del sel de la estrella* [center of the field of the hill of the star].

---

* Much has been written about the origin of the Basque language, but to no avail. Some believe that it was common to all Spaniards; and there are even some who say that the antediluvians spoke Basque. The best critics agree that it is older than all known languages.

** According to Larramendi, it is "hill with trees in a perfect circle with its post in the middle." This is the same as *bustaliza*. In Baztan, it is also called *sel* [the place where the herd is watered].

Legartartecobizcarra: in Castilian, *alto de entre el arenal* [hill in a sandy area].

Legartecogaraycolepoa: in Castilian, *parte superior del collado del arenal* [upper part of the hill in the sandy area].

Mizpiracolarrearenburua: in Castilian, *cabeza del campo del níspero* [head of the field of the loquat].

Olaberrietacoeguia: in Castilian, *loma de la ferrería nueva* [hill of the new ironworks].

Orbaralizardia: in Castilian, *fresnal de Orbara* [ash grove of Orbara].

Osoguicoguruzeareneguia: in Castilian, *loma de la cruz de los lobos* [hill of the cross of the wolves].

Sagarcelayecoerreca: in Castilian, *regata del llano del manzanal* [irrigation ditch of the plain of apple trees].

Urracaritaarana: in Castilian, *vega del avellanar* [plain of the hazelnut grove].

Urriztizavalondoa: in Castilian, *hondo del avellanar* [hollow of the hazelnut grove].

53. Jean Pierre Darrigol

(Lehonza, Lapurdi 1790 – Baiona, 1829)

He studied in Dax and was ordained a priest in 1815. He was a professor of theology in Dax and Bétharram and of ethics in the Seminary of Baiona, where he came to be director. Despite the brevity of his life and work, he was a serious student of the Basque language who attained great influence in his time. He published only one book: *Dissertation critique et apologétique de la langue basque* (Critical Dissertation on and Apology of the Basque Language) (1827). Among other interests, he was one of the pioneering founders of the Academy of the Basque Language, which he was working to organize when he died. As mentioned, he was held in high regard by most of the contemporary Basque scholars of his day and of the next generation in the northern Basque Country, although later his reputation went into rapid decline because of the extravagant nature of his encomiastic defense of Euskara. However, there is one aspect of his contribution to the debate over the Basque language that deserves recognition: orthographic reform. Until then, no standardized written form of Basque had been established, with different authors resorting to the application of Castilian and French norms to Euskara, with varied success.

In Darrigol's time, standards were first imposed that would ultimately end up being those used today: the exclusion of the *v,* the identical sound of the *g* before any vowel, eliminating the forms *gui* and *gue,* the tendency to eliminate the *c,* substituted, depending on the situation, by the *k* and the *z,* and so on. Darrigol was one of the first Basque scholars to defend these ideas. In the northern Basque Country, the first author to put this orthographic reform into practice was Martin Duhalde (1753–1804) in his work, *Meditacioneac gai premiatsuen gainean* (Meditations on Indispensable Themes) (1809). And in 1838, another book was published anonymously that followed this line of orthographic reform: *Andre Mariaren ilhabethea* (The Virgin Mary's Month). As for the peninsular Basque Country, it was necessary to wait until 1883 for José Francisco de Aizkibel to opt for a similar standard in his *Diccionario vasco-español* (Basque-Spanish Dictionary).

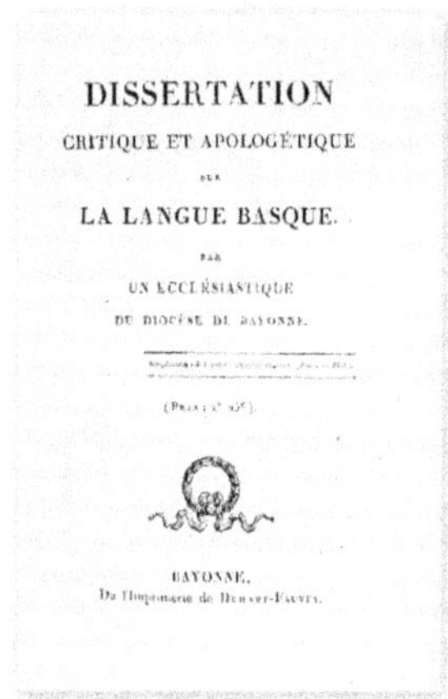
DISSERTATION
CRITIQUE ET APOLOGÉTIQUE
LA LANGUE BASQUE.
UN ECCLÉSIASTIQUE
DU DIOCÈSE DE BAYONNE.
BAYONNE.

Selected Text(s):

Dissertation critique et apologétique de la Langue Basque, par un eclésiastique du diocèse de Bayonne [Critical Dissertation on and Apology of the Basque Language, by an Ecclesiastic in the Diocese of Baiona] (Bayonne: Duhart-Fauvet, 1827), 125–26, 158–62.

If it is true that the secrets of human language are profound and that the mechanism of the verb in particular presents a divine character in each language, we are not afraid to say that this quality is especially remarkable in Basque conjugation. Even if what we have said to this point were insufficient to justify our assertion, it will be overwhelmingly demonstrated by the most interesting verbal system that exists in human language.

If we claim the most extensive influence imaginable, the most complete action possible of one subject on another, such is the first value and essential function of our active verb. Embodying both singular and plural pronouns for all three persons; exhausting with extraordinary economy all the combinations that are mathematically possible among the six personal pronouns by presenting them first two by two, then three by three; expressing with astonishing facility an enchanting variety, a rapidity of expression that is unequaled, all the respective attitudes or situations these diverse pronouns are capable of adopting, used both as subject and complement, as direct or indirect complement—such is the fascinating mechanism and singular richness of this incomparable verb.

. . .

Had the Basque language preserved nothing of its ancient splendor but its system of conjugation, that would be enough, one scholar [Fleury Lécluse, in his *Manuel de la langue basque*, page 86] has said, to make that beautiful language worthy of study: but it is far from true, we might add, that its system of verbal conjugation is the only beautiful aspect of itself that this language has salvaged from the ravages of time; it preserves many other vestiges of its ancient splendor, which we have already discussed, and which it may be useful to summarize here briefly.

It is not the case with Basque, as with so many other languages that are far removed from beautiful nature and have to multiply nuances of their primitive sounds; this language only makes distinctions in its phrases between essential and major nuances, so it does not have to pile up the number of its vowels or create excessive accents.

It has remained close to beautiful nature with regard to the sounds articulated and their consonant signs, in the way it either retains the ancient and natural articulations, which are lost in other languages, or rejects other articulations that are both difficult and modern. Among the ancient articulations it preserves, the full and nourished sound of the *s* is honorably represented, similar to the Chaldean *ssodé*, as are the three aspirants *ph, kh, th*, exactly as they were in the language of the ancient Greeks and Hebrews and as they are found naturally in exercising the organs of speech. Among the alembicated sounds that Basque rejects are the consonants *v, x, z, g, j*, pronounced in the manner of the French and other modern peoples.

The radicals of the Basque language are remarkable for the simplicity of their substance, which is often only a single syllable through that just temperament of value that, consisting in a meaning attained but indeterminate, makes our radicals resemble so many logical genres by the flexibility granted them by this way of being and according to which they allow adjectives, nouns, adverbs, comparatives, diminutives, augmentatives, superlatives, etc. to be defined in the most convenient way possible.

Grammarians, utterly preoccupied with considerations of form, count eight different kinds of words, according to Boethius; but the philosophers, who are only concerned with reality, only acknowledge two, the noun and the verb: *Grammatici quia vocum figuras considerant, ideò octo orationis partes speculantur: philosophi autem cùm rem tantùm contemplentur, sola nominis et verbi speculatione indigent* [Grammarians, because they take account of the shapes of words, foresee eight parts of speech; philosophers, as they only foresee the thing, only need to speculate on the noun and the verb]. That was the thought of Priscien: *Partes orationis*, he said, *sunt secundum dialecticos duæ, nomen et verbum* [The parts of speech, according to the Dialectics, are nouns and verbs]. We should not forget that this division, recognized as being truly philosophical, is the division indicated by the Basque language. It offers no less philosophy in each of the two species taken separately. We have already discussed this, so it is not necessary to repeat it here.

To express some essential attribute of the object named, or one of its more sensible qualities, or its usage or intent, while setting aside gender differences, thus avoiding many problems without the least loss of clarity; and using them without determination of number in a way that is as useful in practice as it is theoretically consistent with the fundamental laws of language; to determine singular or plural and to move from one to the other in the simplest and most uniform way imaginable; to confirm the value of the article and the precision it confers on the word without trailing after it a long and embarrassing train of monosyllables; to encompass, through declension alone, all the relations that other languages express either through prepositions, or irregular declensions, or both combined—these are the most striking advantages of our appellative words, and consequently of everything except the verbs. To reconcile, to a degree surpassing any other known conjugation, the verbal system in the simplest way imaginable, and to discover in a system so simple the way to supply, not only what is necessary but also stylistic elegance; to use only two verbs, and with those two verbs to link all the possible propositions, and to represent all the respective situations that the different subjects and the different complements of the verb can produce; to exhaust all the possible combinations that can exist between the seven pronouns; and to do all this effortlessly, powerfully, and quickly—these are some of the remarkable qualities of Basque conjugation.

To be exempt from the difficulties arising from the law of gender agreement, to limit agreement of number and case to the simplest terms, to include all the rules of dependence in a well-known usage of a single declension—these are the least of the advantages offered by the syntax of our language.

To arrange words according to thought, to imitate by their arrangement the tranquil nature of contemplative ideas; or even to follow our sentiments in their impetuousness, in their digressions, in that disorder that makes them transcend, as if it were an obstacle, the stages through which the idea proceeds step by step; to touch on the elements of discourse in the order most convenient to understanding, or let them flow with the harmony or fire of the imagination, or for the purpose of affecting or guiding; and consequently to lend themselves, with utmost perfection, to every gender and every circumstance—these are the advantages of our syntax.

Whether the Basque language, even if it had preserved nothing of its ancient splendor but its system of conjugation, is worthy of study, we will leave that up to the experts to judge how many advantages which have been set forth in this essay, render it worthy of their attention.

54. Joaquín Irizar y Moya, known as "le vieux de Vergara" [the old man from Bergara],

(Bergara, Gipuzkoa, 1793 – Bergara, 1897)

The descendant of a noble family from Bergara, he was mayor of the town and Leader of the Provincial Government of Gipuzkoa in 1827. As he himself observed, he had an excellent education as a young man. Subsequently, he entered the military academy, attained the rank of Lieutenant of Artillery, and was stationed in Mallorca, later becoming a professor in that same corps in Segovia. He served from 1813 to 1827, the year in which he received his law degree, married, and was elected leader of the Provincial Government of Gipuzkoa. King Carlos of the House of Bourbon, his wife the Princess of Beira, the Count of Montemolin, and General Espartero were all guests in his palatial estate, named Irizar, in Bergara, where the historical 1839 Treaty that ended the first Carlist War (and a Basque civil war) was signed. Ideologically, Joaquín Irizar allied himself with the most conservative and traditionalist paradigms, as is obvious from the titles of his books: *Études d'un antiquaire por la defense de Dieu, de la religion et du Pape* (An Antiquarian's Studies in the Defense of God, Religion and the Pope) (1862–66), *Sobre el matrimonio civil. A las Cortes y a los otros mil que harán bien en leerme. Odium Christi* (On Civil Matrimony: To Parliament and the Thousands of Others Who Would Do Well to Read What I Write. Hatred of Christ) (1871), and *Memoria sobre lo absurdo del Sistema Métrico Decimal* (Memoir on the Absurdity of the Decimal Metric System) (1869–70). In connection with this last topic, he even wrote a letter to the Spanish Prime Minister at the time, Práxedes Sagasta, exhorting him to abolish the new metric system. He was not, however, the only Basque author who opposed the metric system; the bard Iparraguirre, for instance, sang songs in support of this idea. As we can see, then, Irizar's traditionalist perspective spanned a number of social topics.

Another detail that revealed his ideological sympathies was his choice of a pseudonym, "the old man from Bergara," which had been the surname adopted by an ancestor of his who fought in the wars of Granada almost four centuries earlier. However, his book *De l'eusquère et des erdere ou de la langue Basque et ses derivés* (On the Basque Language and the Non-Basque Ones, or on the Basque Language and Its Origins), betrayed a symptom of his contradictory and independent character. This is because he dedicated it to the Carlist leader Tomás Zumalacarregui, yet in it he also revealed a desire for the future Queen Isabel II (favored by the liberals) to take him under her patronage. In effect, there are constant examples of non-alignment and independence in all of his work. The Carlist War obliged him to take residence in France, and in fact, his book on the Basque language, *De l'eusquère et des erderes . . .*, was published in Paris and written in French, although it seems as though he had started it in Bergara. In the work, using Basque as his excuse for writing, he takes the opportunity to speak on all sorts of topics. Likewise, in other publications of his on topics apparently far removed from linguistics, for example, the decimal metric system or the port of Pasajes (Pasaia) in Gipuzkoa, he devoted long chapters to Euskara.

The purpose of his work is not linguistic, and it is even less an apology for Euskara, but ultimately religious. In fact, he does not show any great enthusiasm for the language, but instead offers a pessimistic and devastating portrait of it. Not only does he describe the brutal reduction in the number of speakers during his own lifetime, as well as offering a very low estimate of the percentage of those who speak it (between one-third and one-fourth of the population), but he is persuaded that the language will disappear, perhaps before the end of the century. For this reason, he recommends that it is time to devote as much research as possible into the Basque language before it dies out. That does not preclude Irizar from being convinced that the Basque language was the primitive language spoken in Paradise and that a "triumvirate" of authors (Larramendi, Astarloa, and Erro) have offered sufficient proof of that fact. Withal, for him what mattered was not the more or less peerless quality of Basque, but that the existence of this primal language would demonstrate the truths of Genesis and of the entire Catholic religion.

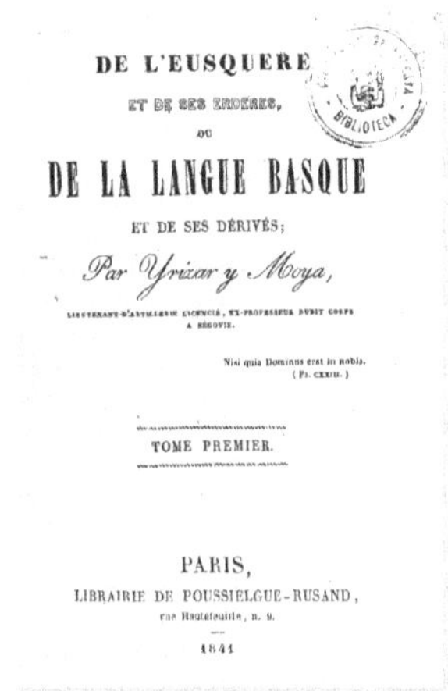

DE L'EUSQUERE

ET DE SES ERDERES,

OU

DE LA LANGUE BASQUE

ET DE SES DÉRIVÉS;

Par Yrizar y Moya,

LIEUTENANT-D'ARTILLERIE LICENCIÉ, EX-PROFESSEUR DUDIT CORPS À SÉGOVIE.

Nisi quia Dominus erat in nobis.
(Ps. CXXIII.)

TOME PREMIER.

PARIS,

LIBRAIRIE DE POUSSIELGUE-RUSAND,

rue Hautefeuille, n. 9.

1841

SELECTED TEXT(S):

De l'eusquère et des erderes ou de la langue Basque et de ses derivés [On the Basque Language and the Non-Basque Ones, or on the Basque Language and Its Origins], vol. 1 (Paris: Poussielgue-Rusand, 1841), 7, 15–17, 33–34, 77–78, 80–82, 104–06.

Important Notice

The object of this work being the defense of the Apostolic Roman Catholic religion, I believe that it is important for me to say that I am an Apostolic Roman Catholic, and that I therefore submit the entirety of my work to the Church, to the Holy Father, and other competent authorities, but I also ask that lesser authorities delay in judging my work until it is finished, or in large part complete, because if it is possible that I have fallen into thousands of errors and illusions, I believe that I have not committed any against the faith, so great is my respect for it.

. . .

Some of the fanatic native speakers of the [Basque] country make many foolish claims for this language. Some even think that Adam spoke Euskara, which is not impossible if indeed it is the original language; and that he spoke it exactly as it is spoken in our villages today, which is far more difficult to accept because it is spoken one way in Bizkaia and another in Navarre, one way in Gipuzkoa and another in the Basque Country of France, as is particularly evident in the pronunciation, because the original elements undergo slight alterations that lead the outsider into error; and I can speak of this with some authority because, being a native of the center of the Basque Country, I find myself lost when I have had to speak with different Basque speakers, and even more so with people from Lapurdi or natives of France.

As I find such exaggerations annoying, perhaps because they are errors I myself make, I greatly disapproved of Basque, or Euskara, because it was so poorly defended and by such impertinent amateurs. Because of this I have been greatly prejudiced against this language for many years, not because I believed that the Basque language was inferior to Spanish, French, or Latin but because I did not believe that it lived up to their exaggerated claims, and especially because of the frivolity with which they accepted absurd nonsense as proof instead of facts or rational arguments. But whatever my opinion of the Basque language, the strong feeling I have always had for old books and for the comparison of languages, even if for no other purpose than to read a story by Balzac or Frédéric Soulié, obliged me to study and examine my maternal language, and I saw in it beauties that astonished me and filled me with the greatest admiration; but although in this I may have been completely fair and objective, whatever my personal feelings, at least I believed it was one of the most distinct and varied languages spoken in the world given its greater or lesser perfection under circumstances lost forever to memory, because it is still a great mistake even to think that it would be possible to prove something so impossible.

. . .

All things considered, when we see that the last civil war [the first Carlist War, 1833–39] has attracted the attention of the whole world, it seems that we can say without fear of seeming arrogant that it is time to consider and resolve the matter. But if we add to that that Euskara is losing every day more and more of her influence, that this language has completely disappeared from Araba, that she has lost much ground in Bizkaia, that in Navarre she is only spoken on the borders and in the mountains, and that in France too she is spoken less each day and is increasingly limited to the confines of the Pyrenees, we will see that if this problem is not addressed and resolved immediately, she will be lost forever. What resistance can the tiny Province of Gipuzkoa offer to this unhappy state when day and night the French and Spanish encroach further in every direction? I do not wish to be a prophet of doom, and for me the extinction of Euskara is a terrible disaster, but I do not see how she can survive another century of encroachment by the Spanish language; let us see if she even lasts until the end of this century, because the speed with which she was obliterated in Araba was truly frightening. I repeat, then, that this is not only the appropriate time for addressing the problem, it is the only time; so despite my passion for this language, if I do not succeed in drawing attention to her beautiful qualities, I guarantee that I and all those who have been witness to her many perfections will be sadly disappointed. *Absit, absit* [Should it ever be absent], may God spare us such a sadness!

. . .

Concerning the Primitive Language

If we consider the question of the primitive language we will find it so simple, and so inseparable from other equally important questions that we will address later, that the matter could not possibly be more urgent. Wiseman is Catholic, and the other Basque authors he cites are Catholic, as are the two in the footnote, Larramendi and Erro, yet of the sources that I have defended, only Wiseman cites Astarloa. Now, for a Catholic the question is quite natural, for knowing that there was an original language, that it survived the flood, and that it survived for many years after that, because the men on the plains of Sumer were capable of conceiving grand projects, and of carrying them to their conclusion, then he must ask himself: Is it inevitable that there should still be abundant traces of the primitive language in the world? I do not know; but it is not improbable and certainly not impossible. Could it possibly be part of the design or decree of Providence to reveal that language in time? It would seem likely, because a discovery of that nature would confirm a thousand truths about religion. The first and most important benefit would be a new demonstration of the true history of Genesis, and consequently of the truth of the Judaic religion and, subsequently, of Christianity. The second would be that through such a revelation it would be demonstrated that all men are brothers; because it is likely that in that language there would be the capacity to nourish and bind together all the other languages and unite them into a family, so to speak, which would be a presumption or an irresistible indication that all men descended from a single couple or marriage.

. . .

Astarloa, Erro, and Larramendi, then, might have fallen into error and failed to reach their goals even if they were not suffering hallucinations, falling into the category of men like Sorrequieta and the Abbot of Bidassouet, that is, Charlemagne and Louis XV, Caesar and Carlos II of Spain; although one who brings together names so distant and different from each other in terms of their individual literary merit can, nonetheless, be accused of undue haste.

In proof of this, Wiseman himself says that the opinion of the Academy of Saint Petersburg is that the languages that exist today are merely dialects of a language that has been lost; but many lost things are found every day. If Mr. Champollion is correct, it turns out that the intelligence of the hieroglyphics was lost but is no longer; so it might happen also that this primitive language was unknown, but that it was not lost; because it might happen that the nucleus of that language is to be found in Euskara, Hebrew, or Sanskrit, although the scholars have not yet had the honor of deciphering them. In this way, in the last century we have seen many so-called original or independent languages appear, which later were seen to have important connections with others.

. . .

But Astarloa and his friends can count Wiseman himself as an ally when they say that the Basque language is the primitive language. In effect, it is enough to glance at his ethnographic chart to know that the Basque language is unique; because although the other languages occupy vast territories, Euskara occupies only a small region; and because within that space only ten percent of the inhabitants speak Basque, it follows that she occupies a small area, whereas other linguistic families occupy countries totally out of proportion with her tiny area.

In such a case, the ordinary course of human logic would be either to presume innumerable fine qualities in something, a language say, that was similar, or else to disparage it. The former must have been the mistake made by Larramendi, Astarloa, and Erro, whereas the latter was the mistake made by Traggia and others like him. Whichever the case, my aim is not to deny Traggia's merit as a writer, although his opposition to the Basque Country has led him to make the most absurd claims.

. . .

We can add to what we have said above, an argument that corroborates what the three colleagues sought to prove, that languages are closer to perfection in their infancy than they are later; but the Hebrew language seemed paltry even in its cradle, whereas Euskara, thirty or forty centuries later, seems to be endowed with most remarkable qualities, not only in the opinion of the three Basque linguists, but also according to her critics. But by that very argument, we must assume that she has suffered some loss over the course of so much time; and if we judge by comparison, based on Grimm's observations about German, she must have suffered great loss; and if, despite this, she is far superior to Hebrew, it is clear that her claims of being the primitive language, unfounded as they may be, are still sounder than those of Hebrew, proving without doubt that these Basque linguists are not simply deluded visionaries.

. . .

From the foregoing, it is clear that my opinion is that the authors mentioned above were not just visionaries; I still reserve the right to return to this subject to analyze it more thoroughly at the proper time. In effect, they have been on a quest for something whose non-existence has not been demonstrated, and they have, consequently, as much right to be considered just as careful as the prudent Molitor, without my having to acknowledge, on those grounds, that they have proven that the Basque language is the primitive language, although I do agree that they have resolved each of the three great questions they set out to resolve; these being, on the part of Larramendi, to provide Euskara with a grammar and a dictionary, which he did; on the part of Astarloa, to prove that Basque was the primitive language of Spain, which he did, demonstrating without any doubt that the Basque language predated the arrival of the Phoenicians, the Greeks, the Romans, the Goths, the Arabs, or any other nation mentioned in history. As for Mister Erro, he attempted to read the ancient Spanish coins that had been categorized as unknown, and he has read them. Thus, all three have achieved their goals, although in secondary matters of great importance; if you wish, they may have been mistaken.

55. Victor Hugo

(Besançon, 1802 – Paris, 1885)

His father was a military officer and because of constant changes in his postings, Victor Hugo lived in a number of different places in Spain, Italy, and France during his childhood. After 1815, he lived in Paris where his education was complemented by a precocious dedication to literature. He wrote poetry (*Odes and Ballads*), theatrical pieces (*Cromwell, Hernani*), and novels (*Les Misérables, L'Homme qui rit, Notre-Dame de Paris*). His political posture, favoring a socially concerned republicanism, brought him into conflict with the French Empire and forced him into exile in Belgium. He was a determined defender of freedom in every area, from art to politics, as well as for the individual. His literary influence was enormous, and he came to be regarded as the leader of romanticism after the publication of *Cromwell* (1827), whose preface is regarded as the foundational manifesto of that movement.

Among many other genres, he cultivated one that was much in vogue among the romantics; the travel journal. Between 1838 and 1840, he traveled through Switzerland, Provence, Alsace, and the Rhine; and in 1843, he visited what was considered to be one of the most romantically exotic places in Europe: the Pyrenees. He dedicated a large part of this journey to the Basque Country and produced some extraordinarily fine observations that are, always in a passionate and idealized tone, quite characteristic. Clearly, he perceives here a cultural unity of the Basque people that transcends all political-administrative divisions, recognizing in the language as the basis of identity in a nation without any official status; the Basque language is, for the Basques, "a country, almost a religion." However, the "natural constructs" that constituted nations based on culture, were of course in conflict with the prevailing nation-state configurations, which Hugo has no doubt will prevail. Equally interesting is Hugo's political interpretation for explaining how a "natural democracy" like that of the Basques ended up allying itself with the absolutist reaction against the new liberal system in the context of the first Carlist War.

VICTOR HUGO ILLUSTRÉ

EN VOYAGE

ALPES ET PYRÉNÉES

Selected Text(s):

En voyage. Alpes et Pyrenées [On a Journey: The Alps and the Pyrenees] (Paris: Heltzel, 1890), 62–63.

This is Gipuzkoa, this is the ancient land of the *Fueros*; these are the old free Basque provinces. They speak some Castilian, but mainly they speak Basque.

. . .

Beyond this, I add a remarkable quality worthy of study: that here a deep, secret bond, which has never been broken, unites—despite treaties, despite these diplomatic borders, despite the natural borders of the Pyrenees—all the members of the mysterious Basque family. The old word Navarre is not a word. One is born Basque, one speaks Basque, one lives as a Basque and one dies a Basque. The Basque language is a country, I almost said a religion. You speak one Basque word to a mountaineer in these mountains; hearing that word, you cease to be a man for him; now you are his brother. The Spanish language is as foreign here as the French language. Undoubtedly, this Basque unity tends to grow smaller and will finally disappear. Great states must absorb small ones; that is the law of history and of nature. But it is remarkable that this unity, so fragile in appearance, has survived for so long. France has seized one side of the Pyrenees; Spain has seized the other; neither France nor Spain has succeeded in uprooting the Basque people. Beneath the new history imposed on it after four centuries, it is still perfectly visible, like a crater beneath a lake.

Never has the law of molecular adhesion under which nations are formed struggled more energetically against the thousand causes of every order that dissolve and recompose those great natural formations. I would like, let me say in passing, for the makers of history and the makers of treaties to study a bit more than they have habitually done this mysterious chemistry by which humanity is made and unmade.

This Basque unity leads to strange results. Thus, Gipuzkoa is an old country of communes. The ancient republican spirit of Andorra and Biguères has expanded after a century into the Jaizkibel Mountains, which are therefore the Jura of the Pyrenees. Here people lived under a Charter, whereas France suffered under the extremely Christian absolute monarchy and Spain under the absolute Catholic monarchy. Here, from time immemorial, the people chose the mayor, and the mayor governs the people. The mayor is the magistrate, the mayor is the judge, and he belongs to the people. The priest belongs to the Pope. What is left for the King? The soldier. But if he is a Castilian soldier, the people will reject him; if he is a Basque soldier, the priest and the mayor will own his heart, the king will own nothing but his uniform.

On first sight, it would seem that a nation such as this was admirably suited to receive new ideas from the French. Wrong. Old freedoms fear new freedoms. The Basque people have experienced it.

At the beginning of this century, the Spanish Parliament, for any and all purposes, and often to no purpose, made amendments, decreeing Spanish unity. The Basque constituency revolted. The Basques, driven back into their mountains, began the war of the North against the South. The day the throne broke with the Spanish Parliament, it was in Gipuzkoa that the beleaguered and defeated royalty took refuge. The country of rights and privileges, the nation of the *fueros*, cried out: Long live the true king! Ancient Basque freedom made common cause against the revolutionary spirit with the ancient monarchy of the Spains and the Indies.

And beneath that apparent contradiction, there was a profound logic and true instinct. Revolutions—we must insist on this—are no less brutal to ancient freedoms than were the ancient powers. They rendered everything new, and placed everything under a new framework; because they were working for the future, they took the measurements for the future of Europe from the present. This created the immense generalizations which are, so to speak, the cadres of the nations of the future that accommodate themselves with such difficulty to the old peoples, and which have so little regard for old ways, old laws, old customs, old freedoms, old borders, old languages, old habits, old authorities, old bonds that link everything together, old principles, old systems, old realities.

In revolutionary language, the old principles are called prejudices; the old realities are called abuses. That is both true and false at the same time. Whether they are republican or monarchical, old societies are replete with abuses, just as old men are full of wrinkles and old buildings with ruins; but it would be necessary to distinguish, to pull up the brambles and respect the building, to eradicate the abuses and respect the state. This is what revolutions do not know, do not want, [and] cannot do. Make distinctions, choose, prune—they are like the weather. They do not come to weed the field, but to make the earth tremble.

A revolution is not a gardener; it is the breath of God.

It passes by once, and everything collapses; it passes by again, everything comes back to life.

So revolutions mistreat the past. Everything rooted in the past fears them. In the eyes of revolutions, the ancient Spanish royalty was an abuse, the ancient Basque mayor another. The two abuses sensed the danger and united against the common enemy; the king's power depends on the mayor. And this is how it happened that the ancient Republic of Gipuzkoa ended up fighting for ancient Castilian despotism against the Constitution of 1812, to the great astonishment of those who see only the surface of things.

56. François-Xavier Michel Gerber, known as Francisque-Michel

(Lyons, 1809 – Paris, 1887)

From the time he was young, with only an undergraduate education, he was devoted to literature and the study of a wide variety of subjects, which endowed him with an encyclopedic level of knowledge and culture. He tirelessly published newspaper articles as well as books, and in particular, he produced critical editions of unpublished medieval texts. As a result, François Guizot, the Minister of Education, commissioned him to go to Great Britain in search of old, unpublished French texts. Among others, Michel discovered a manuscript in Oxford, which he subsequently published, of the *Chanson de Roland* (Song of Roland), an epic poem recounting the Battle of Roncesvalles

(Roncevaux in French, Orreaga in Basque) in Navarre; now regarded as one of the earliest major works of French literature. At the age of thirty, having published more than forty books, he decided to standardize his academic status and began to study humanities at the University of Bordeaux. Subsequently, he took a doctorate with one thesis in Latin on Virgil and another in French on various marginalized peoples living in the Pyrenees. In 1842, he was named Professor of Foreign Literature at the same university, but he devoted himself primarily to practical endeavors and especially to the publication of an astonishing number of books. His interests, as indicated, were many and diverse, but tended toward what we would characterize today as folklore (ballads, various argots) and the daily lives of ordinary people (gypsies, beggars, outcasts, and heretics living in the Pyrenees). In all these endeavors, Francisque-Michel was strongly influenced by the Romantic Movement.

And, if Europeans regarded any group of people in the mid-nineteenth century as exotic or romantic, it was the Basques. Michel came in contact with the Basque Country from various perspectives in the course of his tireless reading and research through the Basques' appearance, for example, as Pyrenean outcasts, in the battle of Roncesvalles (where it was they, not the Saracens as stated in the poem, who defeated the rearguard of Charlemagne's army), and in maritime commerce, and he decided to make it the object of more thorough study. First, he published a new edition of Oihenart's proverbs in 1847, followed, in 1857, by a work synthesizing Basque culture: *Le Pays Basque, sa population, sa langue, ses moeurs, sa literature et sa musique* (The Basque Country: Its Population, Language, Way of Life, Literature and Music). If Iztueta can be considered the first Basque folklorist to write in his own language and therefore address his work to his fellow Basques, Michel stands out as the great promoter and advocate of Basque culture in France as well as internationally. In many intellectual circles, even those in which Humboldt's studies had gone unnoticed, the originality and appeal of Basque culture was first presented in his book. Critical and methodical, Michel offered a panorama of popular and cultured literary production, as well as the language and other ethnographic characteristics of the country, although he could not avoid including in his repertory of old songs the apocryphal ones of Lelo and Altabiscar. His critical appraisals of the opinions and verdicts expressed by various authors concerning Euskara are of great interest, as is his personal opinion concerning the current sociolinguistic status of the Basque language.

LE

PAYS BASQUE

FRANCISQUE MICHEL

PARIS

LONDRES ET EDIMBOURG

SELECTED TEXT(S):

Le Pays Basque, sa population, sa langue, ses moeurs, sa littérature et sa musique [The Basque Country: Its Population, Language, Way of Life, Literature and Music] (Paris: Didot, 1857); reprint (Donostia: Elkar, 1994), 7–15, 467.

Euskara, or the Basque Language

The Basque language, a source of such pride to those who speak it today, but which a noted linguist [Alfred Maury] says is now little more than a patois, was spoken, even during the Middle Ages, only by the people living in the mountains of northern Spain and southwestern France. And it is incorrect to say, as one of the most important historians of Navarre [José Moret] insists, that in 1167 it was the national language of the country. If we examine the document he cites, but surely misunderstands [*Liber rotundus ecclesia Pompelonensis* (Round Book of the Church of Pamplona)], describing a recitation of the coronation of King Carlos III in 1389, it is clear that, at least at the end of the fourteenth century, the national language of Navarre was the Roman language because the sermon delivered by the king, and presented as the language of Navarre, is written in that language [as cited in José Yanguas y Miranda's *Diccionario de Antigüedades de Navarra . . .*].

The language of the Basques does not seem to have been written at all during the Middle Ages,[1] which is not surprising when you remember how rare it was, before the twelfth century, for vulgar languages to be used except for the daily routine of life. But it is hard to understand why none of the many writers who have spoken about Navarre and the other Basque provinces, for example, the troubadour Guillaume Anelier, who is so free with details about the history of the former at the end of the thirteenth century, have said nothing about a language so different from those derived from Latin, except to point out its strangeness.

. . .

The opinion linking Euskara to the languages of ancient Iberia has generally prevailed; but other language groups have also had their day. One of those [by George Borrow, in his *The Zincali, or An Account of the Gypsies of Spain* (1841)], which writers have tried to resuscitate several years ago, consists of identifying Basque as a Tartar dialect; but apparently, there is no basis for this at all. Fifteen years before Borrow, one of the great scholars of that period [Julius Heinrich Klaproth], equally as competent as the English missionary, conducting a comparison of Basque with the Asiatic languages, [and] principally with those categorized as Semitic, had no hesitation in declaring that he had not discovered any recognizable bonds of kinship between the dialect in question, and the language of the Basques.[2] It will be necessary, then, to

1. The author of *Un Voyage d'Espagne* [A Journey to Spain], written in the year 1655 and published in Paris in 1666, Intro., p. 4, goes even further when, pp. 5–6, he states definitively concerning the end of the western chain of the Pyrenees: "They speak a language there that is only understood by those from that country; moreover, it is so poor that a single word can mean several things, and for that reason it cannot be used for commerce; it is not written, and the small children learn Castilian or French in school."

2. *Mémoires relatifs a l'Asie...* [Memoirs Relating to Asia...], vol. 1 (1826), 214–34 . . . A compatriot and contemporary of Klaproth, Christian Gottlieb Arndt, in his work titled *Ueber der Ursprung un die Verschiedenurtige Werwandtschaft der Europäischen Sprachen* . . . [About the Origin and Different Relationships between European Languages . . .] (1818), 20, attempted to prove that Basque belonged to the same family as Finnish and Sami, and that Celtic was linked to it by some of its roots. Rasmus Christian Rask, too, in his *Ueber das Alte und die Echtheit der Zend-Sprache* . . . [About the Antiquity and Authenticity of the Zend language . . .] (1826), 69, has attempted to link Basque to Finnish. Recently, Maury has come upon some connections he finds convincing, at least initially. After having observed that in Basque declension is effected through postposition, as in the Ugric-Tartar languages, that its conjugation is equally similar to that of these

.../...

categorize everything [Mathieu de] Bastide [in his *Dissertation sur les Basques* (Dissertation on the Basques) (1786)] and the Abbot d'Iharce de Bidassouet[3] have written about the kinship of this language with Hebrew and Phoenician, as pure speculation, and to renounce Leibniz's hope of discovering the cradle of the Basque language in Africa,[4] which encouraged Mr. Eichhoff [in *Parallèle des langues de l'Europe et de l'Inde* (The Similarity of the Languages of Europe and India) (1836)] to assume that the ancestors of the Cantabrians came from the western part of Asia where the Chaldean languages originated; it seems to me that such a hope has as little basis in fact as William Humboldt's claim of kinship between Euskara and Greek.[5]

.../...

languages, and that the Basque verb has very close analogies with that of the North American languages, he concludes as follows: "Euskara, then, seems to provide a link between the American language and Ugric-Tartar, and what confirms this is that certain very distinct peculiarities are common to Basque and to some of the languages that are spoken from northern Sweden to the far end of Kamchatka, and from Hungary to Japan." *La Terre et l'Homme* . . . [Earth and Man . . .], 460.

3. *Histoire des Cantabres, ou des premiers colons de toute l'Europe* [History of the Cantabrians, or the First Inhabitants of All Europe], etc., vol. 1 (the only one published) (1825). From pages 242–409, the author attempts to demonstrate the superiority of the Asiatic Basque language over all ancient and modern languages; he almost goes so far as to say that God spoke Basque in the Earthly Paradise: "I do not know if Euskara . . . was the language of the Eternal Father; I would not be so bold as to assert that the Eternal Father spoke Basque; but what is certain is that the noun *Arc,* which in Basque is *arkh, arkha, arche,* and that of the kind of wood of which the Arc or arkha had to have been built, are Basque words, words from Euskara." Here is how the dignified Abbot concludes: "We can conclude, then, that there is no language in the universe that is closer to the language which the Eternal Father inspired in Adam."

4. "If it turned out that there were many Basque words in the Copt language, this would confirm . . . that the ancient language of Spain and Aquitaine could have come from Africa." Letter XXI to Mr. Mathurin Veyssiere la Croze, *Opera omnia* [Complete Works], vol. 5 (1768), 503 . . . The Berber language offering, like Basque, the phenomenon of complete isolation, similar features could have implied some kinship between the Berbers and the Basques; but the comparison of the languages of these two peoples has proven precisely the opposite, because no analogy has been found between them, either in similarity of words or grammatical forms, which, in conjugation, is strikingly reminiscent of the languages of North America. See the article by Klaproth on the dissertation of the Abbot Darrigol, in the *Bulletin des sciences historiques* [Bulletin of Historical Sciences], vol. 17, 340, 341.

5. In a letter dated December 12, 1801, this scholar wrote to Wolf: "I am constantly discovering more and more Greek in Basque." *Wilhelm von Humboldt's gesammelte*

.../...

Despite the foregoing, I want to join the Abbot Darrigol [in his *Dissertation critique et apologétique de la langue basque* (Critical Dissertation on and Apology of the Basque Language)] in pointing out this fact, quite easy to prove, that there are very few languages, if any, in which the vocabulary evokes the biblical tradition to the same degree. In effect, it is not necessary to distort the roots of Basque words to discover in them traces of the creation, the flood, the promised Messiah, etc. Quite the contrary, in Euskara, *aste* (week), means, in its true sense "beginning," and each one of the days leads us back to that meaning: Monday, *aste-lehene* (first beginning); Tuesday, *aste-artia* (mid-beginning); Wednesday, *aste-azkena* (end of the beginning); Thursday, *orz'eguna* (*orzu*, "behold," *eguna*, "the day"; a word, which can be broken down into *egi, eki,* "sun", and *duna*, a flexional ending indicating possession); finally, Saturday, in the dialect of Zuberoa, *nazken* or *azken-eguna* (last day). The year, in Basque, is *urthe*, which means "inundation, periodic time corresponding to an inundation, to the flood," the starting point of the post-Diluvian era.

The eldest son of Noah was named *Sem*: in Basque, *semé,* which means "son." [The word] sister, is expressed *ereba*: broken down, you have *ar-eba*, (Eve of the male); *eba* being the root of "cut, remove, lift out"; *Jaincoa*, ordinarily translated "the Lord of the heavens," "the good master on high," presents, as do *Jainco*, *jinco, jingo*, the true indeterminate future of the verb "to come," which we could translate as "the one who is to come," "the awaited," and the same with many other words.

Results such as these are no doubt quite remarkable; but is that any reason to reject them? No, because they are authorized by the Basque language and modern criticism has certainly not abolished the right to interpret words by their roots. Now, what is the source of this power of Basque words to signify? Who can explain it? Many have tried.[6] Most

.../...

Werke [Works Compiled by Wilhelm von Humboldt] vol. 5 (1841–46), 240, letter 62. Several authors have claimed that the Greeks inhabited the coastline of the Bay of Biscay; but the facts do not support this opinion, and, as the Basque proverb says, *ustea, ez yakitea* [opinion is not knowledge]. On this point, see the discussion of P. Gabriel de Henao, bk. 1, chs. 57 and 58 of his *Averiguaciones de las antigüedades de Cantabria* [Investigations into the Antiquities of Cantabria], 336–46.

6. Here, I will only cite the work of Thomas de Sorreguieta, the first part of which is titled: *Semana hispano-bascongada, la única de la Europa, y la más antigua del*

.../...

recently, one of our colleagues [Adolphe Pictet, in an article published in the *Bibliothéque universelle de Genève* (Universal Library of Geneva) (1854)], reviving the system of Esteban de Garibay, as so many others have done, placed the origin of the Basques in the exact birthplace of a people in Asia[7] where, he says, ancient names, perfectly in harmony with Euskara, were abundant; but Mr. Adolphe Pictet [in his *De l'Affinité des langues celtiques avec le sanscrit* (The Affinity of the Celtic Languages With Sanskrit (1837)], who, following the lead of Susmilch [*Histoire de l'Académie . . . de Berlin* (History of the Academy . . . of Berlin) (1745)] and James Cowles Prichard [in *The Eastern Origin of the Celtic Nations proved by a Comparison of their Dialects with the Sanskrit, Greek, Latin, and Teutonic Languages* (1831)],[8] has placed the first Celts in that part of the world, refuses to acknowledge the presence there of the first Basques, whom some have suggested originated along side them.[9] He has rudely reprimanded the professor from Bordeaux, who, in this circumstance, has lost more ground than partisans in the heart of the Lower Pyrenees have. There, the same proof and the same

---

.../...

orbe [The Spanish-Basque Week, Unique in Europe and the Oldest on Earth] (1804), in particular part 4. The second part, published in the same year, carries this title: *Monumentos del bascuence, ó prosecucion de los precedents del asteá, eguná, illá, urieá y demas* [Monuments of the Basque Language, or an Investigation into the Precedents of the Words *asteá*, *aguná*, *illá*, *urieá* and Others].

7. For example, these writers see in the noun *Aralar*, which is the name of a high mountain situated between Navarre and Gipuzkoa, a reference to the mountains of Armenia, as in the noun *Araxes*, a nearby stream that cuts through the Valley of Larraun, a reminder of a famous river [the Ares]; they are still trying to identify the name *Gorbea* or *Gorbeya*, used to designate another mountain that separates the province of Araba from Bizkaia, with that of a mountain range in that same Asian country; but first, as Father Gabriel de Henao is careful to observe, *Averiguaciones de las antigüedades de Cantabria* [Investigations into the Antiquities of Cantabria], bk. 1, ch. 1, 11n20, the name of the range is different; furthermore, as Academy member Traggia correctly notes, *Diccionario geográfico-histórico de España* [Geographical-Historical Dictionary of Spain], sec. 1, vol. 1, 419, col. 2, derivations based on close similarities are more ingenious than sound.

8. Cf. Bopp, "Ueber die eltischen Sprachen vom Gesichtspunkte der vergleichenden Sprachforschung . . ." [About Elite Languages from a Comparative Research Perspective . . ."], *Abhandlungen der Berliner Akademie aus dem Jahre 1838* [Essays of the Academy of Berlin in the Year 1838), in vol. 4, *Philologisch-historisch Abtheilung* [Philological-Historical Department] (1839), 187–272.

9. J. Augustin Chaho, *Lettre à M. Xavier Raymond sur les analogies qui existent entre la langue basque et le sanscrit* [Letter to Mr. Xavier Raymond about the Analogies that Exist Between the Basque Language and Sanskrit] (1836).

hypotheses have been accepted, supported by the negative hypotheses furnished by futile combinations that have been put forth at random to demonstrate that Basque was descended from Hebrew and from the Punic language. They have gone so far as to claim that Euskara is one of the primitive languages fallen from the sky at the foot of the famous Tower of Babel to separate the human race by the confusion of languages, and to group it together by families or tribes destined to occupy and inhabit this or that region of the world. The Basques, as we can see, have abandoned the interpretation of the Abbot d'Iharce de Bidassouet, who insinuates, although timidly, that God and our first parents may well have spoken their language in the earthly paradise; but more intensely than ever they present it as a primitive language. As they interpret it, Euskara, which has hardly any literature at all and has scarcely been developed, would be an ancient vestige, an ancient example of those first languages dropped from on high. Carrying that logic to its extreme, it is better that no influence, no human science, has ever affected Basque, which, by that very token, has not had to resist the ravages of time, that is, the loss of words that would have been all too quickly replaced by borrowings from neighboring languages. For example, it could not be doubted that it would have adopted a number of Latin words during the time when the Basques were in contact with the Romans; but those words are for the most part modified by the genius of the language. The same observation is made regarding the Spanish and French terms that are found in it. We can find, equally, a number of words which, undoubtedly, are of Germanic origin; those were probably introduced into Basque in the period of Visigoth domination. But all of those foreign elements are merely imported into the language, which essentially and basically differs from all known languages, although it does possess some roots in common with them, among others with the Finnish languages and those of northern and central Asia, namely Turkish, a kinship that comes from the primitive connection that exists between the roots of all the world's languages rather than from any kinship with some particular family.

Pierre d'Axular

Except for a few scattered poems and pastoral poems, there is hardly any poetry in French Basque except for translations of the Holy Scripture and the Imitation of Jesus Christ, and other small books of piety. The Spanish Basques are far richer in that respect. We should not, however, accuse those in France of being more ignorant or less skillful: the penury of works written in their language is explained by the fact that barely a hundred thousand people speak it, divided fairly equally among three dialects. A book composed in one of these dialects would only reach a rural population of around thirty thousand, among whom we would find scarcely a hundred lovers of reading, so the writer would be wasting his time, his effort and the cost of publication. In reality, there are only a few devotional works, whose sale could cover the cost of printing, with nothing left for profit.

It is not my purpose to look for merit in that kind of book, which are worth neither more nor less than those of that genre that circulate in our rural areas; but I should point out a genre that rises considerably above that level, and which provides tangible proof that what we have said about the richness and other qualities of Euskara is no exaggeration.

Axular's *Gueroco guero* [sic] is an initial demonstration in that direction.

57. Antoine Abbadie Thompson

(Dublin, 1810 – Paris, 1897)

Born in Ireland, his mother was Irish, his father was from Zuberoa. When he was three, he and his family moved to Toulouse, where he began his studies, specializing in physics. A characteristic example of the nineteenth-century scientific polymath, his preferences within a vast range of interests were oriented toward astronomy, geography, and linguistics. Between 1837 and 1848, he traveled through Ethiopia gathering linguistic and ethnographic data. Throughout his life, he traveled to many other places, both for the purpose of exploration and to carry out physical or astronomical experiments. A member of several geographic and philological academic societies, he was one of the founders of the *Societé Linguistique* (Linguistic Society) of Paris. Although he was constantly on the move, from Norway to Santo Domingo, by way of Alexandria, after 1849, his primary residence was in his castle Abadia, near Hendaia (Lapurdi). Abbadie felt a deep identification with the Basque people, and became one of those most crucially responsible for the defense, promotion, and dignification of the Basque language. In part, this loyalty to things Basque came from his father, Michel, who was a passionate student and promoter of Euskara. Despite his privileged economic and social position, Antoine

Abbadie practiced a romantic populism that led him to dress in traditional Basque fashion (with beret and sandals) and engage in peasant diversions, such as *pelota* or Basque handball. Additionally, his cult of the body and physical fitness made him a consummate sportsman and an excellent swimmer.

Abbadie was, above all, a promoter and a Maecenas or generous benefactor. His proselytizing spirit in favor of the Basque language encouraged other scholars to both study it and publish their writings on the subject. Abaddie inspired, among others, Prince Napoleon, Darrigol, Duvoisin, Arturo Campión, and Pierre Loti, and of course, he maintained correspondence with many other lovers of Basque who did not need encouragement, such as Chaho.

Besides the work on the Basque language that he wrote in collaboration with Chaho, and other works on grammar and orthography, Abbadie's most important labor in relation to the Basque language was his sponsorship and encouragement of the *Juegos Florales* (Literary Competitions), which were financed by his estate (until well after his death) in the period 1853–1901. Ideologically, Abbadie intended these festivals of Euskara to inspire a twofold "flowering" or regeneration of the Basque people: linguistic and physical. He wanted to see the simultaneous development of strong bodies through the practice of popular sports and the enrichment of the Basque language through songs and poetic compositions. Therefore, it was not exclusively a matter of literary competitions, but of festivals in which declamations were mixed with games of *pelota*, performances by *bertsolariak* or versifiers, popular sports and dances, together with agricultural and fishing exhibits. In this, they were quite different from other similar Literary Competitions during that period organized elsewhere in Europe. Moreover, it should be noted that Abbadie's festivals predated other such gatherings; for example, he first organized the Basque-language celebrations six years before the Catalan *Jocs Florals*, which were to be so important in the linguistic renaissance of Catalonia. Furthermore, the poets who attended these contests were by no means literary professionals, but aficionados of literature who in some cases (Felipe Arrese and Jean Baptiste Eliçamburu, for example) ended up becoming quite famous poets. These Basque-language festivals (in both the northern and southern Basque Country) did not, perhaps, succeed in creating a body of poets and writers sufficient to pull Basque literature out of the slough in which it was mired, but at least they managed to honor and popularize the language, which for the first time was exhibited publicly in a respectful and dignified manner.

Selected Text(s):

(with Augustin Chaho), *Études grammaticales sur la langue euskarienne* [Grammatical Studies of the Basque Language] (Paris: Arthus Bertrand, 1836).

In pointing out to the readers the flaws of the grammarians who have preceded us, we have resisted the impulse to characterize their systematic expositions of our language with blindness or negligence. Euskara, different in this regard from all the other languages of Europe, belongs to the family of polysynthetic languages that are so rich and varied in the primitive races of America and which in the ancient world are to be found only in the aboriginals of Spain and southern France.* Man's mind seems to experience great difficulty in moving from these languages to the grammatical forms of the Semitic or western languages in which the sentence is analyzed through composition and in which the derivatives rarely exceed words of more than seven syllables. We are aware of the great difficulties experienced by the Jesuits of Mexico when they tried to use the Spanish language to teach the indigenous peoples. Those reverend fathers wisely concluded from this that it was easier to make the different tribes learn a common indigenous language because it had great rapport in its grammar with all the other languages of America. Similarly, Euskara resembles this kind of metaphysical system, whose physiognomy seems bizarre initially, but easily understood

* This opinion is based on the grammars of the known languages; it is to be hoped, however, that languages as perfect as ours will be discovered among the many languages still to be studied in Asia and Africa.

once that initial hurdle is overcome and one manages to grasp its deep structure in a nuanced manner. Although the mind may then enjoy that structure, it requires further effort to grasp the relationships between that system and those with which it is more familiar. This is the case with the Basque language. As much pleasure as there is in knowing it intimately, it is equally painful to appreciate it from the perspective of French grammar. Only after translating it, does such difficulty cease. Unless one has long practice, or a clear and philosophical mind, it is impossible to translate directly from French to Basque; it is like a new country to which one must become acclimatized gradually.

The reader, then, will already have anticipated the difficulties inherent in our grammatical synthesis. Every book proceeds by linear stages, and the form of exegesis exposes us to the same inconvenience inherent in the classifications of natural sciences in which the table of lateral relationships, so multiple and so important, is relegated to secondary importance. The mind is quite capable of conceiving all the relationships and affinities, but speech only proceeds in straight lines.

To avoid these inconveniences, as well as to satisfy a way of thinking that will seem sure and philosophical to us, we have chosen a new method for our exposition. Our studies will be classified according to the three final characteristics of language: suffixes, declensions and conjugations, that is, the three modifications of the word depending on its qualities, its position, and its relationships.

Unfortunately, we have had to reject the grammatical system that comes down to us from the ancients, and which has been more or less developed and perfected by so many authors. It is ingenious and has the advantage of being generally known and quite well understood; but it lends itself poorly to making generalizations about analytical languages, is utterly antipathetic to those that proceed by synthesis, and especially the Basque language.

. . .

We have tried to appreciate objectively the character of Euskara, in both its beauties and in its imperfections, for no human language is perfect; we have attempted to restrain the inevitable enthusiasm we bring to the definition of the language of our forefathers. Far from wishing to isolate Euskara from the thousands of modes of speech spread across the earth, we have sought out analogies, for the laws of humanity are the same everywhere. It is not reasonable to attribute to the Creator anything but a unique plan in the development of thought, through speech; and if the Basque language presents a distinct physiognomy, we must regard it as something washed ashore in the course of protracted invasions. We will offer a few remarks about the languages whose grammars present analogies with Euskara.

. . .

In judging the principal languages of the two hemispheres as similar based on these few analogies, we believe we have said enough to encourage the philologists to pursue these relationships. Their efforts will not be fruitless, we are sure. Many beautiful works have already been dedicated to the grammar and etymologies of the grand family of Indo-Germanic languages. The science has one more step to take: it must eventually show how language is formed, is perfected gradually, even how alphabetical writing has slowly emerged from the chaos of the hieroglyphics through the mediation of phonemes. To the extent that linguistic imperfection allows, we will hazard some thoughts on this enormous question.

As we can see through the education of the deaf-mute, every language starts with concrete nouns; then we learn to generalize through the slow emergence of abstract nouns and qualifiers, the cases and endings found in the vestiges of all languages. As with the language of so many black peoples, this is the way backward nations stammer out their ideas.

To arrive at the verb, instead of the preposition, there had to be great development in a nation. Abstract nouns for present or past existence combined with abstract nouns for persons must have formed the first elements of conjugation, that is, the present and the past. The forms *niz* (*ni iz*), *nintzan* (*ni izan*), show traces of the noun that is based with the *iz*, the essence or base of the verb. Was it then necessary to go back in time to invent the perfect, the pluperfect, etc.? The noun for accomplished existence, *izan* [being, existence], is added to the general idea *iz* or to oneself, thus forming a superlative of the past. From here, *izan niz*, *izan nintzan*, "I have," "I have been." The modifications of the verb to express the relations of the persons can be developed in the same way. Once we had the verb "be," we were able to combine it with verbal nouns to express the ideas of action. This development is natural, positive, and must have been initiated in the infancy of society.

The third stage of languages is seen in the syncopated forms through which the verbal noun is interpolated in the developed verb. Basque offers us a few initial examples, but the word condensed in this way still preserves all the inflexions through the complex relations of subjects to rules. From there, to advance to the forms of the analytical languages, the transition is easy to grasp. The inflexion of the verb agrees with that of the regime; thus, we say *galdu ditut indarrac* (I have lost my strengths), or more precisely, (I have lost them my strength). Little by little, always expressing the noun independently, we are liberated from an overly precise verbal inflexion specifying the personal subject of little use alongside the noun.* At the same time, the declension is divided. The cases were expressed first through prefixes, then by way of separate prepositions. Finally, the detached article ends up providing some of the precision lost by changing the original rule. The languages of the black races, Basque, Latin, and French will successively depict this transformation in the way the thought is expressed. The Georgian language shows the transition from one stage to the next through postpositions, which can be declined separately, forming adverbs of time and place, and by the conjugation of its verbs, which does not follow a uniform system.

Another equally serious question is posed by the philologist. What pains of creative thought, what wars, internecine convulsions, or outside influences have shattered the organized coherence so damaged in most languages, but so simple and prolific in Euskara? "A remarkable thing in Basque is that this language rejects all changes so perfectly," such are the words of [Wilhelm von] Humboldt. We will add that this language resembles a kind of savage algebra: its elements are simple, its combinations many, its results satisfying; its principles and its composition lead only to the smallest number of insoluble questions. But, in order to develop such grand and simple principles did it not require an enormous moral superiority or a great confidence in the future of its physical and political life? Were not the irregularities in syntax and grammar of other languages caused by admixtures imposed by invasions? Or could they have been manipulated to plunder the most salient characteristics of other languages, thus growing rich on the spoils by an instinct of domination? What is the physical or moral circumstance that freezes and fixes a language in such a moment of its formation? These questions can only be answered theoretically; because the data is lacking, because languages have not been sufficiently examined in their different stages of creation, from the horde that uses a paltry vocabulary to the nation that speaks through the mouth of its great writers.

Whatever the case, we are tempted to believe that through the progressive movement of the human spirit, languages obey two tendencies which it would be interesting to study in their relations with the elo-

* We see evidence of this genesis in what are labeled active verbs, in the difference of their inflexions compared to those of the essential verb that generates them. Also, the verb "to be" turns out to be irregular in almost all other languages.

quence of the word and the metaphysics of thought. Unlike before when unexpected needs were expressed by a small number of roots that were already known but subjected to new combinations, new words now come from outside with their ideas that were previously unknown, and the unity of the primitive grammar is shattered by the introduction of words that resist declension, irregular verbs and exceptions in syntax. Nations whose origins are the most complex, languages that are most heterogeneous because of their borrowings, seem to be called to shape the future of humanity. Alloys prevail as in the physical. Synthetic languages are born of nature that initially conceives a single source; analytical languages are produced either by a long habit of differentiation and abbreviation or by the violent effect of an outside invasion. Languages of analysis have taken what rises to the top. The law that produces and rules these phenomena no doubt has its harmonies and its grand purpose.

We do not wish to hide what is hypothetical about these ideas, deciding that it was more useful to mention them than to silence them. Some elevated spirit will know how to appreciate them in their true value; perhaps they will inspire some useful research; perhaps some great truth will come of it.

58. Jean Martin Hiribarren

(Azkaine [Ascain], Lapurdi, 1810 – Baiona, Lapurdi, 1866)

Ordained in 1833, he served as parish priest in Urruña (Urrugne) and Bardoze (Bardos), in Lapurdi. In 1865, he was named honorary Canon of the Cathedral of Baiona. He published some minor works in Basque on migration and religious topics, and left many unpublished writings, among them a grammar and a Basque to French dictionary. But the work that brought him fame and a renowned place in Basque-language literature was *Eskaldunac* (The Basques) (1853), a poem composed of more than five thousand verses. Rather than an epic poem, its tone is that of a sketch of customs expressing a love of things Basque in general and from Lapurdi in particular. Quite devoted to the Basque language, he took part in a debate that was very redolent of his era: namely, that of the orthographic stabilization of written Basque and the necessity of choosing between *ç* and *z*, *c* or *k*, and so on.

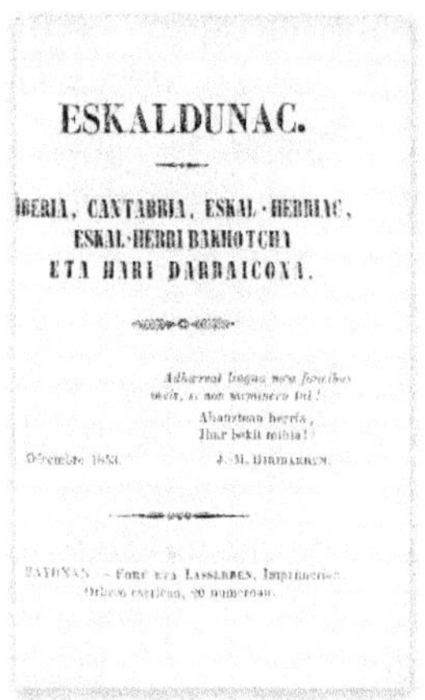

ESKALDUNAC.

IBERIA, CANTABRIA, ESKAL-HERRIAC,
ESKAL-HERRI BAKHOTCHA
ETA HARI DARRAICONA.

SELECTED TEXT(S):

Eskaldunac. Iberia, Cantabria, Eskal-Herriac. Eskal Herri bakhotcha eta hari darraicona [The Basques: Iberia, Cantabria, The Basque Regions, and Everything Concerning Each of the Basque Regions], (Baiona: Fore et Lasserre, 1853), 3–7.

To Begin, Two Words for the Basques

The ancient things of which I'll write,
most countrymen will cherish,
it's no easy task, they know this,
long gone, the past's a dark cloud.

All this time in the home of our ancestors,
few know whence they've come,
what our forebears did to remain here,
how they defended their land with the gun.

Look at all those children, the years spent
at school at the expense of their parents,
learning to speak foreign tongues,
and not Basque, or much else besides.

So there were many great French kings,
they know of them in that language,
if that's all they've learnt, we might
just as well burn their houses down now.

Many think that speaking Basque
is not worth two cents!
Oh most beautiful, eternal tongue
who will sing you're peerless on this earth!

The Spaniards want to speak Spanish,
the French French, thorns and all;
why do the Basques give up Basque,
and search for other things to waste time on?

Isn't it just as easy to learn something else
and add it to the Basque they already know?
None of us has our own Basque name
they were buried in books, lost in time.

The jealous Latin, Spanish, and French have tried,
with all their might, to weaken the old Basque;
since none spoke it, it was easy to besmirch it:
Oh, this century can never repay the debt it owes us!

Those without money can't learn a thing,
for without it there's no French schooling;
they say all good books are in French;
the Basques don't have books or cash!

I have mentioned books, written abroad,
and not those to aid prayer in the church,
such good, holy books exist in abundance;
clouds don't darken the soul's luminosity.

The exploits of others are spread far and wide
but the Basques' virtues are mentioned by no one;
perhaps in some remote city, an Enlightened Basque man,
lost in the crowd, may miraculously be found.

For any country it is a source of shame
to be without a leader in their midst;
this is what is happening to our youth today
because no one has told them about their origins.

Inconceivable how much ignorance there is
in this, the oldest country on earth;

let light shine on your shadows, Basques,
this is the age of the Enlightenment.

Mumbling French is not the same as speaking it;
better to be silent than talk like a fool.
Do not give anyone the chance to laugh at you;
better to do something else with your time.

Today we invite all Basques
to begin enriching their spirits
so future generations know
what their ancestors were capable of.

Many are doing the right thing in our country;
in most houses people find consolation in labor,
and bear the pain of their wounds in silence;
in this manner they are spreading goodness.

The worst books in the world have been written;
it would be best if all of them were burned;
like serpents they live among the roses,
awaiting the time to bite innocent souls.

It's time to throw mud on the faces of those
who hunger after these malevolent books;
let us sing together: country, labor, virtue;
I shall be the first to sing loudly.

IBERIA

No one in the world is like a Basque;
for centuries we stood alone;
others have come to mingle in our landscape,
the blood in our veins flows clear like glass.

Oldest country, yours is the glory;
no other people stand as high as you;
never, never forget your Basque ancestry;
abandon now and forever the influence of Spain!

59. Jean Pierre Duvoisin, known as "Captain Duvoisin"
(Ainhoa, Lapurdi, 1810 – Ziburu [Ciboure], Lapurdi, 1891)

He spent his childhood in Ezpeleta (Espellete) and began his studies in the Seminary of Larresoro (Larressore), excelling because of his love of literature, geography, and history. After dropping out of the Seminary, under complex circumstances following the death of his father and the revolution of 1830, he decided to take up the profession of his father and enlisted in the Customs Service, reaching the rank of captain. He coordinated this work with an interest in Basque culture in general and in particular the language, initiating at an early age his primary area of activity in this field: translation. Specifically, he translated into other dialects, or provided translations from, the Basque of Lapurdi. These works included *Les Aventures de Télémaque* (The Adventures of Telemachus) by François Fénelon, *Afectos sobre los Ejercicios del Padre San Ignacio* (Feelings about the Exercises of Saint Ignatius) by Agustín Cardaberaz, the *Diálogos basco-castellanos . . .* (Basque-Castilian Dialogues . . .), also known as *Solasak* (Words) by Agustín Pascual Iturriaga, the *De Imitatatione Christi* (Imitation of Christ) by Thomas à Kempis, several chapters of the Quixote, and especially, fulfilling an assignment given him by Prince Bonaparte, the Bible—*Bible saindua edo Testament zahar eta berria* (The Holy Bible, or the Old and New Testament) (1859). In fact, his encounter with Bonaparte and the decision to broaden the group of his collaborators changed Captain Duvoisin's life, as he ended up abandoning his work in the Customs Service to dedicate himself exclusively to research on Euskara. He also published some works specifically related to the Basque language: *Étude sur la declinaison basque* (Study on Basque Declensions) (1866), *Études sur la langue basque* (Studies on the Basque Language) (1874), and *De la formation des noms dans la langue basque* (On the Formation of Nouns in the Basque Language) (1874). Finally, he also wrote an original and interesting book titled *Laborantzako liburua, edo bi aita semeren solasak laborantzaren gainean* (A Book of Agriculture, or Two Fathers and Sons' Agricultural Words) (1858). At his death, he left thousands of unpublished pages on topics related to the Basque language, literature, and culture. His ideas on the Basque language attempt to establish criteria based on scientific analysis. He did not, however, reject metaphysical and "philosophical" arguments related to the presumed primitive language as superior to that spoken at the time; the latter of which was assumed to be only a pale reflection of the original after suffering centuries of deterioration because of revolutions and barbarism. The influence of Chaho and Astarloa are palpable in his linguistic concepts.

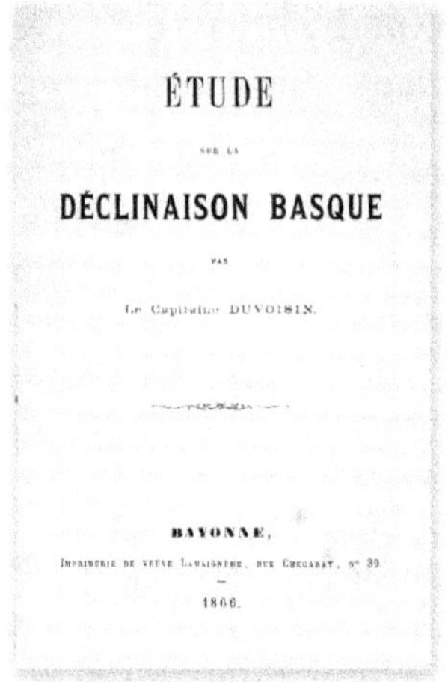

ÉTUDE

SUR LA

DÉCLINAISON BASQUE

PAR

Le Capitaine DUVOISIN.

BAYONNE,

Imprimerie de veuve Lamaignère, rue Chegaray, n° 39.

1866.

SELECTED TEXT(S):

Étude sur la declinación basque [Study on Basque Declensions] (Bayonne: Veuve Lamaignére, 1866), 47–51.

19

General Considerations

Leibniz speculated and Doctor Young attempted to prove by lexical comparisons that the Basque language originated in Egypt and belongs to the same trunk as Coptic. Julius Klaproth uses the same procedure as Young to connect Basque with the Semitic languages, and he believes he has established their common kinship. Cardinal Wiseman finds curious analogies between Basque and some American dialects, for instance, the lack of some of the same letters, the tendency to combine the same consonants and similar complication in the system of conjugation.

Lexical indices are always uncertain, and their value is seriously diminished when the grammatical comparison fails to corroborate it. Abstracting from religious belief, and considering everything from the philosophical point of view, human language must have been subject from the beginning to a universal and constant law, applicable at all times, in all places and among all peoples. From this, we can deduce that all languages, and each one in particular, share a common basis. Science has confirmed this rational premise by innumerable proofs. So, it is not surprising that we can find in Basque certain analogies with other languages, especially the more ancient ones.

Phonetically, Basque is far from being an indigent language. Without traversing the spectrum of all of its dialects, or speaking of intermediate sounds, the language of Lapurdi has only five vowels, two semivowels, five aspirated letters, twenty simple consonants, and eighteen compound ones. Of the latter, in truth, several do not seem to be natural. It has been shown through the study of its declensions that the language has a marked tendency, not to merge, but to separate similar phonemes, either vowels or consonants, and the analysis of the words leaves no doubt about this.

As for the verb, philology seems to understand the mechanism more clearly than the essence. The Basque verb is not a word we can grasp and classify as we can others. It comes about through the combination of personal pronouns with certain flexional endings and characteristic letters; it's like a spirit dressing a body into which it infuses life. Basque will offer in its grammar a marvelous conjugation; but you will not find the verb in its dictionary. The Basque verb is the antithesis of what we call the verbal noun, the base of a system in favor today and, we believe, destined to fall from use once the synthetic languages succeed in isolating their elements by returning to origins and breaking down their verbs. Now, what in Basque is as clear as day will be suddenly veiled in other languages; the spirit of the verb, detached from its envelope, will cease to be perceptible and will have vanished, leaving behind it the inert elements from which life has been removed. The verbal noun is a fiction; verb is spirit.

The study of Basque will not be lacking in use for the advance of science. To the knowledge of conjugation and declension, it would be necessary to add another: knowledge of the internal structure of the words. From the beginning, the system is divided into two branches: the formation of roots and the formation of compounds; the two have different procedures. In the roots, euphony guides the ordering of the vowels and the consonants; in the compound words, the attachment of one or several flexional endings to the root is effected according to a law of derivation, although not without the intervention of euphony in the harmony of the parts.*

To consider Basque in its apogee, as is the case with all the ancient languages, we have to go back to the time of the cradle of humanity and beware of prejudices that still pervade the works of many philologists.

---

* There are many Basque suffixes. To define them and determine their use is a labor that demands time as well as reflection. The author of this study has assembled most of them; he anticipates that he will be able to publish the results of his investigations eventually.

Man is as powerless to create a language as he is to create the smallest molecule. He assembles and separates, combines and takes apart; he wants to make something from nothing. This truth is as constant in the moral order as in the physical order; man works from a base that has been given to him. Nowhere is this truth stronger, more obvious, or more palpable than in the history of language. Down through the centuries, revolutions and barbarism have extinguished light and contributed to spreading shadows over human intelligence. It is in vain that periods of darkness are followed by radiant days; in vain do brilliant writers struggle to perfect the language, they can lift it to its lost glory. And we disdainers of the past, glorying in our century, are forced by the weight of an imposing truth to admit that the modern language, as a system, as genius, or in its grandeur, is far inferior to that of the peoples whose kings slept on the skins of animals. Despite all our advantages, the genius of the Romans frightens us; they never conquered Mount Cenis, as we are about to do, but we cannot vie with their language. Yet, that language was but the palest ghost or image of a more perfect language. Spirituality is the prism through which the shattered rays of divine inspiration penetrate. Reason itself must pay homage to this truth that comes to give its hand to philosophical truth. Philosophical truth is affirmed and imposed before any demonstration, before logical proof, because we must have faith in the laws of harmony and conceive of order as the essential condition of being.

Grammar, which represents, beneath all of its sensible forms, the genius and rules of a language, will show us the various aspects of the Basque language and its internal organism. But, to understand the nature of its speech, to measure the distance separating this language from others, and to grasp their affinities, it is necessary to enter the more extensive domain of metaphysics. Grammar stops at the forms; by contrast, metaphysics only makes use of the sensible to explain the idea, whose realm she alone traverses.

In metaphysics, the word is not multiple; it is one as the idea is one. The idea changes; the word is transformed, but there are no more words than there are species of ideas. Synthetic unity must serve as a point of departure for grammatical analysis. Basque has maintained this characteristic unity; it contrasts with languages boasting an erudite classification for their rich variety of words. But is that not somewhat artificial? Has it not been acknowledged that articles, adverbs, prepositions, and conjunctions are words that have been disfigured? Basque cannot make such distinctions; it does not accept this classification, and observation proves that this would be alien to it; this truth was established long ago.

(See Darrigol, *Dissert.*, p. 22; Abbadie, *Prolegomena*, p. 4.; Chaho, *Gram.*, p. 8).

The noun is the only true word.

The importance of the Basque language in antiquity is necessarily measured by the people who spoke it. Historical, architectural, and numismatic monuments have demonstrated that Basque was the primitive language of the Iberian Peninsula, the islands of the western Mediterranean, and extensive areas of Gaul and Italy, and it is probable that it was widely spoken in other countries. The distinguished Wilhelm Humboldt has provided a system of proof drawn from the language itself and from ancient ethnography. His work is known throughout the scientific world, and in view of his authority it would undoubtedly be superfluous to seek further proof that Basque was the language of a great people. Furthermore, from the scientific point of view, the development of its grammatical system renders any contrary opinion untenable.

For how many centuries has Basque been spoken in Western Europe? It would be impossible to say. In the distant mists of the dawn of history, we can envision the barbaric hordes migrating from north to south. The Basques took refuge and survived in the steepest and most rugged places in Spain. The Romans in turn came to dominate the mixed populations from the earlier conquest. Again, the North sent down its hordes, and the Roman colossus was brought down. Wherever the conquerors imposed their yoke, nationalities perished. At one extremity of the known world, the Basque dwelling in the mountains, inspired by an exalted love for independence and favored by physical obstacles, continue to resist the incessant and repeated efforts to invade their territory. This is how the Basques survived generation after generation and preserved a language that dates from prehistoric times.

What is particularly characteristic about this language is the regularity of word-formation, declension, and conjugation—that, amid an extraordinary abundance of transmutations. This regularity stands in stark contrast to the anarchy afflicting the most celebrated languages. The explanation of the alterations in Greek and Latin is a thorny subject fraught with conjecture. The comparison of these languages with those of Indian origin has produced some happy results. Basque, on the contrary, can be fathomed and explained from within. "The richest language," Jolivald said, "would be one in which each idea would be rendered by a different term, in which each nuance of the idea would be expressed by specific modifications, such as different suffixes and flexional endings, etc." (*Encycl. Cath.*, s.v. "Gramm."). This theory is the system on which the Basque language is constructed. There, each root carries with it and engenders new words appropriate for the expression of various kinds of effusions of the idea presented within the root.

Basque is the standard bearer of primitive languages, a living vestige of antiquity. Linguists do not seem to have understood this; scientific progress leads them back to a problem that they neglected.

60. Joseph Augustin Chaho [Xaho] Lagarde

(Atharratze [Tardets], Zuberoa, 1811 – Baiona, Lapurdi, 1858)

The son of the Scrivener of Atharratze, he was brought up in a family oriented toward literature, with several of his younger brothers also being writers. He began his studies in the Seminary for minors in Olorón, where he graduated in rhetoric, and enrolled in Pau (Béarn) to study finance. His family was closely connected to that of Abbadie, and it was probably this link that led Chaho to move to Paris when he was only twenty years old. There he became involved with Charles Nodier's esoteric movement that was frequented by romantics (such as Victor Hugo and Alexander Dumas) with whom he also established relations. He also began studying oriental languages and is said to have mastered Sanskrit. From his first public appearances, he showed himself to be a fierce polemicist, attracting much attention. In 1834, he published three works that served as his debut: the first, *Paroles d'un voyant* (Words of a Visionary) as a response to *Paroles d'un croyant* (Words of a Believer) by H. F. Robert de Lammenais, which advocated a certain accommodation between liberal ideas and Catholicism. Chaho advocated a strong critique of Christianity and proposed a theoretical alternative in which he was already immersed: that of the visionary. The second work, *Paroles d'un biscaïen aux libéraux de la reine Christine* (Words of a Bizkaian to the Liberals of Queen Cristina), was his first venture into politics. Here, he proclaimed his solidarity with the Carlist cause in the recently initiated civil war; not, of course, for its absolutist character but for its defense of the *fueros* and Basque identity. The third, in which he further developed the aforementioned positions of the visionary and a defense of Basque identity, was titled *Azti-Beghia. Agosti-Chaho Bassaburutarrac Ziberou herri maïtiari, Parisetic igorriric, beste hanitchen aïtzindari arguibidian-Goiz-izarra* (The Visionary Eye: The Man from Basaburua [Zuberoa], Agustin Chaho, to the Beloved People of Zuberoa. Sent from Paris, Precursor of Many to Come, on the Path of Light of Morning Star [Venus]).

His political positions were radical. He was a republican, Jacobin, fiercely anticlerical, a utopian with an anarchist touch, and a Basque nationalist. This mix was, moreover, seasoned by a strong romantic and esoteric quality that turned out to be too intense even for the turbulent and revolutionary times in which he lived. Despite his progressive inclinations, he was by no means a partisan of Marx or of Fourier. However, he claimed that the traditional flag of the Cantabrians (that is, the Basques) had two stripes, a red and a black one, similar to that adopted by the Spanish Anarcho-Syndicalists, and one wonders whether this was, perhaps, just a coincidence or consciously thought up.

In 1836, he traveled to Navarre to acquire first-hand knowledge of the first Carlist War. He could have enlisted as a volunteer if his dedication and support for the Carlist cause had been unambiguous, but his differences with the absolutist and clerical cliques of Don Carlos could not have been greater. He traveled as a romantic observer to an exotic place, no matter how persistently he proclaimed the cultural and even political identity of the Basques on both sides of the Pyrenees. The parallelism with Byron's journey to Greece was reinforced by the all too famous portrait that Chaho painted of himself dressed in the Navarrese style, just as the British poet had had himself painted in the Greek style. Although initially it seems that he was well received by the Carlists, who were always anxious for support from outside and believed they were dealing with a French supporter of Don Carlos, Chaho was finally denounced as a revolutionary and anti-religious agent and expelled from the Carlist-controlled zone. However, his stay in Navarre lead to the publication of one of his most interesting books, the *Voyage en Navarre pendant l'insurrection des Basques* (Journey to Navarre during the Basque Insurrection) (1836). It is a completely romantic text; a mixture of travelogue to an exotic site, ethnological analysis, social commentary, political proclamation, linguistic commentary, and fictional novel. Of course, the Carlist military leader, Zumalacárregui, as well as all the Basque characters that appear in the novel are completely idealized and configured as archetypes: the shrewd smuggler, the virtuous military savior of his country, the honorable farmer, and so on.

In the same year, 1836, together with his friend and protector, Antoine Abbadie, he published the *Études grammaticales sur la langue euskarienne* (Grammatical Studies of the Basque Language), in which comparisons are established between the Basque languages and Sanskrit, something he had already pointed out in the *Voyage.* In 1838, he founded the *Revue des Voyans* (Visionary Review) in Toulouse and might have been initiated as a Freemason. In 1840, he moved to Baiona and established contact with the printer Lespés, with whom he published (between 1844 and 1852) what constitutes an authentic journal of propaganda and ideological agitation: the newspaper *Ariel*. This publication would go through a number of subtitles: *Courrier des Pyrénées et de l'imbecilium Club de Paris* (Mail from the Pyrenees and the *Imbecilum* Club of Paris), *Courrier des Pyrenées, Cantabrie et Navarre* (Mail from the Pyrenees, Cantabria and Navarre), *Courrier de Vasconie* (A Column from the Basque Country) and *Le Republicain de Vasconie* (The Republican from the Basque Country). As a supplement, there appeared in 1848 the first newspaper written in Euskara: the *Üscal-Herrico Gaseta* (Basque Country Gazette), which only lasted for two issues. Like its author, the newspaper *Ariel* was Republican, anticlerical, and Basque nationalist, with references to current events in both parts of the country. Additionally, in the *Üscal-Herrico Gaseta* an important linguistic topic was broached: that of the necessity for a unified literary language.

After the revolution of 1848, he became directly involved in politics, becoming a member of the Municipal Council of Baiona and the National Guard, as well as the General Council of the Pyrenees. He presented himself as a candidate to the French Legislative Assembly, receiving 3,453 votes, just 127 short of those needed to win a seat. Indeed, the *bertsolari* (versifier) Pierre Topet (known as *Etchahun*) composed some propagandistic verses supporting his candidacy in the electoral campaign. Yet with Napoleon III's coup d'état and the promulgation of the Second Empire in 1851, Chaho, like other progressives, was persecuted and had to go into exile, settling in Gasteiz (Vitoria), Araba. He returned to Baiona in 1853 and died five years later at the age of forty-seven. His secular funeral ceremony was the first ever celebrated in the Basque Country.

Chaho was an author fully integrated into the intellectual currents of his time. Specifically, he was the only Basque Romantic perfectly contemporary with the movement, whereas other Basque Romantic authors were influenced by Romanticism much later, some forty or fifty years after its apogee. Complex and contradictory, we would have to add to his facets as a nationalist, visionary, and social revolutionary another fully romantic persona: the creator of legends. In the same line as Walter Scott (*Ivanhoe*), Victor Hugo (*Hernani*), Prosper Mérimée (*Carmen*), Lord Byron, Gustavo Adolfo Bécquer, and Goethe, Chaho provided some of the foundational legends of greatest force for the forging of a new Basque mythic construct. In serial format in *Ariel*, he published "Lelo ou la Navarre il y a 500 ans" (Lelo, or Navarre Five Hundred Years Ago), and especially the legend of Aitor.

HISTOIRE PRIMITIVE

EUSKARIENS - BASQUES,

CHAHO.

M. DCCC. XLVII.

A MADRID, A BAYONNE,

Selected Text(s):

Histoire primitive des Euskariens-Basques: langue, poésie, moeur et caractère de ce peuple; introduction à son histoire ancienne et moderne (Primitive History of the Basque-*Euskariens*: Language, Poetry, Way of Life, and Character of This People; Introduction to Their Ancient and Modern History] (Bayonne: Jaymebon, 1847), 2, 75, 77–78, 80.

The Basques speak a language that they call *Eskuara, Euskera,* or *Uskara*, depending on the dialect: so the people living in the mountains call themselves *Eskualdun, Euskeldun,* or *Uskaldun*, to the exclusion of any other name, this being the only one used among the native speakers, to such an extreme that illiterate Basques are still unaware for the most part that their ancestors were ever known at any time in history by any name other than *Euskariens. Eskualdun*, in Basque definition, means "the man, or the people, who have or possess or speak the Basque language." In their language, the Basques use the word *Eskualherri* (land of *Eskuara* or the *Euskariens*) to designate all of the provinces of the territory that they occupy between Asturias, Old Castile, Aragón, Béarn, and French Gascony.

. . .

The name Iberia comes from the Ibero or Ebro River, just as [the word] Muscovite in French comes from Moscow. Does this mean that the Muscovites of Peter the Great were not the same people as the Russians of Emperor Nicholas? And because we commonly refer to them as

Russians and Muscovites, is it any less true that they speak a dialect of the Slavic language? Are they not true Slavs? In the same way, the Pyrenean Iberians, called Cantabrians, Vascons, Vascongados, Basques, speak Euskara and are Euskariens. But, says Mr. Du Mége, no author from antiquity has ever called the people of the mountains and their language by these names. Nothing could be truer; and not only the Greek and Latin authors, who had every good reason not to know them, have made the mistake of omitting them, but even Basque authors themselves, to the point that in the excellent *Dissertation* by the Abbot Darrigol, published in 1827 and laurelled by the Institute of France, that noun "Basque" [*Eskuara*] is not cited even once.

This little mystery demands an explanation. Authors and philologists of the mountains writing in Latin, Castilian, or French, always refer to the national language as Cantabrian, Vascon, Vascongade, Vascuense, and Basque; and it should be noted that in more than fifty volumes published over two centuries in Navarre and in Bizkaia, the true and popular name does not surface anywhere; it is not mentioned even once. In retaliation, in the oldest improvisations, in all the books written in Euskara, the original name is used exclusively, and the Latin, Roman, Castilian, and French names, which we call *edarien* [non-Basque], are proscribed.

. . .

The Euskariens, as a border population between two great Empires, Gaul and Spain, have always, ever since the invasion of the people from outside, spoken two and sometimes three languages in addition to the national language. Given the originality and eccentric character of the mountain language, it is conceivable that the Celts, the Gauls, the Phoenicians, the Greeks, the Romans, and all people of hyperborean origin, might have invented specific names to designate the Euskarien tribes. Thus the names Iberia, Cantabria, and Vasconia were admitted into the history to which the Euskariens, too poor, too occupied in war and agriculture, did not contribute any literature of their own. The Montagnards [mountainous people, namely Basques], to whom the languages of their confederates and their enemies were quite familiar, adopted without difficulty those exotic names. This was necessary, because they were unable to persuade foreign peoples to accept or use theirs. They would say, for example, using Latinate terms, Iberia, Cantabria, or Vasconia, to designate their own land, all the more willingly because the word *Eskualherri* [the Basque Country], complex in its meaning, is absolutely unsusceptible to declension.

. . .

The Euskariens, when they speak Latin, Castilian, Gascon, or French, always call themselves, even when speaking with each other, Iberians, Cantabrians, Vascones, Basques, Vascongados, and Vascos. And their glorious ancestors did almost the same thing, but not because they did not know their language, Euskara, and their legitimate name, *Eskualdun*. Even today, for the Montagnards, the names Zuberoa, Upper and Lower Navarre, Lapurdi, Gipuzkoa, Araba, and Bizkaia are lumped together in Latin, Castilian, Romance, and French as Iberia, Cantabria, Vasconia, the Basque Country, and the land of the Basques; but in the national language, in Euskara, the territory of the seven provinces reverts to what the entire southwestern region of Europe used to be called by the primitive Iberians, that is: the land of the Euskariens, *Eskual-Herria*!

61. Justo Barbagero—The Creation of the Diocese of Vitoria and the Basque Language

The political fragmentation of the Basque Country was traditionally linked to an even greater fragmentation in terms of ecclesiastical administration. Holding ourselves to the chronological period which this study comprises, namely that period between the sixteenth and the nineteenth centuries, the northern Basque Country was divided into three dioceses: that of Baiona, which included Lapurdi and part of Lower Navarre; that of Dax (in Landes, Gascony) which included the northern part of Lower Navarre; and that of Oloron (Béarn), which consisted of the towns of Zuberoa. As for the southern Basque Country, the diocese of Pamplona-Iruña included most of Navarre and the entire eastern part of Gipuzkoa, while that of Calahorra (La Rioja) included the Deba valley in Gipuzkoa, the entire central and eastern parts of Bizkaia, and almost the entire province of Araba. However, the western part of Bizkaia and some of the northeastern towns of Araba fell under the jurisdiction of the diocese of Santander. After 1785, Tudela (Tutera) in Navarre and the territory around it had its own bishop. Finally, the valleys of western Araba were part of the diocese of Burgos.

During the French revolutionary process in the late eighteenth and early nineteenth centuries, an effort was made to accommodate the new administrative reality of the departments with those of the dioceses, initially suppressing that of Baiona and keeping that of Oloron for all the departments of the Lower Pyrenees. Baiona was restored as a see in 1801, and after 1822, it comprised the entire department, namely, the three Basque territories plus Béarn. On the other side of the border, the reforms took a little longer. In the Concordat of 1851 between the Holy See and the Spanish state, the territorial realignment of the bishoprics was anticipated. Special priority and relative urgency were given to the Basque case (the bishopric of Ciudad Real was not established until 1876, for example, and that of Madrid-Alcalá in 1885), with the creation of a new diocese to include the three chartered territories of Araba, Gipuzkoa, and Bizkaia, with its see in Vitoria (Gasteiz), the capital of Araba. This diocese was inaugurated in 1862, and its first bishop was Don Diego Mariano Alguacil. In 1949, after the last Spanish Civil War (1936–39), Bizkaia and Gipuzkoa were declared "traitorous provinces," and among other repressive measures the Basque diocese was broken into three parts, with sees in Vitoria, Bilbao, and Donostia-San Sebastián.

The creation of the diocese of Vitoria had to be done at the cost of the parishes that were inserted between those mentioned earlier: specifically, 108 parishes would be eliminated from the bishopric of Pamplona-Iruña, which had nearly 120,000 parishioners; 101 parishes from the bishopric of Santander, with some 31,000; 34 from Burgos with 6,500; and 553 parishes from the diocese of Calahorra with 225,000, this latter one being by far the most severely affected. As one would imagine, there was considerable resistance by the ecclesiastical dignitaries of these bishoprics to the creation of the Basque diocese. Among these, the opinion expressed by Justo Barbagero, the abbot-elect of the collegiate Church of Santo Domingo de la Calzada (La Rioja), in a memoir sent to the Minister of Justice, on August 5, 1861, is of interest.

The difficulties which Barbagero enumerated as problematic for the constitution of the new miter in Vitoria were, in general, fairly inconsistent and spoke of the enormous population increase that would beset the city, the difficulties of communication in a mountainous country, and the lack of respect that the parishioners would have for a new see compared to the tradition and prestige of those in Pamplona-Iruña and Calahorra. But where the abbot truly came to the fore with arguments of substance was in the political consequences such a decision would entail. In general terms, he proceeded to emphasize the distinct *foral* character of the Basque territories, whose potential capriciousness regarding independence would be better left unstirred by even greater motives (in this case ecclesiastical) regarding Basque identity; in other words, it was better to keep them divided. But what is most interesting for our purposes is the clear identification Barbagero makes between language and politics. In his view, the main factor of national unity or disunity is the possession of one or several languages, and the creation of the Basque diocese would necessarily contribute to the revitalization of the Basque national language (which was in decline at the time), leading to the formation of a nationality distinct from the Spanish and encouraging political division.

Selected Text(s):

Justo Barbagero, *Memoria o consideraciones sobre la reunión de las tres Provincias Vascongadas en un solo obispado, con la silla episcopal en Vitoria* [Memoir or Considerations on the Merging of the Three Basque Provinces into a Single Bishopric, with Its Episcopal See in Vitoria] (5 August, 1861), Archive of the Ministry of Justice, no. 4027, cited in Francisco Rodríguez De Coro, "Un documento excepcional del Ministerio de Justicia contra la creación de la diócesis vasca, 1861" [An Exceptional Document of the Ministry of Justice Opposing the Creation of the Basque Diocese, 1861], *Scriptorum Victoriense* [On the Writers of Vitoria-Gasteiz] 25 (1978), 321–334.

The preceding observations are based on principles of law, equity, moral, and religious standards, and must not be ignored. The fourth and final pertains to the political order and is of such great importance that it merits more detailed treatment.

It is worth noting that, despite the passing of so many centuries since the Reconquest, the successive formation of the three kingdoms of Castile, Aragón, and Navarre, as well as their union in a single and indivisible monarchy of which the Basque provinces form an integral part, no effort has been made to establish in them an Episcopal see, or even to unite the three provinces into a single bishopric. This inaction cannot be ascribed to indifference on the part of their inhabitants, as if in ancient times they had been less religious and less patriotic than other Spaniards; nor to the lack of piety and zeal on the part of our Catholic monarchs, who have always been so generous in founding and endowing churches to promote the faith and attend to the spiritual needs of their subjects; nor to the fact that there were fewer obstacles of distance for the good government of those provinces by the bishops established in Castile; nor to any resistance of these people to give up or allot the necessary part of their territory to this purpose; nor, finally, to the lack of precedents for the establishment of new sees, in different epochs and for reasons that seemed to be even less justified. In the sixteenth century, the bishopric of Valladolid was established in a limited space with respect to the rights of nearby churches; with even more narrow constraints, that of Tudela in Navarre was constructed at the end of the last century; and that of Santander was established in the middle of that century with jurisdiction over a large part of Bizkaia and some towns in Araba. That would have been the opportune moment to try to establish a bishopric in the provinces if there had not been very powerful reasons not to do so—and even to close off forever the very possibility of doing so.

And these reasons could not have been other than the very ones now put forth for uniting the three provinces into a single bishopric: the fact that special legislative measures would be taken to guarantee equality in customs and traditions. This special legislation would give the three provinces a kind of independence, making their bond with Spain very precarious were the bonds linking them to the crown not strengthened by the canonical connection constraining them and making them dependent on Castile. This is not to suggest that we worry that their inhabitants would even consider the idea of rebelling against our kings and breaking the bonds that unite them to the noble Spanish nation; the honor and prestige they derive from those bonds are a sufficient guarantee of their loyalty for now; but governments must foresee and guard against contingencies of every kind that might come about in the future, such as a new dynastic challenge, a European war, or any other political challenge or dissidence that, igniting passions and blinding reason, might cause them to neglect or fail in their obligations. If the administrative independence and special laws they enjoy now were to be combined with a new spiritual and ecclesiastic independence, they would have everything they need to govern themselves and to be totally independent.

The extraordinary force of ecclesiastic dependence for the maintenance of the proper submissiveness of these provinces, and to make the very possibility of a permanent break with the Spanish monarchy unthinkable, was made evident during the last civil war [the first Carlist War]: with communications cut off with the capitals of their diocese, the exercise of Episcopal jurisdiction frustrated, and despite the provision by His Holiness of procedures authorizing the appointment of an apostolic delegate, even then the faithful inhabitants by force of habit and respect for their diocesan prelates chose to support them, and even without the need for Papal encouragement of a crusade, they doubted their own self-worth if they did not conduct themselves as usual.

Equality of customs and traditions: this is the principle being evoked at this moment for political annexations in violation of all law and justice, and by that same token differences in traditions and customs could be invoked as justification for separation. So instead of maintaining this difference of customs among the Basque peoples with respect to those of Castile and Navarre, efforts should be made to extend good customs and eradicate bad ones in all of the provinces, facilitating communication and interaction instead of raising barriers through the demarcation of a new bishopric. To achieve this goal (which our kings must have considered to be of grave importance) and to remove the main obstacle militating against the union of all the peoples into a single nationality, they have sought to limit the use of the Basque language, requiring that Castilian books be used for instruction in all schools, and using other means for making the use of this language universal. The clergy have contributed substantially to its adoption throughout the country because of the need to use it in their relations with the capitals of the dioceses and communication with their prelates. By persisting in these methods, and because of greater contact and familiarity with Castilians during the war, the Basque language had nearly disappeared; in entire regions bordering on Castile, they neither speak nor understand it. It is used with the same frequency as Castilian in towns inside the territory which have some degree of commercial activity; and reduced to its purity in the final entrenchments in the mountains and isolated farmsteads, it would soon die out by attrition if it were not revived by the establishment of a diocese embracing the three provinces with this very purpose in mind. If the Basques have a bishop who speaks their language, a municipal council and parishioners who speak their language, pastoral missions, sermons and books in their language, they will identify with it more and more. They will try to extend it throughout the boundaries of the three provinces, winning back the lost ground and making it their national language; and if the greater attachment is added to this, they would acquire their customs, traditions, and *fueros,* which to a certain extent authorize and sanction its use, we will have contributed to the formation in Spain of a separate nationality and a base for political separation for those who in the future may wish to invoke the principle of nationalities.

For these reasons, which the Government of His Majesty will be able to appreciate appropriately, the creation of an Episcopal see in Vitoria, or in any other place in the provinces from which the title of "Basque Bishop" can originate, is not to be recommended.

62. José María Iparraguirre Belardi

(Urretxu, Gipuzkoa, 1820 – Itsaso, Gipuzkoa, 1881)

Iparraguirre was a popular poet, a cider- and coffeehouse singer far removed from sophisticated literary circles, and fully immersed in the art of oral improvisation known as *bertsolaritza* [versifying]. His own life is a model of vagabondage and painful survival, always on the verge of economic ruin, incarceration, and exile, either for political reasons or as a social outcast: an individual, like all those of his class, who was intensely embarrassing to the authorities and to power of any kind. His parents were confectioners in Urretxu, but when Iparraguirre was a child, they moved to Madrid. However, at the tender age of thirteen, when the first Carlist War broke out, he returned to the Basque Country to enlist in the army of Don Carlos, becoming a member of his personal guard. After the Treaty of Bergara (1839), he decided to go into exile. First, he went to France, but in spite of his Carlist sympathies, he soon came under the influence of the (ultimately unsuccessful) 1848 liberal revolution. He spent his time singing the Marseillaise in cafes in the heart of the reactionary Second Empire, for which he was imprisoned and once again sent into exile. This time, he went to England, where he joined an opera company. Becoming even more politicized, he was imbued with the demand for recuperation of *foral* rights that was increasing at that time, and returned to Madrid. There, in 1853, he premiered one of his pro-*fueros* songs, the *Guernicaco arbola* (The Tree of Gernika), which won sudden and enormous popularity, becoming the de facto anthem of the *foral* movement as well as a national anthem par excellence. But when he began performing this anthem throughout the province of Gipuzkoa he was arrested and sent into exile in Santander. He subsequently moved on to Portugal and, later, to the Americas.

There he lived off and on in Argentina and Uruguay, and worked at a wide variety of jobs, including that of a shepherd. After the abolition of the *fueros* at the conclusion of the second Carlist War in 1876, he returned to the Basque Country. A legendary figure, his return voyage was financed by popular donation, and during his old age, he lived on a pension granted him by the Basque Provincial Governments.

His ideological position was somewhat surprising. In part, it was a straightforward product of his Carlist *foral* militancy, but it also displayed universal and fraternal ideas acquired during his experience in France, which were often contradictory to the former sympathies. What seems beyond all doubt is his practical defense of Basque culture. He performed his entire repertoire in Euskara, and linked the language to the maintenance of the traditional political-juridical order. He even went to the point of dedicating some of his songs to it, for instance *Biba Euskera!* (Long Live Euskara!), a song of pure glorification and apology, and *Arren, ez bedi galdu Euskera* (Never Let Euskara Die), a pathetic cry of alarm at the possible disappearance of the language. In these songs, in addition to references to the classic defenders of the language (Astarloa, Erro, and Larramendi, for example) he mentions Basque researcher José Francisco de Aizkibel (Azkoitia, 1798–1865) who became a well-known scholar during his life, especially by virtue of publishing a Basque to Castilian dictionary.

Selected Text(s):

Biba Euskera! [Long live Euskara!]; *Arren ez bedi galdu euskera* [Never Let Euskara Die], in *Jose Maria Iparragirre. Erro-urratsak* [Jose Maria Iparragirre: The Original Steps], ed. Gontzal Mendibil, vol. 1 (Igorre: Keinu, 1999), 279, 314.

Long Live Euskara!

There's a man in Spain
whom we must love;
he's Don Francisco Aizkibel,
Father of Basques.
He's a man of integrity
and wisdom;
let us pay homage
to our master.

For over twenty years
he's lived in Toledo,
and in all that time this son
of Izarraiz has never slept,
working on his books
night and day
to keep our beloved Euskara
from falling into oblivion.

Down with Arabic and Hebrew
and all the other languages,
my friends:
long live Euskara!

Cross on our chest,
flag in our hands,
let us sing to the heavens:
We are Basques!

To live in peace
in our mountains
we have to speak Euskara
in every council meeting.
Then the name of those who speak Basque
will win great renown
throughout the world
in centuries to come.

Never Let Euskara Die

Today we see Euskara dying away,
our beautiful, beloved language.
It's a shame our good Basque brothers
feel no shame!
Today we never hear them mention
Larramendi, Astarloa...
If you think about it,
nothing could be worse.

We've lost our way,
we've lost our language...
at this rate, in a hundred years
we'll have forgotten our name!
What were Erro and Aizkibel like?
No one remembers them now.
Our Euskara... alas!... If she dies
then we're not Basques any more!

How can we be silent or forgive?
In centuries to come
they'll be right to ask:
where are your traditions?
Sure, they're sorry, I mean...
any Basque with a sense of shame,
as our wisest men said
long ago.

Many wise men
in Paris and London
try to find old books
in Euskara...
[Louis] Lucien [Bonaparte] is there, restless prince
who's one of us now,
lover of all things Basque,
first among the wise.

For Christ's sake, my brothers,
don't let our Euskara die!

If we lose her... we're lost,
we and our sons.
So always speak in Euskara
old and young alike.
Don't let them say
we're Basques without a heart.

63. Nicolás Soraluce Zubizarreta

(Zumarraga, Gipuzkoa, 1820 – Donostia-San Sebastián, 1884).

During the first Carlist War, his family decided to send him to Argentina to keep him away from the trouble. There he devoted himself to a number of business matters. Although he returned to take up residence in Donostia, he maintained contact with Latin America, serving as Uruguayan consul there. He combined business affairs with public life (as lawyer for the General Councils of Gipuzkoa between 1851 and 1863) and with study and research, especially in history. In fact, Soraluce became one of the most rigorous and balanced historians of his era. He was one of the main experts of the time on the *foral* system, which bore fruit with the publication of an updated legislative compilation of Gipuzkoa: *Fueros de Guipúzcoa, títulos adicionales y consideraciones, reglamentos, sumario histórico* (*Fueros* of Gipuzkoa, Additional Titles and Considerations, Regulations, Historical Summary) (1866). However, his most famous works, also historical in nature, were *Historia de la M. N. y M. L. Provincia de Guipúzcoa precedida de la guía descriptiva y plano de la misma* (History of the M[ost] N[oble] and M[ost] L[oyal] Province of Gipuzkoa Preceded by the Descriptive Guide and Map of the Province) (1864) and the *Historia General de Guipúzcoa* (General History of Gipuzkoa) (1869).

A latecomer to the Basque-Iberian concept, the situation of the Basque language worried him, especially at a moment of clear retreat when the specter of its possible disappearance was becoming all too evident. His position coincided with that of the majority of liberal authors of the era: a language reduced to rural areas was incompatible with progress, so steam engines and their like would end up destroying it. Or, expressed another way, the rustic status of Euskara doomed it, and there was no possibility of developing it in the urban and industrial world.

LOS IBEROS Ó SEAN EUSKAROS

Y EL EUSKARA.

MEMORIA

PUBLICADA EN LOS NUMEROS 20 Y 21 DE LA REVISTA EUSKARA.

PAMPLONA:
IMPRENTA DE JOAQUIN LORDA,
Mercaderes, 19.
1879.

SELECTED TEXT(S):

Los iberos ó sean euskaros y el euskera. Memoria publicada en los números 20 y 21 de la Revista Euskara [The Iberians or Basques and Euskara: Memorandum Published in Numbers Twenty and Twenty-One of the *Euskara* Journal) (Pamplona: Joaquín Lorda, 1879); reprint, as "Memoria sobre la lengua vascongada leída en el Ateneo de San Sebastián el mes de octubre de 1879" [Memorandum of the Basque Language Read in the Athenaeum of San Sebastián in the Month of October 1879], in Juan Mañé y Flaquer, *El Oasis. Viaje al País de los Fueros* [Oasis: Journey to the Country of the *Fueros*], vol. 2, *Viaje por Guipúzcoa al final de su etapa foral (1876)* [Journey through Gipuzkoa at the End of Its *Foral* Period (1876)] (Bilbao: Villar, 1969), 449–450, 469–471.

Memorandum of Don Nicolás Soraluce on the Basque Langauge

Gentlemen:
At this time, I am going to keep the promise I announced and pledged myself to fulfill after my presentation before this Athenaeum during its meetings on the evenings of this last March 31 and April 4 on the topic introduced by the gentleman Don Joaquín Jamar, and which was discussed during that meeting and those preceding it, and which is the following:

> "Is it important to make an effort to preserve the Basque language?"

The person introducing this topic arrived at the following conclusion:

> "The Spanish Basque-Navarrese nation numbers approximately eight-hundred thousand inhabitants, of whom six hundred thousand speak Castilian, a relatively small number of these speak Basque as well, while the remaining two hundred thousand speak only Euskara. An effort should be made, therefore, not to impose the Basque language on the six hundred thousand Basque-Navarrese citizens, but to teach the smaller group to speak Castilian."

Concerning this specific conclusion of Mister Jamar, while accepting it as a topic for further discussion, I too expressed my opinion moments before Don José de Goicoa, President of the Section of Literature and Fine Arts, closed the debate, as described in Article 14 of the proceedings.

His opinion was the opposite of that of Mister Jamar and the gentlemen José Manterola, Andrés Egoscozábal, Serafín Baroja and the author of these lines, all of us participants in those debates.

In taking part in these debates on the aforementioned session of last April 4, and suggesting as a topic for the following academic term for those interested in expressing their written opinion pro or con, I offered a number of philological-historical-philosophical considerations, among them the idea that because this is the only provincial capital in which the Iberian or Basque language is still spoken, such a circumstance demanded that more consideration be given to the discussion.

I introduced Mister Jamar's conclusion as a written motion to be taken up in the meeting of this same Athenaeum on the evening of April 7; subsequently, as noted in Article 22 of the aforementioned Proceeding, the President approved the motion and the Athenaeum also approved it in one of the last meetings of the first Academic term.

Such are the antecedents of the question that will be the topic of my present address before this illustrious Athenaeum.

. . .

The Euskara Association of Navarre, in its literary contest celebrated last July in Elizondo, and by the distinguished Municipality of Donostia [San Sebastián] in that city this past September, both attracted many contestants, especially the September event in which thirty-three manuscripts of poetry and prose were submitted, in addition to the twelve Basque improvisational poets, and five others who served as judges.

Taking into account as well the contests, also in Euskara, from the other side of the [River] Bidasoa [that is, in the northern Basque Country] in previous years, thanks to Mister Antoine d'Abbadie, one of the most distinguished advocates of Basque culture, we have clear evidence that the Basque-Navarrese Country on both sides of the Bidasoa welcomes these literary award competitions celebrating the ancient and venerable Basque language, while at the same time, demonstrating the enthusiasm and desire for the cultivation of Euskara inspiring them.

If these interested parties were to abstain, either partially or completely, from participating in this project, then Gipuzkoa, alone or with the support of Donostia, should accept the cost of carrying it to its successful conclusion.

It is likely that this would involve little if any sacrifice, but even if this should turn out to be considerable, we should not be intimidated. We would be more than compensated by the proportionately enormous prestige it would bring to us among national and foreign corporations and linguists throughout the world now and in the future.

It is well known that once an Academy is constituted, the leadership responsible for its direction and successful operation is enormously important. Happily, our country boasts a man of scientific and general knowledge, as extraordinary as he is modest, who on the many occasions when he has been called on to demonstrate his skill in debate has always and everywhere succeeded in raising his flag atop the highest peak.

And so great was his reputation in this regard that in one of the capitals (the most important and the one most crucial to the glory of the Basque people), his talents having been acknowledged previously in the nation's capital, he was invited to apply as distinguished professor with almost certain prospects of successful candidacy.

There is no doubt that a majority of the intelligent and dedicated students of the Basque-Navarrese Country, who have over time shown their high regard for his candidacy, would happily lend their support to the achievement of the noble and illustrious purpose of such an endeavor.

Nor would the advocates of Euskara and Basque culture who have been made aware of his exceptional knowledge hesitate to offer their support, and others too will at the very least contribute their grain of sand or good will: I mean those of us approaching the age of sixty or who are even older.

And, how can we doubt that a Prince [Louis Lucien Bonaparte], who has for over a quarter of a century been engaged in a project as interesting as it is praiseworthy regarding Basque philology, all the while serving on numerous occasions as Maecenas, and who if he is noble by birth is no less distinguished for the excellence of his enlightenment, and whose innumerable translations, writings and editions that I cited in my *Catálogo de obras eúskaras* [Catalog of Basque Works], also appear, fully annotated, in the French edition of Humboldt's *Averiguaciones . . .* [Inquiries . . .]—how, I repeat, can we doubt that such a man would bring honor through his name, intelligence, and experience to matters in which his knowledge and love of Basque culture would equally lead us to consider the aforementioned gentleman, Abbadie?

Obviously, a positive recommendation might well be ventured about this.

Wars, the scourge of humanity diminishing man, always leave in their wake traces of unpleasant memory for the present and the future.

The kind of literary war I hope to inspire, based on what is yet unknown or shrouded in confusion in my chosen field of study, always begins by setting aside the current state of knowledge and, when it reaches its happy conclusion, it sheds light satisfying to everyone without prejudice to anyone.

From the province that was the protector of the wholesome tendency of this last effect, as well as others equally beneficent and plausible, as I have indicated, and which personify the basic arguments of Larramendi and Peñaflorida, respectively, we can only expect that it will now follow the same example and tendency it has followed for over a century in connection with this endeavor which, conferring as much glory as light, it will cause to shine on the Basque-Navarrese Country in particular.

Donostia, which also does not shrink away either when it comes to analogous cases, as it is now demonstrating on behalf of the improvement and enhancement of its people, also sought, in 1877, to glorify the memorable authors of those unforgettable sessions that took place in Zubieta in 1813, soon to be commemorated by a monument being erected in their honor, will grow brighter in prestige each day as those events recede into the past; yes, Donostia will honor its pledge.

It is now time, therefore, because it has been honored as province and as capital with the glory and opportunity to serve as the last refuge and repository of a monument from time immemorial, it is time for it [Donostia] to put into play all the resources needed to carry out without delay the project to which this chapter is dedicated.

These, then, are my thoughts, my wishes, my excitement.

Despite the thousands of years that have elapsed, however, this does not keep me from anticipating the end that awaits her as limit, as has befallen other languages, with little likelihood of surviving the fate that in nine or ten centuries has generally befallen the nation; not because she lacks elements that are as rich as they are philosophical, but because, first, as time goes by, the area in which the primitive language of Spain is spoken are more limited each day; because both inside and outside the primary schools the children have been forbidden to use it all during this century, because Spanish and French are gradually absorbing both sides of the Bidasoa, and finally, because two powerful means of communication are joining the fray: the steam engine and the electric telegraph, as I pointed out in chapter three of the second volume of my *Historia general de Guipúzcoa* [General History of Gipuzkoa].

But between this and our complicity and declaration of her possible and imminent disappearance, as some expect, there is an enormous distance.

No, let us not imitate that terrible ancient greeting which, in essence, embodies the pagan ideal, so justly rejected by Christianity, and which the gladiators, moments before going out to sacrifice their lives reciprocally in the stadiums of Rome for the entertainment of the public, pronounced these fateful words before Caesar: *Morituri te salutant* [We who are about to die, salute you].

Let us do just the opposite, sacrificing all of our resources so that our descendants will bless us, and in blessing us they can point to our legacy with noble pride, saying:

Here stands the most important monument of the Iberians or Basques, a righteous people who lived in great numbers thousands of years ago.

Donostia, October 24, 1879.

64. Antonio Cánovas del Castillo

(Málaga, 1828 – Santa Águeda [Arrasate-Mondragón], Gipuzkoa, 1897)

His father was a schoolteacher who would have preferred him to study science and business, but from an early age, he preferred literature. When he was still in his teens, he founded the weekly paper, *La Joven Málaga* (Young Málaga). When his father died, he moved to Madrid with the support of Serafín Estébanez Calderón (his mother's cousin), studying law and working in the offices of the Madrid-Aranjuez railroad. Early on, he achieved great renown as a writer, in three separate fields: literature (*La Campana de Huesca* [The Huesca Bell]), historical essay (*Historia de la decadencia de España, Estudios del reinado de Felipe V* [History of the Decline of Spain, Studies of the Reign of Felipe V]), and journalism, writing for *La Patria* (The Nation).

After 1854, however, his activities clearly shifted toward politics. An early member of *La Unión Liberal* or Liberal Party, he held a number of offices under Leopoldo O'Donnell, in the State Department, as well as those of Foreign Affairs and Treasury. He combined all of this with research into historical topics, which allowed him to establish a solid body of historiographical work, including *Relaciones de Roma y España en el siglo XVI, Bosquejo histórico de la Casa de Austria* (Relations between Rome and Spain in the Sixteenth Century, Historical Sketch of the Bourbon Dynasty). After the 1868 Revolution in Spain, the dethronement of Isabel II, and the various phases of the six-year upheaval—the brief reign of Amadeo of Savoy and the equally short-lived (1873–74) First Republic—Cánovas created a revised constitutional formula for the country based on the British bicameral system, imposing a mathematical revolving rhythm to the exercise of power. The fundamental objective of this peaceful alternation between two powerful liberal parties—termed Conservative and Liberal—was to avoid the direct intervention by the army in politics through the proclamation of decrees, as had been the habitual practice until then. After 1892, the political situation became extremely complex: in Catalonia, autonomist and Anarchist movements, through both social and direct action, challenged the power of the Spanish state from within; while externally, the remnants of the Spanish Empire in Cuba and the Philippines were dismantled after the intervention of the United States in the Spanish-American War in 1898. The iron hand exercised by Cánovas against the Anarchist movement, with exemplary executions of militant anarchists in Montjuich (Barcelona), made him the target of this movement. As a consequence, while vacationing in the summer spa of Santa Águeda, near Arrasate-Mondragón in Gipuzkoa, he was assassinated by the Italian anarchist Miquele Angiolillo.

His relationship with the Basque Country is important, if only because he was head of the government that made the decision to decree the abolition of the *fueros* of Bizkaia, Gipuzkoa, and Araba in 1876. His ideas on the Basque Country, its language, and its culture, were reflected in the extensive prologue he contributed to Miguel Rodríguez Ferrer's book *Los Vascongados. Su país, su lengua . . .* (The Basque Provinces: Their Country, their Language . . .) (1873), at the height of the second Carlist War when the First Republic was still functioning.

Selected Text(s):

Prologue to *Los Vascongados. Su país, su lengua y el Príncipe L. L. Bonaparte, con ilustraciones y comprobantes sobre sus antigüedades, sus principales nombres históricos, su literatura euskara, su bibliografía vasca, sus artistas y obras de arte, su música, sus danzas, sus supersticiones, su organización social antigua y moderna, condición de sus respectivas clases, sus Fueros, carácter que estos presentan y perduración de sus partidos actuales, con el influjo que tuvo este país en nuestras conquistas y descubrimientos ultramarinos* [The Basque Provinces: Their Country, Their Language and the Prince L. L. Bonaparte, with Illustrations and Proof of Their Antiquities, Their Principal Historical Names, Their Literature Written in Euskara, Their Basque Bibliography, Their Artists and Works of Art, Their Music, Their Dances, Their Superstitions, Their Ancient and Modern Social Organization, the Condition of Their Respective Classes, Their *Fueros* and the Influence These Have on Basque Character, and the Survival of Their Current Parties, as Well as the Influence this Country Had on Our Conquests and Discoveries Overseas], by Miguel Rodríguez Ferrer (Madrid: J. Noguera, 1873), xii–xiv, xxix–xxx.

I believe a day will come when those honorable provinces acknowledge that in their current relations with the other provinces of Spain they are unintentionally violating the clearest juridical principles. Forming a gradual and successive alliance over time for the providential purpose of constituting state and nation, this does not imply an obligation on the non-Basque regions of Spain to remunerate with the profits of their own labor the general services which their privileged and exempt brothers need and require neither more nor less than they do. And it is even less appropriate that the other Spaniards should be considered to be under a perpetual obligation to risk their lives in defense of the moral and material interests, which the Basques enjoy equally through the state or common nation, unless this is a mutual relationship with equal obligations for all. It is undoubtedly true that, over time, they have been granted systems of obligations that were from the outset unilateral and perpetually advantageous to one region of the country; but they have been equally burdened with something far worse, servitude and slavery. Today, such obligations are not tolerated, but neither are civil and public privileges; and my reasons for saying this are not particular to one school of thinking or another, but based on principles unanimously accepted today by civilized peoples, whatever their political perspective.

But nothing I have just said about privileges extends to the local autonomy, to any specific administrative regime, to any internal organ, in short, to any of the three Basque provinces. Far from wanting such institutions to be eliminated from there, I would like to see them extended, if possible, to the rest of Spain. The local freedoms of the Basques, like all those engendered and created by history, benefit those who enjoy them, and do not harm anyone, unless it is regarded as harmful because of the righteous envy it arouses in others. In this regard, I am in complete agreement with the opinions held by my distinguished friend Don Miguel Rodríguez-Ferrer, in the book for which I write these pages. And with that debt of conscience and obligation paid in full, I am entitled to give free rein from now on to the vital affection inspired in me by the land, the memories, and even the *fueros* themselves, to the extent that they are the product of local legislation and above all the patriarchal and industrious customs of those noble provinces.

. . .

The Basque (or Bizkaian, or whatever you want to call him) being enclosed in his solitary language, which is totally unknown in other nations, and being even more isolated in his impassable mountains, has until now defied the impetuous current of new ideas, not allowing them to infiltrate except slowly and gradually into his mind, and only then after having carefully digested and assimilated them. The same can be said for his language which, obeying the necessities of the times, has allowed some new words into its vocabulary, from Latin, German, Spanish, French, and probably Celtic and other even older languages; but only through the very narrow opening in the shutter that is cautiously opened at nightfall, like one of those small doors in a fortress, in such a way that in its outline, foundation, and general profile the structure of that language remains unchanged and integral.

For some time now, the proud modern mind, over-stimulated by such mysteries, and even offended by such resistance, has been employing the powerful means now available to it to persuade that remarkable race—which defends its mountains from attack the way it defends its language from foreign ideas—to surrender or at the very least reveal to the insatiable curiosity of the epoch the secret of its origin, its earliest connections, and its successive interactions with other races over the long centuries before the world suddenly became aware of its existence. Vain endeavor! Linguistic research into the historical classification of the Basque language or Euskara could be summed up today in this conclusion, which as everyone knows originated with the original wise man, to wit: "Know that nothing can be known." And the worst part is that there is no shame at all in naively confessing that about the Basque language. No one knows if it comes from the north or from the south; no one knows if its source is Aryan or Semitic, or whether it is totally original and autonomous; and although everyone persists in borrowed words in it, every day less and less is known about its origin and lineage. Where linguistics cannot go, experimentally, neither can induction.

. . .

Although those peaceful Iberian tribes lived apart in this way from all outside influences, generally having no knowledge of warring peoples, or being understood by them, kings, warlords, and entire nations passed by their mountains without stopping, caring little about such a land, inhospitable at the time, or the people who lived there. It is well known that neither the Romans nor the Visigoths, nor the Arabs or even the first Christian kings, felt the least temptation to settle there and chop their way through those forests, axe in hand, to rip them out and steal a few feet of planting soil from the rocks that barely nourish the roots, when there were such large quantities of good soil by the Ebro River, and even more and richer soil from the Ebro on southward. So, the Basques lacked everything needed to fight wars, not to mention their lack of inclination to do so.

In short, as I see it, there never was any true political independence in the Basque provinces, as has been and still is claimed by their natives, because they accepted Romans and Visigoths without resistance as their masters, as well as those early Christians who founded kingdoms in the mountains to fight against the Moors; no one ever even conceived of the idea of oppressing and tyrannizing them, or trying to seize their narrow, stony precincts, their lumber, their fish, or even their totally patriarchal form of government, which they had already adopted when feudalism appeared with the emergence of the ambitious monarchies of the Middle Ages. And if from that time and through the centuries they have indeed preserved intact their language, their customs, and the purity of their Iberian race, the reason for this is clear to me, and that is because they have never drawn attention or attracted to themselves the implacable iron of the conquerors, for their power, their riches, or even their arrogance. I will say more, and that is that if the Basques had been as unruly through time as they seem to be now, not only would they have felt the iron hand of the conquerors in centuries of oppression and barbarism, but that even in the modern age, and under the scepter of the Spanish Monarchy, they would not have been as fortunate as they have been; rather, their privileges would have suffered the same fate as those of Aragón, Catalonia, and even Navarre, which are certainly not provinces lacking in resolve and courage. If the Basques had demonstrated the dangerous and anti-Spanish independence of Navarre in the days of Fernando the Catholic; had they, in the days of the House of Austria, generously offered asylum and protection from arrest to ministers who opposed the king, such as Antonio Pérez; or risked themselves as Catalonia did, accepting a foreign king and protecting dynasties in opposition to the majority of the national vote, which was the case of the dynasty of Austria at the beginning of the previous century; then they might well swear that their particular pacts of alliance with Castile or their armed forces were insufficient to preserve intact their current privileges during the unitary and leveling revolution that has been underway in the peninsula for centuries, for the purpose of constituting one state and one Spanish nation. Some of the services Basques now deny, they had already denied in those times; but on the other hand, they formerly offered other services that they refuse to offer today, manifesting above all a conduct that is irreconcilable with order and peace.

65. Victor Bernard Derrecagaix

(Baiona, Lapurdi, 1833 – 1915)

Although he was born in Baiona, he was originally from Sohüta (Chéraute) in Zuberoa. He studied in Senpere (Saint-Pée-sur-Nivelle) in Lapurdi, and then in Paris. He later became a professional soldier, reaching the rank of brigadier general, and took part in the Crimean War (1854–56), in the campaign to put down the uprising in Algeria, and in the Franco-Prussian war of 1870. While in Africa, he had specialized in the study of topography and geography and later, in 1867, after transferring to the French division headquarters in Paris, he initiated a literary career parallel to his military service. His work included different aspects of his profession, such as recording military campaigns, military biographies, discussing military strategy, and applied cartography, and he also wrote *Mes souvenirs* (My Memoirs) (1921). From 1887 on, he taught in the Advanced War College. Later he dedicated himself to something that was of profound interest to him and that formed an essential part of the educational heritage of the military officers of his day: cartography and geodesics. He was also appointed director of the Army's Cartographic Service.

We are interested here in an 1876 article on the Basque people in which he posits Basque originality in three fundamental aspects: language, physical anthropology, and geography, three pillars that confer on this people Asian connections that can be traced back to remote antiquity. Elsewhere, he responds with geographical arguments (although without naming it) to the 1867 article by Elisée Reclus predicting the disappearance of the Basque people. Derrecagaix admits that, given the historical dynamic they are living, inevitable changes will occur, among them the removal of the *fueros*, but that this should, in no way, imply the disappearance of the people themselves. To defend this hypothesis, he contrives a geographic argument related to the conditioning character of the environment: that mountain people tend to reinforce their identity and maintain their independence, unlike the people of the plains; thus, their sense of individuality keeps them from being swallowed up by other communities.

Selected Text(s):

"*Notice sur les Basques*" [Note on the Basques], *Bulletin de la Societé de Géographie* [Bulletin of the Geographical Society] 11 (1876), 401–38.

Finally, the Basques have a separate language, which is not a regional dialect or a language derived from any specific languages, but a language complete in itself, with combinative characteristics, which in other respects has certain analogies (of which we will speak later) with certain languages of Asia, and above all, with dead languages.

All of these circumstances make of them a kind of exception, in the sense that they arouse the curiosity of scholars and lead their investigations toward a past that the night of time enshrouds in darkness.

In effect, where do these men come from, whom destiny relegated to the confines of two large countries, whose character and customs surprise us and whose language bears no resemblance to that of any other people? This is the problem that, gradually, contemporary science investigations have had to address.

. . .

A moment's reflection suffices to see that the opinions expressed constitute an important body of facts, some representing perceptible realities, others remaining in a state of simple hypothesis. The latter can however acquire a certain level of probability, paving the way to convictions that could ultimately prove to be true.

These facts are of three kinds: some derive from linguistics; others involve the physical characteristics of the Basque race, subjected to rigorous analysis by anthropologists; some are provided by geology. So then, the source of these observations inspires a certain level of confidence.

. . .

1) Facts relative to the origin of the Basques, derived from linguistics and corroborated by history and geography.

The Basques are descendants of the Iberians.

The Iberians were a great people who came to Europe in an era considered as the most ancient in historical times.

They occupied Spain and, probably, the south of Gaul and the large western islands of the Mediterranean, and perhaps North Africa.

When the Phoenicians explored the Mediterranean basin, they confirmed the existence of Iberians on the peninsula. These explorations took place between the nineteenth and the thirteenth centuries before Christ.

The traditions of this epoch tell us that they arrived by way of North Africa.

The numerous traces of their language discovered by the ancient peoples of this region and of Egypt make us suspect that they had been there for a long time and in an epoch before the most ancient Egyptian dynasties; in other words, more than 2,400 years before Christ.

Their language is mixed, in some locutions, with the ancient dead language of the first Brahmins, which places its origin on the high plains of central Asia, not far from Northern Hindustan, and demonstrates its kinship with the most ancient Hindu dynasties. Chronology places the existence of the latter around the year 3,000 before Christ.

2) Facts relative to the origin of the Basques, derived from anthropology.

A race with a brachicephalic skull inhabited Europe before the Indo-European races who now occupy it (history records the presence of the latter in Greece twenty centuries before Christ).

The Basques are descendants of that race; but their skulls show signs of admixture with the races of North Africa.

According to the classification of [Jean Louis Arman de] Quatrefages, the Chude and Caucasian sub branches of the Halophile branch of the white, or Caucasian, stem also show a resemblance to the same race.

This means that the trace is picked up again in Finland, among the Estonians; in the region of Orenburg, among the Votyaks; in northeastern Siberia, among the Chukchi; in Georgia and Circassia, among the Georgians and the Cherkess people; finally in North America, among the inhabitants of the countries near the Pacific as far as Mexico.

Basques, like these Finnish and Caucasian groups, probably came from the high plains of central Asia.

As for the data provided by geology, they establish, simply, even in the Basque Country itself, the existence of a race more ancient than that preceding them, who lived in the Stone Age and were contemporary with the reindeer era.

In summation, it seems to us that the previous presentation of studies and observations is sufficiently conclusive to provide serious evidence about the past and the origin of the Basques. For us, this evidence can be stated as follows:

The contemporary French Basques settled to the north of the Pyrenees only at the end of the sixth century A.D.

They are descendants of the Iberians who formerly occupied Spain, and who were there ten centuries before Christ and spoke Basque.

These Iberians belonged to a race that inhabited Europe before the Indo-European peoples, and who arrived there as a consequence of emigrations from central Asia, as did those who came after them.

A number of signs allow us to further suppose that the emigrations of the Iberians came from North Africa, and that they were interrupted because of the establishment of settlements that endured for long periods.

Let us add that the migrations of a people can be considered as evidence of a conquering power or of a need for expansion determined by the search for a comfortable way of life obliterated by circumstances. However, the perfection of the language reveals a rather advanced level of civilization.

It would seem, in our opinion, that before their tribes inhabited the European lands, the ancestors of the Iberians must have constituted a strong and numerous population in central Asia, which, because of its position, had contact with peoples of the Arian race who were their neighbors. Hence the analogies between Basque and Sanskrit.

We can only hypothesize about the chronological date of the existence of this population, and yet it has been established that they were in Europe more that twenty centuries before Christ, and that the language with which Basque has the closest analogy was spoken in the north of Hindustan more than three thousand years before our era.

From all of the preceding, it can be deduced that the Basques are, at least along with the Estonians and some tribes from the Caucasus, the most ancient peoples of Europe.

To conclude, it remains to be seen if they are destined to disappear, as some authors claim, and if their language will inevitably be lost and converted in the near future into a dead language, the final vestige of our earliest existence.

Concerning this matter, it is difficult even for the most erudite scholars to life up the veil of the future. The Basques are already disappearing, some people say. This is not our opinion.

Emigration can reduce the population of this race; their relations with neighboring peoples can gradually increase the fusion of races. All of this is possible, but there is a powerful factor that militates against their disappearance. I am speaking of their geographical isolation. Only the peoples of the plains intermingle in the bosom of conquering nations or human groups that surround and penetrate them.

In contrast, races of identical origin whom destiny isolated in mountainous regions, even those most accessible, preserve an indelible seal and forge an unbreakable resistance and vitality against any fusion with their neighbors. This is something that is repeated in all corners of the world. The Swiss, the Tyroleans, the Montenegrins, and the Afghans, have always preserved an autonomy, an individuality all their own. This is because of the difficulty of communication in mountainous countries, to the pride, the love of independence that long residence in a place develops, to physical strength, to the moral value which climate, the ruggedness of the terrain, the dangers of existence, and the customs derived from them, give to people living in such regions. There is in their lives an isolation against the forces of nature, a sentiment of individuality as a people and as a country that preserves them not only from the possibility of absorption but also from excessively frequent contact. This is how the Basque lives, and this will suffice to preserve his character and his qualities indefinitely.

There will be changes, undoubtedly; and without going too far, it is probable that the Spanish Basque will lose, as a consequence of this last war [the second Carlist War], what remains of his ancient privileges, which are in any case incompatible with the demands of modern legislation. But it should not be forgotten that if the Spanish Basque has preserved until now certain special rights, the same is not true of the French Basque. Integrated, in effect, for almost a century into our national life, the latter has given much proof of cooperation and adhesion to our beloved country, as have his fellow countrymen. In the navy, in the army, in politics, he has had his representatives who have served the commonwealth generously. And yet, despite this merging of his existence with the nation he has preserved his personality and the original seal of his race. Thus, it can be affirmed that if civilization sometimes destroys the individuality of peoples, this only happens when it comes in contact with societies that are too backward and which adopt its vices without having the resources to resist them. When, on the other hand, it works its influence on a population that is mature enough to receive its benefits, civilization can only better it. The disappearance of such a population, if it occurs, should not be attributed to anything more than a slow action of time, favored by circumstance and by geographic conditions.

There is, then, no reason to fear that our Basques will disappear little by little and gradually lose the characteristics that are innate to them. Everything leads us to believe that they will go on living in their mountains; there they will maintain their love for the land of their ancestors, for the home in which they were born, for their vibrant language, their traditional dress, the exalted virtues of their ancestors—in short, for everything that reminds them that they are descendants of a noble race and that, before they were French or Castilian, they were for centuries the people called *Eskualdunac.*

66. Juan María Eguren Múgica

(Elgeta, Gipuzkoa, (?) 1828 – Vitoria [Gasteiz], Araba, 1880)

There is some question as to whether he was born in Arrasate-Mondragón or Elgeta. He represents the perfect model of the teacher devoted to extending the use of the Castilian language throughout the Basque Country (although particularly in Gipuzkoa) by means of primary schools. He was a teacher and education inspector, first in Gipuzkoa and then in Araba. He published a *Método práctico para la enseñanza del castellano* . . . (Practical Method for Teaching Castilian . . .) intended for use in schools predominantly attended by children whose maternal language was Basque. Eguren's philosophy differed from that of his predecessors, for although the fundamental objective of Pascual Iturriaga and Luis Astigarraga was to save the Basque language by means of bilingual instruction, Eguren essentially advocated the necessity of knowing Castilian and extending it to all citizens, the fate of the Basque language being of secondary importance. For Eguren, the intellectual progress of the young was inevitably linked to the dominant official language, and it was inconceivable to him that this could be achieved through the means of a minority and rural language, such as Basque; he would probably have been quite surprised if he had had the opportunity to see physics textbooks or the classics of philosophy translated into Euskara that were to be published a century later.

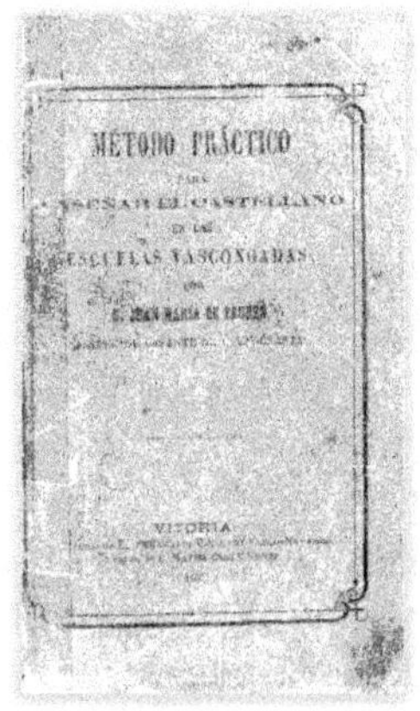

MÉTODO PRÁCTICO

ENSEÑAR EL CASTELLANO

ESCUELAS VASCONGADAS

VITORIA

Selected Text(s):

Método práctico para la enseñanza del castellano en las escuelas vascongadas [Practical Method for Teaching Castilian in Basque Schools] (Vitoria: Semanario Católico Vasco-Navarro, 1867), v–ix, xi–xiv.

Prologue

The importance and even urgent necessity that exists to teach the Castilian language in the schools of Gipuzkoa is universally acknowledged today; consequently, we will offer only a few remarks on this matter, to persuade those who might not yet be totally convinced of this truth.

The vast majority of the children who attend the schools of our country do not understand Castilian because in rural schools, which are the ones that make up most of the Gipuzkoan community, with few exceptions, only Basque is spoken, and even in the more important towns, the Castilian language is still not generally used except among sophisticated people with more advanced education. Therefore, a large proportion of the people in Gipuzkoa usually speak Basque, and consequently, this is the first language the children learn.

It turns out, then, that when they begin to attend school they do not understand Castilian well, and because this is the language in which they learn to read, write, and all the other disciplines, except for Christian doctrine, they do not understand what they are reading and studying, and their intellectual development, where true learning lies, is extremely slow. This explains why teachers in the Basque schools have to work so hard at their painful mission and are so often frustrated by not achieving satisfactory results no matter how hard they work; consequently, public education does not succeed as it should.

It is beyond all doubt, then, that if public education is to progress successfully along the path it has to traverse to reach the goal which the demands of the era have laid out for it, the teaching of the Castilian language must take precedence over all other instruction. Otherwise, not only does education suffer because this circumstance inevitably makes it more difficult, but the people in the towns do not acquire a liking for it because no one likes what they do not understand, and this contributes strongly to the maintenance of the status quo which we must overcome by every means available to us if humanity is to fulfill the high purpose of the perfection of their moral condition.

But it is not only in the schools that Castilian is needed, because the child who attends school will tomorrow be attending classrooms to pursue a career, and will later be practicing a trade or craft of some sort which will oblige him to be in constant contact with persons foreign to the country, or will go off to distant lands to make his fortune or to acquire the means to make a living, which the poverty of the native land and other circumstances make it difficult for him to attain.

. . .

Even the farm workers who never venture beyond the narrow confines of their farmstead, and who consequently have less contact with people who generally speak Castilian and therefore think they do not need to learn it, are more and more frequently forced to find translators to help them read a letter from an absent son, or a receipt or some other document they have to consult, just as when, on leaving their village to conduct business in the city or attend to other matters that inevitably arise in the normal course of life, they have to deal with functionaries or persons who do not understand Basque.

Finally, those who do not understand Castilian find themselves deprived of one of the most powerful tools for intellectual progress—reading; consequently, if for the successful performance of their work, or to make progress in any art or craft, they want to consult a work that deals with such materials, they also lack this tool, because nothing is written in Basque. Outside the tiny confines of our country, this language is of no use, so those who do not speak or understand Castilian are foreigners in their own country.

. . .

Method

that must be followed in the Basque Schools
in order to teach Castilian to the children
and how to use this book to achieve this end

It being the case that the teaching of Castilian must precede all other instruction in the schools for the children of our country so they can benefit from the instruction they will receive later in various disciplines, it is beyond doubt that the teacher must allot a certain amount of time and work on this task each day in the school curriculum.

It might well be the case that in some communities it will be necessary to devote more time to this objective than in others, because in rural towns, consisting of more or less isolated farmsteads, towns without streets, as they say, Castilian is much less common and less used than in more important towns that, because of their location, or the industry in which their inhabitants work or other circumstances, have more active and frequent contact with those who speak this language. For this reason, only the teacher, being aware of the special circumstances of the community in which he lives, can determine precisely the amount of time he needs to devote to the exercises that we are going to review and how much or how little importance to give them, although we are convinced that they will be useful even in large towns where the children speak Castilian, because it is obvious that they are unaware of most of the words they use.

So to get them to learn this language in the schools, the old methods are inadequate. They used to forbid the children from speaking Basque by giving a ring to anyone who violated this rule and punishing the child who had the ring in his possession at the end of the week. And because at the same time they usually made no effort to teach them to speak Castilian in the school, it turned out that there were always children punished on Saturdays because no matter how hard the child tried to keep from breaking the rule, it was impossible for him to avoid it.

Let us then consider the method that should be used in the schools to teach Castilian.

. . .

At the same time that we are using this method to attempt to teach Castilian in the school, it is also necessary that this language be spoken in it routinely and that Basque be used only when it is absolutely necessary to explain something to the children, because otherwise our efforts to achieve this goal will be undermined.

The children can also be motivated in other ways to get used to speaking Castilian outside the school, and one way is to dictate two or three sentences to those in the fourth section on Saturday so that on Monday they can bring them to class translated and written, offering a small prize to the one who does best in this task. By this and other strategies that occur to the teacher, much can be accomplished. We are not unaware that part of this effort is wasted when dealing with communities where almost no one speaks Castilian, for in such places the child does not hear this language until he returns to school, and because most of the time he is away from school, the teacher's work is made even more difficult.

In these places, the results will be naturally more gradual and the problem more difficult, but by no means impossible, because no matter how frequently we tell ourselves that it is, there's an immense distance from difficulty to impossibility.

...

Here are the conclusions that follow what we have said so far:

That the teaching of Castilian in the Basque schools should be considered one of the crucial elements of the program.

That it is important to leave room in the scheduling of time and work for the purpose of this endeavor.

That to achieve this, it will be important to group the children into four large sections that can be subdivided into the necessary groups without any of them being older than ten.

That each one of the groups of the first section should focus on committing to memory the first part of this method that covers the Basque to Castilian dictionary, either in its entirety or just the part which the teacher believes is most important and necessary; the second section should do the practical exercises on the declinations included in the second part of this method; the third section should focus on the conjugation exercises that constitute the third part; and the fourth, the translation exercises that cover the last part of this method.

67. Elisée Reclus

(Sainte-Foy-la Grande, Gironde, 1830 – Thourout, Belgium, 1905)

Elisée Reclus was one of the most interesting French geographers of the nineteenth century, with two vast and ambitious works that complement each other: *Géographie Universelle* (World Geography) (1875–1894) and *L'Homme et la Terre* (Man and Earth) (1905–1908). A member of the First International and a militant anarchist, he was condemned for his participation in the Paris Commune (1871) and was saved from prosecution thanks to pressure on his behalf from the world scientific community. The nucleus of his work is based on the relation between nature and society. His analyses focused on the search for equilibrium between man and the environment, the class struggle, and the sovereign will of the individual. He conjoined a deep respect for minority cultures and nationalities and a fierce critique of imperialism, with a confidence in the fusion of the races in a common project, emphasizing what united people over what separates them.

He focused on the Basque case, which for him constituted a paradigm of a distinct and magnificent traditional culture based on respect, equality, independence, resistance to feudal and monarchical oppression, individual rights and freedoms, and a particular culture whose language was its most outstanding feature. Of course, Reclus linked the Basque language and culture to the traditional peasant world, finding no place for it in industrial civilization, and thus regarded it as fated to disappear under the wheels of the locomotive, the *avant garde* of progress. The approaching ethnic and cultural fusion that Reclus announced would imply the loss of language and nationality for the Basque people as the price for becoming integrated into a new project for universal progress.

SELECTED TEXT(S):

"Les Basques. Un peuple qui s'en va" [The Basques. A Vanishing People], *Revue de deux mondes* [Two Worlds Journal] 68 (March 1867), 1; reprint, as "Los vascos. Un pueblo que se va por Eliseo Reclus (1867)" [The Basques: A Vanishing People, by Elisée Reclus (1867)], trans. and ed. "Martín de Anguiozar" [pseud.], *Revista Internacional de los Estudios Vascos* 20 (1929), 71–72.

Only recently has the existence of their language been threatened with extinction again. Administration and political centralization, industry, commerce, social mobility—everything, even advances in education, is converging against them to suffocate their noble language.

Anyway, it is not through violence that French and Spanish are replacing Basque; they conquer the country, but without annexing successively the villages closest to the borders into their realm; only here and there do they seize a few farms that pass through their hands as purchases. All around the Basque language, as around all the dialects spoken in France, the ideal limit remains the same, but nonetheless, the language is perishing. Modified by a constant phenomenon of intussusception, it mixes with foreign words that are incompatible with its genius, it loses its elegant turns of phrase and tries to accommodate itself more and more to the spirit of the foreigners who come to settle in the country; it continuously loses its originality and gradually becomes a patois. Every highway that penetrates into Basque territory also drills a hole into the language itself. Serving as agents for merging populations as well as a means of transport for merchandise, the railroads from Baiona [Bayonne] to Gasteiz [Vitoria], from Bilbao to Miranda, from Altsasu [Alsasua] to Pamplona [Iruña], exert the most sinister influence on the purity of the language, and soon, the locomotives on the lines of the Aldude region [Les Aldudes], passing through the most remote valleys of the Basque Country, will be even more terrible machines of destruction for Euskara. Sooner or later, the Basque Countries on both sides of the Pyrenees, completely crisscrossed in every direction by lines of communication, will belong to foreigners as much as to the natives themselves, and the latter, obliged to learn two languages at once, will end up abandoning the one that is least useful.

Although Basque patriots naturally have good reason to complain about the inexorable necessity of things, it is also true that each new advance will be fatal for the maintenance of the dialects of Euskara that are spoken on both sides of the Pyrenees. The thing that most effectively now protects the Basque against the encroachment of French and Spanish is the total ignorance in which the people remain even today. The inhabitants of some of the steep ravines of the mountains have no curiosity at all about the outside world, and current events scarcely register in their communities. They do not read newspapers; they never open a book, except for a collection of prayers or an almanac bought at a fair now and then. A large number of children do not even attend primary school, and the teacher who teaches them French or Spanish has to use a somewhat mixed dialect of Euskara. You can imagine what the state of public education is in a country in which parents, frustrated at having a lazy or stupid son who is not even capable of becoming a good worker, console themselves with a saying that has become proverbial: "We'll make a priest or a schoolteacher out of him!" Fortunately, it will not be long before knowledge becomes accessible to those people who are by nature so mentally keen and expansive. In this century of prodigious activity, in which the "struggle to survive" dooms those who fall behind, the Basques too will learn to march at an ever more rapid pace, but it will be at the cost of their nationality and their very language. Nothing will remain of their magnificent language, one of the wonders of the past, but lexicons, grammars, a few pastoral odes, badly written modern tragedies, and songs of debatable antiquity.

As if they sought to hasten the imminent disappearance of this distinct group that still constitutes a race within the human race, Basques are emigrating in great numbers, leaving behind empty places that are then partially occupied by people from Béarn, Frenchmen, and Spaniards.

. . .

For the past thirty years, the Basques have set their sights on the New World; that is, within the space of a single generation one quarter of the able-bodied men have abandoned their native country. Each year, despite the wars and revolutions in the provinces of River Plate, the flow of emigration continues ever more rapidly, and in certain villages of the Pyrenees, it bodes to become a veritable flight. Is it conceivable, when the nation is vanishing, that the language, divided anyway into several dialects that are very different from each other could resist the pressure from two invading languages that are laying siege to it? Also, six hundred thousand, which is the number of Basques who are estimated to speak their mother tongue, is an exaggeration, and this will be greatly reduced in the near future. To conclude, Euskara will be erased from among the languages of Europe just as Cornish, Erse [Irish Gaelic], Manx, and Welsh were and then, along with the language, the ancient customs and vestiges of ancient nationality will also disappear.

Certainly, on contemplating the disappearance of this last surviving group from the ancient Iberian world, it is impossible to keep from feeling a sense of sadness, because among the human races, Basques were truly one of the most noble and in many aspects, their social state was even superior to ours. This is in no way a paradox: the history and laws of the Pyrenees offer clear evidence of the preeminence, which their rectitude, their generosity, their passionate love for independence, and their respect for the individual gave them, over other neighboring societies. Unique among all the peoples of Southern Europe, the Basques knew how to make themselves respected by the Romans, and they never became their slaves; they made their way through those long and sorrowful centuries of the Middle Ages without ever allowing themselves to be dishonored by servitude. The wretched and barbaric serfs who lived all around them, convinced in their shameful abjection that freedom was a privilege of the nobility, considered them gentlemen, and in truth, all Basques were noble, as much and more than the haughty barons of the courts of France and Spain, because their rights were not dependent on a master, the least infringement of these being subject to immediate retaliation. If they had sovereigns, at least they forced them to meticulously observe their sworn oath, and on more than one occasion, they made it their duty to apply the death penalty stipulated by their local constitutions against those in violation. Masters of themselves, they carefully abstained from meddling in the affairs of their neighbors. If the King of Castile or France invited them to follow him, they first ascertained whether the war was legitimate, and if it seemed unjust to them, not a single mountain man left his valley. Although the history of Europe was one long series of assassinations, they lived in peace; each year the districts situated on opposite sides of the Pyrenees pledged perpetual friendship to one another, and their ambassadors, each it turn, solemnly placed a symbolic stone on a pyramid constructed by their ancestors in the middle of the pastures near the port.

All of those small republics, whose isolation would have made them easy prey for conquerors, were fraternally united in a grand federation, and each of them was pledged to "sacrifice all their property and their lives" to maintain the common nation "in law and justice" *Irurac bat* "the three are one," is the lovely motto of the Basque provinces. In the national assemblies that were held outside beneath the shade of the oak trees, everyone's vote had the same weight as everyone else's. Strangest of all, in an epoch in which the barbaric peoples of Europe treated their women with such fierce disdain, the Basques reserved for them that degree of deference that so scandalized Strabo eighteen centuries earlier; in several valleys, as today in the American state of Kansas, the female citizens offered their advice and spoke as freely as the men. Local chronicles have recorded sessions in which a woman, opposed by everyone, persisted in maintaining a position which, to be fair, was often the most logical and convincing.

The one thing above all others that demonstrates the clear superiority of the sparsely populated Basque society over the neighboring populations, in terms of the quality of its civilization, is the great respect it has always evinced for the human being. Every Basque was absolutely inviolable in his home, and in that fortified castle, protected by the respect of everyone, he enjoyed a greater degree of personal security than the Frenchman of the Middle Ages at the foot of the altar or the Englishman of our days with the all his privileges of *habeas corpus*. If other Iberians, free like him, presented an accusation against his person before a council, his home was not, for that reason, any less sacred to everyone; proud and confident, cap on his head, staff in his hand, and with all the dignity of his peers who were going to judge him, he would approach the oak of Gernika where audiences were held, nature all around him, in view of the mountains and the sea, beneath the thick foliage of a tree ten centuries old that served as seat for the assembled examiners. It was there that the Basque, standing before his judges and his accusers, would respond as a free man to his equals. No one, unless he was convicted of a crime, could be deprived of his home, his horse or his weapons; there was never any infringement on his personal freedom. Further, the absolute freedom of his person was for the Basque life itself; to avoid prolixity, this is why so many young men flee the draft and why each year thousands of men are uprooted from our authoritarian and formalist society to go off to breathe the fresh air of the Pampas in the New World. Augustin Chaho, whom one might call the last of the Basques, a name he himself gave to Zumalacarregui, chose to lock himself in a tiny room on the fifth floor of a house in Baiona rather than suffer the humiliating vigilance of over-zealous agents in streets and walkways: this man who, after being set free, remained for more than a year with no other view than that of the narrow rooftops of the city, and finally died for lack of air and movement without having been able to finish the great works he had begun about the Basque language.

. . .

Races, like chemical elements, must be dissolved to form combinations and acquire new properties. On entering modern society, from which they had lived apart in other times, the Basques will have to sacrifice the purity of their type, their beautiful language, the memories of their glorious history, and perhaps even their name; many of them will in this way take the risk of entirely losing their national originality and, no longer possessing anything but copied habits and thoughts, they will enlist in that vulgar herd of men who renounce all initiative; but in our half-barbaric society in which teaching has not advanced beyond a rudimentary state and where the most important social phenomena are still achieved at random, this chief factor of the absorption of a race by neighboring nations could not take place without carrying with it numerous temporary disadvantages. In revenge, the Basques too, as they become ever more a part of the modern world, will join the common endeavor for the good of all, and in so doing, they will enter into a civilization superior to the one that was so dear to them. Now, they will no longer have to continue the quest for their own freedom. It is not through titles of nobility granted them by the *fueros* and treaties that they have a right to respect for their person, but through their qualities as free and equal men. Their ideal no longer confines itself to the narrow horizon of their mountains, because it is not absolutely and only beneath the tree of Gernika where justice should be carried out, but also in every place on earth where a group of human beings happen to find themselves.

Moreover, the qualities of the Basque race will by no means disappear as a consequence of the fusion of the Basques with the surrounding peoples; they will extend to a greater number of individuals and facilitate the coming together of mankind. Thus the people of Béarn, descended from the Iberians but counting equally among their ancestors the Celts and Romans, are the natural intermediaries between the Basque and the other inhabitants of southwestern France. Similarly, most of the people of Bordeaux, of such graceful and delicate features, so light on their feet, are no less Iberian than Gaul and, through a phenomenon frequent among all mixed races, there are those among them who are sometimes extraordinarily reminiscent of the type of the Basques in the Pyrenees. If traces of the Delaware and the Cherokee can sometimes be seen in the North American, although the blood of the red-skinned race is mixed in such miniscule proportions compared with that of the colonists in the New World, who are of pure race, how much more visible must the Iberian influence be on those French peoples produced through the admixture of Celts, Franks, Romans, and anonymous autochthonous peoples? It would also be difficult to ascertain in what proportion the Phoenicians, Jews, Moors, Gypsies, Goths, and Celts have modified the Iberian base of the inhabitants of Spain; but despite the diversity of all these elements, the fusion nonetheless decreased definitively, and no matter how great their national vanities might be in the future, it is ever more impossible to deny the integration into the great human fraternity of this mixed race produced by the union of so many races that were in ancient times different and hostile to one another.

From this point of view, the gradual mixture of Basques with the other peoples of Western Europe is one of the most remarkable facts of history. For their physical characteristics, language, traditions, and customs, these men undoubtedly constitute a race apart. The do not descend from the Aryan stem in which many wise men, motivated by a harmful sense of pride, see the only truly human race, the only one worthy of the lights and the joys of freedom, and yet the aboriginal Basques can enter human society on a firm footing; they are already our brothers in blood and intelligence, they share our destinies without being in any way inferior to us. And, although at the foot of the Pyrenees this fusion of races of completely different origin is taking place, we see analogous intersections occurring in the new continent of America between reds, blacks, and whites from all corners of the earth. Say what you will, those *mestizos*, whose ancestors came from every continent, have no less vitality than the Aryans of Europe and Asia, and their hearts are exalted enough to allow them to found and maintain free societies. For those of us who seek unity of the human race, not in the past but in the future, this alliance that grows ever more intimate between the different families of men is the principle of unity that will end up transforming all the peoples of the earth into a single humanity. As many small rivers from opposite directions pour down into the same valley to form a great river, just so do races that were born on different continents come together, and sooner or later the men will recognize each other as brothers, with the same sense of their rights and the same ideal of justice and virtue.

68. Felipe Arrese Beitia

(Otxandio, Bizkaia, 1841 – Otxandio, 1906)

He is another of those incarnations of the popular bard that were so prolific in the Basque Country in the nineteenth century, such as José María Iparraguirre and Pierre Topet ("Etchaun"). Arrese was sent to Gasteiz (Vitoria) to study design and when he returned home, he became a professional sculptor of religious images, which led to his being known popularly as the *santugiñe* (saint-maker). He knew the Basque Country like the back of his hand because his craft took him incessantly throughout its provinces to sculpt images of saints. He was a well recognized and popular figure and, true to his profession, he was an extremely pious individual. Moreover, his political sympathies clearly favored the *fueros* and the defense of the Basque language was a fulcrum of his thought and poetry. An autodidact whose education consisted of constant but systematic reading, Arrese wrote poetry without bringing it to public notice until he had his grand opportunity on the occasion of the literary competitions sponsored by Abbadie, which were held for the first time in the southern Basque Country in 1879, in the town of Elizondo (Navarre). Arrese was not only awarded first prize but also won sudden and remarkable fame, thanks to his poem "*Ama Euskeriari azken agurrak*" (Final Farewell to Our Mother Euskara). This is not all that surprising if we consider the topic and the circumstances in which the event was held. The *fueros* having been recently abolished, Arrese's poem dealt precisely with linking *foral* abolition to the death of the Basque language: a national elegy that conveyed literally the state of mind in which a good part of the Basque population found itself. In the following years, Arrese won prizes in these literary competitions as many as fourteen times in a row. Ideologically, he therefore posits a web of connections between the Basque language, which he called "*Paradisuko izketa*" (The language of Paradise), Tubal, the *fueros*, and the Tree of Gernika.

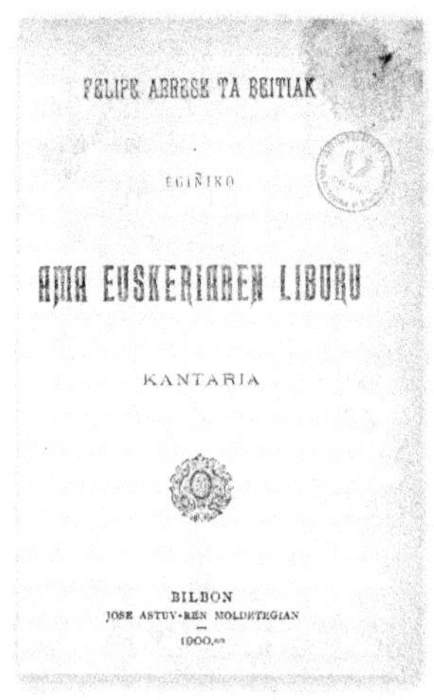

FELIPE ARRESE TA BEITIAK

EGIÑIKO

AMA EUSKERIAREN LIBURU

KANTARIA

BILBON
JOSE ASTUY-REN MOLDETEGIAN
—
1900.an

Selected Text(s):

Ama Euskeriari azken agurrak!!! [Final Farewell to Our Mother Euskara] (Bayonne: Lamaignère, 1880); reprint, in *Enciclopedia General Ilustrada del País Vasco* [General Illustrated Encyclopedia of the Basque Country], Cuerpo B, Arte, Lengua, Literatura [Section B, Art, Language, Literature], vol. 1 (San Sebastián: Auñamendi, 1978), 468–71.

Final Farewell to Our Mother Euskara!

My beloved old Mother,
ancestral mother of Euskara,
behold your faithful son who comes
to bid you his last farewell.
Unable to prevail in such a long battle,
you've grown very old;

beaten down with wounds,
now you're going to die.

Deep sorrow grieves me
on this sad occasion,
because I see our beloved land
Castilianized;
if you don't believe it,
come and look, Tubal;
but no, you would not recognize
your child.

Where, where are your sons,
your *Fueros*, your lovers of Euskara?
Where, oh father Tubal,
where are your illustrious descendants?
Where the laws
of your fine and loyal sons?
Where shall my eyes
weep now?

The laws of our elders
bid us grim farewell,
and we are left as orphans
stripped of our rights;
if we had loved our Euskara
as we should have,
our admirable customs would have been preserved
in their purity.

Without any doubt,
our descendants
will be right to say
we were crazy fools;
they'll know
of the freedoms we enjoyed with Euskara
and that because we became infatuated with Castilian,
they were lost to us forever.

Blessed crags
and blessed mountains,
until now you've been
the guardians of our *fueros*;

you Basques ever high on the peaks
but not the towns;
behold what Castilian has wrought at last.

Down here on the plains I hardly ever see
any loyal sons of Tubal,
and we only hear
Castilian spoken now;
this is why my heart
is pierced with pain,
because I no longer have hope
that our Euskara can be revived.

To hate Euskara
and want to enjoy the *fueros*
seems like pure foolishness to me;
perhaps that could be possible,
but my heart tells me no;
I think our rights are dead
if Euskara isn't revived.

For it's through our own failure
that we've put this lovely, sweet, and gentle language
at risk of perishing at the doors of death;
if someone doesn't take pity
to restore her to health,
our mother Euskara
will soon leave this world.

She sent so many brave sons
across the ocean,
and just as many across the land,
fierce in war;
many admirable men
who wrote and spoke Basque;
they all died, and now
our beloved Euskara must die.

Look at her, laying at the foot
of the Tree of Gernika
in anguish and agony, almost at death's door,
without being able to breathe properly.

Seeing her like that, will nobody
take pity on her? Will her sons not come
to save her?

Ay, dear Mother!
It seems to me that the sons of today have forgotten,
because no one comes forth
to help you in your anguish.
Die, then, alone and abandoned,
oh language of Paradise,
after suffering through six thousand years
so much cruel and bitter pain.

Alone here in such painful agony,
how can I help you, Mother?
Sigh and groan, dissolve in tears,
stretched out at your feet;
I beg forgiveness for all your sons
with all my heart,
and help you give up your spirit
in the hands of the Lord.

Go stainless from the world,
go pure from the world,
go from this world never having worshipped
an ox or a cow;
you always abhorred and trampled
on idols,
and now, true to your father,
surrendering your lives to your Lord.

Euskara has died! Euskara has died!
She's closed her eyes forever.
Weep, Araba! Weep, Gipuzkoa!
Weep, Bizkaia!
Weep cliffs! Weep mountains!
Until the springs dry up,
source of so many remedies
for pains and ills!

Weep, our brothers from Navarre
and the Basques from France!

Tear your clothes to shreds with me;
forget the history and tales
of our elders,
and let the new Castilians
take their places.

And what, oh heavenly tree,
has become of your green foliage?
I see your branches naked,
dry and without acorns.
How terrible! The Castilian worm
has devoured your roots,
and your heart, and your guts,
everything but the bark.

Are you still standing, crags?
Have you not yet fallen, mountains?
Are you still gushing forth
treasures like Muskiz [a town in Bizkaia]?
Turn-turning windmills, pound-pounding mills,
sending water gush-gushing from fountains,
stocking rivers and seas with fish?

It's too much. Crumble, great rocks;
mountains, don't pour out lavish gifts
to bury Euskara, our dead language.
Crash down, peaks; ravines, fill up with rocks;
come, arid Castilian steppes;
rivers, dry up; seas, drain dry.
Farewell, Basque valleys.

My people, the centuries
will remember you forever;
there'll never be another race
as noble as you;
some enemies will sully
your name in vain;
[but] your true and only God
will keep you pure.

69. Casimiro Jausoro

Known to have been a Bizkaian who settled in Madrid and who experienced the Basque Country only at a distance and nostalgically, it remained, however, at the forefront of his mind politically. To judge by the works he published, he appears to have had a scientific background. These short books had the particular characteristic that they were written in verse in order to be more amenable for a wider audience. He addressed various subjects, including astronomy, physics, geography, and hygiene. In his chapter on nostalgia for the homeland, he published a book (in 1870) of reminiscences about the carnival of Bilbao. His distance from the Basque Country enabled him to maintain an independent political stance concerning specific party ties. Despite the enormous media coverage (centered in Madrid) during the second Carlist War, that heaped ridicule on the Basque administrative system, there were also initiatives that defended this same system from the Spanish capital itself. One such initiative was the *La Paz* (Peace) newspaper, and Jausoro became deeply involved with the controversy from the outset. He took a stand by publishing a book, *El Fuero y la Revolucion. Defensa de las Instituciones vascongadas* . . . (The *Fuero* and the Revolution: A Defense of the Basque Institutions . . .) (1872), dedicated to Ramón Ortiz de Zárate, in which he addressed the way in which the nation was configured and its relationship to the maintenance of the *fueros*. Jausoro was, of course, a *foral* sympathiser; what is more, he considered the Basque *foral* system to be the best possible arrangement, situated as it was halfway between the reactionary conservatism of the moderates and the revolutionary republicanism of the progressives. As such, he proposed the construction of a Spanish political system based on a unique federal republic that would recover the *foral* systems of the old kingdoms and counties; in other words, rather than abolishing the Basque *foral* system, it would be extended throughout Spain's lands. Moreover, following a traditional line of defense of the *foral* system—the notion of the Basques' original independence, the mythic battle of Arrigorriaga between Bizkaia and Castile, and the notion of the consensual, voluntary incorporation of the basque provinces into the Kingdom of Castile through pacts—the evidence that Jausoro adduced as the most conclusive regarding this time-honored *foral* autonomy was the survival of the Basque language.

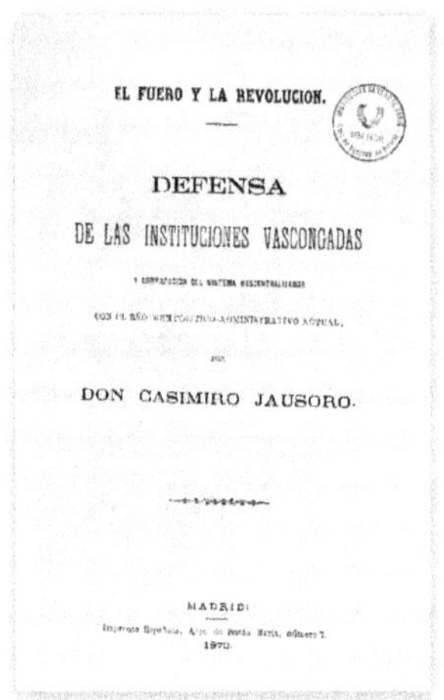

EL FUERO Y LA REVOLUCION.

DEFENSA

DE LAS INSTITUCIONES VASCONGADAS

DON CASIMIRO JAUSORO.

MADRID:

SELECTED TEXT(S):

El Fuero y la revolución: defensa de la instituciones vascongadas y comparación del sistema descentralizador con el régimen político-administrativo actual [The *Fuero* and the Revolution: A Defense of the Basque Institutions and Comparison of the Decentralized System with the Current Politico-Administrative Regime] (Madrid: Imprenta Espanola, 1872), 31–33, 35–36, 38–39, 40–42, 100–101.

We need not trouble ourselves too much in seeking evidence of Basque autonomy, when one of the main pieces of evidence is in plain sight and is fully convincing: the Basque language itself.

A nation's language is, so to speak, the first thing that constitutes its origin: its comparison with other tongues allows us to gain an understanding of the relationships it has maintained and the conquests it has undergone.

After conquering the known world, the Romans gave it their laws, tastes, customs, and language. There are obvious signs of their domination in the languages of the lands where Latinate people have lived. The languages of the different nations born of this race are the descendants of a common language no longer in use, and the analogies that exist among them demonstrate perfectly that there was once a time when all of these nations were united under a single power.

In Spain itself, apart from the Castilian language, there are many dialects specific to each province or ancient kingdom. The origin of all of these dialects becomes immediately clear as one deduces the Roman influence upon them, because all the words in these languages are Latin, with the exception of certain Arabic terms, and the modifications undergone by these languages as they became dialects are not so substantial as to obscure their common origin in the slightest, even when these changes are intensified by the particular accent of each region.

Basque is the only language that differs entirely from all others, with which it has no point of contact whatsoever. No one is certain of exactly where it came from; some date it back, no less, to the first inhabitants of Spain, believing it to have been the universal language of Spain until it was wiped out as the peninsula was invaded by one group of conquerors or another.

Be that as it may, Euskara is unique to this country even today, because with the exception of some relatively large cities and the towns bordering Castile, Castilian is barely known. This clearly shows that the various conquerors did not overrun, and did not even know, that remote region. Otherwise, would they have refrained from influencing the physical conditions and even the behavior of the inhabitants of Castile? Would we not have encountered traces of Roman domination as evident as those found in the other regions of the Iberian Peninsula?

. . .

If Basques retain their original language, their timeless customs, their music—whose character and rhythm is found in no other—and even the physical makeup that distinguishes them from other Spaniards, we are forced to agree that they have not been exposed to the same experiences as the rest of the inhabitants of Spain, and this has set them apart as a people.

The character and customs of the three provinces are also proof of their autonomy: they are the same as those—yesterday, and those of yesterday are the same as they have been for time immemorial. No society in the world is more attached to the usages and customs of its elders.

If the ancient monarchs of Asturias or León, Navarre or Castile, ever ruled or subjugated the country at any time, it must, in any case, be readily admitted that these protectorates, *accepted by the Basque Country*, made no impression whatsoever on the centuries-old institutions and the independent government of the Basque people.

Nor does history have anything at all to tell us about the Arab occupation, which proves that they either never set foot on that [Basque] land or limited themselves to making a number of incursions into it, being forced to retreat by not daring to undertake a conquest whose success they had good reason to doubt and contenting themselves with crossing the territory's flattest portion, which borders on Castile.

If we were impassioned apologists for our country, which would certainly not be an odd thing for anyone, we could enjoy ourselves by allowing our enthusiasm to lead us into the formulation of suppositions that would in all probability be much better grounded than those formulated by our adversaries. But, aware that affection blinds, we prefer not to do this, certain in the knowledge that it will be easier for us to persuade people's minds another way.

So let us restrict ourselves to the impartiality of history, trusting that this will be more than sufficient to demonstrate that country's right, now as before, to its freedoms.

. . .

Even if we were to presume (and we would be presuming a great deal) that the monarchs of Castile, León, or Navarre ever took over any part of the Basque Country, it cannot be said that the country, therefore, belonged to them by right of conquest, nor that from the time it first fell under their rule to the point when its the natives shook themselves free from the yoke of that alien domination, could the Basque Country be considered to have been part of the invading king's realms.

When a peace treaty is signed between two countries following a war, the captured strongholds or territories are returned to the nation to which they belonged; or if the victor, not too inclined toward generosity or too demanding, ambitious, or needy, refuses to return them, the lost territory does not lose its nationality as long as the passing of time has not erased the race or the society to which it is, so to speak, bound by ties of blood. Furthermore, if that nation, despondent at one point, is fortunate again at another and recovers what it has lost, surely no one can say that the recovered part, like the whole of the nation that has regained its independence, is not free of obligations or of the need to acknowledge foreign rights.

Because of the fact that Spain came under the sway of Napoleon (for a short time, happily) and Napoleon placed his brother Joseph on the throne and disposed of the country's destiny as he pleased, can it therefore be said that Spain belongs to France, and that consequently the latter has rights over the former? Never, for this would be absurd.

The provinces found themselves in a similar situation. Presuming (and I repeat, it is a great deal to suppose) that, faced with a lack of good news, the neighboring king had forcibly and unlawfully taken hold of some portion of Basque territory (never rightfully, for the king was never voluntarily acknowledged as its ruler) and that he had done so not to incorporate it into his realm but rather because the Basques needed a military leader to protect them from foreign aggression, this king could ill afford to grant them such protection if he were not sufficiently powerful. Furthermore, it would have been natural for them to acknowledge the authority and certain rights inherent in his lofty position and rank.

. . .

Hungary lies in the Austrian heartland, yet the Austrian Emperor is merely the king of the Hungarians, much in the same way that the King of Spain has always been *Lord* of the Basque provinces following their respective annexations to the Crown of Castile, through the election of Alfonso VIII as Lord of Gipuzkoa in 1200, and of Alfonso XI as Lord of Araba in 1332.

After all, we must not lose sight for an instant that these annexations were voluntary. In other words, the two provinces were independent from Castile before being incorporated into it, and it mattered not at all whether they had previously belonged to it or not; by agreeing to annexation, all [the Basques] had done was to choose the lord that suited them best.

Bizkaia's situation was different. When Bizkaia ratified its union with Castile, it continued with its system of hereditary succession of its lords, a system which it had the power to replace with an electoral one as necessary, but which it did not do away with at that time. Bizkaia, we have said, did no more than acknowledge Don Juan I as a descendant of its earlier lords, which had been the case before his elevation to the throne of Castile, and by virtue of the hereditary custom, which it had the power to reject, the province continued to acknowledge the kings of Spain as its lords.

We have thus answered those who refute Basque autonomy by basing their arguments on alleged conquests and dominations of that country by the kings of León, Castile, or Navarre to arrive at the conclusion that if the Basque provinces had belonged to any of those [foreign] kingdoms that were later fused into a single one, then that territory belonged to Castile whether it liked it or not.

. . .

For this reason, it is of great importance to emphasize the historic fact of the *independence of the three provinces* upon becoming voluntarily and definitively incorporated into Castile, and the right of these provinces to their own internal autonomy.

It turns out that there existed a perfect state of independence at the time of the origin of the Basque Country's right to its particular system and situation.

Moreover, apart from what we have already said, this right is even more ancient from our perspective, as we shall endeavor to show.

. . .

In summary: we perceive the constitutional system practiced to date as deplorable; the unitarian or federal republic that has been posited following the course of modern ideas which, godless and arrogant as they are, endeavor to place paltry human reason above a Supreme Being, the lord of all creation, seems to us to be even worse.

The manner of government that we deem most fitting for all of the provinces of Spain is the system employed in the Basque provinces, because whether the system arises from Basque customs or whether the customs arise from the system, it has always freed the Basque people from tyranny.

We do not want the system of *yesterday*, that is, excessive centralization caused by circumstance, as the only measure to safeguard public order, a system that at certain times might have brought greater harm through the remedies it sought to apply than did the evils it hoped to combat. Now that the cause of that centralization has vanished, which gave excessive authority to the executive power, we seek a return to the system of *yesteryear*, to the rights and laws of the people, to the decentralization and administrative autonomy that are its most precious and only true freedoms. We want, in a word, for Spain to be as happy, perhaps even happier if this were possible, than the three Basque provinces with their *fueros* are in the eyes of a dedicated *foral* sympathiser, and we want those same provinces to be eternally joined to Spain by a bond of brotherhood, trusting that this generous, just, and magnanimous nation will protect them in return for a loyalty that has never been gainsaid, and will always safeguard its legitimate rights symbolized by that beautiful and eloquent slogan: "Union, Peace, and *Fueros*."

Madrid, September 1871.

Bibliography

Libraries consulted

Azkue Library, Euskaltzaindia (Royal Academy of the Basque Language), Bilbao.

Universidad Pública de Navarra-Nafarroako Unibertsitate Publikoa (Public University of Navarre) Library, Pamplona-Iruña.

Basque Library, Fundación "Sancho el Sabio," Vitoria-Gasteiz.

Basque Library, Labayru Institute, Seminario Diocesano de Bizkaia, Derio.

Koldo Mitxelena Library, Donostia.

Foral del Señorío de Bizkaia Library, Bilbao.

Biblioteca Digital del Señorío de Bizkaia. At http://www.bibliotecaforal.bizkaia.net

Liburutegi Digitala. Eusko Jaurlaritza/Fundación "Sancho el Sabio." At http://www.euskadi.net

Primary Material

Abbadie Thompson, Antoine, and [Joseph] Augustin Chaho. *Études grammaticales sur la langue euskarienne*. Paris: Arthus Bertrand, 1836.

Abendaño Eztenaga, Miguel. Prologue to *De divina scientia et predestinatione. In civitate lassionensi vulgo San Sebastián*. San Sebastián: Martín de Huarte, 1674.

Agramont, Pedro de. *Historia de Navarra 1632*. Pamplona: Mintzoa, 1996.

Aguirre, Martín de. *Responsum de succesione Regni Portugaliae pro Philippo Hispaniarum Rege Principum omnium potentissimum*. Venice: Franciscum Ziletum, 1581.

Alemán, Mateo. *Ortografía castellana*. Mexico City: Academia Mexicana, 1609.

Alonsótegui, Miguel. "Crónicas de Vizcaya, 1577." In *Historia General de Vizcaya, comprobada con autoridades y copias de escrituras y privilegios fehacientes, 1787* by Juan Ramón de Iturriza y Zabala, 60. Reprint, Bilbao: Cipriano Lucena, 1885.

———. *Tratado que muestra la vida miserable que padece el hombre.* 1561. Edited by Pedro de Ortúzar. Bilbao: Diputación Foral de Vizcaya, 1970.

Aramburu, Miguel de. *Nueva recopilación de los Fueros, privilegios, buenos usos y costumbres, leyes y ordenanzas de la Muy Noble y Muy Leal Provincia de Guipúzcoa.* Tolosa: Bernardo de Ugarte, 1696.

Araquistáin, Juan Venancio de. *Tradiciones vasco-cántabras.* Tolosa: Imprenta de la Provincia, 1866.

Arce de Otalora, Juan. *Summa nobilitatis Hispaniae, ac immunitatis regiorum tributorum, causas, ius, ordinem, iudicium, et exusationem breuiter complectens: nunc postermo recognita, atque infinitis prope locis emendata, nouisque additionibus acta.* Salamanca: Juan Bautista Terranova, 1570.

Archu, Jean Baptiste. *Uskara eta Franzes Gramática, Uskalherrietaco haurrentzat eguina.* Baiona: Fore et Lassarre, 1853.

Argaiz, Gregorio de. *Población eclesiástica de España, y noticia de sus primeras honras, halladas en los escritos de S. Gregorio obispo de Granada, en el chronicon de Hauberto Monge de S. Benito, ilustradas por el maestro fray Gregorio de Argaiz, Chronista de la misma Religión. Dedicadas a la Majestad Suprema, y Soberana de Dios, Trino y Uno.* Madrid: Melchor Sanchez, 1667.

———. *Corona real de España por España fundada en el crédito de los muertos y vida de San Hyeroteo, obispo de Atenas y Segovia, por el Maestro Fray Gregorio de Argaiz, monge y cronista del Orden de San Benito. Dedicada a la Reyna nuestra señora Doña Mariana de Asturia, madre y tutora de Carlos el Deseado, Rey de España y Nuevo Mundo, y única Governadora destos reynos.* Madrid: Melchor Alegre, 1668.

Arrese Beitia, Felipe. *Ama Euskeriari azken agurrak!!!* Bayonne: Lamaignère, 1880. Reprint, in *Enciclopedia General Ilustrada del País Vasco.* Cuerpo B, Arte, Lengua, Literatura. Vol. 1, 468–71. San Sebastián: Auñamendi, 1978.

Astarloa, Pablo Pedro. *Apología de la lengua Bascongada o ensayo crítico-filosófico de su perfección y antigüedad sobre todas las que se conocen: en respuesta a los reparos propuestos en el Diccionario geográfico histórico de España, tomo segundo, palabra Nabarra, por* . . . Madrid: Gerónimo Ortega, 1803. 2nd ed. Bilbao: Pedro Velasco, 1883.

———. *Discursos filosóficos sobre la lengua primitiva o Gramática y análisis razonada de la Euskara o Bascuence*. Madrid: Gerónimo Ortega, 1803. 2nd ed. Bilbao: Pedro Velasco, 1883.

———. *Reflexiones filosóficas en defensa de la Apología de la lengua bascongada o Respuesta a la Censura del Cura de Montuenga*. Madrid: Cano, 1804.

———. *Carta de un vascongado al señor don Tomás de Sorreguieta, advirtiéndole varias equivocaciones que ha padecido en su obra titulada Semana Hispano-Bascongada*. Madrid: Cano, 1804.

Astigarraga, Luis. *Diccionario manual bascongado y castellano. Elementos de gramática. Para el uso de la juventud* . . . San Sebastián: Ramón Baroja, 1825.

Axular [Pedro de Aguerre]. *Guero bi partetan partitua eta berezia, lehenbicicoan emaitenda, aditcera, cenbat calte eguiten duen, luçamendutan ibiltceac, eguitecoen gueroco utzteac. Bigarrenean quidatcenda, eta aitcinatcen, luçamenduac utciric, bere hala, bere eguin bideari, lothu nahi çaicana*. Bordele [Bordeaux]: Guillen Milanges, 1643.

Barbagero, Justo. *Memoria o consideraciones sobre la reunion de las tres Provincias Vascongadas en un solo obispado, con la silla episcopal en Vitoria*. In Francisco Rodríguez De Coro, "Un documento excepcional del Ministerio de Justicia contra la creación de la diócesis vasca, 1861," 321–34. Scriptorum Victoriense 25 (1978).

Barreré de Vieuzac, Bertrand. "Rapport du Comité de Salut Publique sur les idiomes, 8 Pluviôse, an II [1794]." In *Une politique de la langue. La Revolution française et les patois: l'enquête de Grégoire*, edited by Michel de Certeau, Dominique Julia, and Jacques Revel, 321–31. Paris: Gallimard, 2002.

Beriayn, Juan de. *Tratado de cómo se ha de oir Misa, escrito en romance y bascuence, lenguajes de este obispado de Pamplona*. Pamplona: Carlos de Labayen, 1621.

———. *Doctrina Christiana en Romance y Bascuence, lenguajes de este Obispado de Pamplona. Compuesta por el Licenciado Juan de Beriayn Abad de Uterga*. Pamplona: Carlos de Labayen, 1626.

Beuter, Pedro Antón [Pere Antoni]. *Primera parte de la Crónica general de toda España y especialmente del Reyno de Valencia*. 1538 (in Catalan). Valencia, 1548.

Cánovas del Castillo, Antonio. Prologue to *Los Vascongados. Su país su lengua y el Príncipe L. L. Bonaparte, con notas ilustraciones y comprobantes sobre sus antigüedades, sus principales nombres históricos, su literatura euskara, su bibliografía vasca, sus artistas y obras de arte, su música, sus danzas, sus supersticiones, su organización social antigua y moderna, condición de sus respectivas clases, sus Fueros, carácter que estos presentan y perduracion de sus partidos actuales, con el influjo que tuvo este pais en nuestras conquistas y descubrimientos ultramarinos,* by Miguel de Rodríguez Ferrer. Madrid: J. Noguera, 1873.

Cardaberaz, Agustín de. *Eusqueraren berri onac: eta ondo escribitceco, ondo iracurtceco, ta ondo itzegiteco Erreglac: cura jaun, ta escola maisu celosoai Jesusen Compañiaco Aita Agustín Cardaberaz-ec esqueñtcen, ta dedicatcen dieztenac.* Pamplona: Antonio Castilla, 1761.

Carlos y Zúñiga, Luis. *Plan de antigüedades españolas, reducido a dos articulos y ochenta proposiciones.* Madrid: Villapando, 1801.

Chaho, Joseph Augustin [Agustín, Agosti]. *Paroles d'un Voyant en réponse aux Paroles d'un Croyant.* Paris: Dondey-Dupré, 1834.

———. *Paroles d'un Biscaïen aux libéraux de la reine Christine.* Paris: Dondey-Dupré, 1834. Translated into Basque and Spanish as *Bizkaiko baten eleak. Palabras de un bizkaino a la reina Cristina.* Bilbao: Likiniano Elkartea, 1999.

———. *Azti begia eta beste izkribu zenbait.* Paris: Dondey-Dupré, 1834. Klasikoak series. Donostia: Euskal Editoreen Elkartea, 1992.

———. *Voyage en Navarre pendant l'insurrection des Basques (1830–1835). Avec portraits et costumes.* Paris: A. Bertrand, 1836. Translated into Spanish as *Viaje a Navarra durante la insurrección de los vascos.* San Sebastián: Txertoa, 1976.

———. "Aîtor: Légende cantabre." *L'Ariel* (1845). Translated into Spanish as *La leyenda de Aitor y otros relatos.* San Sebastián: Orain, 1995.

———. *Histoire primitive des Euskariens-Basques; langue, poésie, moeur et caractère de ce peuple; introduction à son histoire ancienne et moderne.* Bayonne: Jaymebon, 1847.

Conchillos, José. *Propugnáculo histórico y jurídico, Muro literario, y tutelar; Tudela ilustrada y defendida[...] Dedicada a la misma Ciudad de Tudela, primera población de España, por el patriarca Tubal.* Zaragoza, 1666.

———. *Desagravios del Propugnáculo de Tudela contra el Trifauce Cervero, Autor del Bodoque*. Antwerp [false place of publication]: Sebastián Sterlin, 1667.

Conde, José Antonio. *Censura crítica de la pretendida excelencia y antigüedad del vascuence*. Madrid: Imprenta Real, 1804.

———. *Censura crítica del alfabeto primitivo de España y pretendidos monumentos literarios del vascuence*. Madrid: Imprenta Real, 1806.

Court de Gébelin, Antoine. *Monde Primitif analysé et comparé avec le monde moderne, considéré dans son génie allégorique et dans les allégories auxelles conduisit ce génie; precedé du plan général des diverses parties qui composeront ce Monde primitif: avec des figures en talle-douce*. 9 vols. Paris, 1773–82.

Cubillo de Aragón, Álvaro. *El enano de las musas: comedias, y obras diversas: con un poema de las Cortes del León y del Águila, acerca del Búho gallego*. Madrid: María de Quiñones, 1654.

Covarrubias, Sebastián de. "Cantabria." In *Tesoro de la Lengua Castellana o Española*. Madrid, 1611. Reprint, Madrid: Turner, 1977.

Darrigol, Jean Pierre: *Dissertation critique et apologétique sur la Langue Basque, par un eclésiastique du diocèse de Bayonne*. Bayonne: Duhart-Fauvet, 1827.

Dechepare, Bernat: *Linguae Vasconum Primitiae*. Burdigalae [Bordeaux]: Franciscum Morpain, 1545.

Derrecagaix, Victor Bernard. "Notice sur les Basques." *Bulletin de la Societé de Géographie* 11 (1876): 401–38.

Diccionario Geográfico-Histórico de España por la Real Academia de la Historia. Sección I. Comprehende el Reyno de Navarra, Señorío de Vizcaya, y Provincias de Álava y Guipúzcoa. Madrid: Viuda de don Joaquín Ibarra, 1802.

D'Iharce de Bidassouet, Pierre. *Histoire des cantabres, ou des premiers colons de toute l'Europe avec celle des basques, leurs descendants directs, qui existent encore, et leur langue asiatique-basque, traduite, et réduite aux principes de la langue française*. Paris: Julie Didot Ainé, 1825.

D. P. P. A. [Pablo Pedro de Astarloa]. *Versos a la proclamación de nuestro augusto monarca Don Carlos IV (que Dios guarde) ejecutada so el árbol de Guernica el dia 18 de febrero de este presente año de 1789*. Madrid: Aznar, 1789.

Duvoisin, Jean Pierre. *Étude sur la déclinaison basque*. Bayonne: Veuve Lamaignére, 1866.

Echave, Baltasar de. *Discursos de la lengua Cántabra-Bascongada compuestos por . . . Introducese la misma lengua, en forma de una Matrona venerable y anciana, que se quexa, de que siendo ella la primera q. se habló en España, y general en toda ella la ayan olvidado sus naturales, y admitido otras Extranjeras. Habla con las Provincias de Guipúzcoa y Vizcaya, que le han sido fieles, y algunas vezes con la misma España.* Mexico City: Henrrico Martínez, 1607.

Eguren, Juan María. *Método práctico para enseñar el castellano en las escuelas vascongadas.* Vitoria: Semanario Católico Vasco-Navarro, 1867.

El tordo vizcaíno, contestación al Búho gallego. N.p.: [1638?]. Reprint, in *Semanario erudito* 12 (1789): 110–210. Reprint, as Appendix 3 of Estanislao Labayru, *Historia General de Bizcaya*, ed. Andrés Mañaricúa, 49–184. 1895–1903. Bilbao: La Gran Enciclopedia Vasca, 1976.

Erro, Juan Bautista. *Alfabeto de la lengua primitiva de España y explicación de sus más antiguos monumentos, inscripciones y medallas.* Madrid: Repullés, 1806.

———. *Observaciones filosóficas a favor del Alfabeto Primitivo o Respuesta apologética a la Censura crítica del Cura de Montuenga.* Pamplona: Longas, 1807.

———. *El Mundo Primitivo o Exámen Filosófico de la Antigüedad y Cultura de la Nación Bascongada.* Madrid: Fuentenebro, 1815.

Etcheberry, Joannes [of Ziburu]. *Manual Devotionezcoa, edo ezperen, oren oro escuetan erabilltçeco liburutchoa Escarazco versutan eguiña, eta guztiz bi partetan bereçia. Lehenan iracasten direla, Guiristiño Commun batec, iaguiñ behar dituen gauça guehienac: berçean, errateco lituquen, halaber othoiz guehienac.* Bordele [Bordeaux]: Guillen Millances, Erregueren Imprimatçallearenean, 1627.

———. *Eliçara erabiltceco liburua.* Bordele [Bordeaux]: Guillen Millanges, 1636.

Etcheberry, Joannes [of Sara]. "Laburdiri Euscararen Hatsapenac." 1712. In *Obras vascongadas del doctor labortano Joannes d'Etcheberry (1712) con una introducción y notas por Julio de Urquijo e Ibarra*, edited by Julio Urquijo, 1–119. Paris: Paul Geuthner, 1907.

———. *Lau-Urdiri Gomendiozco Carta edo Guthuna.* Baiona: Mateo Roquemaurel, 1718.

Extractos de las Juntas Generales celebradas por la Real Sociedad Bascongada de los Amigos del País en la Villa de Bilbao por setiembre de 1772. Vitoria: Tomás de Robles, 1772.

Fabre D'Olivet, Antoine. *La langue hébraïque restituée*. Paris, 1815.

Fernández de Castro, Pedro [Conde de Lemos]. "Historia del Búho gallego con las demás aves de España" (n.p.: early seventeenth century?). Reprint, in Justo Zaragoza, *Castellanos y vascongados*, 233–64. Madrid: Víctor Sáez, 1876. Reprint, as Appendix 3 of Estanislao Labayru, *Historia General de Bizcaya*, ed. Andrés Mañaricúa, 233–62. 1895–1903. Bilbao: La Gran Enciclopedia Vasca, 1976.

Floreto de anécdotas y noticias diversas que recopiló un fraile dominico residente en Sevilla mediados del siglo XVI. Edited by Francisco Javier Sánchez Cantón. Memorial Histórico Español series 48. Madrid: Real Academia de la Historia, 1948.

Flórez, Enrique. *La Cantabria. Disertación sobre el sitio, y extensión que tuvo en el tiempo de los romanos la región de los cántabros, con noticia de las regiones confinantes, y de varias poblaciones antiguas, Discurso preliminar a la España Sagrada . . .* Madrid: Antonio Marín, 1768. Reprint, Madrid: San Martín, 1786 and J. Rodríguez, 1877.

Fontecha y Salazar, Pedro de. *Escudo de la más constante fee y lealtad*. Bilbao: Diputación de Vizcaya, 1762. Reprint, Bilbao: Juan E. Delmas, 1866; La Gran Enciclopedia Vasca, 1776.

Fueros, Privilegios, Franquezas y Libertades del M. N. y M. L. Señorío de Vizcaya. Bilbao: Biblioteca Bascongada de Fermín Herran, 1897.

Garat, Dominique Joseph. *Origines des basques de France et d'Espagne*. Paris: Hachette, 1869.

———. "Sur l'usage et l'emploi de la langue basque." Gure Herria 4 (1924): 704–06.

Garibay, Esteban de. *Los XL libros d'el compendio historial de las Chronicas y universal Historia de todos los reynos de España*. Antwerp: Christophoro Plantino, 1571.

———. *Ilustraciones genealógicas de los Catholicos Reyes de las Españas, y de los christianissimos de Francia, y de los Emperadores de Constantinopla, hasta el Catholico Rey nuestro Señor Don Philipe el II y sus serenisimos hijos*. Madrid: Luis Sánchez, 1596.

———. *Memorial Histórico Español*. Vol. 7, *Memorias*. Madrid: José Rodríguez, 1854.

Godoy, Manuel. *Memoria del Príncipe de la Paz, o sea cuenta dada de su vida política, para servir a la historia del reinado del Sr. D. Carlos IV de Borbón.* Madrid: Impresa de Sancha, 1836.

González, Tomás. *Colección de cédulas, cartas-patentes, proviones, reales órdenes y otros documentos conciernientes a las Provincias Vascongadas…* 4 vols. Madrid: Imprenta Real, 1829–30.

Gorosabel, Pablo. *Noticia de las cosas memorables de Guipúzcoa.* Tolosa: E. López, 1899–1901. 2nd ed. 3 vols. Bilbao: La Gran Enciclopedia Vasca, 1972.

Grámatica de la lengua vulgar de España. Louvain-Leuven: B. Gavio, 1559.

Grégoire, Henri. "Rapport sur la nécesité et les moyens d'anéantir les patois et d'universaliser l'usage de la langue française, 16 Prairial, an II [1794]." In *Une politique de la langue. La Revolution française et les patois: l'enquête de Grégoire*, edited by Michel de Certeau, Dominique Julia, and Jacques Revel, 331–51. Paris: Gallimard, 2002.

Guichard, Etienne. *L'harmonie étymologique des langues.* Paris, 1606.

Henao, Gabriel de. *Averigüaciones de las antiguedades de Cantabria enderezadas principalmente a descubrir las de Guipúzcoa, Vizcaya y Alava, provincias contenidas en ella, y a honor y gloria de San Ignacio de Loyola, nacido en la primera y originario de las otras dos, patriarca y fundador de la Compañía de Jesús.* 2 vols. Salamanca: Eugenio Antonio García, 1689–91.

Hervás y Panduro, Lorenzo. *Catálogo de las lenguas de las naciones conocidas, y numeración, división, y clases de estas, según la diversidad de sus idiomas y dialectos. Su autor el abate Don Lorenzo Hervás, bibliotecario de NN. SS. P. Pío VII, Volumen V. Continuación del tratado III. Lenguas y naciones europeas: y de la parte II. Naciones primitivas: sus lenguas matrices, y dialectos de estas.* Madrid: Imprenta del Real Arbitrio de Beneficencia, 1804.

Hiribarren, Jean Martin. *Eskaldunac. Iberia, Cantabria, Eskal-Herriac. Eskal Herri bakhotcha eta hari darraicona.* Bayonne: Foré et Lasserre, 1853.

Huarte de San Juan, Juan. *Examen de ingenios para las sciencias. Donde se muestra la differencia de habilidades que ay en los hombres, y el genero de letras que a cada uno responde en particular.* Baeza: Juan Bautista de Montoya, 1575. Reprint, edited by Esteban Torre. Barcelona: PPU, 1998.

Hugo, Victor. *En voyage. Alpes et Pyrenées.* Paris: Heltzel, 1890.

Humboldt, Wilhelm Freicher von. *Berichtigungen und Zusätze zum . . . Mithidates über die Cantabrische oder Baskische Sprache.* Berlin: Voss, 1817.

———. *Prüfung der Untersuchungen über die Urbewohner Spaniens vermittelst der Vaskischen Sprache.* Berlin: Dümmler, 1821. Translated into Spanish by Francisco Echebarria, with a prologue by Arnald Steiger, as *Primitivos pobladores de España y Lengua Vasca.* Madrid: Minotauro, 1959.

———. "Diario del viaje vasco 1801." *Revista Internacional de los Estudios Vascos* 13 (1922): 614–58.

———. "Los vascos. Aportaciones sobre un viaje por el País Vasco en la primavera de 1801." *Revista Internacional de los Estudios Vascos* XIV (1923): 205–50, 373–400 and 15 (1924): 83–137, 262–305 and 391–466. Reprint, as *Los vascos.* San Sebastián: Ediciones Vascas, 1975.

Iñiguez de Ibargüen, Juan, and García Fernández de Cachopín. *Crónica General Española y Sumaria de la Casa de Vizcaya, y su antigua fundación, y Nobleza* (c. 1588). Manuscript in the Biblioteca de la Diputación de Vizcaya.

Iparraguirre, José María. "¡Biba Euskera!" In *Jose Maria Iparragirre. Erro-urratsak,* edited by Gontzal Mendibil. Vol. 1, 279. Igorre: Keinu, 1999.

———. "Arren ez bedi galdu euskera." In *Jose Maria Iparragirre. Erro-urratsak,* edited by Gontzal Mendibil. Vol. 1, 314. Igorre: Keinu, 1999.

Irizar y Moya, Joaquín. *De l'Eusquère et des erdères ou de la langue basque et de ses dèrivés par Irizar y Moya, lieutenant d'artillerie licencié, ex-professeur dudit corps à Ségovie.* 5 vols. Paris: Possielgue-Rusand, 1841–45.

Isla, José Francisco de. *Historia del famoso predicador Fray Gerundio de Campazas, alias Zotes.* 2 vols. Madrid, 1758, 1768. Reprint, Madrid: Editora Nacional, 1978.

Iturriza y Zabala, Juan Ramón. *Historia General de Vizcaya. Comprobada con Autoridades y copias de Escrituras, y Privilegios fehacientes. En la qual se relaciona su población, y posesion perpetua por sus naturales, conservando su primitiva lengua, fueros, franquezas y libertades.* Bolibar-Berriz, 1782–85. Reprint, Barcelona: Viuda e hijos de J. Subirana, 1884. Bilbao: Cipriano Lucena, 1885.

Iztueta, Juan Ignacio de. *Guipuzcoaco dantza gogoangarrien condaira edo historia, beren soñu zar, eta itz neurtu edo versoaquin. Baita berac ongui dantzatzeco iracaste edo instruccioac ere. Obra balio andicoa eta chit premiazcoa, Guipuzcoatarren jostaldia gaitzic gabecoaquin, lendabicico etorqui Españar argüí eta garbi aien oitura maitagarrien gordacaiztceco.* Donostia: Ignacio Ramón Baroja, 1824. Reprint, Donostia: Euskal Editoreen Elkartea, 1990.

———. *Guipuzcoaco Provinciaren Condaira edo Historia ceñetan jarritzen diraden arguiro beraren asieratic orain-arte dagozquion barri gogoangarriac.* Donostia: Ignacio Ramón Baroja, 1847.

Jausoro, Casimiro. *El Fuero y la revolución: defensa de las instituciones vascongadas y comparación del sistema descentralizador con el régimen político-administrativo actual.* Madrid: Imprenta Española, 1872.

Kircher, Athanasius. *Turris Babel.* Amsterdam: Janssonio-Waesbergiana, 1679.

Lahetjuzan, Dominique. *Essai de quelques notes sur la langue basque, par un vicaire de champagne, sauvage d'origine.* Bayonne: Cluzeau frères, 1808.

Lancre, Pierre de. *Tableau de l'inconstance et instabilité de toutes les coses. Où il est montré, qu'en Dieu Seúl gist la vraye Constance, à laquelle l'homme sage doit viser.* Paris: Abel l'Angelier, 1610. Reprint, as *Tableau de l'inconstance des mauvais anges et démons où il est amplement traité des sorciers et de la sorcellerie...* Paris: Jean Berjon, 1613. Reprint, edited by Nicole Jacques-Chaquin. Paris: Aubier, 1982.

Larramendi, Manuel de. *De la antigüedad y universalidad del Bascuence en España.* Salamanca: A. J. Villagordo, [1728?].

———. *Discurso histórico sobre la famosa Cantabria. Questión decidida. Si las provincias de Bizcaya, Guipuzcoa y Alaba, estuvieron comprendidas en la Antigua Cantabria.* Madrid: J. de Zuñiga, 1736.

———. *Diccionario trilingue del castellano, bascuence y latín.* San Sebastián: Bartolomé Riesgo, 1745.

———. *Corografía o descripción general de la M. N. y M. L. Provincia de Guipúzcoa.* San Sebastián: Sociedad Guipuzcoana de Ediciones, 1969.

———. *Conferencias curiosas, políticas, legales y morales sobre los Fueros de la M. N. y M. L.* Provincia de Guipúzcoa. San Sebastián: Caja de Ahorros Municipal, 1983.

Lécluse, Fleury. *Grammaire basque*. Toulouse: Jean Douladoure; Bayonne: L. M. Cluzeau, 1826.

———. [pseud. Lor Urhersigarria] *Plauto políglot o, o sea, hablando libremente hebreo, cántabro, céltico, irlandés, húngaro, etcétera, seguido de una respuesta a la impugnación del Manual de la Lengua Basca*. Tolosa [Toulouse]: J. M. Douladure, 1828.

Leiçarraga, Joannes. *Iesus Christ gure Iaunaren Testamentu Berria. Othoitza ecclesiasticoen forma Catechismea. Kalendrera. ABC edo Christinoen instructionea*. La Rochelle: Pierre Hautin, 1571. Reprint, Bilbao: Euskaltzaindia, 1990.

Le Jumel de Barneville, Marie Cataline [Madame D'Aulnoy]. "Relación del viaje de España." 1679. In *Viajes de extranjeros por España y Portugal*, edited by José García Mercadal, vol. 4, 10–281. Salamanca: Junta de Castilla y León, Salamanca, 1999.

López Madera, Gregorio. *Historia y discursos*. Granada, 1602.

Luzuriaga, Juan. *Paraninfo celeste. Historia de la mystica zarza, milagrosa imagen y Prodigioso Santuario de Aranzazu, de religiosos observantes de nuestro Seráfico Padre San Francisco en la Provincia de Guipuzcoa, de la Region de Cantabria, escríbela, y consagrala a la soberana Reyna de Angeles, y Hombres Maria Santísima Señora Nuestra el M. R. P. Fr. . . .* Mexico City: Viuda de Calderón, 1686. Madrid: Juan García Infanzon, 1690.

Madariaga, Pedro de. *Honra de escribanos*. Valencia: Pedro Patricio Mey, 1565. Reprint, Madrid: Antonio de Sancha, 1777.

Maldonado, Alonso de. *Chronica universal de todas las Naciones y Tiempos*. Madrid, 1624.

Mañé y Flaquer, José. *El Oasis. Viaje al País de los Fueros*. Barcelona: Jaime Jesús Roviralta, 1879–80.

Mantuano, Pedro de. *Advertencias a la Historia del Padre Juan de Mariana*. Madrid, 1613.

Mariana, Juan de. *Historiae de rebus Hispaniae,* Toledo: Pedro Roderico, 1592. Reprint, as *Historia general de España, la compuesta enmendada y añadida por el Padre Mariana, con la continuación de Miniana completada por el Conde de Toreno y la de nuestros días por Eduardo Chao*. Madrid: Gaspar Roig, 1848–51. Madrid: Biblioteca de Autores Españoles, XXX, 1854.

Marineo Sículo, Lucio. *De rebus Hispaniae memoriabilibus*. Burgos, 1496. Translated into Spanish as *De las cosas memorables de España*. Alcalá de Henares, 1539.

Martínez de Isasti, Lope. *Compendio historial de la M. N. y M. L. Provincia de Guipúzcoa.* 1625. San Sebastián: Ramón Baroja, 1850. Reprint, Bilbao: La Gran Enciclopedia Vasca, 1972.

Martínez de Zaldibia, Juan. *Suma de las cosas cantábricas y guipuzcoanas.* Edited by de Fausto Arocena. San Sebastián: Oficina tipográfica de la Diputación de Guipúzcoa, 1945.

Martínez Marina, Francisco. *Ensayo histórico-crítico sobre el origen y progresos de las lenguas: señaladamente del romance castellano.* Madrid: Joaquín Ibarra, 1805.

Masdeu, Juan Francisco de. *Historia crítica de España y de la cultura española*, 20 vols. Madrid: Sancha, 1783–1805.

Mayans y Siscar, Gregorio. *Orígenes de la lengua española: compuesta por varios autores, recogidos por . . .* Madrid: Victoriano Suárez, 1737. Reprint, Madrid: Rivadeneira, 1873.

Mendieta y Retes, Francisco de. *Quarta parte de los Annales de Vizcaya que Francisco de Mendieta, vecino de Bilbao, recopiló por mandato del Señorío.* San Sebastián: Juan Carlos Guerra; Hijos de J. Baroja, 1915.

Mendoza y Bobadilla, Francisco de. *Tizón de la Nobleza Española, presentada al Rey Felipe II el 20 de agosto de 1560.* Madrid: Antonio Luque y Vicens, 1849.

Michel, François Xavier [Francisque-Michel] *Le Pays Basque. Sa population sa langue, ses moeurs sa littérature et sa musique.* Paris: Didot, 1857. Reprint, Donostia: Elkar, 1994.

Moguel y Urquiza, Juan Antonio. *Versiones vascongadas de varias arengas y oraciones selectas de los mejores autores latinos, o demostración práctica de la pureza, fecundidad y elocuencia del idioma Bascuence contra las preocupaciones de varios escritores extraños, y contra algunos bascongados que sólo tienen una noticia superficial del idioma patrio.* Tolosa: F. de la Lama, 1802.

———. *Cartas y disertaciones de don Juan Antonio Moguel sobre la lengua vascongada.* In *Memorial histórico español: colección de documentos, opúsculos y antigüedades que publica la Real Academia de la Historia.* Vol. 7. Madrid: José Rodríguez, 1854.

———. *El doctor Peru Abarca, catedrático de la lengua bascongada en la Universidad de Basarte o Diálogos entre un rústico solitario bascongado y un barbero callejero llamado Maisu Juan.* Durango: Julián Elizalde, 1881. Reprint, as "Separatas de la Gran Enciclopedia Vasca" 4. Bilbao: La Gran Enciclopedia Vasca, 1970.

———. "Apología de la lengua bascuence contra las erradas ideas y conjeturas de don J. Traggia."*Euskal Erria* 25 (1891): 39, 69, 116, 137, 212, 244, 270, 297, 336, 369, 390, 442, 474, 497, 524.

———. "La historia y la geografía de España ilustradas por el idioma vascuence." Edited by Justo Garate, *Euskera* 16, nos. 3–4 (1935): 187–354 and 18, nos.1–2 (1937): 3–64. Reprint, 2 vols. Bermeo: Gaubeka, 1936, 1937.

Moret, José [pseud. Flavio Silvio y Marcelo]. *El Bodoque contra el propugnáculo histórico y jurídico del licenciado Conchillos*. Colonia Aggripina [Cologne, false place of publication]: Severino Clarley, 1667.

———. *Investigaciones históricas de las Antigüedades del Reyno de Navarra*. Pamplona: Pascual Ibáñez, 1766.

Moret, José, and Francisco de Alesón. *Annales del Reyno de Navarra*. Pamplona: Pascual Ibáñez, 1766.

Ocampo, Florián de. *Las cuatro partes enteras de la Corónica de España que mandó componer el Serenísimo Rey don Alonso llamado el Sabio*. Zamora, 1541.

———. *Los cincos libros primeros de la Crónica de España, que recopila el maestro...* Medina del Campo: Guillermo de Millis, 1553.

Oihenart, Arnaud. *Notitia utriusque Vasconiae tum Ibericae tum Aquitanicae*. Paris: Sebastián Cramoisy, 1638. Reprint, translated by Javier Gorosterratzu. Vitoria-Gasteiz: Parlamento Vasco-Eusko Legebiltzarra, 1992.

Oliveira, Fernão de. *Grammatica do Linguagem Portuguesa*. Lisbon: Germãon Galharde, 1536.

Orosius, Paulus. *Historia adversum paganos libri VII, ex recognitione Caroli Zangemeiter*. Lipsiae [Leipzig]: B. G. Tevbeneri, 1889.

Pascual Iturriaga, Agustín: *Arte de aprender a hablar la lengua castellana para el uso de las escuelas de primeras letras de Guipúzcoa*. Hernani, 1841.

———. *Diálogos basco-castellanos para las escuelas de primeras letras de Guipúzcoa*. Hernani, 1842.

———. "Memoria presentada a las Juntas Generales de Gipuzkoa reunidas en Mondragón en 1830, relativa a la conservación de la lengua vascongada." General Archive of Gipuzkoa, Section 1, Neg. 21, Leg. 133. In Joxemanuel Bujanda, *Euskara eskolan eraiki nahi zuen Euskal pedagogo aurrerakoia: Agustin Pascual Iturriaga,*

Hernani, 1778–1851, 178–90. Bilbao: Udako Euskal Unibertsitatea, 1991.

Pasquier, Etienne. *Recherches de la France*. 10 vols. Paris, 1560–1621.

Pérez de Lazárraga, Juan. *Dianea & Koplak*, edited by Patri Urkizu. Donostia: Erein, 2004. Transcription of an unpublished manuscript by Señor de la Torre de Larrea (1564–67). At http://lazarraga.gipuzkoakultura.net/ (accessed February 8, 2006).

Perochegui, Juan. *Origen y antigüedad de la lengua bascongada y de la Nobleza de Cantabria*. Barcelona, 1731. Reprint, as *Origen de la nación vascongada y de su lengua, de que han dimanado las monarquías francesa y española, y la República de Venecia, que existen al presente, lo que se hace demostrable por su propia narrativa y encadenamiento*. Pamplona: Herederos de Martínez, 1760. Reprint, San Sebastián: Roger, 2000.

Picaud, Aimeric. *Liber Sancti Jacobi. Codex Calistinus* (c. 1143), edited by Walter Muir Whitehill. Santiago de Compostela, 1944. Reprint, in *Viajes de extranjeros por España y Portugal*, edited by José García Mercadal. Vol. 1, 153–68. Salamanca: Junta de Castilla y León, 1999.

Pineda, Juan de. *La Monarquía Eclesiástica* o *Historia Universal del Mundo*. Salamanca, 1588.

Platón [Plato]. *Diálogos*. Mexico: Porrua, 1981.

Poza, Andrés de. *De la antigua lengua, poblaciones y comarcas de las Españas en que de paso se tocan algunas cosas de la Cantabria*. Bilbao: Matías Mares, 1587. Reprint, as *Antigua lengua de las Españas*, edited by Ángel Rodríguez Herrero. Madrid: Minotauro, 1959.

Pulgar, Fernando del. *Claros varones de Castilla*. Toledo, 1486. Reprint, edited by J. Domínguez Bordona. Madrid: La Lectura, 1923.

Quevedo, Francisco de. *Premáticas y aranceles generales*. Clásicos castellanos series 56. Madrid: Espasa-Calpe?, n.d.

Reclus, Elisée. “Les Basques. Un peuple qui s’en va.” *Revue de deux mondes* 68 (March 1867): 1. Reprint, as “Los Vascos. Un pueblo que se va por Eliseo Reclus (1867),” translated and edited by “Martín de Anguiozar” [pseud.], in *Revista Internacional de los Estudios Vascos* 20 (1929): 57–83.

Reglamento provisional de las escuelas de instrucción primaria de la M. N. y M. L. Provincia de Guipúzcoa. Azpeitia: Imprenta Excelentísima Diputación a cargo de Pablo Martínez, 1875.

Risco, Manuel. *El R. P. M. Fr. Enrique Florez, vindicado del Vindicador de la Cantabria, Don Hipólito de Ozaeta y Gallaiztegui. Por el P. M. Fr. Manuel Risco, del Orden de S. Agustín.* Madrid: Pedro Marín, 1799.

———. *Tratado de la Vasconia antigua. En que se establecen todas las antigüedades concernientes a la región de los vascones desde los tiempos primitivos hasta los reyes primeros de Navarra.* 2nd ed. Madrid: Real Academia de la Historia; José Rodríguez, 1878.

Rodríguez de Guevara, Alfonso. *Fundación y antigüedad de España, y conservación de la nobleza de Cantabria.* Milan: Pablo Gottardo and Leonardo Poncios, 1586.

Sada y Amézqueta, Juan [pseud. García de Góngora y Torreblanca]. *Historia apologética y descripción del Reyno de Navarra y de su mucha antigüedad, nobleza, calidades, y Reyes que dieron principio a su Real casa, y procuraron sus acrecentamientos . . . dividida en III libros . . . sacada a luz por García de Góngora y Torreblanca.* Pamplona: Carlos de Labayen, 1628.

Sanadon, Barthelemy Jean-Baptiste. *Essai sur la noblesse des Basques, pour servir d'Introduction à l'Histoire générale de ces Peuples. Rédigé sur les Mémoires d'un Militaire Basque, par un ami de la Nation.* Pau: J. P. Vignancour, 1785. Translated into Spanish as *Ensayo sobre la nobleza de los bascongados, para que sirva de introducción á la Historia general de aquellos Pueblos, traducido por D. Diego de Lazcano Presbytero.* Tolosa: Francisco de Lama, 1786.

Santa Teresa, Bartolomé [Bartolomé de Madariaga]. *Plauto Bascongado o El Bascuence de Plauto en su comedia Poenulo, acto V, escena primera, y la impugnación del Manual de la lengua basca impreso en Bayona de Francia, año 1826, por Mr. Lécluse, profesor de las lenguas hebrea y griega.* Santander, 1828.

———. *Anti-Plauto polígloto o Defensa de Plauto Bascongado y de la impugnación del Manual de La Lengua basca de Mr. Lécluse.* Santander, 1829.

Silius Italicus. *De bello punico.* Geneva: Haeredes Iacobu Chouët, 1607.

Soraluce, Nicolás de. *Los iberos ó sean euskaros y el euskera. Memoria publicada en los números 20 y 21 de la Revista Euskara.* Pamplona: Joaquín Lorda, 1879. Reprint, as "Memoria sobre la lengua vascongada leída en el Ateneo de San Sebastián el mes de octubre de 1879." In Juan Mañé y Flaquer, *El Oasis. Viaje al País de los*

Fueros. Vol. 2. *Viaje por Guipúzcoa al final de su etapa foral (1876)*, 449–71. Bilbao: Villar, 1969.

Sorreguieta, Tomás de. *Semana Hispano-Bascongada, la unica de la Europa, y la más antigua del Orbe. Con dos suplementos de otros ciclos, y etimologías bascongadas*. Pamplona: Viuda e hijo de Longas, 1804.

———. *Triunfo de la Semana Hispano-Vascongada y del vascuence contra varios censores filosóficos enmascarados, en tres cartas dirigidas á los literatos Españoles*. Madrid: Viuda de Ibarra, 1805.

Traggia, Joaquín. *Aparato a la Historia Eclesiástica de Aragón*. Vol. 1. Madrid, 1792.

———. "Del origen de la lengua vascongada." In *Diccionario Geográfico-histórico de España por la Real Academia de la Historia*, s.v. "Navarra." Vol. 2, 151–66. Madrid: Viuda de don Joaquín Ibarra, 1802.

Ulibarri, José Paulo de. *Gutun liburua* [early 19th century?]. Edited by Lino Akesolo. Vitoria: Diputación Foral de Álava, 1975.

Uriarte Astarloa, José María. *Pablo Pedro Astarloa (1752–1806) Biografía*. Durango: Durangoko Arte eta Historia Museoa, 2002.

Valdés, Juan de. *Diálogo de la lengua, (1535–36)*. Clásicos castellanos series 86. Madrid: "La Lectura"; Espasa-Calpe, 1928.

Valla, Lorenzo. *Elegantiae Linguae Latinae*. Venice, 1444.

Vargas Ponce, José de. *Estados de vitalidad y mortalidad de Guipúzcoa en el siglo XVIII. Trabajados por el Teniente de Navío don . . .* Madrid: Real Academia de la Historia, 1982.

Villalón, Cristóbal de. *Gramática Castellana. Arte breve y compendiosa para saber hablar y escribir en la lengua Castellana congrua y deçentemente*. Antwerp: Guillermo Simon, 1558.

Viterbo, Annio de. *Comentaria super opera diversorum auctorium de antiquitatibus loquentium*. Rome, 1498.

Yanguas y Miranda, José. *Historia Compendiada del Reino de Navarra*. San Sebastián: Ignacio Ramón Baroja, 1832.

———. *Adiciones al Diccionario de Antigüedades de Navarra por . . .* Pamplona: Javier Goyeneche, 1843.

Zabaleta, Miguel de. *Relación verdadera de la jornada que su Majestad el Rey don Filipe Tercero de España, hizo a la Provincia de Guipúzcoa*. Logroño: Matías Mares, 1616.

Zalacain, Gerónimo. *Iracurtzaren asierac edo lenasteac euscalerrico aurrentzat.* Tolosa: P. Gurruchaga, 1875.

Zamácola, Juan Antonio. *Historia de las Naciones bascas de una y otra parte del Pirineo septentrional y costas del mar Cantábrico desde sus primeros pobladores hasta nuestros días.* Auch: Viuda de Dupret, 1818.

———. *Perfecciones analíticas de la lengua vascongada e imitación del sistema adoptado por el célebre ideologista don Pablo Astarloa en sus admirables "Discursos filosóficos sobre la primitiva lengua."* Bilbao: Casa de Misericordia, 1822.

Zaragoza, Justo, ed. *Castellanos y vascongados. Tratado breve de una disputa y diferencia entre dos amigos, el uno castellano, de Burgos, y el otro vascongado, en la villa de Potosí, reino del Perú, documento hasta ahora inédito publicado por Z.* Madrid: Víctor Sáinz, 1876.

Secondary Material

Agulhon, Maurice. *Marianne au combat (imagerie et symbolique républicaines en France de 1789 à 1880).* Paris: Flammarion, 1979.

Aitzol [José María Ariztimuño]. *La muerte del euskera o los profetas de mal agüero. Refutación documentada de las predicciones y opiniones antivascas emitidas por D. Miguel de Unamuno en las Cortes Constituyentes el 18 de septiembre; por don Pío Baroja en Barcelona el 28 de septiembre y por D. Ricardo Baroja en el Instituto Politécnico de Irun el 26 del mismo mes de este año de gracia de 1931* [1931]. At http://www.euskaraz.net/donostia/gorosti/testuak/00061.htm (accessed February 8, 2006).

Alarcos Llorach, Emilio. "Una teoría acerca del castellano." *Boletín de la Real Academia Española* 21 (1934): 202–28.

Alonso, Juan, and Antonio Arnaiz Villena. *El origen de los vascos y otros pueblos mediterráneos.* Madrid: Complutense, 1988.

Altuna, Patxi: "Aita Larramendiren bizitza." In *Manuel Larramendi. Hirugarren mendeurrena, 1690–1990.* Edited by Joseba Andoni Lakarra, 3–26. Andoain: Andoaingo Udala; Euskaltzaindia; Gipuzkoako Foru Aldundia; Eusko Jaurlaritza, 1991.

Altzibar, Xabier. "Euskaldunen nazio eta hizkuntza (1770–1830)." *Euskera* 31, no. 1 (1986): 17–45.

Apesteguía, Juan. "Joaquín de Lizarraga." *Gran Enciclopedia de Navarra.* Vol. 7 (1990): 89–90.

Arana Martija, José Antonio. "Louis Lucien Bonaparte: Visión lingüística de Europa en el siglo XIX." In *Los Escritores*. Vitoria: Sancho el Sabio, 1996.

Arano Bereño, Ander, et al. *Iparragirre*. Bilbao: Euskaltzaindia, 1987.

Aranzadi, Juan. *Milenarismo vasco: Edad de oro, etnia y nativismo*. Madrid: Taurus, 1982.

Areitio, Darío de. *El gobierno universal del Señorío de Vizcaya*. Bilbao: Junta de Cultura Vizcaína, 1943.

Arocena, Fausto. *Garibay*. Zarauz: Icharopena; Ayuntamiento de Mondragón, 1960.

Azurmendi, Joxe, et al. "Wilhem Von Humboldt: investiga en Vasconia, 1801." Special issue, *Revista Internacional de los Estudios Vascos* 48, no. 1 (2003).

Barandiaran, José Miguel de. "El euskera en Álava a fines del siglo XVIII." *Revista Internacional de los Estudios Vascos* 17 (1926): 464–67.

Bazán, Iñaki, ed. *El historiador Esteban de Garibay*. San Sebastián: Eusko Ikaskuntza, 2001.

Bilbao, Jon. *Eusko Bibliographia. Enciclopedia General Ilustrada del País Vasco*. 9 vols. San Sebastián: Auñamendi, 1970–75.

Borst, Arno. *Der Turmbau von Babel. Geschichte der Meinungen über Ursprung und Vielfalt der Sprachen und Völker*. Munich: Deutschen Taschenbuch Verlag, 1995.

Branet, Alphonse, and Jean Barada. "Notes sur Juan Antonio Zamàcola." *Revista Internacional de los Estudios Vascos* 17 (1926): 453–63.

Breva Claramonte, Manuel. "Las ideas lingüísticas del siglo XVIII en Lorenzo Hervás: la descripción de las lenguas del mundo." In *Euskalaritzaren historiaz (I): XVI–XIX. Mendeak*, edited by Ricardo Gómez and Joseba Labaka, 327–40. Donostia: Diputación Foral de Gipuzkoa, 1992.

Bujanda, Joxemanuel. *Euskara eskolan eraiki nahi zuen Euskal pedagogo aurrerakoia: Agustin Pascual Iturriaga, Hernani, 1778–1851*. Bilbao: Udako Euskal Unibertsitatea, 1991.

Caballo, Guglielmo and Roger Chartier, eds. *Histoire de la lecture dans le monde occidental*. Paris: Seuil, 1997. Translated into Spanish as *Historia de la lectura en el mundo occidental* (Madrid: Taurus, 2001).

Caro Baroja, Julio. *Los vascos y la historia a través de Garibay (Ensayo de biografía antropológica).* San Sebastián: Txertoa, 1972.

———. *Sobre la lengua vasca y el vasco-iberismo.* San Sebastián: Txertoa, 1979.

———. *La casa en Navarra.* Pamplona: Caja de Ahorros de Navarra, 1982.

———. *Vasconiana.* San Sebastián: Txertoa, 1986.

———. *Las falsificaciones en la Historia (en relación con la de España).* Barcelona: Seix Barral, 1992.

Caussat, Pierre, Dariusz Adamski, and Marc Crépon. *La langue source de la nation. Messianismes séculiers en Europe centrale et orientale (du XVIIIe au XXe siècle).* Liège: Mardaga, 1996.

Cavalli-Sforza, Luigi Luca. *Genes, pueblos y lenguas.* Barcelona: Crítica, 2000.

Celaya, Gabriel. *Iberia sumergida.* Madrid: Peralta, 1978.

Certeau, Michel de, Dominique Julia, and Jacques Revel, eds. *Une politique de la langue. La Revolution française et les patois: l'enquête de Grégoire.* 1975. Paris: Gallimard, 2002.

Cohn, Norman. *The Pursuit of the Millennium: Revolutionary Millenarians and Mystical Anarchists of the Middle Ages.* Rev. ed. New York: Oxford University Press, 1970. Translated into Spanish as *En pos del Milenio* (Barcelona: Barral, 1971).

Dávila Balsera, Paulí. *Lengua, escuela y cultura. El proceso de alfabetización en Euskal Herria, siglos XIX y XX.* Bilbao: Universidad del País Vasco-Euskal Herriko Unibertsitatea, 1995.

———, ed. *Enseñanza y educación en el País Vasco contemporáneo.* Donostia: Universidad del País Vasco-Euskal Herriko Unibertsitatea; Kutxa, 2003.

De Benito Pascual, Jesús. "La Real Sociedad Bascongada de los Amigos del País y las escuelas de primeras letras (1771–1793)." In Luis Mª Areta Armentia and Jesús de Benito Pascual, *Las ideas pedagógicas de los ilustrados vascos.* Vitoria-Gasteiz: Servicio Central de Publicaciones, Gobierno Vasco, 1990.

———. *La enseñanza de las primeras letras en Gipuzkoa (1800–1825).* San Sebastián: Diputación Foral de Gipuzkoa, 1994.

Del Amo, Carlota. "El debate sobre la lengua vasca en los periódicos madrileños a comienzos del siglo XIX." In *Actas del Congreso La Lengua y los Medios de Comunicación*, edited by Joaquín Garrido

Medina. Vol. 2, 602–11. Madrid: Universidad Complutense de Madrid, 1999.

Desgraves, Jean-Louis. *Le livre en Aquitanie XVe–XVIIIe siècles*. Biarritz: Atlantica, 1998.

Duhart, Mixel. "Dominique Joseph Garat 1749–1833." *Bulletin de la Société de Sciences, Lettres et Arts de Bayonne* (1992–93): 148–49.

———. *Yo, Domingo José Garat*. San Sebastián: Txertoa, 1997.

Dubois, Claude-Gilbert. "L'Imaginaire historique et ses manifestations dans l'historiographie du XVIe siècle." *Storia della Storiografia* 14 (1988): 68–95.

———. *L'imaginaire de la nation, 1792–1992*. Bordeaux: Presses Universitaires de Bordeaux, 1991.

Echenique, Mª Teresa: *Historia lingüística vasco-románica*. Madrid: Paraninfo, 1987.

Eco, Humberto [Umberto]. *La búsqueda de la lengua perfecta*. Barcelona: Crítica, 1999.

Eliade, Mircea. *Le mythe de l'éternel retour: Archétypes et répétition*. Paris: Gallimard, 1951. Translated into Spanish by Ricardo Anaya as *El mito del eterno retorno. Arquetipos y repetición*. Madrid: Alianza, 1989.

Elías de Tejada, Francisco. *El Señorío de Vizcaya (hasta 1812)*. Madrid: Minotauro, 1963.

Elías de Tejada, Francisco, and Gabriella Percopo. *La Provincia de Guipúzcoa*. Madrid: Minotauro, 1965.

El Libro Blanco del Euskara. Bilbao: Euskaltzaindia, 1978.

Enciclopedia General Ilustrada del País Vasco. 51 vols. San Sebastián: Auñamendi, 1979–.

Enciclopedia General de Navarra. 11 vols. Pamplona: Caja de Ahorros de Navarra, 1990.

Erize Etxegarai, Xabier. *Nafarroako Euskararen Historia Soziolinguistikoa (1863–1936). Soziolinguistika historikoa eta Hizkuntza Gutxituen Visitas*. Iruña: Nafarroako Gobernua, Hezkuntza eta Kultura Departamentua, 1997.

Estévez Rodríguez, Xosé. *La historiografía guipuzcoana, desde Zaldivia a Gorosabel, sobre la adhesión de Gipuzkoa a Castilla*. Koldo Mitxelena Kulturunea, http://www.gipuzkoakultura.net/euskera/index.htm (accessed February 8, 2006).

Etxenike, Karmele. "Apuntes sobre el vascoiberismo actual." *Euskonews & Media* 54 (November 12–19, 1999), http://www.euskonews.com/0054zbk/frgaia.htm (accessed February 8, 2006).

Fernández Albaladejo, Pablo. "Manuel de Larramendi: la particular historia de Guipúzcoa." *Saioak* 1 (1979): 148–56.

Frazer, James George. *Folk-Lore in the Old Testament: Studies in Comparative Religion, Legend, and Law.* 3 vols. London: Macmillan and Co., 1918. Translated by Gerardo Novás into Spanish as *El folklore en el Antiguo Testamento.* Madrid: Fondo de Cultura Económica, 1981.

Garate, Justo. *La época de Astarloa y Juan Antonio Moguel.* Bilbao: Diputación de Vizcaya, 1936.

———. *Viajeros extranjeros en Vasconia.* 1942. 2nd ed. Buenos Aires: Ekin, 1989.

García Mercadal, José, ed. *Viajes de extranjeros por España y Portugal.* 6 vols. *Desde los tiempos más remotos hasta comienzos del siglo XX.* Salamanca: Junta de Castilla y León, 1999.

García-Sanz Marcotegui, Ángel, Iñaki Iriarte López, and Fernando Mikelarena Peña, eds. *Historia del navarrismo (1841–1936). Sus relaciones con el vasquismo.* Pamplona: Universidad Pública de Navarra-Nafarroako Unibertsitate Publikoa, 2002.

———, ed. *Memoria histórica e identidad. En torno a Cataluña, Aragón y Navarra.* Pamplona: Universidad Pública de Navarra-Nafarroako Unibertsitate Publikoa, 2004.

Geografía histórica de la lengua vasca. Auñamendi series. Zarauz: Icharopena, 1960.

Gilmont, Jean-François. "Reformas protestantes y lectura." In *Historia de la lectura en el mundo occidental*, edited by Guglielmo Caballo and Roger Chartier, 415–68. Madrid: Taurus, 2001.

Gil Novales, Alberto, ed. *Diccionario biográfico del Trienio liberal.* Madrid: El Museo Universal, 1991.

Gómez, Ricardo and Joseba Lakarra, eds. *Euskalaritzaren historiaz (I): XVI–XIX. Mendeak.* Donostia: Diputación Foral de Gipuzkoa-Gipuzkoako Foru Aldundia, 1992.

Goñi Gaztambide, José. *Historia de los Obispos de Pamplona. IX. Siglo XIX.* Pamplona: Universidad de Navarra; Gobierno de Navarra, 1991.

Gorostiaga Bilbao, Juan. *Épica y lírica vizcaína antigua.* Bilbao: Centro Estudios Vascos de Falange Española, 1952.

Gorrotxategi, Joaquín. "Andrés de Poza y el euskera." In *Euskalaritzaren historiaz (I): XVI–XIX. mendeak*, edited by Ricardo Gómez and Joseba Lakarra, 107–28. Donostia: Diputación Foral de Gipuzkoa-Gipuzkoako Foru Aldundia, 1992.

Goyhenetche, Manex. *Les basques et leur histoire. Mythes et réalités.* Baiona: Elkar, 1993.

———. [Goihenetxe]. "A. d'Oihenart historien: Aspects de son profil social, politique, culturel." In *Oihenarten Laugarren Mendeurrena*, 497–508. Bilbao: Euskaltzaindia, 1994.

Guerra, Juan Carlos. *Viejos textos del idioma. Los cantares antiguos del euskera.* San Sebastián: Martín y Mena, 1924.

Hansen-Love, Ole. *La révolution copernicienne du langage dans l'œuvre de Wilhelm von Humboldt.* Paris: J. Vrin, 1972.

Hastings, Adrian. *The Construction of Nationhood: Ethnicity, Religion and Nationalism.* Cambridge: Cambridge University Press, 1997.

Hernández Mata, Amelia. "Antoine d'Abbadie eta garaikideen sare intelektuala." In *Antoine d'Abbadie 1897–1997. Congrès International (Hendaye, 1997)*, 231–62. Donostia: Eusko Ikaskuntza; Bilbao: Euskaltzaindia, 1998.

Historia de una ciudad, Vitoria. Vitoria: Bankoa, 1977.

Hobsbawm, Eric J. *Primitive Rebels: Studies in Archaic Forms of Social Movement in the 19th and 20th Centuries.* Manchester: Manchester University Press, 1959. Translated into Spanish by Joaquín Romero Maura as *Rebeldes primitivos. Estudio sobre las formas arcaicas de los movimientos sociales en los siglos XIX y XX* (Barcelona: Ariel, 1968).

Hobsbawm, Eric J., and Terence Ranger, eds. *The Invention of Tradition.* Cambridge: Cambridge University Press, 1983.

Hourmat, Pierre. *L'enseignement primaire dans les Basses-Pyrénées au temps de la monarchie constitutionnelle, 1815–1848.* Anglet: IPSO, 1973.

Intxausti, Joseba. "El Euskara: de su mito a la conciencia nacional. Hizkuntzaren kontzientzia eta eskea, historian." In *Euskal Herria. Errealitate eta egitasmo. Realidad y proyecto*, edited by Joseba Intxausti. Vol. 1, 361–86. San Sebastián: Caja Laboral Popular, 1985.

———. *Euskara, euskaldunon hizkuntza.* Donostia: Elkar, 1992.

Irigarai, Jose Angel. *Euskera eta Nafarroa.* Pamplona: Aranzadi, 1973.

Jimeno Jurío, José María. *Navarra, historia del euskera.* Tafalla: Txalaparta, 1997.

———. *Navarra, Gipuzkoa y el euskera.* Pamplona: Pamiela, 1999.

Juan Bautista Erro y Azpiroz, 1773–1854. San Sebastián: Diputación Foral de Guipúzcoa, 1954.

Juaristi, Jon. *Euskararen ideologiak.* Vol. 1. *Etorkiak.* Donostia: Kriselu, 1976.

———. *La tradición romántica. Leyendas vascas del siglo XIX.* Pamplona: Pamiela, 1986.

———. "La gnosis renacentista del euskera." In *Euskalaritzaren historiaz (I): XVI–XIX. mendeak*, edited by Ricardo Gómez and Joseba Lakarra, 129–72. Donostia: Diputación Foral de Gipuzkoa-Gipuzkoako Foru Aldundia, 1992.

———. "Las fuentes ocultas del romanticismo vasco." In *Euskalaritzaren historiaz (I): XVI–XIX. Mendeak*, edited by Ricardo Gómez and Joseba Lakarra, 341–66. Donostia: Diputación Foral de Gipuzkoa-Gipuzkoako Foru Aldundia, 1992.

———. *El linaje de Aitor. La invención de la tradición vasca.* Madrid: Taurus, 1998.

———. *El bosque originario. Genealogías míticas de los pueblos de Europa.* Madrid: Santillana, 2000.

Julia, Dominique. "Lecturas y Contrarreforma." In *Historia de la lectura en el mundo occidental*, edited by Gugielmo Caballo and Roger Chartier, 415–68. Madrid: Taurus, 2001.

Kintana Goiriena, Jurgi. "Euskarazko historiografia (I): aurrekariak eta lehen pausuak (XVI-XIX mendeak)." *Kondaira* 0 (2003): 1–38. At http://www.kondaira.com/kondairao/Euskarazko%20historiografia.pdf (accessed February 8, 2006).

Lafon, René, and Gilberte Reicher. *Bernard Dechepare, sa vie et son œuvre.* Paris: Maisonneuve, 1948.

Laka, Itziar. "Astarloaren hizkuntzalaritzaz." *Anuario del Seminario de Filología Vasca "Julio de Urquijo"* 23, no. 1 (1989): 75–86. Reprint, in *Euskalaritzaren historiaz (I): XVI–XIX. mendeak*, edited by Ricardo Gómez and Joseba Lakarra, 367–78. Donostia: Diputación Foral de Gipuzkoa-Gipuzkoako Foru Aldundia, 1992.

Lakarra, Joseba Andoni, ed. *Manuel Larramendi. Hirugarren mendeurrena, 1690–1990.* Andoain: Andoaingo Udala; San Sebastián: Diputación Foral de Gipuzkoa, 1991.

———. "Larramendirekin aurreko hiztegigintzaren historiaz: aztergai eta gogoeta." In *Euskalaritzaren historiaz (I): XVI–XIX. mendeak*, edited by Ricardo Gómez and Joseba Lakarra, 275–312. Donostia: Diputación Foral de Gipuzkoa-Gipuzkoako Foru Aldundia, 1992.

Larrañaga Elorza, Koldo. "Oihenart y el tema de los orígenes vascos." *Vasconia* 24, no. 1 (1996): 115–43.

———. "Cantabrismo en Navarra." *Príncipe de Viana* 59 (1998): 447–79.

Lázaro Carreter, Fernando. *Las ideas lingüísticas del siglo XVIII.* Madrid: Crítica, 1985.

Legarda, Anselmo de. "Primera frase vasca impresa conocida, en Torres Naharro, 1513." *Boletín de la Real Sociedad Bascongada de los Amigos del País* 7 (1951): 41–48.

———. *Lo "vizcaíno" en la literatura castellana.* San Sebastián: Biblioteca Vascongada de los Amigos del País, 1953.

Leoné Puncel, Santiago. *Los fueros de Navarra como lugar de la memoria.* San Sebastián: Fundación para el Derecho Histórico y Autonómico de Vasconia, 2005.

Lida de Malkiel, María Rosa. "Túbal primer poblador de España." *Ábaco* 3 (1970): 11–47.

Llano Gorostiza, Manuel. "Francisco de Mendieta y su cuadro sobre el Besamanos de la Jura de Guernica." In Jacinto Gómez Tejedor, Francisco Sesmero Pérez, and Manuel Llano Gorostiza, *Tres estudios sobre Guernica y su comarca*, 139–221. Bilbao: Diputación Provincial de Vizcaya, 1970.

Madariaga Orbea, Juan. *Historia social de Bergara en su época preindustrial.* Bergara: Ayuntamiento de Bergara, 1991.

———. "Expresiones culturales y mentales en la Euskal Herria de los siglos XVI al XIX." *Revista Internacional de los Estudios Vascos* 46, no. 1 (2001): 203–323.

———. "Espacio doméstico y espacio sepultural en Euskal Herria, siglos XVI al XIX." In *Casa, familia y sociedad*, edited by José María Imícoz, 429–87. Bilbao: Universidad del País Vasco-Euskal Herriko Unibertsitatea, 2004.

———. "Predicación y cambios culturales en la Euskal Herria de los siglos XVIII–XIX." In *Euskal Herriko Erlijiosoen Historia. Familia eta Institutu Erlijiosoen Euskal Herriko Historiaren I. Kongresuko Aktak*, edited by Joseba Intxausti. Vol. 1, 489–525. Oñati: Arantzazu E. F., 2004.

Mañaricúa, Andrés de. *Historiografía de Vizcaya (Desde Lope García de Salazar a Labayru)*. Bilbao: La Gran Enciclopedia Vasca, 1971.

———. *Polémica sobre Vizcaya en el siglo XVII: El Búho gallego y el Tordo vizcaíno*. Bilbao: La Gran Enciclopedia Vasca, 1976.

Michelena, Luis [Koldo Mitxelena]. *Textos arcaicos vascos*. Madrid: Minotauro, 1955.

———. *Historia de la literatura vasca*. Madrid: Minotauro, 1960.

———. *La lengua vasca*. Durango: Leopoldo Zugaza, 1977.

———. "Guillaume de Humboldt et la Langue Basque." In *Euskalaritzaren historiaz (I): XVI–XIX. mendeak*, edited by Ricardo Gómez and Joseba Lakarra, 379–94. Donostia: Diputación Foral de Gipuzkoa-Gipuzkoako Foru Aldundia, 1992.

Mikelarena Peña, Fernando. "Protonavarrismo, libros y bibliotecas privadas durante el Antiguo Régimen." In *Memoria histórica e identidad. En torno a Cataluña, Aragón y Navarra*, edited by Ángel García-Sanz Marcotegui, 89–125. Pamplona: Universidad Pública de Navarra-Nafarroako Unibertsitate Publikoa, 2004.

Miranda García, Fermín, and Eloísa Ramírez Vaquero. "Pedro de Agramont y la *Historia de Navarra*." In Pedro de Agramont y Zaldivar, *Historia de Navarra, 1632*, xiii–xil. Pamplona: Mintzoa, 1996.

Monreal Zia, Gregorio: "Anotaciones sobre el pensamiento político tradicional vasco en el siglo XVI." *Anuario de Historia del Derecho Español* 50 (1980): 971–1004.

———. "Larramendi: madurez y crisis del régimen foral." In *Manuel Larramendi. Hirugarren mendeurrena, 1690–1990*, edited by Joseba Lakarra, 91–135. Andoain: Andoaingo Udala; San Sebastián: Diputación Foral de Gipuzkoa, 1991.

Múgica, Serapio. "Garibay como vascófilo y etimólogo." *Revista Internacional de los Estudios Vascos* 23 (1932): 620–25.

Munárriz Urtasun, Eufrasio de: "El cambio de apellidos en la vieja Navarra." *Revista Internacional de los Estudios Vascos* 14 (1923): 401–03.

Munita Loinaz, José Antonio. "Esteban de Garibay (1533–1599) y el 'Compendio Historial.'" *Mundaiz* 16 (1980): 13–23.

Ninyoles, Rafael Lluis. *Idioma y poder social*. Madrid: Tecnos, 1972.

Nora, Pierre, ed. *Les lieux de la mémoire*. 3 vols. Paris: Gallimard, 1984–1987.

Oihenarten Laugarren Mendeurrena. Bilbao: Euskaltzaindia, 1994.

Olender, Maurice. *Les langues du paradis: Aryens et sémites, un couple provedentiel*. Paris: Seuil, 1989. Translated into Spanish by Vicente Villacampa as *Las lenguas del Paraíso. Arios y semitas una pareja providencial* (Barcelona: Seix Barral, 2001).

Otazu y Llana, Alfonso de. *El "igualitarismo" vasco: mito y realidad*. San Sebastián: Txertoa, 1973.

Oyharçabal, Beñat. "Les premières grammaires du basque." *Bulletin du Musée Basque* (Baiona) (1989): 453–72.

———. "A. Abbadieren euskal gramatikari buruzko ideiak eta ordu arteko euskal gramatikagintza." In *Antoine d'Abbadie 1897–1997. Congrès International (Hendaye, 1997)*, 431–51. Donostia: Eusko Ikaskuntza; Bilbao: Euskaltaindia, 1998.

Patlagean, Evelyne. "L'histoire de l'imaginaire." In *La nouvelle histoire*, edited by Jacques Le Goff, 249–69. Paris: Retz-CEPL, 1978.

Peillen, Txomin. "L'oeuvre de P. Larramendi: cristallisation de mythes historiques et culturels basques." *Bulletin du Musée Basque* 118 (1987): 131–66.

Pereira de Queiroz, María Isaura. *Historia y etnología de los movimientos mesiánicos*. Madrid: Siglo XXI, 1969.

Poliakov, Léon. *Le mythe aryen. Essai sur les sources du racisme et des nationalismes*. Brussels: Complexe, 1987.

Rodríguez Herrero, Ángel. *Ordenanzas de Bilbao. Siglos XV y XVI*. Bilbao: Ayuntamiento de Bilbao, 1948.

Román del Cerro, Juan Luis. *El desciframiento de la lengua ibérica "en ofrenda de los pueblos."* Alicante: Aguaclara, 1990.

———. *El origen ibérico de la lengua vasca*. Alicante: Aguaclara, 1993.

Sánchez Carrión, José María [pseud. Txepetx]. *Lengua y pueblo*. San Sebastián: Elkar, 1980.

———. *Un futuro para nuestro pasado: claves de recuperación del Euskera y teoría social de las Lenguas*. 2nd ed. San Sebastián: Seminario Julio Urquijo; 'Adorez eta Atseginez' Mintegia, 1991.

Sánchez-Prieto, Juan María. *El imaginario vasco. Representaciones de una conciencia histórica, nacional y política en el escenario europeo 1833–1876*. Barcelona: Eiunsa, 1993.

San Martín, Juan. "Juan Antonio Mogel eta Urkiza. Bere bizitza ta lanak." *Euskera* 5 (1960): 26–50.

———. "Puntualizaciones sobre el euskera de Urraul alto (Navarra)." *Cuadernos de Sección. Lengua y Literatura*, Eusko Ikaskuntza, 3 (1984): 453.

Sarasola, Ibon. *Euskal Literaturaren Historia*. Donostia: Lur, 1971.

Saroïhandy, Jean Joseph. "Oihenart contra Garibay y Morales." *Revista Internacional de los Estudios Vascos* 13 (1922): 448–55.

Schlieben-Lange, Brigitte. *Idéologie, révolution et uniformité de la langue*. Liège: Pierre Mardaga, 1996.

Soboul, Albert, ed. *Dictionaire historique de la Révolution française*. Paris: Presses Universitaires Françaises, 1989.

Soria Sesé, Lourdes. *La historiografía castellana sobre la incorporación de Gipuzkoa a Castilla*. Koldo Mitxelena Kulturunea. At http://www.gipuzkoakultura.net/euskera/index.htm (accessed February 8, 2006).

Tellechea Idígoras, José Ignacio. *Autobiografía y otros escritos*. San Sebastián: Sociedad General de Ediciones y Publicaciones, 1973.

Temprano, Emilio. *La selva de los tópicos*. Madrid: Mondadori, 1988.

Thomas, Ceiwin H. "The Welsh Language." Journal of the Faculty of Arts (Malta University Press) 3, no. 2 (1966): 73–101.

Torrealday, Joan Mari. *Euskal idazleak gaur. Historia social de la lengua y la literatura vascas*. Oñati: Jakin, 1977.

Tovar, Antonio. *La lengua vasca*. 2nd ed. San Sebastián: Biblioteca Vascongada de los Amigos del País, 1954.

———. *El euskera y sus parientes*. Madrid: Minotauro, 1959.

———. *Mitología e ideología sobre la lengua vasca*. Madrid: Alianza, 1980.

Txillardegi [pseud. José Luis Álvarez Emparanza]. *Lingua navarrorum*. San Sebastián: Orain, 1996.

Uriarte Astarloa, José María. *Pablo Pedro Astarloa (1752–1806) Biografía*. Durango: Durangoko Arte eta Historia Museoa, 2002.

Uribe Villegas, Oscar. *Situaciones de multilingüismo en el mundo*. Mexico City: Universidad Autónoma de México, 1972.

Urkiza, Julen and Luis Baraiazarra. *Frai Bartolome Santa Teresa. Idazlan guztiak*. 2 vols. Bilbao: Euskaltzaindia, 2000.

Urkizu, Patri. *Agosti Chahoren bizitza eta idazlanak, 1811–1858*. Bilbo: BBK-Euskaltzaindia, 1992.

———. "Anton Abbadia, hizkuntzalari, literatur kritikari eta mezenas." In *Antoine d'Abbadie 1897–1997. Congrès International (Hen-*

daye, 1997), 63–70. Donostia: Eusko Ikaskuntza; Bilbao: Euskaltzaindia, 1998.

———, ed. *Historia de la literatura vasca*. Madrid: UNED, 2000.

———, ed. *Joan Perez de Lazarraga. Dianea & Koplak*. San Sebastián: Erein, 2004.

———. "Cosas de antaño. Los Sinodales de Calahorra (1602 y 1700)," *Revista Internacional de los Estudios Vascos* 14 (1923): 335–52.

Urquijo, Julio de. "La Crónica Ibargüen-Cachopín y el Canto de Lelo." *Revista Internacional de los Estudios Vascos* 13 (1922): 83–98 and 232–247.

———. "Sobre algunos escritos de D. Joaquín de Irizar y Moya." *Revista Internacional de los Estudios Vascos* 13 (1922): 99–101.

Valverde, Lola. "Antoine d'Abbadie eta mende amaierako mugimendu euskaltzalea." In *Antoine d'Abbadie 1897–1997. Congrès International (Hendaye, 1997)*, 289–303. Donostia: Eusko Ikaskuntza; Bilbao: Euskaltzaindia, 1998.

Veyrin, Philippe. "Un bascophile ignoré L'abbé Dominique Lahetjuzan (1766–1818)." *Gure Herria* (1923): 657–65 and (1924): 564–73.

Villasante, Luis. *Historia de la literatura vasca*. Bilbao: Sendo, 1961.

———. "El colegio de Misioneros franciscanos de Zarauz (1746–1840)." *Scriptorium Victoriense*, Victoriense 21 (1974): 281–330.

Vinson, Julien. *Essai d'une bibliographie de la langue basque*. Paris, 1891–1897. Facsimile edition, *Anuario del Seminario de Filología Vasca "Julio de Urquijo."* Suppl. no. 9 (1984).

Vovelle, Michel, ed. *Les images de la revolution française*. Paris: Publications de la Sorbonne, 1988.

Yaguello, Marina. *Catalogue des idées reçues sur la langue*. Paris: Seuil, 1988.

Yrizar, Pedro. *Pablo Pedro de Astarloa, conferencia de D. Pedro de Yrizar*. Madrid: Real Sociedad Bascongada de los Amigos del País, 1999.

Zabala, Antonio. *Euskal erromantzeak*. Oiartzun: Auspoa-Sendoa, 1998.

Zabalo, Joseph. *Xaho, el genio de Zuberoa*. Tafalla: Txalaparta, 2004.

Zamanillo, Edelmio. *Lectura y traducción de la lengua de los iberos*. Zaragoza: Ibercaja, 1988.

Zelaieta, Ángel. *Foruak eta Euskal literatura*. San Sebastián: Haranburu, 1978.

Zubiaur Bilbao, José Ramón. *Las ideas lingüísticas vascas en el siglo XVI (Zaldibia, Garibay, Poza)*. San Sebastián: Universidad de Deusto, 1990.

———. "Garibai hizkuntzalari." In *Euskalaritzaren historiaz (I): XVI–XIX. mendeak*, edited by Ricardo Gómez and Joseba Lakarra, 173–82. Donostia: Diputación Foral de Gipuzkoa-Gipuzkoako Foru Aldundia, 1992.

———. "Teorías y mitos históricos acerca del euskera." In *Mitos, Teorías y Aspectos del Lenguaje*, edited by Iñaki Beti and José Ramón Zubiaur, 83–98. San Sebastián: Universidad de Deusto, 1996.

Zulaika, Joseba. *Del Cromañón al Carnaval. Los vascos como museo antropológico*. San Sebastián: Erein, 1996.

Index

www.ingramcontent.com/pod-product-compliance
Lightning Source LLC
LaVergne TN
LVHW010049110826
845155LV00028B/258